THE UNITING STATES

THE UNITING STATES

The Story of Statehood for the Fifty United States
Volume 3: Oklahoma to Wyoming

Edited by
Benjamin F. Shearer

GREENWOOD PRESS
Westport, Connecticut • London

Library of Congress Cataloging-in-Publication Data

The uniting states: the story of statehood for the fifty United States/edited by
  Benjamin F. Shearer.
      p. cm.
    Includes bibliographical references and index.
      ISBN 0-313-33105-7 (v. 1 : alk. paper) — ISBN 0-313-33106-5 (v. 2 : alk. paper) —
    ISBN 0-313-33107-3 (v. 3 : alk. paper) — ISBN 0-313-32703-3 (set : alk. paper)
      1. Statehood (American politics). 2. U.S. states. I. Shearer, Benjamin F.
JK2408.U65 2004
320.473'049–dc22   2004042474

British Library Cataloguing in Publication Data is available.

Library of Congress Catalog Card Number: 2004042474
ISBN: 0-313-32703-3 (set)
        0-313-33105-7 (Vol. I)
        0-313-33106-5 (Vol. II)
        0-313-33107-3 (Vol. III)

First published in 2004

Greenwood Press, 88 Post Road West, Westport, CT 06881
An imprint of Greenwood Publishing Group, Inc.
www.greenwood.com

Printed in the United States of America

The paper used in this book complies with the
Permanent Paper Standard issued by the National
Information Standards Organization (Z39.48-1984).

10 9 8 7 6 5 4 3 2 1

Contents

List of Maps

Maps

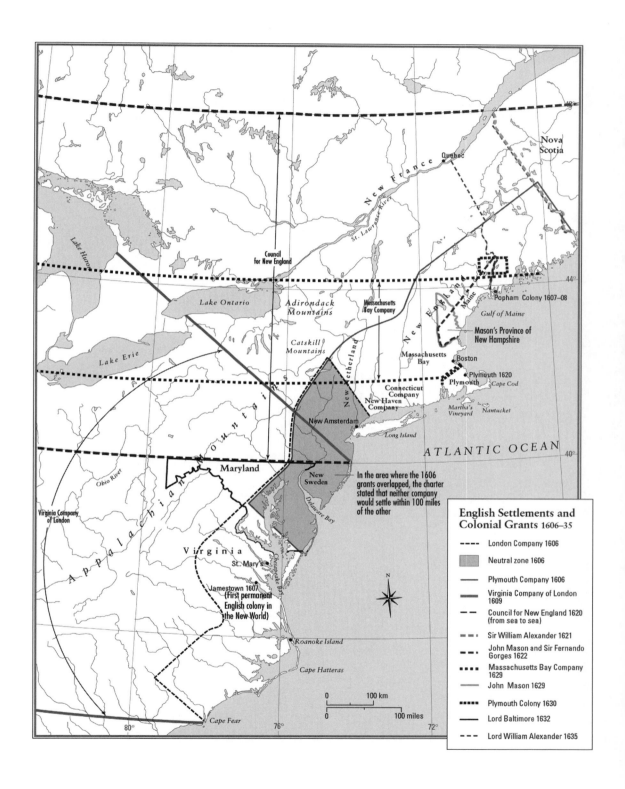

English Settlements and
Colonial Grants 1606–35

- - - - - London Company 1606
▨ Neutral zone 1606
——— Plymouth Company 1606
——— Virginia Company of London 1609
– – – Council for New England 1620 (from sea to sea)
–·–·– Sir William Alexander 1621
– ·· – ·· – John Mason and Sir Fernando Gorges 1622
·········· Massachusetts Bay Company 1629
——— John Mason 1629
▪▪▪▪▪ Plymouth Colony 1630
——— Lord Baltimore 1632
- - - - Lord William Alexander 1635

In the area where the 1606 grants overlapped, the charter stated that neither company would settle within 100 miles of the other

Council for New England

Massachusetts Bay Company

Popham Colony 1607–08

Mason's Province of New Hampshire

Massachusetts Bay

Boston

Plymouth 1620

Plymouth

Cape Cod

Martha's Vineyard

Nantucket

Connecticut Company

New Haven Company

New Amsterdam

Long Island

ATLANTIC OCEAN

New Sweden

Delaware Bay

Maryland

Virginia Company of London

Virginia

St. Mary's

Chesapeake Bay

Jamestown 1607 (First permanent English colony in the New World)

Roanoke Island

Cape Hatteras

Cape Fear

Ohio River

Appalachian Mountains

Lake Erie

Lake Ontario

Lake Huron

Adirondack Mountains

Catskill Mountains

New Netherland

New England

Maine

Gulf of Maine

Nova Scotia

Quebec

St. Lawrence River

New France

0   100 km
0   100 miles

N

80°   76°   72°

40°

44°

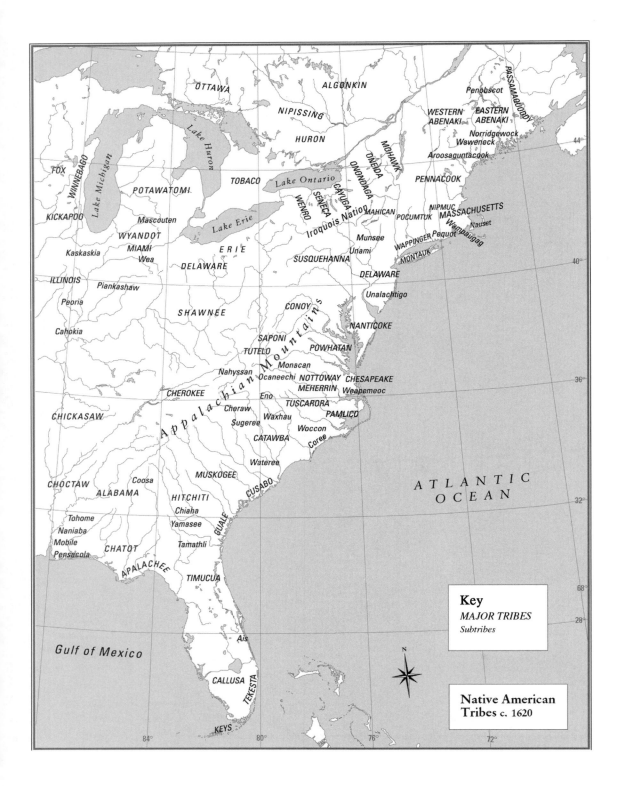

OTTAWA

ALGONKIN

Penobscot

PASSAMAQUODDY

NIPISSING

WESTERN ABENAKI

EASTERN ABENAKI

HURON

Norridgewock

Wawenock

Aroosaguntacook

FOX

WINNEBAGO

Lake Huron

TOBACO

Lake Ontario

ONONDAGA

MOHAWK

ONEIDA

PENNACOOK

POTAWATOMI

KICKAPOO

Lake Michigan

Mascouten

Lake Erie

WENRO

SENECA

CAYUGA

Iroquois Nation

NIPMUC

MASSACHUSETTS

MAHICAN

POCUMTUK

Wampaug

Nauset

WYANDOT

MIAMI

Wea

ERIE

Munsee

WAPPINGER

Pequot

Kaskaskia

DELAWARE

Unami

MONTAUK

ILLINOIS

Piankashaw

SUSQUEHANNA

DELAWARE

Peoria

SHAWNEE

CONOY

Unalachtigo

Cahokia

NANTICOKE

SAPONI

TUTELO

POWHATAN

Nahyssan

Monacan

CHEROKEE

Oceaneechi

NOTTOWAY

CHESAPEAKE

MEHERRIN

Weapemeoc

Eno

Cheraw

Waxhau

TUSCARORA

CHICKASAW

Sugeree

PAMLICO

CATAWBA

Woccon

Coree

Wateree

ATLANTIC OCEAN

CHOCTAW

Coosa

MUSKOGEE

CUSABO

ALABAMA

HITCHITI

Chiaha

GUALE

Tohome

Yamasee

Naniaba

Mobile

CHATOT

Tamathli

Pensacola

APALACHEE

TIMUCUA

Gulf of Mexico

Ais

Key

MAJOR TRIBES

Subtribes

CALLUSA

TEKESTA

N

Native American Tribes c. 1620

KEYS

xiv

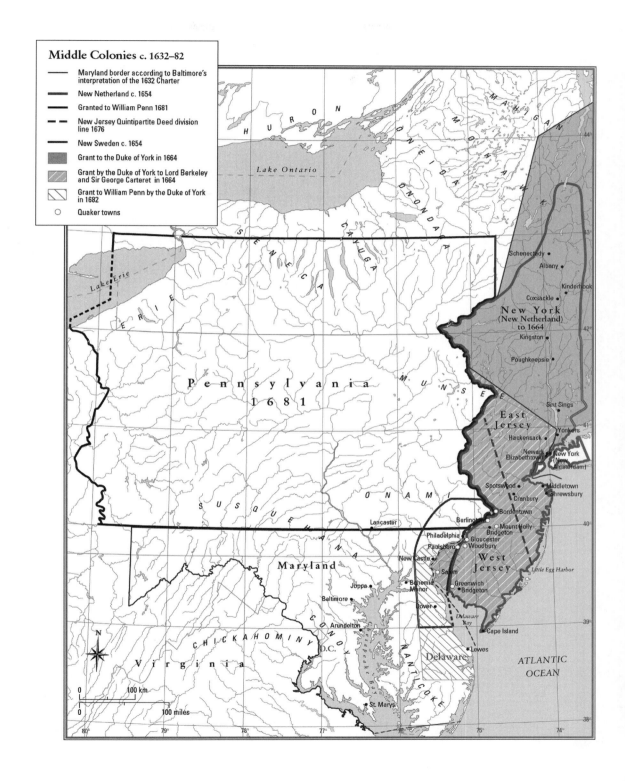

Middle Colonies c. 1632–82

— Maryland border according to Baltimore's interpretation of the 1632 Charter

— New Netherland c. 1654

— Granted to William Penn 1681

-- New Jersey Quintipartite Deed division line 1676

— New Sweden c. 1654

Grant to the Duke of York in 1664

Grant by the Duke of York to Lord Berkeley and Sir George Carteret in 1664

Grant to William Penn by the Duke of York in 1682

○ Quaker towns

HURON

Lake Ontario

M O H A W K

S E N E C A

C A Y U G A

O N O N D A G A

E R I E

Lake Erie

M U N S E E

O N A M I

Pennsylvania
1681

S U S Q U E H A N N A

Schenectady

Albany

Kinderhook

Coxsackle

New York
(New Netherland)
to 1664

Kingston

Poughkeepsie

Sint Sings

East
Jersey

Yonkers

Hackensack

Newark   New York
Elizabethtown (New
           Amsterdam)

Spotswood   Middletown
  Cranbury   Shrewsbury

Lancaster

Burlington
Bordentown

Philadelphia Mount Holly
  Bridgeton
Paulsboro Gloucester
         Woodbury

New Castle   West
  Salem   Jersey   Little Egg Harbor

Maryland

Joppa

Baltimore

Bohemia
Manor   Greenwich
         Bridgeton

Dover

Arundelton

D.C.

St. Marys

Delaware   Delaware
            Bay

Cape Island

Lowes

Lewes

ATLANTIC
OCEAN

N

C H I C K A H O M I N Y

Virginia

C O N O Y

N A N T I C O K E

Chesapeake Bay

0   100 km

0   100 miles

44

43

42

41

40

39

38

80°   79°   78°   77°   76°   75°   74°

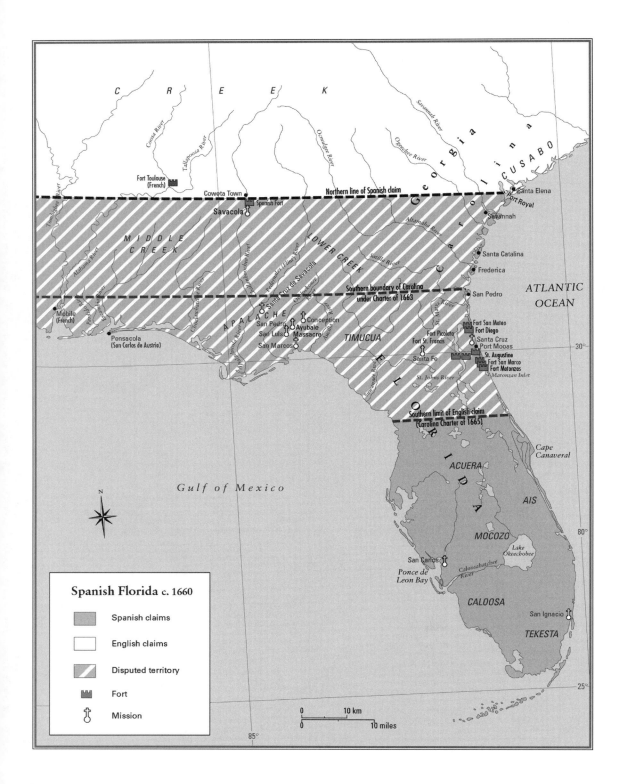

Spanish Florida c. 1660

Spanish claims

English claims

Disputed territory

Fort

Mission

C R E E K

CREEK

Coosa River

Tallapoosa River

Oxmulgee River

Ocechee River

Savannah River

Georgia

Carolina

CUSABO

Fort Toulouse
(French)

Coweta Town

Savacola

Spanish Fort

Northern line of Spanish claim

Santa Elena

Port Royal

MIDDLE
CREEK

Tombigbee River

Alabama River

Alabama River

Chattahoochee River

LOWER CREEK

Altamaha River

Savannah

Flint River (Flint)

Santa Cruz de Savacola

Sarilla River

Santa Catalina

Frederica

APALACHE

Fort Toulouse River

San Pedro

Pedernales (Flint) River

Conception

Santa Fe River

San Pedro

Southern boundary of Carolina
under Charter of 1663

San Pedro

Mobile
(French)

Pensacola
(San Carlos de Austria)

San Pedro

San Luis

Ayubale
Massacre

San Marcos

TIMUCUA

Suwannee River

Fort Picolata

Fort St. Francis

Santa Fe

Fort San Mateo
Fort Diego

Santa Cruz
Port Mooss

St. Augustine

Fort San Marco
Fort Matanzas

Matanzan Inlet

ATLANTIC
OCEAN

30°

F L O R I D A

St. Johns River

Southern limit of English claim
(Carolina Charter of 1665)

Gulf of Mexico

ACUERA

Cape
Canaveral

AIS

MOCOZO

Lake
Okeechobee

80°

N

CALOOSA

San Carlos

Ponce de
Leon Bay

Caloosahatchee
River

San Ignacio

TEKESTA

0   10 km

0   10 miles

85°

25°

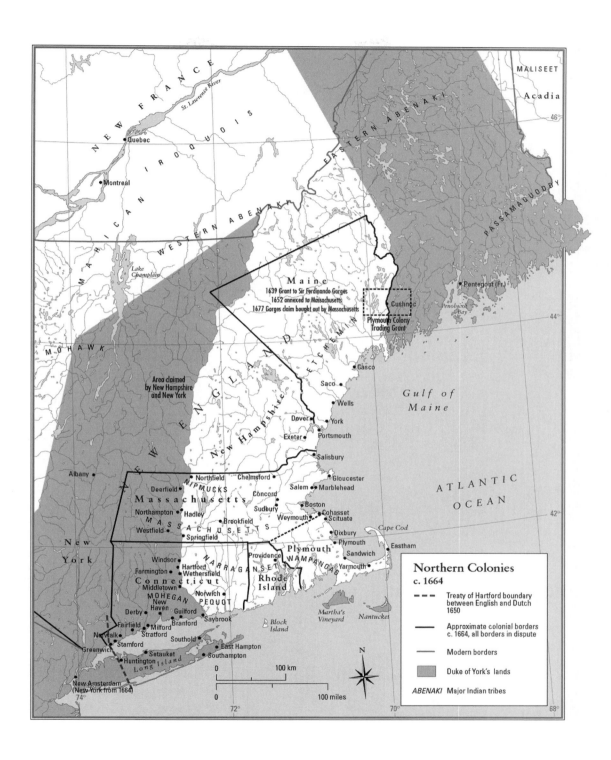

MALISEET

Acadia

NEW FRANCE

St. Lawrence River

AMERICAN IROQUOIS

• Quebec

• Montreal

EASTERN ABENAKI

PASSAMAQUODDY

WESTERN ABENAKI

MOHAWK

Lake Champlain

Maine
1639 Grant to Sir Ferdinando Gorges
1652 annexed to Massachusetts
1677 Gorges claim bought out by Massachusetts

Cushnoc

• Pentegout (Fr.)

Penobscot Bay

Plymouth Colony
Trading Grant

46°

44°

Area claimed
by New Hampshire
and New York

ETCHEMIN

• Casco

• Saco

Gulf of
Maine

• Albany

NIPMUCKS

New Hampshire

• Wells

• Dover • York
• Exeter • Portsmouth

• Salisbury

NEW ENGLAND

• Northfield • Chelmsford

• Gloucester

• Deerfield

Massachusetts

• Concord • Salem • Marblehead

ATLANTIC
OCEAN

New
York

• Northampton • Hadley
MASSACHUSETTS
• Westfield • Springfield

• Sudbury
• Brookfield

• Boston
• Weymouth • Cohasset
• Scituate

42°

• Windsor

NARRAGANSETT

• Duxbury

Cape Cod

• Hartford
• Farmington • Wethersfield
Connecticut
• Middletown
MOHEGAN
• Norwich
New PEQUOT
• Derby Haven
• Fairfield • Milford • Guilford
• Stratford • Branford
• Norwalk
• Stamford Southold
• Greenwich
• Setauket
• Huntington Long Island

Providence
WAMPANOAG

Rhode
Island

• Plymouth • Eastham
Plymouth
• Sandwich
• Yarmouth

Block
Island

Martha's
Vineyard

Nantucket

East Hampton
• Southampton

New Amsterdam
(New York from 1664)

74°

72°

N

0   100 km

0   100 miles

70°

68°

Northern Colonies
c. 1664

- - - - Treaty of Hartford boundary
between English and Dutch
1650

——— Approximate colonial borders
c. 1664, all borders in dispute

——— Modern borders

▓▓▓ Duke of York's lands

ABENAKI Major Indian tribes

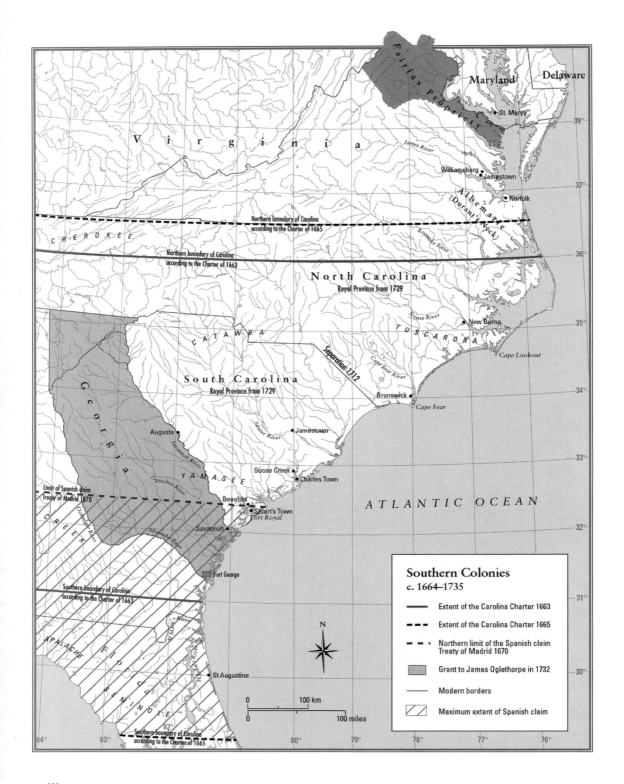

Maryland

Delaware

Fairfax property

St Marys

V i r g i n i a

James River

Williamsburg • Jamestown

A l b e m a r l e
(Durant's Neck)

• Norfolk

Roanoke River

Northern boundary of Carolina
according to the Charter of 1665

C H E R O K E E

Northern boundary of Carolina
according to the Charter of 1663

North Carolina
Royal Province from 1729

C A T A W B A

Neuse River

• New Berne

T U S C A R O R A

Cape Lookout

South Carolina
Royal Province from 1729

Separation 1712

Cape Fear River

Brunswick

Cape Fear

G e o r g i a

Augusta •

Savannah River

Y A M A S E E

Ogeechee River

Santee River

Jamestown •

Goose Creek •
• Charles Town

A T L A N T I C   O C E A N

Limit of Spanish claim
Treaty of Madrid 1670

C R E E K

Ocmulgee River

Beaufort •
Stuart's Town •
Port Royal

Altamaha River

Savannah •

Fort George

Southern boundary of Carolina
according to the Charter of 1663

A P A L A C H E

F L O R I D A

S E M I N O L E

St Augustine •

Southern boundary of Carolina
according to the Charter of 1665

N

Southern Colonies
c. 1664–1735

——— Extent of the Carolina Charter 1663

– – – Extent of the Carolina Charter 1665

– · – Northern limit of the Spanish claim
Treaty of Madrid 1670

████ Grant to James Oglethorpe in 1732

——— Modern borders

▨▨▨ Maximum extent of Spanish claim

0   100 km
0   100 miles

84°   83°   80°   79°   78°   77°   76°

31°

30°

32°

33°

34°

35°

36°

37°

38°

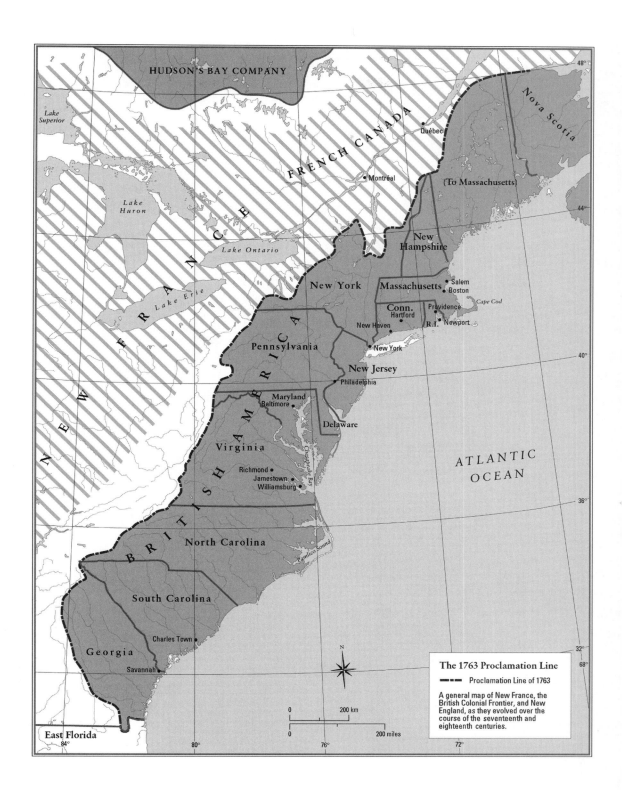

The 1763 Proclamation Line

- - - Proclamation Line of 1763

A general map of New France, the British Colonial Frontier, and New England, as they evolved over the course of the seventeenth and eighteenth centuries.

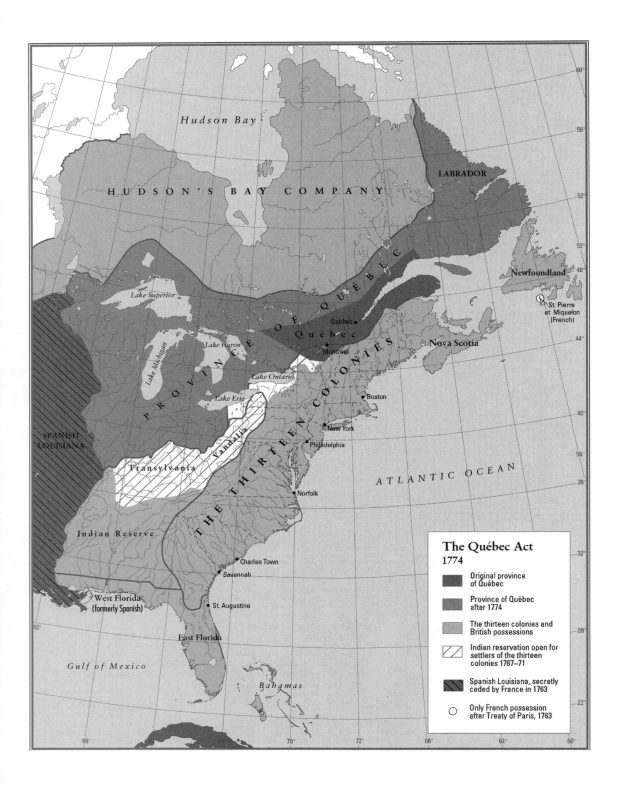

The Québec Act
1774

Original province of Québec

Province of Québec after 1774

The thirteen colonies and British possessions

Indian reservation open for settlers of the thirteen colonies 1767–71

Spanish Louisiana, secretly ceded by France in 1763

Only French possession after Treaty of Paris, 1763

Hudson Bay

HUDSON'S BAY COMPANY

LABRADOR

Newfoundland

St. Pierre et Miquelon (French)

PROVINCE OF QUÉBEC

Lake Superior

Lake Huron

Québec
Québec

Montréal

Nova Scotia

Lake Michigan

Lake Ontario

Lake Erie

THE THIRTEEN COLONIES

Boston

New York

Philadelphia

SPANISH LOUISIANA

Vandalia

Transylvania

Norfolk

ATLANTIC OCEAN

Indian Reserve

Charles Town

Savannah

West Florida (formerly Spanish)

St. Augustine

East Florida

Gulf of Mexico

Bahamas

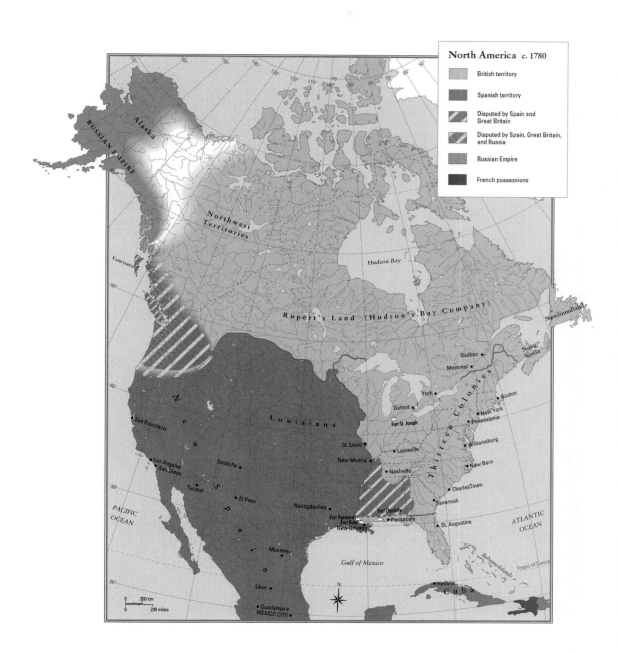

North America c. 1780

British territory

Spanish territory

Disputed by Spain and
Great Britain

Disputed by Spain, Great Britain,
and Russia

Russian Empire

French possessions

RUSSIAN EMPIRE

Alaska

Northwest
Territories

Vancouver

Hudson Bay

Rupert's Land (Hudson's Bay Company)

Newfoundland

Québec

Nova
Scotia

Montréal

York

Boston

Detroit

New York

Fort St. Joseph

Philadelphia

Louisiana

St. Louis

Louisville

Williamsburg

San Francisco

New Madrid

New Bern

Santa Fe

Nashville

Los Angeles

CharlesTown

San Diego

Tucson

Savannah

El Paso

Nacogdoches

Fort Charlotte

PACIFIC
OCEAN

Fort Panmure

Pensacola

ATLANTIC
OCEAN

Fort Bute

St. Augustine

New Orleans

Monterey

Gulf of Mexico

Bahama Islands

Tropic of Cancer

Léon

Havana

Cuba

200 km

200 miles

Guadalajara

MEXICO CITY

N

Thirteen Colonies

N e w   S p a i n

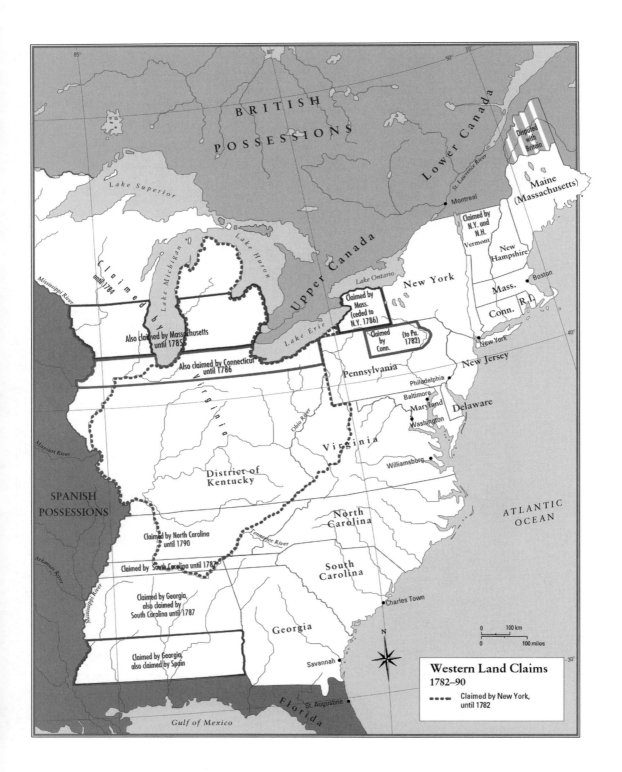

BRITISH POSSESSIONS

Lower Canada

Upper Canada

Lake Superior

Lake Michigan

Lake Huron

Lake Ontario

Lake Erie

Montreal

St. Lawrence River

Maine (Massachusetts)

Disputed with Britain

Claimed by N.Y. and N.H.

Vermont

New Hampshire

Boston

Mass.

Conn.   R.I.

New York

Claimed by Mass. (ceded to N.Y. 1786)

Claimed by Conn.

(to Pa. 1782)

Claimed until 1784

Also claimed by Massachusetts until 1785

Also claimed by Connecticut until 1786

Virginia

Mississippi River

SPANISH POSSESSIONS

Missouri River

Arkansas River

Mississippi River

Pennsylvania

Philadelphia

Baltimore

Maryland

Washington

Delaware

New Jersey

New York

Ohio River

Williamsburg

District of Kentucky

Virginia

North Carolina

Claimed by North Carolina until 1790

Tennessee River

Claimed by South Carolina until 1787

Claimed by Georgia, also claimed by South Carolina until 1787

South Carolina

Charles Town

Georgia

Claimed by Georgia, also claimed by Spain

Savannah

Florida

St. Augustine

Gulf of Mexico

ATLANTIC OCEAN

N

0   100 km
0   100 miles

**Western Land Claims
1782–90**

- - - - Claimed by New York, until 1782

BRITISH

NORTH AMERICA

Lower Canada

Disputed with Britain

Lake Superior

Montreal

Maine
(to Mass.)

Mississippi River

N o r t h w e s t   T e r r i t o r y

Ceded by Virginia 1784

Lake Michigan

Lake Huron

Upper Canada

Vt.

N.H.

Lake Ontario

New York

Boston

Mass.

Ceded by Massachusetts 1785

Lake Erie

Conn.

R.I.

New York

Ceded by Connecticut 1786

Ceded by Conn. 1800

Pennsylvania

New
Jersey

Ohio River

Philadelphia

Baltimore

Washington

Md.

Delaware

ATLANTIC
OCEAN

N

Virginia

Williamsburg

L o u i s i a n a
Ceded by Spain to France 1800

Ceded by Virginia 1789
(Kentucky)

Missouri River

Ceded by North Carolina 1790
(Tennessee)

Tennessee River

North
Carolina

Arkansas River

Ceded by South Carolina to Georgia 1787

Mississippi River

Ceded by Georgia 1802

South
Carolina

0   100 km
0   100 miles

Charleston

G e o r g i a

Western Land Cessions
1782–1802

– – – Boundary of territory
ceded by New York 1782

——— Boundary of territory
ceded by Virginia 1784

Original thirteen states
by 1782

Lands ceded by individual
states to the federal
government with date

Spanish possessions

British possessions

Ceded by Spain 1795

Savannah

Spanish Florida

St. Augustine

Gulf of Mexico

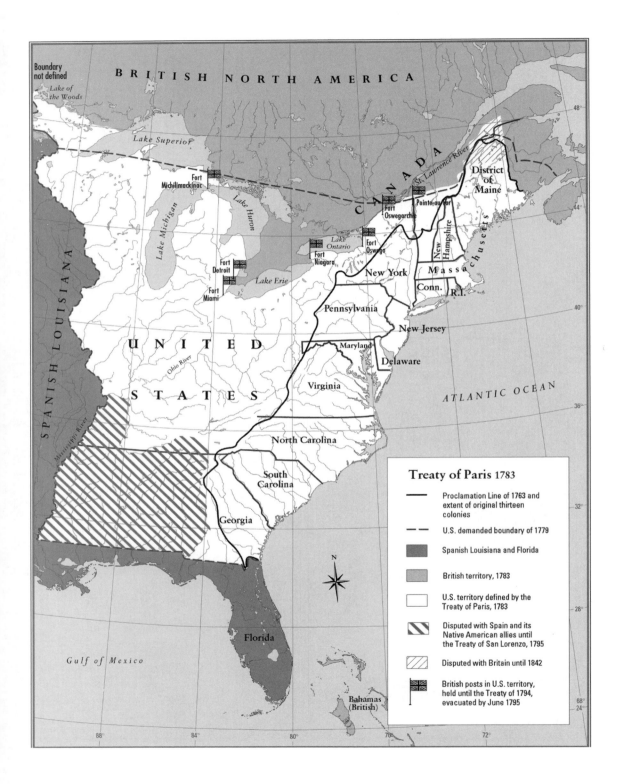

Boundary not defined

BRITISH NORTH AMERICA

Lake of the Woods

Lake Superior

SPANISH LOUISIANA

Fort Michilimackinac

Lake Michigan

Lake Huron

CANADA

St. Lawrence River

Pointe-au-Bar

District of Maine

Fort Oswegatchie

New Hampshire

Fort Niagara

Lake Ontario

Fort Oswego

Massachusetts

Fort Detroit

Lake Erie

New York

Conn.

R.I.

Fort Miami

Pennsylvania

UNITED

Ohio River

Mississippi River

STATES

New Jersey

Maryland

Delaware

Virginia

ATLANTIC OCEAN

North Carolina

South Carolina

Georgia

N

Florida

Gulf of Mexico

Bahamas (British)

48°

44°

40°

36°

32°

28°

24°

88° 84° 80° 76° 72°

Treaty of Paris 1783

— Proclamation Line of 1763 and extent of original thirteen colonies

--- U.S. demanded boundary of 1779

Spanish Louisiana and Florida

British territory, 1783

U.S. territory defined by the Treaty of Paris, 1783

Disputed with Spain and its Native American allies until the Treaty of San Lorenzo, 1795

Disputed with Britain until 1842

British posts in U.S. territory, held until the Treaty of 1794, evacuated by June 1795

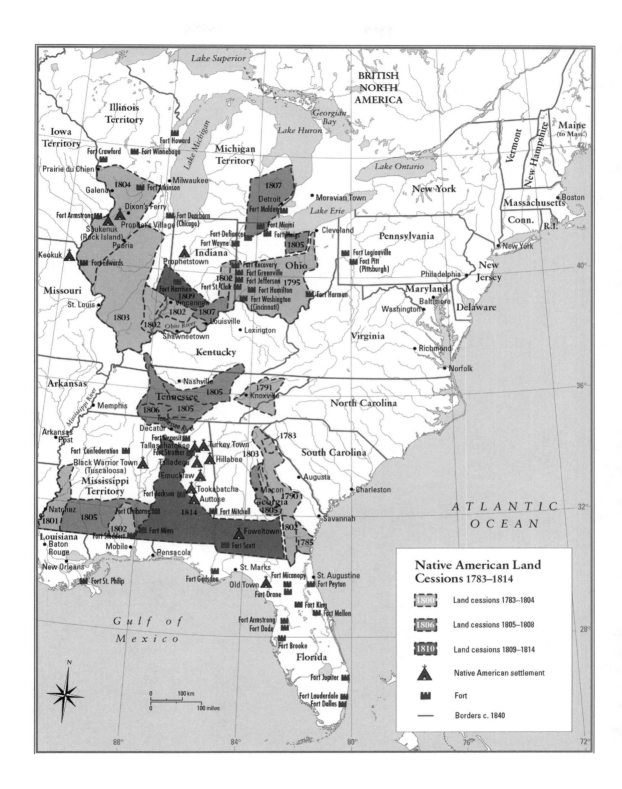

Native American Land
Cessions 1783–1814

1800	Land cessions 1783–1804
1806	Land cessions 1805–1808
1810	Land cessions 1809–1814
▲	Native American settlement
⚏	Fort
—	Borders c. 1840

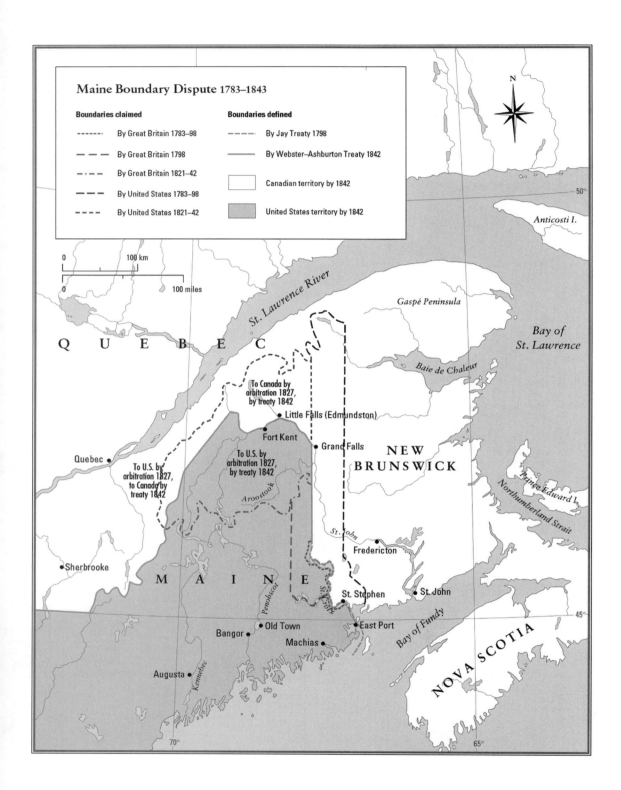

Maine Boundary Dispute 1783–1843

Boundaries claimed

- - - - - - By Great Britain 1783–98
— — — By Great Britain 1798
— · — · By Great Britain 1821–42
— — By United States 1783–98
- - - - By United States 1821–42

Boundaries defined

— — — By Jay Treaty 1798
——— By Webster–Ashburton Treaty 1842

□ Canadian territory by 1842
▨ United States territory by 1842

0   100 km
0   100 miles

N

Anticosti I.

QUEBEC

St. Lawrence River

Gaspé Peninsula

Bay of St. Lawrence

Baie de Chaleur

To Canada by arbitration 1827, by treaty 1842

Little Falls (Edmundston)

Fort Kent

To U.S. by arbitration 1827, by treaty 1842

Grand Falls

NEW BRUNSWICK

Quebec

To U.S. by arbitration 1827, to Canada by treaty 1842

Aroostook

Prince Edward I.

Northumberland Strait

Sherbrooke

MAINE

Penobscot

St. John

Fredericton

St. John

St. Croix

St. Stephen

Bangor

Old Town

East Port

Machias

Bay of Fundy

NOVA SCOTIA

Augusta

Kennebec

50°

45°

70°

65°

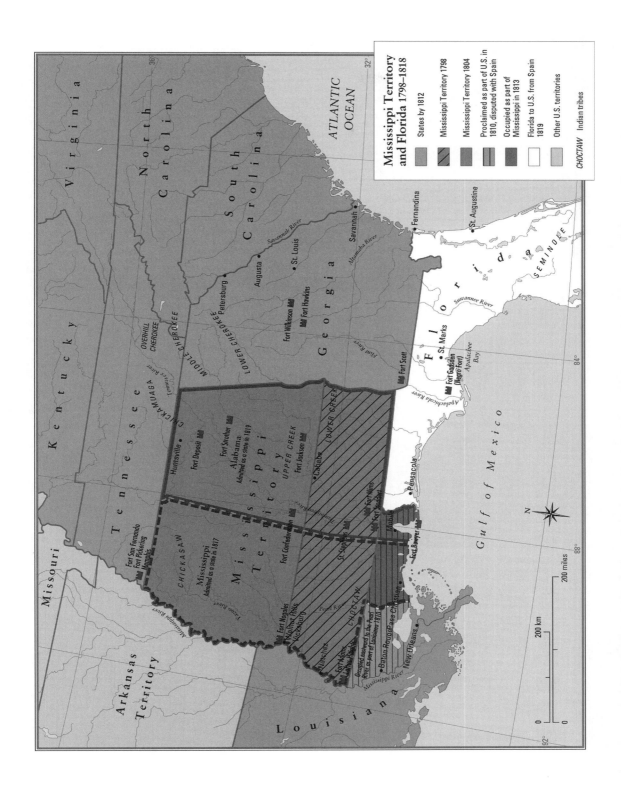

Mississippi Territory and Florida 1798–1818

States by 1812

Mississippi Territory 1798

Mississippi Territory 1804

Proclaimed as part of U.S. in 1810, disputed with Spain

Occupied as part of Mississippi in 1813

Florida to U.S. from Spain 1819

Other U.S. territories

CHOCTAW Indian tribes

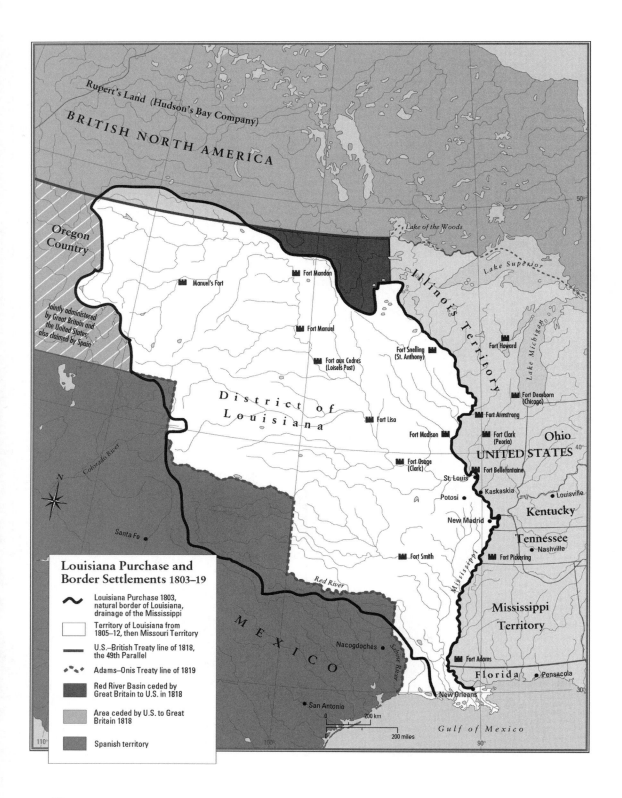

Louisiana Purchase and Border Settlements 1803–19

~ Louisiana Purchase 1803, natural border of Louisiana, drainage of the Mississippi

☐ Territory of Louisiana from 1805–12, then Missouri Territory

— U.S.–British Treaty line of 1818, the 49th Parallel

•°•° Adams–Onis Treaty line of 1819

Red River Basin ceded by Great Britain to U.S. in 1818

Area ceded by U.S. to Great Britain 1818

Spanish territory

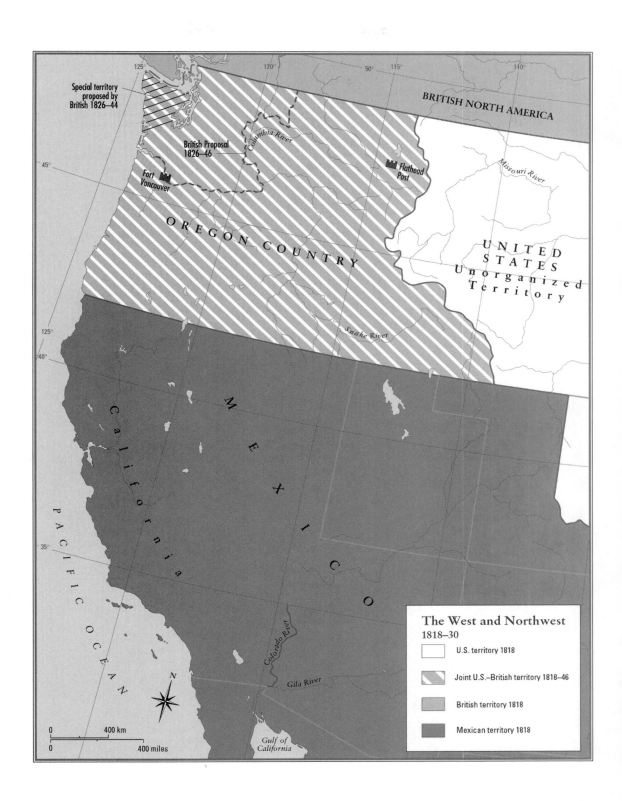

Special territory
proposed by
British 1826–44

British Proposal
1826–46

Columbia River

BRITISH NORTH AMERICA

Missouri River

Flathead
Post

Fort
Vancouver

O R E G O N   C O U N T R Y

UNITED
STATES
U n o r g a n i z e d
T e r r i t o r y

Snake River

M   E   X   I   C   O

California

PACIFIC OCEAN

Colorado River

Gila River

N

400 km

400 miles

*Gulf of
California*

The West and Northwest
1818–30

☐ U.S. territory 1818

▨ Joint U.S.–British territory 1818–46

▦ British territory 1818

▦ Mexican territory 1818

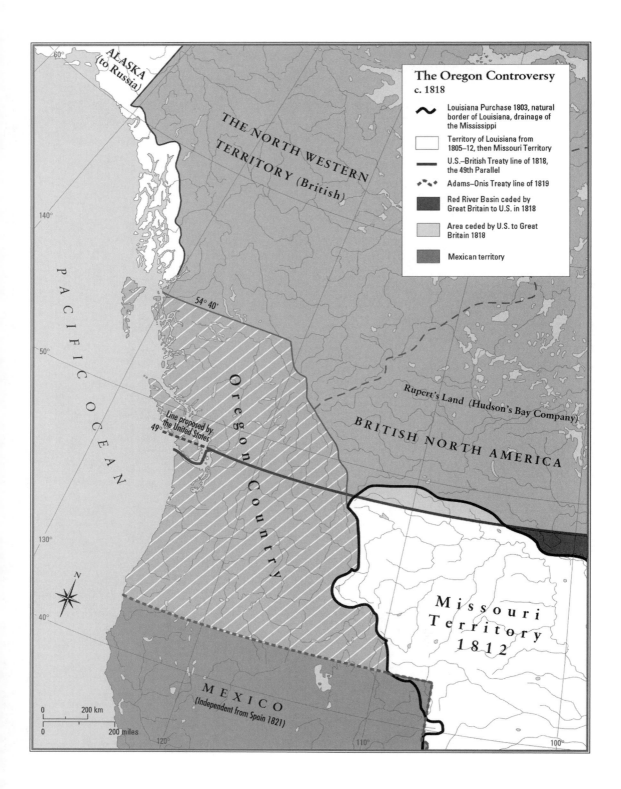

The Oregon Controversy
c. 1818

～ Louisiana Purchase 1803, natural border of Louisiana, drainage of the Mississippi

▢ Territory of Louisiana from 1805–12, then Missouri Territory

━ U.S.–British Treaty line of 1818, the 49th Parallel

◆•◆• Adams–Onis Treaty line of 1819

▨ Red River Basin ceded by Great Britain to U.S. in 1818

▨ Area ceded by U.S. to Great Britain 1818

▨ Mexican territory

ALASKA (to Russia)

THE NORTH WESTERN TERRITORY (British)

PACIFIC OCEAN

54° 40'

Oregon Country

Line proposed by the United States 49°

Rupert's Land (Hudson's Bay Company)

BRITISH NORTH AMERICA

Missouri Territory 1812

MEXICO (Independent from Spain 1821)

N

0   200 km
0   200 miles

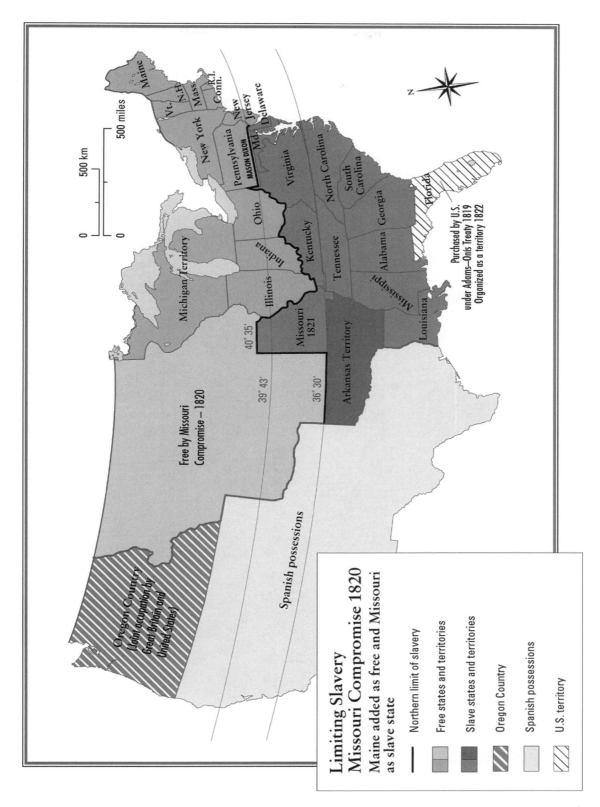

Limiting Slavery
Missouri Compromise 1820
Maine added as free and Missouri
as slave state

— Northern limit of slavery

Free states and territories

Slave states and territories

Oregon Country

Spanish possessions

U.S. territory

Free by Missouri
Compromise – 1820

40° 35'

39° 43'

36° 30'

Missouri
1821

Arkansas Territory

Michigan Territory

Illinois

Indiana

Ohio

Kentucky

Tennessee

Mississippi

Alabama

Georgia

Louisiana

Maine

Vt.

N.H.

Mass.

R.I.

Conn.

New York

Pennsylvania

MASON DIXON

New
Jersey

Delaware

Md.

Virginia

North Carolina

South
Carolina

Florida

Purchased by U.S.
under Adams–Onis Treaty 1819
Organized as a territory 1822

Oregon Country
(Joint occupation by
Great Britain and
United States)

Spanish possessions

N

500 miles

500 km

0

0

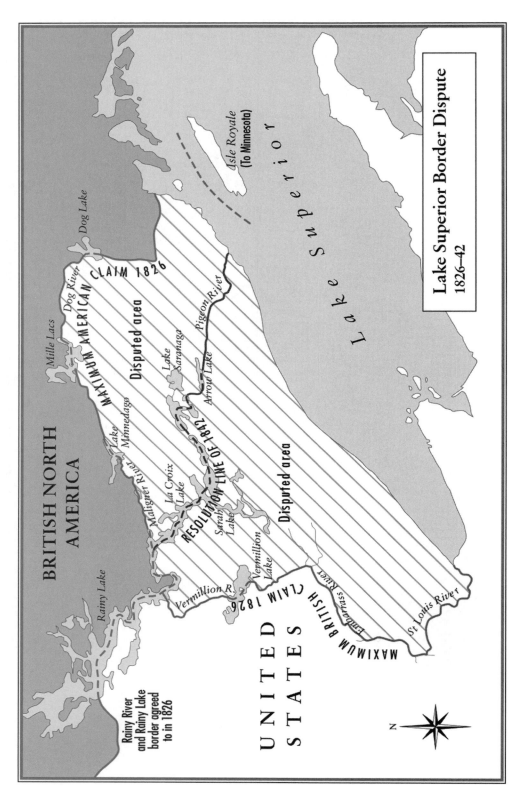

Lake Superior Border Dispute
1826–42

Lake Superior

Isle Royale
(To Minnesota)

BRITISH NORTH
AMERICA

Dog Lake

Dog River

MAXIMUM AMERICAN CLAIM 1826

Disputed area

Mille Lacs

Pigeon River

*Lake
Saranaga*

*Lake
Minnedago*

Arrow Lake

RESOLUTION LINE OF 1842

Maligner River

*La Croix
Lake*

*Sarah
Lake*

Disputed area

Rainy Lake

*Vermillion
Lake*

Vermillion R.

MAXIMUM BRITISH CLAIM 1826

Embarrass River

St. Louis River

UNITED
STATES

Rainy River
and Rainy Lake
border agreed
to in 1826

N

xxxii

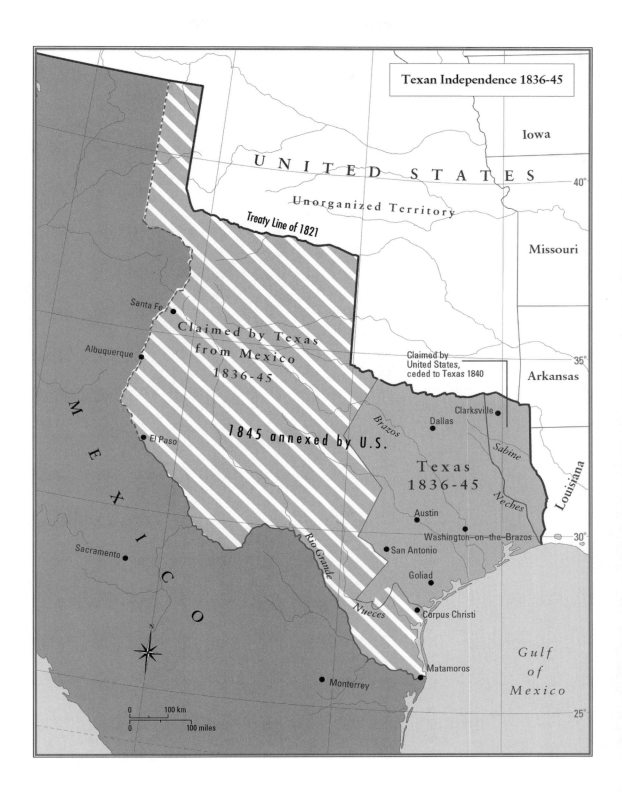

Texan Independence 1836-45

Iowa

UNITED STATES

Unorganized Territory

40°

Treaty Line of 1821

Missouri

Santa Fe

Claimed by Texas
from Mexico
1836-45

Albuquerque

Claimed by
United States,
ceded to Texas 1840

35°

Arkansas

M
E
X
I
C
O

El Paso

1845 annexed by U.S.

Brazos

Dallas

Clarksville

Sabine

Texas
1836-45

Neches

Louisiana

Sacramento

Rio Grande

Austin

Washington-on-the-Brazos

30°

San Antonio

Goliad

Nueces

Corpus Christi

Gulf
of
Mexico

Matamoros

Monterrey

0   100 km
0   100 miles

25°

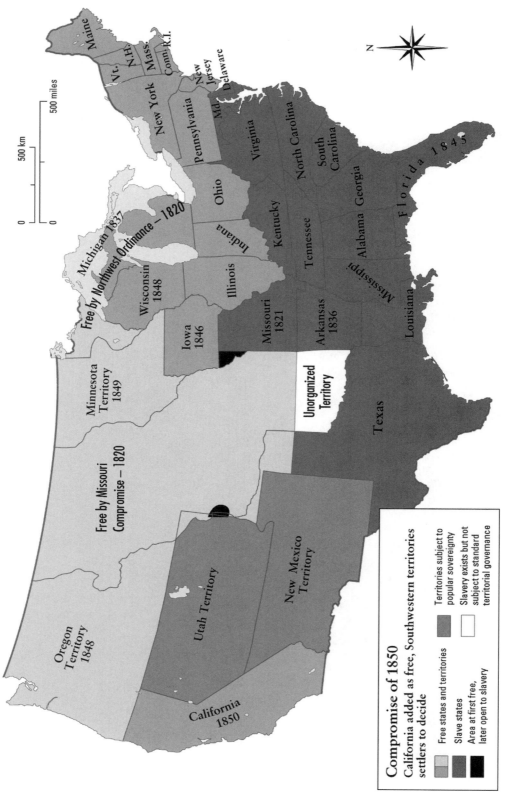

Compromise of 1850
California added as free, Southwestern territories
settlers to decide

Free states and territories

Slave states

Area at first free,
later open to slavery

Territories subject to
popular sovereignty

Slavery exists but not
subject to standard
territorial governance

Oregon
Territory
1848

California
1850

Utah Territory

New Mexico
Territory

Minnesota
Territory
1849

Free by Missouri
Compromise – 1820

Unorganized
Territory

Texas

Iowa
1846

Missouri
1821

Arkansas
1836

Louisiana

Mississippi

Alabama

Georgia

Florida 1845

Michigan 1837

Free by Northwest Ordinance – 1820

Wisconsin
1848

Illinois

Indiana

Ohio

Kentucky

Tennessee

North Carolina

South
Carolina

Virginia

Pennsylvania

Md.

Delaware

New York

New
Jersey

Maine

Vt.

N.H.

Mass.

Conn. R.I.

N

500 miles

500 km

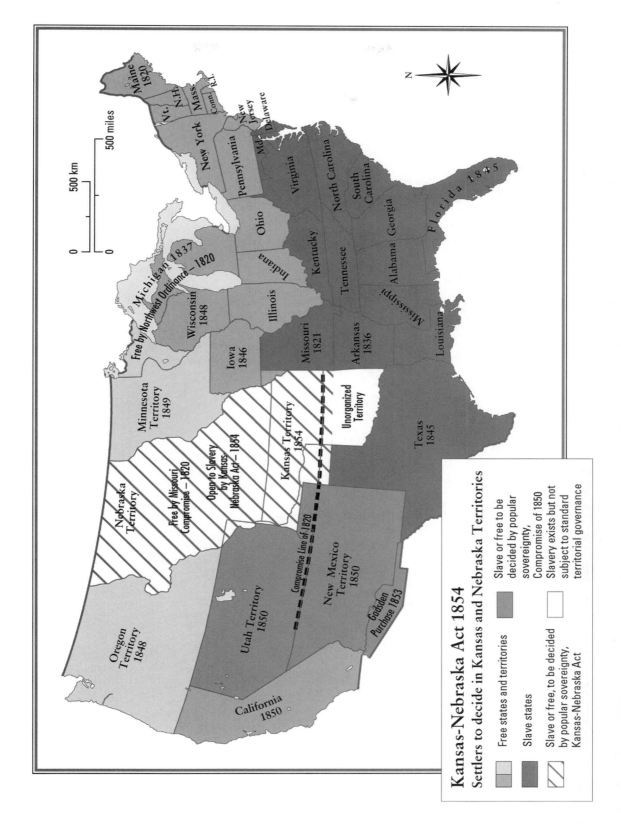

Kansas-Nebraska Act 1854

Settlers to decide in Kansas and Nebraska Territories

Free states and territories

Slave states

Slave or free, to be decided by popular sovereignty, Kansas-Nebraska Act

Slave or free to be decided by popular sovereignty, Compromise of 1850

Slavery exists but not subject to standard territorial governance

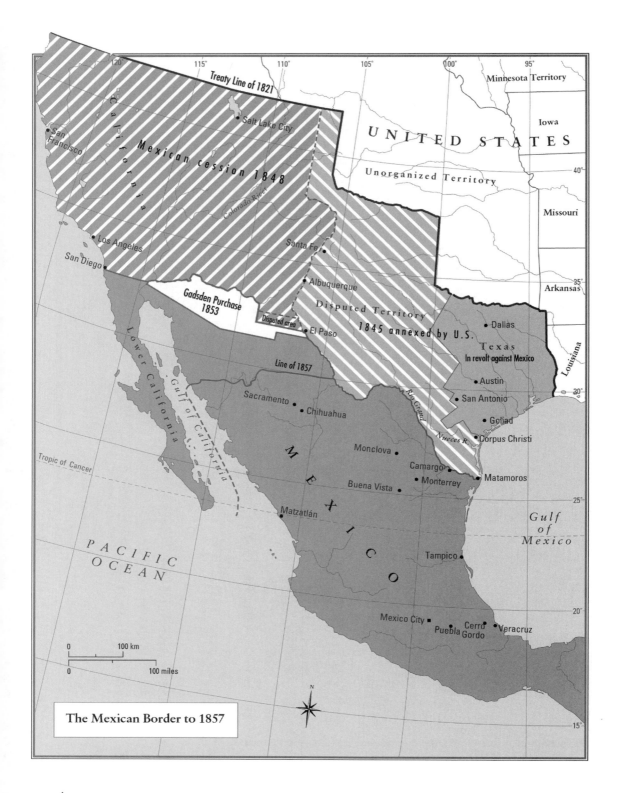

The Mexican Border to 1857

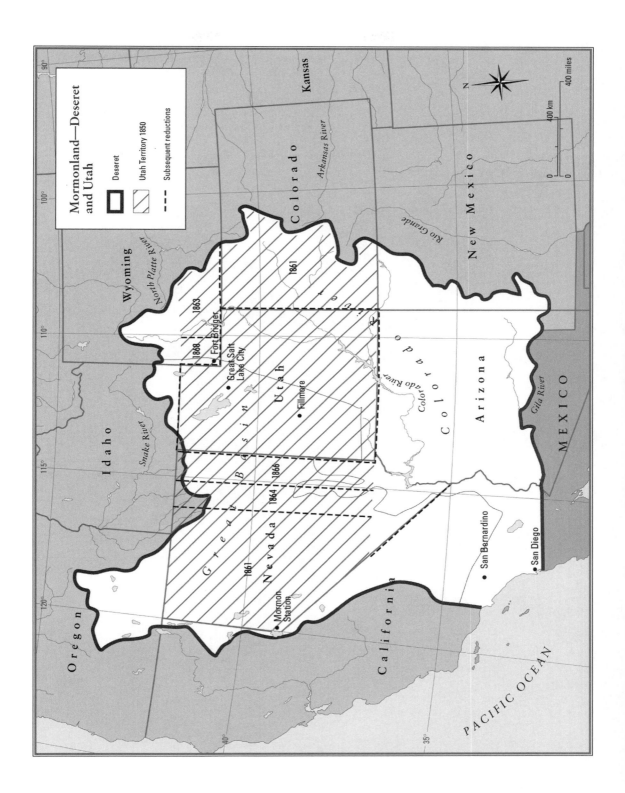

Mormonland—Deseret and Utah

- Deseret
- Utah Territory 1850
- Subsequent reductions

N

400 km
400 miles

Kansas

Colorado

Arkansas River

New Mexico

Rio Grande

Wyoming

North Platte River

1863

1868

Fort Bridger

Great Salt Lake City

Utah

Fillmore

Colorado River

Colorado

Arizona

Gila River

MEXICO

Idaho

Snake River

1861

Great Basin

1866

1864

Nevada

1861

Mormon Station

San Bernardino

San Diego

California

Oregon

PACIFIC OCEAN

90°

100°

110°

115°

120°

40°

35°

1790

MINNESOTA

WISCONSIN

MICHIGAN

Territory Northwest
of the Ohio River
1787

Conn.
Res.

IOWA

ILLINOIS INDIANA OHIO

KANSAS MISSOURI

WEST
VIRGINIA

KENTUCKY

VT.

N.H.
1788

MASSACHUSETTS 1788

NEW YORK
1788

CONN.
1788 R.I.
1790

PENNSYLVANIA
1787

NEW
JERSEY 1787

MD.
1788 DELAWARE
1787

VIRGINIA
1788

TENNESSEE

NORTH CAROLINA
1789

Territory
South
of the
Ohio River
1790

OKLAHOMA ARKANSAS

SOUTH
CAROLINA
1788

MISSISSIPPI

GEORGIA
1788

TEXAS

LOUISIANA

FLORIDA

United States Territorial Growth
1775–1960

	British Territories
	Union States
	U.S. Territories
	Spanish Territories
	Disputed Areas
	Special Status Areas

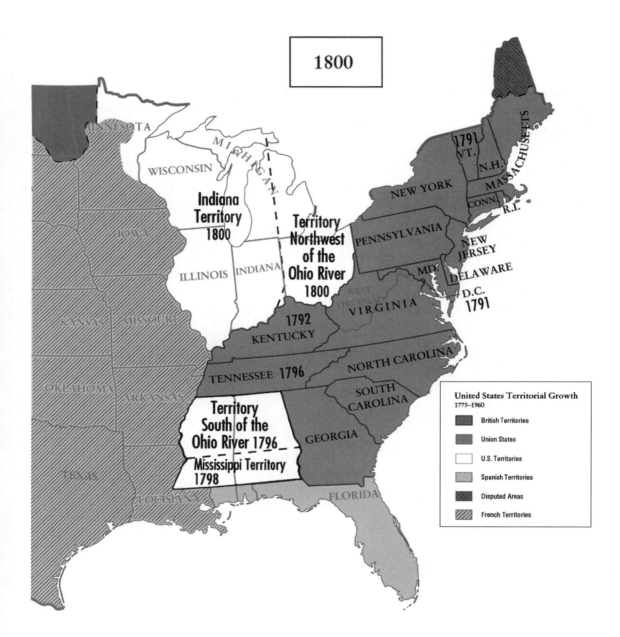

1800

Indiana
Territory
1800

Territory
Northwest
of the
Ohio River
1800

Territory
South of the
Ohio River 1796

Mississippi Territory
1798

MINNESOTA

WISCONSIN

MICHIGAN

IOWA

ILLINOIS   INDIANA

KANSAS   MISSOURI

OKLAHOMA   ARKANSAS

TEXAS

LOUISIANA

1791
VT.

N.H.

NEW YORK

MASSACHUSETTS

CONN.

R.I.

PENNSYLVANIA

NEW
JERSEY

MD.   DELAWARE

D.C.
1791

WEST
VIRGINIA   VIRGINIA

1792
KENTUCKY

TENNESSEE 1796

NORTH CAROLINA

SOUTH
CAROLINA

GEORGIA

FLORIDA

United States Territorial Growth
1775–1960

British Territories

Union States

U.S. Territories

Spanish Territories

Disputed Areas

French Territories

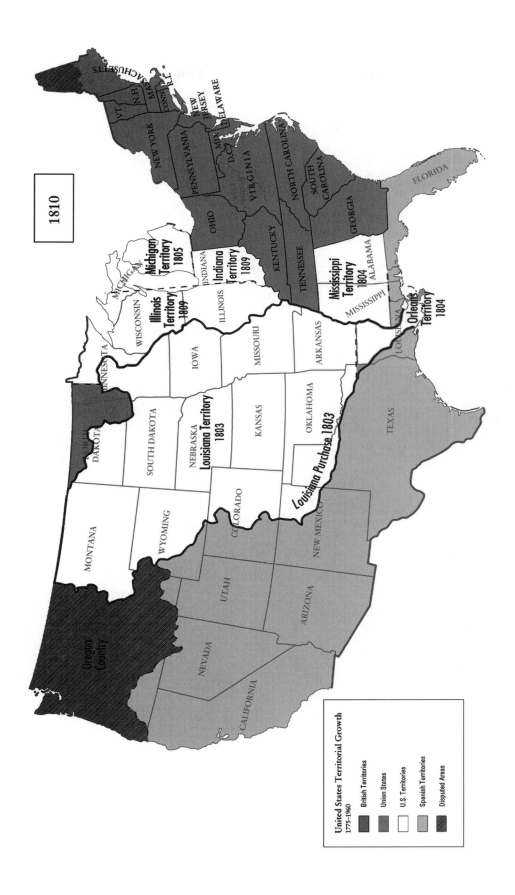

United States Territorial Growth
1775–1960

British Territories
Union States
U.S. Territories
Spanish Territories
Disputed Areas

1810

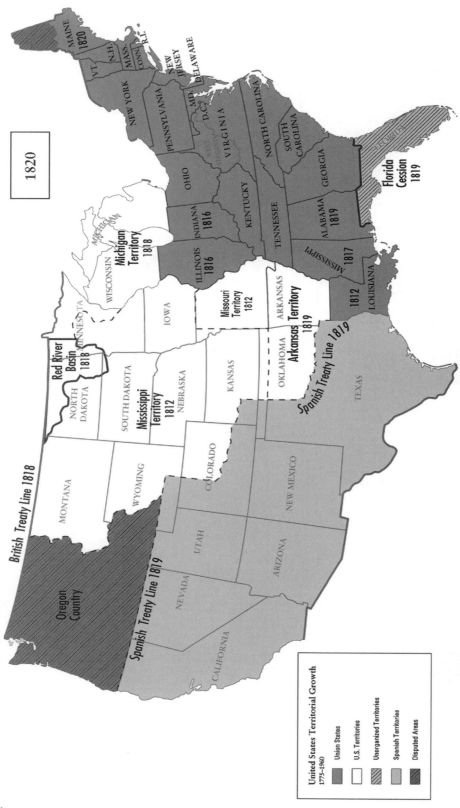

United States Territorial Growth
1775–1960

Union States
U.S. Territories
Unorganized Territories
Spanish Territories
Disputed Areas

1820

MAINE 1820
VT.
N.H.
MASS.
CONN.
R.I.
NEW YORK
NEW JERSEY
DELAWARE
PENNSYLVANIA
MD.
D.C.
VIRGINIA
WEST VIRGINIA
OHIO
NORTH CAROLINA
SOUTH CAROLINA
GEORGIA
KENTUCKY
TENNESSEE
ALABAMA 1819
MISSISSIPPI 1817
Florida Cession 1819
INDIANA 1816
ILLINOIS 1816
LOUISIANA 1812
MICHIGAN TERRITORY
Michigan Territory 1818
WISCONSIN
IOWA
Missouri Territory 1812
ARKANSAS
Arkansas Territory 1819
OKLAHOMA
Spanish Treaty Line 1819
MINNESOTA
Red River Basin 1818
NORTH DAKOTA
SOUTH DAKOTA
NEBRASKA
KANSAS
Mississippi Territory 1812
British Treaty Line 1818
MONTANA
WYOMING
COLORADO
NEW MEXICO
TEXAS
Oregon Country
Spanish Treaty Line 1819
UTAH
ARIZONA
NEVADA
CALIFORNIA

xlii

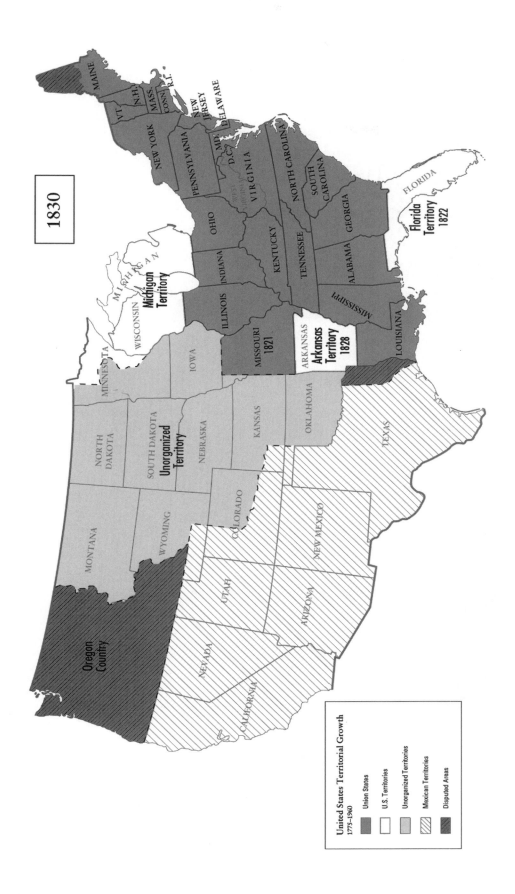

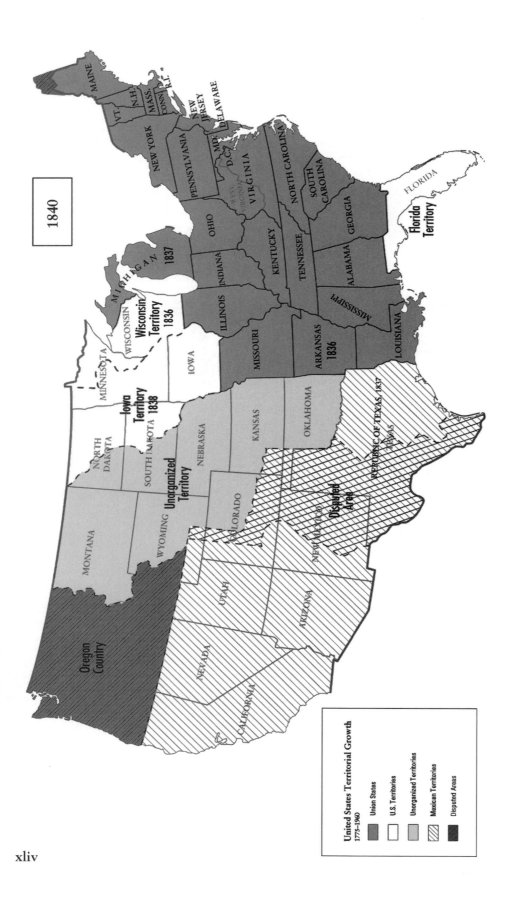

1840

United States Territorial Growth
1775–1960

■ Union States
□ U.S. Territories
▨ Unorganized Territories
▧ Mexican Territories
■ Disputed Areas

MAINE
N.H.
VT.
MASS.
CONN.
R.I.
NEW YORK
NEW JERSEY
DELAWARE
PENNSYLVANIA
MD.
D.C.
WEST VIRGINIA
VIRGINIA
NORTH CAROLINA
SOUTH CAROLINA
FLORIDA
OHIO
KENTUCKY
TENNESSEE
GEORGIA
ALABAMA
Florida Territory
MICHIGAN 1837
INDIANA
ILLINOIS
MISSISSIPPI
LOUISIANA
WISCONSIN
Wisconsin Territory 1836
MINNESOTA
MISSOURI
ARKANSAS 1836
IOWA
Iowa Territory 1838
NORTH DAKOTA
SOUTH DAKOTA
Unorganized Territory
NEBRASKA
KANSAS
OKLAHOMA
REPUBLIC OF TEXAS 1837
TEXAS
Disputed Area
MONTANA
WYOMING
COLORADO
NEW MEXICO
Oregon Country
NEVADA
UTAH
ARIZONA
CALIFORNIA

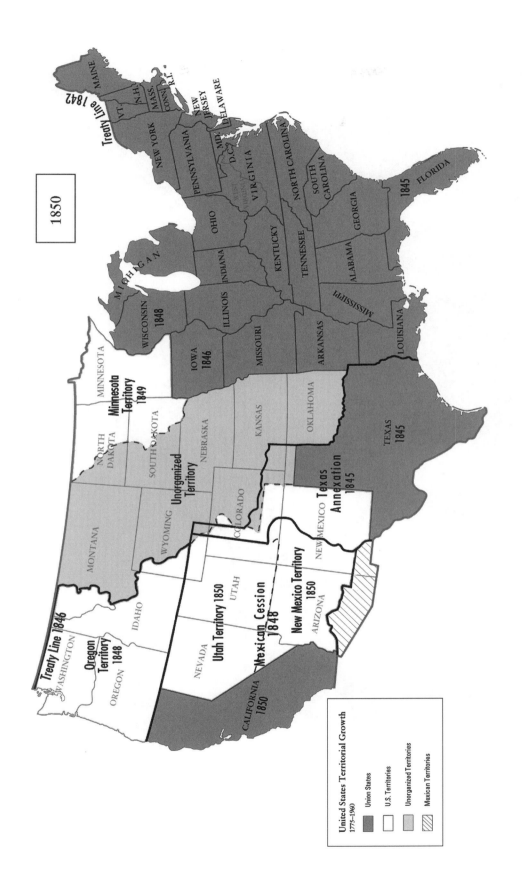

1850

United States Territorial Growth
1775–1960

- Union States
- U.S. Territories
- Unorganized Territories
- Mexican Territories

Treaty Line 1842

MAINE

VT.
N.H.
MASS.
CONN.
R.I.

NEW YORK
NEW JERSEY
PENNSYLVANIA
MD.
DELAWARE
D.C.
WEST VIRGINIA
VIRGINIA
OHIO
NORTH CAROLINA
SOUTH CAROLINA
KENTUCKY
TENNESSEE
GEORGIA
ALABAMA
MISSISSIPPI
FLORIDA
1845

MICHIGAN

WISCONSIN
1848
ILLINOIS
INDIANA

IOWA
1846
MISSOURI
ARKANSAS
LOUISIANA

MINNESOTA
Minnesota
Territory
1849

NORTH DAKOTA
SOUTH DAKOTA
NEBRASKA
KANSAS
OKLAHOMA
TEXAS
1845

Unorganized
Territory

WYOMING
COLORADO

MONTANA

Texas
Annexation
1845
NEW MEXICO

Utah Territory 1850
UTAH
Mexican Cession
1848
New Mexico Territory
1850
ARIZONA

IDAHO

NEVADA

CALIFORNIA
1850

Treaty Line 1846
WASHINGTON
Oregon
Territory
1848
OREGON

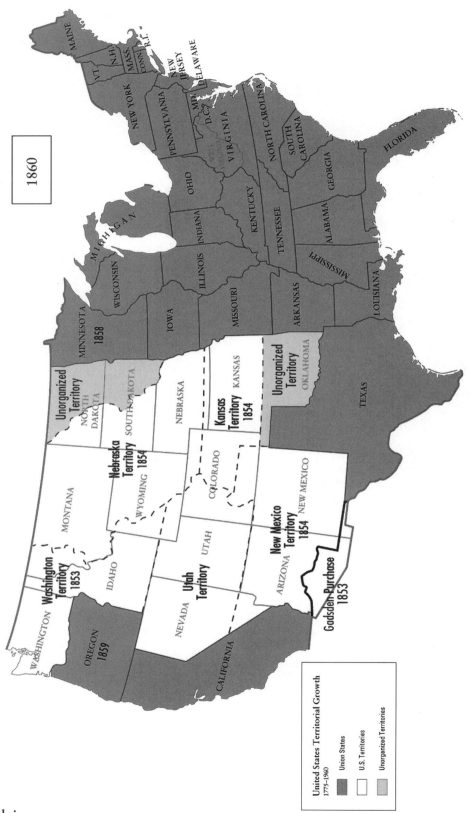

United States Territorial Growth
1775–1960

Union States
U.S. Territories
Unorganized Territories

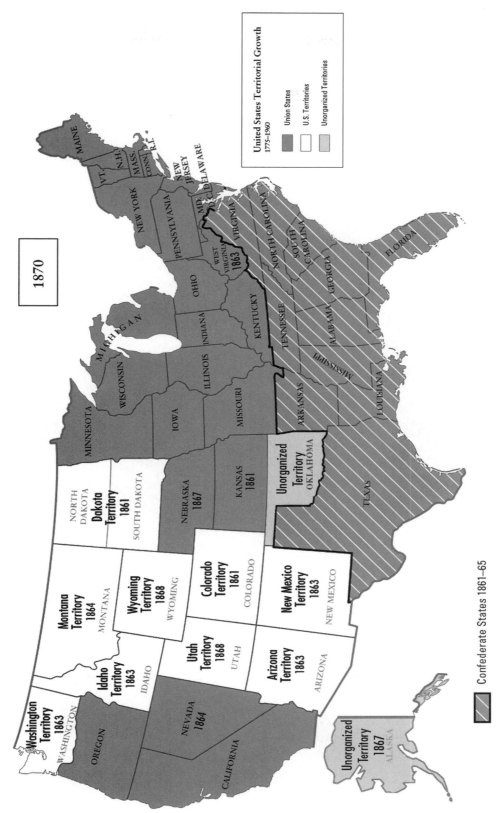

United States Territorial Growth
1775–1960

Union States
U.S. Territories
Unorganized Territories

1870

Confederate States 1861–65

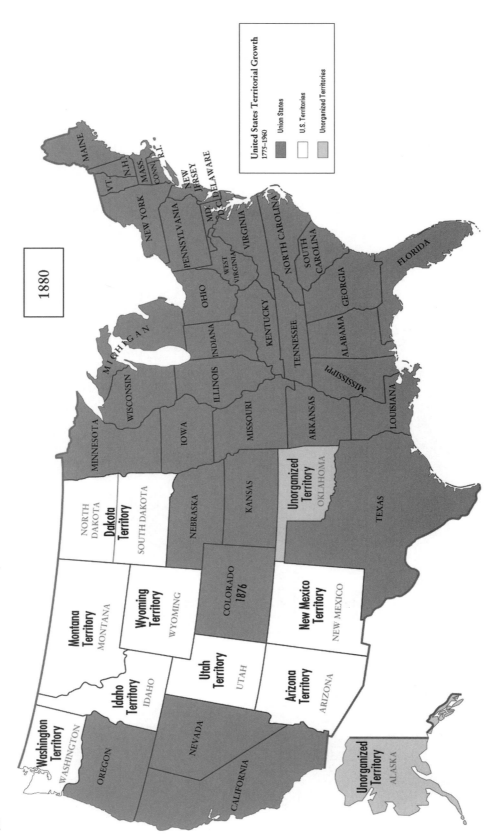

1880

United States Territorial Growth
1775–1960

■ Union States
□ U.S. Territories
▨ Unorganized Territories

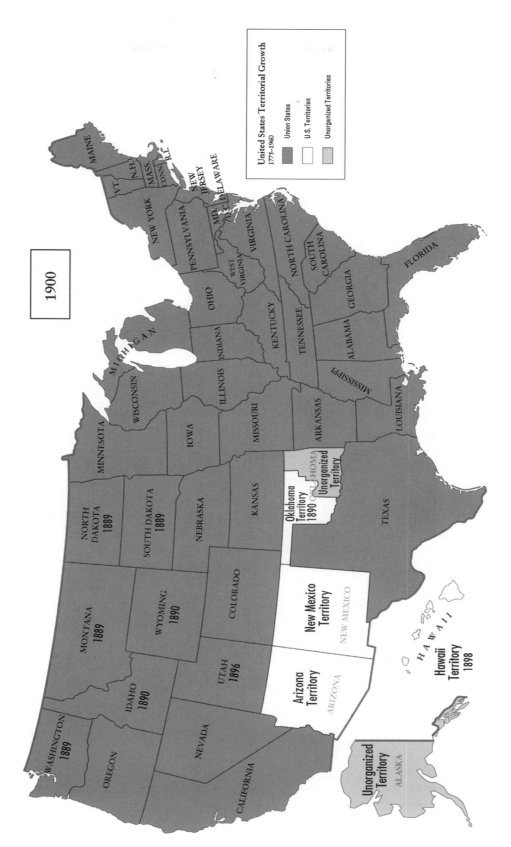

United States Territorial Growth
1775–1960

- Union States
- U.S. Territories
- Unorganized Territories

1900

MAINE
VT.
N.H.
MASS.
CONN.
R.I.
NEW YORK
NEW JERSEY
PENNSYLVANIA
MD.
DEL.
DELAWARE
D.C.
WEST VIRGINIA
VIRGINIA
OHIO
KENTUCKY
NORTH CAROLINA
SOUTH CAROLINA
TENNESSEE
GEORGIA
ALABAMA
FLORIDA
MICHIGAN
WISCONSIN
INDIANA
ILLINOIS
MISSISSIPPI
LOUISIANA
MINNESOTA
IOWA
MISSOURI
ARKANSAS
NORTH DAKOTA 1889
SOUTH DAKOTA 1889
NEBRASKA
KANSAS
Oklahoma Territory 1890
OKLAHOMA
Unorganized Territory
TEXAS
MONTANA 1889
WYOMING 1890
COLORADO
New Mexico Territory
NEW MEXICO
WASHINGTON 1889
IDAHO 1890
UTAH 1896
NEVADA
Arizona Territory
ARIZONA
OREGON
CALIFORNIA
HAWAII
Hawaii Territory 1898
Unorganized Territory
ALASKA

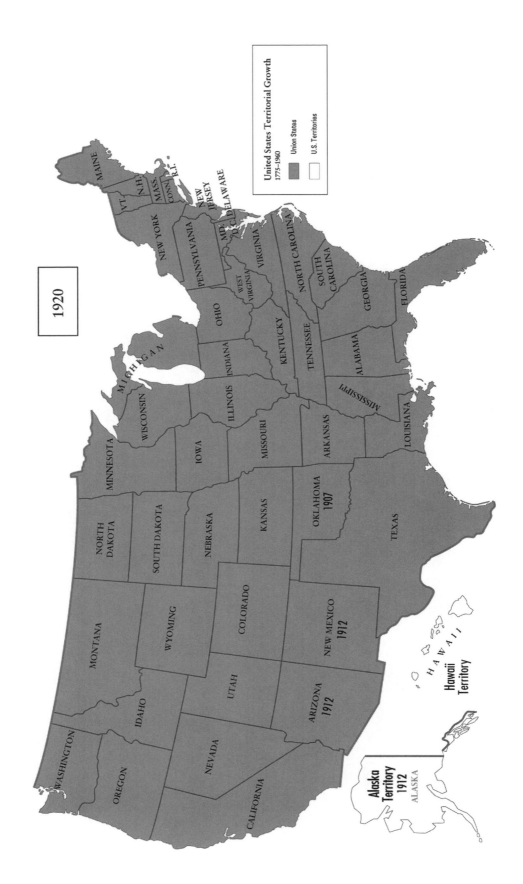

1920

United States Territorial Growth
1775–1960

Union States
U.S. Territories

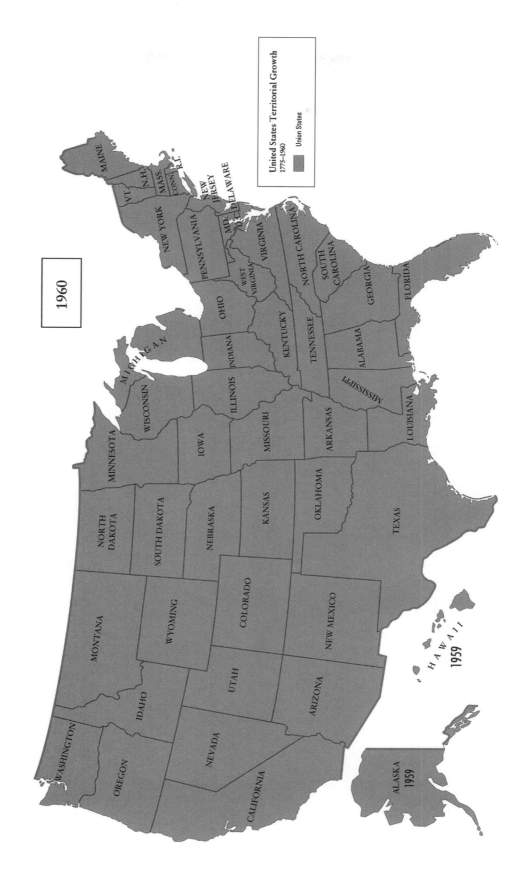

United States Territorial Growth
1775–1960

Union States

1960

MAINE
VT.
N.H.
MASS.
CONN.
R.I.
NEW YORK
PENNSYLVANIA
NEW JERSEY
MD.
DELAWARE
WEST VIRGINIA
VIRGINIA
NORTH CAROLINA
SOUTH CAROLINA
GEORGIA
FLORIDA
OHIO
KENTUCKY
TENNESSEE
ALABAMA
MISSISSIPPI
INDIANA
ILLINOIS
MICHIGAN
WISCONSIN
MINNESOTA
IOWA
MISSOURI
ARKANSAS
LOUISIANA
NORTH DAKOTA
SOUTH DAKOTA
NEBRASKA
KANSAS
OKLAHOMA
TEXAS
MONTANA
WYOMING
COLORADO
NEW MEXICO
IDAHO
UTAH
ARIZONA
WASHINGTON
OREGON
NEVADA
CALIFORNIA
HAWAII
1959
ALASKA
1959

THE STATE OF OKLAHOMA

Admitted to the Union as a State: November 16, 1907

Kerry Wynn

INTRODUCTION

Oklahoma entered the Union in 1907 as the forty-sixth state, preceded by Utah and followed by New Mexico. The statehood process of Oklahoma was complicated by the difficulties of uniting two territories, the Indian Territory and the Oklahoma Territory, under one state government. American control of the Indian Territory began in the 1820s, when the federal government established an "Indian Country" as a new home for Native American groups dispossessed by American expansion. After the Civil War, treaties reduced the Indian Territory to the area that is now the state of Oklahoma. The establishment of Oklahoma Territory in 1890 further reduced the Indian Terri- tory to the eastern portion of the future state. The debate over the proposed state of Oklahoma included not only how and when Oklahoma Territory would become a state but also whether it would be united with the Indian Territory. At the turn of the twentieth century, Oklahoma Territory was organized in a similar fashion to other U.S. territorial governments. Its constit- uents were mostly American citizens and members of Native American nations from the western plains. The Indian Territory, on the other hand, was ruled by the Cherokee, Choctaw, Creek, Chickasaw, and Seminole nations. The admission of Oklahoma to the Union united these "Twin Territories" under a single government with a state constitution that reflected contemporary political currents.

The history of Oklahoma encompasses a long period of change in American ideas about race, Native American policy, and political party organization. Its original founding as the Indian Territory reflected the virulence of the Native

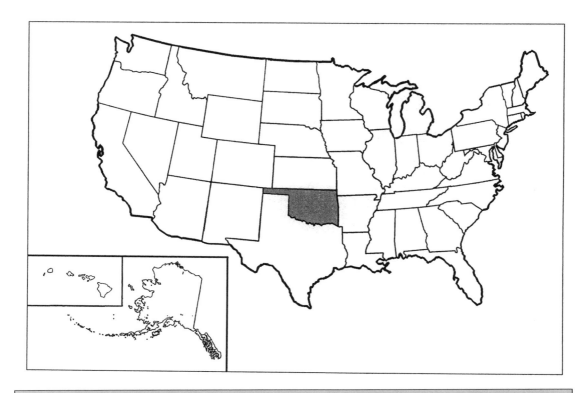

Oklahoma

Territorial Development:

- The United States obtains future Oklahoman Territory from France through the Louisiana Purchase, April 30, 1803
- Future territory of Oklahoma organized as a part of the Louisiana Territory (the District of Louisiana for a time in 1804), 1804–1812
- Reorganized as a part of the Missouri Territory, 1812–1834
- Portions of the Missouri Territory reorganized into the Indian Territory through the Organic Act, 1834
- The United States obtains more lands containing future Oklahoman Territory through the annexation of Texas, December 29, 1845
- The United States reorganizes portions of the Missouri Territory into the new U.S. Territory of Oklahoma, May 2, 1890
- Oklahoman and Indian lands consolidated, and Oklahoma admitted into the Union as the forty-sixth state, November 16, 1907

Territorial Capitals:

- Guthrie, 1890–1907

State Capitals:

- Guthrie, 1907–1910
- Oklahoma City, 1910–present

Origin of State Name: Allen Wright, a Native American missionary who spoke Choctaw, composed the word out of the two Choctaw words "ukla," meaning "person," and "huma," meaning red.

First Governor: Charles N. Haskell
Governmental Organization: Bicameral
Population at Statehood: 1,657,155
Geographical Size: 68,667 square miles

American policy of the Jacksonian era, which demanded the removal of all Native American groups living east of the Mississippi River. After the Civil War the U.S. policy of establishing reservations and forcing the acceptance of new boundaries reduced the size of the Indian Territory as Native American tribes from the western plains settled on lands in western Indian Territory. American expansion constantly shaped the history of Oklahoma. American settlers insisted that lands in the Indian Territory be opened to non-native settlement, and in 1889 the first of these lands were offered to homesteaders. By the turn of the twentieth century, American settlers who were not citizens of any of the nations of the Indian Territory had flooded the lands of the five nations established there. The agitation of these new settlers tied the Indian Territory to the Oklahoma Territory as the statehood process proceeded.

Although supporters of Oklahoma Territory and American citizens fought for the statehood of Oklahoma (often including the Indian Territory in their campaign), many members of the Native American nations of the Indian Territory were opposed to the joint statehood of the two territories. Indeed, many Native American residents of what is now Oklahoma had protested against the establishment of the Oklahoma Territory and against the settlement by Americans on lands set aside for Native Americans. To force the Indian Territory into the United States, Congress passed laws and directed the negotiation of treaties that would dismantle the sovereign governments of the Cherokee, Choctaw, Creek, Chickasaw, and Seminole nations. This legislation ended tribal landholding and made any excess land available for settlement by whites. Leaders of the Indian Territory proposed a constitution for a separate state to be made out of the Indian Territory. Although the elite of the Indian Territory joined the new state of Oklahoma eagerly and established their influence within that new state, many mourned the end of the Indian Territory. Factions within several nations opposed the changes that accompanied statehood.

Oklahoma's territorial history and its path to statehood also reflect the political and social currents of the late nineteenth and early twentieth centuries. The tension between Republicans and Democrats, which reflected regional differences between northern and southern states, affected both the territorial government of Oklahoma and the state's constitutional convention. Many residents of Oklahoma and the Indian Territories supported alternative political movements such as Populism and Socialism. Populism found a stronghold in these two territories, where small farmers felt increasingly vulnerable to market forces and the power of large conglomerates. The Socialist Party also gained a footing in Oklahoma, mostly as a protest against entrenched political corruption. Progressivism likewise enjoyed support in the new territories. In fact, the Oklahoma constitution incorporated many of the Progressive reforms that had been enacted in the legal codes of other states.

The debates in the U.S. Congress over the admission of Oklahoma and the Indian Territories to the Union elucidated all these political and social strands. Congressmen demonstrated their biases—northern against southern, eastern against western, Democrat against Republican. For many years, bills submitted in favor of statehood for Oklahoma languished in Congress. In 1906, when the enabling legislation for the state of Oklahoma passed, Democrats dominated the constitutional convention. These men constructed a constitution that reflected Progressive ideas of reform of government. The Oklahoma constitution is extremely lengthy and comprehensive. It was intended to guarantee that many of the abuses of capitalism would be impossible in the new state. The prominence of Democrats, however, resulted in part from their platform of white supremacy, and some of the constitutional process foreshadowed racial discrimination to come.

TERRITORIAL GOVERNMENTS

The Twin Territories share a history that is quite different from the histories of other territories and states. In the 1880s, their history began to diverge, and the western and eastern halves of the area that is now Oklahoma took on very different aspects. The United States acquired a claim to the land that is now the state of Oklahoma in 1803 as part of the Louisiana Purchase. At that time, the western and southern borders of the territory were in dispute, but the Adams-Onís Treaty of 1819 between the United States and Spain resolved that problem and set the southern and most of the western borders of what would become Oklahoma. The panhandle, often referred to as "No Man's Land," was added to the territory at a later date. Between 1803 and the Civil War, the United States carved territories and then states out of the area gained in the Louisiana Purchase, but the area of Oklahoma remained outside the United States long after many of these territories gained statehood.

Until the 1880s, the entire area of what is now Oklahoma remained an "unorganized" territory, meaning that the United States had established no territorial government there. This land was controlled by Native American nations. In the 1880s, American settlers clamored for the chance to settle on lands in the Indian Territory. In 1889, the federal government answered these calls by opening the first of several areas in the Indian Territory to non-native settlement. In 1890, Congress passed the Oklahoma Enabling Act, carving the Indian Territory in half and establishing a U.S. territorial government in the western portion.

The Creation of the Indian Territory

At the time of the Louisiana Purchase, a number of Native American groups lived and hunted within what have become the present borders of Oklahoma. These groups included the Osage, Quapaw, Wichita, Caddo, Kiowa, and Comanche. Bands of eastern Native Americans also hunted in the area.[1] In the 1820s an area encompassing the contemporary states of Oklahoma, Kansas, and Nebraska was designated as Indian Country by the U.S. government. The United States set aside these lands as a location to resettle various tribes the American government hoped to remove from within state and territorial boundaries. This provision exemplified the goal of the United States to annex increasing amounts of land to accommodate American settlers who had already been moving west into lands controlled by Native American groups. To facilitate American expansion and the creation of new territories and states in the Old Northwest Territory, the federal government engaged in the conquest of Native American lands.

With the presidency of Andrew Jackson, this removal policy targeting Native American groups entered a new phase. Jackson ardently supported removing Native American nations to areas outside of the established borders of the United States and concentrating them in the Indian Country. The Indian Removal Act, passed by Congress in 1830, provided funds to the executive branch to negotiate treaties exchanging eastern land for areas in the west. Throughout the 1830s, federal representatives carried out an aggressive campaign to remove all Native American groups from the land east of the Mississippi and to resettle them in the Indian Country. During the 1830s and after, this area of Native American settlement came to be known as the Indian Territory. The Indian Territory was never an organized territory of the United States in the same manner as other territories that passed through a territorial stage before statehood. The Indian Territory, in all phases of its existence, was ruled by independent Indian nations, not by a territorial government elected by U.S. citizens. Before Oklahoma's statehood, more than sixty Native American groups had been resettled on the lands that eventually comprised the state.

Among the first groups resettled in the Indian Territory were the Cherokees, Choctaws, Chickasaws, Creeks, and Seminoles. American observers of the time often referred to these nations as the "Five Civilized Tribes." The designation "civilized" was attributed to them because of such factors as the constitutional governments established by these nations, the numbers of their citizens that converted to Christianity, the existence of English-language education, and the lifestyle of some citizens, who were slaveholding planters. In the early nineteenth century, the Five Tribes made their homes in the southeastern United States. Throughout the nineteenth century, however, the desire of American settlers for land led to successive treaties that greatly reduced the landholdings of these nations. In return for ceding this land, the individual nations received guarantees that the United States would respect their sovereignty.

Between 1820 and 1832, each of these five nations signed treaties with the United States, agreeing to surrender its land in the east and relocate to the Indian Territory. Within each nation, however, significant contingents of men and women refused to move west voluntarily. Some of the treaties had been signed by small contingents of the tribes, and many Native Americans did not feel bound by the stipulations of the treaties. When Andrew Jackson observed the unwillingness of the southeastern tribes to move, he ordered the forced removal of the Five Tribes from the Southeast and their transportation to Indian Territory. Each nation suffered extreme casualties during these journeys.

After their removal from the Southeast, each of the Five Tribes established governments in Indian Territory. All but the Seminoles based their governments on written constitutions, and each established representative governments, court systems, and educational institutions. Choctaw leaders drafted a new constitution in 1834 to replace the one they had written in 1826 in Mississippi. The Choctaw nation was divided into three districts, each of which elected a chief to govern for a four-year period. By the time of the Civil War, the office of principal chief had been added to these three district chiefs. The Choctaws also elected a national council, which met yearly. The Choctaw nation had a supreme court and district courts in addition to a police force. In 1837, by the Treaty of Doaksville, the Chickasaw nation united with the Choctaw nation. By 1855, however, the Choctaws and Chickasaws agreed upon a treaty separating the two nations again. The Chickasaw constitution created after the separation established the position of governor, a bicameral legislature, and a court system.

The Creek nation was divided into the Upper Creeks and the Lower Creeks, a division dating back to their lives in the east. The Creek government was organized by towns. Each town had a local chief and a council. There were also two national chiefs and a national council, which met annually. After 1833, the Seminoles became part of the Creek nation. In 1856, these nations separated, and the Seminole government, which was not based on a written constitution, was structured around towns ruled by local chiefs and legislatures. The Creek nation adopted its first constitution in 1859. This constitution established a national council and maintained two principal chiefs and assistant chiefs. The people of the Cherokee nation suffered an extreme amount of factionalism once they settled in their new home. There was a great deal of controversy about the legitimacy of the treaty, and supporters and opponents of the treaty were at odds over the form of the new government. In addition, a group of Cherokees (the Old Settlers) had already settled in Indian Territory when the majority of the Cherokees (the Ross Party) arrived. In 1839 the Cherokees established a new constitution under which they were to hold elections for principal chief every four years. They established a bicameral legislature and a system of courts with a supreme court at the top.

Just as the Five Tribes were resettled in the area that is now Oklahoma, many other tribes were resettled in the area that is now Kansas, joining the men and women who already lived there. The Kansas-Nebraska Act of 1854, however, limited the Indian Territory to the area that is now the state of Oklahoma. Kansas and Nebraska were organized as territories on their way to becoming states. The Native American tribes settled within the boundaries of the new Indian Territory signed agreements with the United States that reduced their lands further. After the Kansas-Nebraska Act, future removals were sent to the area that is now Oklahoma, and the term "Indian Territory" referred to a diminishing area.

The Civil War in Indian Territory

During the Civil War, the members of the Five Tribes were divided among themselves as to which side to support. Many professed loyalty to the Union, but others were swayed by their connection to the South and their slaveholding system. The governments of the Five Tribes signed treaties to ally themselves with the Confederacy. After the war, as part of their treaties with the United States, the Five Tribes relinquished the lands in the western half of the Indian Territory to the U.S. government. This land was used for the resettlement of additional Native American tribes who had already been resettled once in Kansas, as well as for numerous other tribes from other parts of the United States. The treaties of 1866 also required the Five Tribes to work toward a common government for the eastern half of the Indian Territory. Although they never established a common government structure, the five nations did meet periodically in international councils.

While the Five Tribes rebuilt their governments in the eastern half of the Indian Territory, the United States resettled many groups of Native Americans in the western half of the territory. These groups included the Sauk and Fox, Potawatomi, Absentee Shawnee, Iowa, and Kickapoo, among others. Reservations were established for these groups and for the Kiowa, Comanche, Apache, Cheyenne, and Arapahoe. The federal government struggled to force the last four groups to submit to life on reservations. Until the middle of the 1870s, these tribes and the U.S. government waged bloody conflicts. Some of these conflicts were thinly disguised military massacres of Native American men and women. By 1874, military action had forced most groups to consent to live on the reservations they had been assigned by treaties.

American Settlement

By the 1880s, a significant contingent was beginning to lobby the U.S. government to open unoccupied lands in the Indian Territory to American settlement. Railroad interests, which wished to capitalize on the land grants that accompanied their expansion, had been lobbying Congress long before this time to organize the western half of the Indian Territory for American settlement. In the late 1870s and 1880s, Americans hoping to settle in the Indian Territory as small farmers added their voices to the demand. By this time, many of the public lands of the West had been offered up by the U.S. government and settled by Americans. Settlers who had not gained a stake in these lands were anxious to take advantage of the farmland of the Indian Territory.

The independent Native American nations of the Indian Territory and associations of cattle ranchers who leased portions of the territory from them opposed any settlement by non–Native American homesteaders in the Indian Territory. Native Americans throughout the territory pointed out that the federal government had set aside the Indian Territory so that it would not be overrun by American settlement, as other areas held by Native Americans throughout the United States had been overrun in the past. The treaties signed by many of these nations stipulated that, after their relocation, they would not be enclosed in any territory or state. The encroachment of white settlers on lands set aside for Native American nations violated the sovereignty of those nations settled in the Indian Territory and threatened the independent governments that the United States had promised to respect.

The cattle ranchers of the Indian Territory also resisted the opening of the Indian Territory to settlement. Beginning in the 1870s, cattle ranchers—mainly men from Texas—had established themselves in the central and western areas of the Indian Territory. Some cattlemen occupied the territory without legal title to the land, claiming areas that the federal government had purchased but had not used for settlement. Other ranchers paid taxes to the Cherokee nation for the use of their surplus lands in the western Indian Territory or leased land from various tribes throughout the western half of the territory. Both the ranchers of the Indian Territory and the Native American nations within its boundaries sent representatives to Washington, D.C., to lobby against the opening of the Indian Territory and the organization of a territorial government.

In the late 1870s, promoters of American settlement in the Indian Territory began to encourage individual settlers and politicians to seek the opening of lands gained from treaties with the Five Tribes after the Civil War. E. C. Boudinot, a citizen of the Cherokee nation and an associate of a railroad company, wrote a letter to the *Chicago Times* on February 17, 1879, advertising the existence of what have been referred to as the "Unassigned Lands."[2] The Unassigned Lands encompassed a large portion of the western half of the Indian Territory and had been ceded by some of the Five Tribes in the treaties of 1866. Boudinot encouraged the opening of these lands to settlement by American citizens. Later that same year, Levi Woodward, a U.S. Indian agent at the Sauk and Fox agency, reported that he had seen an increasing number of Americans (mostly men) passing through, intending to establish settlements in the Indian Territory. Woodward alerted the U.S. government because he felt that this movement was "assuming formidable and apparently large proportions."[3]

Throughout the 1880s, the illegal movement of American settlers into the Indian Territory continued. The promoters of American settlement in the Indian Territory came to be known as "boomers." The most zealous of these boomers was David L. Payne, who organized groups of would-be settlers who repeatedly crossed the border into the Indian Territory to establish "colonies." American military forces removed these settlers from the territory each time they crossed the borders. Between 1879 and his death in 1884, Payne organized multiple forays into the Indian Territory. President Arthur issued proclamations against this settlement, but Payne's followers, under the leadership of David L. Couch, continued to invade the territory. In addition to these organized group efforts, individuals sought to settle in the territory as well.

On the heels of these illegal efforts to settle in the territory, several proposals to open it to legal settlement appeared in Congress in the 1880s. On January 6, 1888, Representative William Springer of Illinois introduced one of the most successful of these proposals. Springer's bill would open certain lands in the Indian Territory to American settlement and establish a government for a Territory of Oklahoma. The Committee on Territories approved of a revised form of Springer's bill, and both houses debated the matter at length. By the end of the congressional session in 1889, however, the bill was stalled in the Senate by opposition to the opening of the Indian Territory to American settlement.

Near the end of the Fiftieth Congress in the spring of 1889, supporters of the opening of the Indian Territory added an amendment to the Indian Appropriation Bill for that year. The amendment approved the opening of some parts of the Indian Territory formerly in the possession of the Creek and Seminole nations for homesteaders. The bill passed Congress and was signed into law. The Unassigned Lands, also called the "Oklahoma District," were to be opened to settlement. Before the lands in the Indian Territory could be distributed, however, any remaining Creek and Seminole claims to the land had to be extinguished. For this purpose, U.S. representatives entered negotiations with Creek and Seminole representatives, agreeing that $1.25 per acre be paid for these lands. The land specified by the Indian Appropriation Act included more than 2 million acres.

On March 23, 1889, President Benjamin Harrison declared that the lands specified in the Indian Appropriation Act could be claimed by eligible settlers beginning on April 22, 1889. The settlement of the first set of public lands in Oklahoma took the form of a "land run." Land runs had very little precedent in the United States. Generally, the process of settlement occurred at a much slower pace. In the Indian Territory, however, would-be settlers greatly outnumbered homestead plots, and they had been given a month's notice to reach the Oklahoma District by the time of its opening. In preparation for settlement, surveyors marked off plots for homesteads and towns. Federal troops kept prospective settlers out of the territory until noon on April 22. These hopeful settlers gathered at all of the boundaries of the lands to be distributed. At the appointed time, the borders of the territory were opened, and the settlers flooded it on horses, wagons, and trains. Historians estimate that between 60,000 and 100,000 people entered the territory on April 22.[4] Each settler claimed a homestead or town lot.

Some settlers did not abide by the rules of the land run. Groups of people called "sooners" crossed the boundaries before the appointed time to assure their choice of lots. The claims of sooners created problems in determining the legal ownership of plots. Often, both a sooner and a participant in the land run claimed the same piece of land. By the conditions of Harrison's proclamation, anyone who crossed the line and settled before the appointed time was not to receive any land. The time when a settler arrived was, however, often difficult to prove, and some resorted to violence to bully others to abandon claims. President Harrison had authorized the use of federal troops to avert violence in the process of settlement. For the most part, this goal was achieved. The conflicting claims continued, however, and could lead to long legal battles to determine ownership of the land.

Settlers claimed lands in the western half of the Indian Territory according to the provisions of the Homestead Act of 1862. This act distributed public lands in the western United States to men or women in 160-acre plots. In return for the land, the settler had to live on the land for five years and improve the land by building homes or cultivating crops. At the end of those five years and with the payment of the fees covering the work of land offices, the homesteader would receive the title of the land. Proponents of the Homestead Act aimed to settle the American West with small, independent farmers.

The demand to make more land available in the Oklahoma Territory caused the allotment of several Indian reservations under the provision of the General Allotment Act of 1887. Often called the Dawes Act, this legislation provided for the division of communally held tribal lands among the individual members of each tribe. This process was a component of the assimilation program of the federal government, which assumed that landownership would "civilize" Native Americans and prepare them for citizenship in the United States. Under the Dawes Act, federal officials surveyed tribal lands and distributed homesteads to individual tribal members. Any "surplus" land remaining after the allotment was purchased by the federal government and opened to settlement by American citizens. The federal government created a commission, often referred to as the Jerome Commission, to negotiate with the Native American nations of the Oklahoma Territory to determine the terms of the sale of their surplus land. Further land runs were held in 1891 to settle Sauk, Fox, Potawatomi, Shawnee, and Iowa lands; in 1892 to settle Cheyenne-Arapahoe lands; in 1893 to settle the Cherokee Outlet; and in 1895 to settle Kickapoo lands. After the final run, the government moved to a lottery system to settle the Kiowa, Comanche, Wichita, Caddo, and Apache lands in 1901.

The Creation of Oklahoma Territory

When the Unassigned Lands were opened, Congress made no provision for a territorial government. Until 1890, the Territory of Oklahoma did not exist. The residents of the various towns set up provisional governments for local issues and formed committees of local people to provide justice. Temporary town governments usually included a limited number of elected officials and peacekeepers. Settlers established subscription schools, educational facilities supported not by the government but by funds raised by participating families.

The governments created by settlers were limited in their ability to govern, and some had little legitimacy. In addition, there was no overarching territorial structure to ensure uniformity of government or justice.

To address these problems, Congress passed the Oklahoma Organic Act on April 23, 1890, and President Harrison approved the bill on May 2. The Organic Act was based on Senate Bill 895, one of three proposals for the government of the Oklahoma Territory. The Organic Act set the limits of the Territory of Oklahoma, which included the area of the Indian Territory except those lands owned by the Five Tribes and the Quawpaw Agency. At this time, Congress also attached "No Man's Land," the land that forms the Oklahoma Panhandle, and Greer County, which at this time was also claimed by Texas. The Organic Act stipulated that as further lands were opened by the allotment process, these lands would be attached automatically to the Territory of Oklahoma.

The Oklahoma Organic Act also established a government for the Oklahoma Territory. It stipulated that the president of the United States would appoint a governor, secretary, three supreme court justices (who would also function as district judges), an attorney general, and a marshal. It also asked the settlers of the Oklahoma Territory to elect a twenty-six-member House of Representatives, a thirteen-member council, and a delegate to the U.S. Congress. The Organic Act mandated the temporary use of the laws of Nebraska and the division of the territory into seven counties. Guthrie was chosen as the capital city of the Oklahoma Territory. Debate about changing the location of the capital arose throughout the territorial and early statehood periods. Part of the Organic Act applied to the Indian Territory and stipulated that the U.S. court there was to be divided into three sections, each of which would have three commissioners.

The government established by the Organic Act met in August of 1890. The first legislature contained Republicans, Democrats, and members of the People's Party Alliance. The legislature passed provisions for a public school system and institutions of higher education. The legislators were perhaps most concerned with allocating the spoils of the new territorial institutions. They spent a great deal of time arguing over where territorial institutions should be placed. President Harrison appointed George W. Steele the first governor of the territory.

In addition to the Organic Act, another congressional measure promoted settlement in the Oklahoma Territory. In 1901, Congress passed the Free Homes Bill, a measure proposed by Dennis Flynn, a delegate to Congress from the Oklahoma Territory. The Free Homes Bill aided the settlement of Oklahoma by making the homesteads distributed by the federal government free of charge to the homesteader. Previously, the homesteader had paid a price that averaged around $1.25 an acre for land, to reimburse the federal government for its payment to purchase the title from the Native American group that laid claim to the land. Congress had entertained and passed relief bills as temporary measures to aid the Oklahoma homesteaders, who were often unable to pay the price. The Free Homes Bill provided a permanent solution to the problem, assisting settlement.

Dismantling the Indian Territory

In the 1890s, as the Oklahoma Territory grew in the western half of what would become Oklahoma, the federal government worked to dismantle the sovereign Indian nations of the Indian Territory in what would become the eastern half of the state. The Five Tribes had been exempted from the provisions of the Dawes Act, but, as land hunger increased, the federal government began to pressure these nations to allot their lands. As the nineteenth century ended, all the nations of the Five Tribes possessed communally owned lands. Although members of the tribes owned their houses or buildings and the products of the land on which they lived, the land was held by each nation, not by individual men and women. Policymakers in the federal government viewed individual landholding as an important step in breaking up tribal governments. They pushed the allotment process and landownership as the first step in a process of "civilization" that would make Native American men and women citizens of the United States.

White and African American settlement in the Indian Territory influenced the government's opinion about the necessity of breaking up the governments of the Five Tribes. After the Civil War, increasing numbers of American citizens had moved into the Indian Territory. Some of these men and women resided legally in the Indian Territory because they were given permits to live there by the individual nations. Others were squatters, living on land they could not legally own. By the turn of the century, white American citizens greatly outnumbered Native Americans who lived in the Indian Territory. These American citizens created problems in the Indian Territory because they were not citizens of any of the Indian nations who governed that territory and therefore were not entitled to attend the schools or use the services of the nations involved. These Americans protested the lack of social services available to them because they did not belong to any of the five governments.

During the 1890s, the federal government attempted to negotiate treaties that would allow the Indian Territory to be added to the Union as part of a state. In 1893, an amendment to the Indian Appropriation Bill for that year authorized the creation of a commission to negotiate with the Five Tribes to extinguish their communal titles to land. On November 1, 1893, the Senate confirmed the members of the Commission to the Five Civilized Tribes. This commission came to be referred to as the Dawes Commission because the chairman of the commission was Henry L. Dawes, a former U.S. senator from Massachusetts. The federal government expected the Dawes Commission to negotiate an end to the autonomous governments of the Five Tribes and provide for the allotment of their land. The Dawes Commission eventually became the tool the federal government used to accomplish all the tasks that needed to be performed for allotment to take place. The commission helped to determine citizenship in the Five Tribes, and it completed the paperwork for enrollment and allotment.

Many members of the Five Tribes strongly opposed the Dawes Commission and allotment. Initially, the leaders of each nation refused to meet with the Dawes Commission, stating their opposition to a change in governments of the territory. Elements emerged within the Five Tribes supporting allotment, however, and the federal government placed continued pressure on the tribes to negotiate. After 1896, the federal government authorized the Dawes Commission to create lists of citizens in all of the nations as a preparatory step for allotment, despite the opposition of the tribal governments. As the process of determining citizenship progressed, representatives of most of the nations agreed to meet with the Dawes Commission.

Throughout the process of negotiating treaties, the federal government in Washington passed measures that infringed upon the sovereignty of the Five Tribes, regardless of their process of treaty negotiations. In 1897, Congress attached yet another amendment to an Indian Appropriation Bill for the purpose of limiting tribal sovereignty. This bill effectively ended the tribal court systems by extending the jurisdiction of the federal courts in the Indian Territory to all of its inhabitants, tribal citizenship aside. This act also mandated the approval of all new legislative acts within the Five Tribes by the president of the United States. These two measures were a great blow to tribal sovereignty and were passed by the U.S. Congress even though the Five Tribes had not agreed to these limitations.

Congress passed an even more extreme measure when it approved "An Act for the Protection of the People of the Indian Territory, and for other purposes" on June 27, 1898. This act is generally referred to as the Curtis Act, because it was sponsored by Charles Curtis, a Republican representative from Kansas. The Curtis Act was intended to ameliorate what were seen as the poor conditions of American citizens in the Indian Territory who were not citizens of any of the nations and to provide for the dissolution of tribal governments. The Curtis Act mandated surveys of towns and broadened the rights of town residents, encouraged the establishment of free public schools, and abolished the tribal courts. It also mandated the dissolution of tribal governments in the Indian Territory by March 4, 1906.

The Five Tribes resisted allotment and tribal dissolution to varying degrees. The Creeks were the most visibly and adamantly opposed to allotment, but segments of each nation resisted the division of communal lands. Chitto Harjo spearheaded a movement in the Creek nation that became known as the Crazy Snake Rebellion. In the Cherokee nation, the Keetoowah Society protested allotment by refusing to register. Federal authorities quickly quashed overt resistance to the processes of the Dawes Commission. The Crazy Snake Rebellion was controlled quickly, and the members of the Cherokee nation who refused to register were jailed until they complied.

Still, lawmakers persisted in putting pressure on the Five Tribes, proceeding as if they would inevitably be annexed to the Union at a not-so-distant point in the future. In 1901, Congress passed a law making all Native Americans in

Indian Territory citizens of the United States. Congress would later pass legislation that American citizenship did not negate tribal citizenship, but the citizens of the nations of the Indian Territory had always prided themselves on not being American citizens. Many enjoyed the status of belonging to their indigenous nation outside of "the states." Citizenship was granted to these groups in 1901 with an eye to their participation as American citizens, not as members of Native American nations.

DEBATE OVER STATEHOOD

Debates over statehood took many forms in the years between 1890 and 1906. Congress, divided by party loyalties and sectional biases, prevented the admission of the Oklahoma Territory to the Union for a decade. Proposals for statehood also took many forms during these years. The admission of the Oklahoma and the Indian territories as separate states was proposed, as was the joint statehood of the two. For many years Congress did not entertain any of these proposals. By 1905, however, legislators had decided on joint statehood. The issue was later muddied by the addition of Arizona and New Mexico to the bill for Oklahoma statehood. Partisan wrestling then began anew.

Even more than in Congress, the debate in the territories occupied the minds and newspapers of their citizens. Residents of the Oklahoma Territory and the Indian Territory at first argued for individual statehood, but eventually the call for joint statehood subsumed this current. Many segments of society, particularly in the Indian Territory, remained staunchly attached to the idea of the independence of the two territories, but others called for the admission of the territories on the quickest terms possible.

The Debate in Congress

Beginning in 1892, delegates from the Oklahoma Territory and congressmen from established states introduced multiple bills for Oklahoma statehood. Citizens of the Oklahoma Territory, in particular, enthusiastically supported statehood for their territory. Until 1906, Congress blocked all bills on this issue. There was concern that Oklahoma would not have the funds to administer its own affairs as a state because of its lack of taxable lands. Homesteads were untaxed for a period of time, and land held by Native Americans under the allotment act was exempt from taxation for an even longer period. Also, some critics noted the small land base of the territory. The Oklahoma Territory was significantly smaller than other western states and territories. Finally, one of the most vexing questions was the issue of the Indian Territory. Congressmen wondered if the members of the Five Tribes were suited for citizenship and waited for the disposition of tribal affairs before they would agree to statehood for the Indian Territory.

Between 1892 and 1906, representatives and senators proposed at least a dozen bills to admit the Oklahoma and the Indian territories to the Union as one or two states. Until the Fifty-seventh Congress, all bills proposed for the statehood of the Oklahoma and the Indian territories died in committee. During the Fifty-seventh Congress, Dennis Flynn proposed a bill for the single state-hood of the Oklahoma and the Indian territories that made its way through the House but failed to pass in the Senate. In the next congress, Bird McGuire, a delegate from Oklahoma, introduced a bill for the statehood of the Oklahoma Territory without the Indian Territory. This bill passed the House, but the Senate added the Indian Territory to the provisions of the bill, and the House refused to accept the change.

One of the main conflicts over the admission of the Oklahoma Territory to statehood revolved around its relationship to the Indian Territory. There was a great deal of debate over whether the two would be united and admitted as one state or admitted to the Union separately. This debate was compounded by the insistence of many that the Indian Territory should not be made into a state at all, but that the United States should respect the treaties it had made with the independent nations of the Five Tribes. The supporters of the admission of the two territories as one state were referred to as supporters of "single statehood." The supporters of the admission of the two territories as two separate states became known as supporters of "double statehood."

Debate in Congress also concerned the unique nature of the Indian Territory and the responsibility of the federal government to respect its treaties with Native American nations. Although some congressmen seemed concerned at the discarding of treaties signed in good faith, others showed more interest in the "civilization" and the "advancement" of Native American citizens. During the 1906 debates, one representative spoke of the "act of dishonor" the govern-ment committed by breaking its treaties and pointed to the promises of sover-eignty the government had made, but another representative insisted that to "civilize the Indian your must give him a white citizen for a neighbor."[5] This attitude marked a change in the dominant trend in the Native American policy of the United States. Instead of attempting to force Native American groups onto communally held reservations, government officials were now urged to encourage the integration of Native American men and women into American society, sometimes forcibly.

Political influence also intruded on the question of statehood. There was speculation among some that the territories had opposite political leanings. Many assumed that the Oklahoma Territory would form a state dominated by Republicans and that the Indian Territory would be controlled by Democrats. Republicans in Congress, however, still feared that Oklahoma would be swayed to a Democratic position. If so, with the Indian Territory, there would be two Democratic states instead of one. There was disagreement as to whether a combined state would lean to the Republican or the Democratic side. A great deal of sectional discord also existed. Northerners reacted against a state that leaned toward the South. Easterners resisted the addition of one, let alone two, new western states from the Oklahoma and the Indian territories. The factionalism between eastern and western states complicated the statehood of Oklahoma and the Indian territories even further because the fates of the two territories were also tied to the future of the territories of Arizona and New Mexico.

At the beginning of the Fifty-ninth Congress, statehood bills for the territories originated in both houses. In the House of Representatives, Edward Hamilton of Michigan introduced an omnibus bill for the admission of Oklahoma and the Indian territories as a single state and the admission of Arizona and New Mexico as one state. Considerable debate surrounded this bill, but much of that debate was caused by the proposal to admit Arizona and New Mexico as a single state. By this point congressmen seemed to take for granted that the Oklahoma Territory and the Indian Territory preferred to be admitted as one state.

When the debate on this bill took place, many politicians based their decisions on party alliance. As one Republican declared, "I am a Republican, and I do not propose to shift the leadership of this House to the handful of Democrats on the other side."[6] Eastern Republicans hoped to limit the representation of western Democrats in the federal government. Although the main topic of debate was now the admission of Arizona and New Mexico, the same question had been asked repeatedly about the Indian Territory and Oklahoma. Eventually, the Hamilton statehood bill did pass Congress, but only after it was amended to allow Arizona and New Mexico to vote on whether they wished to enter as one state.

The Debate in the Territories

In the Oklahoma Territory, there was significant support for both single and double statehood. Many men promoted statehood for Oklahoma by any means, with or without the attachment of the Indian Territory. By 1905, however, the single-statehood movement was the more visible. On June 12, 1905, supporters of single statehood held a convention at Oklahoma City that drew delegates from both the Oklahoma and the Indian territories. They submitted the resulting petition for statehood to Congress.

The Sequoyah Constitution

Many leaders of the Indian Territory protested the joining of Oklahoma and the Indian territories into one state. On November 14, 1901, for example, the legislature of the Cherokee nation passed a "Memorial...Protesting Against the Proposed Union of Indian Territory, and Especially of the Cherokee Nation, with Oklahoma." This memorial argued against single statehood, which was being promoted throughout both territories. The memorial referred to the subsuming of the Cherokee nation into a state without its consent as a "dangerous menace to our common property interests and in direct violation of the most solemn treaty pledges made to us by the United States." They "denounced" the single-statehood movement as "fundamentally wrong and unjust to the Cherokee Nation and its People."[7]

In 1905 the chiefs of the Cherokee, Choctaw, Seminole, and Creek nations called for a convention to discuss the possibility of admission of the Indian Territory into the Union as a separate state. One hundred fifty-seven delegates from around the Indian Territory met on August 21, 1905. Pleasant Porter, principal chief of the Choctaw nation, served as president of the convention. The other chiefs, or representatives sent by those chiefs, participated as vice presidents. Some of the most prominent participants were white men who had married Native American women. Others were members of the Five Tribes who hoped to prove their political prowess to constituents. The delegates at this convention approved a constitution for a state to be called Sequoyah, named after the man who invented the Cherokee syllabary.

A few men are generally given credit for drafting most of the Sequoyah constitution—Charles N. Haskell, William H. Murray, W. W. Hastings, John R. Thomas, and Robert L. Owen.[8] As statehood approached, these men became prominent leaders of the Democratic Party in both territories. The Sequoyah constitution strengthened their claim to power because it incorporated many of the changes they wished to see in the Oklahoma constitution. The first part of the constitution included specific guarantees of individual rights, expanding the federal Bill of Rights to approximately thirty sections. The constitution followed the convention of establishing three branches of government. It also directed the first legislature consider the topic of women's suffrage, established schools and a university, enacted protective measures for miners, prohibited the sale of alcohol, and (in its longest section) regulated corporations. The Sequoyah constitution, however, stipulated that separate schools must be maintained for African American children.[9]

The voters of the Indian Territory approved the Sequoyah constitution on November 7, 1905. More than sixty thousand people voted in the election, approving the constitution by a large majority.[10] Voters in this election also selected four delegates, two Democrats and two Republicans, to take the constitution to Congress. The U.S. Congress, however, had already reached consensus on the issue of statehood, preferring proposals that mandated joint statehood for the two territories. To many participants in the Sequoyah convention, this decision came as no surprise. Many men in both territories suspected that Congress would bring the Oklahoma and the Indian territories into the Union together, and the increasing number of single-statehood conventions threw their support behind that plan.

Although the Sequoyah constitution was not accepted by the U.S. Congress, it benefited the leaders of Indian Territory when it came time to participate in the joining of the two territories. The Sequoyah convention provided an arena where the future state leaders from the Indian Territory could meet and establish political relationships. The constitution also set a precedent for the inclusion of new, progressive ideas about government. Much of the Sequoyah constitution was included in the eventual Oklahoma constitution. Finally, the Sequoyah movement protested the inclusion of the Indian Territory in the state of Oklahoma. Although many undoubtedly assumed that single statehood would win the day, others surely hoped that their plea for a separate state would be heeded.

The Oklahoma Enabling Act

Congress passed the Oklahoma Enabling Act on June 16, 1906. This act joined the Oklahoma and the Indian territories and directed their citizens to elect delegates to a convention to draft a constitution. Fifty-five delegates were to be sent by each of the territories, and two were to be elected by the Osage nation. The Enabling Act instructed these delegates to establish a republican form of government and to guarantee religious freedom and the right to vote regardless of race. The act also stipulated that prohibition be mandated in the Indian Territory and the Osage nation for twenty-one years. Guthrie, the capital of Oklahoma Territory, was to be the state capital until 1913, when the citizens of the state could elect to move it elsewhere.

The Enabling Act authorized men over the age of twenty-one, both American citizens and members of Native American groups within the boundaries of the proposed state, to vote. The governor, the chief justice, and the secretary of the Oklahoma Territory were to apportion the Oklahoma Territory into election districts, and they were to appoint a committee to do the same in the Osage nation. In the Indian Territory, the commissioner to the Five Civilized Tribes and two judges of the U.S. court in the Indian Territory were to establish the districts. The two territories responded to the enabling law, electing delegates and convening a constitutional convention.

POLITICS

The political structures of the Oklahoma and the Indian territories differed greatly until statehood. In the western half of the future state, many national political parties battled for dominance, but in the eastern half, tribal governments held elections in which their own parties participated. Whereas the national political parties had meaning for the residents of the Indian Territory and many hoped to play prominent roles in those parties at statehood, elections in the Indian Territory functioned within separate party systems. Participation in tribal government was limited to citizens of the nation, so the American citizens living in the Indian Territory could not vote in these elections.

The federal government increasingly attempted to assert its influence over the Indian Territory after the Civil War. An Indian agent at Muskogee provided federal services to all of the nations. White settlers who were not citizens of the various nations focused their political attentions on gaining federal positions in the Indian Territory. The men who filled these positions were also appointed by the president of the United States, and, therefore, were usually Republicans. Many of the American settlers in the Indian Territory, however, were southerners who were loyal to the Democratic Party. After statehood, many members of the Five Tribes, with their southern roots, joined the Democratic Party.

Despite the differences between the two territories, common factors tied them together. In both places, the Republican Party controlled patronage positions. Sectional biases, north and south, helped to determine party affiliation. The reform movements supported by farmers and laborers persisted in both territories. The majority of residents in both places had settled within the last few generations, claiming land that was purchased or stolen from the Native American groups who became their neighbors. Throughout the two territories, the members of these Native American nations persisted in making their agendas known to the state and federal government. Sadly, racism directed at African American residents also permeated both territories, with the segregationist impulse increasing as statehood neared.

Political Parties in the Territories

In terms of territorial political offices, the Republican Party dominated the appointed and elected government of Oklahoma Territory. Seven of the eight delegates elected to the U.S. Congress were Republican, and the majority of elected offices in the territory went to Republicans as well.[11] The Republicans enjoyed great support because of the prevalence of settlers from northern areas of the United States and the votes of African American settlers in the territory. The appointed officials in the territory were also often Republican because Republicans occupied the White House for thirteen of the seventeen years of the Oklahoma Territory's existence. Eight of the nine governors of the Oklahoma Territory were Republican.

Throughout the territorial period, however, the Democratic and Populist parties were quite active, and they kept the Republican Party from dominating the politics of Oklahoma. Of the eight legislatures elected during Oklahoma's territorial phase, Republicans controlled only three.[12] Republicans generally claimed a plurality of the seats but often lacked a clear majority. The Populists were a major force in limiting the dominance of the Republican Party. Whether alone or allied with each other, the Democratic and Populist forces swayed the votes of many Oklahomans in the 1890s. By 1902, however, the participation of the People's Party in elections decreased.[13]

The Socialist Party also appeared in Oklahoma, running candidates first in the elections of 1900. Socialists rejected much of the structure of party politics that engaged Republicans and Democrats. Whereas the two main parties often engaged in partisan issues, avoiding debate on weightier topics that might divide their constituencies, the Socialist Party supported a platform that called for several reform measures. Included in these reforms were "universal suffrage, the initiative and referendum, tax reform on a graduated basis, the eight-hour day on public works, compulsory education with state-supplied texts, and the acceptance of some forms of state enterprise."[14] When the Oklahoma constitution was written, it contained some of these reforms, also called for by later Progressive reformers. Although the Socialist Party remained small, it influenced the politics of other parties.

In addition to these political parties, special interest groups of farmers and laborers also played prominent roles in the politics of the Oklahoma and Indian territories and in the constitutional convention. Miners in the eastern part of the state joined the United Mine Workers Association in the late 1890s. Peter Hanraty, later the vice president of the constitutional convention, was a leader of this union. As the twentieth century began, Oklahoma workers formed increasing numbers of labor unions. In 1903 these groups joined together under the umbrella of the Twin Territories Federation of Labor.

Farmers also united in larger groups to protest the uncertainty of their situation. They faced the problems of growing indebtedness, lack of capital, and the instability of transportation. The Farmers Alliance formed branches in the Oklahoma and the Indian territories during the 1890s. Later, the Farmers' Union joined farmers together in protest. The Farmers' Union worked mainly to counter the economic pitfalls of the capitalist system through cooperative efforts, but leaders of the Farmers' Union did move into politics. Farmers and laborers joined in suggesting their own agenda for the constitutional convention.

By the end of the territorial period, the Republican Party in Oklahoma had been weakened by resentment at patronage politics and the debates surrounding statehood. Oklahoma residents also resented the tendency of presidents to appoint leaders for the territory who came from other states. Even among Republicans, the division between those who whole-heartedly supported the national party and those who sought what they believed to be best for the Oklahoma Territory created factionalism within the Republican Party there. This factionalism outlived the specific context of its origin—the Free Silver issue of the 1890s—to become a serious division between two wings of the Republican Party.[15]

Political Parties and Racism

The Republican Party's popularity among white residents of the Oklahoma Territory also waned at the turn of the twentieth century as the Democratic Party turned toward what one historian has called "a politics of race."[16] The Republican Party in Oklahoma owed much of its success to the support of African American voters. In return, Republicans ran black men for local elective offices and rewarded African American supporters with patronage positions. African American individuals and communities also maintained an active, vocal presence in the Republican Party. In this respect, Oklahoma Territory was quite different from the southern states from which many of its residents came. In states throughout the South after Reconstruction, white individuals and governments, particularly within the Democratic Party, attempted to take away the rights of African Americans. Southern states enacted "Jim Crow" laws, obstructed African American voting and landholding, and used violence to enforce a racist, one-party system.

Although Oklahoma was, by comparison, a politically free society for African American men, racism still permeated the political system in many ways. Increasingly during the 1890s, Democrats used racial politics to draw white Oklahomans to their political party. Democrats employed arguments that played on the fear of racial equality between African Americans and whites to pressure white voters into voting with their race instead of with their political party.

These arguments also proved fruitful for Democrats in the Indian Territory. Before the Civil War, many members of the Five Tribes held slaves. After the Civil War, as a part of their treaties with the United States, the tribes were asked to accept the freedmen of their individual nations as equal citizens. Each nation accomplished or resisted this task to a varying degree. The Seminole and Creek nations integrated freedmen in their societies to the greatest degree. Freedmen participated in Seminole government in prominent positions. At the other end of the spectrum, the Cherokee and Choctaw nations had given freedmen the right to vote but often obstructed that right and barred them from serving in public office. The Chickasaw nation refused to adopt its freedmen at all. Even though the Democratic Party might have been resisted in Indian Territory, some of its racial arguments maligning African Americans worked there as well.[17]

By the time of statehood, some members of the Republican Party had turned away from the egalitarianism that characterized the attitudes of members who sought racial equality. The Republicans began to split into factions, one supporting segregation and discrimination against African Americans and one still seeking their participation. As the constitutional convention approached, the Republican Party was crippled by this fundamental disagreement in its ranks. Those who were left to defend African American civil rights could not mount an effective resistance to the segregationist designs of the Democrats.

Democrats fought for segregation. In 1901, they successfully pushed a law mandating separate schools through the legislature. Although other measures, such as segregated rail cars, had failed to pass, de facto segregation was instituted in many situations. At the time of the constitutional convention, the Democrats made their ultimate designs known. When they produced "Suggestions for a Platform" in preparation for the convention, the second suggestion noted that the Democrats "favor[ed] laws providing for separate schools, separate coaches and separate waiting rooms for the negro race."[18]

THE CONSTITUTION

At the November 4 elections for delegates to the Oklahoma state constitutional convention, the Democratic Party won a definitive victory over the Republican Party, sending one hundred Democratic delegates compared with only twelve Republicans. This showing resulted not only from the strong Democratic support in the Indian Territory, but also from resentment at the patronage Republicans had enjoyed in the Oklahoma Territory. There was also dissatisfaction with the Oklahoma Territory government and irritation at the selection of territorial appointees made by the federal government. Federal positions in the Indian Territory had also largely gone to Republicans in those years, so dissatisfaction in both territories was often directed against a Republican government.

As statehood neared, the Progressive movement became more prominent in Oklahoma politics. As a national movement, Progressivism had already captured the interest of other areas of the country. Progressivism is the term historians have used to describe a myriad of political and social movements that occurred between the 1890s and the 1920s. In the United States the Progressive movement arose in response to the conditions caused by industrialization and urbanization and sought, through various means, to ameliorate the problems of American society. Concerns of the Progressive movement included distrust of corporations and the concentration of political and economic power, movements for prohibition and women's suffrage, and attempts to alleviate poor working conditions. Reformers of the Progressive era generally thought that it was possible to solve society's problems through careful study and concerted effort.

By the turn of the century, residents of the Twin Territories were highly skeptical of the motives of trusts—huge conglomerates accused of controlling markets—because of their alleged price fixing and abuses of the public's good faith. The railroads were the most prominent examples of trusts in the Oklahoma and the Indian territories, and residents there had complained about the railroads' abuses for years. Many Progressives were also involved with the issue of consumer safety. Their pronouncements carried a working-class tone of pride in manual labor and agriculture. Factions of small businessmen, farmers, and laborers supported Progressive ideas. Charles N. Haskell, the future governor of the state of Oklahoma, categorized workers as "producers" and trusts as "parasites," a delineation that has stuck in Oklahoma's mythology.[19]

The constitutional convention convened on November 20, 1906. The men of the Sequoyah Convention played a prominent role. The delegates elected men to the offices of the convention as one of their first orders of business. William H. "Alfalfa Bill" Murray of Tishomingo was elected president of the proceedings, Peter Hanraty of McAlester was elected vice president, and John Young of Lawton was elected secretary. Other prime positions were allotted to men who served as the chairmen of committees for drafting the various provisions of the constitution. Much of the constitution was drawn from documents such as the Sequoyah constitution or suggestions made by labor and agricultural groups, which had gained support even before the convention. Charles N. Haskell, a participant in the Sequoyah Convention and the future governor of Oklahoma, also played a prominent role in the convention as a negotiator and coordinator of the Democratic Party.

The Oklahoma constitution created by the delegates maintained many of the standard features of state constitutions. It established three branches of government with powers that balanced each other, a guarantee of individual rights, and an infrastructure for the state. The elections for governor were to be held in years that were not years of presidential elections, and the governor was not allowed to serve two consecutive terms. The legislative branch was to be the strongest, with members of the House of Representatives serving two-year terms and members of the Senate serving four-year terms. The constitution also incorporated some new political tools, including the power of initiative and referendum for the state's voters. The power of initiative meant that when 8 percent of the voters in the state signed a petition, they could propose legislative measures, and 15 percent could propose a constitutional amendment. The power of referendum meant that 5 percent of voters signing petitions for a referendum on an act of the legislature could force a vote on the issue. The constitution also stipulated that primary elections were to be held to nominate candidates for public office. Although it was not included in the original draft of the constitution, a prohibition amendment was submitted to the voters at the time of the vote on the constitution.

Initiative and referendum and the new primary structure were intended to make the government answerable to the people. Other measures regulated business and commercial interests. The constitution established several positions for inspectors and commissioners of labor and charity. A large proportion of state offices were made elected positions. Again, as in the Sequoyah constitution, a long section detailed the restrictions upon corporations. Convict and child labor were also prohibited by the constitution, and the eight-hour day was instated for laborers on public works projects and mining operations.[20]

Three issues engendered debate among the participants at the constitutional convention, and all three were eventually not included or were settled outside the official constitutional document. The issue of women's suffrage drew a great deal of attention from several factions. Women in the Oklahoma Territory had the right to vote in school elections, but as statehood approached, suffragists lobbied to widen those voting rights to include the right to vote in all state elections, as in a few other western states. Men such as Robert Owen, Peter Hanraty, and Henry Cloud argued in favor of women's suffrage, but its opponents proved stronger. After much debate, women's suffrage was not included in the new constitution, and the right of women to vote in school elections was maintained only by the smallest of margins.[21]

Prohibition also consumed time at the convention. The Enabling Act had mandated that the former Indian Territory must prohibit alcohol for at least the next two decades. The problem for the constitutional convention was whether to institute prohibition in the western portion of the state. In the end, prohibition was not included in the constitution itself, but it was submitted to the voters as a separate issue in the same election. In this election, prohibition passed, and it was instituted for the entire new state of Oklahoma.

Some delegates at the convention also pushed the inclusion of Jim Crow laws to discriminate against African American residents of Oklahoma. Murray's opening speech to the convention stressed, among other issues, that he believed the issue of racial equality to be an odious one. Murray's beliefs left no room for compromise, because they condemned African American industry and advancement and pronounced African American men unfit for political participation.[22] The necessity of federal approval of the constitution influenced Democratic leaders to avoid Jim Crow clauses in the constitution, but they promised to enact such legislation in the first years of statehood. The Oklahoma constitution did reveal the centrality of race and the distinctive race relations of the state of Oklahoma. Article 11, Section 23 of the constitution is a "Definition of Races," stipulating "Whenever in this constitution and laws of this State, the word or words, 'colored' or 'colored race,' 'negro,' or 'negro race' are used, the same shall be construed to mean or apply to all persons of African descent. The term 'white race' shall include all other persons."[23]

On April 19, 1907, the members of the constitutional convention passed and signed a version of the Oklahoma constitution. At that point, William Murray sent a letter to President Roosevelt, asking him to comment upon the constitution because the entry of Oklahoma into the Union depended on the president's approval. Murray assured Roosevelt that his "expression of disapproval...would enable the Convention to eliminate the objectionable provisions, if any, and would thus subserve the interests of every citizen in this State, irrespective of party, creed, or color."[24] Considering his opening statement and the position of the Democratic Party against racial equality, Murray's comments seem disingenuous, but it was known that the president would not accept a constitution that discriminated on the basis of color.[25]

After the disbanding of the first session of the convention, the members met two additional times for shorter sessions. On September 17, 1907, the election was held on the constitution. Over two hundred fifty thousand men voted in the election, and the constitution passed by a vote of 180,333 to 73,059.[26] The separate measure on prohibition in the state passed by a smaller margin. In the same election, Charles N. Haskell won the position of governor for the new state. Although the major battle was between Haskell, the Democratic candidate, and Frank Frantz, the Republican candidate, the Socialist candidate, C. C. Ross, received almost ten thousand votes. The Democrats swept the September elections, claiming majorities in both the House and the Senate and in other elected offices throughout the state.

FEDERAL APPROVAL

The Oklahoma constitution drew attention from all around the United States. During the campaign for the ratification of the constitution, nationally prominent men visited Oklahoma to campaign for its approval or disapproval. William Howard Taft toured the state to speak against the adoption of the constitution on behalf of the Republicans, who considered the constitution to be a product of the Democratic Party. William Jennings Bryan traveled around Oklahoma to speak on the good points of the new constitution and to recommend it to voters.

President Theodore Roosevelt disliked the progressive reforms of the Oklahoma constitution and is reputed to have been so unimpressed by its reforms that he referred to its creators as "a zoological garden of cranks."[27] After the first draft had been finished, Roosevelt asked the attorney general, Charles Joseph Bonaparte, to report on the legality of some parts of the Oklahoma constitution. Roosevelt suspected that parts of the Oklahoma constitution violated the national Constitution and the Enabling Act. Bonaparte eventually informed Roosevelt that his objections were not enough justification for opposing the constitution.[28]

More distressing to Roosevelt and other Republicans were the accusations of gerrymandering, the favorable rearranging of election districts, leveled against the Democratic majority at the constitutional convention. The Enabling Act had designated specific counties that would also serve as the congressional districts of the new state. The constitution, while retaining the names of these counties, redrew their boundaries, changing the composition within them.[29] The objection to this alleged gerrymandering led Roosevelt to call for a federal census of the proposed state to be held before the election to ratify the constitution. Roosevelt stated his opposition to the passage of the constitution in the event that the gerrymandering was shown to have occurred. The federal census, however, showed no evidence of an intentional redrawing of the districts.[30] Therefore Roosevelt accepted the constitution.

On November 16, 1907, President Theodore Roosevelt issued a proclamation welcoming the state of Oklahoma to the Union. In celebration of the occasion, Oklahomans planned a gala celebration at Guthrie to commemorate statehood and to inaugurate the new governor. Charles N. Haskell presided over the "marriage" of the two territories and received his commission to lead the new state. The reconciling of the different constituencies of the new state continued after this point, but there would always be those for whom the statehood of Oklahoma connoted the end of their sovereign governments. It would take several decades for the tribal governments of Oklahoma to be reinvigorated and for the dual citizenship of many Oklahomans to become a reality. Others saw this event as the culmination of decades of work toward statehood and the participation of Oklahoma in the United States.

SUMMARY

Thus, the Oklahoma and the Indian territories were brought together as a single entity. These two areas were first a part of the United States in the 1820s as a portion of the Indian Country, a space set aside for the resettlement of Native American groups. Between the 1830s and the 1880s, the federal government forced multiple tribes to settle on the lands of the Indian Territory, promising to respect their governments and allow them to remain outside of an organized American state.

The pressure of boomers and business interests eventually overwhelmed the government's restriction on settlement. In 1889, lands in the Indian Territory were opened to settlement, and in 1890, the Territory of Oklahoma was created. The agitation for statehood then began. First, the movement in both territories insisted upon separate statehood, but later the call for a single state gained sway in the territories and in Congress.

In Congress, partisan politics slowed the movement for statehood and eventually dictated the terms on which the state would enter the Union. The Republican-dominated Congress picked up the call for single statehood. Using the Oklahoma question in an attempt to admit Arizona and New Mexico as one state, Congress passed an omnibus bill dealing with all four territories. This bill created the state of Oklahoma and called for the convention that would eventually draft the new constitution. This constitution owed much to the dominance of the Democratic Party, which derived both from Progressive reforms and from racial politics.

The history of the creation of the state of Oklahoma is unique and telling. For many decades, there was no thought of turning the area that is now Oklahoma into a state. The land was to be set aside for the settlement of indigenous peoples who had been forced out of their homes in other states. By the turn of the twentieth century, the respect of the American government for the independence and sovereignty of the Native American nations in the Indian Territory was waning. The United States retracted its promise of sovereignty to these peoples, dismantling their governments and forcibly making American citizens of their populations. Throughout this process, voices were raised in protest against American encroachment and political maneuvering.

For many American settlers, however, the story of Oklahoma's statehood contained only positive tones. The opening of land in Oklahoma and the land run of 1889 are celebrated as part of the state's unique history. The territorial government, although comprising major blocks of Republicans and Democrats, consistently incorporated demands from third parties. Agricultural and labor interests maintained a strong presence in the Twin Territories and were able to insert protections for their livelihoods in the Oklahoma constitution. Congress heard the demands of Oklahomans and admitted Oklahoma to the Union.

The factors that created Oklahoma produced a multiethnic state with rich agricultural and mineral resources. Significant populations of whites, blacks, and

Native Americans settled within its boundaries. Tribal governments existed in conjunction with territorial and state governments. The competition for resources often produced inequality, but all Oklahomans fought to have their rights respected and their needs met by the new state.

NOTES

1. Arrell M. Gibson, *The History of Oklahoma* (Norman: University of Oklahoma Press, 1984), p. 27.

2. Ibid., p. 95.

3. Senate Executive Document, No. 20, 45th Cong., 1st Sess., p. 21, as quoted in Joseph B. Thoburn and Muriel H. Wright, *Oklahoma: A History* (New York: Lewis Historical Publishing Company, 1929), p. 511.

4. Thoburn and Wright, *Oklahoma: A History*, p. 546.

5. Representative Beall of Texas, 59th Cong., 1st Sess., *Congressional Record* 40 (2) (January 24, 1906): 1514; Delegate McGuire of Oklahoma Territory, ibid., p. 1567.

6. Representative Grosvenor of Ohio, ibid., p. 1501.

7. The Cherokee National Government to the Secretary of the Interior, January 22, 1902, transcript located in the Foreman Collection, vol. 12, Oklahoma Historical Society, Oklahoma City.

8. Danney Goble, *Progressive Oklahoma: The Making of a New Kind of State* (Norman: University of Oklahoma Press, 1980), p. 192.

9. "The Constitution of Sequoyah," in *The Oklahoma Red Book* (Oklahoma City: Democrat Printing Company, 1912), pp. 623–674.

10. Goble, *Progressive Oklahoma*, p. 193.

11. James R. Scales and Danney Goble, *Oklahoma Politics: A History* (Norman: University of Oklahoma Press, 1982), pp. 4, 5.

12. Ibid., p. 4.

13. Worth Robert Miller, "Frontier Politics: The Bases of Partisan Choice in Oklahoma Territory, 1890–1904," *The Chronicles of Oklahoma* 62 (4) (Winter 1984–1985): 429–446.

14. Goble, *Progressive Oklahoma*, p. 112.

15. Ibid., pp. 99–104.

16. Murray Wickett, *Contested Territory: Whites, Native Americans, and African Americans in Oklahoma, 1865–1907* (Baton Rouge: Louisiana State University Press, 2000), p. 168.

17. Ibid., pp. 168–175.

18. "Suggestions for a Platform," reprinted in Goble, *Progressive Oklahoma*, pp. 230–233.

19. Goble, *Progressive Oklahoma*, pp. 181–183.

20. "Constitution of Oklahoma," in *The Oklahoma Red Book*, pp. 40–120.

21. Louise Boyd James, "The Woman Suffrage Issue in the Oklahoma Constitutional Convention," *The Chronicles of Oklahoma* 56 (4) (Winter 1978–1979): 379–392.

22. Speech of William H. Murray, in *Proceedings of the Constitutional Convention of the Proposed State of Oklahoma, held at Guthrie, Oklahoma, November 20, 1906, to November 16, 1907* (Muskogee: Muskogee Printing Co., [n.d.]) (hereafter cited as *Proceedings of the Constitutional Convention*), pp. 15–25.

23. "Constitution of Oklahoma," *Oklahoma Red Book*, p. 112.
24. *Proceedings of the Constitutional Convention*, p. 455.
25. Wickett, *Contested Territory*, pp. 193–194.
26. Gibson, *History of Oklahoma*, p. 124.
27. Goble, *Progressive Oklahoma*, p. 203.
28. Elting E. Morrison, ed., *The Letters of Theodore Roosevelt* (Cambridge: Harvard University Press, 1952), 5:673.
29. Ibid.
30. Ibid., p. 784.

BIBLIOGRAPHY

Goble, Danney. *Progressive Oklahoma: The Making of a New Kind of State.* Norman: University of Oklahoma Press, 1980.

Miller, Worth Robert. *Oklahoma Populism: A History of the People's Party in the Oklahoma Territory.* Norman: University of Oklahoma Press, 1987.

Proceedings of the Constitutional Convention of the Proposed State of Oklahoma, held at Guthrie, Oklahoma, November 20, 1906, to November 16, 1907. Muskogee, OK: Muskogee Printing Co., [n.d.].

Thoburn, Joseph B., and Muriel H. Wright. *Oklahoma: A History of The State and Its People.* New York: Lewis Historical Publishing Company, 1929.

Wickett, Murray. *Contested Territory: Whites, Native Americans and African Americans in Oklahoma, 1865–1907.* Baton Rouge: Louisiana State University Press, 2000.

THE STATE OF OREGON

Admitted to the Union as a State:
February 14, 1859

Melinda Marie Jetté and Tim Zacharias

INTRODUCTION: THE QUESTION
OF STATEHOOD IN A NATION DIVIDING

Statehood became an issue of importance for Oregon settlers beginning in the late 1840s, with the settlers often feeling that their aspirations for equal stature in the Union were subject to the mercurial nature of party politics in the nation's capital. This question of statehood for a distant territory in the Far West was much more than a story of political squabbles, however. Oregon entered the national scene just as regional differences in the United States began to rend the national political fabric. In the years leading up to the Civil War, Oregon shifted from being a small, overlooked territory removed from the center of power and assumed a role alongside Kansas in the larger fate of the nation. For Oregonians, and for Americans, the question of statehood for Oregon reached a crescendo in the late 1850s.

Soon after Oregon delegates elected as the "state" legislature met in early July 1858, La Fayette Grover and Delazon Smith hastily departed from Salem, Oregon's capital, en route for Washington, D.C., three thousand miles away. The legislature had elected Smith and Joseph Lane, then Oregon's territorial delegate in Washington, as their national senators, whereas Grover had won the representative seat in the June election. Because Congress had yet to pass an Enabling Act, Oregon was not officially a state, and Lane, Grover, and Smith were faced with the task of justifying Oregonians' pre-emptive action in producing and approving a state constitution. Thus, when the second session of the Thirty-fifth Congress opened in December 1858, the pressing mission for Oregon's congressional delegation was to break through the geographic isolation

Oregon

Territorial Development:

- The United States and Great Britain sign a temporary treaty for joint tenancy of the Oregon Country, October 20, 1818
- The United States obtains formal title to all land in the Oregon territory south of the 49th parallel from Great Britain through the Oregon Treaty, June 15, 1846
- Oregon, carved out of the much larger Oregon Territory, is organized as a U.S. territory, August 14, 1848
- Oregon admitted into the Union as the thirty-third state, February 14, 1859

Territorial Capitals:

- Oregon City, 1848–1851
- Salem, 1851–1855
- Corvallis, 1855
- Salem, 1855–1859

State Capitals:

- Salem, 1859–present

Origin of State Name: "Oregon" may have come from the French-Canadian word "ouragan," meaning "storm" or "hurricane." It is also possible that it comes from the Spanish word "orejon," meaning "big ear," which was given to a number of the tribes of the region, or from the Spanish word "oregano," or, wild sage, which grows in eastern Oregon.

First Governor: John Whiteaker
Governmental Organization: Bicameral
Population at Statehood: 52,456
Geographical Size: 95,997 square miles

and the national political wrangling then hindering the territory's petition for statehood.

A convention meeting in Salem had produced a constitution in September 1857, and voters ratified it that November, but statehood depended on congressional approval. Bills supporting the admission of both Minnesota and Oregon had been introduced during the first session of the Thirty-fifth Congress, but Oregon's admission to the United States proved more nettlesome than that of Minnesota, which became a state in May 1858. Both of these free northern territories sought statehood during the nation's sectional crisis. By the 1850s, the socioeconomic changes wrought by the emerging industrial capitalism in the North, based on free labor, were increasingly at odds with the southern agricultural economy dependent on black slave labor.

During the 1840s and 1850s, policies of coexistence that had emerged in the decades following the American Revolution (1775–1783) faced intense challenges from both regions looking to settle territories in the trans-Mississippi West. Southerners increasingly viewed the free labor system of the North as a direct threat to the South's economic stability and "distinct" culture. Northerners increasingly saw slavery threatening both the free labor of white men and republican democracy itself. Additionally, abolitionists advocating an outright ban on slavery constituted a vocal, growing minority that challenged the feasibility of maintaining a compromise with the southern position. The Fugitive Slave Act and the Compromise of 1850, by which Congress attempted to preserve the status quo, only served to exacerbate the growing division and animosity between the two regions.

The specific controversies that delayed Oregon's admission to the Union reflected the fracturing of the national political culture. While approving a state constitution in November 1857, Oregon's white male electorate also voted to ban slavery and to exclude free blacks from Oregon. Oregonians were also strongly Democratic, although there were a number of loosely organized anti-Democrat groups. Given this political landscape, Republicans in Congress hesitated to admit Oregon as a state for fear that Oregon's Democratic representatives and senators would side with southern Democrats on national issues. Meanwhile, Southerners were just as wary of admission because of Oregon's long-standing opposition to slavery in the territory. To comprehend the controversy over Oregon's admission to the Union in the 1850s fully, it is important to trace both the history of the Pacific Northwest in relation to the national political culture and the history of local political battles within the region itself from the turn of the nineteenth century.

THE OREGON QUESTION

The uncertainty over Oregon's future that La Fayette Grover and Delazon Smith faced on their journey to Washington, D.C., in the summer of 1858 was not new. During the first half of the nineteenth century, Oregon's place within the United States remained unsettled. In 1803, both the United States and Great Britain laid claim to the original Oregon Country, the vast region west of the Rocky Mountains that stretched from Russian Alaska to Spanish California. The British and American claims to the territory were codified in the Convention of 1818. This agreement outlined a plan for joint occupancy for the region, allowing both American and British citizens free movement there.

For the first three decades of the century, American interest in the Oregon Country was limited to select groups, including some national statesmen such as Thomas Jefferson, eastern maritime merchants, Rocky Mountain fur trappers, Protestant missionaries, and "Oregon boosters" such as Hall Jackson Kelley and Thomas Hart Benton. As a result, the Hudson's Bay Company, a London-based fur trade firm, maintained a virtual commercial monopoly in the vast region. By the early 1840s, however, changing geopolitical realities in North America led to a shift in British and American positions on the Oregon Country. With a decline in the fur trade, the Hudson's Bay Company progressively shifted the focus of its Pacific Coast commercial operations from Fort Vancouver on the Columbia River to Fort Victoria on Vancouver Island. Beginning with the emigration of 1843, Americans in large numbers left the Mississippi Valley on the two-thousand-mile overland route from Independence, Missouri, to Oregon. These Oregon Trail emigrants were motivated by a number of factors, including a desire to leave poor economic and social conditions in the Midwest and to seek a new start in a region that promised "free land" and a salubrious climate. By 1848, 11,500 overland emigrants had made the voyage to Oregon.

On the national level, the election of 1844 brought into office an expansionist president, James K. Polk, whose campaign slogan touted "the occupation of Oregon and the re-annexation of Texas." During Polk's presidency, the United States experienced the largest territorial expansion since Thomas Jefferson negotiated the Louisiana Purchase in 1803. Whereas Texas, the Southwest, and California were annexed following the Mexican War (1846–1848), Oregon was acquired through negotiations with Great Britain. In the American press, the issue facing Polk was ostensibly whether he should insist on acquiring the entire Oregon Country from the southern border of Russian Alaska to California. Despite the expansionist slogan, "54°40' or fight," that gained popularity after the election of 1844, the crux of the Oregon Question dividing the United States and Great Britain was the area of present-day Washington State.

For several decades the American government had proposed extending the international border along the 49th parallel from the Rocky Mountains to the Pacific Coast. British officials had rejected this line on several occasions. Like the Americans, the British retained an interest in the deep-water port of Puget Sound and in the free navigation of the Columbia River, both of which provided important transportation routes into the interior. From December 1845 through late April 1846, Congress engaged in a heated debate over the Oregon Question, always returning to the question of whether the United

States should compromise on the 49th parallel. If the two countries could not reach an accord, the possibility of armed conflict loomed in the background. After Polk finally received approval from Congress to negotiate for the lower portion of the original Oregon Country, the United States and Great Britain agreed on the 49th parallel as the international border. Under the international boundary treaty, signed on June 15, 1846, the Oregon Country became the region south of the 49th parallel that included the present-day states of Oregon, Washington, Idaho, and parts of western Montana and Wyoming.

OREGON'S PROVISIONAL GOVERNMENT

Although the international treaty was signed in 1846, Oregon did not gain territorial status until August 1848 and did not have a territorial government until March 1849. Before the institution of the territorial government, civil affairs in Oregon came under the jurisdiction of a provisional government. The Oregon provisional government, established in 1843 following a series of meetings in the Willamette Valley, produced a political culture that influenced Oregon's attempt to enter the Union in the 1850s. The provisional government brought together representatives of the various European-American groups that had re-settled Native American lands in the Pacific Northwest, including New Englanders, Midwesterners, French-Canadians, and former mountain men. Because most of the American emigrants came to Oregon by the Oregon Trail, the largest percentage of the settler population hailed from the midwestern border states, creating a similar sociopolitical climate in the Northwest.

The midwestern sociopolitical culture supported the populist principles of Jacksonian democracy, with a fervent belief in the notion of popular sovereignty and an antipathy toward non-white minorities, especially blacks and Native Americans. The Compact Theory, the basis for nineteenth-century notions about popular sovereignty, had a long history in the United States, dating back to the early colonial period in New England. Under the Compact Theory, the citizenry retained an inalienable right collectively to form a "compact" that would govern civil affairs and protect private property. In addition, it was believed that both women and non-whites naturally lacked the qualities necessary for conducting civil affairs. Oregon's isolation in the Far West ensured that these presuppositions went largely unchallenged.

Voters in Oregon approved the formation of a provisional government and enacted organic laws for the region beginning in 1843. The provisional government, which was initially comprised of a legislature and an executive committee, was later modified to include a legislature and a governor. The provisional government's organic laws, which developed over several years, were based on the laws of Iowa and the Northwest Ordinance of 1787. They codified the

European-American settlers' positions on important issues of the day, including slavery, Native American rights, and landownership.

In accordance with the Northwest Ordinance of 1787, the 1843 Organic Act outlawed slavery and involuntary servitude. In June 1844, however, the provisional legislature enacted a series of additional measures sponsored by a recent Missouri immigrant, Peter Burnett, who later became California's first state governor. One measure stipulated that free blacks must depart within three years of their arrival in Oregon. If such individuals did not leave within the prescribed time, they would be subject to trial and public flogging. These positions were a reaction to the Comstock Affair of May 1844, which had resulted in the deaths of several Native Americans and whites at Willamette Falls. European-American settlers believed that James Saules, a free African American, was the instigator of the incident, heightening white fears about racial violence. The anti-black measures were modified in December 1844, when African American indenture replaced the whipping provision, and were eventually repealed in 1845. The provisional legislature's repeal of the anti-black laws was the result of a moderate stance on the part of newly elected legislators rather than a major shift in racial attitudes among the majority of the white population, and the support for such anti-black measures remained prevalent throughout the Oregon Country. European-Americans in the region were strongly opposed to the presence of African Americans, slave and free, because they viewed African Americans as a threat to social and economic order.

As for Native American rights, the 1843 enactment contained provisions of the Northwest Ordinance of 1787 recognizing the indigenous inhabitants' prior title to lands then being re-settled by the in-coming European-Americans. The organic laws also recognized the Native Americans' theoretical right to due process. These provisions received strong support from the former fur trappers, both American and French-Canadian, who were married to native women and who constituted another visible minority in the Willamette Valley. The Organic Act, however, also stated that the provisional government would reserve the right to authorize "lawful wars" against Native American groups, presumably to protect settlers inhabiting former Native American lands.

Concern over landownership arose immediately because of the lack of treaties in place respecting the regional Native Americans' title to their traditional territories and the lack of statutes in place regulating land issues between settlers themselves. "Claim jumping" was a serious concern in the 1840s as emigrants continued to stream into in the region. In response to settlers' concerns, although without consulting with local Native American groups, the Oregon provisional government instituted a land law that recognized preemptive land claims and required settlers to register their claims with the government. These measures were intended to give settlers a legitimate means to gain legal title to their land under a future American administration, and a delegate was sent to Congress to lobby for federal codification of this land policy in the extension legislation.

OREGON BECOMES A TERRITORY

During the decade before 1848, American residents of the Oregon Country, together with a number of French-Canadians, sent several petitions to the U.S. Congress. One such petition, drafted at a general meeting held in the Willamette Valley on March 4, 1845, expressed the settlers' desires for Native American treaties and federal officials to regulate Native American–settler relations, a federal land law and survey, and federal improvements to the overland route to Oregon. Although this petition, like others of this period, was silent on the question of slavery, congressional officials became aware of the anti-slavery stance in Oregon as represented in the provisional government's Organic Law of June 1845.

The settlers' stance on slavery, together with their request for federal expenditures on Native American treaties, land surveys, and road improvements delayed the establishment of a territorial government in Oregon for two years. Following the International Boundary Treaty of 1846, the crux of the issue facing Congress was whether Oregon should be admitted as a free territory consistent with its organic acts. Unfortunately for Oregonians, their requests for territorial status came amid national tensions over territorial expansion, slavery, and the Mexican War (1846–1848). Oregon's status became part of larger national controversy over the future of slavery in the trans-Mississippi West, including territories that might be acquired in the event of a victory over Mexico.

An initial attempt at passing a territorial Enabling Act came on August 6, 1846, when the House of Representatives voted by a margin of more than fifty votes to establish a free territory in Oregon. The measure died, however, after the Senate chose not to act on the bill before adjourning for the summer. Additionally, two days following the initial House vote, Pennsylvania Representative David Wilmot touched off a vitriolic debate over his proviso to an appropriation bill that called for a ban on slavery in any future lands acquired from Mexico. Wilmot's actions brought to the fore a simmering national conflict that was exacerbated by sectional differences over the Mexican War.

Given the political discord in Washington over the Wilmot Proviso, Congress was unable to reach an agreement on the creation of a free territory in Oregon until the summer of 1848. Nonetheless, the question of organizing Oregon as a free-soil territory continued to be debated in the House and Senate during the two-year period following the initial attempt in 1846. In January 1847 and again in February 1848, the House passed bills to organize Oregon as a free territory. The 1847 bill passed by more than ninety votes and the 1848 bill by more than fifty votes. In both instances, the proposed Enabling Act died in the Senate because of opposition from southern Democratic senators, such as South Carolina Senator John C. Calhoun, who sought to remove the free-soil provisions in the Senate bill. By the fall of 1847, while congressional officials continued to battle over the issue of Oregon's future, settlers in Oregon had again become restless for congressional action.

Groups in Oregon sent three additional petitions to Congress during the fall and winter of 1847–1848. The first of these memorials was the Yamhill Petition, sent by settlers and delegates who attended a meeting in the Yamhill district in October 1847. That same fall, Provisional Governor George Abernethy dispatched his handpicked representative, Jessy Quinn Thornton, to Washington with another petition calling for action on organizing a territory. Senator Thomas Hart Benton presented both the Abernethy-Thornton Petition and the Yamhill Petition to Congress in May 1848. These petitions renewed requests for the extension of American governance in Oregon, institution of federal land laws, and federal actions on Native American–settler relations. Given the contentious situation in Washington, these two petitions failed to break the political impasse in Congress with regard to Oregon's future status.

The decisive factor affecting final passage of a territorial Enabling Act was a tragedy that occurred in the eastern portion of the Oregon Country in the winter of 1847. This tragedy, known as the Whitman Massacre, spurred settlers to intensify their pressure on congressional officials. On November 29, 1847, a group of Cayuse tribesmen attacked the Presbyterian Mission at Waiilatpu run by Marcus and Narcissa Whitman. The Whitmans and several other members of the mission were killed, and the survivors were taken hostage. The Cayuse believed they had acted defensively in response to what they perceived as malevolent behavior toward their people by Oregon Trail emigrants and mission officials, particularly Marcus Whitman. Although the survivors were later ransomed through the efforts of Hudson's Bay Company officials and nearby Catholic clergymen, European-American settlers in Oregon were outraged at the acts committed by the Cayuse. In addition to calling up volunteers for punitive action against the Plateau Native American group, the Oregon provisional legislature approved a bill authorizing former fur trapper Joseph L. Meek to travel to Washington, D.C. Meek's mission was to notify President Polk and Congress of the events at the Whitman Mission, to present a new petition requesting organization of a territorial government, and to request military aid for the settlers.

Meek's party departed for Washington, D.C., in March 1848. Traveling with surprising speed, it arrived in Washington in late May of 1848, after only three months on the overland route. Although Joseph Meek, the legislature's envoy, and Jessy Q. Thornton, Abernethy's delegate, represented differing constituencies in Oregon, they both worked for the passage of a territorial Enabling Act during the summer of 1848. On May 29, 1848, bills were again introduced in the House and Senate endorsing a territorial government in Oregon. That same day, President Polk sent messages to both chambers asking Congress for decisive action on the question.

Following the introduction of bills in the House and Senate, more than two months of rancorous debate ensued. Free-soil and anti-slavery supporters in the House pressed for the organization of a free territory in Oregon. In the Senate, Southerners and Northerners furiously debated whether to exclude slavery in

Oregon in the territorial Enabling Act. Several Southerners attempted to amend the Senate bill by removing the free-soil provisions. Others floated a compromise developed by a special Senate committee and originally drafted by John M. Clayton, a Whig from Delaware. Clayton's compromise proposed that Oregon be allowed to ban slavery until a future territorial legislature could decide the matter. A further provision would allow for a legal test case through the territorial judiciary to the U.S. Supreme Court on the question of slavery. Free-soil congressmen refused all compromise, unwilling to bow to any pro-slavery position or one that relied on the Supreme Court to resolve the slavery issue.

Finally, in early August 1848, the Senate withdrew the amendment voiding the free-soil provision and voted to approve the House version of the territorial Enabling Act. The Senate bill passed by a slim majority of 29-25, with voting along sectional lines. All the northern senators voted in favor, and nearly all of the southern senators voted in opposition. Senator Clayton was absent for the vote, and three senators from slave states joined the Northerners in voting for passage of the bill: Thomas Hart Benton of Missouri, Samuel Houston of Texas, and Presley Spruance of Delaware. Congress passed the final version on August 2, 1848, and President Polk signed the bill into law on August 14, 1848.

Forming a Territorial Government

The territorial enactment outlined both the form the new representative government would take and its relationship to the national government. Congress extended the provisions of the Northwest Ordinance of 1787, including the prohibition on slavery. Executive, judiciary, and law enforcement officials were to be appointed by the president and confirmed by the U.S. Senate. These positions included the territorial governor and secretary, the supreme court justice and associate justices, the U.S. attorney, and the U.S. marshal. The legislature consisted of a council of nine delegates and a house of representatives. Congress also declared that the territorial legislature must make laws in accordance with the U.S. Constitution, which were then subject to congressional review. Although Congress did extend all federal land laws, the Enabling Act did not contain a provision for a donation land claim law as previously requested by the Oregon settlers. Congress retained its role as the sole arbiter of treaties and land-title extinguishments involving the local Native American populations and ensured that it alone would decide the future boundaries of Oregon and whether it would be divided into smaller territories. Finally, the Enabling Act recognized that voting rights and elected office would be reserved for citizens of the United States above the age of twenty-one years and for foreigners above that age who had declared their intention to become American citizens.

After the passage of the territorial Enabling Act, President Polk appointed General Joseph Lane, an ambitious Mexican War hero from Indiana, as Oregon's first territorial governor. Polk also appointed Joseph Meek as Oregon's first U.S. marshall. With instructions from President Polk to establish a territorial government as soon as possible, Lane, Meek, and an army detachment of twenty-six men left St. Louis, Missouri, for Oregon in early September 1848. After an arduous trip along the Santa Fe Trail to California, the remaining members of the Lane-Meek party took passage on a boat from California to Oregon, arriving in Oregon on March 2, 1849. Although Provisional Governor George Abernethy had previously announced the passage of the territorial Enabling Act in early February after receiving the news via the Hawaiian Islands, Lane officially proclaimed the establishment of Oregon's territorial government in Oregon City on May 3, 1849.

After appointing Kintzing Prichette as territorial secretary, Lane quickly set to work establishing a functioning territorial government. He announced elections for the first Monday in June 1849 and called for the first meeting of the territorial legislature on Monday, July 16, 1849. Although territorial status soon proved distasteful to Oregonians, Joseph Lane, a Jeffersonian Democrat, remained a popular figure in the territory throughout the 1850s. Oregon voters accepted Lane as one of their own during his short tenure as the first territorial governor, from March 3, 1849, to June 18, 1850.

From the beginning, a major concern for legislators was the nature of Oregon's relationship to the federal government. Accustomed to self-rule under a provisional government and a tradition of Jeffersonian democracy in the Midwest, many Oregon lawmakers had difficulty adjusting to what they considered "colonial" status within the United States. The central grievance involved the fact that executive and judicial offices in the territory were appointed patronage positions of the national executive. Oregon voters and legislators saw the appointed offices as a threat to popular sovereignty, that is, to the right of local people to govern themselves. Because of partisan differences between territorial appointees representing national political interests and lawmakers representing local socioeconomic interests, there was often tension between territorial officials and the legislature throughout the territorial period.

Such friction directly followed the election of 1848, when newly elected Whig President Zachary Taylor appointed John P. Gaines as Oregon's territorial governor in the spring of 1850. News of Gaines's appointment reached Oregon before Gaines arrived on August 18, 1850. Thus, he faced vocal Democratic Party opposition immediately upon taking office. The legislature quickly exerted its authority through a bill calling for the transfer of the capital from Oregon City to Salem. Gaines and his supporters in the legislature and the supreme court denied the legality of the legislature's act. Gaines appealed to Washington, and the controversy was not resolved until Congress enacted a bill recognizing the change. Oregon's second territorial delegate, Joseph Lane, who was elected in 1851 following the death of Oregon's first delegate Samuel Thurston, shepherded the bill through Congress.

Reacting to what they perceived as colonial status within the United States, Oregon settlers pursued several avenues for altering their situation. A few agitated for an independent republic on the Pacific Coast. Although this position never garnered widespread support among Oregon voters, a small group of vocal supporters continued to advocate independence until the start of the Civil War. Other lawmakers effected passage of a territorial resolution calling on Congress to amend Oregon's Enabling Act to authorize the local election of territorial officials. In 1852, after the House Committee on Territories recommended no action be taken on a bill to amend the territorial acts of Oregon and Minnesota for the election of territorial judges, Congress declined to act on the matter.

Another group of settlers believed the best avenue toward self-rule resided in statehood. This group introduced a bill during the first session of the territorial legislature in August 1849. It called for consultation with citizens about their views on the formation of a state government. Although the bill was tabled, the issue of statehood became a regular topic of discussion in the legislature and in the prominent newspapers within the territory. The question of statehood, together with the issue of slavery, remained a central feature in the shifting dynamics that marked Oregon's political culture throughout the 1850s.

OREGON'S POLITICAL CULTURE

Before 1849, Oregon's politics resulted from informal national, ethnic, and religious divisions among groups contesting for the region's material resources. Overt partisanship was discouraged, in keeping with the goal of harmony and consensus idealized in the Protestant ethic of Oregon's significant missionary population. Acquiring territorial recognition, however, instantly injected formal and national components into the factional dynamics. The Democratic Party formally organized in Oregon in 1851 and dominated politics for the next decade. Relocation of the territorial seat of government and the question of statehood provided two central issues the party championed during this period. Whig, Know-Nothing, and Republican efforts attempted to thwart Democratic control, but only the secession crisis temporarily suppressed its influence.

Impetus for Democratic organization resulted from the recruiting efforts of Oregon's first territorial delegate, Samuel R. Thurston. Thurston, a rare Methodist Democrat, won the seat of territorial delegate on behalf of the region's missionary interests to promote the passage of the Oregon Donation Land Claim Act (1850). Originally proposed by Missouri's Senator Linn in 1843, the final measure granted a half section of 320 acres to male settlers (including "American half-breed Indians") and a full section of 640 acres to married couples, with the additional provision that married women would hold their portions of the land grants in their own names.

Thurston's recruiting efforts succeeded in enticing a number of prospects, among them Delazon Smith, a New Yorker who had emigrated to Iowa, and New Englanders Asahel Bush, La Fayette Grover, and Reuben P. Boise. Bush was specifically approached to found a Democratic newspaper in Oregon to facilitate Thurston's reelection as territorial delegate without dependence on former Provisional Governor George Abernethy and the missionary faction.

Bush published the first edition of the *Statesman* on March 28, 1851, but Delegate Thurston succumbed to yellow fever en route to Oregon at Acapulco, Mexico, April 9, 1851. Even before word of the delegate's death reached Oregon, Bush asserted his influence by buying out the interests of other local investors. Bush quickly allied with former governor Joseph Lane, who was running to replace Thurston, but in a manner disguising explicit partisanship, as consistent with the territory's tradition. Once Lane won the election, however, Bush urged formal organization of a Democratic Party.

Bush corresponded regularly with a majority of the territory's appointed and elected Democratic officials. They relied on the *Statesman* to present them favorably, while Bush, in turn, received critical intelligence from around the state that enabled him to select and promote appropriate individuals privately within the party apparatus and publicly for elective office. This pivotal position ensured Bush a gatekeeper role over all newly arrived Democratic appointees, who then achieved local favor or disfavor based upon their relationship with him. George Williams, recently arrived from Iowa as territorial chief justice in 1853, was an important appointee who won Bush's immediate favor.

Bush's association earned the label "Salem Clique," spelled "Cli-que" by the opposition, much as the Martin Van Buren faction of New York Democrats had earned the label "Albany Regency" some two decades earlier. As a network of personal associations, Bush's party control was always tenuous, however. In April 1851, William Bristow, a member of Bush's circle from Eugene, reported that the "thick 'Shells'" were working in the southern Oregon for the purpose of "disorganizing" the party.[1] Bristow's designation of "thick shells" quickly became just the "hards" and "softs" in the vocabulary of the Bush circle: those who adhered to the local party line were the "hards"; Democrats whose actions and voting behavior could not be counted on were known as "softs." Again, these titles were borrowed from the Barnburner and Hunker rivalry in New York state politics of the Jacksonian era. Bush also frequently used the "Know-Nothing" label for any "non-hard" of his party.[2]

The territory's far southern region generally remained out of Bush's sphere of control, as did the northern communities. James K. Kelly, William Farrar, and Asa Lovejoy (one of the original founders of Portland) from the Portland and Oregon City environs were Democratic leaders of the 1850s outside the Bush circle. A Pennsylvania lawyer, Kelly, like Grover, migrated by sea to California in 1850 and then to Oregon in 1851. There Kelly initially became a partner in the law office of Asa L. Lovejoy, originally a Whig from Massachusetts, who became a Democrat in the course of migrating from Missouri in 1845. Farrar hailed from New Hampshire and came to Oregon Territory in 1853 following his appointment as the territory's district attorney. He made his home in Portland, the fastest growing community of the decade. Kelly, because of his ambition to represent Oregon some day on the federal level independent of the Salem Clique, and Farrar, because of his opposition to Portland land schemes on the part of those associated with the Salem Democrats, attempted to create a partisan organization independent of Bush.

The "Salem" portion of the Bush Democrats' label stemmed from the first major partisan contest of the territorial period: relocation of the capital. Bush supported the Salem move because of dissatisfaction over Democratic loyalty among those in the northern region of the Willamette Valley. The Willamette's mid-valley region surrounding Salem comprised more than half of the territory's population, overwhelmingly farmers from the lower Ohio and upper Mississippi valleys steeped in Jacksonian democracy. Meanwhile, settlers from the eastern seaboard and those engaged in a greater variety of professional occupations populated the region around Oregon City and Portland.

Although never formally organized on a territory-wide basis, a handful of influential Whigs participated in the provisional and territorial assemblies. Two of the most respected men in this group were Jesse Applegate and Levi Scott. Applegate had been part of the so-called "Great Migration" of 1843, whereas Scott arrived a year later. Both were members of the party that blazed the southern route into Oregon during 1846. Both eventually settled south of Eugene: Scott founded Scottsburg, and Applegate took a claim near Yoncalla where he developed a close relationship with Matthew P. Deady.

In January 1852, Applegate commended Deady for penning the legislative memorial to Congress requesting popular election of territorial officials. In the same letter, Applegate defended his party against claims that it did not stand for popular rights and asserted personal independence from issues intended as partisan "traps." Applegate's support for popular government included approval of the relocation of the capital.[3] Conversely, fellow Missouri migrant James McBride abandoned the Democratic Party for Whig allegiance over the issue of capital relocation. His son John McBride also joined the Whig party in 1853, and in 1855 the McBrides helped launch the territory's first Republican meeting in Albany.

Two additional Whig partisans influenced political events leading up to the convention: Thomas Jefferson Dryer and David Logan. While editing the *California Courier* in early 1850, Dryer was recruited by a group of Portland businessmen to found an Oregon paper to advocate for their interests. In Portland, he established the *Oregonian*, which appeared on December 4, 1850, some three months before the first issue of the *Statesman*. Despite Dryer's initial promise that his paper would advocate the "great Whig party" along with agricultural and commercial development without being drawn "into individual controversies or local and rival interests," partisan rivalry oozed from every issue of both his and Bush's papers. The journalistic invective of the period soon earned the sobriquet, "Oregon Style."[4]

David Logan was the son of distinguished Whig lawyer, Stephen Logan, of Springfield, Illinois, a member of that state's Whig junto and law partner of Abraham Lincoln. After a brief stint in his father's law office, Logan's intemperance led to a falling out. Logan then volunteered in the war against Mexico in a unit led by Edward D. Baker, who a dozen years later became Oregon's first Republican U.S. senator and a Civil War martyr. Following his discharge, Logan participated in the state's Whig party caucus but was not named to any candidacy. Either pushed by his father or desperate for a new environment from which to seek personal and political redemption, Logan used his father's financial backing to make the migration to Oregon, arriving in 1849 at about the same time as Maryland-bred and Ohio-raised Matthew P. Deady. Both Logan and Deady initially settled thirty miles southwest of Portland in Lafayette.

Within two years, the two faced each other in a territorial election for Yamhill County, which Deady, by then a Clique associate, won by reportedly getting Logan drunk for the stump speech making. Logan then moved to Portland, where he established himself as an exceptionally capable courtroom lawyer and in 1854 won election to the territorial legislature. Shortly thereafter, Deady anonymously penned a letter that appeared in the *Democratic Standard* (a paper just launched by Portland Democrats to compete with the *Statesman*) accusing Logan of raping a Native American girl on the main road of the southern Oregon community of Jacksonville, in front of a crowd at high noon. Logan immediately wrote to refute the charges and privately threatened to kill Deady should they meet in the next round of the judge's circuit court. The threat was never carried out, and little harm was done to either reputation, because Logan figured prominently with Dryer in putting together the only Whig Party convention in Oregon during December 1854.

In the *Oregonian*, Dryer had labeled the capital relocation unconstitutional and factious. He published a lyrical play in serialized form by William L. Adams titled *Treason, Stratagems, and Spoils* which satirized the promoters of relocation as a corrupt, intemperate band of spoilsmen that sought to seduce the electorate into accepting an oligarchic tyranny. For his part, Bush denounced his opponents as "Federalists" and antirepublican promoters of "monopolies, tariffs, and Bank Charters fertiliz[ing] the rich man's soil with the sweat of the poor man's brow."[5]

After losing the relocation effort and sensing the national decline of the Whig Party, Dryer cast about for other coalition-building topics in the pages of the *Oregonian*. He supported the Maine Law movement, linking this position to historic republicanism idealized in the figure of George Washington. Rumors fanned by the *Statesman* respecting Dryer's own intemperance impeded the topics' usefulness as a focal point for anti-Democratic organization, however. By 1853, Bush turned to nativist discourse, although he never officially declared in favor of the anti-Catholic Know-Nothings. The territory's prosecuting attorney, Amory Holbrook, also abandoned his Whig affiliation in May 1854. In Oregon City Holbrook then founded the territory's first secret association of Know-Nothings, frequently referred to at the time as a "wigwam." By 1856, Oregon Know-Nothings followed the national trend by abandoning their secret organizational model and openly campaigned as the American Party.

A number of Oregon's other prominent Whigs and independent-minded Democrats explored nativist politics during the first years of the 1850s. Nativism resonated with many of the territory's early pioneers and those affiliated with missionary efforts. The economic advantage the Hudson Bay Company had held over early American immigrants and the rumors regarding the role of priests in provoking the Whitman attack drew settlers into reactionary political groups. The popularity of the American Party stemmed from its offering an anti-Democratic alternative for the missionaries, Prohibitionists, and "softs" apart from the failed Whig designation. The influence of the nativist coalition peaked in Oregon in 1855 when it was crushed by the legislature's passage of a law requiring public, verbal balloting (known as *viva voce* voting) pushed by Delazon Smith on behalf of the Bush Democrats. Bush had also infiltrated Know-Nothing meetings and later published that party's membership roster, exposing future convention opposition delegates John S. White, John W. Watts, and William Watkins.

Meanwhile, William L. Adams began publishing the *Argus* in Oregon City, using the press the Mission faction had used to launch the region's first paper eight years earlier. Adams's declared purpose was to support the "American side in politics," frequently publishing anti-Catholic and anti-British opinions. As a follower of Virginian Alexander Campbell, Adams adopted an anti-slavery position for the *Argus* but refused to take an explicit editorial stand on statehood. By the spring of 1855, the first Republican Party organizing meeting had occurred in Albany, twenty miles south of Salem, and the *Argus* became the party advocate. During the 1856 presidential campaign, its pages repeatedly advocated, "Free Speech, Free Labor, a Free Press, a Free State and Fremont," as a sign that partisan discourse about slavery was preferable to nativist themes.

Regardless of party, most settlers disliked the restrictions on popular government that came with territorial status and agitated for statehood almost immediately. The slavery issue, in the form of the Kansas-Nebraska Act (1854) and later the Dred Scott decision (1857), only exacerbated the discomfort. By negating the Missouri Compromise of 1820, the Kansas-Nebraska Act threatened to disable the slavery prohibition in Oregon's Organic Law. In an 1853 decision, newly arrived George Williams set free the children of former slave Robin Holmes, who were still owned by local Democratic politician Nathaniel Ford. Williams reasoned that, in the absence of a positive provision in the Organic Law, slavery could not exist in the territory. The mechanism of popular sovereignty enacted by the Kansas-Nebraska Act the following year, however, appeared to create a precedent whereby territories could prohibit slavery only when admitted to statehood. Although personally against slavery, Bush came out immediately in support of the new law, but, in the interest of party consensus, he avoided taking sides on slavery itself.

The election of James Buchanan to the presidency, followed by events in Kansas and the president's response to them, caused many Oregonians, regardless of party, to see a federal conspiracy to force slavery upon them. Applegate and Dryer wrote privately and publicly of this fear, and, despite the defeat of Frémont, Republican Party organizational efforts continued up and down the Willamette Valley. These efforts culminated in another meeting in Albany that adopted a free-state platform on February 11, 1857. Meanwhile, Dryer, who had consistently argued against statehood on the basis that the federal government paid the cost of territorial government administration, made a dramatic turn, declaring in the November 1, 1856, edition of the *Oregonian* that statehood constituted the only means by which Oregonians could decide the slavery issue for themselves. The following April, he was chosen as American Party constitutional delegate by a convention representing Washington and Multnomah counties.

As long as Oregon remained a territory, the slavery question remained a particularly divisive issue among local Democrats. The only solution, as the Kansas-Nebraska Act specified, was through a provision of the state's constitution. The Dred Scott decision further intensified this issue, because the constitutional interpretation outlined by Chief Justice Taney directly contradicted the doctrine Williams had delivered in *Holmes v. Ford* (1853). Statehood represented a means to end this troubling controversy. Oregon's Democratic Party platform of early 1857 reflected this understanding by providing that each member was guaranteed party standing regardless of his "individual conviction of right and policy upon the question of slavery in Oregon."[6] The platform further provided that the decision on slavery would remain outside the constitution until settled by a referendum separate from the ratification vote. After the statewide elections of that June, Judge Williams tested party tolerance by publishing in the *Statesman* a lengthy argument against permitting slavery in Oregon, although his argument was based on economic rather than legal or moral considerations. Meanwhile, Deady declined Bush's offer to submit a pro-slavery commentary.

Local Concerns Regarding Statehood

Beyond the issues of slavery and citizenship, Oregon's agitation for statehood in the 1850s was motivated by two additional local concerns: settling the so-called "Indian problem" and improving commercial transportation to the Far West. As in earlier periods in American history, when European-American settlers in large numbers began moving into the ancestral lands of Northwest Native Americans, conflict between the natives and newcomers soon ensued. The heart of the so-called "Indian problem" was competition over land and resources. As they moved westward, European-Americans carried with them strong imperialist convictions about their natural right to displace indigenous peoples from their traditional lands. The "Indian problem" was the natives' determination to retain their culture and to resist dispossession, to the point of armed conflict if necessary. American immigrants held differing opinions about the fate of the Native Americans in the region. Some believed the Native Americans would eventually die off, others supported "removal" to lands less desirable for European-American settlement, and some extremists held that the Native Americans should be exterminated.

After the events at Whitman Mission in 1847, the United States began to send American troops to the region to "subdue" the Indian threat. Still, incidents of armed conflict between Native Americans and in-coming miners and settlers did erupt into full-scale conflict on several occasions, most notably during the Rogue River War of 1853–1856 and the Yakima War of 1855–1858. The native peoples of the Rogue River region and the Plateau peoples involved in the Yakima War took up arms not only to resist the settlement of their lands by the in-coming settlers but also from frustration over the unfair treaties federal officials were then negotiating. The process was complicated by the Oregon Donation Land Claim Act of 1850, by which Congress offered European-American settlers title to lands not yet under treaty. Another serious problem was the gold rush in the Rogue River region, which brought in thousands of miners to an area where the indigenous inhabitants had long resisted the presence of European-Americans. Ultimately, a combination of superior military force, violence perpetrated by some settler groups, and the effects of disease and starvation subjugated the various native groups. By the late 1850s most of the tribes in the Pacific Northwest had been forcibly relocated onto reservations.

These conflicts, treaties, and forced removals came at a cost both to the Native American communities and the settlers; by 1857 this cost was estimated at $6 million. The federal government hesitated in approving funds for Native American affairs in Oregon, including treaty and reservation funds that were desperately needed, and the reimbursement of debts incurred by settlers and military personnel in fighting the various regional conflicts. Given the financial, social, economic, and moral costs related to Native American–settler relations, Oregonians reasoned that they would be better served by the federal government if they entered the Union. Once a state, Oregon would possess a voting congressional delegation that could more effectively advocate for the necessary appropriations. Despite Delegate Lane's tireless work for congressional reimbursement, many of the debts incurred by the settlers in the Native American wars of the 1850s remained unpaid.

In addition to augmenting federal appropriations for Native American affairs, a voting delegation in Congress might also affect economic progress in Oregon by strengthening commercial transportation links to the Pacific Northwest. The distance between Oregon and the centers of political and financial powers had long been a problem. Since the first calls for improvements to the overland trail in the 1840s, Oregonians were aware of the need for better transportation links with the East. Without a stable market and infrastructure development, Oregon farmers and entrepreneurs would remain at a distinct disadvantage vis-à-vis neighboring California, which had undergone rapid economic development following the gold rush of 1849. By gaining voting members in Congress through statehood, Oregon would have a greater voice in advocating a rail line to the Far West as well as harbor improvements and lighthouses on the Oregon coast.

The Federal Position on Statehood through 1857

Oregonians began advocating statehood in the early 1850s, and in 1854 the territorial legislature sent a memorial to Congress asking for an Enabling Act authorizing a constitutional convention. That year, however, national events precipitated a crisis that would delay Oregon's admission to the Union for another five years. The Kansas-Nebraska Act of 1854 exemplified the growing sectional conflict over territorial expansion and slavery. Senator Stephen A. Douglas of Illinois introduced the act with the support of other Democrats who believed that the measure might resolve the controversy over expansion of slavery. By embodying the notion of popular sovereignty in legislation, the act represented a monumental shift: instead of a policy mandated by Congress, the citizens of the Kansas and Nebraska could decide for themselves whether to permit slavery in their territories. The law repealed the Missouri Compromise of 1820, which had banned slavery in the Louisiana Territory north of 36°30' north latitude (Missouri's southern border). Although support for the doctrine of popular sovereignty was prevalent in the trans-Mississippi West and in theory seemed a method for resolving the slavery issue, the Kansas-Nebraska Act only intensified sectional divisions. By repealing prior limits on slavery, the act opened up new territories for the possible expansion of slavery, which Northerners opposed, and thus ensured a contentious debate over each new territorial or statehood Enabling Act.

During the mid-1850s, Oregon's territorial delegate Joseph Lane attempted to have legislation passed in Congress allowing Oregon to produce a constitution and apply for statehood. Although these attempts at passing enabling legislation did have some support in the House, Lane was unable to garner sufficient enthusiasm for such legislation in the Senate because of the worsening sectional crisis over slavery and especially because of the controversy over the Kansas-Nebraska Act. Lane made an initial attempt in April 1854, when he presented a memorial from the Oregon territorial legislature asking Congress to authorize the territory to draft a state constitution and organize a state government. Lane's proposal sat in committee through the fall and winter of 1854, when it finally reached the House floor. There, representatives engaged in some debate about the size of Oregon's population, suffrage for foreigners, and the slavery prohibition. The Enabling Act passed the House during the second session of the Thirty-third Congress in late January 1855.

In late February 1855, Stephen Douglas brought the House bill before the Senate with an amendment requiring that Oregon have sixty thousand residents before it could be admitted as state. Douglas had added the amendment to placate Southerners opposing the bill because of Oregon's prohibition of slavery. The Senate, however, had only a few days to consider the bill before its scheduled adjournment on March 3, 1855. Support was sufficiently weak that the measure was tabled by a vote of 27-11. As Senator James Jones of Tennessee remarked, southern senators declined to support the act, because it would threaten "the balance of power between the free States and the slaveholding States."[7]

The next year, during the first session of the Thirty-fourth Congress, the issue of Oregon statehood was again introduced in the House and produced energetic debate. Representatives repeated concerns about Oregon's population and the issue of voting rights for foreigners. Representatives Humphrey Marshal of Kentucky and John Letcher of Virginia were successful in having an amendment attached to the Oregon bill requiring that delegates to a constitutional convention must be U.S. citizens. Although the tally of that vote was not reported in the *Congressional Globe*, the bill did finally pass the House in early 1857 with some southern support. Unfortunately for Delegate Lane, he had to report back to Oregon voters in 1857 that Senator Stephen Douglas again failed to bring the Enabling Act to the Senate floor for a vote. Thus, the question of statehood for Oregon would apparently languish for another year. By the spring of 1857, however, news of the Supreme Court's decision in the Dred Scott case created such a reaction among Oregon's settlers that they reversed their stance on a constitutional convention and decided to take matters into their own hands. What so alarmed the electorate in Oregon and in other non-slave regions was the Court's declaration that Congress lacked the constitutional authority to outlaw slavery in the territories.

THE CONSTITUTIONAL CONVENTION OF 1857

Statehood had early popular appeal: nine of the fifteen Oregon counties voted for a convention in the first territorial referendum on the issue in 1854. Support grew in each of the subsequent referendums of 1855 and 1856, with the large populations of Lane, Douglas, and Linn counties (south of Salem) consistently supporting, while the equally populous counties of Yamhill, Marion (ironically encompassing Salem), and Washington (split into Washington and Multnomah by 1855) voted against. The initial majority of 869 against statehood shrank to 415 in the 1855 referendum and to just 249 in 1856.

In addition to three referendums after 1850, the legislature voted on the issue eight times in six years. The legislature meeting in December 1856 again shrugged off the latest voter rejection and quickly approved the ninth resolution in favor of statehood. On December 10, in response to congressional concerns about population and Oregon's eastern boundary extending beyond the Cascade Range, Democratic Governor George L. Curry delivered an address blaming the territory's low population on Congress's failure to provide adequate overland protection. With such protection, he declared, Oregon would draw a sufficient population to qualify for statehood and justify its need for extending its boundary to the Snake River. These concerns about how policy in the East affected Oregon produced a startling 5,938-vote majority for statehood in the referendum of June 1857.

Convention delegates were selected at the same election from six different partisan organizations: Bush (or "Regular") Democrats, National (or "soft") Democrats, Whigs, American or Know-Nothings, Temperance supporters, and Republicans. The electorate chose forty-four Democrats, including a dozen of Bush's closest associates. Sixteen anti-Democrats were also selected, all on the basis of stump positions against slavery and for free-state admission. Only the lone Republican, John McBride, advocated authorizing the delegates to make the decision themselves. Within the territory, the opposition came from either the south or north—from Umpqua County, south of Eugene, or from Yamhill and Multnomah counties in the north—with the exception of three delegates from the Corvallis area (which had developed a rivalry with Bush and Salem-controlled politics): William Matzger (a German-born immigrant), Henry B. Nichols, and Haman C. Lewis.

Beyond the numerical advantage, Democratic dominance began with a caucus meeting at the Salem courthouse, used as the convention hall, on the eve of the proceedings, August 16, 1857. The meeting agreed on a general plan that included the selection of the convention officers, the use of the Indiana Constitution as their model, the selection of the judicial delegates as caucus leaders, and the reaffirmation of the Democrat platform for leaving the slavery issue to a referendum. On the second day of the convention, August 18, the Democratic plan began smoothly with the overwhelming selection of their slate of agreed-upon officers. Matthew P. Deady, the only candidate to openly stump in favor of slavery, was president, and Bush was convention printer. The following day Deady assigned the labor of the convention to eleven standing committees of seven delegates each, granting sixty of seventy-seven places to Democrats. Attorneys received 48.2 percent of the committee appointments (thirty-seven of seventy-seven), although lawyers comprised 31.7 percent of the convention as a whole (nineteen of sixty). Farmers received just 37.7 percent of the rank-and-file positions (twenty-nine of seventy-seven), although they were the single largest occupational group at the convention (twenty-nine of sixty).

Regionally, thirty-three delegates hailed originally from Atlantic states, twenty from trans-Appalachia to the Mississippi River, five from the trans-Mississippi West, and two were foreign immigrants: one each from Germany and Ireland. Forty-one delegates had begun their westward migrations as children or young adults before coming to Oregon. Twenty of the sixty delegates had roots south of the Mason-Dixon Line, but none farther south than Tennessee and North Carolina. More than half of the delegates had arrived in Oregon in 1849 or later. Three-quarters made the overland journey with their families in tow and held an average donation land claim of nearly four hundred acres, about forty acres above the territory's average holding and more than twice the average acreage of their counterparts in the Midwest. They were generally successful men, holding on average $5,364 of real and personal property valuation as compared with an average of $2,295 held by all male residents of the territory. The average residency of the convention members was more than seven years, which contrasted sharply with the residencies of the constitution writers in California (1849) or Nevada (1864), which averaged about three years for the Americans involved. Except for the most recent immigrant representatives or those outside of the Willamette Valley—Marple (arrived 1851, representing Coos Bay), Charles Meigs (1855, representing Wasco County, east of the Cascades), and John Reed (1855, representing Jackson County, bordering California)—the delegates were well acquainted as neighbors and business or professional associates.

The work of the convention lasted five weeks, with final approval on the engrossed document on September 18, 1857. Organizational issues consumed most of the first week's efforts. Because most agreed that by the 1850s constitution writing involved little more than borrowing from the many models of other states, a motion for hiring an official convention reporter at an expense of $300 was withdrawn. In the interest of further efficiency, the Special Committee on Rules provided a forty-minute time limit per delegate on any individual motion. By the third week, September 8, the time limit was reduced to five minutes.

The most difficult of the organizational disputes involved how to assign the Schedule, that part of the constitution governing the transition from territorial status to statehood, including the offering of the referendum on slavery. Bush Democrats led by George Williams and Delazon Smith attempted to transfer these duties to the Judiciary Committee, which Williams chaired. David Logan fought for a more representative committee, offering repeated roll-call divisions on alternate proposals. Unaligned Democrats James Kelly and Cyrus Olney quieted the fray by offering an alternative proposal of a select committee of nine, rather than Logan's offerings of fifteen or of one from each county.

Not until Tuesday, August 25, did the convention settle into its regular routine of receiving committee reports, then reorganizing into the committee of the whole to pass or discuss the reports, and, finally, reconvening as the convention to approve provisions for engrossment or to return proposals back to committee. Week two produced less controversial reception of the militia report and rejections of efforts to reduce the eastern or southern boundaries, but substantial disagreement developed over education matters and the judiciary. Most delegates considered frugality a major virtue. Accordingly, President Deady insisted that state universities were not worth the public expense. As a result, a provision was approved delaying expenditure on a state university for ten years.

The controversy over the judiciary began when committee member David Logan protested that the report given by Judge Williams, the committee chair, did not represent what Logan had seen or voted on in committee. Furthermore, the proposal involved a major consolidation into one county court of the traditional probate courts and county commissions found in the constitutions of midwestern states. The new scheme would give significantly greater powers to elected county judges, who—given Oregon's electorate—would be Democrats. Logan argued instead that the judiciary be expanded to include a municipal court of record rather than consolidated. Furthermore, his proposal for a municipal court revealed specific concern on the part of northern anti-Democrats respecting the inadequate court handling of shady land deals involving Portland property. At the same time that the territorial justices supported consolidation of the courts, they opposed adopting into the bill of rights that portion of the Indiana constitution that guaranteed to juries the authority to determine "the law and the facts." Debate on the report of the Judiciary Committee consumed nearly five days, from August 26 (which included the only night session of the convention) through the morning session of August 31. In the end, a consolidation of the court was effected, although the minority won the concession that the legislature possessed authority to make future reorganizations, and the jury's authority was not diminished.

The judicial plan and the methods used to promote it elicited accusations of unprincipled partisan tyranny from the opposition toward the Democrats. Smith hurled similar charges back at the minority while successfully pushing a motion to limit roll call voting. Apparently sensing his own marginalization, Jesse Applegate offered a motion for leave from the convention. His fellow delegates rejected his motion, but he departed nonetheless.

Week three provided continued debate on judiciary issues and witnessed the development of a new controversy concerning stockholder liability. The overwhelming agrarian interests of the convention advocated unlimited stockholder liability, which would effectively stifle corporate-capitalistic development. Republican John McBride and William Watkins, a Free-Soiler from Jackson County, led the opposition in asserting that incorporation was "the genius of the age" and that America herself and her constitution represented one great corporation.[8] A group of Bush Democrats, meanwhile, championed the benefits of local corporate enterprises that complemented agriculture. Delegates

Grover, Boise, and Williams founded such an enterprise then under construction in Salem—the Willamette Woolen Mills—capitalized with $25,000 worth of subscribed stock. Ultimately, these three men and unaligned Democrats joined with the anti-Democrats to provide the opposition their greatest success of the convention, codifying limited liability into the constitution.

Debate on the judiciary and incorporation continued as the major issues of week four, while a handful other nettlesome issues arose, including constituent petitions on temperance, regulation of foreign immigrants, suffrage, the historically sensitive seat-of-government question, and government support of religion. On Wednesday, September 9, Judge Williams proposed a referendum mechanism granting the state legislature a means of leaving divisive issues to the electorate. Delazon Smith opposed the referendum idea, and it was voted down on a voice vote the following morning. The delegates limited future Chinese immigration and also limited Chinese landowning rights to property held before the constitution was adopted. Opposition efforts to strike out both "male" and "white" as requirements for suffrage lost on voice votes. Although *viva voce* balloting was retained in the constitution, the unaligned Democrats led by James Kelly joined with anti-Democrats to win language that gave the legislature the authority to change the balloting method in the future. After repeated efforts to settle the location of the capital, the convention finally agreed to grant the first legislature the authority to offer a referendum and to delay public expenditure on a capital until after 1865.

During the first week of the convention, the delegates had rejected opening their sessions with prayers by local clergy, and a prohibition on public expenditure for religious services had been incorporated into the adopted report on the bill of rights. On September 8, Hector Campbell, an unaligned Democrat from Milwaukie (just north of Oregon City) and a Massachusetts immigrant, championed an effort to provide chaplains for the legislature and prisons. Despite contradicting provisions adopted previously, Campbell's motion passed both in the committee of the whole and later during the convention's consideration of amendments to Article 1 (the bill of rights). When the convention came to engross Article 1, however, an amendment offered by George Williams to prohibit expenses for religious services passed again, undoing the two previous votes on Campbell's proposal.

The final vote to engross the full document occurred near the end of the fifth week, the morning of September 18, 1857. The three sources recorded the vote with slight differences. the convention *Journal* indicated that eight anti-Democrats were joined by two Democrats William Farrar (of Portland) and Sidney B. Hendershott (of Josephine County) in opposition, while only one anti-Democrat, William Matzger, joined thirty-four Democrats in the affirmative. Nine delegates recorded as absent on final engrossment eventually signed the engrossed document, which was signed by forty-two of the forty-four Democrats and by ten of the sixteen opposition delegates. The placement of the signatures, however, suggests that not all the delegates signed on September

18 or all at the same time. The engrossed and signed copy of the constitution has been preserved in the secretary of state's office in Salem, following its discovery in storage in 1880.

Despite the ideological and partisan divisions, delegates of all persuasions universally adhered to certain principles of American constitutionalism. Rejection of the recording expense resulted from their commitment to borrowing from the existing documents of other states. No debate occurred at all over the tripartite division of governing authority. Although a minor debate did occur over a separate bill of rights, the debate did not indicate any disagreement about the value of incorporating protections for individual rights in fundamental law; rather, the issue involved the proper legal and stylistic method of the incorporation. In the end, the Oregon delegates accepted a fairly extensive list of individual rights and placed it prominently at the beginning of the document because that was the accepted American tradition. The convention's commitment to a referendum on slavery was consistent with the state's established practice of leaving divisive issues to the electorate. Universal white manhood suffrage was unquestioned, whereas free black suffrage was rejected outright. Williams at one point even questioned whether the concept of equality should be included in the bill of rights for fear that it could be construed to mean the equality of whites and blacks. Meanwhile, Logan's proposal to incorporate female suffrage did not even receive a recorded roll-call division. Although today it is hard to understand these positions, they were the standard of almost all of the states at the time. The delegates did reject an effort by their judicial members to delete the provision for a woman's independent property right to her half of the donation land claim, a protection recognized at the time by only one other state—Michigan.

On November 9, 1857, and in accordance to the Schedule, the electorate voted on three questions: adoption of the constitution, slavery, and free black residency. They approved adoption 7,195 to 3,215. Slavery was defeated on a vote of 2,645 approving and 7,727 opposing, and residency for free blacks was also defeated with only 1,081 in favor of admission to 8,640 against.

FEDERAL POSITION ON STATEHOOD, 1858–1859

Despite popular ratification of the constitution in November 1857 and the election the following June of a congressman (Grover) and two senators (Smith, in Oregon, and Lane, already in Washington, D.C.), Oregon's statehood became intertwined with the fight between President Buchanan and Congress over the admission of Kansas. Perceptions of Buchanan's views on slavery, especially what was seen as his attempt to force on Kansas the pro-slavery Lecompton constitution, had been important factors in encouraging Oregonians to pursue statehood. Buchanan further alienated Oregonians by vetoing new homestead legislation. As Polk's secretary of state, however, Buchanan had supported the

U.S. acquisition of Oregon and its future addition as a state. Buchanan also endorsed popular sovereignty and could only accept the product of Lecompton, hoping to appease southerners while trusting that the known free-state majority in Kansas would quickly assert itself to resolve the matter internally without adding to the controversy nationally. Instead, Congress intervened, as House Democrats led by Indiana's William English sponsored a bill requiring resubmission of the Lecompton constitution to the Kansas electorate under the stipulation that a rejection would delay any future consideration of statehood until its population reached ninety-three thousand, the prevailing representative ratio.

In early May 1858, the Senate rejected Buchanan's proposal and adopted the English bill, and two weeks later it took up Oregon's request. Several senators expressed reservations because of the territory's small population and the alien suffrage, black exclusion, and Chinese property-owning prohibitions. Additionally, Congress had a history of mistrust of Oregon requests, stemming from early 1856 reports sent back East by Indian Agent Joel Palmer and General John E. Wool, commander of U.S. military forces in the territory, which blamed the Native American wars of the region on prior settler depredations. In March 1856, Congress had denied Lane's $500,000 appropriation to cover costs of recent Native American conflicts in the territory. Slavery and treatment of the natives involved fundamental questions of national versus state authority, giving Congress sufficient cause to proceed cautiously, but a Senate vote to table the bill until December failed 16-38. The subsequent vote to approve admission then passed 35-17, with the unanimous support of northern Democrats and eleven of the seventeen Republicans. The southern delegation divided evenly, although a slight majority of Democrats from this region approved. Senate acceptance represented a reversal of its votes during sessions in 1854–1855 and in 1857.

Republicans in the House now hesitated to endorse the admission of a decidedly Democratic state, whose policies of black exclusion and discrimination against Chinese seemed to belie free-state attitudes. These concerns led to a postponement of a vote on admission in the House until the December session. By then, and as expected, a full slate of Democrats had been elected to represent Oregon as a prospective state, and they were already in Washington lobbying to be seated. Also, Oregonians had elected a pro-slavery, although Union-loyal, Democrat from southern Oregon as governor, John Whiteaker. In January 1859, the House Republican caucus attempted to use Oregon's admission as leverage to repeal the English bill and to bring about Kansas's admission. Partisan spokesmen attacked from both sides. Democrats criticized the Republicans for their hypocritical delay in admitting a Democratic state, while the Republicans asserted that the Democratic support stemmed from the partisan benefit to be derived from admission rather than from principle.[9]

Further delay resulted, and final debate did not begin until February 10, 1859. Southerners generally spoke in favor of admission. Galusha Grow, a

Republican from Pennsylvania who had championed previous enabling legislation for Oregon, led the opposition. Central to Grow's concerns was the unequal application of population requirements between Kansas and Oregon. Alexander Stephens, a Democrat from Georgia who was becoming a close friend of Joseph Lane, admitted a preference for adequate population but indicated a willingness to make exceptions under House discretion, reversing his position during the earlier enabling debates.[10]

Finally, on February 12, 1859, the House granted statehood on a narrow vote of 114-103. Surprisingly, seventy-three of eighty-eight Republican congressmen voted against the admission of another free state, with Eli Thayer of Massachusetts bravely leading the fifteen in the minority. Southern Democrats approved admission 41-16. These votes, when combined with nearly unanimous approval from northern Democrats, determined the outcome, revealing how perceptions of the strength of Oregon's Democratic affiliation affected congressional decision-making. Beyond the partisan concerns, however, New England Republicans condemned the Oregon Constitution's discriminatory policies toward blacks and Asians. They argued that these provisions violated fundamental rights of U.S. citizens and foreign nationals whom the national government, by its constitution and treaties, was obligated to protect.

Horace Greeley, citing Representative Thayer by name, condemned the fifteen Republicans whose votes aided passage of the admission bill, declaring that those votes would be responsible for electing a pro-slavery president in the election just a year distant.[11] In fact, Oregon's 1860 electorate split in almost exactly the same fashion as the nation, providing Lincoln a popular plurality and the state's three electoral votes.

Meanwhile, President Buchanan, always a supporter of Oregon statehood, had developed a close association with Delegate and Senator-elect Lane. Lane had persuaded the president to let it be known in Oregon that patronage positions would depend on the state's Democrats supporting him (his term would expire in March 1861) and Delazon Smith (whose term would end with the 1859 spring adjournment) for reelection. Thus, Buchanan unhesitatingly signed the admission bill two days after the House vote, on February 14, 1859.

SUMMARY: A NEW STATE IN A NATION DIVIDING

Just as Oregon's statehood produced controversy in the East respecting the balance of power in the sectional and partisan political battle of that era, the sectional crisis rebounded back on Oregon's political scene. Because of Congress's reluctance to confer statehood, the legislature was forced to convene in December under territorial status. Partisan debate over constituent petitions for protecting slaveholding rights soon spilled into the alleyways of Salem. Assemblyman J. H. Lansater, a Marion County Democrat, took such offense at Thomas Dryer for throwing an inkpot at him during floor debate in the assembly that Lansater and several friends afterwards severely beat the *Oregonian* editor.

Meanwhile, the alliance between Delazon Smith and Asahel Bush fractured when the former failed to help the latter bring down Delegate Lane. Bush believed that congressional delay on Oregon statehood resulted from Lane's manipulating the issue for his own political ambition. When Smith departed for Washington in 1858, Bush expected that the short-term senator would obtain the evidence necessary to expose Lane's tactics. In Washington, however, Smith came to admire Lane and defended him in letters to Bush. Bush responded by cutting Smith out of the Clique, forcing the two senators-elect to ally for control of Oregon Democrats, and Lane won Buchanan's promise of patronage for Democrats supporting the Lane-Smith ticket in state elections. Consequently, Lane Democrats dominated the party convention and agreed to support Delazon Smith for the U.S. Senate seat. Bush responded with open attacks on the Lane-Smith coalition and endorsed Senator Stephen Douglas's position on slavery and the territories.

During the special legislative session of May 1859 to select the state's congressional delegation, however, Smith failed to win the Senate when a small cabal of Bush adherents from Salem staged a walkout, effectively depriving the majority of a quorum. Before the walkout Lansing Stout, a Lane-Smith candidate, was chosen as the congressional nominee. In the June general election, Salem Democrats failed to enter a congressional candidate, and Stout defeated the former black-Republican–hating David Logan (now member of that party) by a mere sixteen votes.

Smith's Senate seat remained unfilled. Returning to his home in Albany, Smith began publishing the *Oregon Democrat* in hopes of rallying support, but the splintering of Oregon Democrats only worsened. The state's Buchanan Democrats dominated the next regular state meeting, electing Stout, Deady, and Lane for the upcoming national party convention in Charleston with instructions to endorse Lane for president. Bush's minority, pro-Douglas Democrats countered by joining with the Republicans to deny Lane a return to the Senate. Bush and the Republicans decided to divide the state's representation during the June general election, agreeing not to run candidates in districts where the other party was stronger. By eliminating three-way races, the coalition forced the Lane-Smith candidates into the minority, because eighteen Bush-Douglas Democrats and thirteen Republicans won office, as compared with seventeen Lane-Smith Democrats.

The majority Douglas-Democrat–Republican fusion met in the legislative session of that summer and chose compromise candidates for the U.S. Senate: old Democratic pioneer James Nesmith, and Edward D. Baker, a recent Republican immigrant from California. The final selection came after a delay caused by a handful of Lane-Smith supporters hiding in the barn of Nicolas Shrum, a former nonaligned Democrat of the constitutional convention. As a result,

Lane managed only second place on the Breckenridge ticket, while Smith and Dryer stumped the state as electors for their respective factions: Smith for Breckenridge-Lane and Dryer for Lincoln-Hamlin.

In the November general election, Lincoln carried Oregon's electorate by a mere 270-vote plurality, receiving 5,344 votes to 5,075 for Breckenridge; Stephen Douglas garnered 4,131, and John Bell received just 212. Although Lane supported slavery and southern interests, he ridiculed northern suspicions of secession as partisan imputations against southern patriotism.[12] Lane's miscalculation ended his political viability, and he returned to live out his days at his home near Roseburg. Smith died suddenly on a business trip to Portland just a little more than a week after the 1860 national election. Judge Deady accepted appointment to the federal bench for Oregon and announced that he was removing himself from the Democratic Party, because he now considered himself a Hamiltonian Federalist. The Civil War drove Bush, Boise, and Williams permanently to the Republican side of politics. Grover gravitated to the Union Party during the Civil War before coming back to lead a new organization of Democrats reconstructed on the model of the Salem Clique, which enabled him to achieve first the state governorship and then election to the U.S. Senate in 1878. Grover's political success during this later period derived from his virulent attacks on Asian immigrants and Republican business interests, not unlike the anti-black assaults of the Democratic Party during the 1850s.

A. C. Gibbs became Oregon's first Republican governor in 1862, convening a special session of the legislature in December 1865 to ratify the Thirteenth Amendment's ban on slavery, despite an effort made in the House under direction of Lafayette Lane (the former senator's son) to alter the wording. The same legislature did pass a five-dollar poll tax on "every Negro, Chinamen, and Mullato residing within limits of the state" and authorized labor on public works, with time credited at fifty cents per day in lieu of actual cash payment. The Fourteenth Amendment's grant of citizenship to "persons" along with equal protection and due process guarantees passed in the 1866 regular legislative session by four votes in each chamber, but the 1868 legislature passed a rescinding resolution, withdrawing Oregon's ratification of the amendment. The U.S. Congress simply ignored Oregon's action. The Fifteenth Amendment's proposed guarantee of voting rights for black male adults was rejected by the 1870 Oregon legislature, although the centennial legislature of 1959 passed a ceremonial bill of acceptance.

The first alterations to Oregon's 1857 document were not made until the opening of the twentieth century under Populist energy supplied by an 1880s immigrant, William S. U'Ren. U'Ren, as head of the People's Power League, led the successful effort in the legislatures of 1899 and 1901 to add provisions for the initiative and the referendum. By 1916, nineteen amendments had been adopted through the initiative process, including female suffrage, prohibition, recall by petition, home rule for cities, indictment by grand juries, and abolition of capital punishment. Legislative commissions authorized in 1953 and 1961 submitted recommendations to the state legislature for major revisions to the constitution, focusing on reapportionment procedures, consolidating the executive function and authority, and de-politicizing and professionalizing the local judiciary. These efforts at revision failed, leaving Oregon as one of a handful of states still governed by its original constitution, although it has been amended more than one hundred times and is three times its original length of 11,000 words.

NOTES

1. William W. Bristow to Asahel Bush, April 19, 1851, Asahel Bush Papers, Mss. 581, Oregon Historical Society, Portland.

2. Malcolm Clark, Jr., *Eden Seekers: The Settlement of Oregon, 1818–1862* (Boston: Houghton Mifflin, 1981), p. 280; David Alan Johnson, *California, Oregon, and Nevada, 1840–1890* (Berkeley: University of California Press, 1992), p. 404n.

3. Jesse Applegate to Matthew Deady, January 26, 1851, Matthew Deady Papers, Mss. 48, Oregon Historical Society, Portland.

4. George S. Turnbull, *History of Oregon Newspapers* (Portland: Binford & Mort, 1939), pp. 81–84.

5. William L. Adams, *Oregonian*, February 7, 14, 21, and March 6, 13, 1851; Asahel Bush, *The Statesman*, June 27, 1851.

6. *The Statesman*, April 21, 1857.

7. *The Congressional Globe*, 33rd Cong., 2d Sess., March 3, 1855, p. 1149.

8. *The Oregonian*, September 26, 1857.

9. The minority report on Oregon admission reflecting the Republican caucus position appeared in *The Congressional Globe*, 35th Cong., 2d Sess., January 18, February 10, 1859, pp. 427, 946; Henry H. Simms, "The Controversy Over the Admission of the State of Oregon," *Mississippi Valley Historical Review* 32 (1945): 355–374.

10. Ibid.

11. *The Tribune*, February 1859.

12. Douglas Heider and David Dietz. *Legislative Perspectives: A 150-Year History of the Oregon Legislatures From 1843 to 1993* (Portland: Oregon Historical Society Press, 1995), p. 29; *The New York Times*, November 9, 1860.

BIBLIOGRAPHY

Carey, Charles H. *A General History of Oregon, Prior to 1861*. 2 vols. Portland: Metropolitan Press, 1935–1936.

———. *The Oregon Constitution and Proceedings of and Debate of the Constitutional Conventions of 1857*. Reprint. Portland: Oregon Historical Society Press, 1984.

Clark, Malcolm Jr. *Eden Seekers: The Settlement of Oregon, 1818–1862*. Boston: Houghton Mifflin, 1981.

Corning, Howard McKinley. *Dictionary of Oregon History*. Portland: Binford and Mort Publishing, 1956.

Dodds, Gordon B. *Oregon: A Bicentennial History*. New York: W.W. Norton, 1977.

Douglas, Jesse S. "Origins of the Population of Oregon in 1850." *Pacific Northwest Quarterly* 41 (April 1950): 95–108.

Douthit, Nathan. *Uncertain Encounters: Indians and Whites at Peace and War in Southern Oregon, 1820–1860s*. Corvallis: Oregon State University Press, 2002.

Heider, Douglas, and David Dietz. *Legislative Perspectives: A 150-Year History of the Oregon Legislatures From 1843 to 1993*. Portland: Oregon Historical Society Press, 1995.

Johansen, Dorothy O. "A Tentative Appraisal of Territorial Government in Oregon." *Pacific Historical Review* 18 (November 1949): 485-499.

———, and Charles M. Gates. *Empire of the Columbia: A History of the Pacific Northwest*. New York: Harper & Brothers, 1957.

Johnson, David Alan. *California, Oregon, and Nevada, 1840–1890*. Berkeley: University of California Press, 1992.

Lee, Alton. "Slavery and the Oregon Territorial Issue." *Pacific Northwest Quarterly* 64 (July 1973): 112–119.

McLagan, Elizabeth. *A Peculiar Paradise: A History of Blacks in Oregon, 1788–1940*. Portland: Georgian Press, 1980.

Merk, Frederick. *The Oregon Question: Essays in Anglo-American Diplomacy and Politics*. Cambridge, MA: Harvard University, 1967.

Miles, Edwin. "'Fifty-four Forty or Fight' —An American Political Legend." *Mississippi Historical Valley Review* 44 (September 1957): 291–204.

Pike, C. J. "Petitions of Oregon Settlers, 1838–1848." *Oregon Historical Quarterly* 34 (September 1933): 216–235.

Pletcher, David M. *The Diplomacy of Annexation: Texas, Oregon, and the Mexican War*. Columbia: University of Missouri Press, 1973.

Simms, Henry. "The Controversy over the Admission of the State of Oregon." *Mississippi Valley Historical Review* 32 (December 1945): 355–374.

Woodward, Walter C. *The Rise and Early History of Political Parties in Oregon, 1843–1868*. Portland: J.K. Gill, 1913.

Zacharias, Tim. "Lest We Forget: A Prosopographic Analysis of Oregon's Constitutional Convention of 1857." MA thesis. Washington State University, 2003.

THE COMMONWEALTH OF PENNSYLVANIA

Ratified the Constitution of the United States: December 12, 1787

John David Rausch, Jr.

INTRODUCTION

Pennsylvania was the second state to ratify the new Constitution. In many ways, however, Pennsylvania took the leading role in the debate over the nation's new charter. The convention that wrote the Constitution met in Philadelphia during the summer of 1787. The Pennsylvania General Assembly was the first state legislature to receive the Constitution and the first to call for a state convention. The Pennsylvania press took a leading role in the debate over the new Constitution with many of the articles appearing in Philadelphia papers being reprinted in other states. It was during the debate that the first division of Americans into Federalists and Anti-Federalists appeared. In fact, one of the reasons why Delaware ratified the Constitution before Pennsylvania is that the Pennsylvania convention took time to debate the document at length. The debate occurred because Pennsylvania already had a lively, working two-party system by 1787.

FROM PROPRIETARY COLONY TO INDEPENDENCE

As one of the thirteen original colonies that created the United States, Pennsylvania's history begins as a land grant from the king of England.

William Penn's Charter

The Quaker William Penn is perhaps one of the most famous of the colony builders in American history.[1] He was the son of a British admiral, Sir William

Pennsylvania

Territorial Development:

- British forces acting for the future King James II overpower Dutch defenses and take possession of Pennsylvania, 1664
- Charles II grants Pennsylvania to William Penn, 1680
- Continental Congress approves Declaration of Independence from Great Britain, July 4, 1776
- Great Britain formally recognizes American independence through the Treaty of Paris, September 3, 1783
- Pennsylvania becomes the second state to ratify the U.S. Constitution, December 12, 1787

Capitals Prior to Statehood:

- Trinicum Island, established as the capital of the Pennsylvania colony, 1643
- Chester, 1682–1683
- Philadelphia, 1683–1787

State Capitals:

- Chester, 1787–1790
- Philadelphia, 1790–1799
- Lancaster, 1799–1812
- Harrisburg, 1812–present

Origin of State Name: Charles II gave the state its name by combining the Latin word *sylvania*, meaning "woodland," with William Penn's last name. The state name therefore means, "Penn's woodland."

First Governor: Thomas Mifflin

Governmental Organization: Initially established with a unicameral legislature, but switched to a bicameral system in 1790

Population at Statehood: 433,611

Geographical Size: 44,817 square miles

Penn. King Charles II owed Admiral Penn £16,000. When the admiral died, his son William inherited the claim for the money. Rather than asking the king for money, Penn requested a grant of land in the territory between Lord Baltimore's province of Maryland and the Duke of York's territory of New York. The king signed the charter of Pennsylvania on March 4, 1681. The new colony was named in honor of William Penn's father. It included the land between 39° and 42° north latitude and from the Delaware River west for five degrees of longitude. Although the charter provided for some local self-government, it also provided that the king could revoke provincial laws. In 1682, the Duke of York gave Penn his claim to the lower three counties on the Delaware River, the present state of Delaware, enlarging the original grant.

Penn appointed his cousin, William Markham, to be deputy governor of the colony and sent Markham to North America in April 1681. Remaining in England, Penn drafted his proposed "First Frame of Government," the first constitution of Pennsylvania. In October 1682, Penn traveled to his colony. He visited Philadelphia, created the original three counties of Bucks, Chester, and Philadelphia, and called a General Assembly to meet in Chester on December 4, 1682. This assembly adopted the Great Law on December 7. The Great Law, the fundamental basis for law in Pennsylvania, was a series of statutes enacted to govern the new colony and to implement the vision Penn presented in the First Frame of Government. The statutes provided for a guaranteed liberty of conscience and religious freedom, important to the Quakers.[2] Penn planned to create a bicameral legislature with the upper house, the council, proposing laws to the lower house, the assembly. In 1683, a second assembly revised Penn's First Frame of Government to create the Second Frame of Government. The assembly also joined the Delaware counties to the Pennsylvania colony. Penn returned to England in late 1684 after establishing the foundation for the government of his colony.

After the English Revolution in 1688, Penn was suspected of aiding the Crown. His colony was taken away in 1693. It was restored in 1695 after he was acquitted of treason, a charge that stemmed from his friendship with the deposed King James II. In 1701, Penn reluctantly signed the Charter of Privileges, the document that remained the constitution of the colony until the American Revolution.[3] The charter gave more power to the voters in the colony than Penn desired. In addition, it created a single-house assembly to be elected annually. Men who owned fifty acres of land or who had estates worth at least fifty British pounds could vote. This requirement reduced the political influence of residents of the growing towns in the colony, shifting political power to the landowners in the countryside. Because most of the landowners were Quakers, the charter also increased their political influence. Under the terms of the charter, the assembly could initiate legislation, but the proprietor or the governor could veto legislation. The charter also granted a separate legislature to the three counties in Delaware. Like its predecessor, the charter guaranteed freedom of religion.

Colonial Growth and Development

Although Penn was granted land by the king, he and his heirs chose not to settle any land unless it had been purchased from the Native American inhabitants. All of Pennsylvania except the northwestern corner was settled this way by 1768. The legislature bought the Six Nations' claims to the northwestern corner of Pennsylvania in 1784 and 1789, and the claims of the Delaware and the Wyandot were settled in 1785. One of the most famous and controversial of these purchases was the "Walking Purchase" of 1737.[4] At his death, Penn's sons John and Thomas became the proprietors of Pennsylvania. The colony was becoming a popular destination for immigrants from Europe, and the Penns were making money by selling land that was still the possession of the Native Americans. The brothers needed to establish title to land in the upper Delaware and Lehigh River valleys. In August 1737, the Delawares relinquished ownership of the land, but the purchase remained to be measured. The deed indicated that the purchase extended from a point on the Delaware River near present-day Wrightstown, northwest into the interior "as far as a Man could walk in a day and half," a typical Native American measurement of space. Three men were hired to walk the appropriate amount of time at a very fast pace. The "walk" ended near the present-day borough of Jim Thorpe, much farther than the Delawares had anticipated. They protested and refused to leave until the Iroquois forced them from the land in 1741.

Upon his return to England in 1684, William Penn began recruiting settlers for his colony. He traveled in England, Ireland, and Holland, telling listeners about the colony's freedom of religion. He was quite successful, because a number of people of different ethnic groups began flooding through the port at Philadelphia in the early and mid-1700s. The diverse population affected the colony's politics.

The Quakers were a dominant element among the English population. There were many Anglican settlers as well. The English settled primarily in the southeastern counties around the growing city of Philadelphia. The city grew to become the commercial center for the British colonies.

German-speaking immigrants were the largest group of non-English settlers. Coming largely from the Rhineland, German immigration increased after 1727. By the time of the American Revolution, about one-third of the population of the colony was German. They settled in the interior counties of Northampton, Berks, Lancaster, and Lehigh. German farmers contributed to the growing prosperity of the colony. Mainly Lutheran or Reformed (Calvinist), the Germans found comfort in the colony's freedom of religious conscience. Other Germans were Catholic, Anabaptists, or members of smaller sects. One result of the large German-speaking population was the need to publish important government documents in German. The Declaration of Independence of 1776 was even translated and printed in German.

After 1717, waves of Scotch-Irish immigrants came to the colony because hardships plagued them in Ireland. Primarily Presbyterian, they settled on the frontier, first in the Cumberland Valley and then farther west in central and western Pennsylvania. At the time of the Revolution, the Scotch-Irish comprised about one-fourth of the population in the colony.

Quakers who were Irish and Welsh settled largely in the region around Philadelphia. They were joined in the colony by smaller groups of French Huguenots, Jews from the Spanish Empire, and Irish Catholics. Many immigrant families settled in Pennsylvania for only a short time before moving farther west to the Ohio River Valley.

Slaves were imported into the colony despite the Quaker opposition to slavery. By 1730, about four thousand slaves owned by English, Welsh, and Scotch-Irish colonists had been brought to Pennsylvania. The Pennsylvania Gradual Abolition Act of 1780, the first emancipation statute in the United States, ended slavery in the state. By 1790, the African American population of Pennsylvania was ten thousand.

By 1760, these settlers occupied all of southeastern Pennsylvania and the lower reaches of the Susquehanna River Valley. They had pushed across the Blue Mountains in the western portions of the colony. No ethnic group was in the majority. For example, in Lancaster County in 1750, the Scotch-Irish comprised the largest group at 35 percent of the population. Germans and English each comprised 25 percent of the population. The remainder of the population included smaller groups of Welsh and other ethnic groups. There were few residents of African descent.

The economy of the colony was based largely on agricultural production and trade. Pennsylvania was one of the leading agricultural areas of British North America. Wheat and corn were the leading crops. Small manufacturing also played a role in the economic development of the colony. Sawmills and gristmills were established to take advantage of the many streams. Shipbuilding became an important industry on the Delaware River. The colony also became known for iron manufacture with several leading forges producing pig iron. The Pennsylvania long rifle, a staple of frontiersmen, was created in Lancaster County. Craftsmen in Lancaster County also developed the Conestoga wagon, the prototype for the prairie schooner that carried pioneers to the American West.

Although the diversity and industry in Pennsylvania created a cosmopolitan colony, it also created political conflict. This conflict centered on the differing interests of the proprietor and a more populist political element. The 1701 Charter of Privileges included many features demanded by the populists, including a powerful single-house legislature. The Penn family proprietors, represented in the colony by governors, quarreled with the assembly. The Penns had abandoned Quakerism, whereas the Quakers dominated the assembly until 1756. This conflict resulted in the development of two parties, the Proprietary Party and the Quaker Party. The people of the frontier challenged the residents of the more settled southeastern region for adequate representation in the assembly and for better protection against marauding Native Americans supported by the French.

Events in the 1750s began to foreshadow the end of the proprietary government of Pennsylvania. In 1754, the French and Indian War began in western Pennsylvania. As pacifists, the Quaker and proprietary government had not effectively prepared a suitable defense for the colony. The colony did not participate in the fighting even in 1755 when a British army under General Edward Braddock, aided by the Virginia militia under Colonel George Washington, unsuccessfully tried to remove the French from Fort Duquesne in western Pennsylvania. Only after Braddock's defeat did the Pennsylvania assembly take action in response to an uprising by the Shawnee and Delaware seeking a return of their lands. In April 1756, seven Quaker members of the assembly resigned. This action allowed the assembly to vote to prepare for military action. This vote marked the turning point in the war, and Pennsylvania established more than forty forts on the frontier. A British army that included volunteers from Pennsylvania finally captured Fort Duquesne in November 1758, after the French had deserted it. The British forces renamed it Fort Pitt. The French surrendered in 1763, but the Pennsylvania frontier became subject to a long series of raids by a coalition of tribes led by Pontiac. Although Pontiac's uprising was eventually crushed, it led to an event that showed the disagreement between the proprietary government and the people of Pennsylvania, the "Paxton Boys" incident.

The "Paxton Boys" were Scotch-Irish Presbyterian settlers of the area near present-day Harrisburg. Angered by the inability of the assembly to protect them from Native American attacks, the settlers decided to take action themselves. On December 14, 1763, about fifty men entered the village of Conestoga, a settlement of peaceful Native Americans near Lancaster. The men killed six unarmed natives and tracked an additional fourteen to Lancaster where they, too, were killed. When the assembly agreed to shelter peaceful Native Americans in Philadelphia, the Paxton Boys advanced on the city, pillaging and threatening residents on the way. On February 5, 1764, armed Philadelphia volunteers under the command of Benjamin Franklin met the Paxton Boys in Germantown. Franklin was able to convince the gang to submit their grievances to the government rather than try to overthrow it.

The Paxton Boys' march to Philadelphia spawned a political debate over the causes of the incident. This debate included the publication of the first political cartoons in the colonies. Some observers blamed the Presbyterians for killing unarmed Native Americans when they could not find armed hostile ones. Others criticized the proprietor, John Penn, for not allowing frontier defense to be funded because he did not want his lands taxed. The Quakers were blamed because they would not fight in defense of the frontier, but they did take up arms to defend Philadelphia against fellow whites. The Pennsylvania Germans were attacked as helpless dupes of the Quakers. This incident foreshadowed the conflict in Pennsylvania caused by revolutionary fervor a decade later.

Revolution and the Constitution of 1776

The debate on independence was different in Pennsylvania than in the other colonies.[5] Political activists in the other colonies were working to resist British taxes and trade regulations. In Pennsylvania, the Quakers were trying to get the British to take the colony from the Penn family because the family refused to pay taxes. The Penn family also appealed to the court in an effort to force the Quakers to fight to defend Pennsylvania. The assembly never voted on endorsing independence or remaining with the empire. By the height of the revolutionary fervor in the colonies, the parties representing the proprietor and the Quakers were swept aside by a popular movement to create a new Pennsylvania. In the process, the Charter of Privileges that had governed the colony since 1701 was replaced by a new document.

The radical forces of independence did not have powerful allies in Pennsylvania.[6] Although John Penn did not have a stake in continuing British authority over the colony, he was concerned about how a break with England would affect the status of the 1701 charter and his family's estates in the colony. Quaker and Anglican political leaders in the assembly worked to preserve middle-of-the-road policies that blocked more radical opposition to British measures. The enemies of these leaders called them the "half and half" party because their support came from dissatisfied members of both the Quaker Party and the Proprietary Party. Referring to themselves as "Whigs," because they wanted to identify with British politicians who opposed the strong monarchy, the party was led by men like John Dickinson, a Philadelphia lawyer. He argued in his 1767 pamphlet *Letters of a Pennsylvania Farmer* that England had no power to tax the colonies in any manner. Although this statement appeared radical, Dickinson was more moderate than the firebrands found in the New England colonies. In fact, many of Dickinson's opponents in rural Pennsylvania found him too conservative.

The Whigs' lack of action caused the emergence of a radical lower- and middle-class movement. Whereas merchants and men of the upper classes had once sought elective office, by the early 1770s, artisans and craftsmen campaigned for election. In 1775 and 1776, an alternative political system emerged in Pennsylvania. Younger men of the middle classes, including the astronomer David Rittenhouse, an artist Charles Willson Peale, physicians Benjamin Rush and James Hutchinson, and Thomas Paine, led this system. These men wrote pamphlets and delivered speeches at meetings to mobilize their potential supporters.

In 1774, Governor John Penn refused to call the assembly to select delegates to the First Continental Congress. His refusal caused the creation of committees of correspondence that appointed the delegates instead. The first committees were organized in Philadelphia, but soon committees could be found meeting in towns and villages throughout the colony. Sometimes calling themselves "Associators," these committees operated outside the regular government.

In September 1774, political radicals in Pennsylvania began a campaign to overthrow the conservative government in the colony. The campaign required almost two years of politics.

Two well-organized and vocal parties had coalesced by the spring of 1776. The Moderate Party had the support of the majority of the electorate and was led by John Dickinson, financier Robert Morris, and Dr. Benjamin Rush. This party feared that a revolution would severely damage Pennsylvania's economic structure. George Bryan, Timothy Matlack, James Cannon, Thomas Young, and Thomas Paine led the Radical Party. The Radicals lacked support in the electorate, but they had the support of many of the members of the Continental Congress then meeting in Philadelphia. The Pennsylvania assembly had instructed its delegates to the congress not to vote for independence. The Radicals in the assembly were unable to repeal those instructions.

With majority support in the electorate, the Moderate Party maintained the upper hand during the tumultuous spring of 1776. On May 1, the party kept its majority in the assembly elections. The Radicals, frustrated at their inability to gain the majority, looked to the Continental Congress for help. The Pennsylvania Radicals were able to persuade the Congress to pass a resolution requiring that all colonial governments deriving their power from the Crown should be "totally suppressed":

> That it be recommended to the respective Assemblies and Conventions of the United Colonies, where no government sufficient to the exigencies of their affairs has been hitherto established, to adopt such government as shall in the opinion of the representatives of the people, best conduce to the happiness and safety of their constituents in particular, and America in general. By order of the Congress.

This act of Congress effectively abolished the 1701 charter and undermined the authority of the Pennsylvania assembly.

Seeing their opportunity, the Pennsylvania Radicals met to take steps to form a new government to provide instructions for the delegates to the Continental Congress. On May 20, 1776, four thousand Philadelphians stood in the rain in the State House yard to listen to Thomas McKean, a Philadelphia lawyer. McKean voiced the people's approval of the congress's resolution calling for the dissolution of ties to the Crown and the call for a special constitutional convention to create a new state government. The assembly, also meeting in Philadelphia, was to have no role in creating this new government and, thus, voted itself out of existence on June 14.

A total of 103 delegates from ten counties and the city of Philadelphia convened a provincial conference in Carpenters' Hall in Philadelphia on June 18, 1776. The first entry in the record of the first meeting indicates the reason for the conference:

> This day a number of Gentlemen met at Carpenters' Hall, in Philadelphia, being deputed by the Committees of several of the counties of this Province, to join

in Provincial Conference in consequence of a Circular Letter from the Committee of the City and Liberties of Philadelphia, enclosing the resolution of the Continental Congress of the 15th of May last.

On the second day of the conference, the delegates selected officers and agreed that each county would have one vote, regardless of population. The record reports that the conference voted to have the May 15th resolution of the Continental Congress read twice:

Whereas his Britannic Majesty, in conjunction with the Lords and Commons of Great Britain, has by a late act of Parliament, excluded the inhabitants of these United Colonies from the protection of his crown;
And whereas no answer whatever, to the humble petitions of the colonies for redress of grievances and reconciliation with Great Britain, has been, or is likely to be given, but the whole force of that kingdom, aided by foreign mercenaries, is to be exerted for the destruction of the good people of these colonies;
And whereas it appears absolutely irreconcilable to reason and good conscience, for the people of these Colonies now to take the oaths and affirmations necessary for the support of any government under the crown of Great Britain; and it is necessary that the exercise of every kind of authority under the said crown should be totally suppressed, and all the powers of government exerted under the authority of the people of the colonies for the preservation of internal peace, virtue and good order, as well as for the defense of their lives, liberties and properties, against the hostile invasions and cruel depredations of their enemies.

The delegates then voted to declare the current government "not competent to the exigencies of our Affairs." This action was followed by the drafting of a declaration of independence for Pennsylvania, which was then forwarded to the Continental Congress. The conference set elections for a new assembly, authorized a militia of six thousand men for defense, and called for a constitutional convention to meet as soon as possible. The conference adjourned on June 25, after meeting for a week. On July 2, the Continental Congress voted to declare independence.

The election of delegates to a provincial convention was held on July 8, 1776. Each county was to send eight representatives. Before it adjourned, the provincial conference determined the qualifications of electors. In addition to those persons who already had the right to vote, adult militia members were granted the right to vote and could be elected to the provincial convention. The property requirement for voting was abolished, and residents of the state who were known Loyalists were prohibited from voting. Electors were expected to swear the following oath:

I, _____, do declare that I do not hold myself bound to bear allegiance to George the third, King of Great Britain, and that I will not by any means, directly or indirectly, oppose the establishment of a free government in this province, by the Convention now to be chosen, nor the measures adopted by the Congress,

against the tyranny attempted to be established in these colonies by the court
of Great Britain.

Candidates for the convention had to declare their belief in God, Jesus Christ,
and the divine inspiration of the scriptures.

The provincial convention met for the first time on July 15, 1776. The
body elected Benjamin Franklin to preside. George Bryan, James Cannon, and
Benjamin Franklin are credited with being the primary authors of the Constitution of 1776. The document proclaimed in detail the rights of citizens, expanding the right to vote to all tax-paying free men.[7] Legislative power was
granted to a single-house legislature whose members were elected to one-year
terms. Members of the assembly were limited in the number of terms they
could serve in office. The executive branch was comprised of a twelve-member
Supreme Executive Council. The assembly and council together would elect
one of the twelve men to be president. A Council of Censors was to be elected
every seven years. Working for a year, the Council of Censors would evaluate
the activities of government and "censure" those actions that violated the constitution. Only the Council of Censors could make any changes to the
constitution. The constitution was declared in effect on September 28, 1776,
and elections to the new assembly were called for November.

The constitution of 1776 included one troublesome provision. To participate
in politics, a person had to take a "test oath" affirming loyalty to the constitution. A large portion of the Pennsylvania population could not swear an oath
for religious or political reasons and were blocked from political participation.
In many cases, persons who refused to take the oath paid higher property taxes,
and many had their property confiscated. Among the disenfranchised were
Quakers, Anabaptists, and Mennonites, who chose to remain neutral during
the Revolution.

POLITICS UNDER THE CONSTITUTION OF 1776

Two parties emerged in the Commonwealth of Pennsylvania shortly after
the constitution of 1776 was adopted. The Constitutionalists (or Constitutional
Society) formed out of the Radicals who rallied for the new constitution and
supported the document and its democratic principles. A party called the
Republicans (or Republican Society), the Moderates who had opposed radical
revolution and independence, challenged the Constitutionalists. Throughout most of the decade leading up to the ratification of the new federal
Constitution in 1787, Pennsylvania politics was marked by the conflict
between the two parties. In fact, the conflict continued into the ratification
debate with the Republicans becoming the Federalist supporters of the
U.S. Constitution and the Constitutionalists forming the core of the
Anti-Federalist opponents.

The Constitutionalists

The divisions over the new state constitution reflected geographical and social as well as political differences in Pennsylvania. Geographically, the state was divided between Philadelphia and western Pennsylvania. This division led to social distinctions between urban and rural, merchants and farmers, rich and poor. Although there were exceptions, the Constitutionalists received most of their support from the rural western counties, benefiting from overrepresentation in the assembly. In apportioning representation by county, the constitution made sure that the western counties received more than their share of representatives.

The Constitutionalists are given credit for writing the constitution. Primarily comprised of Scotch-Irish Presbyterians from the rural western counties, their leaders were George Bryan, Timothy Matlack, Benjamin Franklin, and David Rittenhouse. George Bryan served as vice president of the Executive Council and later served as acting president. Timothy Matlack, a leader of the Free Quakers who chose to fight in the Revolution, was a merchant, gambler, and philosopher of the Constitutionalists' cause. David Rittenhouse was an astronomer as well as a politician. In drafting the constitution of 1776, they sought to enact Matlack's guiding principle that "All men are born free and equal." They placed all power of government in the hands of the public, using a single-house legislature with frequent elections and a very limited executive. Assembly deliberations were open to the public, and its proceedings were published.

The Republicans

The Republicans were not anti-democratic, but they were concerned about the excesses of unrestrained democracy. The party's leaders were not as democratic as the Constitutionalists, but they also were not Loyalists. They recognized some problems in the constitution of 1776. Republicans opposed annual elections and the single-house legislature while supporting the general principle of increased popular power. Republican leaders included Robert Morris, James Wilson, Dr. Benjamin Rush, George Clymer, and Thomas Mifflin, and they found the majority of their support in the Philadelphia region. Their opposition to the state constitution was that it was "too loose and Democratic."

Pennsylvania Politics: Constitutionalists versus Republicans

The conflict between the Constitutionalists and the Republicans marked the decade preceding the ratification debate. This conflict spilled over into the debate over ratifying a new federal Constitution. Early in the operation of the constitution of 1776, problems emerged. The single-house legislature became too powerful, and the western counties were overrepresented until a census was taken. The assembly often lacked a quorum, because the requirement that two-thirds of the members be in attendance allowed a minority of members to block action simply by disappearing. The test oath became a subject of debate because it prohibited many religious people in the eastern region, primarily Quakers and members of some German sects, from participating in politics.

The Constitutionalist Party dominated politics during the early years of the war, especially when Philadelphia was occupied or threatened with occupation. The Constitutionalists were better able to rally the people by proving themselves more revolutionary than the Republicans. Many potential Republican supporters were kept out of the polls by the test oath. The assembly under the Constitutionalists moved to tax the Penn family's land holdings. It also revoked the charter of the nominally Quaker College of Pennsylvania. In 1780, the assembly enacted the Gradual Abolition Act, the nation's first law banning slavery.

Constitutionalists controlled the assembly from 1776 until 1782, when the Republicans gained the majority. During this period, a number of Constitutionalist supporters changed their positions to oppose the constitution. James Cannon, one of the authors of the constitution of 1776, disapproved the test oath. Thomas Paine and Timothy Matlack also disliked the oath. David Rittenhouse eventually grew disgusted with politics and turned his attention to astronomy. One of the greatest challenges to the Constitutionalist government was price-fixing and inflation in Philadelphia. The government tried to enforce an embargo against exporting grain, and at the same time they instituted price controls in Philadelphia. The embargoes against exporting grain or importing manufactured goods did not work as long as traders had access to free ports in Delaware. Although the Constitutionalists were unable to correct the economy in Philadelphia, the Republican Robert Morris was having success with his bank and financial plans in saving the Continental Army. Frustrated and embarrassed, the Constitutionalists revoked the charter of Morris's bank. After gaining a majority, the Republicans rechartered the bank.

The war against the British needed to be financed, but Pennsylvanians refused or were unable to pay their state taxes. As a result, the county courts confiscated large amounts of property for failure to pay taxes. Citizens in the counties drew up covenants against the state government, pledging not to purchase confiscated property. They also intimidated anyone who purchased the property and made it difficult for government officials to get to the property to take it away. In Westmoreland County, a gang of tax resisters blocked a road with manure, forcing the sheriff and his men to deal with the stench while they removed the barricade.

Despite the state constitution's promise of widespread political participation, few Pennsylvanians took advantage of their opportunities. The test oath blocked a sizable part of the population, but even after the oath was abolished in 1786, only about one-quarter of all eligible Pennsylvanians voted in elections. Residents participated in politics only when they felt their self-interest threatened.

In the election of 1782, the Republicans gained an edge in the assembly, beginning a period of instability in party control of the legislature. The Constitutionalists regained control in the election of 1784 and maintained their control in the 1785 election. The Republicans earned a slight edge in the election of 1786 but realized that they could not maintain their majority for long. These Republicans began to see that the future of Pennsylvania might be better served with a stronger national government. In March 1786, the assembly responded to Virginia's call for a convention to meet in Annapolis, Maryland, to discuss interstate commerce. The Supreme Executive Council selected Robert Morris, George Clymer, John Armstrong, Jr., Thomas FitzSimmons, and Tench Coxe, all prominent Republicans, to be delegates to the convention. Only Coxe attended the convention in September.

In December 1786, the assembly, controlled by the Republicans, considered the report of the Annapolis convention. After learning that the Virginia legislature had selected delegates to attend a convention in Philadelphia in 1787, the assembly also selected delegates. These delegates were Robert Morris, Gouverneur Morris, Thomas Mifflin, James Wilson, Thomas FitzSimmons, George Clymer, and Jared Ingersoll, all from the city and county of Philadelphia. All except Ingersoll were Republicans. The delegates were instructed to join with other delegates

> in devising, deliberating on and discussing all such alterations and further provisions as may be necessary to render the federal constitution fully adequate to the exigencies of the Union and in reporting such act or acts for that purpose to the United States in Congress assembled as when agreed to by them and duly confirmed by the several states will effectually provide for the same.

In March 1787, the assembly added Benjamin Franklin to the list of delegates. Both parties claimed Franklin as a leader. The newspapers of both parties supported the federal Constitutional Convention during its proceedings, indicating that there was some agreement in the state over the necessity for the convention. After the convention concluded its work, however, divisions based on the previous partisan alignments emerged almost immediately.

THE RATIFICATION DEBATE IN PENNSYLVANIA

The Constitutional Convention was still meeting in the State House in Philadelphia when the eleventh Pennsylvania General Assembly returned for its session on September 4, 1787. For this reason, the General Assembly had to meet in a room upstairs in the State House. The convention ended its work on September 17, 1787, and adjourned after having the Constitution signed by thirty-nine delegates and ordering it reported to Congress and transmitted to the states. On September 18, the Constitution was read into the journal of the General Assembly. After the reading, Benjamin Franklin rose in the assembly and suggested that Pennsylvania cede land to the federal government for a new capital. The General Assembly did not act on Franklin's suggestion or on the new Constitution before recessing for the day. It did not resume consideration of the document until September 24.

Calling a Convention

The contours of the debate mirrored the partisan conflict between the Republicans, soon known as Federalists, supporting ratification and the Constitutionalists, known as Anti-Federalists, opposed to it.[8] Despite widespread support for the Constitutional Convention, debate quickly emerged on whether Pennsylvania should ratify the Constitution. This debate began even before the General Assembly had the opportunity to call a state ratifying convention.

The new federal Constitution was published in newspapers in each of the states, allowing the public to read the plan. The document also was published in German in a pamphlet for the benefit of German-speaking Pennsylvanians. For a few days, there was only praise in the Pennsylvania press for the work of the "Grand Convention." After about a week, one editorialist attacked the plan in the *Freeman's Journal*. Soon the papers were full of editorials attacking and defending the U.S. Constitution. Two sides emerged in this debate: the Federalists and the Anti-Federalists. In Pennsylvania, the Federalists consisted primarily of those who had identified with the Republicans in state politics, whereas the Anti-Federalists grew out of the Constitutionalists.

The Federalists wanted to call a state ratifying convention as soon as possible, especially before the assembly session ended on September 29, 1787. The Anti-Federalists wanted to call the convention after the election of a new assembly on October 9. The assembly had resolved to adjourn on Saturday, September 29. On Friday morning, September 28, Federalist George Clymer introduced resolutions calling for a convention to consider the new Constitution, establishing the procedure for selecting delegates to the convention, and setting the time and place of the convention. Robert Whitehill of Cumberland County, an Anti-Federalist, objected and requested that the matter be postponed because Pennsylvanians had not had time to consider the new frame of government fully. Whitehill also informed the assembly that the Congress had not yet considered the Constitution, and it would be illegal for Pennsylvania to consider it before the national legislature did so. After approving the resolution calling for a convention by a vote of 43-19, the assembly recessed until 4 P.M.

When the Federalists returned at 4 P.M., they found that the nineteen members who had objected to the calling of a state convention were not in their seats. The assembly needed a quorum of two-thirds of its members (forty-six of sixty-nine members), and with only forty-four in attendance the body could not conduct business. The sergeant-at-arms was sent to find the missing members. None of the absent members would agree to return, so the assembly was forced to recess for the evening. During the evening, the resolution from Congress transmitting the Constitution to the states for ratification arrived in Philadelphia from New York. When the assembly met on the morning of September 29, the resolution was read. The members opposed to the ratifying convention still had not taken their seats, and the sergeant-at-arms was sent to find them and present them with the resolution from Congress in the hope their opposition would end. Two members, James McCalmont from Franklin County and Jacob Miley from Dauphin County, were located at Major Alexander Boyd's boarding house. Despite being shown the resolution, the men refused to return to the assembly chamber. A crowd had been collecting outside, and when they learned that the men refused to go, the crowd broke into the house, seized the men, and dragged them through the streets to the State House. The assembly now had a quorum. After the roll had been called, McCalmont rose, complained about his treatment, and asked to be excused. When informed that he would be fined five shillings for missing a meeting of the assembly, he pulled the coins from his pocket, threw them on the clerk's desk, and demanded to be excused. He then tried to leave the chamber but was restrained. The assembly was able to complete its business. The resolution setting November 6, 1787, as the date for electing delegates to a convention to be held in the State House in Philadelphia on the third Tuesday in November was approved by a vote of 44-2. The assembly then adjourned *sine die*.

Before leaving Philadelphia, sixteen of the nineteen signed the "Address of the Subscribers Members of the late House of Representatives of the Commonwealth of Pennsylvania to their Constituents," outlining their objections to the new Constitution. The members identified ten objections. The new Constitution was too costly because it created a government of three branches. It would ruin state governments. Power of taxation was vested in the federal Congress. Freedom of the press was not guaranteed. Trial by jury was abolished in civil cases. The presence of a federal judiciary threatened the power of the state judiciary branches. There was no provision for rotation in office, and the terms of members of Congress were too long. There was no declaration of rights and no provision prohibiting a standing army. The address appeared as a broadside on October 2, 1787. After its publication, a number of writers sought to reply, beginning a public debate on the value of the new Constitution.

THE STATE RATIFYING CONVENTION

Pennsylvania was the first state to call for a convention. After the national debate over the actions of the assembly and the seceding assemblymen subsided, an election campaign began. The Anti-Federalists used the newspapers to clarify and support their position against the Constitution. One of the Anti-Federalists' first editorials was the work of "Centinel." Like Publius and the *Federalist Papers* in support of the Constitution, the Anti-Federalists used pseudonyms. "Centinel" has been identified as the work of George Bryan and his son Samuel.[9]

Bryan was a Scotch-Irish Presbyterian who had migrated to Philadelphia from Ireland as a young man. Soon a leading merchant in the city, he joined with John Dickinson, Robert Morris, James Wilson, William Allen, Joseph Hart, and Thomas McKean to oppose some of the measures Britain imposed on the colonies in the late 1760s. Bryan largely disappeared from politics in the early 1770s after experiencing some business setbacks. In 1776, he reemerged by winning a seat on the Supreme Executive Council. He then became vice president and with the death of the president in 1777, Bryan became the acting president. Bryan soon found himself in the Constitutionalist Party during the height of partisan conflict in Pennsylvania. On October 5, 1787, the first of eighteen essays by Centinel appeared in the *Independent Gazetteer*. In these essays, Centinel appealed to longtime Constitutionalists.

Centinel's concern was that new Constitution would make the states powerless. He demonstrated to his readers how support for the state constitution was linked to opposition to the federal Constitution. The first sentence of Centinel No. 1 read:

> Permit one of yourselves to put you in mind of certain *liberties* and *privileges* secured to you by the constitution *of* this commonwealth, and to beg your serious attention to his uninterested opinion upon the plan of federal government submitted to your consideration, before you surrender these great and valuable privileges up forever.

He argued that the federal Constitution would end the protections granted by the Pennsylvania constitution of 1776: "Your present frame of government, secures to you a right to hold yourselves, houses, papers and possessions free from search and seizure." He then issued one of the first calls for a listing of rights to be added to the Constitution.

Speaking to a meeting in the State House yard in Philadelphia on October 6, Federalist James Wilson countered Centinel's argument point by point. The purpose of the meeting was to nominate candidates for the ratifying convention. Wilson began his speech by illustrating how the state constitutions were different from the proposed federal Constitution:

> It will be proper however, before I enter into the refutation of the charges that are alleged, to mark the leading discrimination between the State constitutions and the constitution of the United States. When the people established the powers of legislation under their separate governments, they invested their representatives with every right and authority which they did not in explicit terms reserve; and therefore upon every question respecting the jurisdiction of the House of Assembly, if the frame of government is silent, the jurisdiction is efficient and complete. But in delegating federal powers, another criterion was necessarily introduced, and the congressional power is to be collected, not

from tacit implication, but from the positive grant expressed in the instrument of the union. Hence, it is evident, that in the former case everything which is not reserved is given; but in the latter the reverse of the proposition prevails, and everything which is not given is reserved.

He also addressed the need for a bill of rights. No bill of rights was necessary, he maintained, because a summary of the reserved powers was not needed. No power was given to the government unless it was expressly granted. The Constitution was the collection of expressed powers. The debate continued at a fevered pitch until the election in November. Although much of the debate was at a high intellectual level, a number of attacks were at the level of name-calling.

On October 9, Pennsylvanians went to the polls to elect members of the assembly in the regular annual election. This election was seen as a referendum on the Constitution. The Federalists (the former Republicans) campaigned against the Anti-Federalists (originally the Constitutionalists) who left the State House rather than vote on the call for a ratifying convention. Despite the campaign, fifteen of the seventeen Anti-Federalists who were eligible to run for reelection were successfully returned to the assembly. The Federalists retained their majority in the chamber by a small margin.

With the completion of the assembly elections, the campaign for delegates to the ratifying convention began in earnest. There were reports that members of the assembly who had supported the Constitution chose not to run for the state convention. No Federalist member of the assembly was elected to the state convention. James Wilson, one of Pennsylvania's delegates to the Constitutional Convention that drafted the new frame of government, was the only one elected to the ratifying convention. Four Anti-Federalist assemblymen and five Anti-Federalist members from the Supreme Executive Council were elected to the convention. They voted against ratification.

Election Day was a great victory for the Federalists, foreshadowing Pennsylvania's eventual ratification. In Philadelphia, a crowd of drunken Federalist supporters went to Major Boyd's boarding house, the residence of a number of Anti-Federalist assemblymen. They broke into the house and broke windows with rocks, threatening the Anti-Federalist legislators. The assemblymen complained to the assembly, which requested that the Supreme Executive Council offer a reward for the apprehension of the rioters. The reward was offered, but no one was ever arrested. In fact, news of the election night riot did not appear in any Philadelphia newspaper.

On Wednesday, November 21, 1787, sixty of the sixty-nine delegates met in the State House in Philadelphia. The convention was to last twenty-two days. The record of the debates of the convention is not complete, although compilers have been able to compare the notes of several delegates and observers. The secretary of the convention kept a journal, and stenographer Thomas Lloyd recorded James Wilson's and Thomas McKean's speeches in shorthand.

Some summaries of the debates appeared in newspapers although some of the newspaper accounts may have been suppressed. The *Pennsylvania Packet*, the *Independent Gazetteer*, the *Pennsylvania Journal*, and the *Pennsylvania Gazette* each published short summaries of each day's activities. The *Pennsylvania Herald* published longer news stories with commentary by its editor and reporter, Alexander James Dallas. Dallas was able to publish the debates of November 27 and 28, the first part of the debates of November 30, and the debates of December 12. Other newspapers copied his reports. On January 6, 1788, he stopped publishing the records of the convention after being fired by the *Herald*. The owner of the paper never explained his action, but the Anti-Federalists charged that Dallas's efforts were suppressed by the Federalists. The *Herald* ceased publication in February 1788.

On the first day of the convention, the delegates selected officers. Frederick Muhlenberg was elected president. He received thirty votes in the balloting, while Thomas McKean received twenty-nine. George Gray received one vote. After a brief debate concerning the proper course of action because no candidate received an absolute majority, Muhlenberg was declared the victor. Robert Whitehill of Cumberland County, William Findley of Westmoreland County, and John Smilie of Fayette County led the Anti-Federalists. The leaders of the Federalists were James Wilson and Thomas McKean, both of Philadelphia.

On November 24, to maintain the focus of the convention on the task at hand, Thomas McKean opened business by making a motion "that the Convention do assent to and ratify the Constitution agreed to on the 17th of September last by the Convention of the United States of America held at Philadelphia." That motion failed, and on November 26 McKean moved that the Constitution be considered article by article. Both factions agreed to the motion.

The Anti-Federalists moved that the Constitution be considered section by section in a committee of the whole. They believed that this process would provide the opportunity for a more free and complete discussion of the document. The Federalists objected, not wishing to "cover the same ground twice." The Federalists also argued that the resolution from Congress transmitting the Constitution to the states only permitted the convention to ratify or reject the entire document, not to amend or reject parts of it. The motion was defeated by a vote of 44-24. On November 27, the Anti-Federalists moved that delegates be allowed to state for the journal their reasons for voting to ratify or reject the Constitution. This motion was defeated 44-22.

After considering the Anti-Federalist procedural proposals, the convention approved McKean's motion to consider the Constitution article by article. Most speakers, nonetheless, chose to discuss the document in its entirety. Only twelve of the sixty-nine delegates actually took part in the debates.

Anti-Federalist speakers argued that the Constitution created a consolidated government, not a federal government. They defined a consolidated government as one "which put thirteen States into one." As evidence, they pointed to the preamble. It stated "We the People," not "We the States." According to the Anti-Federalists, this opening phrase proved that the Constitution was not a compact between sovereign states. Additional evidence was found in the provision that members of Congress would vote as individuals, not by state. The federal government was allowed to tax, thus crowding out the taxing ability of the states. Anti-Federalists feared that state governments would cease to exist on the day that the Constitution took effect. The Anti-Federalists also argued that the federal charter threatened individual liberties because it did not include an explicit listing of rights.

Led by James Wilson, Federalist speakers countered with their defense of the Constitution. Wilson pointed out that a number of state constitutions lacked a bill of rights.

> Whence comes this notion, that in the United States there is no security without a bill of rights? Have the citizens of South Carolina no security for their liberties? They have no bill of rights. Are the citizens on the eastern side of the Delaware less free, or less secured in their liberties, than those on the western side? The state of New Jersey has no bill of rights. The state of New York has no bill of rights. The states of Connecticut and Rhode Island have no bill of rights. I know not whether I have exactly enumerated the states who have not thought it necessary to add a bill of rights to their constitutions; but this enumeration, sir, will serve to show by experience, as well as principle, that, even in single governments, a bill of rights is not an essential or necessary measure.

Wilson continued by arguing that a bill of rights might cause more harm than benefit:

> But in a government consisting of enumerated powers, such as is proposed for the United States, a bill of rights would not only be unnecessary, but, in my humble judgment, highly imprudent. In all societies, there are many powers and rights which cannot be particularly enumerated. A bill of rights annexed to a constitution is an enumeration of the powers reserved. If we attempt an enumeration, every thing that is not enumerated is presumed to be given. The consequence is, that an imperfect enumeration would throw all implied power into the scale of the government, and the rights of the people would be rendered incomplete. On the other hand, an imperfect enumeration of the powers of government reserves all implied power to the people; and by that means the constitution becomes incomplete. But of the two, it is much safer to run the risk on the side of the constitution; for an omission in the enumeration of the powers of government is neither so dangerous nor important as an omission in the enumeration of the rights of the people.

Wilson also presented practical reasons that the Constitution must be ratified. It would be impossible for the United States to achieve economic stability or gain respect from foreign nations without a workable frame of government.

On December 4, the president of the convention, Frederick Muhlenberg, observed that the proceedings had been going on for two weeks. He suggested to the delegates "whether the system under their consideration will not meet with a more full and expeditious investigation, by a general statement of the objections to it, and a subsequent reply to those objections." The delegates accepted the suggestion. William Findley, John Smilie, and Robert Whitehill delivered lengthy speeches detailing their opposition to the Constitution from December 4 until December 8. Thomas McKean responded on December 10, and James Wilson presented his arguments in favor of the Constitution on December 11.

The Anti-Federalists made closing speeches on December 12, after which Thomas Hartley of York County moved to consider McKean's November 24 motion that the Constitution be ratified. Stephen Chambers of Lancaster County seconded the motion. Robert Whitehill then rose and presented seven hundred fifty petitions from residents of Cumberland County. These petitions called on the convention to refrain from ratifying the Constitution without amending it or at least providing a bill of rights. He then moved that the convention adjourn so that the people of Pennsylvania and the delegates to the convention could consider the fifteen amendments he had prepared. Whitehill's motion was defeated by a vote of 46-23, and the fifteen amendments were not made an official part of the record. The convention then considered the motion on the question presented by Hartley and Chambers. The Constitution was adopted by a vote of 46-23. Five days after the convention in Delaware unanimously voted for ratification, Pennsylvania became the second state to ratify the Constitution.

President Muhlenberg had the following resolution prepared for presentation to the Confederation Congress:

> In the Name of the People of Pennsylvania. Be it Known unto all Men that We the Delegates of the People of the Commonwealth of Pennsylvania in general Convention assembled Have assented to, and ratified, and by these presents Do in the Name and by the authority of the Same People, and for ourselves, assent to, and ratify the foregoing Constitution for the United States of America. Done in Convention at Philadelphia the twelfth day of December in the year of our Lord one thousand seven hundred and eighty seven and of the Independence of the United States of America the twelfth. In witness whereof we have hereunto subscribed our names.

The resolution was signed by Muhlenberg and the delegates who had voted to ratify the Constitution.

Before adjourning on December 15, the convention approved a resolution to grant a ten-mile-square parcel of land to the new federal government for a new capital. Another resolution offered Congress the use of any public buildings in Philadelphia until the government had a permanent home. After ordering that five thousand copies of the Constitution and the ratification statement be printed, the convention adjourned *sine die*.

SUMMARY: THE CHANGES IN PENNSYLVANIA

Pennsylvania's ratification of the Constitution was an act packed with controversy. The debates in the state were carried to the ratification conventions of the remaining eleven states. The end of the convention in Pennsylvania did not end the debate in the state, because the Anti-Federalists continued their criticism of the Constitution. Ratification of the Constitution also brought changes to the structure of government in Pennsylvania.

After the ratifying convention approved the Constitution, twenty-one members of the voting minority signed a dissenting address that appeared in the *Pennsylvania Packet and Daily Advertiser* on December 18, 1787. The address was copied in other Pennsylvania newspapers and in papers in other states, becoming a semi-official statement of the national Anti-Federalist movement. The "Address of the Reasons of Dissent of the Minority of the Convention of Pennsylvania to their Constituents" summarized the arguments against the Constitution that had appeared in newspapers and pamphlets since September 1787 as well as the arguments raised by Robert Whitehill, John Smilie, and William Findley in the convention.[10]

The dissenters began by criticizing the secrecy of the Constitutional Convention and pointed out that the convention did not have the authority to write a new frame of government. They reminded their readers of the actions of the assembly to reach a quorum to call for a state ratification convention:

Affairs were in this situation when on the 28th of September last, a resolution was proposed to the assembly by a member of the house who had been also a member of the federal convention, for calling a state convention, to be elected within ten days for the purpose of examining and adopting the proposed constitution of the United States, though at this time the house had not received it from Congress. This attempt was opposed by a minority, who after offering every argument in their power to prevent the precipitate measure, without effect, absented themselves from the house as the only alternative left them, to prevent the measure taking place previous to their constituents being acquainted with the business—That violence and outrage which had been so often threatened was now practiced; some of the members were seized the next day by a mob collected for the purpose, and forcibly dragged to the house, and there detained by force whilst the quorum of the legislature, so formed, completed their resolution.

The "Dissent" also provided a detailed analysis of the objections of the minority to the new Constitution. The minority objected to the document because they did not believe that the single government proposed in the Constitution, with the federal government pursuing foreign affairs and allowing the states the management of their internal affairs, could govern a large republic. The sovereignty of the states would eventually disappear. Finally, the dissenters objected to the absence of a bill of rights. The "Dissent" also published the fifteen amendments Whitehill had offered to the convention on December 12. The delegates had voted not to publish the amendments. Of the twenty-three delegates who voted against ratification, twenty-one signed the "Dissent" address. All the delegates from the counties of Berks, Bedford, Cumberland, Dauphin, Fayette, and Westmoreland were signers and were joined by half of the delegates from Washington and Franklin counties and by Whitehill from Lancaster. In 1807, Samuel Bryan claimed that he wrote the "Dissent" with help from the minority delegates.[11]

Ratifying the Constitution did not end the debate in Pennsylvania. In fact, the level of the debate and violence actually may have increased. The debate centered on the following four issues:

1. The need for amendments.
2. Charges that the post office prevented distribution of Anti-Federalist material.
3. Charges that men such as Robert Morris were corrupt and supported the Constitution to avoid paying the debts owed to the United States.
4. The publication of fake letters by both parties to discredit their opponents.[12]

The debate became violent at the end of December 1787. On December 26, a Federalist celebration of ratification at Carlisle in Cumberland County was broken up by a riot. Anti-Federalists burned effigies of Thomas McKean and James Wilson the next day, provoking more violence. Twenty men were arrested on January 23, but they were soon freed by companies of militiamen from Cumberland County and a few from Dauphin and York counties. On March 20, 1788, the Supreme Executive Council told the state's attorney general to drop the charges against the rioters. News of the riot was published in newspapers in every state.

In January 1788, John Nicholson, the comptroller general of Pennsylvania, started a campaign to have the assembly overturn the ratification vote. In his petition, he requested that the assembly censure the Pennsylvania delegates to the Constitutional Convention for overreaching their authority. He also asked that the assembly refuse to confirm the ratification vote by the state convention. He wanted the assembly to instruct the Pennsylvania delegates to the Confederation Congress to vote against the adoption of the Constitution. More than six thousand people, primarily in the western counties of the state, signed the petition. The assembly adjourned on March 29, 1788, without taking action on the petition.

Although debate waged in the Pennsylvania newspapers changed little about the state's ratification of the Constitution, it had the potential to influence the ratification process in other states, if readers in other states could obtain Pennsylvania newspapers. On January 1, 1788, Ebenezer Hazard, the postmaster general of the United States, with the consent of the Congress, ordered that the mail would be carried by riders on horseback and not by stagecoaches. The stagecoaches were able to carry newspapers without charge to the publishers, but the riders wanted payment to carry the newspapers. Anti-Federalists charged that Hazard changed the regulations to prevent the circulation of Anti-Federalist material.

On July 3, 1788, news that the ninth and tenth states had ratified the Constitution reached Carlisle, Cumberland County. Knowing they could not defeat the Constitution but hoping to have some influence over the development of the new government, Pennsylvania Anti-Federalists circulated a letter calling for the party to meet in a convention in Harrisburg in September. On September 3, 1788, representatives from fourteen counties gathered. Led by George Bryan, they called on the people of the state to abide by the ratification decision and drew up a petition to call a general convention of the states to propose amendments to the Constitution. The First Congress, following popular opinion for a listing of rights, proposed the first ten amendments to the Constitution (the "Bill of Rights") on September 25, 1789. These amendments were ratified by the Pennsylvania assembly on March 10, 1790, and became part of the Constitution on December 15, 1791.

The ratification of the U.S. Constitution created an opportunity for change in Pennsylvania's frame of government, although the Republicans (or Federalists) were careful not to change too quickly.[13] The Republicans built on their majority in the assembly election of 1788, an election overshadowed by the impending elections of members to the new U.S. House of Representatives. The Republicans had tried to alter the constitution of 1776 in 1777, 1778, and 1783–1784 but were unsuccessful, even when they had a majority in the assembly. In June 1788, a writer in the *Pennsylvania Gazette* pointed out that the Pennsylvania court system would need to be changed to bring it into compliance with the new Constitution. The Republicans pointed out the many inconsistencies between the Pennsylvania constitution and the U.S. Constitution but, fearing a Council of Censors controlled by Constitutionalists (Anti-Federalists), did not suggest that the Censors be called.

During the second session of the 1789 assembly, the Republicans decided to act. Thirty Republican assemblymen gathered at a Philadelphia tavern to plan a campaign to appeal to the public for support in changing the constitution of 1776. The next day Gerardus Wynkoop addressed the assembly, calling on the people to indicate whether they wanted a state constitutional convention. He also introduced resolutions specifying the necessary reforms. The current system had become too expensive to operate. As the state grew and more counties were created, the Supreme Executive Council had to increase in size. Wynkoop also argued that the state constitution had to conform to the federal Constitution. The assembly adopted the resolutions calling for a new state constitution by a vote of 41-17. The minority was comprised of Constitutionalists from the rural parts of the state. The resolutions were printed and distributed around the state.

The Supreme Executive Council was asked to join in the resolutions, but it refused on the strength of Constitutionalist arguments that the Council of Censors could make the appropriate changes. The newspaper also did not clearly favor the Republican position, so the Republicans began to doubt whether they could be successful in their call for a constitutional convention.

During the fall session in September, the Republicans moved ahead with their campaign. A committee reported that the people preferred a constitutional convention to the prospect of allowing the Council of Censors to propose alterations. The report concluded by proposing that a convention be called in Philadelphia at the end of November 1789. The Constitutionalists countered with a suggestion that a referendum be called to judge the true strength of public opinion for a convention. The motion was defeated, as was a second Constitutionalist motion proposing that the convention meet in Lancaster instead of Philadelphia. Finally, by a vote of 39-17, the assembly adopted the committee report and called a convention.

The Republicans had adopted a strategy used by the Constitutionalists and the Anti-Federalists: the petition. By September 1789, the party had collected more than ten thousand signatures on petitions calling for a state constitutional convention. The Constitutionalists had used a similar tactic to block a call for a convention in 1779. When the assembly adjourned, members returned to their counties to campaign for the next assembly and to seek seats at the state constitutional convention. Several Constitutionalists asked their constituents not to vote in the convention election, but every county sent a full slate of delegates, including those Constitutionalists.

In late November, the state constitutional convention convened in Philadelphia. The majority of the delegates were Republican. James Wilson, William Lewis, and Thomas McKean led the party. Constitutionalist leaders were Robert Whitehill, William Findley, John Smilie, and James McLene. Thomas Mifflin was elected president of the convention.

Surprisingly, the convention operated in a spirit of cooperation. Party leaders Findley and Wilson met at the start of the convention and reached an agreement: if the Republicans refrained from violent attacks on the constitution of 1776, the Constitutionalists would help to enact the necessary changes. As part of the agreement, the old constitution served as the starting point for proposing amendments.

The new constitution did not increase the property qualification to vote specified in the constitution of 1776. It did abolish the practice of rotation in office and the Council of Censors. It established a senate to create a two-house legislature and vested executive power in a single governor. The governor was given power to veto legislation and to appoint hundreds of officials. Judges could serve for life barring misbehavior and were granted fixed salaries. The debate in the convention centered largely on the details of the provisions. This debate was not partisan; rather, it was ideological, with delegates dividing based on their views of the proper role of government. Aristocratic conservatives usually were defeated by a coalition of more moderate Republicans and the Constitutionalists.

The convention adjourned on February 29, 1790, intending to reconvene on August 9. The second session lasted until September 2, with only minor revisions made to the proposed constitution. The charter was adopted on the last day of the convention. It took effect without being submitted to the people because no one thought that it needed to be. Three years after ratifying a new national frame of government, the Commonwealth of Pennsylvania had a new state constitution.

NOTES

1. The early colonial history of Pennsylvania is summarized in Susan E. Klepp, "Encounter and Experiment: The Colonial Period," in *Pennsylvania: A History of the Commonwealth*, ed. Randall M. Miller and William Pencak (University Park: The Pennsylvania State University Press, 2002), pp. 47–100.

2. A transcription of the Great Law can be found at: http://www. docheritage. state.pa.us/documents/greatlawtrans.asp.

3. A transcription of the Charter of Privileges can be found at: http://www. constitution.org/bcp/penncharpriv.htm.

4. A transcription of the Walking Purchase treaty can be found at: http:// www.docheritage.state.pa.us/documents/walkingpurchasetrans.asp.

5. See William Pencak, "The Promise of Revolution: 1750–1800," in Miller and Pencak, eds., *Pennsylvania: A History of the Commonwealth*, pp. 101–152.

6. The history of the Revolution in Pennsylvania is summarized in Roland M. Baumann, "The Pennsylvania Revolution," available at: http://www.ushistory.org/ pennsylvania/birth2.html.

7. A transcription of the constitution of 1776 can be found at: http://www. docheritage.state.pa.us/documents/constitutiontrans.asp.

8. Primary documents from the ratification debate are collected in Merrill Jensen, ed., *The Documentary History of the Ratification of the Constitution*, vol. 2, *Pennsylvania* (Madison: State Historical Society of Wisconsin, 1976).

9. See Owen S. Ireland, *Religion, Ethnicity, and Politics: Ratifying the Constitution in Pennsylvania* (University Park: The Pennsylvania State University Press, 1995), pp. 36–43.

10. See Ralph Ketcham, ed., *The Anti-Federalist Papers and the Constitutional Convention Debates* (New York: Mentor, 1986), pp. 237–256.

11. Jensen, *The Documentary History of the Ratification of the Constitution*, p. 617.

12. Ibid., p. 642.

13. The history of the constitution of 1790 appears in Robert L. Brunhouse, *The Counter-Revolution in Pennsylvania, 1776–1790* (New York: Octagon Books, 1971), pp. 215–227.

BIBLIOGRAPHY

Brunhouse, Robert L. *The Counter-Revolution in Pennsylvania, 1776–1790*. New York: Octagon Books, 1971.

Graham, George J. "Pennsylvania: Representation and the Meaning of Republicanism." In *Ratifying the Constitution*. Edited by Michael Allen Gillespie and Michael Lienesch. Lawrence: University Press of Kansas, 1989.

Ireland, Owen S. *Religion, Ethnicity, and Politics: Ratifying the Constitution in Pennsylvania*. University Park: The Pennsylvania State University Press, 1995.

Jensen, Merrill, ed. *The Documentary History of the Ratification of the Constitution: Volume 2, Pennsylvania*. Madison: State Historical Society of Wisconsin, 1976.

Ketcham, Ralph, ed. *The Anti-Federalist Papers and the Constitutional Convention Debates*. New York: Mentor, 1986.

McMaster, John Bach, and Frederick D. Stone, eds. *Pennsylvania and the Federal Constitution, 1787–1788*. Reprint. New York: DaCapo Press, 1970.

Nix, Robert N. C., and Mary M. Schweitzer. "Pennsylvania's Contributions to the Writing and Ratification of the Constitution." *The Pennsylvania Magazine of History and Biography* 112 (January 1988): 1–24.

Selsam, J. Paul. *The Pennsylvania Constitution of 1776: A Study in Revolutionary Democracy*. Reprint. New York: Octagon Books, 1971.

THE STATE OF RHODE ISLAND

Ratified the Constitution of the United States:
May 29, 1790

William M. Ferraro

INTRODUCTION

On November 27, 1789, delegates in North Carolina ratified the Constitution, leaving Rhode Island as the only one of the original thirteen colonies outside the new federal government. In their starkly isolated position, reluctant Rhode Islanders became the subjects of intense political and economic pressure as well as easy targets for derision. With a checkered history that many observers viewed as economically opportunistic and religiously eccentric at best or as utterly corrupt and depraved at worst, it was thought that the new Union might survive and prosper perfectly well without the smallest potential state in both land area and population. Clinging rather precariously to the southeastern corner of New England along the narrow finger of water called Narragansett Bay, Rhode Islanders faced the choice of going forward alone and trying to carve out a lucrative exchange point for commerce between the new United States and the rest of the world or joining the larger states in the republican experiment at the risk of forfeiting cherished local prerogatives and freedoms.

COLONIAL GOVERNMENT

Roger Williams began a new settlement that he called Providence at the head of Narragansett Bay in 1636, when he was banished from Massachusetts for criticizing Puritan leaders. He envisioned a community dedicated to "soul liberty," where individuals contested openly for their religious beliefs. A remarkable character, Williams shaped the development of both Providence and the

Rhode Island

Territorial Development:

- Rhode Island chartered by King Charles II, 1663
- Continental Congress approves Declaration of Independence from Great Britain, July 4, 1776
- Great Britain formally recognizes American independence through the Treaty of Paris, September 3, 1783
- Rhode Island becomes the thirteenth state to ratify the U.S. Constitution, March 29, 1790

Capitals Prior to Statehood:

- The Rhode Island state government convened variously in Providence, Newport, Bristol, East Greenwich, and South Kingston from 1663–1854.

State Capitals:

- Newport and Providence, co-capitals, 1854–1900
- Providence, 1900–present

Origin of State Name: The state was probably named "Roode Eylandt," by Adriaen Block, a Dutch explorer, because of its red clay.

First Governor: Arthur Fenner
Governmental Organization: Bicameral
Population at Statehood: 69,112
Geographical Size: 1,045 square miles

Baptist church over the remaining decades of his long life and left a legacy of provocative ideas on government, theology, and Native American linguistics.

Two years after Williams founded Providence, another group of religious seekers settled nearby at the northern end of Aquidneck, the largest island in Narragansett Bay. They named their community Pocasset but soon changed the name to Portsmouth. In 1639 a disgruntled group broke away from Portsmouth, migrated to the southern end of Aquidneck where there was a fine natural harbor, and formed their own settlement, which they named Newport. With the advantages of the harbor, this community quickly outdistanced its older neighbor and rivaled Providence for importance. On the mainland to the west of Newport, Samuel Gorton, another religious seeker and strong personality, initiated a settlement called Shawomet. As it grew, this community became known as Warwick.

Although each of these communities developed its own local government centered around the town meeting of all eligible voters, or "freemen," it soon became essential to unite in some fashion to secure land titles, check hostile Native Americans, counter an aggressive British imperial policy, and expand trade.[1] The first attempt at cooperative government was the Aquidneck Compact. This agreement created an elaborate structure of officials carefully balanced between Newport and Portsmouth and an assembly composed of all freemen eligible to participate in their local town meetings. The Aquidneck Compact government held the theoretical power to address all matters of common interest to the two towns, but real control still rested in the freemen, who displayed a jealous regard for their towns' autonomy. The Aquidneck Compact disintegrated in less than a decade.

In the midst of the Aquidneck Compact government's brief career, Roger Williams successfully negotiated with powers in England for the first instrument of central government that covered all towns in Rhode Island. Williams secured a charter, known as the Patent of 1644, that authorized the towns to form a unified government according to their own local inclinations. Town representatives did not settle upon an acceptable government until 1647. Clearly, freemen in the individual towns retained the upper hand. No legislative enactment, for example, could become law unless each town meeting approved the measure. All four towns received equal representation in the general court, and the decisions of the legislative body could be overturned or varied by the annual general assembly open to all freemen. All government officers stood for election each year.

The several checks proved so restrictive that pressure quickly mounted for reforms that enabled the central government to function meaningfully. Several changes addressed this concern, the most notable being that laws passed by the central government would take effect unless the town meetings vetoed the measure within ten days. No longer was a positive vote needed from each town to implement a general law.

Newport leader William Coddington did not like melding the Aquidneck towns with Providence, and Warwick and believed that the island communities suffered from increased taxation to support the poorer mainlanders. Acting on his displeasure, Coddington procured a commission in London that appointed him governor for life over the islands of Aquidneck and Conanicut in Narragansett Bay. His commission called for assistants nominated by the freemen of Newport and Portsmouth but no legislative assembly.

Coddington's action enraged freemen throughout Rhode Island. His opponents in Newport and Portsmouth hired Dr. John Clarke, a prominent physician and religious leader, to seek an annulment of the outrageous commission. Mainland residents persuaded Roger Williams to act as their agent and to cooperate with Clarke. The pair succeeded in late 1652. English authorities vacated Coddington's commission and reaffirmed the government established under the Patent of 1644.

The revived central government showed greater willingness to assert authority over the towns. For instance, a measure passed to facilitate tax collections from balky towns. Freemen in the towns responded to the assertion of central authority by pushing through measures strengthening their veto power. First, the period for freemen in each town to consider legislation was increased from ten days to twenty. Then a measure passed that nullified any general law within a town if the local town meeting vetoed the act of the general assembly. Finally, the time to consider legislation was extended to nearly three months. The reconstructed review process reasserted the superiority of the towns over the colony government.

A change of rulers in England undermined the patent granted under the ousted regime and left Rhode Islanders in a precarious position. John Clarke again came to the rescue. In 1663, his negotiations resulted in a new charter that maintained Rhode Island as an independent colony and sanctioned the continuing experiment in religious liberty.

The Charter of 1663 received widespread approval in Rhode Island and served as the fundamental law of the colony, and later the state, until 1843. This landmark charter created a sovereign central government that consisted of a governor, deputy governor, ten assistants, six deputies from Newport, four deputies each from Providence, Portsmouth, and Warwick, and two deputies each from all future towns. As a whole, these officers composed the General Assembly, a body that held impressive powers. Unlike the Patent of 1644, the Charter of 1663 conferred no direct political authority upon the towns. The supremacy of Rhode Island's central government even eclipsed British law whenever circumstances rendered it impossible to conform to royal orders or decrees. Semiannual elections, however, retained significant power in the hands of the town freemen.

An anxious time for Rhode Islanders and other colonists occurred between 1686 and 1689 when King James II attempted to establish coercive colonial rule under Sir Edmund Andros. Although compelled to dissolve their existing government and submit to Andros, Rhode Islanders managed to hide their treasured charter and keep local government alive in their town meetings.

The oppressive experiment ended with the flight of King James II from the throne and the arrest of Andros in Boston. Still possessing their charter, Rhode Island's freemen quickly restored their former government.

Renewal of the colony government recommenced the competition for power between the central government and the town governments. Splitting the General Assembly into two chambers in 1696 augmented the strength of the towns. An upper house now held the governor, deputy governor, and assistants elected on an at-large basis, and a lower house contained the deputies elected from the towns. Each house could veto decisions of the other. All money or tax bills, however, originated in the lower house, giving an important prerogative to the town deputies.

Freemen remained zealous guardians of their autonomy and suspicious of their elected leaders. A bill that passed in 1733 ended the longstanding irksome practice that allowed colony magistrates to sit as members of their local town councils. Control over town councils now rested entirely with local town meetings. Not until 1760 did the freemen give up their privilege to vote in person for colony officers on the opening day of the May legislative session. The new law required all to vote by proxy except those slated to serve in the General Assembly. Despite this change, freemen across Rhode Island readily could observe the General Assembly, because sessions rotated among the five counties in the colony. Although dynamic governors like Samuel Cranston, Samuel Ward, and Stephen Hopkins managed to assert the central government's authority with some consistency, all officers of the colony labored in a political environment tilted toward local power lodged in the freemen assembled in their town meetings.

REVOLUTIONARY WAR AND ARTICLES OF CONFEDERATION

Unsurprisingly, freemen wary of centralized authority within their own colony also exhibited little taste for increasingly invasive British imperial policies. New taxes associated with the Sugar and Stamp Acts of the 1760s outraged most Rhode Islanders, who rejected the validity of these measures and tended to maltreat enforcement officials more than other colonists did. Rhode Islanders also engaged in the battle of ideas against British imperialism. Stephen Hopkins and Silas Downer, for instance, wrote influential pamphlets that denied the authority of Parliament over the colonies.[2] Rhode Islanders stepped forward, too, when overt action seemed necessary. A hastily gathered band of men from Providence burned the reviled British revenue cutter *Gaspee* when it accidentally beached in Narragansett Bay in late 1772. This celebrated act of defiance against British authority presaged the revolution soon to come.

Rhode Islanders offered sympathy and support for Bostonians suffering under the Intolerable Acts of 1774 that essentially curtailed all commercial activity in that insurgent city. Freemen in one western Rhode Island town characterized the British policy as "slavery itself, protected and guarded by tyranny, advancing with hasty steps towards this land of freedom and liberty."[3] Preparation for armed resistance appeared to be the only recourse. The General Assembly ordered a monthly drill of all militia companies in the colony in anticipation of war.

As open hostilities with Great Britain approached, Rhode Island officials acted in harmony with the discontented in other colonies. The General Assembly unanimously sent two delegates to the Second Continental Congress with instructions "to co-operate with the other colonies in every proper measure for obtaining a redress of the grievances, and establishing the rights and liberties of all the colonies, upon an equitable and permanent foundation."[4] Two men—Stephen Hopkins and William Ellery—signed the Declaration of Independence and cast the lot of Rhode Islanders with the revolution against British rule.

The Revolutionary War tested the resolve of Rhode Islanders. British troops occupied the island towns of Newport, Portsmouth, Middletown, and Jamestown for nearly three years. British raids ravaged coastal areas, destroying property and unsettling lives. Heavy taxes for war expenses and appeals for relief supplies burdened property holders as the conflict continued year after year. In the towns resistance mounted against tax levies by the central government that were seen as improper and unfeeling exercises of power. By the early 1780s, many Rhode Islanders simply refused to pay these taxes, and town treasurers were jailed for their inability to collect levies.

High taxes to cover debts persisted even after the climactic British surrender at Yorktown. This situation dampened jubilation over the final achievement of independence and kept Rhode Islanders suspicious of centralized government authority. Rhode Island's delegates in the Continental Congress eyed warily all measures that might further intrude the national government into state or local affairs. The Rhode Island delegation's votes against impost bills stopped passage of this important source of revenue until a heavily amended version carried in early 1786. These contrary stances attracted harsh criticism from proponents in other states and isolated Rhode Island politically as calls arose for a constitutional convention to correct the defects in the Articles of Confederation.

Despite uniting with the other colonies in the Revolutionary War, Rhode Islanders still valued their local autonomy. As a framework for united government, the Articles of Confederation catered to this sentiment. Submitted by Congress to the states for ratification in November 1777, the Articles of Confederation received swift approval from the General Assembly in Rhode Island only three months later because it reserved sovereignty to each state and backed up the rhetoric with clauses that gave the states the power to control trade and taxes. Furthermore, any adjustment to the Articles of Confederation required the unanimous agreement of all states, with each holding one vote.

Quite conscious of the state's small size, aggressively defensive of its prerogatives and autonomy, and satisfied with the legal protections given each state under the Articles of Confederation, Rhode Island leaders saw no pressing reason to promote the movement for a new government that gained momentum in early 1787. In response to the formal call for a constitutional convention, a clear majority in the lower house of the General Assembly decided against sending delegates. Two subsequent votes in the General Assembly ended with the same result, although the breakdown of ballots between the upper and lower house changed each time. In choosing this course, Rhode Island legislators ignored the advice of its two congressional delegates and the desires of several prominent merchants. Some of these merchants sent a letter of protest to the convention explaining their disagreement with the legislature's decision. The action also provoked Virginia's great advocate for constitutional reform, James Madison, who wrote to a friend denouncing Rhode Island for "the wickedness and folly which continue to reign there."

Others shared Madison's scorn. One of Thomas Jefferson's correspondents firmly believed that the absence of a Rhode Island delegation from the Constitutional Convention was a blessing rather than a curse: "All the States have elected representatives except Rhode Island, whose apostasy from every moral, as well as political, obligation, has placed her perfectly without the views of her confederates; nor will her absence, or nonconcurrence, occasion the least impediment in any stage of the intended business." Even some Rhode Islanders joined the chorus of denunciation. One of these disgruntled residents wrote to George Washington

> [T]he measures of our present Legislature do not exhibit the real character of the state. They are equally reprobated & abhorred by gentlemen of the learned professions, by the whole mercantile body, & by the most respectable farmers & mechanics. The Majority of the administration are composed of a licentious body of men, destitute of education & many of them void of principle. From anarchy & confusion they derive a temporary consequence & this they endeavor to prolong by debauching the minds of the common people whose attention is wholly directed to the abolition of debts, public & private.[5]

Undeterred by such pressure, Governor John Collins of Rhode Island rebuked those who condemned his state in a defiant letter to the president of Congress: "Our conduct has been reprobated by the illiberal, and many severe and unjust sarcasms propagated against us; but, sir, wen we state to you the reason, and evince the cause, the liberal mind will be convinced that we were actuated by that great principle which hath ever been the characteristic of this state,—the love of true constitutional liberty, and the fear we have of making innovations on the rights and liberties of the citizens at large." In the end, no voice represented Rhode Island during the hot summer of verbal sparring and eventual written compromises. This fact, however, did not prevent dismay from arising in the state when it was seen that the proposed Constitution dramatically strengthened the executive branch and substantially augmented the power of large, heavily populated states over smaller ones.[6]

THE CONSTITUTIONAL RATIFICATION QUESTION

In 1788, ratification of the Constitution by nine states brought into existence the new government of the United States and placed Rhode Islanders in a dilemma. They could choose to remain outside the new government and attempt to survive and even thrive as an entrepôt, or trading intermediary, between the United States and other nations. Alternatively, they could ratify the Constitution and be absorbed into a Union that could trample upon their cherished autonomy. Looming over these choices was the very real threat that the new federal government might dismiss Rhode Island's claim to sovereignty, dismantle the local government, and incorporate the land area and people into some neighboring state or states.

Local Dynamics

Existing party divisions in Rhode Island framed the ratification debate. The "Country" Party opposed the new Constitution. This party's core belief was an apprehension or "jealousy" of centralized power distant from the people being governed. The Country Party won adherents throughout the state, but its greatest strength came from the inland and most agrarian towns. The Mercantile Party favored ratification. Its members advocated broad economic development and tended to be wealthier residents of the more urban areas. In terms of national party divisions then taking shape, Mercantile Party adherents advocated the Federalists, and Country Party supporters fell in behind the Anti-Federalists.[7]

The Country Party slogan—"To Relieve the Distressed"—encapsulated its appeal to Rhode Islanders. Its message struck political and economic chords. Politically, the Country Party promised to end rule by callous or isolated officials and to return the process of government to the people. This commitment took concrete form in the reliance of party leaders upon "instructions" from their constituents. Beginning with their mercurial rise to power in 1786, Country Party leaders regularly sent legislation to the freemen in the towns for local consideration before taking final action. The Country Party also advocated reapportionment in the General Assembly to represent better the growing population of new towns restricted to two representatives by the Charter of 1663. Economically, the Country Party advanced and enacted a paper money program based on real estate mortgage loans that increased currency in the state and eliminated both burdensome taxes and state debt. (This funding scheme angered many outside Rhode Island.) Importantly, many Mercantile Party adherents took out loans under the paper money program to assist their personal financial dealings. Their unwillingness to give up individual advantage contributed to the delay in Rhode Island's entrance into the new Union.[8]

National Dynamics

It was impossible for Rhode Islanders to weigh only local concerns during the ratification struggle. National leaders clearly indicated that stark and painful consequences would follow after a formal rejection of the new Constitution. The surest penalty would be duties placed on all Rhode Island commerce, in effect treating the state like a foreign nation. Restrictions could also be placed on movement across Rhode Island's borders. National leaders balanced these ominous possibilities with the encouraging prospect of a bill of rights that would be added to the Constitution to guarantee and safeguard local and individual privileges that many Rhode Islanders believed the new, more powerful central government eliminated or put in dire jeopardy. Rhode Islanders eagerly contributed their ideas to the active national debate in newspapers and pamphlets on the best amendments to compose a bill of rights.

Less obvious than these threats or ongoing constitutional debate was the private jockeying for salaried positions in the new federal government, an activity known as "patronage-seeking," or simply, patronage. The national government established under the Constitution created a large number of federal jobs. Custom houses to manage trade and collect duties employed assessors, weighers, gaugers, and other officials. Post offices in every city and town needed postmasters. The new federal court system required judges, attorneys, and marshals. Some of these positions kept the employee in the state; others required relocation to the national capital. Political advancement and financial rewards motivated men to seek these patronage positions. Political leaders valued the ability to control access to offices as a way to consolidate or expand their hold on power.

Aspirants for patronage wrote to President George Washington asking for appointments while controversy raged in Rhode Island over ratification of the Constitution. Jeremiah Olney, who knew Washington from Continental Army service, was among the first to make an appeal. The language of his letter was typical.

> The State of Rhode-Island, tho' it has hitherto refused, will undoubtedly ere long adopt the federal Constitution, when a Collector must be appointed for the State. It is an Office I am anxious to obtain: if your Excellency should be under no engagement in consequence of a prior application; and your knowledge of my Character will, in your own estimation, warrant my appointment to it, I will endeavour to manifest my Gratitude by an upright, impartial, and faithful discharge of the Trust reposed in me; which I am sure would be infinitely more pleasing and satisfactory to a Mind, like yours, fraught with the sincerest Wishes for the public Weal, than any private testimony thereof could possibly prove.

Olney eventually secured an appointment, and many other aspirants followed his lead.[9] If Rhode Island did not ratify the Constitution, there would be no patronage for Rhode Islanders. The hunger to secure patronage undoubtedly drove many to redouble their efforts to overcome the Country Party's opposition to ratification. Indeed, some could argue that patronage coming to Rhode Island after ratification could be used to reconcile Country Party adherents disappointed with the result.[10]

Confrontation

In October 1787, the General Assembly set the stage for an arduous ratification process by refusing to vote on the proposal to convene a state convention to decide the issue. Citing the need to proceed with caution on such a momentous question, the Country Party majority ordered one thousand copies of the proposed Constitution printed and distributed among the towns. This action was designed to give all freemen the chance to review the document and reach their own conclusions concerning its merits after mature deliberation. The Country Party trumpeted this action as in perfect keeping with their localist ideology. On the other hand, Mercantile Party members deemed the move dilatory and evasive. Outside observers saw the action as further evidence of the political depravity and waywardness that held Rhode Islanders in a tight grip.

Taking advantage of its momentum, the Country Party majority used its leverage when the General Assembly met again in February 1788 to question the propriety of calling a ratifying convention and then choosing to present the matter of ratification directly to the freemen for discussion and decision in town meetings. Eager to secure wide and fair participation, the law urged the most thorough warning of all potential voters and outlined a special method of balloting. Each man must voice his vote aloud and have his name and vote recorded by the town clerk. All votes could then be verified upon a final accounting in the General Assembly. The law designated late March as the time for voting.

Mercantile Party backers who wanted a statewide convention composed of delegates from each town expressed their disapproval with the Country Party plan by boycotting the town meetings called to consider the Constitution. Besides indicating their dissatisfaction, this course also shrewdly camouflaged the exact extent of the Mercantile Party's weakness in relation to its stronger political adversaries. Without a meaningful opposition in the field, Country Party adherents overwhelmingly defeated ratification by a tally of 2,711-243.

An outside observer explained the result to a friend in private correspondence. The commitment in Rhode Island to the state paper money program to eradicate debt ranked as the foremost factor. Once this program was completed, support for the Constitution likely would increase. Current opposition also stemmed from the status of slaves under the new government. Many wanted slaves to be taxed the same as white men and not counted for purposes of representation in Congress. Rhode Islanders also desired that direct taxes be proportioned by the quantity of produce exported from each state rather than by its population. Self-interest clearly motivated each objection.[11]

One of the few largely rural towns to register any significant number of votes in favor of ratification was Portsmouth. Twelve freemen in that town ignored the boycott and voted for the Constitution. Sixty of their townsmen joined the majority. Differences of opinion in Portsmouth would loom very large as the ratification process in Rhode Island traveled its long road.

Supporters of the Constitution across Rhode Island rallied after this initial defeat. Residents in the commercial seaports of Newport, Providence, and Bristol took the lead in this effort. Petitions sent to the General Assembly earnestly entreated for the gathering of a deliberative convention to conduct a sustained discussion of the proposed Constitution. These pleas went largely unheard. The Country Party retained its hold on the state government after the April election and blocked any formal debate or discussion on ratification during the May and June legislative sessions.

Popular expressions of discontent now added to the petition movement. New Hampshire became the ninth state to ratify the Constitution, and the new United States now would come into existence. Providence residents planned to mark this achievement with grand festivities on the Fourth of July. Organizers sent invitations far and wide with the idea of using the occasion to develop better rapport between partisans split over the ratification issue. Both sides rejoiced in the nation's independence from Great Britain, and it was thought that some structure of compromise could be fashioned on this foundation. All good intentions went awry. Country Party enthusiasts from distant towns viewed the celebration as a ploy to undermine their unity and trick them into a disastrous error. Those who came to Providence from the country towns arrived filled with anger rather than charitable feelings. Armed confrontation was avoided only through the quick decision by celebration organizers to drop events provoking the ratification question and to focus all activities on independence.

Tensions in Rhode Island clearly were on the rise when the General Assembly reconvened in Providence that October. Advocates of the Constitution succeeded in getting a vote on a motion for a ratifying convention, but they lost, 40-14. Discussion over amendments to the Constitution advanced by other states became more prevalent in the aftermath of this defeat. Any hopes for a rapid change of heart among the Country Party majority were misguided. The General Assembly defeated two more motions for a convention by similar majorities. The first vote came in December. The second occurred in March 1789. Riding this steady wave of support, the Country Party again carried the state government in the April elections.

Country Party enthusiasm, however, dulled under growing outside pressure. An increasingly impatient Congress had begun to pass bills establishing the nation's revenue and financial systems. Unless Rhode Island ratified the Constitution, it stood to realize none of the benefits of these measures and to suffer painful penalties and encumbrances. Commercial interests in Rhode Island vigorously resumed their petitioning of the General Assembly. Unable to turn a deaf ear to the growing din, the General Assembly again voted on a motion for a ratifying convention in June. The motion failed, but the Country Party mustered a smaller majority than previously. This outcome attracted more pressure from Congress. Only after considerable haggling did Congress decide against penal duties on products shipped from North Carolina and Rhode Island, the two states still pondering ratification. This reprieve would end on January 15, 1790.[12]

At the September 1789 session of the General Assembly, a recharged Mercantile Party minority persuaded the Country Party majority to pass an act that mandated freemen to call town meetings to provide specific instruction to their legislative representatives on the question of whether to hold a ratifying convention. Freemen in the country towns remained staunch in their opposition. The vote in a new General Assembly resulted in another defeat for Constitution proponents, 39-17.

By the start of the next session of the General Assembly on January 11, 1790, Rhode Islanders faced the double predicament of having just four days before the imposition of harsh duties on their domestic products and being the only one of the original thirteen states not to have ratified the Constitution. (President Washington emphasized this latter point in a private letter of December 27 to a Rhode Island friend, discretely urging favorable action on ratification.[13]) On January 15, the lower house agreed to call a ratification convention, 34-29. The upper house postponed its decision until the next day and then voted 5-4 against the motion. With anxiety mounting, the General Assembly decided to reconsider the subject the following morning. That day was Sunday, and only an extraordinary situation would compel the transaction of legislative business on the Sabbath.

The lower house again acted first, passing a new motion for a ratification convention, 32-11. The upper house then took up the issue. Missing from their number was a member who was a Baptist minister, and the vote concluded in a 4-4 tie. The bill then went to Governor John Collins for his tie-breaking ballot. A Country Party stalwart since the start of the ratification ordeal, Collins now thought it best to look beyond particular local interests and to work toward the common good of the nation. He therefore voted in favor of holding a convention and wrote in glowing terms of this result to President Washington.

> This Event gives me the most sincere pleasure, as there is every Reason to hope that the Accession of this State will in a short Time not only entitle the Citizens

thereof to all the Benefits of the Federal Government, but as it will render the Union complete, and affords a rational and pleasing prospect that the Thirteen States which by their United exertions, at the expence of their common blood and treasure obtained liberty and Independence, will be again joined in the firmest Bands of Friendship, under a Constitution calculated to secure to them the great Objects for which they fought and bled.

The decision to hold a convention averted an immediate crisis and convinced Congress to extend Rhode Island's reprieve from revenue law duties until April 1, 1790.[14] Collins fared less well. The Country Party renounced his decision and nominated another candidate at the next gubernatorial election.

CONVENTIONS AND A NARROW RESOLUTION

The bill for a convention directed the towns to elect delegates who would assemble in South Kingston on the first Monday in March.[15] This convention could debate all aspects of the Constitution and cast a binding vote for or against ratification. A still-strong Country Party worked hard to secure delegates opposed to the Constitution. Having achieved its long-sought object of a convention, the Mercantile Party worked equally hard to elect delegates who would push through any remaining obstacles and adopt the Constitution.

Portsmouth had been one of the most divided towns. After electing delegates to the ratifying convention at a town meeting held February 8, 1790, the freemen there again assembled in large numbers on February 27. A majority of freemen at this meeting formally withdrew their allegiance from the Country Party and indicated their support for the Constitution. The election of Giles Lawton, Jr., who had voted for the Constitution in the referendum almost two years earlier, as town meeting moderator confirmed the shift in local sentiments. A five-man committee—three of whose members could be identified as longstanding Mercantile Party adherents—then composed a lengthy set of instructions to the town's four delegates describing the position of the new majority in favor of ratification.

The new majority in Portsmouth gravely prefaced their instructions by noting that sure disaster would overwhelm the state and its people if the convention rejected the Constitution. Financial prospects weighed heavily on their minds, and they compiled a list of economic evils and disadvantages sure to burden them if they remained separate from the Union. Some discretion was given to the delegates as far as agreeing to a temporary adjournment and proposing amendments to the Constitution. None, however, could misinterpret their principal charge, which was to adopt the Constitution as quickly as possible so that suffering in the town would cease.

The surge of sympathy in Portsmouth for the Constitution may be explained by a growing confidence among the local population that the central government would not use its powers rapaciously or invidiously. In their instructions to the delegates, Portsmouth's freemen acknowledged the flourishing commerce in neighboring states and credited the new Union with this happy condition. They fervently believed that similar benefits would come to them after ratification. Portsmouth residents with damage claims from the British occupation during the Revolutionary War also may have spurred this shift away from the Country Party. A stronger central government would control vastly more resources—financial, legal, and diplomatic—and the likelihood of receiving monetary compensation would improve dramatically. A new enumeration of damage victims listed 166 people, a meaningful percentage of the town's population. Finally, religious influences may have encouraged the swing. Quaker leader Moses Brown, a member of a prominent merchant family in Providence, wrote a detailed letter to the Quakers in Portsmouth urging them to accept the Constitution. The opinion of such a respected leader commanded serious consideration, and enough devout Quakers lived in Portsmouth to make a difference in local political councils.

The new attitude toward the Constitution evident in Portsmouth and elsewhere in the state did not lead to immediate ratification. When the convention gathered in South Kingstown, delegates still differed over constitutional provisions preserving slavery and the national government's power to levy taxes. One of the convention members, Theodore Foster, a Mercantile Party adherent from Providence, kept a contemporaneous journal that, despite the haste and sketchiness of many entries, provides the fullest account of the proceedings.[16] Foster's notes clearly show that neither side quailed before the arguments and contentions of the other. It quickly became apparent that reaching some compromise would be difficult.

The proceedings began with a sharp exchange over the adoption of a rule that would allow the indefinite postponement of a final vote on the main question of ratifying the Constitution. Country Party supporters pushed vigorously for this parliamentary point. Mercantile Party sympathizers, who evidently knew that they controlled enough votes to defeat this gambit, displayed remarkable restraint and patience throughout the dispute. Job Comstock, a very vocal Anti-Federalist from East Greenwich, advanced his view with great fervor on the grounds of "fair play." Foster recorded Comstock's elaboration: "He wants not to trick any Body. Wishes to act agreeable to the Wishes of the People. The Voice of the People is the Voice of God. If it was the best Constitution it would be a bad one if disagreeable to the Minds of the People, and he will not agree to it till the Minds of the People are reconciled to it." After listening to Comstock, Federalists quashed the proposal by a vote of 39-27. After appointing a committee to draft a bill of rights and amendments, the delegates adjourned until the afternoon.

Foster's notes resume with the deliberations on the morning of March 3. Debate then centered on the mode of direct taxation prescribed by the Constitution. Henry Marchant, a Federalist from Newport, acknowledged legitimate concerns about a system of taxation based on population rather than on the value of products but adopted a long-range perspective to put a brighter tinge on the issue. New England states would not grow in population as fast as new states to the west. The prescribed mode of taxation was sure to lessen the future burden placed on Rhode Islanders. Joseph Stanton, a staunch Anti-Federalist from Charlestown, countered with a strong appeal to present reality. Stanton remarked pithily that "20 Planters in the southern States are worth 30 of Us," suggesting the inequity of a tax system that benefited those who controlled great property and wealth at the expense of small farmers. Stanton's argument prompted agreement from Nathan Miller, but this Federalist from Warren dismissed all objections to the Constitution at this moment as untimely.

This debate on the fairness of taxes went back and forth, hinging on whether future advantages outweighed present disadvantages and whether a just estimate of taxes owed by each individual in Rhode Island ever could be obtained. In the course of the debate, Federalists defended the legitimacy of taxation by the national government against counter arguments by their opponents. George Hazard, a Newport delegate, spoke most colorfully in favor of taxes to reduce debt: "This Debt of 54 Millions of Dollars is like a Cloud cast upon us—it eats like a Canker Worm Night & Day."

William Bradford, a Federalist from Bristol, tried to calm the increasing storminess of the exchanges by refocusing attention on the principal issue of ratification and the inability of anybody to predict the future precisely. Foster noted that Bradford proclaimed his support for the Constitution despite flaws and then appealed to God: "He does not know whether it will appear perfectly right in the Eyes of him who sees through all things." Debate then fizzled without resolution.

The convention next examined provisions in the Constitution for the election of senators and representatives. John Sayles, a Smithfield delegate, opened the debate with a strong expression of Country Party ideology: "Congress never ought to have the Power of altering the Mode of Election. It ought to be Reserved to the People." Federalist sympathizers indicated that Congress would not meddle with state prerogatives unless there were extraordinary reasons. No sensible basis existed for fears. Apparently mollified, Anti-Federalists continued the review of the Constitution.

Nothing struck a nerve until the section on presidential veto power. Foster recorded in his notes: "Jos. Stanton objects to the Power of the President to reject a Bill—says that he has the Power of one Third of Congress." Henry Marchant responded for the Federalists. Eliminating or reducing the veto power would unsettle the delicate and essential system of checks and balances that prevented either the executive or legislative branch from becoming overbearing and tyrannical. He closed with a plea: "This the most beautiful Part of the Constitution—we ought to be careful how we destroy it."

Other Federalists chimed in with their support for the veto. Nathan Miller wanted nothing changed. "There are Two Interests in this Government—a Northern & Southern Interest. The President to hold the Balance—Therefore let Two Thirds of Congress determine." Benjamin Bourn, a Providence delegate, suggested that the president could not veto legislation arbitrarily. He must state his objections in writing and is ultimately responsible to the people at another election. Bourn also noted that the Massachusetts Constitution provided for an executive veto. Joseph Stanton, however, remained unmoved, and said "there is a Disposition in all the Race of Adam to assume Power. It may be observed." Unable to reach agreement, the delegates referred the matter of the presidential veto to the committee to draft amendments and adjourned until the afternoon.

The section in the Constitution preventing prohibition of the overseas slave trade until 1808 provoked controversy in the afternoon session. Joseph Stanton disapproved any measure that tended to encourage "the African trade." Job Comstock, Stanton's fellow Anti-Federalist, condemned the slave trade as "iniquitous. Righteousness exalteth a Nation but Iniquity is a Reproach to any People." Federalists avoided the moral question and instead pointed out the inconsistency inherent in the Anti-Federalist position. On almost every issue, they wanted to limit the power of the national government. Now, when it came to slavery, they wanted the national government to be able to act aggressively to curtail the practice. Most ominously, as Jonathan J. Hazard, a South Kingstown delegate, observed, an obstinate demand to end slavery immediately by amendment would doom the nascent Union. "The southern states will separate from us before they will agree to this Alternate proposed."

Anti-Federalists persisted in their denunciations and created divisions in the Federalist ranks. William Barton, a delegate from Providence who desperately wanted to ratify the Constitution, struggled to reconcile his conflicting desires. With wrenching diction, he expressed his wish that "all men may be free" and that the delegates show their love of the Constitution by formally disapproving the slave provisions. His appeal elicited a reply from Jonathan Hazard that attacking slavery "will be Stabbing to the Vitals of the S. States." He urged his fellow delegates to "Let the southern states alone.... We cannot injure one order of Men without injuring all." Unimpressed, Anti-Federalist spokesman Joseph Stanton read aloud the "Beautiful" preamble of the Constitution and asked the convention, "Why in the Name of Common Sense should not this Liberty be extended to the Africans?"

The debate lurched along until the president turned discussion back to the main point of slave importation and reasserted the claim that any attack on slavery "will disaffect the Southern States." His intervention did little to redirect or focus deliberations. Delegates raised legal and biblical precedents without leading toward any substantial agreement. A combination of frustration and exhaustion finally brought this debate to an inconclusive end. A few complaints over the obscure meaning of the prohibition against "capitation" taxes closed out the day.

Reconvening the next morning, the delegates moved along easily until they reached the section of the Constitution concerning the amendment process. William Barton praised the article as one that "ought to be written in Letters of Gold." Jonathan Hazard, main defender of the slavery provisions, differed: "We want a Constitution not to be altered. The Rich and powerful States will be uneasy till they alter it for their Benefit. That so far from thinking the Clause ought to have been written in Letters of Gold—he is sorry it was ever written in Letters with Ink and is sorry that it has appeared as a Part of the Constitution." Federalists generally supported the amendment process as a way to convince Anti-Federalists that problems with the new government could be overcome in due time by change in the fundamental law.

A motion to consider the amendments Congress already had proposed to modify the Constitution then passed and opened new channels of debate. James Sheldon, a Richmond delegate, proposed that states as well as Congress should be precluded from making any law respecting religion. This proposal launched a brief discussion on the history of legislation concerning religion and the freedom of conscience. The delegates seemed to conclude that it was adequate to place prohibitions only on the national government.

The convention then moved from amendments proposed by Congress to amendments proposed by other states. Foster recorded no significant discussion or queries. These preliminaries led to the appointment of a committee to draft amendments. The delegates then adjourned until the afternoon.

Foster's notes resume with the afternoon session on March 5. The business at hand was the report from the committee appointed to draft amendments. A large crowd had gathered to witness the deliberations. Foster sensed the importance of the occasion: "Thus Life Passes and carries along the Tide of Time to land us in Eternity—of what consequence will then be all this Parade?" Parliamentary maneuvering occupied the first stages of the session. Job Comstock, the unbowed Country Party adherent and Anti-Federalist, motioned "that the Bill of Rights and Amendments be Referred to the People at large to have their Opinion & Sentiments thereon." Comstock's obviously dilatory motion was declared out of order after yet another typical exchange of well-worn views by the opposing sides.

A review of the proposed amendments then took place. Dispute arose over the appropriate manner to represent and tax slaves. Fear that any action on this issue put the ability of the states to unite under one government in imminent peril overshadowed the specifics of the exchange. Federalist William Bradford contended that the wisest course would be to steer clear of this intractable obstacle. "It seems that we are too Jealous. We ought to enter into the Govt. on a Broad Basis. Happy if the Southern States do not overrun the Eastern States—it will tend to attract their Attention to the Matter." His view eventually prevailed. The delegates postponed further consideration of the contentious subject.

Significant debate on the proposed amendments began again the next morning. The usual differences of opinion filled the air without settling any point of real consequence. The slave trade provoked another acrimonious set of charges and countercharges. Job Comstock again tried to refer the issue of a bill of rights to "the People" of the state for their direct consideration. Exasperated delegates adjourned until the afternoon without reaching a decision on Comstock's revived motion.

Nothing changed upon the resumption of proceedings. The delegates remained divided on critical components of the Constitution and the whole matter of amendments. Much apprehension still existed that the Constitution and national government imperiled local autonomy and personal liberty. To the amazement of many convention participants and observers, disagreement still raged as to whether the delegates even had the authority to adopt the Constitution.

Seeing no other viable option, the delegates began to debate the merits of an extended adjournment. Nathan Miller ranted against such a course and ended with the wish that "he had the Eloquence of Demosthenes." Miller and his Federalist compatriots could not dissuade a majority. Without a vote on ratification, the Country Party delegates secured an adjournment of the convention until May in Newport. This first session made clear that a schism persisted between agrarian interior towns and their commercial counterparts located along the coast.

Foster recorded no utterance from any of Portsmouth's four delegates, but all four voted for the motion to adjourn the convention. Divisions and uncertainties among the delegation may explain their silence. Two of them had voted against ratification at the referendum in March 1788, and it can be assumed that they still harbored personal reservations against the Constitution. Another was a Quaker who had been the first inhabitant of Portsmouth to emancipate a slave under the manumission law passed by the General Assembly in 1784. His moral beliefs may have disinclined him to advocate a Constitution that protected the institution of slavery in several essentials and put him at odds with the instructions of his fellow townspeople that were rooted primarily in economic concerns. The fourth delegate had no discernable political background and may have been selected as a neutral figure acceptable to both the local Country and Mercantile factions.

The new majority in Portsmouth showed no tolerance for diffidence and equivocation by their delegates. At a town meeting in late April 1790, the assembled freemen repeated their instructions favoring ratification and prohibited their delegates from agreeing to another adjournment. Given the obvious dissatisfaction with these delegates, it is surprising that no recorded effort was made to choose replacements. An accommodation with Country Party diehards may explain the decision to keep the same delegation.

The state ratifying convention reconvened at Newport on May 25, 1790. The gathering felt severe pressures from the national government. Just a few days earlier, the Senate had passed a bill potentially disastrous to Rhode Island commerce under the guise of checking smuggling. This bill probably would have passed the House if not for help from an unlikely source. John Page, a congressman from Virginia who earlier had spoken out against sanctions upon Rhode Island, condemned all coercion as unfair and unwise. Elaborating,

Page contended that the Union would achieve real strength only if the states joined willingly and upon the merits of the Constitution. Legislation to restrict trade served no good purpose. Foreign nations would think that the Union was not the free choice of its citizens, and the completion of the Union probably would be delayed longer by the justifiable repugnance of Rhode Islanders to overbearing tactics. Page's argument convinced enough of his colleagues to postpone action on the measure.[17]

Closer to home, additional pressure came from the freemen in Providence. At a town meeting convened the day before the ratifying convention resumed deliberations, these freemen voted to secede from Rhode Island and make an independent arrangement with the United States unless the Constitution won approval. Although they took no formal steps, Newporters also spoke in ominously similar tones.

Such urgent concerns sparked five days of frantic debate and maneuvering among the delegates at the ratifying convention. Inconclusive discussions led to a vote on May 28 for a lengthy adjournment. It failed by a majority of nine. On May 29, the delegates finally cast ballots on the question of ratification. No one could be sure of the result until the final tally showed a vote of 34-32 in favor of the Constitution. Federalists rejoiced at their success. Anti-Federalists resigned themselves to defeat.

Anti-Federalist delegates generally proved steadfast in their opposition, but a critical shift occurred in the delegation from Portsmouth. One of their number moved for an overnight adjournment late in the afternoon of May 28 to consult with his constituents. This erratic action in light of recent instructions prompted the hasty gathering of a town meeting on the morning of May 29. Angry Portsmouth freemen reiterated their instructions calling for ratification without delay. Although they were not sufficiently exasperated to unseat their reluctant delegate and send a replacement, the assembled freemen expressed their firm belief that failure to adopt the Constitution immediately would bring evil consequences, and they assigned a messenger to deliver copies of their instructions to the leader of the town delegation and the president of the ratifying convention.

Despite their unequivocal instructions, only two of Portsmouth's delegates voted for ratification. A longstanding opponent of the Constitution ignored his fellow townspeople and voted against ratification. The fourth delegate, the Quaker evidently torn between his moral opinions and political obligations, absented himself from the convention at the time of the decisive ballot. His presence may have reduced the final margin in favor of ratification to one and set in motion other deals or defections that could have led to rejection of the Constitution as well as untold complications. Portsmouth freemen expressed their displeasure with the recalcitrant Anti-Federalists by purging all Country Party sympathizers from town offices at the next election, including the delegate who defied instructions with his vote against ratification.

FEDERAL APPROVAL

The secretary of the state convention sent President Washington unofficial notice of the favorable action immediately upon ratification of the Constitution. "I have the pleasing satisfaction of informing your Excellency that the Constitution of the United States of America was this day ratified and adopted by the convention of the People of this State, agreeable to the recommendation of the general Convention, assembled at Philadelphia, and the consequent resolution of Congress thereon."[18] Word of Rhode Island's ratification ended all consideration of punitive legislation. Steps began instead to implement the Constitution in the newest member of the Union.

On June 9, official notification of Rhode Island's vote in favor of the Constitution was addressed to President Washington. This document included a lengthy statement on the new government as well as twenty-one suggested amendments to the Constitution. The appended material was meant to clarify and safeguard essential liberties and privileges and to set the new Union on the best possible future course.[19]

Several striking comments marked the assessment of the Constitution. Convention delegates asserted "the right to the free exercise of religion" and commended regular elections for executive and legislative officials as a sound way to prevent oppressive rule. They desired suffrage for "all men" firmly attached to the community and warned against any violation of freedom of speech or the press as ultimately hazardous to essential liberties. Also applauded were trial by jury and related checks on government policing powers, including the right of the people "to keep and bear arms."

To ensure that their understanding of the Constitution's operation was in fact accurate, convention delegates welcomed amendments that would remove all doubts. Several amendments are particularly noteworthy. Convention delegates sought a guarantee of sovereignty to each state with an explicit reservation of "every power, jurisdiction and right, which is not by this Constitution expressly delegated to the United States"; protection of existing state paper money programs from any federal interference; prohibitions against military conscription, poll taxes, and monopolies; a system of direct taxation that gave priority to state legislatures; and the authority for state legislatures to recall senators and elect replacements. The seventeenth proposed amendment denounced the slave trade as "disgraceful to the cause of liberty and humanity" and urged Congress to pass laws that speedily ended slave imports. In keeping with this desire for amendments, the Rhode Island General Assembly approved the Bill of Rights without contention during June.[20] These ten amendments did not cover every item of interest to Rhode Islanders, but such a good start left little reason to mount vocal or concerted opposition.

Congress acted promptly to approve the favorable ratification vote in Rhode Island. Before the end of June, the House and Senate passed legislation that instituted federal judicial and treasury officers in the new state. No controversy or debate delayed these measures.[21]

RECONCILIATION

The exhausting ratification struggle left no energy or taste for a battle over a new state constitution. Rhode Island's venerated colonial charter still held wide appeal. Leaving it in place began the process of healing local divisions and allowed politicians to concentrate on their adjustment to the new national government.

Both those who had supported and those who had opposed the Constitution now competed for federal patronage.[22] By a combination of design and luck, a balance resulted that left neither side totally happy nor embittered. The General Assembly elected one senator from each faction. Joseph Stanton from Charlestown in the southern portion of the state had been a prominent Country Party leader. Theodore Foster hailed from Providence and counted an array of merchants among his friends. Besides his politics, Foster's selection benefited from his marriage to a sister of the sitting Anti-Federalist governor, Arthur Fenner, Jr. Rhode Island's sole seat in the House of Representatives went to Benjamin Bourn, a Providence lawyer aligned with the old Mercantile Party. Bourn faced feeble opposition from increasingly disorganized Anti-Federalist adherents, and his election demonstrated the superiority Federalists then maintained in the state.[23]

Federalists again demonstrated their relative strength by securing a majority of the new federal positions in the state. Perhaps the most disappointed person was former governor John Collins, the Country Party leader whose scruples moved him to cast his deciding vote for the ratifying convention that eventually brought Rhode Island into the Union. His emotional request to be appointed collector of customs at Newport elicited no sympathy. Abandoned by his former party and unappreciated by his erstwhile Federalist opponents, Collins received no reward for sacrificing his political career.[24]

The most highly publicized act of reconciliation was President Washington's visit to Rhode Island. Washington very publicly had avoided Rhode Island in an earlier tour of New England, and no observer missed the snub. The president first attempted to improve relations in a letter of June 4 to Governor Fenner acknowledging Rhode Island's ratification vote:

> Since the bond of Union is now compleat, and we once more consider ourselves as one family, it is much to be hoped that reproaches will cease and prejudices be done away; for we should all remember that we are members of that community upon whose general success depends our particular and individual welfare—and, therefore, if we mean to support the Liberty and Independence which it has cost us so much blood & treasure to establish, we must drive far away the dæmon of party spirit and local reproach.

His official response to the ratifying convention praised its action as one "which unites under one general Government all the branches of the great American family; and I doubt not but it will prove as auspicious to the good people of your State as it is pleasing to other parts of the Union." Washington journeyed to Rhode Island during August 1790. The president spoke on several occasions in Newport and Providence and received courtesies at every turn. The symbolic importance of Washington's visit cannot be overstated. His presence in Rhode Island salved old wounds and helped unite the widely despised outcast with her sister states. None could doubt the strong message that little Rhode Island was to be treated as an equal.[25]

SUMMARY

Rhode Islanders never experienced their worst fears after ratification. The state retained its identity and a considerable degree of local autonomy. Local advocates for the Constitution as a replacement for the Articles of Confederation had been sustained by their hopes for improved economic fortunes and outlasted their opponents who focused more on philosophical issues of power and control. Although the state's paper money program to reduce debt after the Revolutionary War clearly played a significant role in the reluctance to ratify the Constitution, it must not overshadow other influences, both local and national. Rhode Islanders cherished their rights and privileges under the Charter of 1663 and did not want to forfeit them to an intrusive national government. The Constitution continued to protect slavery, and an awakening abolitionist sensibility in the state found association with such a government objectionable.

Approval of the federal government finally came after it became apparent that Congress would impose harsh penalties and burdens on Rhode Island's commerce and crush the state's ability to exist as a separate entity. Prospects for patronage jobs under the federal government motivated Federalists to continue the fight for ratification during the gloomy stretches of Anti-Federalist ascendancy. The reality of patronage then helped settle scores among Rhode Island's factions. Finally, President Washington's tour of the state in August 1790 made citizens in Rhode Island and across the nation recognize that the ratification battle had ended and that all needed to concentrate on bringing about the anticipated benefits of union.

NOTES

1. The summary of Rhode Island colonial government that follows compresses the account in William M. Ferraro, "Lives of Quiet Desperation: Community and Polity in New England over Four Centuries: The Case of Portsmouth and Foster, Rhode Island" (Ph.D. diss., Brown University, 1991), pp. 10–27.

2. Stephen Hopkins, "The Rights of Colonies Examined," reprinted in *Records of the Colony of Rhode Island and Providence Plantations in New England,* ed. John Russell

Bartlett (Providence: various publishers, 1856–1865), 6:416–427; Carl Bridenbaugh, ed., *Silas Downer: Forgotten Patriot: His Life and Writings* (Providence: The Rhode Island Bicentennial Foundation, 1974).

3. Bartlett, *Records of the Colony of Rhode Island*, 7:283.

4. Ibid., 7:267.

5. Paul H. Smith, ed., *Letters of Delegates to Congress, 1774–1789* (Washington: Library of Congress, 1976–2000), 24:196–197, 255–257, 310–313, 333–334.

6. Bartlett, *Records of the Colony of Rhode Island*, 10:258–259.

7. For a Mercantile Party advocate's colorful review of the competing ideologies, see Dorothy Twohig, et al., eds., *The Papers of George Washington: Presidential Series* (Charlottesville: University Press of Virginia, 1987–), 4:410–412.

8. This overview compresses the account in Ferraro, "Lives of Quiet Desperation," pp. 189–203.

9. Twohig et al., eds., *The Papers of George Washington*, 1:398–400; 3:596–597; 4:11–12, 102–103; 5:18–24, 149–150, 166–168, 194–195, 220–222, 414–419.

10. Earlier important studies of ratification in Rhode Island fail to mention the role of patronage. See Frank Greene Bates, *Rhode Island and the Formation of the Union* (New York: Columbia University, 1898); Irwin H. Polishook, *Rhode Island and the Union, 1774–1795* (Evanston: Northwestern University Press, 1969); Patrick T. Conley, *Democracy in Decline: Rhode Island Constitutional Development* (Providence: Rhode Island Historical Society, 1977).

11. Smith, *Letters of Delegates to Congress, 1774–1789*, 25:217–218.

12. Linda Grant DePauw et al., eds., *Documentary History of the First Federal Congress of the United States of America, March 4, 1789–March 3, 1791* (Baltimore: Johns Hopkins University Press, 1972), 8:389–398; Twohig et al., eds., *The Papers of George Washington*, 3:565–567; 4:12–15.

13. Twohig et al., eds., *The Papers of George Washington*, 4:451–452; 5:1–2.

14. Ibid., 5:7–8, 66–67.

15. The subsequent presentation follows the account in Ferraro, "Lives of Quiet Desperation," pp. 207–217, and Ferraro, "Localism in Portsmouth and Foster during the Revolutionary and Founding Periods," *Rhode Island History* 54 (3) (August 1996): 80–84.

16. See Robert C. Cotner, ed., *Theodore Foster's Minutes of the Convention, Held at South Kingstown, Rhode Island, In March, 1790, Which Failed to Adopt the Constitution of the United States* (reprint, Freeport, NY: Books for Libraries Press, 1970). All quotations for the debates during the convention are from this source. Some spelling has been changed to improve clarity.

17. DePauw et al., eds., *Documentary History of the First Federal Congress*, 1:311–314; 9:795–803; 13:1446–1447, 1458–1463; Twohig et al., eds., *The Papers of George Washington*, 5:406–411.

18. Twohig et al., eds., *The Papers of George Washington*, 5:439–440.

19. DePauw et al., eds., *Documentary History of the First Federal Congress*, 1:355–362; Twohig et al., eds., *The Papers of George Washington*, 5:500–505.

20. Bartlett, *Records of the Colony of Rhode Island*, 10:380–382; DePauw et al., eds., *Documentary History of the First Federal Congress*, 1:388–389; Twohig et al., eds., *The Papers of George Washington*, 5:572.

21. Joseph Gales, comp., *The Debates and Proceedings in the Congress of the United States* (Washington: Gales and Seaton, 1834), 2:2290–2293 (known more familiarly as *Annals of Congress*).

22. Twohig et al., eds., *The Papers of George Washington*, 5:457–458, 497–499, 506–509, 516–517, 528 529, 531–536.

23. DePauw et al., eds., *Documentary History of the First Federal Congress*, 14:812–822.

24. Twohig et al., eds., *The Papers of George Washington*, 5:419–420.

25. Ibid., 4:585–586; 5:470, 536–537; 6:279–288, 299–305, 673–675.

BIBLIOGRAPHY

Bartlett, John Russell, ed. *Records of the Colony of Rhode Island and Providence Plantations in New England.* 10 vols. Providence: various publishers, 1856–1865.

Bates, Frank Greene. *Rhode Island and the Formation of the Union.* New York: Columbia University, 1898.

Conley, Patrick. *Democracy in Decline: Rhode Island Constitutional Development.* Providence: Rhode Island Historical Society, 1977.

Cotner, Robert C., ed. *Theodore Foster's Minutes of the Convention, Held at South Kingstown, Rhode Island, In March, 1790, Which Failed to Adopt the Constitution of the United States.* Reprint. Freeport, NY: Books for Libraries Press, 1970.

DePauw, Linda Grant, et al., eds. *Documentary History of the First Federal Congress of the United States of America, March 4, 1789–March 3, 1791.* Baltimore: Johns Hopkins University Press, 1972–, vols. 1, 8, 11, 13, 14.

Ferraro, William M. "Localism in Portsmouth and Foster during the Revolutionary and Founding Periods." *Rhode Island History* 54 (3) (August 1996): 67–89.

Polishook, Irwin H. *Rhode Island and the Union, 1774–1795.* Evanston, IL: Northwestern University Press, 1969.

Smith, Paul H., ed. *Letters of Delegates to Congress, 1774–1789*. Washington, DC: Library of Congress, 1976–2000, vols. 24, 25.

Twohig, Dorothy, et al., eds. *The Papers of George Washington: Presidential Series.* Charlottesville: University Press of Virginia, 1987–, vols. 1, 3–6.

THE STATE OF SOUTH CAROLINA

Ratified the Constitution of the United States: May 23, 1788

Matthew H. Jennings

INTRODUCTION

South Carolina became the eighth of the United States of America when it ratified the Constitution on May 29, 1788, roughly a month after Maryland and three weeks before New Hampshire. The seemingly easy choice to join the Union belied the fact that South Carolina, first as a colony and later as a state, was anything but united within its own borders. A century of hard-fought English colonization, the establishment of plantation agriculture, and the recent War of Independence had left deep, even permanent scars on South Carolina society, slicing along lines of region, class, and, most importantly, race. South Carolina's profound divisions shaped its past and continue to haunt its present. The region's journey to statehood—and the battles over the federal Constitution—cannot be understood without a well-developed sense of the experiences of the people who lived and died in colonial South Carolina.

COLONIAL SOUTH CAROLINA

For most of South Carolina's human history, the region was occupied by Native Americans. When Spanish explorers moved through the region in the middle of the sixteenth century, they encountered and exploited diverse peoples whose polities ranged in size from the Mississippian paramount chiefdom at Cofitachequi (near present-day Camden), to the forerunners of the modern Cherokee, Catawba, and Creek tribes, to the autonomous villages that dotted the resource-rich Atlantic coast. The Spanish made several *entradas*, or military

South Carolina

Territorial Development:

- The Carolina Colony is separated from the Commonwealth of Virginia and King Charles II grants the land to eight English gentlemen who had helped him to the throne, 1663
- Carolina is divided into the two separate colonies of North Carolina and South Carolina, 1711
- South Carolina is made a Royal Providence, 1729
- Continental Congress approves Declaration of Independence from Great Britain, July 4, 1776
- Great Britain formally recognizes American independence through the Treaty of Paris, September 3, 1783
- South Carolina becomes the eighth state to ratify the U.S. Constitution, May 23, 1788

Capitals Prior to Statehood:

- Charleston, 1670–1788

State Capitals:

- Charleston, 1788–1790
- Columbia, 1790–present

Origin of State Name: Like North Carolina, South Carolina was first named in honor of Charles IX of France and subsequently so called in honor of Charles I and Charles II of England, both of whom made out grants to the area.

First Governor: Charles Pinckney
Governmental Organization: Bicameral
Population at Statehood: 249,073
Geographical Size: 30,109 square miles

expeditions, into the greater Southeast, but their attempts at planting colonies were unsuccessful. It is a common misconception that the Spanish were interested solely in conquest, whereas the English were mainly concerned with building colonies. In the early decades of colonization, both European powers engaged in both sorts of colonial activity. The Spanish, under Pedro Menéndez de Avilés, established a town and a fortress at St. Augustine in the 1580s, but their influence on the native peoples of South Carolina remained slight. Franciscan missionaries did proselytize several native communities in the Sea Islands, but these missions declined throughout the seventeenth century, as did the Spanish influence on the region as a whole.

The Native American population of what became South Carolina was large and strikingly diverse. Colonial history is often written as though a homogenous group of Native Americans waited patiently to be "discovered" by Europeans. In South Carolina, the years leading up to colonization were turbulent. Larger governmental structures (like the chiefdom at Cofitachequi) declined through disease and emigration, and new, smaller polities took their place. When the English landed at what they called the Ashley and Cooper rivers in 1670, they entered a shattered world. Their entry would transform the remnants of this world into something altogether distinct: a violent, multicultural society based on trade and plantation slavery.

South Carolina entered the English colonial world at a comparatively late date. The mainland colonies to the north and the island colony of Barbados to the south had been flourishing for decades. Charles II's recently restored monarchy had furthered English colonial interests by adding New York and securing England's hold on Jamaica. Those who had supported Charles II during Oliver Cromwell's reign could safely call in royal favors. Anthony Ashley Cooper (soon-to-be Lord Shaftesbury), a friend of the king, led a renewed English drive to colonize the region. By the late 1660s, Shaftesbury had drawn up the Fundamental Constitutions that purported to establish a utopian, hierarchical society in South Carolina. It bears mentioning that Shaftesbury's personal secretary was philosopher John Locke, although it is unclear what effect, if any, Locke had on the famous document. The actual English settlement of South Carolina did not, however, occur along the lines drawn up by Shaftesbury.

Sensing an opportunity to increase their personal fortunes, planters from overcrowded Barbados moved into South Carolina's swampy lowcountry and tried to recreate the society they had left behind on Barbados in which a small white population ruled over a large unfree labor force. Although Anthony Ashley Cooper was no opponent of a stratified society, his plan had called for settling in orderly towns, following the model of the Massachusetts Bay Colony. South Carolina's earliest white settlers spread out dangerously thinly along the coastal rivers and quickly began to exploit local Native Americans in trade and as slaves while arming friendly tribes as a defensive measure.

If it is possible to argue that race relations were ever relatively peaceful in South Carolina, the case could be made for the years between 1670 and 1680.

After this initial "feeling-out" period, Carolina's Native American traders engaged in activities that would eventually bring native and white populations to open hostility. Native Americans recognized the threat posed by aggressively expanding settlements. Native fields, for instance, were particularly vulnerable to the herds of cattle that roamed the colony's hinterlands. Native reactions to English colonization were complex and culturally appropriate. In the Westo War (1680), the Tuscarora War (1710), and the Yamasee War (1715), Native Americans fought both alongside and against the English. The Yamasee, for instance, proved remarkably adept at raiding Florida's missions for Native American slaves in the opening decade of the eighteenth century. The Yamasee War, as devastating as it was to native and non-native Carolinians alike, led to a temporary respite from the endemic violence that marked the colony's early years. The defeated Yamasees and their allies removed to the periphery of the English colonial world. Scholars have estimated the "east of the mountain" native population in South Carolinas declined from 10,000 in 1685 to 5,100 in 1715. The number continued to drop precipitously as a result of disease, emigration, and violence, and one 1790 source suggests that fewer than five hundred Native Americans lived within the borders of South Carolina.[1]

South Carolina's early economy was diverse; whites and a few native and African slaves raised cattle and harvested naval stores, but it soon became clear that rice was South Carolina's surest cash crop. Using African expertise and labor, South Carolina's planters built a flourishing rice-centered economy. Rice production in Carolina was striking for two main reasons. The first was the sheer wealth that it brought to the colony's planter class. On the eve of the War for Independence, nine of the ten wealthiest Americans were from South Carolina, and the area surrounding Charleston was almost four times wealthier than any other mainland county.[2] The second was that rice farming increased the colony's reliance on slave labor. The colony's black population skyrocketed in the first half of the eighteenth century. This development prompted one European settler to remark that South Carolina was "more like a negro country than one settled by white people."[3] Thanks at first to rice (and later cotton) production, Africans and their descendants outnumbered white South Carolinians in the lowcountry throughout the colonial and antebellum period of the state's history. Although other crops, most notably indigo, were produced with modest success, Carolina's future as a colony was intimately tied to rice.

Rice growing in South Carolina produced an extremely volatile political culture. White planters had perched themselves at the top of a large, restive labor force. At the same time that they appreciated their slaves' contribution to their pocketbooks, they lived in constant fear of rebellion and attacks by Native Americans. This dicey situation might have united white South Carolinians politically, but South Carolina's colonial politics were anything but united. As soon as white people arrived in the region, long-lasting political factions developed. Many of the first white settlers were Barbadian planters, whose goals for Carolina (namely personal profit, no matter the risk) often ran counter to those of the proprietors. The two groups clashed over land distribution, the administration of the Native American trade, and the repayment of debts owed to the proprietors. These issues persisted through several of South Carolina's early administrations and eventually contributed to the demise of the proprietorship in the 1710s and 1720s. Religious differences provided another source of tension between proprietors and settlers. The proprietors, whose membership consisted of Quakers, and other Dissenters as well as Anglicans, insisted upon an official policy of tolerance, whereas the Barbadians staunchly opposed any measures that would weaken the Church of England. It is difficult, if not impossible, to separate spiritual and material issues in the political world of colonial South Carolina. The proprietors attempted to ease growing tensions by promoting a Barbadian, Sir John Yeamans, to the post of governor in 1674. Yeamans died shortly thereafter, and the council chose Joseph West to replace him. West left the Barbadian planters—known as the Goose Creek men because their plantations ranged along Goose Creek— alone for the most part, and they ran the council and the colony's Commons House of Assembly, a governing body based on the English parliamentary model.

The conflicts over land and trade in South Carolina proved to be the longest lasting. The proprietors, particularly Anthony Ashley Cooper, had envisioned a precisely surveyed network of towns and plantations. South Carolina's river-studded coastline frustrated early surveyors, and later surveyors did not bother trying. Settlers found the land they wanted and claimed it, either by legal title or as squatters. This practice made it impossible to enforce a system of rent collections by which the proprietors could recoup their investments. Still more frustrating to the proprietors were the impunity and arrogance with which the settlers treated their Native American neighbors. The proprietors particularly abhorred the brisk Native American slave trade that had grown up around the city of Charles Town. The proprietors claimed the profitable trade in deerskins as their exclusive province, but independent traders largely ignored this claim. Following the Westo War, the traders took over the trade monopoly, further lessening the chances that the proprietors would ever see any return on their initial investments. By the 1680s, the proprietors owned a colony that did not make any money and did not follow the rules they had painstakingly laid out for it.[4]

Political infighting was a staple of colonial life in South Carolina. In the 1680s the proprietors, in an effort to reassert their slipping control over the colony, began a successful campaign to attract settlers, many of whom were Presbyterians and Baptists. The proprietors also attempted to reform the Native American trade and the system of land distribution, all of which brought renewed conflict within the colony itself. Dissenting families formed the proprietary party; earlier Anglican settlers made up their most forceful opposition. In one striking 1690 incident, the Goose Creek men chose their own governor to replace the one appointed by the proprietors. This insubordination went all but unpunished. The proprietors suspended the unpopular Fundamental Constitutions and went about another round of governmental reforms.

After a decade-long respite, factionalism ripped South Carolina again in the early 1700s, and again the conflict centered on religion and the Native American trade. In 1700, the palatine, or lead proprietor, began to push for the establishment of the Church of England, a move that offended many of the colony's residents because it would disqualify dissenters from holding public office. At the same time, the colonial government moved to reform the uncontrolled Native American trade. A series of hotly contested assembly elections resulted in rapid shifts of power and the alienation of the defeated party. A botched invasion of Spanish St. Augustine in the first decade of the 1700s resulted in the removal of the governor who had led the expedition, and riots followed. The Anglican Church was officially established in 1706 but seems to have had relatively little effect on the government of the province.

It would be difficult to imagine proprietary government in South Carolina as anything but a dismal failure. The proprietors failed to understand the situation that their settlers had created, and the settlers mistrusted any moves made by the proprietors. The Yamasee War, which erupted in 1715, brought proprietary shortcomings to the fore and eventually led to the demise of proprietary government. The colonists, under attack from a number of justifiably disgruntled tribes, looked to the proprietors for assistance, but none was forthcoming. The proprietors' inaction and ineffective style of government united colonists across factional lines, and, in what is known as "the Revolution of 1719," the colonists took control of South Carolina's government. Within a decade, the Crown had bought out the remaining proprietors' shares, and the transition to royal government was complete.

Royal government did bring some stability to colonial politics, as did the establishment of the buffer colony of Georgia to the south. Disputes still occurred, most notably between the Commons House of Assembly and the council, but none of these matched the crises of the proprietary regime. The slave rebellion at Stono (1739) and the War of Jenkins' Ear (1739–1742) also helped to unify the governing planter class. Still, the political atmosphere throughout the colonial period of South Carolina's history was elitist and rancorous. This trend continued into the Revolutionary War and beyond.

That the backcountry and lowcountry planters often mistrusted each other's intentions is a given for the period leading up to the American Revolution. Still, by the middle of the eighteenth century, most of the lowcountry elite shared a political outlook known as "country" ideology and were remarkably unified in their application of this philosophy to their plantations, politics, and their view of society. Country ideology was one of the driving forces behind the movement toward American independence—think of John Locke's famous "life, liberty and property"—and planters, because they were both property holders (that property included slaves) and burdened by debt, were particularly receptive to it. Country thought has been described masterfully by historians T. H. Breen and Robert M. Weir.[5] At its heart, country philosophy was an elitist view that decried class conflict, instead emphasizing friction between the representatives of the people and the executive. Robert Weir, in an influential 1969 article, argued that South Carolina reflected the ideal "country" system more closely than any other mainland colony. The colony's elite was particularly small, geographically compact, and unbelievably prosperous. They feared slave rebellion almost to the point of paranoia, and they took local autonomy and personal liberty, not for their slaves but for themselves, very seriously. From this perspective, although radical groups like the Sons of Liberty were active in Charleston, the coming of the Revolution was an elite, conservative undertaking.

Like the other colonies of mainland British North America, South Carolina was generally left to run its own affairs in the first half of the eighteenth century. Many scholars use the phrase "benign neglect" to describe British imperial policy during this period.[6] The end of the worldwide conflict known as the Seven Years' War (often referred to as the French and Indian War in America) in 1763 brought the British Empire into closer contact with its colonies. British officials, recognizing anew the economic importance of the colonies and their precarious position at the periphery of the empire, attempted to tighten their control over the colonies. In South Carolina, as in the other colonies, this tightened control was unpopular. In response to the Stamp Act of 1765, a vigorous protest movement, the Sons of Liberty, developed in Charleston. Charleston's artisans and mechanics responded to the Stamp Act vociferously. On October 19, they hanged an effigy of a stamp collector—complete "with a devil at its right hand and a boot with a head stuck upon it on its left"—and announced that "whoever shall dare attempt to pull down these effigies, had better been born with a stone about his neck, and cast into the sea."[7] A solemn funeral procession followed, which featured the burial of a coffin labeled "American Liberty." The mob ended the day by searching the houses of suspected stamp distributors, including that of merchant Henry Laurens, who would later help to oust the royal governor and serve as president of the Continental Congress. Similar protests marked the Townshend Duties, but it bears mentioning that not all white South Carolinians supported the growing protest movement, foreshadowing the difficulties of the Revolutionary War period.

The Revolutionary War fractured South Carolina society deeply. Much of the revolutionary fervor was confined to Charleston. Loyalists and patriots vied for control of the backcountry, which had been thickly settled in the decades leading up to the Revolution. Its recent settlement produced a fiercer resistance to the patriot cause. Moreover, tensions had always run high between the backcountry and the lowcountry. In the 1760s, "Regulator" movements sprang up that attempted to enforce laws in the backcountry and equalize power between the colony's two main regions. By the time of the Revolution, some backcountry planters supported independence; many Quakers and Germans, along with some Presbyterians, Anglicans, and Scotch-Irish, remained neutral or loyal, although some paid lip service to revolutionary ideals. In Charleston, influential men were found on both sides of the revolutionary struggle, but the supporters of independence had the upper hand, a trend rooted in the acceptance of country ideology and general political harmony among lowcountry planters. In late 1775, the royal governor moved his offices to a ship in Charleston harbor, effectively abandoning the city to the revolutionaries. At approximately the same time, Loyalist (Tory) and revolutionary (Whig) militias were fighting each other for control of the pivotal backcountry.

Most members of Charleston's elite were reluctant revolutionaries, and, not surprisingly, the War for Independence took on a remarkably conservative character. South Carolinians fought mainly to protect their rights and property. The idea of a democratic society was anathema to most of the influential patriots. This conservatism reared its head in 1779, when the Continental Congress suggested that white Carolinians arm their slaves to protect against a British attack. Slaveowners were horrified by the idea and voted it down. In 1780, British forces captured Charleston, and backcountry Tories felt increasingly comfortable in making their position known. After a series of defeats in the South, most notably at Cowpens and Yorktown, the British evacuated Charleston in 1782. The victorious revolutionaries offered leniency to most former Loyalists, restoring their property. South Carolina's planters were economically tied to the fortunes of the British Empire, even though their political fate rested in American hands. Leniency on the part of lowcountry planters bred resentment within South Carolina, and the speed with which wealthy South Carolinians went back to business as usual with British trading houses was disturbing as well.

REVOLUTIONARY HANGOVER

The Revolutionary War did little to heal the divisions between lowcountry and backcountry in South Carolina. It also did little to ease the fears of the planter elite of slave rebellion and general class disorder. More importantly, the prosecution of the war had cost South Carolina dearly in economic terms, and the resulting financial crisis shook the young state to its core. The lowcountry elite sought to pacify backcountry and middle-class dissent while it tried to ensure that wealthy white landowners would continue to dominate politics. As South Carolina recovered from the War for Independence, it faced a new set of crises that brought regional divisions to the fore. In the midst of all this turmoil, the state picked delegates to attend a convention in Philadelphia, originally called to revise the Articles of Confederation.

In the aftermath of the Revolutionary War, South Carolinians, whether they had supported or opposed independence, faced the daunting challenge of rebuilding their state. Whig and Tory militias had ranged throughout the state during the war, torching the farms and plantations of their enemies. Charleston itself remained largely intact, but the outlying areas and the only backcountry town of any real significance, Camden, were in ruins.

(Incidentally, it was in the aftermath of the American Revolution that the spelling "Charleston" replaced "Charles Town." Although the precise reason for the shift is unknown, scholars have speculated that the change indicated a rejection of all things British or a spelling that more closely reflected the way the name was pronounced.) Before the official end of the war, in 1782, a new state legislature convened at Jacksonborough, a small town outside of Charleston. The Jacksonborough assembly passed a series of laws designed to bring order to the state and punish South Carolina Loyalists. The legislature voted to assess fees on the estates of persons who had nominally supported the British cause and to confiscate the property of those who were more fervently Loyalist. At first glance, the acts seem incongruous with the otherwise conservative revolutionary movement in South Carolina. In practice, the acts had a limited application. The list of landowners to be punished dropped rapidly from seven hundred. In the end, fewer than four hundred estates were confiscated, and the Jacksonborough assembly punished a handful of lowcountry planters and Charleston professionals, leaving Loyalists in the backcountry basically untouched.

The state treaty signed by South Carolina when the British withdrew favored lowcountry planters much more strongly than the 1783 Treaty of Paris did. Planters would be able to recover slaves confiscated by the British, and debts to British merchants would have to be settled by lawsuits. The Treaty of Paris stated that "no lawful Impediment" could be raised to prevent British creditors from recovering the money owed them.[8] The state treaty essentially rewarded those who had done the least to oust the British. Although the treaty was broken at a relatively early date and was supplanted by the Treaty of Paris, it demonstrates that in the aftermath of the Revolution, the governor and legislature favored forgiveness and the protection of property over punishment. Ordinary citizens—artisans, mechanics, and yeoman farmers who had lost family members and property in the war—were justifiably outraged by measures that acted as though no war had taken place. By the terms of an agreement with British merchants, subjects of the Crown could even become citizens and serve on juries.[9] Even more egregiously, British merchants stood to profit from the rebuilding of the infrastructure their king's armies had destroyed.

Christopher Gadsden, a Charleston merchant who had supported the patriot cause from an early date and had been jailed during the British occupation, led a chorus of protests against the developing postwar order. He worked to raise taxes on slaveowners and opposed the agreement that allowed British merchants to operate without constraint in Charleston. His legislative battles failed to make any headway, and protesters took to the streets of Charleston to show their dissatisfaction. From 1783 to 1785, violence periodically erupted in the city as angry artisans and mechanics, the muscle behind the independence movement, railed against British merchants and the South Carolina gentry who allowed them to do business. These riots smacked of class conflict. The planters and merchants were forced to make some concessions.[10]

Among these concessions was the incorporation of the city of Charleston. Residents in the city could now govern themselves, and several artisans were elected to the city council. Debtors also benefited from policies that allowed them to repay debts with land and a new loan program. Tensions between the backcountry and Charleston slackened. In the wake of the Revolution, judges sent to the backcountry faced humiliation and physical abuse at the hands of debtors. One judge was forced to eat a writ he was trying to serve, and a mob even burned a courthouse to the ground. Other judges riding their circuits had mud and manure thrown at them. In 1785, new counties (and county courts) were created in the backcountry, and the state legislature voted, over strong opposition, to move the state capital to a more central location: Columbia. South Carolina's leadership intended for the state to be an aristocratic republic. Through conciliatory actions, the state's elite was able to avoid open rebellion, such as ripped western Massachusetts during Shays's Rebellion in 1786.

Many backcountry South Carolinians were not considered in the formation of the state government. From 1759 to 1761, as a minor theater of the French and Indian War, South Carolina had battled against the Cherokee in an effort to push Native Americans beyond the line of white settlement. This effort, although it did manage to establish a line on a map between South Carolina and Native America, ignored the fact that other Native Americans lived and worked within the borders of the colony. The Catawba, who had been loosely allied with South Carolina, fought on the British side during the French and Indian War against the Cherokees and who supplied the patriots during the War for Independence, were excluded from state politics. Fortunately for the Catawba, South Carolina's Native American policy after the Revolutionary War was one of benign neglect. Although the Catawba were ignored, they were not the victims of campaigns of extermination and racial violence, as occurred further to the north.[11]

SOUTH CAROLINA IN THE CONSTITUTIONAL CONVENTION

With order temporarily established in the backcountry and merchants, traders, and planters generally at truce in the lowcountry, the state legislature elected five delegates to the Constitutional Convention, four of whom eventually reached Philadelphia. Three of the four were lawyers, and all were wealthy slaveowners from Charleston and its immediate environs, prompting one historian to remark that "Charleston and the surrounding parishes were represented in Philadelphia; South Carolina was not."[12] All four had advanced the cause of independence during the war, and all four had served in the South Carolina state legislature. Pierce Butler, Henry Laurens, Charles Pinckney, Charles Cotesworth Pinckney, and John Rutledge were chosen, although Laurens declined to serve, citing his advanced age and ill health. In terms of South

Carolina's own regional divide, only one of the four, Pierce Butler, had occasionally supported the backcountry. As one historian put it, the delegates were "not only...men of wealth, but they had been chosen by men of wealth."[13] Their behavior during the convention demonstrated their desire to protect their—and their constituents'—hard-earned position at the top of society. Still, what the group lacked in diversity, they made up in talent. William Pierce of Georgia, another delegate to the 1787 convention, made brief but telling character sketches of each of the South Carolina delegates:

- John Rutledge—"Highly mounted at the commencement of the late revolution. Distinguished rank among the American worthies. This Gentleman is much famed in his own State as an Orator, but in my opinion he is too rapid with his public speaking to be denominated as an agreeable orator."
- Charles Cotesworth Pinckney—"A gentleman of Family and fortune in his own State. He has received the advantage of a Liberal education, and possesses a very extensive degree of legal knowledge. When warm in debate he sometimes speaks well, but he is generally considered an indifferent orator."
- Charles Pinckney—"A young Gentleman of the most promising talents. He is altho' only 24 ys of age, in possession of a very great variety of Knowledge. Government, Law, History, and Phylosophy are his favorite studies. He speaks with great neatness and perspicuity, and treats every subject as fully, without running into prolixity, as it requires."
- Pierce Butler—"Mr. Butler is a character much respected for the many excellent virtues which he possesses. But as a Politician or an Orator, he has no pretensions to either. He is a Gentleman of Fortune, and takes rank among the first, in South Carolina. He has been appointed to Congress, and is now a Member of the Legislature of South Carolina. Mr. Butler is about 40 years of age, an Irishman by birth."[14]

Pierce Butler (1744–1822) was born in Ireland, the third son, who could hope to receive no inheritance, of an Anglo-Irish baronet, a member of the House of Commons. His military record was impressive. Butler received his first commission at the age of eleven, and by the time he was fourteen was serving in North America during the Seven Years' War. Butler was wounded in the assault on the French fortress at Louisbourg. He continued to serve with distinction, attaining the rank of major in 1766, until 1773, when he sold his commission and began a career in politics. In 1771, he married Mary "Polly" Middleton, daughter of the fabulously wealthy slave trader and plantation owner Thomas Middleton. Middleton's great wealth came to Butler through his maternal grandmother, Mary Bull. Within a year after Butler's marriage, Mary Bull died, and Pierce Butler gained entry into a world that he had admired, the glamorous life of Charleston's elite. Butler became master of a number of plantations and hundreds of slaves. Throughout his life he continued to acquire both, and when he died in 1822, he owned nearly six hundred slaves and thousands of acres of valuable plantation land both near Charleston and in Georgia. After his plantations were damaged in the fighting, he reluctantly joined the side of the patriots. Butler served in the American military as well, attaining the post of adjutant-general of South Carolina's forces in 1779.[15]

Pierce Butler's turn to politics was a natural one. Born in Ireland, he had served the British Crown, and believed himself able to understand British motivations and to anticipate future British moves. His wealth and connections in the lowcountry and beyond carried a certain amount of political responsibility as well. In 1776 he served in the South Carolina assembly as a representative from the Beaufort District. After the war, Butler continued to serve his local district, fighting for debt relief. He was one of the few lowcountry politicians who advocated moving the state capital from Charleston and increasing the representation of the backcountry, although he did so as the result of a personal dispute. Before being selected to represent South Carolina at the Philadelphia Convention, he had served in the Confederation Congress as well.[16]

Charles Pinckney (1757–1824) was twenty-nine years old when he went to Philadelphia, but he was a member of one of South Carolina's most influential families and was well versed in the business of national politics. His father, Colonel Charles Pinckney, had at first opposed the movement toward independence but later supported it actively. When Charleston fell to the British, the elder Pinckney reversed himself again, leading to punitive taxes on his estate when the British evacuated the city. In 1779, Charles enlisted in the military, assuming the post of lieutenant of the Charleston militia and aiding in the siege of Savannah. Also in 1779, he served in the state legislature. When the British took control of Charleston, Charles was imprisoned and held until June 1781.

Pinckney had recouped many of his losses by 1784, and South Carolina elected him to the Confederation Congress in New York. He became a staunch advocate of expanding Congress's powers under the Articles of Confederation and eventually of scrapping the Articles and devising a new, more centralized form of government for the United States. After the convention, Pinckney served in a number of state and national roles, as four-time governor of South Carolina, U.S. senator, and minister to Spain. His allegiance to Thomas Jefferson—Pinckney was the head of Jefferson's party in South Carolina—came at a high personal cost, because his cousin Charles Cotesworth was John Adams's vice presidential candidate. Personally, Pinckney was vain and egocentric. In his determination to be the youngest delegate to the convention, he lied about his age and claimed to be twenty-four.[17]

Charles Cotesworth Pinckney (1745–1825), Charles Pinckney's second cousin, was born in Charleston in 1745, but like many members of South Carolina's ruling elite, he received most of his formal education in England.

Pinckney took to politics and the law at an early age: he studied at Christ Church College, Oxford, and read law at the Middle Temple at the same time. (It bears mentioning that one of the reasons that Pinckney was in England in the first place was because his father, who had been appointed chief justice of South Carolina was removed from the post to make way for a corrupt royal appointee. Pinckney could have remained in London as a wealthy lawyer and perhaps could even have participated in politics, but he chose to join South Carolina's planter aristocracy instead.) Pinckney returned to Charleston in 1770 to run his plantations and practice law. Pinckney denounced the Stamp Act and supported John Wilkes, a vocal critic of George III; both actions placed him firmly in the ideological camp of the patriots. Pinckney's revolutionary fervor was never in doubt, even though it took on the conservative tint of the other leading gentlemen of South Carolina. He wrote in 1780 that "I entered into this Cause after much reflection, and through principle, my heart is altogether American."[18]

During the Revolutionary War, Pinckney served repeatedly on South Carolina's Council of Safety and in the state legislature. His major contribution to the war effort, however, was of a more military nature. He attained the rank of brigadier general, served as an aide to George Washington, and participated in most of the war's southern battles, including the failed defense of Savannah and Charleston and an abortive raid on British East Florida.[19] His property was confiscated, but he managed to regain his fortune through a good rice crop in the 1780s. Pinckney, like other well-to-do revolutionaries, was offered lenient treatment by the British if he renounced his beliefs, but he flatly refused, landing him in prison and on parole. He believed in a strong central government and shared many of the framers' distrust for full-blown democracy.[20] When George Washington toured the South in 1791, he offered Pinckney a spot on the Supreme Court. Evidently, Washington was impressed with the conservative patriotism of the lowcountry. Pinckney refused, citing the need to rebuild his personal fortune. In 1794, Washington asked him to join his cabinet as secretary of war, but he declined that position as well. A devout Federalist, he was John Adams's vice presidential candidate and was candidate for president himself twice during the first decade of the nineteenth century, but he lost all three elections. Pinckney did serve as minister to France and was one of the diplomats involved in the XYZ Affair. He fervently supported the cause of education in South Carolina as a charter member of the board of South Carolina College. General Pinckney's patriotism was legendary. He once famously effused, "If I had a vein which did not beat with the love of my country, I myself would open it. If I had a drop of blood that could flow dishonorably, I myself would let it out!"[21]

The head of the delegation was John Rutledge (1739–1800), a longtime American nationalist who had taken part in the Stamp Act Congress and the First Continental Congress. Born in or around Charleston in 1739, his formal training was as a lawyer in London, and his high social position combined with a drive to succeed made him one of the most influential men in South Carolina. Rutledge returned to South Carolina in the 1760s and profited enough through his law practice that, at the outbreak of war, he owned five plantations and had land holdings totaling more than thirty thousand acres. He also trained several lawyers, including his younger brother Edward. His political career, probably a given considering his profession and wealth, began just two months after his return from England, when he was elected to the Commons House of Assembly.

Rutledge was one of the royal governor's most determined opponents. In fact, he led a group of legislators that withheld the governor's salary. During the Stamp Act crisis, Rutledge continued his earlier practice of defending rights of American citizens against what he saw as tyranny. Rutledge, and South Carolina, played a large role in the Stamp Act Congress that met in New York in 1765. During the crisis that precipitated the War for Independence, Rutledge charted a moderate course and favored reconciliation with Britain, although he would not tolerate any infringement on American rights. Rutledge's position drew the ire of more radical revolutionaries like Patrick Henry of Virginia. Beginning in 1776, Rutledge served as president of South Carolina, but he resigned in 1778 while a democratic constitution was being considered. Like many of his rank and generation, Rutledge mistrusted popular rule and vetoed any measures that altered the original 1776 South Carolina constitution, which he viewed as a temporary document. Rutledge ended up being elected governor, from which position he surveyed the fall of Charleston to the British. His estate was confiscated by the British. He never regained his pre-war fortune, and he seems to have focused mainly on politics after the end of the war, serving briefly in the U.S. Supreme Court and for several years as chief justice of South Carolina's supreme court. He was offered the position of U.S. chief justice, but the Senate rejected his appointment. From 1792 until his death in 1800, Rutledge battled mental illness brought on by the death of his wife.[22]

South Carolina's contribution to the framing of the 1787 Constitution far exceeded its geographic leverage and proportion of the population. South Carolina in 1787 was America's wealthiest state and the one most dependent upon slave labor to maintain and increase its wealth. In fact, the other members of the convention referred to the South Carolina delegation as "nabobs," indicating their wealth, prestige, and love of luxury. The delegation to Philadelphia, all of whom profited personally from slavery, was keenly aware of these facts, and they were loath to compromise on the issue of the slave trade. In forming their arguments, they laid the tentative groundwork for a philosophy that would espouse states' rights even as they participated in the creation of a strong, centralized national government.

South Carolina's entrenched lowcountry elite mistrusted even wealthy backcountry planters and considered the backcountry a political backwater, in much the same way that they dismissed the pleas of ordinary Charlestonians. The state's delegates to the Constitutional Convention viewed South Carolina as a small aristocratic republic with themselves at the seat of power. They tried to impose their perspective on the convention as a whole, with mixed results. All four delegates believed passionately that a new constitution was necessary to correct the problems of the Articles of Confederation. They believed equally passionately that the new government should be left in the hands of an entrenched elite and that the Revolution had become "too revolutionary."[23] On the matter of representation, for instance, the South Carolina delegation fought at every turn to reduce the role that ordinary citizens played in government. They opposed the direct election of senators and representatives, supporting their stance by "contending that the people were less fit Judges," as Charles Cotesworth Pinckney put it. Pinckney also felt that the state governments would be destroyed if the people were allowed to choose the federal House of Representatives. The South Carolinians used phrases like "proper characters" and "had some sense of character" to describe themselves and the other men assembled in Philadelphia, noting that these men of honor and virtue were elected by legislatures and not by the people.[24] The South Carolinians' efforts to empower state legislatures to select members of Congress failed, as did another of their motions that would have left each individual state to decide how to select congressmen and senators.[25] The South Carolinians also opposed a measure that would prevent the same person from holding federal and state posts concurrently. They argued that able men might choose state government over federal, thereby robbing the federal level of valuable insight and talents. The South Carolina delegation succeeded in striking the clause.

The material wealth of South Carolina was earned mainly at the expense of the state's slaves, who numbered 107,094 in 1790. The white population in the first U.S. census was 141,979. The South Carolinians who participated in the Constitutional Convention would brook no compromise on slavery, and their influence, along with that of the delegation from Georgia, far exceeded what one would expect from states perched on the edge of an American empire that was beginning to frown upon slavery.[26] In the late eighteenth century, South Carolina and Georgia, wedged in between the Creeks and Spanish Florida, needed the protection of a federal military much more than, say, Massachusetts needed the shipping revenues from the transport of slaves. George Washington recognized as much when he wrote of Georgia (although the same could be said of South Carolina), "If a weak State, with powerful tribes of Indians in its rear & the Spaniards on its flank, do not incline to embrace a strong *general* Government there must, I should think, be either wickedness, or insanity in their conduct."[27] In the end, although abolitionist sentiment was strong in some circles, northern states chose quite literally not to make a federal case out of slavery, allowing the domestic institution and its concomitant international trade to continue uninterrupted.

Northern and southern bluster on the issue of slavery was abundant, but neither side was willing to back its rhetoric with decisive action. Delegates from South Carolina and Georgia averred that slaves ought to be counted as white people when it came to determining representation. Gouverneur Morris, a native New Yorker representing Pennsylvania, replied that white Pennsylvanians would revolt if placed on equal footing with slaves. Morris further argued that slavery was "a nefarious institution, the curse of heaven on the states where it prevailed."[28] Rufus King of Massachusetts condemned any proposed constitution that protected slavery. The delegates from South Carolina responded in kind. The question, quipped John Rutledge, was "whether the southern states shall or shall not be parties to the Union."[29] Charles Cotesworth Pinckney stated the case plainly enough: "South Carolina and Georgia can not do without slaves."[30] Charles Pinckney looked to history for his moral justification of slavery. He argued that the institution had existed throughout "all ages," and, citing such civilized nations as ancient Greece and Rome and modern France, England, and Holland, noted that "one half of mankind have been slaves."[31] The entire South Carolina delegation argued that slaves should count equally to white people for the purposes of representation. Because the new American government would be supported and funded by men of property, men with more property should have more sway in the government.

Fierce rhetoric aside, most moral and religious arguments for and against slavery met their end in the harsh light of materialism. As John Rutledge put it, the central issue was profit: "Interest alone is the governing principle of nations."[32] The Constitutional Convention finally agreed upon what has become known as the "three-fifths" compromise: three-fifths of a state's enslaved population would be counted for purposes of representation, and the international slave trade would be outlawed in 1808. Lesser-known articles provided that a two-thirds majority of congressional votes would be needed to pass matters of trade and navigation through the federal government and limited the tax on imported slaves to $10 a head.[33] Although the late eighteenth-century national debate over slavery was silenced shortly after it began, the institution continued to grow, numerically if not geographically, and eventually led South Carolina and twelve other slaveholding states to secede from the Union, sparking the Civil War.[34]

South Carolina's delegates had succeeded in protecting the state's dearest assets, private property, including slave property, and the right to control the state's own destiny. The South Carolina delegation, more than any other, went to Philadelphia to protect their home state from federal meddling. The Pinckneys, Rutledge, and Butler were confirmed patriots and committed nationalists, but they were also members of South Carolina's elite, and they saw little paradox in the two positions. Later generations of white South Carolinians would resurrect their arguments to protest Jacksonian era tariffs in the Nullification Crisis, in the election of Abraham Lincoln in 1860, and in the federal school desegregation brought about by *Brown v. Board of Education* in 1954. In a way, the seeds of states' rights philosophy were sown in Philadelphia by the South Carolina delegates.

RATIFYING THE FEDERAL CONSTITUTION

The math appears simple enough at first glance. In May 1788, South Carolina's ratifying convention approved the Constitution by a wide margin of 149-73, and South Carolina became the eighth state to join the Union. The easy victory for South Carolina's Federalists belied their minority status within the state. Aedanus Burke, an Anti-Federalist judge from Charleston, although he served the entire state, claimed that the Constitution was ratified "notwithstanding of the people do from their souls detest it." This viewpoint was not confined to Anti-Federalists. John Wilson, a North Carolina Federalist, estimated that a majority of South Carolinians opposed the document.[35] How, then, did the Federalists succeed in forcing their will on the Anti-Federalist majority in the state? The answer lies in the division that had troubled South Carolina since its very founding as an English colony: the division between the lowcountry, including Charleston, and the rest of the state.

The General Assembly, which had replaced the Commons House of Assembly when South Carolina became a state, voted in the winter of 1787–1788 to hold the ratifying convention in Charleston in May. Although Charleston was the state's only significant city, the question squeaked by on a single vote, 76-75, reflecting the rising political power of the backcountry. Lowcountry areas that bordered North Carolina and Georgia often voted with the Anti-Federalists outside of Charleston.[36] The delegates to the convention were chosen according to the apportionment rules that governed General Assembly elections. The system gave solidly Federalist Charleston and its environs a distinct advantage. The backcountry, with a white population of 111,534, had 88 seats in the state legislature. The lowcountry, with a white population of just 28,644, had 145 seats.[37]

Edward Rutledge, younger brother of John, a staunch Federalist and future governor of the state, wrote to John Jay: "I hope the Friends of Federal Government may be as successful in New York as they have been in South Carolina. We had a tedious but trifling opposition to contend with."[38] It is unclear whether Rutledge's remarks were intended to be ironic, which is not likely, but upon closer inspection the opposition was neither trifling nor tedious. Eloquent Anti-Federalists from the backcountry and even a few from Charleston pleaded their case in public forums. People with less access to print and power staged demonstrations throughout the state. James Lincoln, a representative of the Ninety Six District next to Georgia and the Cherokees, asserted in January of 1788 that South Carolina was exchanging a "well-formed" democracy for a lowcountry aristocracy: "What have you been contending for these ten years past? Liberty! What is Liberty? The power of governing yourselves. If you adopt this Constitution, have you this power? No: you give it into the hands of a set of men who live one thousand miles distant from you."[39] Lincoln opposed the Constitution because it lacked a bill of rights and because he, like other backcountry planters, already mistrusted the intentions of the state government dominated by Charleston. Why add another layer of government that was even farther away and understood life in the southern backcountry even more poorly?

The *State Gazette of South-Carolina* put opposition to ratification into verse form:

> Some alterations in our fabric we
> Calmly propos'd, and hoped at length to see—
> Ah, how deceived!—these heroes in renown
> Scheme for themselves—and pull the fabric down—
> Bid in its place Columbia's tomb-stone rise
> Inscrib'd with these sad words—*Here Freedom Lies!*[40]

In this portrayal, the delegates to the Constitutional Convention are the "heroes in renown," patriots who turn out to be nothing more than self-serving Charleston lawyer-planters. Aedanus Burke, a judge and legislator who initially opposed ratification but later supported it, accused Charlestonians of wining and dining the opposition into submission: "The merchants and leading men kept open houses for the back and low country members during the whole time the Convention sat." Burke added that the decision to hold the convention in Charleston was a crushing blow to Anti-Federalists, because there were "not fifty inhabitants who were not friendly to it." Burke also blamed the Charleston press, labeling printers "journeymen, or poor citizens, who are afraid to offend the great men."[41] After the Constitution was ratified, Burke reported a rumor that activists in the backcountry painted coffins black and interred them, revisiting symbolic ground that had inspired the revolutionary fervor of the 1770s. A pamphlet war broke out between the two sides. Charles Cotesworth Pinckney blamed northern Anti-Federalists, who, he claimed, "had been most mischievously industrious in prejudicing the minds of our citizens against the Constitution."[42] Accusing outside (read, northern) agitation for South Carolina's problems was a trend that would continue throughout the nineteenth century.

Rawlins Lowndes, a rare Charleston Anti-Federalist, opposed the Constitution because of the limits it placed on slavery, an institution that he viewed as essential to South Carolina's economic survival. "Why confine us to twenty years, or rather why limit us at all?" he argued. "They [the northern states] don't like our slaves, because they have none themselves, and therefore want to exclude us from this great advantage."[43] According to Lowndes, the Constitution not only threatened slavery but also allowed for a permanent imbalance between northern and southern states. The United States would not be a true republic, Lowndes claimed, so long as northern members of Congress could control navigation and trade laws to the detriment of states that needed to continue to import slaves in perpetuity.

South Carolina's Anti-Federalist movement turned on three major issues. All Anti-Federalists in the former British colonies feared a strong centralized government. In South Carolina, where slave-based plantation agriculture ruled, planters saw in the Constitution the potential for the federal government to regulate the practice of slavery. Just as farmers in the western parts of Massachusetts and Pennsylvania feared the control that a federal government might give to eastern commercial interests, backcountry planters, already struggling against an unreceptive state government, did not want to put the national government in the hands of the Charleston elite. Finally, South Carolina had passed debtor relief legislation that flew in the face of proposed federal laws by violating the sanctity of contracts.[44] Backcountry planters, whose ranks were swelling, took pains to avoid being drowned under the rising tide of support for the Constitution.

South Carolina Federalists tried to answer the arguments of the Anti-Federalists. David Ramsay, a leading proponent of ratification, wrote off Lowndes's critiques as narrow-minded jealousy of New England, suggesting that Lowndes had "not one continental or foederal [sic] idea in his head nor one of larger extent than that of a rice barrel."[45] The men who had attended the Philadelphia convention made more salient points. Charles Pinckney and John Rutledge pointed out that both northern and southern interests had accepted compromises in the convention, and the resulting document could make both sections rich. They also noted that the southern states' populations were growing more rapidly than those of the northern states. Virginia, the Carolinas, and Georgia could eventually dominate national discourse. Even more tellingly, the convention did not really mount much of an assault against slavery. It had provided that the external slave trade would end in 1808 but did nothing to stop the internal trade in slaves and nothing to stop individual slaveowners in South Carolina from practicing slavery.

A wide economic gulf existed between the lowcountry planters and even the wealthiest backcountry planters. Simply put, Federalists were wealthier than Anti-Federalists. A higher percentage of Anti-Federalists owned public securities, but Federalists' overall property holdings were greater in number and worth more. Federalist planters owned an average of sixty-six slaves, whereas Anti-Federalists owned an average of thirty-four. Thirty-five Federalists owned more than one hundred slaves; only four Anti-Federalists could make the same claim. As one historian put it, "the more property a delegate [to the ratifying convention] owned, the more likely he was to be a Federalist."[46]

The delegates to the ratifying convention were, with few exceptions, lowcountry planters and lawyers who accepted Federalist arguments at face value. Several Anti-Federalists recognized they had little to gain by opposing the Constitution and grudgingly accepted it. Aedanus Burke wrote that opponents should take the new government "as we take our wives, 'for better, for worse.'"[47] The result was textbook materialism. The areas that had the most to gain from the Constitution supported it most fervently. The Charleston delegates ratified the Constitution by a count of 73-0; in Beaufort, the margin was 14-0; in Georgetown, 12-1. Other lowcountry parishes voted 22-15 in favor of the Constitution. The backcountry, not at all surprisingly, voted 57-28 against ratification.[48] The convention then adjourned but not before proposing several amendments that dovetailed nicely with South Carolina's steadfast insistence upon states' rights. The proposed amendments stipulated that states would control the election procedures for federal offices, they would retain all powers not specifically granted to the federal government, and they prohibited direct taxation except in cases of extreme urgency.[49]

At the same time that South Carolinians were determining what sort of state South Carolina would be, and whether it would be one of the United States, forces were working to ease tensions between the backcountry and Charleston. Charleston was by far South Carolina's largest and wealthiest city, but by the 1780s, the backcountry population had surpassed that of the lowcountry. This fact, combined with the ease by which Charleston had fallen to British forces during the War for Independence, led the state legislature to contemplate a move. The proposed move brought out the worst in the many lowcountry planters and lawyers, several of whom resorted to class-based arguments. One state senator asked, "Had not the people in that part of the country hoisted the banner of defiance against the Laws? Was this then a place where new ones could be made with propriety?" The obvious answer followed: "Certainly not."[50] Another senator proposed to name the new capital "Town of Refuge," since there would be "no sheriff,...the laws would be laughed at, and...the lawless would gather" there.[51] Several sites were considered, and after a moderate amount of political wheedling Columbia was voted to become the new state capital. In 1786, when the vote was taken, Columbia was a not an actual city. Like the federal district in Washington, Columbia was carefully surveyed before it was inhabited, and lots were sold to prominent Carolinians. In fact, the name "Washington" lost to "Columbia" by four votes when it came to naming the new state capital. The state legislature moved to Columbia in 1790, although many important state offices maintained operations in both Columbia and Charleston.[52] In 1790, from its new seat in Columbia, the government of South Carolina began to hammer out the specifics of political life in the state. Old geographical, economic, and political divisions continued to haunt the proceedings.

SOUTH CAROLINA SEARCHES FOR ORDER IN THE NEW REPUBLIC

The decade after the Constitution became the law of the land was a heady time for those who had urged its ratification. Federalists dominated all the branches of government and only slowly did any formidable opposition begin to develop.[53] In South Carolina, a similar situation obtained, though Anti-Federalists did occasionally manage to win elections. South Carolina, as it had been after the War for Independence, was also faced with an economic crisis. One prominent South Carolinian, Ralph Izard, hoped for a rejection of "idle discussions about amendments" and for real, practical actions that would ame-liorate South Carolina's "embarrassed and disgraceful situation" as it pertained to finance.[54] South Carolinians elected several men to the first U.S. Congress who had opposed ratification, a situation that blurred the lines between Federal-ist and Anti-Federalist and indicated that South Carolina politics was returning to normal. Lowcountry planters squared off repeatedly against the rising class of backcountry planters. Backcountry planters had hoped that shifting the capital from Charleston to Columbia would increase their role in government. Unfortunately for them, the move did not have the desired effect. The South Carolina constitution of 1790 did little to ease regional tension within the state.

Lowcountry Federalist planters and lawyers, already unhappy about having to travel to Columbia, began a private smear campaign against the back-country, calling backcountry politicians, who were becoming more Jeffersonian, "yahoos" and "a parcel of illiterate second rate fellows."[55] Such comments show that the small amount of goodwill built up during the War for Independence and shortly thereafter had been spent. William Loughton Smith, a prominent Charleston Federalist, insisted that the new capital would "shed a malig-nant influence on all the proceedings of the Legislature."[56] Not surprisingly, conflict erupted over economic issues and representation.

Political discourse in the 1780s pivoted on the issue of debtor relief, and the lowcountry dominated the discussion. Planting large amounts of any crop ensured that planters would go into debt, but lowcountry planters had enough property to secure larger loans. Although planters in both sections of the state owed money, the lowcountry planters were in a better position to pay it back. Backcountry legislators proposed several measures, including the issuance of large amounts of paper money as loans to smallholding farmers and backcountry planters. Although the legislature did allow for some loans, they attached a property qualification that was beyond the means of many backcountry citizens. A valuation bill that might have aided backcountry planters was similarly rejected. The financial acts of 1788 worked in favor of those with substantial amounts of property, the planters who lived near Charleston.[57]

The topic of representation, long a thorn in the side of the under-represented backcountry, which contained about 80 percent of the state's white popula-tion, came up early and often as legislators debated a new state constitution. Backcountry legislators fought for reapportionment based on population. Not surprisingly, lowcountry politicians, most notably Charles Cotesworth Pinckney, argued that representation should be based on taxes paid, one category that would assure the continued dominance of Charleston and its environs. Even a compromise that would allow combined population and tax representation was pushed aside. The political map after 1790 looked remarkably similar to those of earlier decades. Lowcountry legislators believed that they had protected their power base and had carefully eliminated backcountry influence through legislation. Still, there were cracks in the façade, particularly as more money and property began to flow through the backcountry.

The 1790 constitution reflects a state in a time of flux, and it is remarkable that the document aged so well, surviving with minor revisions until 1865. Lowcountry planters remained in control of politics at the state level, but propertied backcountry citizens began to flex their political muscle as well. The constitution of 1790 replaced Revolutionary-era governments that had changed little since colonial times. The 1776 constitution, for instance, created a bicameral legislature in which the people elected the lower house, the lower house elected the upper house, and both houses together elected a powerful governor, called the "President of South Carolina." The Anglican Church, preferred by most Charleston-area planters, remained established. Substantial property requirements kept power firmly in the hands of the lowcountry elite. Subsequent revisions and constitutions did little to alter these features; the backcountry eventually received slightly more votes, but nothing close to its proportion of the population.[58]

The constitution of 1790 retained property requirements, indicating that South Carolinians still equated wealth and the ability to engage in political discussions. Members of the lower house were to own five hundred acres of land and ten slaves or an estate worth £150. To qualify for the state senate, a man had to own one thousand acres and twenty slaves or an estate worth £300. A moderate amount of property, fifty rural acres or a town lot, was required to vote. The governor lost his absolute veto power, and the legislature elected him. The South Carolina constitution of 1790 established the legal basis for a slaveholding aristocracy that would last until the Civil War. The state legislature, composed almost entirely of slaveowners, was the dominant force in state politics. It made laws, elected U.S. senators, and chose presidential electors in addition to filling all the county-level positions throughout the state. More innovative aspects of the constitution included total religious toleration. Anglicans still dominated Charleston, although other denominations held sway elsewhere, and enough diversity existed so as to make any formal bias toward Protestantism seem antiquated.[59]

How was this document received in the backcountry, and what role did the rising backcountry elite play in the new government? The answer demonstrates that slowly, but surely, the backcountry was emerging as a force to be reckoned with in state politics. The backcountry's rise dovetails nicely with the rise of Jeffersonian Republicanism as a national political force. With Columbia as the state capital, attendance rates rose for backcountry legislators and dropped for those from the lowcountry. The number of representatives from the Charleston area declined, and representatives from Beaufort and Georgetown occasionally voted with the backcountry. The backcountry would have to wait until 1808 for fairer apportionment. Thanks in large part to the property requirements for public officeholders, the constitution of 1790 made progress toward the unifying South Carolina's planter class.[60] Still, contemporaries, and more than a few modern historians, viewed the document as a striking confirmation of the dominance of the lowcountry.

Within four years of the state constitutional convention, backcountry planters were tired of the status quo and moved to reform the constitution, although these efforts were not rewarded for some time. Their political outlook, although largely similar to that of the lowcountry planters, was informed by one major difference. The leading men of the backcountry represented a large class of independent yeoman farmers who owned few if any slaves and whose interests were divergent from Charleston's merchants, lawyers, and the great planters. In 1800, slaves made up 84 percent of the lowcountry population, not counting Charleston. In the same year, slaves composed 17 percent of the population in the backcountry. The economy of the backcountry was based solidly on small-scale agriculture, whereas larger plantations dominated the coastal areas of the state. Although both backcountry and lowcountry leaders were republican, that is, they subscribed to the tenets of country ideology, backcountry planters leaned further in the direction of democracy, touting the voice of the people. Lowcountry planters, although revolutionary in 1776, were not especially tolerant of democracy. Their beliefs tended toward an aristocracy of talent, not birth.[61]

In 1794, a group of influential backcountry planters formed the Representative Reform Association in Columbia. As one might conclude from the group's name, it intended to reform the apportionment of representatives in the state legislature. Sister committees grew up throughout the backcountry. Under a pseudonym, a member of the association pointed out the differences between the backcountry and the lowcountry: the backcountry had a healthy climate and preferred low taxes and small government expenditures, whereas the lowcountry was swampy, unhealthful, and prone to extravagance. The initial drive failed. Later campaigns stressed the large number of slaveholders in the backcountry and the interests they shared with the lowcountry elite. This effort too was defeated.[62]

Lowcountry representatives continued to fear the backcountry for a number of reasons. Charleston-area planters were convinced that, because slavery was not a dominant factor in the backcountry, the region was hostile to the institution. Although some backcountry congregations were openly abolitionist or ambiguous on the subject, many were outspoken advocates of the continuation and expansion of slavery. In the 1790s, support of the French Revolution functioned as a sort of political litmus test, and the backcountry supported it solidly. As ever, coastal planters were wary of any increase in democracy and were terrified by the radical phase of the French Revolution. When the French government recognized the independent nation of Haiti in 1793, it must have seemed from Charleston as though the entire order of society was under attack. Historian Walter Edgar has accurately referred to the recurring sectional tension as "festering like an unlanced boil."[63]

Following the XYZ Affair, in which American diplomats were snubbed by the French, backcountry pro-French sentiment slackened considerably. Still, tensions continued to flare over reapportionment and entered a new arena: higher education. Charleston area planters tried to promote the cause of statewide unity by proposing that a public university be constructed in Columbia. South Carolina College was founded over the objections of two backcountry counties and eventually served to unite young men from all over the state. At the same time, inland planters, allying themselves with emerging Jeffersonians from around the country, finally succeeded in gaining access to real political power. In 1808, the constitution of 1790 was amended. Finally the backcountry was awarded additional seats in the state legislature. A new political landscape developed that shaped antebellum South Carolina politics for decades to come. Instead of the traditional lowcountry-backcountry rivalry, new tensions developed between areas heavily invested in slaves and those less so. The old money, lowcountry elite had finally given in after dominating South Carolina since its founding as an English colony in 1670.[64]

EPILOGUE: TOWARD A MORE SOLID SOUTH CAROLINA AND FUTURE "STATEHOODS"

It is tempting to view the easing of regional tensions as a collapse of the coastal aristocracy, but this view oversimplifies the situation. Charleston-area planters had succeeded in molding parts of the backcountry in the lowcountry's image. Large backcountry plantations, based on tobacco and increasingly on cotton, reflected the values of their lowcountry cousins. New generations of wealthy leaders, with names like Hampton and Calhoun, pushed Carolina into the Jacksonian era, all the while espousing states' rights philosophy borrowed from the revolutionary generation. Many opponents of slavery, including Presbyterians, Methodists, and Quakers, moved north, making it even easier for white South Carolinians, even those who did not own slaves, to support the institution in the years leading up to the Civil War.

It is equally tempting to celebrate 1808 as a watershed moment for democracy, but two large groups of people were not even part of the electorate. By the census of 1820, African Americans once again outnumbered whites in South Carolina, a trend that continued throughout the nineteenth century. In the strictest sense of the word, South Carolina was fundamentally undemocratic and remained so until the end of the Civil War forced the state to reconsider its position. Women did not gain full citizenship rights until the early twentieth century. Of course, South Carolina was not alone on either of these counts, but any treatment of South Carolina's journey toward statehood would be incomplete without accounting for multiple future "statehoods" that forced the state's government to reflect its population more closely.

South Carolina joined the rest of the United States when it ratified the federal Constitution on May 29, 1788, but its history before and after that momentous occasion was anything but united. Within South Carolina itself, regional tensions, racial divisions, and economic disparity, all of which had deep roots in the area's colonial history, made unity more an abstract concept than a practical reality for much of the state's history.

NOTES

1. Peter Wood, "The Changing Population of the Colonial South," in *Powhatan's Mantle: Indians in the Colonial Southeast*, ed. Peter Wood, Gregory A. Waselkov, and M. Thomas Hatley, 38–39 (Lincoln: University of Nebraska Press, 1989).

2. Walter Edgar, *South Carolina: A History* (Columbia: University of South Carolina Press, 1998), pp. 151–153; Alice Hanson Jones, *Wealth of a Nation to Be: The American Colonies on the Eve of Revolution* (New York: Columbia University Press, 1980), pp. 170–171, 377–379.

3. Samuel Dyssli, a Swiss settler, wrote from Charleston to his family on December 3, 1737. The letter appears in R. W. Kelsey, ed., "Swiss Settlers in South Carolina," *South Carolina Historical and Genealogical Magazine* (hereafter cited as SCHM) 22 (3) (July 1922): 85–91. The quotation appears on p. 90.

4. M. Eugene Sirmans, *Colonial South Carolina: A Political History, 1663–1763* (Chapel Hill: University of North Carolina Press, 1966), p. 35.

5. See T. H. Breen, *Tobacco Culture: The Mentality of the Great Tidewater Planters on the Eve of Revolution* (Princeton: Princeton University Press, 1985) especially pp. 3–39; Robert M. Weir, "'The Harmony We Were Famous For': An Interpretation of Pre-Revolutionary South Carolina Politics," *William and Mary Quarterly* 26 (4) (October 1969): 473–501.

6. Robert M. Weir, the dean of colonial South Carolina historians, uses the term "salutary neglect." See Weir, *Colonial South Carolina: A History*, 2nd ed. (Columbia: University of South Carolina Press, 1997), p. 265.

7. Richard Walsh, *Charleston's Sons of Liberty: A Study of the Artisans, 1763–1789* (Columbia: University of South Carolina Press, 1959), p. 37.

8. See Jerome J. Nadelhaft, *The Disorders of War: The Revolution in South Carolina* (Orono: University of Maine at Orono Press, 1981), p. 89.

9. Nadelhaft, *The Disorders of War*, pp. 94–95.

10. Edgar, *South Carolina: A History*, p. 247.

11. See James H. Merrell, *The Indians' New World: Catawbas and Their Neighbors from European Contact Through the Era of Removal* (Chapel Hill: University of North Carolina Press, 1989), pp. 221–125.

12. George C. Rogers, Jr., *Evolution of a Federalist: William Loughton Smith of Charleston, 1758–1812* (Columbia: University of South Carolina Press, 1962), p. 145; Quotation appears in Edgar, *South Carolina: A History*, p. 248.

13. Ernest M. Lander, Jr., "The South Carolinians at the Philadelphia Convention, 1787," SCHM 57 (3) (July 1956): 134–155. Quotation appears on p. 134.

14. Quoted in Malcolm Bell, Jr., *Major Butler's Legacy: Five Generations of a Slaveholding Family* (Athens: University of Georgia Press, 1987), pp. 76–77.

15. Clinton Rossiter, *1787: The Grand Convention* (New York: Macmillan, 1966), p. 133.

16. Bell, *Major Butler's Legacy*, pp. 69–71.

17. Rossiter, *1787: The Grand Convention*, pp. 132–133. See also Robert M. Weir, "Charles Pinckney" in *American National Biography*, ed. John A. Garraty and Mark C. Carnes, 533–536 (New York: Oxford University Press, 1999).

18. Quoted in Marvin R. Zahniser, *Charles Cotesworth Pinckney: Founding Father* (Chapel Hill: University of North Carolina Press, 1967), p. 22.

19. For a recent treatment of the Revolutionary War in the South, see Walter Edgar, *Partisans & Redcoats: The Southern Conflict that Turned the Tide of the American Revolution* (New York: William Morrow, 2001).

20. Rossiter, *1787: The Grand Convention*, pp. 131–132.

21. Quoted in Catherine Drinker Bowen, *Miracle at Philadelphia: The Story of the Constitutional Convention, May to September 1787* (Boston: Little, Brown and Company, 1966), p. 76.

22. Rossiter, *1787: The Grand Convention*, pp. 130–131.

23. Nadelhaft, *The Disorders of War*, p. 178.

24. Ibid.

25. Alexander Hamilton pointed out that the South Carolinians intended to remove people from the process of selecting their representatives. See ibid.

26. No scholarly consensus exists on this important issue, but in the wake of the Revolutionary War several northern states did away with slavery, and in Virginia, the state with the most slaves, anti-manumission acts were repealed, and individual slaveowners did grant large numbers of slaves their freedom.

27. George Washington to Samuel Powel, January 18, 1788, quoted in Gary B. Nash, *Race and Revolution* (Madison, WI: Madison House, 1990), p. 28.

28. Quoted in Bowen, *Miracle at Philadelphia*, p. 201.

29. Ibid.

30. Edgar, *South Carolina: A History*, p. 249.

31. Bowen, *Miracle at Philadelphia*, p. 203.

32. Ibid., p. 201.

33. Rossiter, *1787: The Grand Convention*, pp. 215–218.

34. For treatments of the national debate over slavery and race, see Nash, *Race and Revolution*, and Winthrop D. Jordan, *White Over Black: American Attitudes Toward the Negro, 1550–1812* (Chapel Hill: University of North Carolina Press, 1968).

35. Both men are quoted in Nadelhaft, *The Disorders of War*, p. 180.

36. Walter, *South Carolina*, p. 250. The backcountry districts voted fifty-seven to two against.

37. Mark D. Kaplanoff, "How Federalist Was South Carolina in 1787–1788?" in *The Meaning of South Carolina History; Essays in Honor of George C. Rogers, Jr.*, ed. David Chesnutt and Clyde N. Wilson (Columbia: University of South Carolina Press, 1991), p. 92n. Nadelhaft's numbers are similar, but he includes only Charleston, Beaufort, and Georgetown in his calculation, giving the lowcountry two fewer seats.

38. Edward Rutledge to John Jay, June 20, 1778, quoted in Nadelhaft, *The Disorders of War*, p. 180.

39. Quoted in Rachel N. Klein, *Unification of a Slave State: The Rise of the Planter Class in the South Carolina Backcountry, 1760–1808* (Chapel Hill: University of North Carolina Press, 1990), p. 168.

40. Quoted in Nadelhaft, *The Disorders of War*, p. 185. Emphasis is in the original.

41. Burke to John Lamb, June 23, 1788, quoted in Rogers, *Evolution of a Federalist*, p. 156.

42. Quoted in Kaplanoff, "How Federalist Was South Carolina in 1787–1788?" p. 74.

43. Quoted in Klein, *Unification of a Slave State*, p. 168.

44. Edgar, *South Carolina: A History*, p. 251.

45. Quoted in Kaplanoff, "How Federalist Was South Carolina in 1787–1788?" p. 79.

46. The statistics mentioned are based on the findings of Forrest McDonald, *We The People: The Economic Origins of the Constitution* (Chicago: University of Chicago Press, 1958). The numbers and the quotation can be found in Nadelhaft, *The Disorders of War*, p. 183.

47. Quoted in Rogers, *Evolution of a Federalist*, p. 157.

48. Nadelhaft, *The Disorders of War*, p. 180.

49. Edgar, *South Carolina: A History*, p. 252.

50. Quoted in Klein, *Unification of a Slave State*, p. 144.

51. A. S. Salley, "Origin and Early Development," in *Columbia: Capital City of South Carolina, 1786–1936* (Columbia: R. L. Bryan, 1936), pp. 1–13, quotation appears on p. 3.

52. Ibid., pp. 1–13.

53. See Stanley Elkins and Eric McKitrick, *The Age of Federalism: The Early American Republic, 1788–1800* (New York: Oxford University Press, 1993).

54. Nadelhaft, *The Disorders of War*, p. 191.

55. Quoted in Edgar, *South Carolina: A History*, p. 254.

56. Quoted in Klein, *Unification of a Slave State*, p. 144.

57. Nadelhaft, *The Disorders of War*, pp. 199–200.

58. David Duncan Wallace, *The History of South Carolina* (New York: American Historical Society, 1934), 2:168–170. In 1778, the Anglican Church was disestablished as a gesture of wartime friendship between the state's two regions. See also Nadelhaft, *The Disorders of War*, p. 202.

59. Ibid., p. 350.

60. Klein, *Unification of a Slave State*, p. 146.

61. Ibid., pp. 149–159.

62. Edgar, *South Carolina: A History*, p. 258; Klein, *Unification of a Slave State*, pp. 217–230.

63. Edgar, *South Carolina: A History*, p. 259.

64. Klein, *Unification of a Slave State*, pp. 238–268.

BIBLIOGRAPHY

Bell, Malcolm, Jr. *Major Butler's Legacy: Five Generations of a Slaveholding Family.* Athens, GA: University of Georgia Press, 1987.

Chesnutt, David R. and Clyde N. Wilson, ed. *The Meaning of South Carolina History: Essays in Honor of George C. Rogers, Jr.* Columbia, SC: University of South Carolina Press, 1991.

Clowse, Converse D. *Economic Beginnings in Colonial South Carolina, 1670–1730.* Columbia, SC: University of South Carolina Press, 1971.

Edgar, Walter. *South Carolina: A History.* Columbia, SC: University of South Carolina Press, 1998.

———. *Partisans & Redcoats: The Southern Conflict that Turned the Tide of the Revolution.* New York: William Morrow, 2001.

Gallay, Alan. *The Indian Slave Trade: The Rise of the English Empire in the American South, 1670–1717.* New Haven, CT: Yale University Press, 2002.

Haw, James. *John & Edward Rutledge of South Carolina.* Athens, GA: University of Georgia Press, 1997.

Klein, Rachel N. *Unification of a Slave State: The Rise of the Planter Class in the South Carolina Backcountry, 1760–1808.* Chapel Hill, NC: University of North Carolina Press, 1990.

Landers, Ernest M., Jr. "The South Carolinians at the Philadelphia Convention, 1787." *South Carolina Historical Magazine* 57 (3) (July 1956): 134–155.

Littlefield, Daniel C. *Rice and the Making of South Carolina: An Introductory Essay.* Columbia, SC: South Carolina Department of Archives and History, 1995.

Meleney, John C. *The Public Life of Aedanus Burke: Revolutionary Republican in Post-Revolutionary South Carolina.* Columbia, SC: University of South Carolina Press, 1989.

Merrell, James H. *The Indians' New World: Catawbas and Their Neighbors from European Contact Through the Era of Removal.* Chapel Hill, NC: University of North Carolina Press, 1989.

Morgan, Philip D. *Slave Counterpoint: Black Culture in the Eighteenth-Century Chesapeake & Lowcountry.* Chapel Hill, NC: University of North Carolina Press, 1998.

Nadelhaft, Jerome J. *The Disorders of War: The Revolution in South Carolina.* Orono, ME: University of Maine at Orono Press, 1981.

Rogers, George C. *Evolution of a Federalist: William Loughton Smith of Charleston, 1758–1812.* Columbia, SC: University of South Carolina Press, 1962.

Sirmans, M. Eugene. *Colonial South Carolina: A Political History, 1663–1763.* Chapel Hill, NC: University of North Carolina Press, 1966.

Underwood, James Lowell. *The Constitution of South Carolina.* 2 vols. Columbia, SC: University of South Carolina Press, 1986.

Wallace, David Duncan. *The History of South Carolina.* 4 vols. New York: The American Historical Society, 1934.

Walsh, Richard. *Charleston's Sons of Liberty: A Study of the Artisans, 1763–1789.* Columbia, SC: University of South Carolina Press, 1959.

Weir, Robert M. *Colonial South Carolina: A History.* 2nd ed. Columbia, SC: University of South Carolina, 1997.

Zahniser, Marvin R. *Charles Cotesworth Pinckney: Founding Father.* Chapel Hill, NC: University of North Carolina Press, 1967.

THE STATE OF SOUTH DAKOTA

Admitted to the Union as a State: November 2, 1889

John E. Miller

INTRODUCTION

"IT'S A GO," the Huron *Daily Huronite* jubilantly headlined on February 21, 1889, regarding congressional passage of the Omnibus Bill the day before. Along with South Dakota, three other states—North Dakota, Montana, and Washington—would be entering the Union as soon as they fulfilled the requirements of the enabling legislation, including the adoption of a constitution. Rumors that President Grover Cleveland might veto the legislation failed to dampen the revelry that broke out across Dakota Territory during the next several days. The president, contrary to speculation, signed the bill into law the following day, and the process for admission of South Dakota commenced. It had been a long, frustrating struggle, lasting an entire decade to arrive at this point, and southern Dakotans were losing their patience by the end of the 1880s. Looking back on the decade toward the end of 1889, the Pierre *Free Press* editorialized, "The present year will soon draw to a close. It has been an eventful one to Dakota, or perhaps we should say to the Dakotas. It has seen the close of the territorial condition and the inauguration of state governments. It has seen long delayed hopes realized."[1]

TERRITORIAL GOVERNMENT

Ironically, although statehood for South Dakota was delayed beyond the time that it normally would have come, territorial status was achieved prematurely and without the close scrutiny that it deserved. Between the first towns organized in the region in 1857 and the emergence of Dakota Territory, only

South Dakota

Territorial Development:

- The United States obtains future South Dakotan territory west of the Missouri River from France through the Louisiana Purchase, April 30, 1803
- The United States obtains more land containing future South Dakotan territory east of the Missouri River from Great Britain through the Joint-Occupancy Treaty, 1818
- Future territory of South Dakota organized as part of the Louisiana Territory (or the District of Louisiana for a time in 1804), 1804–1812
- Reorganized as part of the Missouri Territory, 1812–1834
- East of the Missouri River, the future territory of South Dakota is reorganized as a part of the Michigan Territory, 1834–1836
- East of the Missouri River, the future territory of South Dakota is reorganized as a part of the Wisconsin Territory, 1836–1838
- Reorganized as a part of the Iowa Territory, 1838–1846; becomes unorganized territory, 1846–1849
- Reorganized as a part of the Minnesota Territory, 1849–1858
- West of the Missouri River, the future territory of South Dakota is reorganized as a part of the Nebraska Territory, 1854–1861
- Reorganized as the Dakota Territory, March 2, 1861
- Dakota Territory divided into North Dakota and South Dakota, and South Dakota admitted into the Union as the fortieth state, November 2, 1889

Territorial Capitals:

- Yankton, 1861–1883
- Bismarck, 1883–1889

State Capitals:

- Pierre, 1889–present

Origin of State Name: South Dakota received its name from the Sioux tribe whose name means "allies," or "friends."

First Governor: Arthur C. Melette
Governmental Organization: Bicameral
Population at Statehood: 328,808
Geographical Size: 75,885 square miles

four years intervened. Establishment of the territory in March 1861, just two days before Abraham Lincoln was inaugurated, was an afterthought at a time when congressional attention was heavily focused on the crisis of disunion following Lincoln's 1860 election. The Northwest Ordinance of 1787 required a population of five thousand adult males for a territory to be admitted, and the large expanse of Dakota Territory in 1861, which included all of present-day North and South Dakota and most of Montana and Wyoming, probably failed to meet that qualification. Amidst the disruption existing in the nation's capital during the weeks leading up to Fort Sumter, as one southern state after another seceded from the Union, opposition to admitting Dakota Territory receded.

Before this, the Democratic South had objected to the entry of another territory that excluded slavery, and northern Republicans had wanted to ensure that any new territory would exclude the "peculiar institution" from it. With many southern states having seceded by early March, the issue was of less concern, and northern Republicans as a consequence apparently no longer felt the need to have a specific guarantee against slavery included in the legislation. The three population concentrations in 1861 centered on Yankton and Sioux Falls in the south and Pembina in the north. Amid confusion and in great haste at the end of the session, Congress established the new territories of Dakota, Nevada, and Colorado. Outgoing President James Buchanan signed the legislation creating Dakota Territory on March 2, 1861, just two days before his term expired. Considerable credit for making Dakota a territory must go to J. B. S. Todd and his business partner Daniel Frost, who together took the lead in establishing Yankton and several other settlements along the Missouri River during the preceding two years. Todd's kinship with Mary Todd Lincoln, wife of the president-elect, worked in his favor and may have influenced Yankton's being designated as capital of the new territory. Montana broke off from this territory in 1864, and Wyoming achieved territorial status in 1868.

DISCONTENT WITH TERRITORIAL STATUS

As was predictable, citizens of Dakota Territory grew increasingly resentful of their inferior status in the Union as time went by. They disliked being governed by outsiders whom they viewed as corrupt political hacks, considered themselves to have colonial status, and yearned for self-rule. Over time there was an increasingly large gap between their political status and their social and economic status.

For almost a quarter of a century after the Civil War, only two new states succeeded in gaining admission to the Union—Nebraska in 1867 and Colorado in 1876. Minnesota, Dakota's neighbor to the east, had waited only nine years for statehood after becoming a territory. Colorado's period of waiting had been fifteen years, a little more than half the time it would take South Dakota. By 1880 at least, when more than eighty thousand southern Dakotans were counted in the decennial census, the region easily met the standard of sixty thousand required for admission to statehood under the provisions of the Northwest Ordinance. With an average of one thousand new settlers arriving in the southern part of the territory every week at the height of the Great Dakota Boom during the early 1880s, the population of southern Dakota grew to 262,000 by 1885. During the second half of the decade, as drought conditions appeared and immigration tapered off, growth proceeded at a slower pace. The 1890 census counted 348,600 in the new state of South Dakota.

As early as 1877, the Yankton *Press and Dakotaian*, the chief newspaper in the territory, commented, "We are so heartily disgusted with our dependent condition, with being snubbed at every turn in life, with having all our interests subjected to the whims and corrupt acts of persons in power that we feel very much as the thirteen colonies felt when they flung away their dependent condition and asserted their position among nations."[2] Many things conspired to lead Dakota residents to resent their putative colonial status by the late 1870s and to begin contemplating a statehood drive. They were tiring of carpetbag government and the corruption and scandal that often accompanied it. With the territorial capital at Yankton "stolen away" from them in 1883 and moved to Bismarck by the machinations of Governor Nehemiah Ordway, residents in the southeast especially were disaffected and were determined to sever connections with the northern part of the territory and to gain statehood. Several towns centrally located in southern Dakota, including Pierre, Huron, and Watertown, hoped to become the capital of a new state. Territorial politicians such as Arthur Mellette, Richard Pettigrew, Gideon C. Moody, and Hugh J. Campbell hoped for state or national office, especially the governorship and U.S. Senate seats. Republicans in general resented what they perceived as Democratic selfishness and perfidy, believing statehood to be the only way around it. Finally, disparate groups of reformers, primarily prohibitionists, suffragettes, and educators who were determined to protect the school lands, considered statehood to be a means of achieving their goals. Almost without exception, the advocates of statehood for southern Dakota linked that goal with division of the territory between north and south.

The idea of splitting the territory between east and west might have seemed logical to many, but it never really got off the ground. The greatest agitation for it occurred after gold was discovered in paying quantities in the Black Hills in 1874 and thousands of miners rushed in during the next several years. Consideration was given to splitting off the Black Hills and the surrounding area around it into a state called "Lincoln," but momentum for the idea quickly faded, and little more was heard of the proposition by the early 1880s.

OBSTACLES TO STATEHOOD

The exceptionally long delay in achieving statehood resulted from a variety of factors that together effectively blocked momentum for bringing South Dakota into the Union. Not everyone was interested in the territory becoming a state.

Many people and certain corporate interest groups saw specific advantages in territorial status.

Railroad companies feared the possibility of effective regulation if South Dakota became a state. During the last decade of territorial status, as new lines criss-crossed Dakota, the railroads exerted major influence in the legislature and felt confident of their ability to block effective regulation by that body. With the Northern Pacific operating in the northern part of the territory and the Chicago and North Western system and the Chicago, Milwaukee, and St. Paul involved in the south, the transportation lobby in the Dakota Territory reputedly had a hand in selecting each of the last five territorial governors. Moreover, eastern and foreign investors, who were able to earn as much as 20 percent interest on their money in what was termed "the investor's paradise," were loath to invite the possibility of effective regulation if South Dakota became a state. With 299 banks in the territory, Dakota hosted more banks than eight other states combined. During the 1880s, for example, New Hampshire banks lent out $25 million in western lands and business, much of it going into Dakota.

In addition to these groups, political figures in Washington, D.C., and in various states who had their fingers on the strings of patronage feared that ending territorial status would deprive them of political jobs to dispense. Several of Dakota Territory's early governors were in-laws of U.S. senators and prominent Dakota territorial politicians. Political appointees such as Nehemiah Ordway of New Hampshire, governor of the territory from 1880 to 1884, desired to hold onto the power they enjoyed as long as southern Dakota remained a territory. Agricultural groups were not so much opposed to statehood as apathetic about it. This lack of interest was crucial, because almost all the population earned its living from the land. The 1880s, the period of the statehood struggle, also witnessed the emergence of organized farm protest in the state and the rise of the Farmers Alliance. The Farmers Alliance later merged into the Populist movement during the 1890s, but its role was insignificant in the battle for statehood. Farmers generally failed to perceive a direct link between their struggle for independence from financial interests and the efforts of statehood advocates, who sought independence from outside political control. As a result, they played little role in the campaign for statehood.

There was also a regional flavor to the conflict. Proponents of statehood largely resided in the southern sector, particularly in the southeastern part of the territory. Not until late in the process did residents of the north get excited about the advantages of entering the Union. People in the Black Hills, whose non–Native American population was almost entirely a result of the gold rush, took small interest in the statehood campaign. Regional rivalries served as the context for politics in the Dakota Territory during the decade of the eighties. The three sections—southeast, Black Hills, and north—remained geographically remote from each other. Although railroads rapidly penetrated the eastern part of the territory during the Great Dakota Boom of 1878 to 1886, the Black

Hills remained accessible only by foot or animal transportation until the latter year, and people traveling between the southeastern part of the territory and places in the Red River Valley or elsewhere in the north usually took a roundabout rail route through St. Paul. Politically, this remoteness frequently manifested itself in shifting alliances in which the Black Hills section allied itself either with southeastern Dakota or the northern part of the territory in opposition to the third section. North and southeast generally saw their interests as being at odds with each other.

PARTY POLITICS AND THE ISSUE OF STATEHOOD

The decades after the Civil War witnessed highly charged political skirmishing between Republicans and Democrats all across the nation, and it is not surprising that partisan bickering influenced the situation in Dakota. Political issues naturally turned themselves into partisan ones, which only increased the likelihood that they would involve conflict.

Much of the reason for sectional conflict in Dakota Territory was that Republicans firmly dominated the south, whereas Democrats offered more competition in the north, especially after Governor Nehemiah Ordway established a political alliance with Burleigh County sheriff, Alexander McKenzie of Bismarck. They took the lead in engineering the removal of the capital from Yankton to Bismarck in 1883. The outrage felt in Yankton and elsewhere in southeastern Dakota at what appeared to be a dishonest and nefarious betrayal stimulated the rapid rise of the statehood movement in the south and reinforced longstanding sentiment in the south that statehood should come only after the territory had been divided.

Ultimately, party politics played the most significant role in the controversy over statehood and was the pole around which conflict rotated during the 1880s. Democrats, simply put, viewed admission of southern Dakota and the likely addition of two U.S. senators and an equivalent number of congressmen into Republican party ranks in Washington as being contrary to their party's interests. Even worse than admission of a single state would be the splitting of the territory and the entry of two Republican states. Therefore, the Democrats' fallback position was to support the admission of Dakota as a single state, which would add only half as many Republican senators. More to the point, they fully realized that Republican advocates of statehood in the southern part of the territory were committed to division of the territory as a prerequisite to statehood and would refuse to entertain the possibility of entering the Union as a single state. Therefore, so long as the only viable option remained admission as a single state, southern Dakotans would balk at it, and the Democrats' goal of delaying statehood would be achieved. Democrats in Washington, with a few exceptions toward the very end of the controversy, followed this line, whereas Democrats in Dakota Territory, both in the north and the south, expressed somewhat more ambivalence about what they wanted to achieve or were willing to accept.

ORIGINS OF THE STATEHOOD MOVEMENT

A variety of factors coalesced during the early 1880s to ignite the campaign for statehood. These issues included the Black Hills gold rush, railroad construction, population growth, economic prosperity, growing resentment of outside political control, and a desire for reform.

Before 1879, little effective effort was made in Dakota Territory to launch a drive for statehood. During the previous decade, several modest moves in the direction of splitting the territory had been tried. The first official call to divide the territory occurred when the 1871 legislative session unanimously memorialized Congress to make a division along 46° north latitude, leaving "Dakota" as the southern portion and renaming the area to the north "Lincoln" or "Chippewa." At this time the area around Pembina in the far north was the only part of northern Dakota Territory represented in the legislature, because no other area had any significant population when apportionment was done in 1868. The building of the Northern Pacific Railroad through Fargo to Bismarck by 1873 intensified sentiment for division not only in Dakota, but also among Minnesota business interests, who stood to benefit from increased settlement to the west of them. A bill introduced in the U.S. Senate in 1872 by Minnesotan Alexander Ramsey to split the territory along the 46th parallel passed that body but stalled in the House of Representatives. It presaged the pattern of similar future initiatives, especially after Democrats took over control of the House. In 1872, with Republicans still safely in control of both houses, arguments that division would entail unnecessary expenses and that the population did not justify statehood carried the day. Most of the approximately twenty-five thousand people inhabiting the territory at the time were concentrated in southeastern counties in a triangle between the Big Sioux and Missouri rivers.

Initial failure, however, did not prevent frequent subsequent efforts to split the territory in two. At the outset, interestingly, the north seemed more enthusiastic about the proposition. That situation soon changed, however. In 1874, a bill introduced by Dakota's nonvoting Congressional delegate, Moses Armstrong, to split Pembina from the northern half of the territory was defeated by the House, most of whose members seemed to believe that the area would never attract enough people to warrant statehood. Again in 1877 a proposal for division was debated in the U.S. Senate. The novelty this time was that Nebraska Senator Alvin Saunders called for a north-south line along the one-hundredth meridian, including the Black Hills in the new Territory of Lincoln. Again, Congress was not receptive.

That same year, with as many as twenty-five thousand people lured to the Black Hills by the gold rush, the first public push in the direction of statehood occurred at a meeting in the capital at Yankton. Several men who later became leaders of the statehood movement, including William Henry Harrison Beadle, George H. Hand, and George W. Kingsbury, played prominent roles in the proceedings. The assembly unanimously endorsed a statement crafted by the resolutions committee asserting, "There is every reason, geographical, political, topographical, legal, commercial, and in the best permanent interests of all its people and the general welfare of the nation, why the southern half of Dakota should be admitted as a State."[3] By this time, southern Dakotans had arrived at the opinion that statehood, when it came, should come only after division had occurred. Their general concern lay with their own more populous area, leaving it to the northern section to make it on its own once it was ready to do so. A resolution to that effect was passed by the territorial legislature in 1879, when it memorialized Congress to divide the territory in two, simultaneously voicing its objection to the idea of admitting the entire territory as a single state.

Now, eighteen years after Dakota had become a territory, the statehood movement jelled. Many things converged around this time to boost momentum. The Black Hills gold rush stimulated a major influx of immigrants into the southern part of the territory. The end of the economic depression of the mid-1870s, coupled with the decisions of the Chicago and North Western and the Milwaukee railroads to build into Dakota, sparked the Great Dakota Boom, during which the population of southern Dakota multiplied about four times. By the early 1880s, Dakotans were wearying of corrupt, carpetbag government, and then from 1880 to 1884 they got Nehemiah Ordway as governor, by most estimates the most venal and devious of all of Dakota Territory's Washington-appointed public officials. Despite Ordway's distinguished appearance and sanctimonious manner, he was a grasping, scheming self-aggrandizer who stopped at nothing to promote his own self-interest. He arrived at Yankton with a far-reaching plan to build a vast political machine and to use his office to enrich himself through land speculation, county-seat manipulation, bribery, and other kinds of venality.

Added to these problems were resentment at the way the federal government was handling Native American affairs and a growing concern about the power of monopolistic corporations and especially the railroads. Much of the blame for the situation was ascribed to the failures of the territorial system of government. Statehood might provide the means for effective regulation. Finally, there was the matter of the Native American reservations and the presidentially appointed agents placed in charge of managing them. That many of the agents engaged in corrupt practices to benefit themselves was clear, but Dakotans resented what they considered to be heavy-handed attempts by Secretary of State Carl Schurz and others to remedy the situation and believed that some of the agents were not treated fairly.

Objective conditions made Dakota ripe for a statehood drive. Its citizenry, or at least its local political leadership, had reached a condition of maturity impelling them toward a more independent status. The psychological foundations of statehood were being laid day by day. By 1879, enough wealth had accumulated in the territory that it could begin funding institutions that had previously been postponed, such as insane asylums, penitentiaries, universities, and normal schools. That year, Yankton was designated as home of an insane asylum. Under Governor Nehemiah Ordway, the legislatures of 1881 and 1883 authorized a variety of new territorial institutions. Lawyers, merchants, land dealers, and town boosters were present in profusion at these legislative sessions, seeking political plums that might benefit their own communities. Confident that the territory would eventually be divided, legislators distributed the new institutions between the northern and southern sections. A university in Vermillion, originally authorized in 1862, was funded. In addition, agricultural colleges were established in Brookings and Fargo, and normal schools were located at Springfield, Madison, and Watertown. Watertown later failed to fulfill its obligation of providing eighty acres of land for the school, thereby losing its privilege.

By 1879, and increasingly evident during the next several years, the foundations were laid for a movement advocating statehood for southern Dakota. People were offended by what appeared to be federal persecution of Indian agents. They were concerned about the growing influence of the railroads that were entering the area. The territory was growing in wealth and prosperity, and its population was on the verge of exploding. About three hundred new towns emerged during the years of the Great Dakota Boom, 80 percent of them along railroad lines. A new sense of geographical sectionalism, separating southeastern Dakota, the Black Hills, and the northern part, infused the thinking of residents in the territory. Those in the southern part of the territory increasingly believed that they deserved independent status for themselves. All that was necessary was a political vehicle for the expression of these sentiments.

THE KEY PLAYERS IN THE STATEHOOD MOVEMENT

Every political movement requires effective leadership if it is to succeed. The campaign to achieve statehood for South Dakota benefited from the leadership of men such as Joseph Ward and William Henry Harrison Beadle. In a variety of ways, they demonstrated creativity, farsightedness, and devotion to duty, but, as might be expected, self-interest also played a prominent role in the process.

Although scattered efforts to win the vote for women were building momentum in the United States by the 1880s, the statehood movement that brought South Dakota into the Union in 1889 remained almost entirely an all-male enterprise. Its leadership consisted of a small elite consisting mostly of town dwellers—businessmen, bankers, lawyers, ministers, newspaper editors, and other members of the middle class. Although Dakota Territory was overwhelmingly agricultural, few farmers became involved in the drive for statehood. The core group of leaders referred to themselves as the 20 percent of the population who were not involved in farming. Few were recent immigrants; most of them traced their ancestry back several generations in America. Most came from families that had migrated across the northern tier of states, from New England or New York and on through the upper portions of the Old Northwest before arriving in Dakota. They were typically Protestant in religion and Republican in politics. Democrats, in general, remained skeptical of or absolutely opposed to the idea of statehood. The Democrats who did support statehood generally favored the idea of a single state, which went strongly against the desires of statehood advocates residing in southern Dakota. Members of the Grand Army of the Republic, Civil War veterans who played a major role in Republican Party politics, were active in the movement. Howard Lamar, the foremost historian of Dakota Territory, estimates that the entire group of leaders numbered fewer than two hundred and that no more than a dozen of them were politically popular.[4]

According to lore, the birth of the statehood drive occurred at a famous Thanksgiving dinner held in Yankton in 1879. Most prominent in the assemblage that day was the Reverend Joseph Ward, a Congregational minister and the founder of Yankton College. Ward rightly earned a reputation as "the father of the statehood movement," and his statue stands today as one of two from South Dakota in the rotunda of the national Capitol. Coming from Massachusetts and a graduate of Andover Theological Seminary, he reflected the reform spirit that figured prominently among a number of members of the core leadership group. An expression of the New England conscience, he harbored "contempt for the territorial system, and for the graft and misgovernment with which the system was connected."[5]

Also present at the Thanksgiving dinner were General William Henry Harrison Beadle, territorial superintendent of public instruction, and Judge Hugh J. Campbell, U.S. attorney for Dakota, both members of Ward's congregation and his close friends. These three men were the key figures in inaugurating the statehood drive. Beadle's statue later joined Ward's in the Capitol rotunda. His motives, like Ward's, were reformist in nature. An Indiana native, he was aware of how that state's school lands, granted under the provisions of the Land Ordinance of 1785, had been squandered by corrupt or short-sighted government officials over the years. Service as Dakota Territory's surveyor general from 1869 to 1873 reinforced his determination to protect the school lands for their intended purpose—providing revenue for the running of the educational system. He was determined to write a clause into the constitution forbidding the sale of the school lands for any bid less than $10 an acre. He also was interested in general reform and in guaranteeing the integrity of the political system.

The third member of the trio, Hugh J. Campbell, a Yankton lawyer, harbored mixed motives in pushing for an end to territorial status. He was a sincere and unrelenting advocate of division and statehood, but he also was highly ambitious politically, hoping to be rewarded for his efforts by a seat in the U.S. Senate. He was a crusader and an idealist, a born fighter, whom some considered to be a little too mystical in his approach. He emerged as the chief theorist of the statehood movement by reviving the hoary constitutional doctrine of interposition, which had been used by Southerners before the Civil War in their effort to protect slavery from federal intrusion.

Another key member of the leadership group was Governor William A. Howard of Michigan, but he was aged and ill and died in 1880, too soon to have any significant impact. Alonzo J. Edgerton, chief justice of the territorial supreme court after 1880 and a former U.S. senator from Minnesota, participated in hopes of returning to the Senate. Two other rising Dakota politicians also possessed high political ambitions, and both, unlike Campbell and Edgerton, were able to realize them. Richard J. Pettigrew, a Sioux Falls lawyer and a native of Vermont, built a political following during the seventies and eighties. Elected as territorial delegate in 1880, he tangled with the Ordway regime in the next election and was forced out of the position, but he remained a force to be reckoned with, going on to become one of South Dakota's most prominent political figures over the course of its history. His Sioux Falls political machine and his own political savvy carried him into the U.S. Senate immediately upon statehood in 1889. Watertown lawyer Arthur C. Mellette, an Indiana native, was a close personal friend of Senator Benjamin Harrison and benefited hugely from that political connection. Following the example of other politicians and businessmen involved in the land business, he was able to increase his wealth and to make useful political connections through his multiple land dealings. Like many other politicians during the 1880s, he hoped that the coming of statehood would enhance his political prospects. Unlike many of them, he lived to see his ambitions fulfilled.

ORGANIZING FOR STATEHOOD

The drive for statehood was more an elitist than a democratic process. A small group of leaders took responsibility, and the largest group in the territory, farmers, was hardly represented at all. Organized pressure groups played a prominent role in developments.

Statehood clubs and committees of correspondence emerged locally during the early 1880s.[6] In 1882, an organization was established to push the statehood process. Conventions meeting simultaneously in Sioux Falls and Fargo elected slates of delegates to travel to Washington, D.C., with petitions to split the territory and admit the southern part as a state. Soon, the Ward-Beadle group began to collaborate with Judge Edgerton and others to protect the school lands and promote the movement. Out of this collaboration emerged a bipartisan Citizen's League hoping to establish local units in every county. At a convention held in Canton in June, 193 delegates from fourteen southern counties formulated plans for a statehood campaign. Judge Campbell served on the rules committee of the convention, and Joseph Ward became secretary of the executive committee of the new organization.

The Citizen's League promoted a bill that was passed by the 1883 legislature calling for a constitutional convention, but Governor Ordway vetoed it. The removal of the capital from Yankton that year and Ordway's machinations sparked a political rebellion in Yankton and in the south generally that year, prompting the executive committee of the Citizen's League to go call a delegate convention to meet in Huron in June to work out a plan of action. That convention, defying the governor's veto, scheduled a constitutional convention to meet in Sioux Falls on September 4 to draft a constitution and to set in motion the process of applying for statehood.

In two weeks' time, the Sioux Falls convention completed its work. Acting without official authorization, it operated as an extralegal body. By this time, however, southern Dakotans possessed an elaborate constitutional theory worked out by Attorney General Campbell justifying statehood, whatever the arguments or forces that might be arrayed against them. Campbell reasoned that because southern Dakota met the legal requirements for statehood—its population now being several times the minimal figure of sixty thousand— it possessed the right to declare itself a state without waiting for Congress to act. Relying upon the U.S. Supreme Court's decision in the Dred Scott case, Jefferson's and Madison's Kentucky and Virginia Resolutions, and John C. Calhoun's arguments on states' rights, the Yankton lawyer ingeniously adapted the old doctrine of interposition to his own uses. Rather than using it to protect slavery and defend the right of secession, as southern states had done before the Civil War, Campbell twisted it to insist that South Dakota already was a state and simply needed to have that fact recognized. "We are a state" constituted both a legal-constitutional theory and a battle cry for the South Dakota statehood advocates. Not many legal scholars, politicians, and impartial observers outside the territory were much impressed by the reasoning involved, however.[7]

If Campbell's constitutional arguments persuaded few who were not already convinced, the delegates who declared for statehood at Sioux Falls represented, by and large, an elite group of political leaders and the "best elements" from the southern part of the territory. Of the 125 delegates in attendance, there were 42 lawyers, 31 farmers, 13 newspaper editors, 11 real estate agents, 5 clergymen, and 23 in other businesses and professions. All but seventeen had been born in the United States, and only two of those had been born outside the North. They were relatively young, with an average age of thirty-five. Along with Campbell, Beadle, and Ward, other prominent territorial political figures including George Kingsbury, Gideon C. Moody, Wilmot C. Brookings, and former governors Newton Edmunds and John Pennington were in attendance. This was no group of neophytes. Their generally conservative cast of mind was demonstrated in the constitutional document that they drafted, containing no radical innovations. In large part, the ideas that went into it were copied from other states.

ISSUES INVOLVED IN CONSTITUTION MAKING

The issues involved in constitution making were only peripherally related to the question of statehood itself. Reform-minded zealots had more influence in the process than did average citizens, but counter pressures and inertia prevented some reform measures from winning easy success.

Incorporating the usual bicameral legislature, the new constitution imposed major limitations on the legislature's taxing and spending powers as well as on the governor's powers to act and to veto legislation. These restrictions derived in part from the lavish spending that had occurred during the 1883 legislative session. Three issues stood out most prominently in the deliberations, and these three remained of primary interest right through the final adoption of a state constitution at the time of admission in 1889. The first related to the protection of the school lands. William H. H. Beadle had done his homework well and exercised his persuasive powers effectively. The document adopted by the delegates included the clause that Beadle had insisted upon, prohibiting school lands from being sold for less than $10 an acre. It called for a perpetual fund to hold any funds from land sales; the perpetual fund in turn would distribute interest from principle to support schools. The resulting "Dakota System" was later adopted by the other states that came into the Union under the Omnibus Bill of 1889.

The other two major issues, prohibition and women's suffrage, were left unresolved for the time being, the delegates considering them too controversial for inclusion in the document. Notable also for their omission were provisions placing restrictions on railroads, banks, and monopolies, the issues that most interested the farm population of the territory. This failure reflected the absence of a large contingent of agrarian delegates at the convention. With farmers poorly represented at the convention, strong measures for agrarian relief were unlikely. In turn, by avoiding those issues in their deliberations, the convention insured that many, if not most, of the farm elements in Dakota would remain apathetic, if not hostile, to the idea of statehood. This original 1883 constitution, with some modifications, became the basis for the constitution that was finally adopted in 1889.

FAILURE TO OBTAIN CONGRESSIONAL APPROVAL

The period between 1883 and 1888 turned out to be frustrating to Dakota advocates of statehood, because Democrats in Congress effectively blocked every initiative they put forward. Every two years or so a new constitutional convention met, and just as regularly its recommendations were set aside because of partisan political maneuvering.

That the Sioux Falls convention of 1883 had acted without legal authority and in defiance of Governor Ordway's veto made it less likely that its action would gain approval from Congress. The turnout at the polls in October for voting on the constitution reinforced the unlikelihood of its obtaining congressional approval. Although the ratio approving the constitution was almost two to one (12,336 to 6,814), the proportion of eligible voters casting ballots was disappointingly low. The low turnout was reason enough for the Democratic majority in the House of Representatives to turn down South Dakota's application for statehood. Republicans had enjoyed a brief two-year period of dominance in the lower house after the 1880 election, but the 1882 contest returned a Democratic majority (197 to 118) to that body, and they maintained their hold with smaller majorities after the 1884 and 1886 elections. With Republicans enjoying generally slim margins in the U.S. Senate during the period, bills for division and statehood for South Dakota received favorable consideration there. After Benjamin Harrison went to the Senate from Indiana in 1881, he became South Dakota's ardent champion there. Democrats in the House, however, wishing to prevent the admission of new Republican members of Congress, continually blocked any initiatives to admit South Dakota. Senator Harrison's bill to admit South Dakota passed the Senate on a strict party vote in December 1884, but it never got to a vote in the House during the short session ending March 4, 1885.

The 1885 legislature again passed a bill authorizing a constitutional convention, but by this time Nehemiah Ordway was gone from the governor's office, replaced by Chester Arthur's appointee, Gilbert Pierce. Pierce was a debonair playwright and newspaperman from Chicago who had been managing editor of the *Inter Ocean* before he took over as leading editorial writer for the *Evening News*. Statehood enthusiasts were pleased when Pierce signed into law a bill authorizing a second constitutional convention in Sioux Falls. The Democratic Grover Cleveland had moved into the White House in the meantime, however, making it unlikely that any bill admitting South Dakota would pass muster in Washington. Cleveland, to his credit, tried to avoid appointing spoilsmen and unpopular hacks to territorial political offices and allowed the Republican Pierce to remain in the governor's chair for two years before replacing him with a Democratic appointee. But Cleveland, no more than his fellow Democrats, wanted to admit another Republican state that would add to that party's representation in Congress. The matter was especially crucial, because the party balance in the Senate was tenuous, with Republicans holding slim majorities in that body during the late 1880s. Meanwhile, ex-Governor Ordway moved to Washington, D.C., where he served as a Democratic lobbyist for the Northern Pacific Railroad. He worked to block any move to make South Dakota a state, because the Bismarck political and business interests that he represented wanted to retain that town's status as capital of a large territory. The chances for advancing statehood were getting worse rather than better, it seemed.

The constitutional convention that convened in September 1885 met again in Sioux Falls and was a virtual repeat of the session held two years earlier. Many of the same delegates were back, and the leadership remained in the same hands, as was reflected in the choice of Judge Edgerton as chair of the meeting. Only a few minor changes were made in the 1883 constitution, the delegates' attention this time being focused on gaining approval from Congress for their work and working out acceptable compromises on several issues being pushed by the reformers. The convention decided to submit the prohibition question to a separate vote of the electorate rather than incorporate it in the constitution itself. The same approach was used to resolve the issue of minority representation urged upon them by Democrats. That party wanted the constitution to include provisions giving minority parties a say in governing the state, rather than letting strict majority rule determine election outcomes. Advocates of women's suffrage failed to obtain a similar vote for their cause, however. Nor were proponents of the initiative and referendum successful in getting on the ballot.[8]

The cautious, conservative tenor of the gathering was exemplified in a statement on women's suffrage by Gideon Moody, a dominant figure at the conference: "We have got to pass the gauntlet of all criticism of our enemies, powerful here, but still more powerful out of this commonwealth. Let us be prudent; let us be conservative; let us make liberal provision for submitting all these provisions to the people when the time comes. But let us try no new untried experiments now."[9]

The convention also went part way toward implementing Hugh Campbell's "We Are a State" philosophy by providing for a slate of state officers to be elected. The state officers and legislative representatives so selected were intended to be symbolic rather than actual officeholders. One month later, the same delegates reassembled as a state Republican Party convention to nominate legislative representatives and people for congressional posts as well as a full slate of state officials, including Arthur C. Mellette for governor. In November, voters south of the 46th parallel again trooped to the polls, this time approving the constitution by a margin of 25,226 to 6,565. Prohibition was adopted by a narrow margin. The voters overwhelmingly approved the offered slate of governmental officials, starting with "Governor" Mellette, put forward by the nominating convention; for state capital they chose Huron, which garnered 12,695 votes to Pierre's 10,574. Sioux Falls (with 3,338 votes), Chamberlain (3,170), Alexandria (1,374), and a scattering of other towns (602) trailed in the balloting.

The "legislature" that was not a legislature convened in the Huron Opera House in December along with the "governor" who was not a governor and other state "officials" and "judges," and they proceeded to "elect" two U.S. "senators," Alonzo J. Edgerton and Gideon C. Moody. Congress, however, was not impressed by the display and refused to act on the proposal from southern Dakota that it be immediately admitted to the Union. Again, the ratio of votes (about two to one in favor of admission) was impressive, but the turnout was light, and Democrats in Congress had no more reason to want a new Republican state in the Union than they had earlier.

Senator Harrison of Indiana, South Dakota's friend in the Senate, introduced a bill to admit South Dakota under the Sioux Falls constitution of 1885. Senator Matthew Butler of South Carolina took up the cudgels for the Democrats, demanding a committee inquiry into the authority under which the so-called legislature had been elected. Senator George Vest of Missouri joined him in pressing the case of Democratic opponents of admission. Republicans, including Samuel McMillan of Minnesota and Preston Plumb of Kansas, however, joined Harrison in arguing for the legitimacy of the convention and the virtue of its cause. Butler introduced a substitute measure that would have admitted the entire territory as a state. This bill, it was rumored, had been provided to the senator ready-made by ex-Governor Ordway and other opponents of division. Such an outcome, however, was completely unacceptable to the mostly Republican southern Dakota statehood contingent. The Senate passed Harrison's bill in February 1886 by a vote of 32-22, with only one Democrat, Senator Daniel Voorhees of Indiana, voting for it. In the House, Representative William D. Hill, an Ohio Democrat and a member of the Committee on Territories, championed division of the territory and statehood for South Dakota. In January 1886, meanwhile, President Cleveland met with a delegation of South Dakota statehood proponents, including Mellette, Moody, and Edgerton, but to no effect. Partisan political considerations, as usual, defeated statehood dreams in the House. In Sioux Falls in May, a Dakota State League was organized to carry on the fight, taking over leadership from the Dakota Citizen's League.

During the second congressional session, beginning in December 1886 and continuing into the new year, a contingent of congressional Democrats led by Congressman William Springer of Illinois, the chairman of the House Committee on Territories, adopted a new strategy to minimize possible political fallout from the Dakota issue. Instead of dividing the territory and admitting the southern half, he proposed admitting all of Dakota as a state along with Montana, Washington, and New Mexico. Heavily Republican Dakota and Washington would thus be balanced by presumably Democratic Montana and New Mexico. Dakota Territory Governor Louis K. Church, a New York lawyer who had recently been appointed to the office by his friend and fellow New Yorker, President Grover Cleveland, indicated his support for the idea, as did other members of his party in the territory and Ordway Republicans. Some Democrats, however, and the regular Republican organization in Dakota stoutly opposed the idea. Republicans in the Senate also rejected it, and many Democrats in the House of Representatives were less interested in the Democratic complexion of New Mexico than in the racial background of its population and its less-developed institutions.

Once again, the 1887 legislative session in Bismarck proposed to divide the territory along an east-west line, this time along the 7th standard parallel. This division, unlike the 46th parallel, had the advantage of following the lines already laid out by the surveyors in platting the original townships. This provision for division was not attached to a statehood proposal, a fact that may have hurt its chances more than helped them, because the vote in November in southern Dakota resulted in a favorable margin of only 29,826 to 15,535. In northern Dakota Territory, the results were 8,830 in favor to 18,007 against. Obviously, the statehood movement had reached an impasse.

THE TURNING POINT: THE 1888 ELECTION

For the forces committed to South Dakota statehood, the major turning-point occurred with the results of the 1888 election, which brought a Republican president back into the White House and also returned Republican majorities in both houses of Congress. So long as Democrats controlled either the presidency or one of the houses, they could block entry of new Republican states. Once that advantage was gone, victory for the statehood forces became virtually inevitable.

At the start of 1888, Dakota Territory was entering its twenty-eighth year of territorial status. Few Dakota residents could have anticipated the speed and ease with which statehood now was achieved after such a delay. Partisan politics explained Congress's failure to act up to now. It would also be responsible for the final victory. The year began with one more intense debate in Congress on the issue. Four separate bills for the admission of Montana, Wyoming, Washington, and South Dakota were reported out of the Senate Committee on Territories in April. The Platt Bill, named after committee chairman Orville Platt of Connecticut, provided for the division of Dakota Territory along the 46th parallel, the admission of South Dakota as a state, and the formation of a new Territory of North Dakota.

Democrats in the Senate countered with an Omnibus Bill that would have included New Mexico, a way, by their calculations, to maintain a more even balance between the two parties in that chamber. Arguments in favor of South Dakota's admission reiterated old claims that the territory's population justified such an action, that self-government was being denied to its citizens, that appointed officials were imposing outside rule on its people, and that such conditions bred fraud and corruption. To admit all of Dakota as a single state was unfeasible and unfair. The distances involved would make participation in government impossible for those without substantial resources. It would make for a government of the rich, court and legislative sessions would be inaccessible, and there was a danger that such a large entity would become "An Imperial State." Senator Platt cited Benjamin Franklin's contention that the proprietary government of Pennsylvania had been corrupt because of the veto power of appointive governors. Corruption always attended appointive officers. Dakota was now supporting its own government and no longer needed assistance from the federal government.

Senator Cushman K. Davis of Minnesota noted that now much of the opposition to statehood for South Dakota came from southern Democrats who had seceded from the Union in early 1861, just at the time that Dakota

Territory was being established. After the Civil War, these southern states had been readmitted with dispatch, whereas South Dakota continued to be denied its rightful place among them. Senator John Sherman of Ohio summed up the attitude of Republican champions of South Dakota when he noted, "Why should not South Dakota be admitted? In the name of heaven, why? Simply because the Democratic party did not want that state to be admitted? There is no use in going beyond that."[10] In the end, the Platt Bill passed the Senate along strictly party lines, 26-23, after a substitute bill for admission of the entire territory as a single state had been voted down by an identical margin.

The minority Republicans in the House managed to achieve something they had not been able to do since 1883, obtaining a hearing on the Dakota question and a debate on its merits. A strategic maneuver to attach statehood bills for Dakota, Washington, and Montana to a privileged resolution for a change in the rules brought the issue to the floor, where a lively debate occurred. Democrats in the House, like their counterparts in the Senate, sought admission for Dakota as a whole, along with Montana, Washington, and New Mexico. Up until this time, such stalling tactics had succeeded in preventing any action that would have brought South Dakota in as a state.

The election of 1888 changed all that. Benjamin Harrison's victory over Grover Cleveland and the Republican capture of both houses of Congress for the first time since 1875 made it certain that statehood for South Dakota would come quickly after the new administration took office. Congressional Democrats therefore wasted no time in changing their approach. Aware that they would no longer be able to block statehood for South Dakota, they now decided to support the proposal so as to reap some of the credit for bringing it in. The result was passage of the Omnibus Bill admitting four states simultaneously—South Dakota, North Dakota, Montana, and Washington. New Mexico would have to wait until 1912 to gain admission.

Southern Dakotans were cheered by the Republican nomination of Benjamin Harrison, who during the preceding decade had been their champion in the upper house of Congress. The senator ran a typical front-porch campaign, welcoming delegations of citizens who came to visit him at his home in Indianapolis. He relied on the party organization to get his message out to the electorate around the country. To one of these groups he noted that Dakotans were being "disfranchised and deprived of their appropriate influence in the electoral college only because the prevailing sentiment in the territory is Republican."[11] The party's national platform that year called for the immediate admission of South Dakota, whereas the Democratic platform continued its support for a single state.

The Democrats, under Congressman Springer, remained hopeful after the election that they might get admission of Dakota as a single state or at least get New Mexico added to the list of new states entering the Union. Both initiatives were designed to keep the Republican advantage in Congress to a minimum. But that was not to be. Republicans could afford to be patient now, knowing that they would soon have majorities in both houses. Understanding the situation, many Democrats thought they should salvage what they could. Samuel S. Cox of New York, a Jeffersonian Democrat then serving his thirteenth term in the House, played the key role in breaking the logjam in the House. A pragmatist with greater knowledge of state making than any of his colleagues, urged his fellow representatives to put aside partisanship and to seek a practical solution to the problem. He called for the admission of all the territories that had been under consideration except Utah and New Mexico. Now the process moved inexorably forward. The House passed the Omnibus Bill by a vote of 133 to 120. Following a number of conferences, the bill, put together largely by Congressman Springer in the House and Senators Butler, Cullom, and Platt in the Senate, moved toward passage.

On February 20, 1889, a week and a half before Harrison's inauguration, Congress finally passed the Omnibus Bill. It required the calling of constitutional conventions for the new states of South Dakota and North Dakota, the election of delegates, and final ratification of the documents that those bodies would draw up. Two days later, President Cleveland signed the bill into law. Rejoicing in southern Dakota commenced, but people there still had a job to do. The constitutional convention meeting in Sioux Falls on July 4 fulfilled its task expeditiously. Hardly anything in the 1885 document had to be modified except changing the dividing line from the 46th parallel to the 7th standard parallel and adding the prefix "South" to the name. The prohibition controversy was again resolved by providing for a separate ballot to be held on the issue. A vote on women's suffrage was delayed until a year after statehood was achieved. Beadle's school lands principle was again incorporated into the document, so the reformers were partially appeased. The delegates also reapportioned judicial and legislative districts and provided for splitting territorial property, debts, and records between the two states.

On October 1, 1889, voters went to the polls and overwhelmingly ratified the constitution, 70,131 to 3,267. They also approved constitutionally mandated prohibition by a much narrower margin, 40,234 to 34,510. A proposal for minority representation failed to pass. They chose Arthur C. Mellete for governor and other Republicans for state offices, selected a heavily Republican group of delegates for both houses of the bicameral legislature, and approved Pierre as a temporary state capital until a vote could be taken the following year on a permanent location. President Harrison, faced with the duty of signing documents admitting both North and South Dakota into the Union on November 2, deliberately shuffled the papers so that no one could know which one had priority. As the president put it, "They were born together; they were one and I will make them twins."[12] By general practice, however, North Dakota, which comes first in the alphabet, has been counted as the thirty-ninth state and South Dakota as the fortieth. In this regard, at least, after years of playing second-fiddle to its southern neighbor, North Dakota achieved precedence. Two weeks later, the new South Dakota legislature met in Pierre and proceeded to select two U.S. senators, Gideon Moody and Richard Pettigrew. The two men drew straws to determine who would get the two-year term and who would get the six-year one; Pettigrew wound up with the full term. For Mellette, Moody, and Pettigrew, the resolution of the statehood struggle brought along with it the kind of political preferment they had sought. Hugh J. Campbell, the "theorist" of the movement, came up empty-handed.

OTHER ISSUES AT THE TIME OF STATEHOOD

Gaining admission was certainly the most important event in South Dakota during the year of statehood in 1889, but it was not the only thing on people's minds. At least five other issues were also in the forefront of the electorate's thinking: growing agricultural distress and the question of how to address it, prohibition, women's suffrage, the location of the new state capital, and the desire to reduce the Great Sioux Reservation to open it up to further white settlement.

The group of the population that had demonstrated least interest in the battle for statehood, farmers, was also by far the largest. During the 1880s, Dakota Territory remained an agricultural frontier region. The towns that emerged and grew up during the Great Dakota Boom during the first half of the decade had as their primary and often their only function the provisioning and servicing of their surrounding agricultural hinterlands. Rapid settlement of the region had accompanied unusually wet seasons during the late 1870s and early 1880s, but in 1886 drought began to set in, and weather conditions worsened in subsequent years. Along with dry weather came erratic markets and softer prices for agricultural products. Farmers were being squeezed, and they sought targets for their wrath. The railroads, which had been so crucial to the boom in the first place, attracted much of their criticism. Protest groups began to emerge to do battle for the farmers' interests.

A territorial Farmers Alliance emerged in 1885, becoming the springboard for farm protest. The legislature that year created a railroad commission, but it proved to be ineffective. By the end of the 1880s, agitation for third party action was mounting, and in June 1890 in Huron an Independent Party was established, the forerunner of the Populists. South Dakota was in the forefront of populism, but the leaders of that movement and the leaders of the statehood drive were in large measure two separate groups.

The weakness of the farm advocates in politics was revealed by their failure to get their candidates selected for any of the high offices that became available with statehood. The new governor, Arthur C. Mellette, was a lawyer without any direct ties to the Farmers Alliance, and the two U.S. senators, Gideon C. Moody and Richard F. Pettigrew, likewise were lawyers who reached out for support from agrarians but had no intimate ties with them. They and the businessmen, lawyers, and editors who controlled the Republican Party machinery were less interested in addressing the farmers' needs than in controlling them politically so as not to embarrass themselves in their efforts to keep things smoothly running. "Mellette's correspondence after 1888 dealt with little else but the problem of controlling the farmers," writes Howard Lamar, "and it is damaging revelation of the small vision of these men that they were never once prepared to grant that the farmer had any right to enter the political forum as an equal."[13] The relatively light turnouts at the polls for the constitutions of 1883 and 1885 and for the proposal to divide the territory in 1887 reflected the apathy of the agrarian element of the population and the farmers' sense that statehood had little relevance for them and their effort to solve their economic problems.

Even when members of the political oligarchy attempted to address problems facing farmers, their efforts were not always welcomed. During the summer and fall of 1889, as the final process toward statehood worked itself out, drought conditions and poor farm prices hit the agrarian population hard. As land values declined, farmers left the land. Governor Mellette visited the counties in the greatest difficulty and traveled to Chicago to solicit donations for the distressed farmers as well as for town dwellers who depended on the farmers' business for their livelihood. His efforts were often not appreciated. The Sioux Falls *Argus-Leader* blamed the governor for tarnishing the image of the state by seeking outside help, berating the "scandal mongers" with their stories of "destitution in South Dakota." The Pierre *Free Press* worried that exaggerated stories about suffering in South Dakota might deter some people from wanting to move there but reassured people that no "permanent harm" would result from it.[14] Truth about conditions seemed to be less important to these editors and other South Dakota boosters than a favorable image of the state, regardless of its authenticity.

Another hotly debated issue in Dakota during the year of statehood was prohibition. The 1883 constitution had avoided the issue, and the 1885 version had turned it over to a popular vote. Wanting to ensure the best possible chances for admission in 1889, the constitutional convention had deflected potential controversy by providing for a separate ballot on the question of whether to include prohibition in the constitution. As elsewhere in the United States, the temperance issue generated heated controversy in Dakota during the late nineteenth century, dividing people along gender, class, occupational, ethnic, and religious lines. The Flandreau *Enterprise* captured the significance of the question when it commented in May, "The hardest political fight that Dakota has ever experienced is now opening. It is the fight over the question of constitutional prohibition."[15]

Early in the year, the territorial legislature passed a prohibition bill only to have it vetoed by Governor Church, who stated his opinion that the issue should be resolved through the constitutional process when statehood was achieved. A big two-day prohibition conference in Huron in March planned an organized drive to get a prohibition clause included in the constitution. The chairman of the executive committee placed in charge of the campaign was Visscher V. Barnes of Yankton, an ambitious Republican politician who had previously lived in De Smet and who would later be immortalized in Laura Ingalls Wilder's *Little Town on the Prairie*.

A clear-cut party division existed between the forces promoting and opposing prohibition, Republicans lining up with the former and Democrats with the latter. Most Republican politicians, beginning with Arthur C. Mellette, enthusiastically supported prohibition. They hosted a rally for the cause at their party convention that year before endorsing its inclusion in the constitution in their platform. They had the full support of the Women's Christian Temperance Union and most of the Protestant church bodies. Democrats, on the other hand, remained either skeptical about or opposed to a measure that they believed restricted individual freedom and would be impossible to enforce. German-Americans and especially German-Russian immigrants voiced their strong opposition to the proposal, and liquor dealers put together an active organization designed to prevent their own elimination. In voting to approve the constitution in October, the electorate also approved prohibition, but seven years later they repealed it.

The third major issue facing South Dakotans in 1889 was women's suffrage. Like prohibition, it generated constant controversy during the later years of the nineteenth century, and, in fact, the two propositions were closely linked. Many of the people in the forefront of the prohibition campaign were also prominent in the women's suffrage movement. Likewise, the ethnic groups, liquor interests, and politicians who opposed prohibition also were generally against giving women the ballot, because they correctly perceived that once women got the vote, they would likely move to ban liquor. Recognizing the potential political pitfalls of the issue, however, the Republican Party, like their Democratic counterparts, did not support it. It was not only men, however, who either shied away from advocating women's suffrage or actively opposed it. Some of the strongest opposition came from women who believed that "a woman's place was in the home."[16] Most of the religious denominations likewise either actively or passively opposed the granting of suffrage. Only the Methodists came out in support of it, and their motive was to link the issue with the drive for prohibition.[17]

What made the battle over women's suffrage particularly noteworthy was the decision of veteran women's rights campaigner Susan B. Anthony to interject herself into the contest and carry her message to the public. Several other prominent suffrage advocates, including Anna Howard Shaw and Carrie Chapman (later Catt), also spent time criss-crossing the state. Controversy seemed to attend their movements, because resistance to granting equality to women remained strong. Some of the suffragettes' problems, however, were their own doing. Differences over strategy split them. Based on long experience, Anthony argued for divorcing the suffrage drive from advocacy of prohibition, although she supported both causes. Marietta Bones of Webster, a leading

South Dakota suffragist, on the other hand, insisted on linking the issues. Further exacerbating internal tensions was a conflict over financial control, because Bones asserted that Anthony had misappropriated $40,000 of funds that had been entrusted to her for the suffrage campaign. In the end, the all-male electorate refused to grant women the vote on election day in 1890 by a margin of two to one.

No issue besides the question of statehood itself generated more heat and controversy during this period than the location of the capital of South Dakota.[18] Huron had led the contestants in the straw poll conducted in 1885. With actual admission into the Union, the battle was engaged all over again. Voters were charged with selecting a temporary capital while voting for the constitution in 1889, with the permanent capital to be designated by vote the following year. In this contest, the two leading candidates, Huron and Pierre, pulled out all the stops in desperate bids for primacy. Businessmen and politicians in both towns believed that becoming the capital city would bring financial ascendancy. Boosters in Pierre, a town that counted 3,235 residents in the 1890 census, predicted that they would number one hundred thousand in several decades' time if they got the designation. Huron residents, no less interested in capturing the crown, went to even greater lengths of spending, orating, deal-making, and outright vote-buying to try to win the designation. In the end, the hopes and dreams of the contestants look dubious. A half-century after being named the capital, Pierre still had not reached the ten thousand mark.[19]

Several other towns entered the competition: Watertown, Sioux Falls, Mitchell, and Chamberlain. All of them were less centrally located, however, than Pierre and Huron, and that hurt their chances. Indeed, the major issue in the contest was which town possessed the greatest geographic advantage. On its face, Pierre would seem to have carried this debate hands down, but Huron advanced some rather ingenious arguments to try to prove that it, in fact, deserved that designation. Pierre, Huron's supporters pointed out, sat across the Missouri River from the Great Sioux Reservation, and that put it on the edge of a "vast and desolate wasteland." Its location in the middle of the rich agricultural region of East River South Dakota made Huron the "most accessible" town from every part of "civilized" South Dakota, its proponents contended. They had maps that purported to show that even people in the Black Hills had easier access to Huron than to Pierre, because they could get there by railroad through northern Nebraska rather than having to travel by horse or wagon across the Great Sioux Reservation to Pierre.[20]

Only those who were already convinced would probably have accepted that argument, but Huron had some other advantages on its side. Newspapers were subsidized, city lots given away, drinks and theatre tickets handed out, rallies and parades organized, little boxes of soil handed out, and bets covered, all to influence votes. Many observers alleged that votes were literally bought.

None of it was enough. In the final balloting, Pierre defeated Huron by a tally of 27,096 to 14,944, with the other towns lagging behind.

Being designated the state capital was a great victory for Pierre, whose residents celebrated both after the preliminary vote in 1889 and then again a year later when that decision was confirmed in the second vote. But Pierrites in 1889 were at least as interested in reducing the size of the Great Sioux Reservation to their west so that more white settlers could move onto it. They hoped to profit substantially as an outfitting and jumping-off point for homesteaders moving out onto lands where the buffalo had once roamed, followed by Dakota who had depended on the hunt for their economic survival. During the 1880s, calls for opening the reservation intensified as the campaign for statehood picked up speed. "The opening of the Sioux Reservation means more to Pierre than anything else," editorialized the Pierre *Free Press* in 1885.[21] By 1889, the opening of the reservation and the granting of statehood were firmly linked in the public mind all over South Dakota as events that would bring major benefits to the entire area. For people in Pierre, having Pierre named as state capital would top it off. The Yankton *Telegram* noted that "the two events, the opening of the reservation and the location of the capital at Pierre, will do more to develop South Dakota than anything that has ever happened, and are next in importance to the division and admission of Dakota as two states."[22]

The Great Sioux Reservation, set aside under the terms of the Treaty of Fort Laramie of 1868, had already been reduced significantly in 1877 as punishment for the Native American defeat of George Armstrong Custer and the Seventh Cavalry at the Battle of the Little Big Horn the previous year. Efforts to "civilize" the Dakota and to convert them into peaceful, industrial farmers had made little progress in the meantime. The general assumption of whites in the territory was that the Native Americans did not need all of the land they nominally owned on the reservation and that much of it should be opened to white settlement and development. The general feeling was that the Sioux had plenty of land to give away, were too indolent to use what they had, and were undeserving of it in any case.

After several failures to obtain approval from three-fourths of the adult male Dakota to alienate more of their land, as was required under the provisions of the Treaty of Fort Laramie, Congress proceeded to draw up another treaty in 1889, this one for the purchase of 9 million acres in an "L" shape west of the Missouri River.[23] Much of the summer was taken up in visiting the various agencies on the reservations seeking to persuade, or, at times, browbeat the various subtribes of Teton Sioux to "touch the pen," that is, to give their approval to the treaty. The Rapid City *Daily Journal* voiced an opinion commonly held among the white population in an editorial. "The Sioux will never again be asked what shall be done for them by the government. They will be treated as the irresponsible, irrational creatures that they are. Congress will legislate for them without asking their opinions. The reservation will be opened. It must be opened."[24]

The pressure and intimidation worked. By early August the requisite number of signatures had been obtained. As they waited for statehood to become final, people in Pierre and also people around the territory prepared to move into areas that had formerly been held by the Dakota. The implications of this land grab only gradually became evident. Resentment over the hard-handed methods used by government officials to gain the Dakota's approval fed into approval for the Ghost Dance movement that swept over the reservation the following year. The result was the Wounded Knee Massacre at Pine Ridge, in southwestern South Dakota, on December 30, 1890. As many as three hundred Dakota, many of them women and children, were cut down by bullets from the rifles and machine guns of the same Seventh Cavalry that had fought with Custer at the Little Big Horn.

CONCLUSION

Jubilation over statehood, then, was mixed with confusion, fear, and ambivalence during 1889 and 1890. After a decade of postponement and growing resentment on the part of Dakota's southern citizenry, final entry into the Union was welcomed with great jubilation. Several other developments in the state—controversies over prohibition and the vote for women, the selection of a state capital, the reduction of the Great Sioux Reservation and the aftermath of that action, and economic distress and agrarian political revolt—made the situation in South Dakota a complicated one. It was a memorable time but one that invited repression of memory as well as celebration.

NOTES

1. Huron *Daily Huronite*, February 21, 1889; Pierre *Free Press*, November 14, 1889.

2. Quoted in Howard R. Lamar, *Dakota Territory, 1861-1889: A Study of Frontier Politics* (New Haven: Yale University Press, 1956), p. 205.

3. George W. Kingsbury, *History of Dakota Territory*, vol. 2 (Chicago: S. J. Clarke Publishing Company, 1915), p. 1611.

4. Lamar, *Dakota Territory*, p. 244.

5. Carrol G. Green, "The Struggle of South Dakota to Become a State," *South Dakota Historical Collections* 12 (1924): 508.

6. Ibid., p. 508.

7. Lamar, *Dakota Territory*, pp. 222–225.

8. B. E. Tiffany, "The Initiative and Referendum in South Dakota," *South Dakota Historical Collections* 12 (1924): 331–371.

9. Lamar, *Dakota Territory*, p. 252.

10. Quoted in Kingsbury, *History of Dakota Territory*, 2:1825.

11. Ibid., 2:1853–1854.

12. Ibid., 2:1935.

13. Lamar, *Dakota Territory*, p. 267.

14. Quoted in John E. Miller, "More Than Statehood on Their Minds: South Dakota Joins the Union," *Great Plains Quarterly* 10 (Fall 1990): 214–215.

15. Quoted in Huron *Daily Plainsman*, May 25, 1889.

16. Dorinda Riessen Reed, *The Woman Suffrage Movement in South Dakota* (Pierre: Commission on the Status of Women, 1975), pp. 20–47; Cecelia M. Wittmayer, "The 1889–1890 Woman Suffrage Campaign: A Need to Organize," *South Dakota History* 11 (Summer 1981): 206.

17. Dennis A. Norlin, "The Suffrage Movement and South Dakota Churches: Radicals and the Status Quo, 1890," *South Dakota History* 14 (Winter 1984): 314–315, 320.

18. John Elmer Dalton, "A History of the Location of the State Capital in South Dakota," Governmental Research Bureau, University of South Dakota, Report No. 14 (January 1945); "Capital and Capitol History of South Dakota," *South Dakota Historical Collections* 5 (1910): 175–182.

19. Dalton, "A History of the Location of the State Capital in South Dakota."

20. For maps, see Miller, "More than Statehood on Their Minds," pp. 211–213.

21. Pierre *Free Press*, September 24, 1885.

22. Yankton *Telegram*, quoted in Pierre *Free Press*, August 22, 1889.

23. Herbert T. Hoover, "The Sioux Agreement of 1889 and Its Aftermath," *South Dakota History* 19 (Spring 1989): 56–94.

24. Rapid City *Daily Journal*, quoted in Pierre *Free Press*, November 1, 1888.

BIBLIOGRAPHY

Gibson, Arrell Morgan. "State-Making in the New West." In *The West in the Life of the Nation*. Lexington, MA: D. C. Heath and Company, 1976.

Green, Carroll G. "The Struggle of South Dakota to Become a State." *South Dakota Historical Collections* 12 (1924): 503–540.

Kingsbury, George W. *History of Dakota Territory*. 2 vols. Chicago: The S. J. Clarke Publishing Company, 1915.

Lamar, Howard R. *Dakota Territory, 1861–1889: A Study of Frontier Politics*. New Haven, CT: Yale University Press, 1956.

Miller, John E. "More Than Statehood on Their Minds: South Dakota Joins the Union." *Great Plains Quarterly* 10 (Fall 1990): 206–217.

Pomeroy, Earl. *Territories and the United States, 1861–1890: Studies in Colonial Administration*. Philadelphia: University of Pennsylvania Press, 1947.

Remele, Larry. "'God Helps Those Who Help Themselves': The Farmers Alliance and Dakota Statehood." *Montana: The Magazine of Western History* 37 (Autumn 1987): 22–33.

Robinson, Doane. *History of South Dakota*. 2 vols. Logansport, IN: B.F. Bowen and Company, 1904.

Schell, Herbert S. *History of South Dakota*. Lincoln: University of Nebraska Press, 1975.

THE STATE OF TENNESSEE

Admitted to the Union as a State: June 1, 1796

Mark R. Cheathem

INTRODUCTION

The history of the state of Tennessee was similar, in many ways, to that of Kentucky, admitted as the fifteenth state in the Union on June 1, 1792. Richard Henderson's Transylvania Company, which played a prominent role in the permanent settlement of middle Tennessee, was also instrumental in settling Kentucky, which originally was part of Virginia's western frontier. Like Kentucky, Tennessee faced indifference from its state of origin, in its case, North Carolina; significant Native American problems; and neglect from the federal government. All three issues convinced Tennesseans that their best hope for survival on the frontier was statehood.

TERRITORIAL GOVERNMENT

Early Settlement in East Tennessee

Archaeologists believe that Paleo-Indians moved into what is now Tennessee as early as thirteen thousand years ago. European exploration of the region, however, had to wait until 1540, when Spanish explorer Hernando de Soto's expedition moved west across the Appalachian Mountains from North Carolina. Spain failed to follow up de Soto's journey with further expeditions, leaving the area free for French and English exploration in the late seventeenth century. Both countries laid claim to the territory, but France's defeat in the French and Indian War in 1763 left Britain in control.[1]

It was not until the late 1760s that permanent white settlement began in what became Tennessee. This migration into the trans-Appalachian region was

Tennessee

Territorial Development:

- Great Britain cedes future territory of Tennessee on September 3, 1783, with the Treaty of Paris
- The United States passes the Northwest Ordinance: territorial claims inherited from colonial charters ceded to the public domain, July 13, 1787
- Organized along with the future state of Kentucky as part of the Southwest Territory, May 26, 1790
- Southwest Territory is limited to the land comprising the future state of Tennessee after Kentucky achieves statehood, June 1, 1792
- Tennessee admitted into the Union as the sixteenth state, June 1, 1796

Territorial Capitals:

- Rocky Mount, 1792–1794
- Knoxville, 1794–1796

State Capitals:

- Knoxville, 1796–1812
- Nashville, 1812–1817
- Knoxville, 1817–1819
- Murfreesboro, 1819–1826
- Nashville, 1826–present

Origin of State Name: The Cherokee applied the name "Tanasi" to two small villages that bordered the river of the same name, and it is from this word, whose original meaning is unknown, that the state gets its name.

First Governor: John Sevier
Governmental Organization: Bicameral
Population at Statehood: 105,602
Geographical Size: 41,217 square miles

in opposition to Britain's Proclamation of 1763, which sought to restrict colonial settlement west of the Appalachian Mountains. Encouraged by reports of rich land and excellent game hunting, settlers, most of whom came from the colonies of North Carolina and Virginia, ignored the British edict and poured across the Appalachian Mountains into the Holston River region in what is now east Tennessee. They established four distinct communities there: North Holston, Watauga, Carter's Valley, and Nolichucky. After the Lochaber Treaty, negotiated between Great Britain and the Cherokee in 1770, proved unsuccessful in restricting the further movement of these whites into Cherokee territory, the British authorized an official survey of the boundaries in the Holston area. The survey team, led by Virginian John Donelson, found that three of the four white settlements in the disputed area were located outside British colonial authority and in violation of the legal boundaries specified in the Lochaber Treaty. The residents of Watauga, Carter's Valley, and Nolichucky were ordered to disband their communities and move off Cherokee land.[2]

The Watauga Association

Settlers in the three disputed communities responded by forming the Watauga Association in 1772. Their original intention was not to establish an independent state free from British authority but to maintain control of the lands on which they had settled. The association established a constitution, called the Watauga Compact, based on Virginia law, and a government consisting of five elected judges, who performed executive, judiciary, and legislative functions. During the four years of its existence, the leaders of the association settled judicial disputes, organized a militia, and successfully convinced the Cherokee to let them lease their land for ten years.[3]

When the Revolutionary War began in 1775, the association reorganized itself into the Washington District and appointed a thirteen-member committee to govern the newly named region. In 1776, this committee sent petitions to Virginia and North Carolina requesting annexation. The petition to North Carolina recounted the history of the Watauga Association, assuring the North Carolina government that its members were not "a lawless mob." Their argument apparently convinced North Carolina's leaders, who authorized the association to send five representatives to the state's constitutional convention that November. Once the North Carolina constitution was in place and elections were held, the state legislature voted in 1777 to name the former Watauga communities Washington County, solidifying their placement under the state's jurisdiction.[4]

Early Settlement in Middle Tennessee

The Watauga Association's success in the Holston region spurred white settlers' interest in the Cumberland River area, which the Cherokee also controlled, in what is now middle Tennessee. In March 1775, North Carolina district judge Richard Henderson, who owned the Transylvania Land Company, negotiated the Treaty of Sycamore Shoals with the Cherokee. Henderson's company obtained nearly twenty million acres, including modern-day middle Tennessee, for a pittance. The treaty allowed the British to convince those Cherokees who opposed the land cession to fight against the western settlers. This hostility, born out of white land greed and native resistance to further intrusion on their land, continued throughout the Revolutionary War and after.[5]

Cherokee defiance failed to stop permanent white settlement of the Cumberland region. Eager to protect his land claims there, Richard Henderson asked John Donelson, the Virginia surveyor, and James Robertson, one of the leaders of the Watauga settlement, to explore the area north of the Cumberland River and, if they found it viable for permanent settlement, to establish a community there. In the spring of 1779, Robertson made his initial foray into the Cumberland Basin, penetrating as far as the French Lick on the Cumberland River. He returned to the Holston settlements convinced that permanent establishment near the Cumberland was feasible and should be undertaken immediately. Fired by Robertson's enthusiasm, Henderson and Donelson agreed to pursue the endeavor. In the fall of 1779, Robertson took his party by land, crossing through the Cumberland Gap into present-day Kentucky, then traveling south to the Cumberland region that he had found so habitable. They arrived at the French Lick in December and began building Fort Nashborough, site of what is now the state capital of Nashville. Meanwhile, Donelson's party set out in December 1779, following the Tennessee River through the present-day states of Tennessee, Alabama, and Kentucky. Once in Kentucky, they took the Cumberland River southeastward and met up with Robertson at Fort Nashborough in April 1780.[6]

The Cumberland Compact

Although considered part of North Carolina's Washington County, the Cumberland settlers decided that the two hundred miles between their settlements and the county court made establishing a governing body a necessity. So, on May 1, 1780, 256 men in the settlements signed the Cumberland Compact. This document established a council of twelve "conscientious and [deserving] persons," or judges, to be elected from the eight Cumberland settlements, referred to in the compact as "stations." It authorized the twelve judges to govern the settlements and settle disputes. The agreement was especially democratic. All "free men…over the age [of twenty] one years" were allowed to vote, and if "the people in general [were] dissatisfied" with those elected, they could simply "call a new election at any of the said stations, and elect others in their stead." The compact also established a militia and compelled all men over the age of sixteen to serve if needed.[7]

Seemingly intent on avoiding another Watauga Association movement, North Carolina paid close attention to the Cumberland settlements in the

1780s. In 1783, the state organized them into Davidson County and allowed residents to elect two representatives to the North Carolina legislature. One of the representatives, James Robertson, convinced powerful North Carolina land speculator William Blount to submit legislation changing Fort Nashborough's name to Nashville and making it the county seat. Two years later, Davidson County was divided to create a new county, Sumner County. In 1788, Tennessee County was created by subdivisions of both Davidson and Sumner Counties. Together these three counties made up North Carolina's Mero District.[8]

The use of the name "Mero" for the North Carolina district indicated that Cumberland residents were not completely satisfied with North Carolina's efforts. The state government seemed unconcerned about Native American attacks, which the Cumberland settlers believed were being encouraged by the Spanish in Louisiana, and about Spanish threats to close off American trade on the Mississippi River. Finding their appeals to the North Carolina government unanswered, Robertson and other Cumberland leaders moved to woo the Spanish. Robertson introduced the legislation naming the three Cumberland counties after the Spanish governor of Louisiana, Don Estevan Miro. (The misspelling of his name was an inexplicable mistake.) Robertson and other Cumberland leaders, including justice of the peace and land surveyor Daniel Smith, opened correspondence with Spanish officials concerning the Native American attacks and navigation rights on the Mississippi. The Cumberland settlers used their intrigues with Spain to prompt North Carolina into concentrating more on its western settlements.[9]

The Creation of the State of Franklin

Dissatisfaction with the North Carolina government had also reemerged in the Holston settlements and led leaders there to attempt establishing an independent state. Several factors contributed to the movement. The division of the Washington District into three counties, Washington, Greene, and Sullivan, gave residents and leaders greater political organization and local control. In an attempt to generate revenue, the Confederation Congress in Philadelphia encouraged states to cede their western lands to the central government, which would then sell them. The Confederation Congress additionally indicated a desire to form new states out of the western lands. North Carolina refused to follow the congress's recommendation and in 1783, began selling title to its western lands. This decision stimulated interest in the western frontier among North Carolina land speculators, who controlled the state legislature, and potential landowners. This interest, coupled with the indifference of other North Carolinians to the western part of the state, convinced North Carolina in 1784 to cede its land to Congress with the understanding that all land claims would be honored.[10]

Taking advantage of North Carolina's indifference toward its trans-montane lands, John Sevier, Arthur Campbell, and other western frontier leaders immediately moved to establish a separate state. In August 1784, these leaders met at Jonesboro. The forty attendees, who selected Sevier as their chairperson, voted unanimously in favor of statehood. The group also elected delegates to a convention, set to meet in December of that year, that would draw up a state constitution. In November 1784, however, the North Carolina legislature decided to repeal its land cession to the Confederation Congress. This result placed the independence movement brewing on the western frontier in the position of deciding whether to remain loyal to North Carolina or to continue pursuing statehood.[11]

The leaders of the movement chose independence. On December 14, forty-three delegates assembled in Jonesboro and began drawing up a provisional constitution. They rationalized their actions by alluding to the 1784 cession, the willingness of Congress to form new states, the inability of North Carolina to defend its western inhabitants against Native American attacks, and geographical necessity. Their final reason, they believed, provided the only necessary justification: "We unanimously agree that our lives, liberties and property can be more secure and our happiness much better propagated by our separation; and consequently that it is our duty and inalienable right to form ourselves into a new and independent state." The provisional constitution included a declaration of rights, which emphasized that "all political power is vested in and derived from the people," and plans for political representation, suffrage, and government organization and powers. The delegates voted to name the proposed state after the famous American statesman, Benjamin Franklin, and also selected provisional government officers, most importantly naming John Sevier as governor.[12]

The December meeting revealed significant support for a new state, but it also demonstrated that divisions existed among the delegates. The vote for statehood, which went 28-15 in favor of independence, showed a clear lack of unanimity. Sevier in many ways typified the reluctance of some delegates. He feared that forming a new state would harm his speculative ventures. Yet he also worried that failing to support the state of Franklin would lead to his political and economic ostracism if the independence movement succeeded. So, in the words of one historian, Sevier "opposed the movement until he saw that it would proceed without him and then grasped the reins of power." Although Sevier held a unique position of power, other delegates also seemed to fear the effect of independence on their futures but apparently dreaded even more missing the opportunity that Franklin's existence might provide them.[13]

The next year, tensions between the Franklin leaders and the North Carolina government escalated. The first General Assembly of Franklin met in March 1785 and began its business of government. The meeting provoked North Carolina Governor Alexander Martin to threaten the use of his state's militia to end the Franklin movement, a move that Sevier and the Franklin leaders denounced. Richard Caswell's ascension to the governor's chair in North Carolina eased the strained relations somewhat, but it did not keep Franklinites from sending a representative, William Cocke, to the Confederation Congress to negotiate for their state's admission into the proposed Union. A noted North Carolina lawyer and politician, Cocke failed in his primary mission when only seven of the required states voted in favor of Franklin's inclusion. He and other Franklin leaders took heart, however, from the positive response expressed by many congressional members.[14]

Unfortunately for Cocke, Sevier, and other Franklin supporters, the proposed state never achieved independence. A meeting of Franklinites in November 1785 failed to produce a permanent constitution, although the General Assembly continued to meet over the next few years, appointing government officials and even negotiating treaties with the Cherokee. At the same time, however, North Carolina moved more aggressively to reduce support for Franklin. Anti-Franklin members of the state legislature appointed Franklinites to their body, hoping to tie them more closely to North Carolina. In 1787, the state agreed to forgive western residents of the state (meaning those in the Franklin counties) for back taxes that they owed. Any hope that Franklin leaders expected from the 1787 meeting of the states in Philadelphia, Pennsylvania, was dashed when the delegates wrote into the U.S. Constitution a stipulation that current states had to approve the formation of new states within their borders. The Franklin movement staggered on until 1789, but it effectively ended the previous year, when Sevier's term as governor expired and no new elections took place. The Franklin experiment had failed to help frontier settlers realize their desire for a separate state.[15]

The Creation of the Southwest Territory

By the time North Carolina entered in the Union as the twelfth state in 1789, it was once again ready to rid itself of its western lands and their trouble-making residents. The establishment of the state of Franklin had faltered, but frontier leaders spent 1788 and 1789 renewing communications with the Spanish. They were presumably trying to ascertain if Governor Miro was still interested in extending his nation's claim over the region. At the same time, frontier settlers also began petitioning the North Carolina government to cede the western lands on which they lived to the new federal government. Their motivation was not simply independence, greed, or jealousy, although those reasons also played a role in the request. Native American attacks had increased, and frontier settlers were once again looking for government help in defending their homes.[16]

North Carolina leaders listened and, on December 22, 1789, ceded the state's western lands to the United States. The decision made sense on many levels. Frontier settlers wanted the federal government to provide the political stability and military protection that North Carolina could not and would not give them. North Carolina needed to relieve itself of a financially draining and politically volatile region. The federal government hoped to use the ceded lands to generate revenue through land sales, drive off troublesome Native Americans, and give it control of territory still threatened by the British and the Spanish.[17]

A precedent for creating a territory from the western lands was already in place. In 1787, Congress had passed "An Ordinance for the government of the territory of the United States North west of the river Ohio," or the Northwest Ordinance. This legislation gave the federal government control over 265,000 square miles. The ordinance specified that three to five states could be created from the territory; the states of Ohio, Indiana, Illinois, Michigan, Wisconsin, and part of Minnesota were eventually created from the Northwest Territory.[18]

Under the Northwest Ordinance, three stages were required to realize statehood. In the initial stage, the president appointed and the Senate confirmed a territorial governor, a court of three judges, and a secretary. The governor appointed the necessary local officials, controlled the militia, and issued executive orders. The judges oversaw the justice proceedings and, acting in concert with the governor, issued laws. The secretary served as the territory's record-keeper and the governor's aide. Once the territory's population reached five thousand free adult males, the second stage began. At that point, residents of the Northwest Territory would be allowed to elect, by popular vote, representatives to the lower house of a legislature. These representatives would then nominate ten residents, five of whom Congress would select to serve in the upper house, or legislative council. The house and council formed the territorial legislature, also known as the General Assembly, which worked with the governor to produce laws. The Ordinance also directed the General Assembly to elect a delegate to Congress. This territorial delegate had the right to participate in debate but not to vote in the national legislature. To achieve statehood, the population of the territory had to exceed sixty thousand free residents, at which time Congress would consider its application to become a state. If accepted into the Union, the new state would be "on an equal footing with the original States, in all respects whatever." The new state would then be allowed "to form a permanent Constitution and State Government; provided the Constitution and Government so to be formed, shall be Republican."[19]

With that precedent in mind, on May 26, 1790, the U.S. Congress organized North Carolina's ceded lands into "the territory of the United States, south of the river Ohio," more commonly called the Southwest Territory. This new territory was established following the guidelines provided by the Northwest Ordinance. Like its counterpart in the northwest, the Southwest Territory would protect religious freedom and basic civil rights, including the rights of *habeas corpus* and trial by a jury of peers. With "Religion, Morality and knowledge being necessary to good government and the happiness of mankind," the Southwest Territory would also promote "Schools and the means of education." The only substantial difference between the two territories involved slavery. The Northwest Ordinance specifically prohibited slavery and involuntary servitude except as punishment for convicted criminals. It did allow slaveowners to pursue and capture their fugitive slaves. North Carolina's cession act, however, stipulated that "no regulations made or to be made by Congress shall tend to emancipate Slaves." In accepting the land cession, Congress agreed to that condition, thus protecting the institution.[20]

With the legislation in place, President George Washington appointed the territorial officials. For governor, he bypassed John Sevier and instead chose William Blount, a former Revolutionary War soldier, member of the Continental Congress, delegate to the 1787 Constitutional Convention, and representative in the North Carolina legislature. Blount was also a land speculator who owned nearly one million acres of land in the Southwest Territory. Along with his position of governor, Blount was given the title of superintendent of Indian affairs in the Southern Department. Washington appointed Daniel Smith as the territory's secretary and selected John McNairy, David Campbell, and Joseph Anderson as the territory's three judges. Smith was a prominent figure in the Mero District, serving as justice of the peace and general of the district's militia. McNairy was a judge in the Mero District. Campbell had been a prominent member of the Franklin independence movement and was serving as judge in the Washington District when he received his appointment. Anderson, whom Washington appointed when his original choice, William Peery, turned down the offer, had served as an officer in the Revolutionary War. Upon Blount's recommendation, John Sevier took charge of the militia in the Washington District, and James Robertson succeeded Daniel Smith as commander of the Mero District militia.[21]

Governing the Southwest Territory

William Blount established his residence at William Cobb's Washington County home, Rocky Mount, making it the first capital of the Southwest Territory. (The capital would later move 105 miles southwest to White's Fort, the site of Knoxville.) From there, the governor began visiting the Washington District, comprised of Greene, Hawkins, Sullivan, and Washington counties, in the Holston region and the Mero District, consisting of Davidson, Sumner, and Tennessee counties, in the Cumberland region. Blount used the trips to inform residents of the creation of the Southwest Territory. The response he received was usually positive. In the Washington District, residents enthusiastically indicated their support for the Southwest Territory's formation, hoping that it would allow them to begin moving westward. In the Mero District, the residents' excitement was more restrained because of fear that Native American attacks would continue unabated regardless of the change in government.

Blount also made political appointments on his visits. Typically, he retained officeholders in the positions they held, whereas newly created offices went to influential men who supported Blount and the new government. For example, William Cocke, one of the staunchest supporters of the State of Franklin, became the attorney general for the Washington District, and Andrew Jackson, an up-and-coming lawyer in Nashville, received the same position in the Mero District. Both men were strong allies upon whom Blount could depend.[22]

One of Blount's most important tasks was authorizing an official census of the territory's residents. He ordered the militia in the seven counties to gather on the last Saturday in July and "obtain on that day an actual enumeration of the people within the limits" of the county districts. The results were incomplete, according to Blount's own appraisal, but nonetheless surprising. The Washington District contained 28,649 residents, including 2,256 slaves. Greene was the largest county, with Hawkins next in population, then Washington and Sullivan counties. The census even counted 3,619 individuals living south of the French Broad River in Cherokee territory. The Mero District was much smaller, counting only 7,042 residents. Davidson County had the largest population, with Sumner second and Tennessee third. Whereas the number of slaves made up only 7.9 percent of the total population in the Washington District, the 1,161 slaves in the Mero District constituted 16.5 percent of the total population. For territorial government, however, the most important statistic was the 6,271 free white males over the age of twenty-one. This number exceeded the minimum of five thousand necessary for establishing a territorial legislature as provided by the Northwest Ordinance, but Blount made no move to call for elections.[23]

Instead, Blount turned his attention to what he and many others believed was the most pressing issue facing his government: white conflict with Native Americans over land in the Southwest Territory. As superintendent of Indian affairs in the Southern Department, Blount had to resolve problems with two of the four major native groups in the territory: the Creek and the Cherokee. (Of the other two groups, the Chickasaw, had predominantly friendly relations with white settlers, and the Choctaw had removed themselves from events in the Southwest Territory several years previously.) The Creek particularly opposed the Cumberland settlement in the Mero District. Ignoring the 1785 Treaty of Hopewell, in which the Cherokee had agreed to allow the Cumberland settlements to exist, the Creek had made life extremely difficult for those settlers. Their frequent raids disrupted life for residents of Nashville and surrounding communities. Fearing that the Spanish were encouraging the natives' violence, President Washington attempted to resolve the problem by inviting Creek representatives, including their flamboyant mixed-blood chief Alexander McGillivray, to New York for a peace conference. The resulting Treaty of New York, signed in August 1790, aimed to put an end to hostile relations. The Creek pledged their loyalty to the United States, agreed not to form alliances with other nations, and promised to report troublemakers in their midst. In return, the United States pledged to maintain the existing boundaries of the Creek people, to allow them to punish white trespassers, and to assist them in agricultural endeavors.[24]

Although the Creek were troublesome, the Cherokee presented a larger problem for Blount and residents of the Southwest Territory. The Treaty of Hopewell had not succeeded in resolving tensions between whites and Cherokees. Instead, they grew worse when white settlers moved onto Cherokee land south of the French Broad River and North Carolina's government established Greene and Hawkins counties outside the boundaries of the treaty. With the Northwest Territory engulfed in combat between the United States and Native Americans, President Washington, Secretary of War Henry Knox, and members of Congress pressed Blount to sign a new treaty with the Cherokee that would keep the United States from having to fight wars in two regions. Blount agreed and sent emissaries to the Cherokee asking them to meet for a peace conference. Representatives for both sides assembled on the Holston River from late May to early July of 1791. By the end of the negotiations, the two groups had reached familiar terms. The Cherokee agreed, among other things, to give up more land and to allow "free and unmolested use of a road from Washington district to Mero district, and of the navigation of the Tennessee river." In exchange, the United States promised to pay the Cherokee an annuity of $1,000, gave them the right to punish white individuals settling illegally on Cherokee land, and prohibited U.S. citizens from trespassing on Cherokee hunting grounds.[25]

Neither treaty, however, ended the hostility between whites and Native Americans. Tensions in the Mero District ran especially high over the next few years. In August 1791, leaders there sent a memorial to President Washington asking him for more federal protection from native attacks. Secretary of War Knox responded to their request, recommending that Blount use the territory's militia for defense and urging him to punish white settlers who violated the treaties. Blount failed to make the suggested changes, and in September 1792, warriors from the Chickamauga towns attacked Buchanan's Station, a small settlement just outside of Nashville. White settlers were able to repel the assault, which one historian has called "the last major Indian attack on the Cumberland." Periodic skirmishes and raids continued, however, increasing the Mero District's residents' resentment toward the United States.[26]

The Washington administration based its decision not to send federal troops to assist the Southwest Territory on several factors, including lack of resources, fear of united Native American military action in the Northwest Territory, and concern about Spanish encouragement of Native American violence. In 1791, the United States was fighting Native Americans in the Northwest Territory and simply could not spare any military support for protection against what it considered minor attacks on the southwestern frontier. A major American defeat in November 1791 only increased the federal government's reluctance to help Blount's government and its willingness to make concessions to Native American requests. One such request came in late December 1791, when a delegation of Cherokee chiefs unexpectedly arrived in Philadelphia for a meeting with President Washington. They demanded amendments to the Treaty of Holston, including provisions for more money for their annuity and more stringent punishment of trespassers on their land. The administration gave them those concessions and even ordered Blount to furnish the chiefs protection as they returned home. The retirement of Spanish Governor Don Estevan Miro in late 1791 also caused the Washington administration some anxiety. His replacement in Louisiana, Luis Carondelet, made clear his desire to stop further American settlement to the west and announced his intention to organize the southern Native American groups into a defensive military alliance.[27]

All these actions alarmed leaders and residents of the Southwest Territory. A petition from residents of Tennessee County to James Robertson clearly indicated the fear that they felt. We "have much to dred from the Indians as the Spring Season Approaches," the petition read. "The Recent Murders & ravages Committed by them on our Frontiers, too evidently proves their Intentions on this quarter." Governor Blount did not ignore these pleas for help. In 1792, he held two separate conferences with Native American representatives, hoping to create friendly relations. The attack on Buchanan's Station in September 1792 and other clashes between whites and Native Americans, however, helped to end those diplomatic efforts. The arrival in February 1793 of a company of federal troops was too little, too late. Frontier settlers had determined to take other action.[28]

In early June 1793, Governor Blount set out for Philadelphia on a mission to convince President Washington to act militarily against the Southwest Territory's Native Americans. Before leaving, he ordered an armed expedition against a group of Cherokee warriors that had been raiding settlements in the eastern part of the territory. Ignoring Blount's directives not to enter Cherokee territory, the expedition's leader, Captain John Beard, and his men killed nearly a dozen natives, none of whom seemed to have been part of the raiding party. Daniel Smith, acting as governor in Blount's absence, immediately condemned the killings and apologized to Hanging Maw, the Cherokee chief whose village had been attacked and whose wife had died in the carnage. Blount tried to use Beard's raid to convince President Washington to change his administration's attitude toward the Native American problem in the Southwest Territory, but the president remained unyielding in his advocacy of a defensive posture. The result of Beard's excursion and the federal government's inaction was several months of attacks by both sides, although the Cherokee bore the brunt of the fighting. John Beard, defiant in the face of a pending court-martial because of his earlier mission, led another raid against a Cherokee town, and John Sevier, under orders from Daniel Smith, launched a massive attack on the Cherokee town of Etowah in October.[29]

When Blount returned to Knoxville, which had been the territory's capital since 1791, he faced an angry populace. Residents of the Southwest Territory were furious at the federal government's treatment of their situation. They were also unhappy with their governor's inability both to convince the Washington administration of their plight and to stop the native attacks. Residents also complained that laws requiring local officials to send revenue to Daniel Smith's office gave the territorial government too much taxation power. All these problems led some frontier residents to leave the territory, moving south into Spanish-controlled areas or north into the state of Kentucky. Some suggested that independence from the national government was their only recourse. Many more began arguing that a territorial legislature would help alleviate their problems.[30]

Formation of the Territorial Legislature

When Blount had reported the results of the 1791 census to President Washington, he had claimed that "the heads of families very generally were opposed to giving in their numbers [for the census]—fearing a General Assembly would shortly be the consequence." The accuracy of his 1791 report is debatable. What is certain is that pressure for a legislature had been growing since the territory's establishment. During the summer of 1793, Blount began to recognize that his political future rested on his response to calls for a territorial legislature. While still meeting with administration officials in Philadelphia, Blount ordered the local militia in the Southwest Territory to canvass their districts and ascertain if eligible voters favored the calling of a general assembly. To government officials back in the territory, he cast himself as looking out for the best interests of the people. "My object in administering the government has been to please the people," he wrote John Sevier. "If the people wished an Assembly I wished them to have it, and still wish it, of the people believe it will be for their benefit."[31]

The people did want a legislature and let Blount know it. An address from the people of the recently created Hamilton District, consisting of the new counties of Jefferson and Knox, seemed to convince Blount to act. On October 19, 1793, the governor set the date of the elections, to take place under the guidelines set by the Northwest Ordinance, for December. The eligible voters of the Southwest Territory would elect thirteen representatives; Washington, Hawkins, Jefferson, and Knox counties would each elect two; Sullivan, Greene, Tennessee, Davidson, and Sumner counties would each elect only one. To be eligible for election, candidates had to be either a U.S. citizen and a resident of the territory or have been a resident of the territory for three years and own at least two hundred acres of property. The elections took place, although not without political squabbling and accusations of fraud, as scheduled.[32]

Based on these criteria, the representatives elected to the General Assembly embodied the upper echelon of white frontier society. Leroy Taylor and John Tipton represented Washington County. William Cocke and Joseph

McMinn served the people of Hawkins County; Alexander Kelly and John Beard won election in Knox County. Samuel Wear and George Dohorty were Jefferson County's designated winners. Voters in Sullivan County elected George Rutledge, and those in Greene County elected Joseph Hardin. Dr. James White, who would later serve as the territory's congressional delegate, represented Davidson County. The other two members of the legislature were David Wilson of Sumner County and James Ford of Tennessee County. Blount ordered them to meet in Knoxville in late February 1794 to begin their business.[33]

The most important task faced by these thirteen representatives in February was that of nominating ten men, from whom President Washington would select five to serve as councilors in the upper house of the General Assembly. According to the Northwest Ordinance, these men had to own five hundred acres of land to be eligible for appointment. The five who were nominated but not selected were William Fort, Richard Gammon, David Russell, Adam Meek, and John Adair. All five of the councilors chosen by President Washington— Stockley Donelson, Griffith Rutherford, John Sevier, Parmenas Taylor, and James Winchester—were land speculators and Blount supporters. Donelson, who was a land speculator, was one of explorer John Donelson's sons, and he also happened to be Andrew Jackson's brother-in-law. Rutherford, who was originally from Ireland, was a land surveyor and speculator. Sevier, of course, was already a prominent land speculator and political figure. Not much is known about Taylor, except that he seemed to be the most unexpected choice of the five. Winchester was an entrepreneur and militia commander in Sumner County.[34]

In addition to submitting nominations for members of the upper house, the thirteen representatives also tended to another important duty. Against Blount's instructions, the representatives composed a petition, which they delivered to the governor, and a memorial, which they forwarded to Congress. The petition requested the territorial government's protection against Native American attacks, noting that since 1791 these attacks had resulted in the deaths of nearly two hundred white residents and the destruction of more than $100,000 worth of property. It asked Blount to consider building a minimum of twenty-four military posts to protect the frontier settlements and to provide militia to support the forts. The memorial noted the threat that Native Americans posed to the settlers in the Southwest Territory and asked the federal government to provide equal protection to their settlements as they did for more populated areas. The house then adjourned, set to meet again as a full legislature, councilors and all, in August 1794.[35]

Blount attempted to use the intervening months to respond to the legislature's concerns. He asked Dr. James White to submit the representatives' memorial to the U.S. House of Representatives, hoping that "efficient measures will be taken to stay the savage hand from the repetition of such horrid acts as [the residents of the Mero District had] too long been compelled to submit to." White did as asked and received promises of assistance both from Congress and Secretary of War Knox. Obtaining delivery of those promises proved difficult, however. In the end, the Southwest Territory received only encouragement to use local militia, six small howitzers with accompanying ammunition, and two hundred "old muskets wanting repair." In the Mero District, Andrew Jackson noted, "this Country is Declining [fast] and unless Congress lends us a more am[ple] protection this Country will have at length [to break] or seek a protection from some other Source than the present."[36]

While representatives of the Southwest Territory were appealing to the federal government for help, the Native Americans about whom they complained were also petitioning Washington's administration for perceived wrongs. In June, a Cherokee delegation visited Philadelphia to ask for changes in the Treaty of Holston. The most important change involved an increase in the annual payment from $1,500 to $5,000. Later that summer, the Chickasaw chief Piomingo led a delegation of his people to Philadelphia to meet with President Washington. The president thanked them for their military support against other Native American groups and promised to reward them for their alliance with a $3,000 annuity.[37]

With Native American relations seemingly improving, the territorial legislature met in Knoxville on August 25, 1794. The thirteen representatives and the five councilors took the oath of office that first day. The next day, the council chose Griffith Rutherford as its president, and the house elected David Wilson as its speaker. In later sessions, the General Assembly selected James White over William Cocke as territorial delegate to Congress, where he would sit in the House as a nonvoting member. Over the course of the session, the legislature met in a private home, in a local tavern, and at the courthouse. The atmosphere of at least one of these meeting places and the perception of frontier rowdiness undoubtedly led the house to pass rules of conduct for its members. Representatives were supposed to cover their heads when seated and were expected to remain seated when someone else had the floor. To have the opportunity to address the other members, representatives had to stand quietly beside their chairs until recognized by the speaker.[38]

With necessary appointments made and preliminary guidelines set, the General Assembly moved on to the business of enacting legislation. The body spent great effort on adopting acts intended to regulate the territory's judicial system, including introducing new schedules for the meeting of county, district, and superior courts and the construction of courthouses in Jonesborough and Nashville. The legislators created a new county, named for John Sevier, out of part of Jefferson County and recognized the city of Knoxville. Additionally, the legislature established Greeneville College, which later became Tusculum College, in Greene County and Blount College, which was the forerunner of the University of Tennessee, in Knoxville.

Money is a concern for any government, and the Southwest Territory's situation was no different. The elected representatives passed property and land tax measures intended to produce revenue for the territorial government. To handle the revenue, the legislature created a treasury department with two treasurers: one representing the east and the other representing the Cumberland settlements. Showing concern for internal improvements, the General Assembly set up a lottery in hopes of raising money to establish a road between the Hamilton and Mero districts. John Sevier, who served on the council, introduced a bill, which the legislature approved, that provided relief for militia members who had been severely injured and for the families of those who had died while in service.

All of these matters were important to the legislators and their constituents, but the main concern remained the uneasy relations with Native Americans. The federal government's generosity and friendliness toward Native Americans in the Southwest Territory had failed to alleviate white settlers' fears concerning Indian hostility. Three days into the legislative session, circumstances brought home the reality of the hostile relations. On August 27, the assembly voted to allow its two Knox County representatives, Alexander Kelly and John Beard, leaves of absence to help determine if rumors of native attack on Knoxville were true. The reports concerning Knoxville proved unfounded, but others did not. On September 8, one of the councilors, James Winchester, requested and was granted a leave of absence to return to Sumner County. His request apparently had something to do with Native American attacks near his home, Cragfont.[39]

A more dangerous encounter occurred just days later. On September 13, a military force of nearly 550 men, under the direction of Major James Ore, set out from Nashville, intent on inflicting devastation on the Chickamauga in the southeastern region of the territory. Ore's men destroyed the Chickamauga towns of Nickajack and Running Water and, with them, any future Chickamauga opposition. James Robertson, commander of the Mero District militia and also a brigadier general in the U.S. Army, had secretly worked to coordinate the attack on the Chickamauga. His complicity in the events led him to resign his position as brigadier general, but he still defended the attack. Governor Blount probably knew of Robertson's plans and may even have participated in formulating them.[40]

Recognizing the widespread anxiety in the Southwest Territory, the legislature on September 15 adopted a memorial to Congress outlining the need for federal intervention. Between February and September, a Knoxville newspaper noted, hostile Cherokee and Creek had killed sixty-seven residents, wounded or captured nearly another three dozen, and stolen almost four hundred horses. The General Assembly, speaking for those it represented, demanded that the Washington administration reconsider its treatment of Native Americans. Treaty making and annuities simply were not working, the legislators complained. "Fear, not love is the only means by which Indians can be governed," the memorial argued.[41]

DEBATE OVER STATEHOOD

The General Assembly was not content merely to wait for Congress to act. On September 5, it asked Governor Blount to conduct a new census the following July. The purpose of the census was to ensure that representation was fairly apportioned. On September 29, the legislature went further. It asked Blount to use the census as a means of determining whether there existed sufficient sentiment among the people to explore statehood. The legislature's reasoning was clear: if the federal government would not give settlers in the Southwest Territory protection, maybe it would defend residents of a new state. When Blount adjourned the General Assembly on September 30, 1794, he and the legislators could claim that the General Assembly's session had been a success. Conflicts with both the federal government and Native Americans over the next several months only confirmed their belief that the avenue to peace and protection was through statehood.

Blount's tense relationship with the Washington administration played a large role in bringing about Tennessee statehood. Governor William Blount was popular among frontier residents, especially since the calling of the legislature, but in 1795 he ran into trouble with Washington's administration. Henry Knox resigned as secretary of war in late 1794. He had enjoyed a good relationship with the territorial governor and understood residents' frustrations, even if he did little tangible to help them. On the other hand, Knox's replacement, Timothy Pickering of Massachusetts, had no sympathy for settlers in the Southwest Territory and was cynical about their motivations, especially Blount's. Pickering believed, with some validity, that part of the settlers' rationale for requesting federal assistance was to seize Native American lands for their own economic and personal gain. According to one historian, "the change from trust to suspicion in the office of the secretary of war would have its role in accelerating the territory toward statehood."[42]

Because Pickering maintained that the federal government would give no help against Native Americans, the Blount government attempted, as it had before, to resolve the situation itself. In November 1794, Blount had met with lower- and upper-town Cherokee representatives and reached a peace agreement. Creek warriors, however, continued to harass white settlements. Blount wrote Pickering in January 1795 that the "blood-thirsty [Creek] Nation, will [n]ever cease to murder and rob those Citizens, until it is severely chastised." The governor used his government's new harmony with the Cherokee to convince them to join the Choctaw, Chickasaw, and white settlers in a frontier war against the Creek.[43]

Blount's actions, however, only served to stir up enmity and violence among the various Native American groups and to bring down the ire of the federal government on his head. The Creek increased their attacks on white settlements in the Mero District and on Chickasaw towns, which were usually less populated and more vulnerable than those of the Cherokee. Blount's scheming with his new Native American allies led President Washington to tell

Chickasaw leaders that the United States would not support a war against the Creek. When white settlers continued to petition the federal government for assistance, and Blount persisted in his intrigues, Secretary of War Pickering addressed Blount in frank terms. "The United States are determined...to avoid war with the Creeks. Congress alone are competent to decide upon an offensive war, and Congress have not seen fit to authorize it. The acts of individuals, and especially of public officers, apparently tending to such an event ought not to be silently overlooked." With this warning Pickering ordered that "all ideas of offensive operations are therefore to be laid aside and all possible harmony cultivated with the Indian tribes."[44]

Surprisingly, in April 1795, the Creek approached Blount's government and sought peace. By that time, however, Blount was turning his attention elsewhere. In early 1795, Dr. James White, the territory's delegate to Congress, had notified Blount that if the Southwest Territory expected to become a state, the governor would have to take the initiative, and the sooner, the better. White informed Blount that Republicans had privately indicated to him that they would support the territory's inclusion as a state. The implication was that if Republicans supported Blount's move toward statehood, then they would expect the people of the new state to vote for Thomas Jefferson in the 1796 presidential election. Blount, who had never enjoyed an especially close relationship with Washington's Federalist administration, heeded White's recommendations and called for the territorial legislature to meet on June 29, rather than in October as originally announced.[45]

Blount made clear in his opening speech to the legislature the reason for assembling it before the previously announced date. He wanted to determine "whether it is, as I have been taught to believe, the wish of the majority of the people, that this Territory should become a State" if it conformed to the guidelines established in the Northwest Ordinance. The governor asked that a census be taken to determine if the territory's free population exceeded the minimum requirement of sixty thousand residents. He also wanted census takers to ask residents if they were interested in the territory's becoming a state.[46]

The General Assembly responded to Blount's request by convening a joint committee consisting of John Sevier and James Winchester from the council and William Cocke, James Ford, Thomas Hardeman, Abraham Landers, Leroy Taylor, and Samuel Wear from the house. The committee's job was to determine if Blount's proposals were the best means of determining the will of the people. Its members decided to adopt Blount's recommendations, and the General Assembly endorsed their decision, with Thomas Hardeman of Davidson County casting the only dissenting vote. In an address to Blount, Sevier conveyed the sentiment of the entire legislature (excepting Hardeman):

The members of the Legislative Council, and of the House of Representatives, beg leave to express to your Excellency their approbation of the object for which they were principally called together; and feeling convinced that the great body of our constituents are sensible of the many defects of our present mode of government, and of the great and permanent advantages to be derived from a change and speedy representation in Congress, the General Assembly of this Territory will…endeavour to devise such means as may have a tendency to effect that desirable object.[47]

The General Assembly conducted other business as well. Legislators authorized the funding of the planned road project between the territory's eastern districts and the western district, which had suffered from stagnation after the proposed lottery failed. They also endorsed the exploration of a joint road project between North Carolina and the Southwest Territory, which would make passage through the Appalachian Mountains more feasible. The legislature also indefinitely extended Dr. James White's tenure as territorial delegate, formed a new county, Blount, out of Knox County, and tabled the militia relief act passed at the previous session.[48]

The most important item on the agenda, of course, was the upcoming census. When the census was taken later in the year (September 15 to November 15), it clearly revealed that the free population exceeded sixty thousand and that the majority of the white residents in the Southwest Territory wanted statehood. Census takers asked each free adult male that they counted: "Is it your wish if, on taking the enumeration, there should prove to be less than sixty thousand inhabitants, that the Territory shall be admitted as a State into the Federal Union with such less number or not?" Out of 9,066 votes, 6,504, or 71.7 percent answered in the affirmative, whereas only 2,562, or 28.3 percent, responded negatively. The question actually proved unnecessary, because the total free population numbered 66,650, more than enough to allow the Southwest Territory to enter the final stage of attaining statehood. The 10,613 slave residents pushed the territory's non–Native American population to 77,263.[49]

THE CONSTITUTION

With the census taken and popular endorsement for statehood clearly revealed, Blount called for the election of delegates to a constitutional convention. Under the legislation passed by the General Assembly, Blount authorized each county in the Southwest Territory to hold elections on December 18 and 19. Free men twenty-one years and older were eligible to vote for five individuals who would represent them at a constitutional convention, scheduled to begin on January 11, 1796.[50]

Support for statehood was not universal, however, and was particularly lacking in the Mero District. When the census was taken, respondents there voted 154 to 748 against statehood. (Strangely, votes from Sumner County were not reported.) The reasons for their opposition were numerous. The territorial legislature had guaranteed sheriffs, who were placed in charge of the census, higher pay if larger numbers of residents were reported. Mero residents believed that provision was unethical and led to inflated figures. Concern that the Mero District would become politically irrelevant because of its small population was another worry. Almost all the population continued to reside in the eastern part of the territory. The eight counties in the Washington and Hamilton districts had 65,338 residents; the three Mero District counties had only 11,924. Six counties in the Washington and Hamilton districts (Hawkins, Knox, Washington, Sullivan, Jefferson, and Green) had populations exceeding 7,600. Sumner, with the largest population in the Mero District, had only 6,370 residents, making it the seventh-largest county in the territory. Some Mero residents also opposed statehood because they desired their own separate state.[51]

Despite this opposition, the counties held their elections and selected fifty-five delegates to attend the convention and formulate a constitution. From Blount County, Joseph Black, David Craig, Samuel Glass, James Greenaway, and John Houston served. Davidson County sent Thomas Hardeman, Andrew Jackson, Joel Lewis, John McNairy, and James Robertson. Representing Greene County were Elisha Baker, Stephen Brooks, Samuel Frazier, John Galbreath, and William Rankin. In Hawkins County, James Berry, William Cocke, Thomas Henderson, Joseph McMinn, and Richard Mitchell won election, as did Joseph Anderson, George Doherty, Alexander Outlaw, Archibald Roane, and James Roddye of neighboring Jefferson County. Voters in Knox County elected John Adair, William Blount, John Crawford, Charles McClung, and James White. Peter Bryan, Thomas Buckenham, John Clack, Spencer Clack, and Samuel Wear represented Sevier County. William C. C. Claiborne, Richard Gammon, John Rhea, George Rutledge, and John Shelby, Jr., made the jaunt from Sullivan County to Knoxville. Taking seats for Sumner County were Edward Douglass, William Douglass, David Shelby, Daniel Smith, and Isaac Walton. Tennessee County sent as its delegates James Ford, William Fort, Thomas Johnston, Robert Prince, and William Prince. Landon Carter, Samuel Handley, James Stuart, Leroy Taylor, and John Tipton represented Washington County.[52]

Many of these delegates were, or eventually became, prominent Tennessee politicians. Joseph Anderson, who was a territorial judge, eventually won election to the U.S. Senate. William Blount had been a North Carolina congressman, was currently territorial governor, and later served as senator. William Cocke later sat in the U.S. Senate, and William C. C. Claiborne served as both senator and congressman from Tennessee and ultimately became governor of Louisiana. Andrew Jackson served as U.S. representative, senator, and president. Joseph McMinn and Archibald Roane were future Tennessee governors. John Rhea served as congressman. Two of the Mero District's most prominent citizens also served as delegates: James Robertson, who had helped found the Tennessee settlements, and Daniel Smith, who later became U.S. senator. Although not an official delegate, John Sevier also attended the convention, participating in an unofficial capacity. Sevier had been a North Carolina representative to Congress and had additionally held the governorship of the State of Franklin. He later became a Tennessee congressman and governor of the state. The governor's half-brother, Willie Blount, who himself later became governor, also worked as a pro-statehood lobbyist at the convention.[53]

Once the delegates convened, they filled official and functional positions for the convention. Blount was elected president by a unanimous vote. William Maclin was appointed secretary. John Sevier, Jr., served as the reading and engrossing clerk, and John Rhea acted as doorkeeper. Daniel Smith, the territorial secretary, governed the convention when Blount was absent and also chaired the committee charged with composing a constitution and an accompanying bill of rights. This committee, which had the most important job of the convention, consisted of two delegates from each county: Joseph Black and David Craig (Blount); Andrew Jackson and John McNairy (Davidson); Samuel Frazier and William Rankin (Greene); William Cocke and Thomas Henderson (Hawkins); Joseph Anderson and James Roddye (Jefferson); William Blount and Charles McClung (Knox); John Clack and Samuel Wear (Sevier); William C. C. Claiborne and John Rhea (Sullivan); David Shelby and Daniel Smith (Sumner); William Fort and Thomas Johnston (Tennessee); and James Stuart and John Tipton (Washington).[54]

The drafting committee accomplished its two major tasks in quick order. On January 15, after only two days of meetings, the committee returned a draft version of the bill of rights. This "declaration of rights," as it was called in the state constitution, listed thirty-two rights granted to the state's residents. It generally followed the U.S. Constitution in guaranteeing basic civil rights, including freedom of assembly, speech, and press; the right to a speedy jury trial, writ of habeas corpus, right to bear arms and to organize a militia; and protection against unreasonable search and seizure, double jeopardy, and quartering of troops in private homes.[55]

There were some notable differences. Religion is one example. Whereas the U.S. Constitution simply declared, "Congress shall make no law respecting an establishment of religion, or prohibiting the free exercise thereof," the Tennessee bill of rights went further in explaining the role of religion in the lives of its citizens. It stated

> that all men have a natural and indefeasible right to worship Almighty God according to the dictates of their own conscience; that no man can, of right, be compelled to attend, erect or support any place of worship, or to maintain any minister against his consent; that no human authority can, in any case whatever, control or interfere with the rights of conscience; and that no preference shall ever be given, by law, to any religious establishment or modes of worship.

The declaration of rights also guaranteed "[t]hat no religious test shall ever be required as a qualification to any office or public trust under this state."

The Tennessee bill of rights also addressed two other areas of concern for the territory's residents. Section 29 of Article 11 proclaimed that "an equal participation of the free navigation of the Mississippi, is one of the inherent rights of the citizens of this state." Because of that inherent right, "it cannot therefore, be conceded to any prince, potentate, power, person or persons whatever." This section was undoubtedly aimed at Spain and France, both of which had claimed complete control over navigation rights on the Mississippi River. Section 31 dealt with a disputed region in the eastern part of the territory. It claimed "that the people residing south of French Broad and Holston, between the rivers Tennessee and the Big Pigeon, are entitled to the right of pre-emption and occupancy in that tract."

Drafting the body of the constitution took only a little longer. On January 27, the committee submitted a constitution for the delegates' consideration. The preamble recognized the authority by which the delegates proposed the constitution—the U.S. Constitution, the land ceded by North Carolina, and the Northwest Ordinance—and declared that *the people* of the Southwest Territory "do mutually agree with each other to form ourselves into a free and independent state, by the name of 'The State of Tennessee'." Contrary to legend, Andrew Jackson had nothing to do with the naming of the state. Daniel Smith had published his book, *Short Description of the Tennessee Government*, in 1793, and the name as applied to the Southwest Territory seems to have dated from that time.[56]

The constitution established a bicameral legislature, called the General Assembly, consisting of a house of representatives and a senate. Both chambers were, of course, "dependent on the people." Bills could originate from either house, and proceedings were to be public, "unless when the business shall be such as ought to be kept secret." Elections for the house and the senate were set to occur every two years, with senators elected from districts and representatives, from counties. To be eligible for election, a candidate for the legislature had to be a free male who was at least twenty-one years old. He had to have resided in the state for three years and own at least two hundred acres of land.

The constitution also made clear the provisions for establishing the executive and judicial branches. Elected by the people, the governor had to meet the minimum qualifications to hold office: be at least twenty-five years of age, own at least five hundred acres of land, and have been a state resident for four years. He could serve three consecutive terms of two years each and after leaving office for a term was eligible for reelection. The governor's only real power lay in his position as commander-in-chief of the state army, navy, and militia, his granting of pardons for criminals, and his authority to "convene the general assembly by proclamation." As for the judiciary, the constitution provided for "judges of the several courts of law and equity," which included "superior and inferior courts of law and equity." The constitution gave the legislature the authority to appoint the judges and establish the courts.

The constitution contained many safeguards against government abuse. State elections were frequent, occurring biennially. Eligibility to vote, at least for males, was largely democratic. Like legislative candidates, they had to be free males at least twenty-one years old. They also had to own a freehold, be a state resident, and be a resident for at least six months in the county in which they wished to vote. These criteria allowed free black males to vote. The constitution provided for the impeachment of government officials, which could occur for "any misdemeanor in office." To guard against exorbitant spending by the new state government, maximum salaries for government officials were set until 1804. State officials in all three branches were required to take an oath of office. Legislators had to promise that they would not support any legislation "injurious to the people, or consent to any act or thing whatever, that shall have a tendency to lessen or abridge their rights and privileges, as declared by the constitution of this state." State officials were not allowed to accept bribes. Violators would find themselves unable to serve in the state government for two years and would "be subject to such further punishment as the legislature shall direct."

Delegates were sufficiently concerned about militia service and religion that they drafted separate articles for each topic. Concerning militia service, the constitution gave members of the militia the right to elect lower-ranked officers, who would then, in turn, elect higher-ranked officers. To protect those men who belonged to pacifist religious sects, the constitution authorized the legislature to pass laws of exemption for those cases. The mixing of religion and public service was another matter to which the delegates gave attention. They prohibited ministers and priests from serving in the legislature, arguing that those men were "by their profession, dedicated to God and the care of souls, and ought not to be diverted away from the great duties of their functions." Contradicting the declaration of rights passed earlier, the main body of the constitution also contained a provision stating, "No person who denies the being of God or a future state of rewards and punishments, shall hold any office in the civil department of this state."

OPPOSITION TO THE CONSTITUTION

The ability of the committee to reach agreement in such a short time indicated the near unanimity of the delegates on crucial issues. There was some dissension, however. A group opposed to the Blount government and to a strong state government, but not to statehood, emerged during the course of the debates. Led by Joseph McMinn, Joseph Anderson, and Alexander Outlaw and possibly numbering as many as fourteen delegates, this opposition group called for the drafting of a declaration of rights, to which the pro-Blount delegates readily agreed. The opposition group also tried unsuccessfully to establish a unicameral legislature and, when that failed, worked to restrict the power of the senate. Its members additionally sought to limit the rights of land speculators. The pro-Blount group responded by including a provision that all land and slaves would be taxed equally. Revealing the convention's overall inconsistency concerning religion, the opposition group wanted to ban clergy from holding any public office but demanded that officeholders believe in "the divine authority of the old and new testaments." In both instances, the delegates reached a compromise.[57]

Despite the work of this opposition group, the delegates were agreed on the goal of statehood, and this consensus allowed them to vote unanimously for the constitution when it was presented to them on February 6, 1796. The delegates believed that their approval and that of Congress was all that was necessary for the constitution to take effect. Certain that Congress's sanction was forthcoming, the convention members empowered Blount to authorize elections for the General Assembly and governorship. The governor responded by setting the elections for the second Thursday and Friday in March 1796. The delegates also wanted Blount to forward the constitution to Philadelphia as soon as possible. He did so almost immediately, sending Joseph McMinn to deliver a copy to Secretary of State Thomas Pickering.[58]

Confident of congressional approval, residents of the new state acted accordingly. Andrew Jackson, who had been one of Blount's strongest supporters at the convention, observed, "The people Generally approve of the Constitution;... Calumny that fiend to virtue has fled, a calm has arrived, imprecations Cease, and Cesar is rendered his due." The elections were held as scheduled, and the General Assembly, consisting of eleven senators and twenty-two representatives, convened in Knoxville, the designated capital of the new state, on March 28. Its members promptly elected James Winchester speaker of the senate and James Stuart speaker of the house. The following day, at a joint session, the election returns were counted, and John Sevier was pronounced the state's first governor. Two days later, at another joint session, William Blount and William Cocke were elected to represent Tennessee in the U.S. Senate. The assembly sent Blount into his new position with the thanks of the people, who were "confiden[t] in your integrity and ability to serve them."[59]

FEDERAL APPROVAL

Although optimism reigned in Knoxville, all was not going smoothly for Tennessee statehood in Philadelphia. Shortly after the state constitution had passed, Arthur Campbell, who had supported the State of Franklin movement in the 1780s, warned President Washington that Congress needed to delay Tennessee's admission "one or two years more" for the "interest and safety of the people." Opposition was more widespread, however, than just this one

Virginian's opinion. When Washington submitted Tennessee's application for statehood to Congress on April 8, its approval met staunch resistance. Federalists in Congress were reluctant to admit Tennessee because they believed that the new state would vote for Jefferson, the Republican candidate in the fall presidential election. Therefore, they moved to delay its admission until after a new president had been elected.[60]

Accomplishing that goal led to a heated battle in both chambers of Congress between Federalists and their Republican opponents. The House of Representatives appointed a five-member committee that, on April 12, endorsed Tennessee's statehood and recommended that it be given "all the privileges enjoyed by the other States of the Union." When the House as a body took up the issue on May 5, however, Federalists worked to quash Tennessee's application. William Loughton Smith of South Carolina was their first spokesman. He argued three points: first, Congress alone had the right to form a state in the Southwest Territory; second, the accuracy of the census taken in the territory was questionable both in number and legality; and, third, some of the provisions in Tennessee's proposed constitution contradicted the U.S. Constitution. Theodore Sedgwick of Massachusetts echoed Smith's reasoning and added his own reservation: the Northwest Ordinance prohibited slavery, and "there were slaves to a very considerable number" in the Southwest Territory. Not all Federalists opposed Tennessee's statehood, however. Robert Goodloe Harper, who was from South Carolina, thought that "the wish of the people ought to be gratified," and Tennessee should be admitted into the Union. His only concern was the number of representatives that it would have.[61]

Republicans, who possessed a majority in the House, defended the actions of the territory's legislature and voters. James Madison, the venerable architect of the U.S. Constitution, argued that denying the people of the Southwest Territory statehood "deprived them of a right essential to freedom—the right of being represented in Congress." The points raised by Federalists, he thought, were minor in scope and inconsequential to the question at hand. Several other Republicans, including Thomas Blount, William Blount's brother, followed Madison's lead in calling for Tennessee's admission as the sixteenth state. When the vote in the House was taken on May 6, Republicans carried the day by a count of 43-30.[62]

Republicans and supporters of Tennessee initially did not fare as well in the Senate, which Federalists controlled. Senators appointed three Federalists—Rufus King of New York, Jacob Read of South Carolina, and John Rutherfurd of New Jersey—to a committee charged with considering Tennessee's application. King, the committee chairman, submitted a report on May 16 that recommended denying Tennessee statehood for the various reasons given by House Federalists. The report did, however, propose that Congress take a census in the Southwest Territory and, once the necessary population was confirmed, admit the state. Federalist senators endorsed the report by a 14-11 vote, effectively ending Tennessee's chances of entering the Union before the fall's presidential election. Subsequent days of debate and proposed amendments failed to change the tenor of the Senate.[63]

With adjournment for both chambers rapidly approaching on June 1, House Republicans attempted to convince the Senate to relent on Tennessee's admission. They introduced an amendment reducing Tennessee's representatives in the House from two to one. At the same time, the House repeated its call for the state's immediate admission. When the Senate received the amended bill on May 30, it refused to concur with the House amendments, leaving Tennessee's statehood hanging in the balance yet again.[64]

The next day, May 31, the House sent a strong message to the Senate, renewing its call for Tennessee's admission and requesting the appointment of a joint congressional committee to resolve the issue. The Senate agreed and appointed Republican Aaron Burr of New York and Federalist Caleb Strong of Massachusetts as its managers. Burr, according to one historian, was instrumental in bringing about the joint committee's recommendation in favor of Tennessee's immediate admission. The Senate agreed to follow the committee's suggestion and passed the bill. On June 1, 1796, President Washington signed the bill that brought Tennessee into the Union as the sixteenth state.[65]

As part of Tennessee's admission, the bill voided the elections that had taken place in March 1796. The Tennessee legislature would have to elect two senators, and Tennessee voters would have to elect another representative. On August 2, the legislature selected William Blount and William Cocke as the state's two senators. In an election held later that fall, Andrew Jackson won a seat in the U.S. House of Representatives.[66]

SUMMARY

Living on the western frontier in the late eighteenth century was no easy task. Settlers who moved across the Appalachians from North Carolina understood the dangers inherent in their migration, but they expected the state and federal governments to assist them politically, economically, and militarily because, regardless of their place of residence, they were Americans. When that expected help proved ineffective or absent, Tennesseans decided that the way to self-preservation lay in becoming a member of the Union. As they correctly surmised, joining the United States as its sixteenth member secured them the various forms of protection that they had sought for nearly three decades.

NOTES

1. John R. Finger, *Tennessee Frontiers: Three Regions in Transition* (Bloomington and Indianapolis: Indiana University Press, 2001), pp. 7–8, 14–15; Paul H. Bergeron

et al., *Tennesseans and Their History* (Knoxville: The University of Tennessee Press, 1999), pp. 8, 21; Stanley J. Folmsbee et al., *History of Tennessee*, 4 vols. (New York: Lewis Historical, 1960), 1:99–100.

2. Bergeron et al., *Tennesseans*, pp. 22–23.

3. W. Calvin Dickinson, "Watauga Association," in *The Tennessee Encyclopedia of History & Culture*, ed. Carroll Van West, 1039–1040 (Nashville: Rutledge Hill Press, 1998); Folmsbee et al., *History of Tennessee*, 1:107–110.

4. Folmsbee et al., *History of Tennessee*, 1:119–123; Bergeron et al., *Tennesseans*, pp. 24–25; "Watauga Petition," July 5, 1776, in J. G. M. Ramsey, *The Annals of Tennessee to the End of the Eighteenth Century* (reprint, Kingsport, TN: Kingsport Press, 1926), pp. 134–138.

5. Ronald N. Satz, *Tennessee's Indian Peoples: From White Contact to Removal, 1540–1840* (Knoxville: The University of Tennessee Press, 1979), p. 64; Bergeron et al., *Tennesseans*, pp. 26–27; "Treaty of Sycamore Shoals," March 17, 1775, available at: Eighteenth-Century History, http://victorian.fortunecity.com/rothko/420/aniyuntikwalaski/treaty/sycamoretreaty.txt.

6. Finger, *Tennessee Frontiers*, pp. 77–82; Samuel C. Williams, *Tennessee During the Revolutionary War* (Nashville: Tennessee Historical Commission, 1944), pp. 104–116.

7. Finger, *Tennessee Frontiers*, pp. 82–83; "Cumberland Compact," May 1, 1780, in A.W. Putnam, *History of Middle Tennessee* (reprint, Knoxville: The University of Tennessee Press, 1971), pp. 94–102.

8. Bergeron et al., *Tennesseans*, p. 34; Finger, *Tennessee Frontiers*, p. 109.

9. Bergeron et al., *Tennesseans*, p. 34; Walter T. Durham, "Daniel Smith," in *Tennessee Encyclopedia*, pp. 856–857.

10. Samuel C. Williams, *History of the Lost State of Franklin*, rev. ed. (reprint, Johnson City, TN: The Overmountain Press, 1993), pp. 19–34; Michael Toomey, "State of Franklin," in *Tennessee Encyclopedia*, pp. 339–340.

11. Williams, *Franklin*, pp. 289–294; and Finger, *Frontiers*, pp. 110–111.

12. "Constitution of the State of Franklin," December 14, 1874, in Williams, *Franklin*, pp. 339–347; Finger, *Tennessee Frontiers*, pp. 112–113.

13. Finger, *Tennessee Frontiers*, pp. 112–113; Carl Driver, *John Sevier: Pioneer of the Old Southwest* (Chapel Hill: The University of North Carolina Press, 1932), pp. 87–88.

14. Williams, *Franklin*, pp. 56–66, 82–89; Alexander Martin to the Inhabitants of Washington, Sullivan, and Greene counties, April 25, 1785, ibid., pp. 67–71.

15. Toomey, "State of Franklin," p. 338; Bergeron et al., *Tennesseans*, pp. 44–45.

16. Williams, *Franklin*, pp. 235–244; Walter T. Durham, *Daniel Smith: Frontier Statesman* (Gallatin, TN: Sumner County Library Board, 1976), pp. 103–119.

17. "North Carolina: Cession of Western Land Claims," in *Territorial Papers of the United States, Volume IV: The Territory South of the River Ohio, 1790–1796* , ed. and comp. Clarence E. Carter, 3–8 (Washington, DC: Government Printing Office, 1936); Walter T. Durham, "Southwest Territory," in *Tennessee Encyclopedia*, pp. 867–868.

18. Durham, "Southwest Territory," pp. 867–868; Walter T. Durham, "The Southwest and Northwest Territories, A Comparison, 1787–1796," *Tennessee Historical Quarterly* 49 (Fall 1990): 189; "Ordinance of 1787," July 13, 1787, in *Territorial Papers of the United States*, vol. 2, *The Territory Northwest of the River Ohio, 1787–1803* , ed. and comp. Clarence E. Carter, 39, 48 (Washington, DC: Government Printing Office, 1934).

19. Durham, "Southwest and Northwest," p. 189; "Northwest Ordinance," pp. 41–45, 49.

20. "North Carolina Cession," p. 7; "Northwest Ordinance," pp. 46–49; "An Act for the Government of the Territory South of the River Ohio," in *Territorial Papers*, 4:18–19.

21. Walter T. Durham, *Before Tennessee: The Southwest Territory, 1790–1796* (Piney Flats, TN: Rocky Mount Historical Association, 1990), pp. 32–33, 42–43; Walter T. Durham, "Daniel Smith," in *Tennessee Encyclopedia*, p. 857; Theodore Brown, Jr., "John McNairy," in *Tennessee Encyclopedia*, p. 594; Carroll Van West, "David Campbell," in *Tennessee Encyclopedia*, p. 118; Folmsbee et al., *History of Tennessee*, p. 190; William Peery to George Washington, [December 24, 1790], in *Territorial Papers*, 4:40.

22. Durham, *Before Tennessee*, pp. 39, 41–46; Finger, *Tennessee Frontiers*, p. 129.

23. William Blount to militia colonels in Southwest Territory, March 7, 1791, Thomas Jefferson to William Blount, March 12, 1791, and census report for Southwest Territory [19 September 1791], in *Territorial Papers* 4:49–50, 52–3, 80–1; Finger, *Tennessee Frontiers*, pp. 129–131.

24. Durham, *Before Tennessee*, pp. 47–48; "Treaty of New York [August 7, 1790]," in *Indian Affairs: Laws and Treaties*, ed. and comp. Charles J. Kapple, 2:25–29 (Washington, DC: Government Printing Office, 1904); John Buchanan, *Jackson's Way: Andrew Jackson and the People of the Western Waters* (New York: John Wiley and Sons, 2001), pp. 79–81, 103–104; Finger, *Tennessee Frontiers*, p. 132.

25. Durham, *Before Tennessee*, pp. 48–52, 55–63; Satz, *Tennessee's Indian Peoples*, pp. 68–69; Finger, *Tennessee Frontiers*, pp. 133–136; "Treaty of Holston [July 2, 1791]," in Kappler, ed., *Indian Affairs*, 2:29–33.

26. Finger, *Tennessee Frontiers*, pp. 132, 135–136; Durham, *Before Tennessee*, pp. 62–64, 80–85; Buchanan, *Jackson's Way*, pp. 131–136.

27. Finger, *Tennessee Frontiers*, pp. 136–137; Durham, *Before Tennessee*, pp. 65–71; Report of Henry Knox to George Washington, January 17, 1792, Amendment to the Treaty of Holston, February 17, 1792, and Henry Knox to William Blount, January 31, 1792, and February 16, 1792, in *Territorial Papers*, 4:111–115, 120, 115–117, 118–119.

28. Petition of Tennessee County to James Robertson [1 February 1792], in *Territorial Papers*, 4:117–118; Bergeron et al., *Tennesseans*, pp. 54–55.

29. Durham, *Before Tennessee*, pp. 129–142; Finger, *Tennessee Frontiers*, pp. 142–144.

30. W. Bruce Wheeler, "Knoxville," in *Tennessee Encyclopedia*, p. 507; Durham, *Before Tennessee*, pp. 142–147.

31. William Blount to George Washington, September 19, 1791, William Blount to John Sevier, May 31, 1793 and June 2, 1793, in *Territorial Papers*, 4:80, 264–266, 267–268; Durham, *Before Tennessee*, pp. 145–146.

32. Durham, *Before Tennessee*, pp. 146–148, 153; "Ordinance from William Blount Concerning Elections," October 19, 1793, in *Territorial Papers*, 4:309–310.

33. "Proclamation of Governor William Blount," January 1, 1794 and "Certificate of Governor William Blount," March 1, 1794, in *Territorial Papers*, 4:319, 329–330.

34. "Act of the Representative Assembly," February 26, 1794 and "Certificate of Governor William Blount," March 1, 1794, in *Territorial Papers*, 4:328, 329–330; Robert V. Remini, *Andrew Jackson and the Course of American Empire, 1767–1821* (New York: Harper and Row, 1977), p. 73; Mabel Pittard, "Griffith Rutherford,"

in *Tennessee Encyclopedia*, pp. 819–820; Walter T. Durham, "James Winchester," in *Tennessee Encyclopedia*, p. 1067.

35. Durham, *Before Tennessee*, pp. 150–152, 165–166; Finger, *Tennessee Frontiers*, p. 145; William Blount to Representatives in the Lower House, March 1, 1794, in *Territorial Papers*, 4:330.

36. Durham, *Before Tennessee*, pp. 152, 154–155; William Blount to James Robertson, March 8, 1794, Report of Congressional Committee for Territorial Defense [April 8, 1794], Henry Knox's report to George Washington, April 11, 1794, in *Territorial Papers*, 4:331–333, 335–336, 337–338; Andrew Jackson to John McKee, May 16, 1794, in *The Papers of Andrew Jackson*, ed. Harold Moser et al., 6 vols. to date (Knoxville: The University of Tennessee Press, 1980–), 1:48–49.

37. Durham, *Before Tennessee*, pp. 156–158; "Treaty with the Cherokee Nation," June 26, 1794, and "Speech to Chickasaws," July 11, 1794 [draft], in *Territorial Papers*, 4:346–347, 349–350.

38. Durham, *Before Tennessee*, pp. 158–161; "Rules of Decorum," August 25, 1794, in Ramsey, *Annals of Tennessee*, pp. 624–625; Jo Tice Bloom, "Early Delegates in the House of Representatives," in *The American Territorial System*, ed. John Porter Bloom, 65–66 (Athens, OH: Ohio University Press, 1973).

39. Durham, *Before Tennessee*, pp. 159–76; Walter T. Durham, *James Winchester: Tennessee Pioneer* (Gallatin, TN: Sumner County Library Board, 1979), pp. 42–43.

40. Finger, *Tennessee Frontiers*, pp. 146–147; Satz, *Tennessee's Indian Peoples*, p. 69; Durham, *Before Tennessee*, pp. 176–182; Terry Weeks, "James Robertson," in *Tennessee Encyclopedia*, p. 803.

41. Durham, *Before Tennessee*, pp. 162–163; "Memorial to Congress," September 15, 1794, in Putnam, *History*, pp. 501–503.

42. Durham, *Before Tennessee*, pp. 163, 188; Finger, *Tennessee Frontiers*, pp. 146–147.

43. Durham, *Before Tennessee*, pp. 184–193; William Blount to Thomas Pickering, January 9, 1795, and January 10, 1795, in *Territorial Papers*, 4:380–381.

44. Durham, *Before Tennessee*, pp. 191–195; Timothy Pickering to William Blount, March 23, 1795, quoted in Durham, *Before Tennessee*, p. 194.

45. Ibid., pp. 188, 197; Folmsbee et al., *History of Tennessee*, p. 207; Finger, *Tennessee Frontiers*, p. 148; Proclamation by William Blount, April 25, 1795, in William Blount, *The Blount Journal, 1790–1796* (Nashville: Tennessee Historical Commission, 1955), pp. 109–110.

46. William Blount to General Assembly, June 29, 1795, in Ramsey, *Annals of Tennessee*, p. 641; Folmsbee et al., *History of Tennessee*, p. 207; Finger, *Tennessee Frontiers*, p. 148.

47. Samuel C. Williams, "The Admission of Tennessee into the Union," *Tennessee Historical Quarterly* 4 (December 1945): 295–296; John Sevier to William Blount, July 7, 1795, in Ramsey, *Annals of Tennessee*, p. 642.

48. Durham, *Before Tennessee*, pp. 199–201.

49. "Census of Southwest Territory [November 28, 1795]," in *Territorial Papers*, 4:404–405; Durham, *Before Tennessee*, pp. 197–198; Folmsbee et al., *History of Tennessee*, pp. 207, 209.

50. "Proclamation by William Blount [November 28, 1795]," in *Territorial Papers*, 4:407–408.

51. "Census of Southwest Territory [November 28, 1795]," in *Territorial Papers*, 4:404–405; Finger, *Tennessee Frontiers*, p. 149; Durham, *Before Tennessee*, pp. 209–210.

52. Tennessee Constitution, February 6, 1796 (Unless noted, all subsequent references in the narrative come from the 1796 constitution).

53. Durham, *Before Tennessee*, p. 253; Bergeron et al., *Tennesseans*, p. 64; individual entries in *Tennessee Encyclopedia*.

54. Durham, *Before Tennessee*, pp. 253, 258–259; Durham, *Daniel Smith*, p. 197; John D. Barnhart, "The Tennessee Constitution of 1796: A Product of the Old West," *Journal of Southern History* 9 (November 1943): 543; Bergeron et al., *Tennesseans*, p. 64; Ramsey, *Annals of Tennessee*, p. 652.

55. Durham, *Before Tennessee*, p. 254; Durham, *Daniel Smith*, pp. 197–198; Ramsey, *Annals of Tennessee*, pp. 652–653.

56. Durham, *Before Tennessee*, pp. 255–277; Durham, *Daniel Smith*, pp. 197–198; Ramsey, *Annals of Tennessee*, pp. 652–653.

57. Barnhart, "Constitution," pp. 543–546; Folmsbee et al., *History of Tennessee*, pp. 210–211; Ramsey, *Annals of Tennessee*, pp. 653–654.

58. Durham, *Before Tennessee*, pp. 257–258; William Blount to Thomas Pickering, February 9, 1796, in *Territorial Papers*, 4:419–420.

59. Andrew Jackson to William Blount, February 29, 1796, in Moser, ed., *Papers*, 1:82–83; William Blount to Thomas Pickering, March 29, 1796, and Address of General Assembly to William Blount [31 March 1796], in *Territorial Papers*, 4:422–423, 423; Durham, *Before Tennessee*, pp. 260–261.

60. Arthur Campbell to George Washington, February 18, 1796, in *Territorial Papers*, 4:420; Durham, *Before Tennessee*, pp. 16, 50; Finger, *Tennessee Frontiers*, p. 150; Bergeron et al., *Tennesseans*, pp. 68–69.

61. Charlotte Williams, "Congressional Action on the Admission of Tennessee into the Union," *Tennessee Historical Quarterly* 2 (December 1943): 297–301; Williams, "Admission of Tennessee," pp. 304–305; *Annals of Congress*, 4th Cong., 1st Sess., April 12, 1796, p. 916; Speech of William L. Smith, May 5, 1796, Speech of Theodore Sedgwick, May 5, 1796, and Speech of Robert G. Harper, May 5, 1796, idem, pp. 1300–1304, 1306–1308, 1304–1306. (Background information on congressional members can be found in the *Biographical Directory of the United States Congress*, available at bioguide.congress.gov.)

62. Speech of James Madison, May 5, 1796, Speech of John Nicholas, May 5, 1796, and Speech of Thomas Blount, May 5, 1796, in *Annals of Congress*, 4th Cong., 1st Sess., pp. 1308–1309, 1309–1311, 1311–1312, idem, pp. 1313–1329; Williams, "Congressional Action on the Admission of Tennessee," pp. 307–308.

63. *Annals of Congress*, 4th Cong., 1st Sess., pp. 91–94; and Williams, "Congressional Action on the Admission of Tennessee," pp. 308–310.

64. *Annals of Congress*, 4th Cong., 1st Sess., pp. 113–115, 1473–1474; Williams, "Admission of Tennessee," pp. 310–311; Williams, "Congressional Action on the Admission of Tennessee," pp. 309–314.

65. *Annals of Congress*, 4th Cong., 1st Sess., p. 116; Williams, "Admission of Tennessee," pp. 311–312.

66. Durham, *Before Tennessee*, pp. 270–271; Remini, *Andrew Jackson and the Course of American Empire*, p. 84.

BIBLIOGRAPHY

Abernethy, Thomas P. *From Frontier to Plantation in Tennessee: A Study of Frontier*. Chapel Hill: University of North Carolina Press, 1932.

Bergeron, Paul H., et al. *Tennesseans and Their History*. Knoxville: The University of Tennessee Press, 1999.

Driver, Carl. *John Sevier: Pioneer of the Old Southwest*. Chapel Hill: The University of North Carolina Press, 1932.

Durham, Walter T. *Daniel Smith: Frontier Statesman*. Gallatin, TN: Sumner County Library Board, 1976.

———. *Before Tennessee: The Southwest Territory, 1790–1796* . Piney Flats, TN: Rocky Mount Historical Association, 1990.

Finger, John R. *Tennessee Frontiers: Three Regions in Transition*. Bloomington and Indianapolis: Indiana University Press, 2001.

Goodstein, Anita Shafer. *Nashville, 1780–1860: From Frontier to City* . Gainesville, FL: University of Florida Press, 1989.

Masterson, William H. *William Blount*. Baton Rouge: Louisiana State University Press, 1954.

Satz, Ronald N. *Tennessee's Indian Peoples: From White Contact to Removal, 1540–1840*. Knoxville: The University of Tennessee Press, 1979.

Williams, Samuel Cole. *History of the Lost State of Franklin*. Rev. ed. Reprint. Johnson City, TN: The Overmountain Press, 1993.

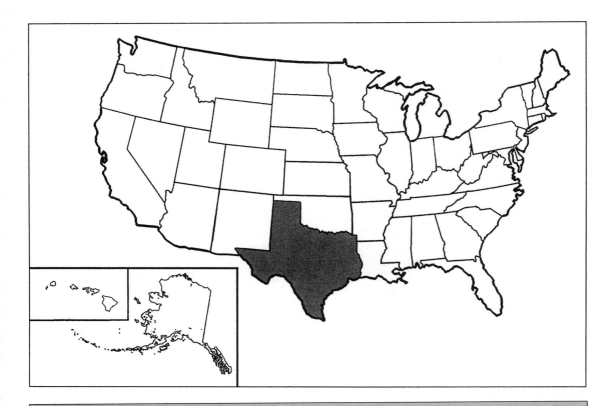

Texas

Territorial Development:

- The United States obtains northern portions of the future state of Texas from France through the Louisiana Purchase, April 30, 1803
- Texan rebels declare independence from Mexican rule in the central and southern portions of the future state of Texas, March 2, 1836
- The Republic of Texas recognized by the United States, March, 1837
- Popularly elected Texan convention votes to accept the U.S. federal government's offer of annexation and membership into the Union, July 4, 1845
- Texas officially annexed and admitted into the Union as the twenty-eight state, December 29, 1845
- Mexico formally recognizes Texan independence and borders with the Treaty of Guadalupe Hidalgo, February 2, 1848

Capitals of the Republic:

- Washington-on-the-Brazos, 1836
- Columbia, 1836
- Houston, 1837–1839
- Austin, 1839–1842
- Washington-on-the-Brazos, 1842–1845

State Capitals:

- Austin, 1845–present

Origin of State Name: The Spanish used the word "teysha," meaning "hello friend," in the language of the Caddo, to refer to friendly tribes in Louisiana, Oklahoma, and Texas. The first Spanish mission, St. Francis of the Texas, was then named after these tribes.

First Governor: J. Pinckney Henderson
Governmental Organization: Bicameral
Population at Statehood: 212,592
Geographical Size: 261,797 square miles

THE STATE OF TEXAS

Admitted to the Union as a State:
December 29, 1845

Jeffrey D. Carlisle

INTRODUCTION

Texas came into the Union in a unique manner. Texas was the only state in the continental United States that was an independent republic before statehood, and it entered the Union as a state, never having gone through the territorial process. The debate over the admission of Texas came during a very turbulent time in American history. Slavery loomed as one of the major issues. Abolitionists and anti-slavery proponents opposed allowing Texas, a vast territory that allowed slavery, to enter the Union, thus expanding slavery immensely. Others argued that annexing Texas would be unconstitutional, that the United States could not absorb a sovereign nation, not to mention the fact that Mexico had not recognized Texas's independence and threatened war if the United States made the attempt. European factors also played a role in the annexation debate. Texas flirted with England, raising the fear that the United States would be blocked from further westward expansion if England gained influence in Texas as it already had in the Oregon country. In the end, the annexation of Texas helped initiate the era of Manifest Destiny, resulting in the Mexican-American War that eventually brought in the rest of the American Southwest. All in all, Texas lay at the heart of a number of important issues facing the United States in the 1830s and 1840s.

BIRTH AND GOVERNMENT OF THE REPUBLIC OF TEXAS

In the Adams-Onís Treaty of 1819, the United States and Spain negotiated the boundaries of the Louisiana Purchase in such a way as to exclude Texas.

In exchange for giving up any claims to Texas, the United States received Florida, and Spain gave up any claim to the Oregon country. American interest in Texas did not stay dormant for long, however. The Mexican government was desperate to settle Texas and, after a fruitless attempt to encourage its own people or Europeans to settle the frontier area, reluctantly agreed to allow Moses Austin and his son, Stephen F. Austin, to settle three hundred Anglo-American families in Texas. The success of Austin's colonists encouraged other Anglos to negotiate deals with the Mexican government. By the 1830s there were ten times as many Anglos living in Texas as there were Mexicans, about thirty thousand Anglos and three thousand Mexicans.

This Anglo flood concerned the Mexican authorities, especially because the immigrants tended to be Protestant even though Mexican law required immigrants to be Catholic, they spoke little if any Spanish, and many of them owned slaves, even while the Mexican government was trying desperately to abolish the institution. When the Mexican government began increasingly to assert its authority over Texas, the Texans rebelled, eventually proclaiming their independence.

Two earlier provisional governments, the Permanent Council, which, despite its name lasted but three weeks, and the Consultation, which drew up a plan for a provisional government, had supported Texas as a separate and independent state within Mexico. Bickering between the provisional governor and the general council led to the calling of a convention for March 1, 1836, with the power to create a new government. Even as the provisional government rejected a declaration of independence, it sent a three-man commission to the United States to seek financial aid and to test the temper of the American people and government concerning the events in Texas. The first commission, consisting of Stephen F. Austin, Branch T. Archer, and William H. Wharton departed Texas, arriving in New Orleans on New Year's Day, 1836.

The level of support for the Texas cause was so overwhelming that Austin, for the first time, united with Archer and Wharton, demanded that the provisional government adopt a declaration of independence without delay. The commission felt sure that it would receive all the aid necessary from the United States. The original plan had been for the commission to return to Texas by early March, perhaps in time to participate in the convention. Illness and poor travel conditions delayed the commission's arrival in Washington until late March.[1]

Meanwhile, in Texas, fifty-nine delegates arrived at Washington-on-the-Brazos on March 1. Delegates were, for the most part younger and more decisive than the men who had served in the Consultation or the provisional government. Almost one-half of the delegates had lived in Texas less than two years. Fifty-two were from the United States, only three were native Mexicans, and two of those had been born in Texas. On March 2 the convention adopted a declaration of independence and then set about drafting a constitution.[2]

The constitution, which was adopted at midnight on March 16, 1836, was modeled on the U.S. Constitution. It established a government of three branches with a system of checks and balances and included a declaration of rights. Among the rights guaranteed by the declaration of rights were freedom of religion, freedom of speech, and of the press, protection from unreasonable searches and seizures, right to a trial by jury, and the right to bear arms. Citizens were also protected from double jeopardy, the suspension of the writ of habeas corpus, excessive bail, excessive fines, and cruel and unusual punishment. The constitution also forbade imprisonment for debt and disallowed monopolies, primogeniture, and entailments.

Terms of office were generally short. Representatives served one year, and senators served three years with one-third being elected annually. The president served a three-year term, with the exception of the first president, who was to serve only two years. A president could be elected to multiple terms but could not succeed himself. The president was commander-in-chief but could not personally command troops in the field without the consent of the congress. Justices of the supreme and inferior courts served four-year terms, were elected by joint ballot of both houses of congress, and could be re-elected. Interestingly, ministers of the gospel and priests were ineligible to hold government office.

The constitution granted citizenship to all persons living in the Republic on the day of the declaration of independence, excluding Africans, descendants of Africans, and Native Americans. All free white emigrants would be entitled to citizenship after a residence of six months once they swore "before some competent authority" their intention to maintain permanent residence within the republic, their support of the constitution, and their allegiance to the Republic of Texas. Those who fled the Republic to avoid participating in the revolution would forfeit their citizenship and all lands that they might hold.

The authors of the constitution were interested in protecting their slave property and addressed the issue in the constitution. Slaves brought into Texas would remain slaves, and the congress could not prohibit emigrants from the United States from bringing slaves with them. Additionally, the congress could not emancipate slaves, nor could slaveowners emancipate slaves without the consent of the congress, unless the slaveowners made arrangements to send the slaves outside of Texas once they were freed. "No free person of African descent, either in whole or in part," was allowed to reside permanently within the Republic without the consent of the congress, and the importation of slaves, except from the United States, was strictly forbidden and considered an act of piracy.

One of the longest sections of the constitution dealt with the distribution of land. All citizens of the Republic as of the declaration of independence would receive land, if they had not already. Each head of household would receive a league (4428 acres) and a labor (177 acres) of land for a total of 4605 acres. Single men seventeen and older would receive one-third of a league

(1476 acres). The constitution then voided several "unjust and fraudulent claims" made before the revolution.

Finally, before it adjourned, the constitutional convention selected an interim government to serve until the constitution could be ratified and a regular government could be elected. David G. Burnet was elected president, and Lorenzo de Zavala was elected vice president. Hearing that Santa Anna's armies were approaching, the convention disbanded, and the interim government fled to the east.[3]

Antonio Lopez de Santa Anna, president of Mexico, personally led several thousand Mexican troops into Texas to suppress the rebellion. At San Antonio he found 187 Texans had fortified the Alamo, an old Spanish mission. For almost two weeks the small band of Texans held out against almost four thousand Mexican troops. On March 6, 1836, the Alamo fell, and the entire Texan garrison was killed. Santa Anna then turned his army eastward in pursuit of Sam Houston, the overall Texan commander, who was roaming east Texas trying desperately to scrape together an army. Fearing Houston was trying to escape into the United States, Santa Anna mounted fifteen hundred of his best troops and sped after Houston's fleeing force. Houston, however, had no intention of reaching the United States. With eight hundred troops, he decided to make a stand at San Jacinto, near present-day Houston, Texas. There, in a battle that lasted eighteen minutes, the Texan forces scored a stunning victory, routing most of the Mexican army and capturing Santa Anna himself.

With Santa Anna under the Texans' control, Houston forced several concessions from the Mexican leader. Santa Anna ordered his troops to evacuate Texas soil, moving south of the Rio Grande, the boundary claimed by Houston. Then, Santa Anna recognized Texas's independence and promised to support these actions when he returned to Mexico. Although the resulting treaties of Velasco were never ratified by the Mexican government and Santa Anna temporarily lost his influence, for all intents and purposes the Republic of Texas was born.

While the convention hammered out the constitution and the armies battled across Texas, the commission of Austin, Wharton, and Archer continued its trip to Washington, D.C. Word of the Texas declaration of independence preceded them in the American newspapers, but no official dispatches were forthcoming. Technically, with the formation of the interim government, the delegates had no authority, because the government that sent them no longer existed. The three men stayed in the United States drumming up support for recognition and monetary aid for Texas, but without official authorization they could accomplish little. By July, the three delegates were back in Texas.[4]

On March 19, 1836, while the first commission whiled away time in Washington, the interim government selected a second commission, made up of George C. Childress and Robert Hamilton, to negotiate with the United States. They arrived in Washington, D.C., as the first commission was departing. Unfortunately, they had left Texas before the battle of San Jacinto and the capture of Santa Anna and had no official accounts confirming the reports in the U.S. newspapers. The commissioners laid their credentials before U.S. Secretary of State John Forsyth and tried to gain support for recognition with unofficial accounts, but Forsyth refused to answer their requests.[5]

On May 26, 1836, the interim government selected yet another pair of commissioners, James Collinsworth and Peter W. Grayson, to replace all previous delegates. The interim government decided that the new negotiators, with first-hand knowledge of the battle of San Jacinto and the negotiations of the treaties of Velasco, would be better able to represent the interests of Texas in Washington. Unfortunately, the third commission, which probably had the best chance for success, arrived in Washington, D.C., four days after Congress adjourned. President Jackson himself was preparing to leave for the Hermitage. Before Jackson departed, however, he met informally with the commission. Jackson informed the commission that a secret agent had been sent to Texas to report on the Republic's condition and that no action could be taken until the informant returned.[6]

Before it adjourned, Congress, for its part, had appeared to be favorably disposed toward recognizing Texas, not because of any action taken by the Texas commissioners but because of petitions sent to Congress by American citizens across the country. From April to July, 1836, when Congress adjourned, memorials and petitions arrived from such disparate states as Connecticut, Mississippi, Ohio, North Carolina, Pennsylvania, and Tennessee, requesting the recognition of the Republic of Texas. Congressmen also showed almost uniform support for recognition but delayed action for two key reasons. First, there was a lack of "official" information concerning the events in Texas. Senator John M. Niles from Connecticut summed up the second issue: if the United States were too hasty in recognizing Texas, and especially if annexation directly followed recognition, it might appear as though the United States had precipitated the revolution to snatch Texas from Mexico. The fact that Texas allowed slavery was only a minor concern at this point.

John Quincy Adams had raised the issue of slavery on the floor of the House on May 7, 1836, when he argued that if the revolution in Texas was simply an effort to extend slavery, which Mexico had abolished, then he was opposed to adding such territory to the United States. Adams's statement raised the ire of southern congressmen, who reminded Adams that it was his treaty of 1819, the Adams-Onís Treaty, which had ceded the United States' interest in Texas, blocking the interests of the southern slaveholding states while expanding dramatically the territory closed to slavery. Adams replied that he had been the last cabinet member to agree to the treaty and did so with great reluctance, and as president he had tried to buy Texas from Mexico for $1 million. At this point the discussion of slavery died out in the House.[7]

In the Senate, on May 23, John C. Calhoun pointed out that "the southern states, owning a slave population, were deeply interested in preventing that country [Mexico] from having the power to annoy them." He then added that "the navigating and manufacturing interests of the North and East were equally interested in making it a part of this Union." Although Calhoun was careful to explain the national interest in Texas, he tied recognition firmly to annexation, seeing the first as ultimately and quickly leading to the second. This position raised a number of objections because several senators saw in it a thinly veiled plan to expand slave territory.[8] Still, even though slavery was a volatile issue, it was not by any means the most important issue at this time, and support or opposition to the recognition of Texas was not drawn upon North-South or slave-free lines.

On June 18, Henry Clay presented a report and resolution of the Committee on Foreign Relations concerning the recognition of Texas. After explaining the methods and process of recognition of a foreign power and the situation in Texas at the current time, the report concluded that

> [T]he independence of Texas ought to be acknowledged by the United States whenever satisfactory information shall be received that it has in successful operation a civil Government, capable of performing the duties and fulfilling the obligations of an independent Power.[9]

On July 1, with an amendment expressing satisfaction with the president's action in having sent an agent, Henry M. Morfit, to Texas to report on the situation, the Senate adopted the report unanimously. As Congress adjourned, recognition and perhaps even annexation seemed to be waiting only for Texas to prove itself independent.

In September, voters in Texas went to the polls to decide several important issues. First, they were to ratify the constitution as it had been written or give the congress the power to amend it. Second, they were to elect a government, including a president, vice president, members of congress, and other officers. Finally, they were to vote on whether they wished to be annexed to the United States. The Texas voters unanimously ratified the constitution, overwhelmingly voted in Sam Houston, the hero of San Jacinto, as president of the new Republic, and voted overwhelmingly, 3277 to 91, in favor of annexation. The Houston government was inaugurated in early October. Immediately Houston set about to gain recognition and annexation as called for in the election. This task fell upon William H. Wharton.

Wharton was commissioned a minister for the Republic of Texas with instructions to gain recognition from the United States and to broach the subject of annexation. He carried with him copies of the declaration of independence, the constitution, and acts and proceedings of the new government to show that it was indeed a *de facto* government. He also carried with him a file of newspaper clippings from the most important newspaper in Texas. Wharton departed for Washington on November 22. As he traveled toward Washington, Wharton noticed a striking change in the attitude of Americans toward Texas. Instead of the overwhelming support he had reported on his first trip, now he noted a building opposition, especially in the northern and eastern presses.[10]

On December 5, 1836, the U.S. Congress reconvened. Jackson's opening message cautiously referred to the Texas issue, but remained noncommittal, although he did promise to have additional information in the near future, once he had received Morfit's report. Meanwhile, Wharton arrived in Washington and was granted an interview with Secretary of State Forsyth but was told that no action would be taken until Jackson presented his information to Congress. Jackson's message with the promised extracts from Morfit's report was presented to Congress on December 21. To almost everyone's surprise and to Wharton's shock, Jackson counseled delay in recognizing Texas.

The government bureaucracy now took over to thwart almost any action on Texas at all. Although Jackson told Wharton that he favored recognition, he felt recognition was Congress's duty; he would concur if the barest majority supported it. Armed with this information, Wharton began pressuring friendly congressmen to take action. On January 11, Robert J. Walker introduced a joint resolution calling for the recognition of Texas, but no action was taken on it. Congress was reluctant to act without another message from Jackson. Because of Jackson's apparent opposition in his message to Congress, many Jackson men feared taking action in opposition to the president. Jackson, for his part, saw no need for a further message, believing that it was Congress's responsibility to take action, which he then would support. Neither Congress nor Jackson seemed willing to take the decisive step.

Wharton eventually discovered the reason for the delay. Martin Van Buren was going to be Jackson's successor, but Van Buren did not have the influence that Jackson carried. Van Buren's supporters realized that the question of annexation would be broached shortly after Texas was recognized, and they also realized that annexation was a divisive subject. Annexing Texas would add to the United States a vast region of slave territory that could conceivably change the balance of power in Congress in favor of the slave states. If annexation became an issue, Van Buren would be forced to come down on one side or the other, thereby alienating the opposition and weakening or perhaps even destroying his control of Congress after the upcoming election. In addition, if a vote on recognition were called for and failed, the failure would embarrass Van Buren's administration before it even entered office.

Finally, on February 18, the House Committee on Foreign Affairs proposed resolutions to recognize the independence of Texas and to appropriate funds for a diplomat. The resolutions were adopted February 28; on March 1, after weeks of delay, the Senate by a vote of 23-19 passed the resolution proposed by Walker on January 11. On his last day as president, Jackson appointed a diplomat, and the recognition of Texas became official. Annexation, which seemed to be only a short time off, would be delayed for almost a decade.[11]

THE DEBATE OVER ANNEXATION

Once Texas was recognized, Texas president Sam Houston immediately began working toward annexation as called for in the Texas elections of 1836. He appointed Memucan Hunt to succeed Wharton in Washington. In August 1837, with the Van Buren administration safely inaugurated and settled, Hunt made his proposal to U.S. Secretary of State John Forsyth. He concentrated his presentation on the benefits of annexation to the United States. Northern industrialists would benefit from widened markets for their goods, southern agriculturalists would benefit by removing competition with Texas sugar and cotton in Europe, and the United States would increase its control of the Gulf of Mexico. Hunt concluded with a veiled threat that if the United States refused annexation, Texas might improve its ties with European countries and therefore might be forever lost to the United States.

Secretary of State John Forsyth replied that the United States could not annex Texas on two grounds. First, he argued that it would be unconstitutional for the United States to annex an independent nation, even with the consent of its citizens. Second, because Mexico had never recognized Texas's independence and was nominally at war with Mexico, annexing Texas would involve the United States in a war with Mexico. In addition, Van Buren had enough trouble on his hands with the Panic of 1837, a financial crisis that hit soon after he took office.[12]

Shortly after Congress came back into session, John Quincy Adams, one of the major opponents to annexation of Texas, proposed a resolution that any information concerning annexation be forwarded to the House, claiming that the American people had a right to know what was going on. He also claimed that a majority of his constituents opposed annexation so stringently that they would prefer disunion to the admittance of Texas.[13] Whether New Englanders actually felt that strongly or not, it is clear that they opposed the addition of Texas because of the expansion of slavery that would result. Throughout September numerous memorials and petitions were presented in Congress opposing the annexation of Texas.

On September 18 Adams proposed adopting a resolution: "The power of annexing the people of any independent foreign state to this union is a power not delegated by the Constitution of the United States to their Congress or to any department of their government, but reserved to the people." The resolution was tabled, and serious discussion concerning Texas was put off to the next session of Congress.

In the second session of the Twenty-fifth Congress, on April 24, 1838, Senator William C. Preston of South Carolina introduced a resolution that called for the United States to "reannex" Texas. Preston followed his resolution with a speech explaining the inability of Mexico to reconquer Texas. He added "proof" that the territory of Texas was at one time part of the United States, hence, the wording in the resolution to "reannex" it. He continued that he found it strange that John Quincy Adams, the leading opponent to annexing Texas, had tried to buy Texas from Mexico during his presidency.

Preston then showed the fallacy of Adams's proposal that annexing a sovereign state would be unconstitutional. He pointed out that Congress is expressly given the power to admit new states and that in fact an area must be organized as a state before it is admitted. New territory had been acquired from both France and Spain, in the form of Louisiana and Florida, respectively. Why then, asked Preston, cannot the United States negotiate the acquisition of territory with Texas, even if it be for the entire realm? Obviously, concluded Preston, the United States could annex new territory and later admit that territory to the Union as states.

Finally, Preston addressed the opposition of the people from the northern and middle states to Texas. He argued that the Northerners' fears that the acquisition of Texas might upset the balance of power in favor of the South were ludicrous. Even with the acquisition of Texas, the southern population would never rival that of the North; thus the House of Representatives was and would remain under the control of the northern states. He concluded that the South stood "entirely on the defensive; we desire *safety*, not power, and we must have it."[14] Preston's lengthy speech demonstrated that the slavery issue was becoming more and more prominent. Northerners became more adamant in their opposition to Texas, and Southerners became more defensive, both sides seeing a conspiracy to wrest or keep power from the other. Preston's resolution was never acted upon.

In the House of Representatives, John Quincy Adams led the opposition to annexing Texas. From June 16, when he reintroduced his resolution declaring the annexation of a sovereign nation to be unconstitutional, until July 9, 1838, when Congress adjourned, Adams spoke almost daily on the issue, preventing the House from taking any action.

Even before the U.S. Congress adjourned, Sam Houston, the Texas president, realizing that Congress would take no action, withdrew Texas's offer of annexation. Other events in Texas dramatically affected the possibility of annexation. Houston's term was ending in December 1838, and, according to the Texas constitution, he could not succeed himself. There were no real political parties in Texas, and none ever developed. Politics generally revolved around personalities, with Sam Houston as the central figure. Texans generally lined up to support Houston or to oppose him. Vice President Mirabeau B. Lamar announced his candidacy for president in early 1838 indicating that he would oppose Houston's policies. Lamar won the election easily, helped by the suicides of the two leading Houston candidates.[15]

In his notes for his inaugural address Lamar discussed his reasons for opposing the annexation of Texas. First, Lamar feared the abolition of slavery if Texas joined the Union. He noted the hostility of northern abolitionists toward Texans in general and loathed the idea of prostrating the Republic, begging for admission, at the feet of those who despised them. Second, Lamar argued that recognition by Britain and other countries would most likely not be forthcoming as long as Texas sought annexation. Foreign powers would be insulted if they recognized Texas only to have it shun their offers of goodwill by joining the United States. Therefore, Texas should halt its attempts to gain annexation by the United States and instead should concentrate on developing ties with other nations to further its independence.[16] Lamar also liked the idea of an independent Texas and had visions of building it into an empire that would stretch to the Pacific Ocean and possibly even conquer Mexico itself in the foreseeable future.

Lamar worked seriously toward gaining European recognition for Texas. As a result, France, which was at the verge of war with Mexico, became the first European nation to recognize Texas in 1839. In 1840 the Netherlands and Britain followed suit, although to win over Britain, Texas had to agree to suppress the African slave trade and to allow Britain to mediate a settlement between Mexico and Texas. In 1841 Belgium also recognized Texas. Unfortunately, Lamar was unable to gain recognition from Mexico, and, as his administration came to a close, open hostility broke out between the two nations.[17]

In the Texas elections of September 1841 Sam Houston ran against Lamar's vice president David G. Burnett. Rather than focusing on the issues, the candidates threw barbs at each other, and the campaign devolved into a mudslinging contest. Houston won re-election 7,508 to 2,574, primarily because of his overwhelming popularity. Once inaugurated, Houston cautiously approached the United States concerning annexation. He appointed Isaac Van Zandt to be Texas's representative in Washington. Van Zandt reported that President John Tyler and the majority of his cabinet supported annexation, but that they were not sure they could gain the two-thirds vote necessary to pass a treaty through the Senate. In fact, Secretary of State Daniel Webster informed Van Zandt that until Texas settled its issues with Mexico and attained Mexican recognition, the United States would be unable to act.[18]

Angered by this information, Houston increased contact with the British. Encouraged, the British hoped to negotiate a settlement between Texas and Mexico, thus encouraging Texas to remain independent. The British knew that one of the issues motivating Texas to seek annexation was the constant threat of an invasion from Mexico. Whether planned by Houston or not, his increased contact with the British gained the worried attention of the United States. The United States feared a British protectorate over Texas, which would bring a decisive halt to the growing idea of Manifest Destiny.

Aware of the British-Texas rapprochement, President Tyler decided to take action. Tyler had assumed the presidency upon the death of Whig president William Henry Harrison. He was a former Democrat, a Southerner, and a slaveowner. He had been placed on the Whig ticket to gain southern support in the 1840 election. Upon his ascension to the presidency, he had quickly alienated the Whigs in his cabinet and in Congress by opposing the national bank and other Whig programs. Thus Tyler quickly became a president without a party. He seized upon the Texas question as a way to regain political support.

After Daniel Webster resigned as secretary of state, Tyler appointed fellow Virginian Abel Upshur to the office. Upshur lobbied among the senators, downplaying the slavery issue and the threat of war with Mexico and emphasizing the British threat, nationalism, and the idea of Manifest Destiny. By the time he began negotiating with the Texans, he apparently felt sure of the success of a treaty. In October 1843 he approached Van Zandt with a proposal to open treaty negotiations. Houston, however, was reluctant to open negotiations without some guarantees. If a treaty were negotiated and then failed to be ratified by the U.S. Senate, Mexico might call off a recently negotiated armistice, and the British might be so offended as to cast off their dealings with Texas, leaving the fledgling Republic in a very dangerous position. Houston wanted assurances that the treaty would pass and that the United States would protect Texas from Mexico until the ratification process was complete. Tyler's administration could do neither with certainty.

Houston's reluctance was almost bypassed when nine-tenths of the members of the Texas congress signed a memorial advocating immediate annexation. Houston tartly reminded the congress of the dangers of failure and that Texas must wait for action by the United States. Under Upshur's guidance the treaty negotiations commenced and were almost complete when, in February 1844, Upshur was killed in an explosion on an American warship. Tyler replaced Upshur with John C. Calhoun, spokesman of the South and an avid expansionist.

Calhoun at first appeared to be a wise choice. He favored not only annexing Texas but also acquiring the Oregon Country. Calhoun put the finishing touches on the treaty, and by April both sides were satisfied.[19] According to the terms of the treaty, Texas would join the Union as a territory. Texas would surrender its public lands and its public property, but in exchange the United States would assume Texas's debt, up to $10 million. The boundaries were left vague, but the United States reserved the right to adjust the boundary as necessary. Texas could apply for statehood as soon as it fulfilled the requirements according to the Constitution.[20]

As word leaked out that a treaty was being negotiated, newspapers in the North and the South began focusing on the issue. Petitions and memorials flooded into Congress both supporting and opposing annexation. The North-South or slave-free split was not complete, however. For example, on April 22, 1844, the day the treaty was presented to Congress by Tyler, petitions favoring annexation were presented from Maine, New York, and Pennsylvania, although the New York petition had signatures divided into columns, one side in support of annexing Texas with slavery and the other only supporting annexation without slavery. Another petition, presented on the same day, also from New York, opposed annexing Texas on any grounds. In general, though, northern states tended to oppose annexation, and southern states supported it.

Tyler presented the treaty to the Senate with a message espousing the major arguments favoring annexation. He stressed that the acquisition of Texas would be valuable to all sections of the country. Northeasterners would benefit from increased intercoastal trade, which would help their shipping industries flourish. Westerners would find new markets for their beef, pork, and horses. Southerners would gain peace and security from both domestic and foreign efforts to disrupt their culture. In addition, Tyler reminded Congress that most Texans were Americans and that Texas had established its independence and had been recognized by European nations. Therefore Mexico would be forced to accept annexation without war. Finally, he emphasized that annexing Texas was necessary to prevent encirclement of the United States by European powers.[21]

Congress spent the next several months debating the treaty. The year 1844 was, however, an election year, and many opposing congressmen were loath to give Tyler a victory that they might be able to save for their own administration. Many also wished to await the results of the election to determine where the American people stood on the issue. Secretary of State Calhoun damaged his own cause by stating in a letter to England, which was published nationally, that Texas must be joined to the United States to protect slavery. This statement, of course, alienated abolitionists and probably cost Calhoun the treaty. Many southern Whigs, who normally would have supported the treaty, followed the party line and voted with their northern brethren to support their party's platform opposing annexation. Many Democrats who were angered at their party's rejection of Van Buren and his replacement with the ardent expansionist Polk joined them. They broke with the party to vote against the treaty. As a result, on June 8 the treaty was decisively defeated 35-16.[22]

Many senators opposing the treaty believed that there would soon be another opportunity to acquire Texas. Thomas Hart Benton, for example, had earlier supported annexation but had voted against the treaty. Two days after the treaty's rejection, Benton explained himself in a speech before Congress. Now that the treaty had been rejected, the way had been cleared for "open, honorable, and successful negotiations," and he was now ready to work toward that end. He saw the treaty as an "insidious scheme of sudden and secret annexation" whose only purpose was to further the political success of Tyler before the election. Despite Benton's flamboyant speech, his motives were as political as those he ascribed to Tyler. Benton simply wanted to deny the Tyler administration a victory so close to the election.

Benton then offered a bill setting out the guidelines for negotiating with Texas. First, the boundaries of Texas should be established, not at the Rio Grande, as Texas claimed, nor the Nueces as Mexico claimed, but between the two rivers, then along the mountains and highlands between the Mississippi River and the Rio Grande. Second, the people of Texas must give some indication that a majority of them desire annexation. Third, Texas should be admitted as a state, but its size should be limited so that it was no larger than the largest existing state. The remaining area claimed by Texas would be admitted with territorial status, divided as equally as possible into two territories. Slavery would be prohibited forever in the northern territory and would be allowed in the southern territory. Finally, the assent of Mexico should be obtained, and any other details would be worked out by the United States over time.

Because adjournment was near, the Senate tabled Benton's proposition without taking any action. Benton's actions, however, set the stage for the dominant issue when Congress reconvened and also foreshadowed the main issue of the election of 1844.[23]

POLITICS AND THE ELECTION OF 1844

During the debate over the rejected treaty, both Henry Clay and Martin Van Buren, the leading candidates in the Whig and Democratic parties, respectively, made a private agreement and came out in opposition to the treaty. They hoped to remove Texas and the controversial slavery issue from the campaign. Although both men left the door open to future annexation, their immediate opposition encouraged Tyler to work toward forming a third party based upon annexation and expansionism.

In May, the Whig Party held its convention and dutifully nominated Clay as its presidential candidate. The party then adopted a platform that emphasized the tariff and utterly ignored Texas. Later that month, the Democratic convention met. Expansionists within the party managed to invoke an old rule requiring a nominee to have two-thirds of the ballots before being declared the candidate. Van Buren could not muster that majority. After several days of fruitless balloting, James K. Polk emerged as the candidate. Polk, a Tennessean, was an avid expansionist and called not only for the "re-annexation" of Texas, but also for the "re-occupation" of Oregon, all the way to its northern boundary. Polk believed that the acquisition of Oregon would help offset any opposition in the North to the annexation of Texas. The Democratic platform killed any chance Tyler had of winning, and he and his supporters were eventually wooed back into the Democratic Party.

There was a third party in the election, however. The National Liberty Party, an abolitionist party, nominated James G. Birney for president. The Liberty Party was adamantly opposed to the annexation of Texas because it would allow slavery to spread.

During the campaign, Clay began to fear that his stance against Texas might cost him important southern support and, thus, the election. In an effort to assure Southerners, Clay published a series of letters in the South explaining that he was no abolitionist and that he would favor annexing Texas if it could be done honorably and without causing war with Mexico. Although the letters were aimed at Southerners, Democrats circulated the letters heavily throughout the North, damaging Clay's standing among abolitionists. Clay later tried to retreat to his original stance against Texas, but the damage had been done.

Polk won the election with 170 electoral votes to Clay's 105. The results were not as decisive as they appeared. Birney's candidacy cut deeply into Clay's support in many northern states, most importantly in New York. In New York and Michigan many abolitionists, disgusted by Clay's waffling, deserted him to vote for Birney. As a result, Polk won both states and the election.

Although Polk's victory was far from a landslide, many people within and without the United States interpreted it as a mandate for annexation. Tyler certainly saw it as such and was determined to make his lame-duck period productive. After his treaty had suffered a decisive defeat in the aftermath of the Democratic convention, Tyler had immediately sent all the correspondence and information pertaining to Texas to the House of Representatives. He proposed an alternate means of bringing in Texas, suggesting a joint resolution of Congress, which required a simple majority of both houses of Congress rather than the support of two-thirds of the Senate as required for a treaty. Congress adjourned on June 17 before action could be taken, and attention was focused on the national election.[24]

In Texas, Houston was angered by the rejection of the treaty. His term was coming to an end, and because he could not succeed himself, his time was limited. The Texas election of September 1844 once again focused on personalities rather than parties. Houston and his supporters rallied around Houston's secretary of state Anson Jones. The opposition threw its support to Vice President Edward Burleson. As in previous Texas elections, the candidates fell to name calling and mudslinging rather than focusing on the issues. Jones was portrayed as a mere puppet of Houston, whereas Burleson was linked to Lamar's failed policies. Annexation was barely mentioned. In the end, Jones won handily, 7,037 to 5,668, benefiting from Houston's popularity.

Before Houston left office, however, he had one more card to play. He instructed President-elect Jones, in his capacity as secretary of state, to contact Texas diplomats in Europe to push forward with negotiations for commercial treaties with England and France. Houston no doubt knew that the information would be perceived by the United States as an indication that it had lost Houston's support and possibly any chance of gaining Texas if the news from Europe was favorable. Jones, as president-elect, feared that such action would kill annexation, which he apparently favored, or might provoke a war between the United States and the European powers, either of which would negatively affect his ability to govern Texas when he assumed office. Therefore, Jones took no action on Houston's instructions.[25]

Meanwhile, with the U.S. presidential election concluded, Tyler waited impatiently for Congress to come back into session. In his annual message of December 3, 1844, Tyler reiterated all of the statements in favor of annexing Texas that he had voiced in his message accompanying the failed treaty of 1844. In addition, however, he pointed out that one of the main objections to the treaty was that it "had not been submitted to the ordeal of public opinion in the United States." The recent election, he argued, had rectified that situation. "The decision of the people and the States, on this great and interesting subject, has been decisively manifested," Tyler claimed. "A controlling majority of the people, and a large majority of the States, have declared in favor of immediate annexation." Therefore, Tyler concluded, Congress should proceed as hastily as possible to achieve this objective. Finally, apparently ignoring Houston's actions, Tyler claimed that the Texans still desired annexation and there should be no legitimate complaint by Mexico should the United States take action.[26]

Both houses of Congress proceeded to discuss the issue. Members of Congress introduced no less than eighteen bills and resolutions to annex Texas. One of the earliest proposals was to incorporate the rejected treaty into a bill and to annex Texas under those terms. Benton reintroduced his bill to the Senate, and Congressman John W. Tibbatts introduced a similar bill in the House. Almost all the bills called for a limit on the size of the state of Texas and for the prohibition of slavery in any part of the Republic north of the Missouri Compromise line. Joseph J. McDowell set out one of the more liberal propositions. He proposed to admit Texas as a state once it developed a constitution and a state government approved by Congress. It could in the future be divided into a maximum of four additional states as the people of Texas deemed necessary. The following day Milton Brown introduced a similar resolution, but with Texas keeping its debt and its public lands.

For a month, Texas dominated the debates within the House. Finally, on January 25, 1845, the House voted on the original resolution and numerous amendments that had been presented. Milton Brown offered a plan that called for admitting the Republic of Texas into the Union as a state with a republican form of government to be created by its population and with the consent of its government. All questions concerning the boundaries of Texas would be settled by the U.S. government. Texas would cede all of its public buildings, fortifications, ports, harbors, navy, armaments, and any other property pertaining to public defense but would retain its public lands, its public funds, and its debt. The United States would deny any responsibilities for the new state's debt. Texas would have the right to create up to four additional states from its territory when the population allowed, with any state formed from the area below the Missouri Compromise line to be admitted with or without slaves, as its residents desired.

Representative Douglass proposed adding that slavery be prohibited in any state formed out of territory above the Missouri Compromise line. Brown accepted the addition, and the House voted 109 to 99 to accept the proposal. After numerous comments and votes on procedures, the resolution was presented in its final form and passed 120 to 98. On Monday, January 27, the Senate received word of the House's action. The Senate delayed action for several weeks before finally resolving to bring the joint resolution before a committee of the whole on February 14.

For nearly two weeks senators presented their views of the issue before bringing the resolution up for a vote on February 27. Senator Walker from

Mississippi offered an amendment to the resolution that would give the president the option of offering to negotiate another treaty with Texas if that were preferable. The amendment squeaked by on a vote of 27-25. An effort by opponents of the resolution to strike the amended resolution was defeated 28-24. At this point Senator Miller proposed replacing the resolution with the proposal offered by Benton in the last session and early in the current session. Benton's proposal would have limited the size of the state of Texas and divided the territory acquired as equally as possible into slave and free portions. Even Benton voted against the measure, and it was defeated 33-11. Finally the Senate voted on the amended House resolution itself, and it passed by the narrow margin of 27-25.

The following day, the House took up the issue of the amended resolution. After a brief discussion and the overwhelming defeat of several proposed amendments, the House passed the Senate version by a larger majority than the original, 132 to 76. It now only remained for the president to sign it to make it official. Tyler signed the bill immediately and ordered Andrew Jackson Donelson, nephew of Andrew Jackson and the American minister to Texas, to offer Texas annexation under the terms of the original House version.[27]

While Congress hammered out the final details of the joint resolution, Britain desperately struggled to block annexation and maintain an independent Texas. Charles Elliot, the British chargé d'affaires in Texas, informed his government that a substantial number of Texan leaders would oppose annexation if they believed they could do so safely. Both Anson Jones and Sam Houston appeared, at least publicly, to oppose annexation. How sincere they were in their convictions is unclear. It is likely that their opposition was a bluff to obtain Britain's help in gaining Mexican recognition of Texas and to increase fears in the United States of losing Texas forever.

The British realized that the greatest threat to Texas independence was a Mexican invasion. Mexico was constantly threatening invasion, although up to that time it had not been able to mount a serious invasion. The British hoped that by convincing Mexico to recognize Texas, Texas might maintain its independence and develop commercial ties with Britain and other European nations at the expense of the United States.

The British and French envoys working together managed to wrest a promise from Jones to delay convening the Texas congress for ninety days. Jones warned them, however, that he could not hold back the growing public support for annexation indefinitely. When Donelson arrived with the American offer, he found Jones averse to calling congress, and even Houston, retired but still influential, gave the resolution a cold reception.

Elliot traveled to Mexico personally to work out an agreement with Mexico. Texas offered to delay any negotiations for annexation for ninety days in exchange for Mexican recognition. The Mexican reply reached Elliot on May 17, 1845. Mexico would recognize Texas on condition that Texas remain independent. If Texas accepted annexation by the United States, the agreement would be immediately nullified. Elliot rushed the Mexican offer to the Texan government, arriving in early June.

Under public pressure Jones called for congress to convene on June 16 and for a special convention elected by the people to meet at the capital on July 4 to determine the future course of the Republic. Elliot arrived with his successfully negotiated treaty just days before congress convened. When congress assembled, Jones laid the two offers before them, the Mexican offer to recognize them if they rejected the offer of annexation, and the joint resolution from the U.S. Congress for annexation and statehood. If there was doubt about the standing of Jones or Houston, there was no doubt on congress's position. The Texas senate unanimously rejected the Mexican treaty, and both houses of congress unanimously accepted the American offer. In addition, they approved elections to be held for the July 4 convention.

A few weeks later, the convention, comprised almost entirely of American-born Texans, met in Austin on the prescribed date. With only one dissenting vote, they adopted an ordinance approving annexation. The delegates then proceeded to draft a state constitution.[28] The constitution was twice as long as the Republic's constitution had been and was modeled on those of many southern states.

THE TEXAS STATE CONSTITUTION

The Texas constitution consisted of thirteen articles. The first article was the bill of rights that guaranteed such typical rights as freedom of religion, speech, and the press. It also included the right to a speedy trial by jury and protections from excessive bail and double jeopardy. Citizens had the right to bear arms and protection from unreasonable search and seizure. Imprisonment for debt was forbidden. Monopolies were prohibited and all "free men" were guaranteed equal protection under the law. Finally, citizens had the right to assemble, and all the expressed rights were guaranteed against the general powers of the government to be forever inviolate.

The second article simply created a government with legislative, executive, and judicial branches. The third article dealt with the legislative branch. All free male citizens over the age of twenty-one, with the exception of Native Americans not taxed and Africans and their descendents, were allowed to vote. U.S. military personnel were also prohibited from voting in Texas elections. The legislative branch consisted of a House of Representatives with at least forty-five but not more than ninety members and a Senate of at least nineteen but no more than thirty-three members.

Members of the House would serve two-year terms, had to have resided in the state at least two years before the election, and had to be at least twenty-one years of age. Senators would be elected to four-year terms, with one-half chosen every other year. Senators had to have resided in the state three years previous to the election and be at least thirty years old. Ministers of the Gospel were prohibited from serving as congressmen. The constitution called for a census to be taken every eight years for the purpose of adjusting the apportionment of congressional representation. The capital would remain in Austin until 1850, at which time an election would determine the permanent seat of government.

Article 4 created the judiciary branch, with a supreme court consisting of a chief justice and two associates. District courts would be created as needed. The justices of the supreme court and the district courts would be appointed by the governor with the advice and consent of two-thirds of the Senate and would serve six-year terms.

Article 5 set up the executive branch. Governors would serve two-year terms but could not serve more than four years in any six-year period. Governors had to be at least thirty and citizens of the United States or Texas at the time of the adoption of the constitution. The governor would serve as commander-in-chief of the state's army, navy, and the militia except when said militia was in the service of the United States. The governor could veto acts of congress but could be overridden with a two-thirds vote in each house. A provision was made to prevent a pocket veto.

Article 6 provided for a militia to be called up by the governor to execute state laws, suppress insurrections, or repel invasions. The next article, the longest in the constitution, discussed general provisions. Many of the thirty-seven sections concerned limitations on the legislature. It banned anyone convicted of bribery, forgery, perjury, or other high crimes from holding public office. Anyone involved in dueling was likewise barred from holding office. Lotteries were prohibited, as were bank corporations. Private corporations were forbidden except when approved by two-thirds of both houses of congress, and the state was prohibited from owning any stock or property in a corporation thus created. The article recognized a woman's private property before her marriage and any gifts she received after marriage as being separate from community property. Finally, the article provided for the method of amending the constitution. A two-thirds vote of each house could propose an amendment that would then be sent to the people for a vote. Upon approval by a majority vote of the people, the next legislature could ratify the proposed amendment with a two-thirds vote in each house and incorporate it into the constitution.

Article 8 dealt with slavery. The legislature was forbidden to pass laws emancipating slaves without the consent of their owners or without compensating owners for their lost property. The legislature could, however, pass laws allowing owners to emancipate their own slaves. Immigrants were free to bring their slave property into the state. Laws were to be created obliging owners to treat their slaves with humanity, to provide them with their basic needs, and to abstain from causing injury to life or limb. Crimes by slaves other than petit theft would be tried by a petit jury. Finally, anyone who maliciously murdered or dismembered a slave would be tried as though the crime had been perpetrated on a free white person, except in the case of insurrection by such slave.

Impeachment was discussed in Article 9. The House of Representatives held the power of impeachment, and the Senate would try any cases. A two-thirds vote was required to convict, and punishment by congress would be limited to removal from office and barring from future officeholding. The official would be vulnerable to additional punishment through the court system.

Education was the issue of Article 10. The article called for the establishment of free schools throughout the state to be supported through property taxes. One-tenth of the state's tax revenues were to be set aside in a perpetual fund for the support of the schools. School property could not be sold, although it could be leased and the proceeds added to the school fund.

Article 11 nullified forged head-right claims or those issued to fictitious persons. The district courts were instructed to remain open until July 1, 1847, to certify head-right claims not already verified by a commission appointed to detect fraudulent claims. Any claims not verified by the specified date would be considered null and void.

Article 12 verified the continued existence of the land office. Article 13, the final article, simply set up the process for easing the transition from Republic to statehood. It set up elections for the people to accept or reject the constitution and also to accept or reject annexation. Upon approval, an election of state officials was to be ordered by the president for the third Monday in December. Officers chosen in this election would serve until the first general election scheduled for November 1847. This article also instructed the president of the Republic to forward the constitution, the results of the election, and all other pertinent materials to the United States for application for statehood. On August 27, 1845, the delegates signed the constitution and presented it to President Anson Jones.[29]

An election was called for October 13, 1845, to allow people to approve the constitution and voice their opinion of annexation. Despite the supposed opposition of Jones and Houston, the election left little doubt of the opinion of the Texas people. Annexation was approved 4,254 to 267, and the constitution was approved 4,174 to 312. Because the American offer was set to expire on January 1, 1846, the documents and election results were rushed to Washington, D.C., where they arrived in early December. President Polk, concerned that the Senate might delay taking action until the deadline passed, recalled Vice President George Dallas from a vacation to preside over the Senate.[30]

FEDERAL APPROVAL

When Congress convened in December, the House took on the issue of Texas statehood early. Most congressmen considered the vote a foregone conclusion. A brief effort was made to delay action, and one congressman proposed to amend the resolution bringing in Texas as a state with slavery prohibited. The amendment was blocked, however, and after a brief debate the House affirmed the resolution on December 16, by a vote of 141 to 56. The House then forwarded the resolution to the Senate for concurrence.[31]

In the Senate, the great orator Daniel Webster preceded the vote with a speech outlining his opposition to the resolution. Webster had not been in Congress the previous session, so he had not participated in the debates, although he had opposed annexation in his actions and speech throughout the country. Now, he probably voiced the opinion of many of the opponents of the resolution. He noted that there was little doubt of the passage of the bill, but he still wanted his comments on record. He believed that the United States endangered itself by acquiring more territory, especially slave territory, and expressed his belief that, although he did not and never had said anything about slavery where it already existed, he could not condone the spreading of slavery nor the admittance of new states with slavery. The founders had never envisioned such a thing. He concluded his relatively brief statement by agreeing with the Massachusetts legislature and the mass of the state's people and reaffirming his own arguments for the last eight years in setting on record his dissent and opposition to the annexation of Texas. After a few more spirited speeches, the Senate, on December 22, voted and passed the resolution 31-13.[32]

After the concurrence of both houses, an official version of the bill was written up and sent to both houses for appropriate signatures. The signed version was then forwarded to President Polk, who signed in on December 29, 1845, making the annexation of Texas official and bringing it into the Union as the twenty-eighth state.

On December 15, 1845, Texas voters went to the polls to elect their state officials. James Pinckney Henderson was elected the first governor of the new state. In a public ceremony in front of the capitol at Austin, on February 19, 1846, Anson Jones gave his farewell address, the Texas flag was lowered, and the American flag was raised. Governor Henderson then gave his inaugural address, and the annexation process was at last complete almost ten years after Texas declared its independence.[33]

Although the process was complete, the controversy and effects of annexation were felt for many years to come. Within a few months the United States was embroiled in a war with Mexico, just as many opponents of Texas had warned. As a result of the war, the United States acquired the rest of the Southwest, including California, large chunks of Arizona, New Mexico, Nevada, Utah, Colorado, and Wyoming, adding almost 1.25 million square miles to the nation.

The Texas boundary, which had been one of the causes of the war with Mexico, was determined by the Treaty of Guadalupe Hidalgo (1848) to be the Rio Grande to its source, then due north to the 42d parallel. Although this agreement ended the boundary dispute with Mexico, it did not create the final boundaries of Texas. Within the area claimed by Texas was the town of Santa Fe with a heavily Mexican population. Historically, as part of Mexico, Santa Fe had been part of the Mexican state of New Mexico. During Lamar's presidency, the Texans had attempted to assert their authority over the area and establish a trade route to the isolated town. The expedition had been a dismal failure. It suffered many hardships in its journey across the deserts and plains of west Texas, and upon its arrival in Santa Fe its members were captured by Mexican forces and hauled as prisoners into Mexico.

As a result of the Treaty of Guadalupe Hidalgo, however, Santa Fe now fell under the jurisdiction of the United States and was still claimed by Texas. Residents of the town wanted no connection with Texas and resisted the incorporation. The issue was finally resolved, along with many other issues throughout the United States, in the Compromise of 1850. In the compromise, Texas gave up its claim to Santa Fe and the surrounding region of New Mexico and in exchange the U.S. government assumed Texas's debt, about $10 million. Thus the boundary of Texas was set at its current location, and the debt question, which had been a big issue in the annexation debates, was finally laid to rest as well.

Besides helping to bring Manifest Destiny to a conclusion in the South, the annexation of Texas also helped the United States in its claim to Oregon. Once Texas joined the Union, the subsequent loss of British influence in the area also loosened Britain's grip on the Oregon Country, hastening a settlement in which the United States gained ownership of half of that region. Thus, Texas helped to open the way for American expansion to the Pacific Ocean.

Finally, the retention of her public domain was perhaps the greatest boon to Texas. The vast tracts of land allowed Texas to construct a large web of railroads across the huge state, to build the largest of all state capitols with funds from land sales, and to endow a state university system. Eventually, Texas would benefit from oil rights off its coastline, which it would claim to possess by virtue of Spanish law. Although Texas lost that battle in the Supreme Court, Congress would later return the oil-rich area to Texas administration.

SUMMARY

From the beginning, the greatest obstacle to annexing Texas was the issue of slavery. Northern abolitionists saw the annexation of Texas, with its huge territory, as allowing the spread of slavery, an abomination that must be stopped at all costs. Other Northerners saw a threat of increasing slave states' power in Congress: Texas was large enough to be divided into several states, perhaps giving the slave states control of the Senate, and, although unlikely, the House of Representatives.

Southerners saw Texas as a safety net. Many felt that the North was becoming too powerful and, with a radicalization of the abolitionist movement, feared that eventually Northerners might begin attacking slavery where it already existed rather than limiting their efforts to stop the spread of slavery. Thus Texas would help the South retain equality in the Senate. Most Southerners denied any threat to the North, pointing out that slavery was forever prohibited in the vast territory north of the Missouri Compromise line. The South, they argued, would never be more powerful than the North and would never threaten to force slavery upon unwilling Northerners, but, they feared, the North might try to impose abolition upon the South.

Most of the other issues in the debate concerning Texas's statehood pale in comparison to the slavery issue, which became at times extremely volatile. The constitutional issue, for example, was never a major factor, although many Northerners appealed to it. They argued that the United States had no power to annex a sovereign nation or could not admit it as a state without going through the territorial process. Southerners effectively negated these arguments by pointing out that there was really no difference in annexing a sovereign nation and annexing (purchasing) Louisiana, which was part of the French Empire. If they could annex part of a country, then why could they not annex an entire country, if it so desired? They continued that, by definition, each new state had to be a "state" before it could be admitted, because Congress had the power to admit new "states." Therefore, the territorial status was unimportant.

On the other side, many supporters of Texas used the bugaboo of a British or French threat in Texas. Were Texas to remain independent, the British would no doubt create close ties with the new Republic and, by asserting themselves, might harm American trade in the area. British influence in Texas might also strengthen its claim to Oregon, thus cutting the United States off permanently from valuable access to the Pacific. Although the British connection was always tenuous at best and probably would not have become a major factor in the foreseeable future, many Americans feared a British-controlled Texas on their border.

Of all the people who opposed annexing Texas, John Quincy Adams was without a doubt the most vocal and able spokesman. He alone helped delay Texas statehood for years. Texas statehood could not be delayed indefinitely, however, because a sense of nationalism and expansionism was growing within the United States. Many Americans looked with desire toward the western half of the continent and saw its acquisition as their Manifest Destiny. By appealing to that desire and to national pride and by asserting that if Texas were lost, the British might gain a new foothold in the West, the supporters of annexation were able to win the day and overcome the slavery issue.

NOTES

1. Ethel Zivley Ratler, "Recognition of the Republic of Texas by the United States," *The Quarterly of the Texas State Historical Association* 13 (January 1910): 167–179.

2. Rupert N. Richardson, Adrian Anderson, and Ernest Wallace, *Texas: The Lone Star State*, 6th ed. (Englewood Cliffs, NJ: Prentice Hall, 1993), p. 109; Randolph B.

Campbell, *Gone to Texas: A History of the Lone Star State* (New York: Oxford University Press, 2003), p. 147.

3. A copy of the constitution of the Republic of Texas can be found at: http://www.law.utexas.edu/constitutions/text.html.

4. Ratiler, "Recognition of the Republic of Texas by the United States," pp. 182–187.

5. Ibid., pp. 195, 200.

6. Ibid., pp. 201–203.

7. Ibid., p. 214.

8. Quotations from the congressional debates before 1838 are taken from *Register of Debates*; quotations from the congressional debates after 1838 are taken from *The Congressional Globe*. Both can be found at: www.loc.gov.

9. *Register of Debates*, 24th Cong., 1st Sess., Senate, pp. 1846–1848.

10. Ratiler, "Recognition of the Republic of Texas by the United States," pp. 223, 230–232.

11. Ibid., pp. 233–253. See also the congressional debates during this time.

12. Eugene C. Barker, "The Annexation of Texas," *Southwestern Historical Quarterly* 50 (July 1946): 53–54.

13. *The Congressional Globe*, 25th Cong., 1st Sess., 1837, p. 23.

14. *Appendix to the Congressional Globe*, 25th Cong., 2d Sess., pp. 555–558. Italics in the original.

15. Campbell, *Gone to Texas*, p. 169.

16. Charles Adams Gulick, Jr., and Katherine Elliott, eds., *The Papers of Mirabeau Buonaparte Lamar*, 6 vols. (Austin, TX: A.C. Baldwin & Sons, 1922), 2:324–327.

17. Barker, "The Annexation of Texas," pp. 55–57.

18. Ibid., pp. 61–63; Campbell, *Gone to Texas*, pp. 175–176.

19. Barker, "The Annexation of Texas," pp. 61–64.

20. The text of the treaty can be found at: http://www.texassovereignty.org/hist/1844.

21. *Journal of the Executive Proceedings of the Senate of the United States of America, 1841–1854* (April 22, 1844), pp. 257–261. The journals of the House of Representatives and the Senate can be found at: www.loc.gov.

22. David M. Pletcher, *The Diplomacy of Annexation: Texas, Oregon, and the Mexican War* (Columbia: University of Missouri Press, 1973), pp. 144–149.

23. *Congressional Globe*, 28th Cong., 1st Sess., pp. 653–657, 660–661, 688.

24. Pletcher, *The Diplomacy of Annexation*, pp. 144–149, 168–171.

25. Campbell, *Gone to Texas*, p. 185; Barker, "The Annexation of Texas," pp. 66–67; Richardson, *Texas: The Lone Star State*, p. 145.

26. *Congressional Globe*, 28th Cong., 2d Sess., pp. 2–6.

27. For the debate, see *Congressional Globe* and the *Appendix to the Congressional Globe* for numerous speeches on both sides of the issue. See also Barker, "The Annexation of Texas," p. 70.

28. Barker, "The Annexation of Texas," pp. 70–72; Pletcher, *The Diplomacy of Annexation*, pp. 190–201.

29. Text of the Texas constitution of 1845 and supporting documents can be found at: http://www.law.utexas.edu/constitutions/text/1845index.html.

30. James L. Haley, "Annexation: Celebrating 150 Years of Texas Statehood" at: http://www.humanities-interactive.org/texas/annexation/annexation_essay.htm, p. 4; Campbell, *Gone to Texas*, p. 186.

31. *Congressional Globe*, 29th Cong., 1st Sess., pp. 39–40, 60–65.

32. Ibid., pp. 88–92. *The Congressional Globe* reports the vote as 31-14, but the *Senate Journal*, 29th Cong., 1st Sess., p. 64, which the author believes is more authoritative, records the vote as 31-13.

33. Barker, "The Annexation of Texas," p. 74; Campbell, *Gone to Texas*, p. 186; "Republic of Texas," *The Handbook of Texas Online*, at: http://www.tsha.utexas.edu/handbook/online/articles/view/RR/mzr2.html.

BIBLIOGRAPHY

Barker, Eugene C. "The Annexation of Texas." *Southwestern Historical Quarterly* 50 (July 1946): 49–74.

Campbell, Randolph B. *Gone to Texas: A History of the Lone Star State*. New York: Oxford University Press, 2003.

"The Handbook of Texas Online," http://www.tsha.edu/handbook/online/.

Smith, Justin Harvey. *The Annexation of Texas*. New York: Baker and Taylor Co., 1912.

THE STATE OF UTAH

Admitted to the Union as a State:
January 4, 1896

John McCormick

INTRODUCTION

Euro-American settlement of Utah began in the summer of 1847 with the arrival of the Mormons, members of the Church of Jesus Christ of Latter-day Saints. Although Utah was then technically under the control of Mexico, it was part of the land the United States captured from Mexico in the Mexican-American War and, with the signing of the Treaty of Guadalupe Hidalgo in February 1848, it officially became part of the United States. Although their thinking on the matter is not entirely clear, the Mormons had evidently come to Utah seeking independence and not necessarily affiliation with either the United States or Mexico. With the victory of the United States in the war, however, Utah would thereafter be either a U.S. territory or a state. Mormons preferred that it become a state, because it would have more control over its own affairs as a state than as a territory. They officially applied for statehood in 1849 as the State of Deseret, but in 1850 Congress granted territorial status instead. Utah applied for statehood six more times over almost fifty years before statehood was finally granted in 1896.

Why did statehood take so long? And why did most of Utah's first six applications not even receive serious consideration? Why did nearly fifty years of what might be called "cold war" develop between the people of the Utah and the people of the United States? The essential answer is this: throughout the nineteenth century Mormons, who always made up the vast majority of Utah's population—always at least 60 percent, and until 1870, more than 98 percent—dominated its economic, political, and civic affairs, and the U.S. government and the American people were deeply suspicious of them. From

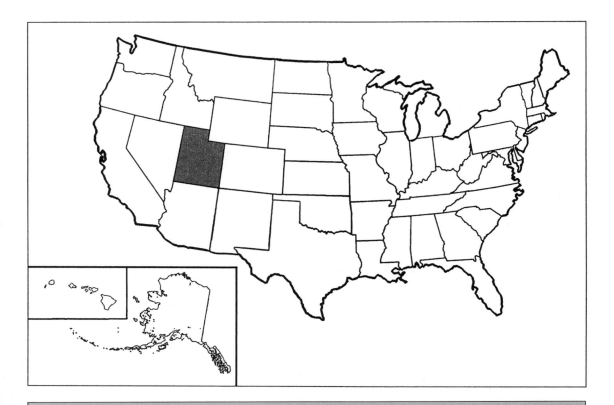

Utah

Territorial Development:

- The United States obtains future territory of Utah from Mexico through the Treaty of Guadalupe Hidalgo, February 2, 1848
- Utah organized as a U.S. territory, September 9, 1850
- Utah admitted into the Union as the forty-fifth state, January 4, 1896

Territorial Capitals:
- Fillmore, 1851–1856
- Salt Lake City, 1856–1896

State Capitals:

- Salt Lake City, 1896–present

Origin of State Name: "Yuttahih" is a word that the White Mountain Apache used to refer to the Navajo people. European settlers believed that the term was used in reference to the Utes, who lived further up the mountain, and the land of the Utes came to be known as "Utah."

First Governor: Heber Manning Wells
Governmental Organization: Bicameral
Population at Statehood: 276,749
Geographical Size: 82,144 square miles

the moment of its founding in New York State in 1830, the Mormon Church was at odds with the larger society in a number of fundamental ways. Given its commitment to theocracy, communitarianism, and polygamy, it interfered with the spread of democratic and capitalistic values and institutions and monogamous practices. It posed a radical challenge to its contemporary society, which believed that the Mormons had to be closely watched and controlled.

Forced to move successively from New York to Ohio to Missouri to Illinois, Mormons came to Utah in 1847, following the murder of their founder and prophet, Joseph Smith, hoping to leave opposition and suspicion behind them. Instead, hostility only intensified. Most Americans continued to see the Mormon Church as a subversive institution threatening American society and believed that statehood could not safely be granted until Utah was "Americanized." Opposition to statehood existed within Utah as well. Mormon leaders initiated and led every effort at statehood, and their church members supported them, but non-Mormons (or "Gentiles," by which Mormons meant anyone not Mormon) opposed them. As Gentile numbers grew, so did their opposition, and Gentile opposition was a crucial reason Utah did not receive statehood for so long. Finally, in the late 1880s, Mormon Church authorities, under enormous pressure from the federal government that threatened them with destruction, or at the minimum, reduction to a small, insignificant sect, made a conscious decision to bring the church into the mainstream of American life. In an apt phrase, Leonard J. Arrington called the decision "The Great Capitulation."[1] Statehood was then possible, and on January 4, 1896, President Grover Cleveland proclaimed Utah the nation's forty-fifth state.

HISTORICAL BACKGROUND

People have lived in Utah since at least 9000 B.C., beginning with those whom anthropologists term Paleo-Indians. Following them over the next 11,000 years were the Great Basin and Plateau Archaic peoples, the Anasazi, the Fremont, the Shoshonean or Numic peoples, and the Navajo. There is no way of knowing how many Native Americans lived in what is now Utah when Mormons first arrived, although historians generally agree they numbered between twenty thousand and forty thousand. By the mid-nineteenth century there were five main groups. Each had developed viable and sophisticated belief systems and ways of living that served them well. The Dine (Navajo) lived in the southeastern part of the state in the Four Corners area. Four groups of Numic peoples lived in other regions of the state: Nimi (Shoshoni) in northern Utah beyond the Great Salt Lake; Nuwuvi (Southern Paiute) in southern and southwestern Utah; Newe (Goshute) west of the Great Salt Lake; and Nucia, or Nuche (Ute), who ranged over about two-thirds of present-day Utah.

Euro-Americans first came into Utah as early as the 1540s, when the Spanish began exploring the northern frontier of New Spain, now the southwestern

United States. The first entry about which much is known occurred in 1765, when a group led by Juan Maria Antonio Rivera arrived in Utah, near what is now Monticello, in the Four Corners area (where present-day Utah, Arizona, Colorado, and New Mexico meet), as part of the Spanish effort to learn more about Spanish territory north of Mexico itself. Eleven years later, in July 1776, two Franciscan fathers, Francisco Atanasio Dominguez and Silvestre Velez de Escalante, set out from Santa Fe with a party of ten in search of a route to the Pacific Coast at Monterey. They spent about six weeks of their two-thousand-mile, five-month journey in Utah, reaching as far west as Utah Valley, forty miles south of the Salt Lake Valley, before heading south and eventually giving up their quest. If they had reached California, Utah's subsequent history would have been much different. It would have been closely tied to Spain, the Catholic Church, and the peoples of the Spanish borderlands, and would not have been as inviting a place for Mormons who sought to escape their contemporary United States.

In the years following the Dominguez-Escalante expedition, others came. Spanish traders periodically pushed into Utah, and they continued after the arrival of the Mormons. In the 1810s a new group began arriving: British, French-Canadian, French, Spanish, and American fur traders, the fabled mountain men who, during the next several decades, established temporary trading posts and thoroughly mapped and explored Utah in their search for beavers. Then, from 1843 to 1844, and again between 1845 and 1847, Captain John Charles Frémont of the United States Army Topographical Corps conducted major expeditions aimed at exploring and opening routes for overland travelers to California and Oregon. In 1846 at least five separate groups of emigrants passed through Utah on their way to the West Coast. The best known was the tragic Donner-Reed party, which became trapped in the Sierra Nevada Mountains by an early winter snowstorm. Of its eighty-seven members, only forty-seven survived starvation and cannibalism.

It was not until 1847 that permanent white settlement of Utah began. In that year, the Mormons arrived. Members of the Church of Jesus Christ of Latter-day Saints, they sought to escape from their contemporary American society and establish a religious utopia, a Bible commonwealth, a literal Kingdom of God on Earth—a perfect society where they would await Christ's second coming—a City of God, a New Jerusalem, the Zion of the New World. These were all terms that they used to describe their project.

THE MORMONS

The Mormon faith began with a teenaged boy named Joseph Smith. Born in Sharon, Vermont, in 1805, the son of an itinerant laborer and farmer, he moved with his family to western New York State in 1816. Four years later, at age fourteen, he claimed to have had a vision in which God the Father and Christ the Son told him the true church of God was no longer on the earth but that, in time, he would help re-establish it. Over the next ten years his visions continued. In March 1830, he published *The Book of Mormon*, a six-hundred-page history of pre-Columbian America that he said he had translated from metal plates that looked like gold buried in a hillside near Palmyra, New York, to which an angel named Moroni had led him. A month later, Smith organized the Church of Christ, later renamed the Church of Jesus Christ of Latter-day Saints. As historian Stow S. Persons has noted, it "shares with Christian Science the distinction of being the most striking indigenous major American religion."[2] Mormons, as they were soon known, exhibited a formidable talent for proselytizing. By the time they arrived in Utah, their church had more than fifty thousand members worldwide, twenty thousand of them in the United States, and was one of the ten largest denominations in the country. By the late nineteenth century, membership had grown to nearly 300,000.

Although a detailed account of early Mormon history and theology is not necessary here, an understanding of certain points is important. Mormons were millennialists. They believed that the return of Jesus Christ and the establishment of the millennial kingdom were at hand, and they expressed those hopes with a real literalness and immediacy. They also saw Joseph Smith and the church presidents who succeeded him as latter-day prophets through whom God revealed His will, the Mormon Church as God's one true church, and themselves as God's chosen people beleaguered on all sides by enemies of the truth. As an elect people, they believed God desired them to "gather" out of a sinful world to a place called "Zion" where they would build the Kingdom of God on Earth, live together in righteousness, and prepare for Christ's coming. The central fact for nineteenth-century Mormons was this sense that they were chosen. For them the concept of a chosen people not only implied but also required the construction of a separated community, a literal and not merely a metaphorical Kingdom of God. The Mormon Church, in other words, did not just aim to teach certain doctrines or to assemble people regularly to hear God's word. Its goal was the establishment of a perfect society, a model upon which all human society would ultimately be organized.

Mormons were clear about the nature of their utopia. In the first place, they envisioned a society devoted above all to discovering and following God's word, a community organized in accordance with religious principles, one integrated and controlled by religious rather than economic sanctions. A religious impulse would infuse every activity, making it difficult, if not impossible, to draw a line between the religious and the secular. Second, their society would be a theocracy. All affairs—not just the religious, but also the political, the social, and the cultural—would be under the direction of religious leaders. Third, it would be a unified society. As Brigham Young, Joseph Smith's successor as Mormon Church president, said, "Except I am one with my brethren, do not say that I am a Latter-day Saint. We must be one. Our faith must be concentrated in one great work: the building up of the Kingdom of God on earth, and our works must aim to the accomplishment of that great purpose."[3]

Fourth, the Mormon utopia would be based on cooperation rather than competition. The emphasis would be on group consciousness and activity rather than on the individual. People would be organized as "one great family of heaven," each person working for the good of the whole rather than for individual self-interest. Finally, Mormons envisioned an essentially egalitarian society, emphasizing again and again that, "If ye are not equal in earthly things, ye cannot be equal in obtaining heavenly things."[4] They believed that, in a revelation to Joseph Smith in February 1831, God had outlined an economic system, variously known as the United Order, the Order of Enoch, or the Law of Consecration and Stewardship, under which everyone had what he really needed, no one had more than he needed, and all were equal in temporal as well as spiritual things. It was this form of economic organization that early Mormons found most appropriate to the state of spiritual perfection they thought was about to dawn.

THE QUEST FOR STATEHOOD

Mormons began settling in Utah in the summer of 1847 when it was still Mexican territory. For the next four years, even after the area became part of the United States in 1848 as a result of the U.S. victory in the Mexican-American War, Mormons governed themselves. For a year and a half or so, a pure theocracy existed. The Mormon Church, believing that God had conferred his priesthood on church leaders, and that they had the right and duty to govern as his representatives on earth, exercised both ecclesiastical and civil authority. Then, in 1849, Mormons created a more formal government, the provisional State of Deseret, and asked that the U.S. Congress recognize it. The State of Deseret operated for nearly two years under Mormon direction until Congress instead created the Territory of Utah by the Territorial Organic Act of September 9, 1850.

In August 1847, barely a month after Mormons arrived in the Salt Lake Valley, church president Brigham Young named, or "called," a three-person Stake Presidency and a twelve-member High Council to serve as both an ecclesiastical and a civil government. Church members accepted the plan at a General Conference in October 1847, leading some historians to term it a "theo-democratic" government. It operated for fifteen months. Meeting regularly, the presidency and the council exercised the executive, legislative, and judicial functions of government. They made laws, provided for their enforcement, and acted as a court of justice to consider all disputes occurring in the settlement. They inaugurated a system of currency, levied and collected taxes, regulated prices, and provided for the construction of a fort, roads, bridges, and a temple. They appointed committees to lay out farmland. They allocated and regulated economic rights and privileges, for example, directing one man to build a gristmill on a mountain stream and setting the amount he was to charge for grinding grain, authorizing another to build a flour mill, directing another to set up a business for tanning leather, and telling another to build a glass factory. Land was neither bought nor sold but belonged to the community as a whole and was given to people on the basis of the "law of stewardship"—"equal according to circumstances, wants, and needs." Water and timber were also owned communally. The assumption was that people were only stewards over their material possessions. Property rights were not absolute but were a collective trust to be used for "the glory of God and the relief of man's estate." Property and human effort had one purpose: the establishment of Zion.[5]

Soon after their arrival in the Salt Lake Valley, Mormons began systematic exploration and colonization of the surrounding area. Intending to settle every-where they could as quickly as possible, they quickly began expanding into every inhabitable region of present-day Utah as well as parts of every sur-rounding state. In the first ten years, they founded nearly one hundred cities and towns, and by the end of the nineteenth century they had established more than five hundred. For Mormons colonization was a great success. For Native Americans, however, it was another story. As historian John A. Peterson observes, Brigham Young's policy was

> to establish settlements on all rivers and streams throughout a tremendously large area and, by thus gaining control of important water resources in a semi-arid region, he hoped to keep gentiles out and establish a huge empire where his people could practice their religion in peace. Unfortunately for the Indians, however, the very spots where Young placed settlements, often rich alluvial plains where rivers exited canyons, were the most productive components of the ecosystems upon which they depended for subsistence.[6]

The result was early and continuing confrontation. The major conflicts were the Walker War of 1853–1854; the Tintic War of 1856; the Battle of Bear River in 1863—when Colonel Patrick Connor's U.S. Army force attacked and destroyed a Shoshoni village and killed more than 250 men, women, and children, more than died in any other single white–Native American confrontation in the United States in the last half of the nineteenth century—and the Black Hawk War of 1865–1872. In the 1860s the federal government began to create reservations for Utah's Native American groups and started the process of moving them there. The full story is a complex one, and historians are just beginning to tell it. It is a story in which Native Americans were not just victims, but were also agents in their own behalf, actors in a complex world of narrowing options, responding in the ways available to them. In any case, from the first, the clear expectation of both Mormons and the federal government was that, as they moved into and expanded throughout Utah, both in terms of numbers and governmental authority, Native Americans would make way for them. In this sense, and overall, the story of the white–Native American experience in Utah was much the same as it was elsewhere in the United States.

With the signing of the Treaty of Guadalupe Hidalgo on February 2, 1848, following the American victory in the Mexican-American War, the United States gained more than one-third of Mexico's territory, more than half a million square miles in all, including areas that are now California, Arizona, New Mexico, Colorado, Nevada, and Utah. More than three hundred years of Spanish and then Mexican control of the area came to an end. The federal government of the United States now had the task of organizing a government for the region, and Utah would become either a territory or a state.

The First Attempt at Statehood: The State of Deseret

In January 1849 Mormon leaders decided to apply for territorial status, the usual path to statehood. They submitted a petition with more than two thousand signatures and sent lobbyists to Washington. By this time, the church's Council of Fifty, which Joseph Smith had organized in 1844 and charged with "establishing the political kingdom of God on earth," had assumed the High Council's governmental functions and took charge of the effort. They may have thought that territorial status would be easier to throw off when the time came for the Kingdom of God to stand alone. They then changed their minds and decided to create a nation-state of their own without the approval of Congress, apparently hoping to present Congress with an accomplished fact, a functioning government that would require only ratification. They faced a dilemma, however. On the one hand, they did not think they had time to go through the steps of calling for a constitutional convention, electing delegates, drafting a constitution, ratifying it, and then petitioning Congress. On the other hand, they knew that statehood would not be granted unless they went through this procedure. Therefore, they named a small committee to meet during the first part of July to write a constitution. They then invented convention minutes and election documents, named members to a legislature, and wrote a memorial to Congress requesting statehood, backdating the convention to March 5 through March 10.

The constitution was modeled on the one under which Iowa had become a state just two years earlier. Because Utah submitted essentially the same constitution in its 1856 and 1862 bids for statehood, it is helpful here to look at it in a little detail. It was relatively brief, only seven printed pages. According to its preamble, "it is a fundamental principle in all Republican Governments, that all political power is inherent in the People; and Governments instituted for their protection, security, and benefit, should emanate from the same." Eight articles then established legislative, executive, and judicial branches of government, prescribed the rules governing elections, established a state militia, provided for a process of amending the constitution, and listed the rights of Utah's citizens. The legislative authority was vested in a General Assembly consisting of a senate and a house of representatives, both elected by the people and holding annual sessions. Members of the house were elected every two years and had to be at least twenty-five years old, free, white male citizens of the United States, and residents of Utah for one year preceding the election. Senators were elected for four years. They had to meet the same requirements as representatives but had to be at least thirty years old. Each member of the assembly was required to "take an oath or affirmation to support the Constitution of the United States."

The executive power was in the hands of a governor, who was to be at least thirty-five years old and was elected for four years, a lieutenant governor, secretary of state, auditor, and treasurer. The judiciary consisted of a supreme court and such inferior courts as the General Assembly might establish. A chief justice and two associate justices were elected for four-year terms by a joint vote of the senate and house. All free, white male residents of the state over twenty-one years of age were eligible to vote, and all able-bodied, free white men between eighteen and forty-five, with some exceptions, were to be armed, equipped, and trained as a state militia.

Article 8 was a "Declaration of Rights." Section 1 specified that "In Republican Governments, all men should be born equally free and independent, and possess certain natural, essential, and inalienable rights; among which, are those enjoying and defending their Life and Liberty; acquiring, possessing and protecting property; and of seeking and obtaining their safety and happiness." Section 2 said that, "All Political power is inherent in the people; and all free Governments are founded in their authority, and instituted for their benefit; Therefore, they have an inalienable and indefeasible right to institute Government; and to alter, reform, and totally change the same, when their safety, happiness, and the public good shall require it." Section 3 dealt with freedom of religion. It said that,

> All men shall have a natural and inalienable right to worship God, according to the dictates of their own consciences; and the General Assembly shall make no law respecting an establishment of Religion, or of prohibiting the free exercise thereof, or disturb any person in his religious worship or sentiments; provided he does not disturb the public peace, nor obstruct others in their religious worship, and all persons, demeaning themselves peaceably, as good members of the State, shall be equally under the protect of the laws; and no subordination or preference of any one section or denomination, to another, shall ever be established by law; nor shall any religious tests be ever required for any office of trust under this State.

The next fourteen articles essentially followed the Bill of Rights of the U.S. Constitution.[7]

The Mormon Church's first president, Brigham Young, and his counselors, Heber C. Kimball and Willard Richards, were elected governor, lieutenant governor, and justice of the supreme court, respectively. Members of the Council of Fifty, most of whom were prominent churchmen, filled other state offices and selected ward bishops as local magistrates. The proposed state, called

"Deseret"—a *Book of Mormon* word interpreted as meaning "honey bee" that connoted the orderly, harmonious society God intended—covered a vast area about twice the size of Texas and nearly four times the size of Utah today. It included virtually all of what are present-day Utah, Nevada, and Arizona, large parts of Idaho, Wyoming, Colorado, Oregon, and New Mexico, and a strip of seacoast in Southern California near San Diego. Because President Zachary Taylor was a Whig, and Democrats controlled both houses of Congress, the convention named John M. Bernhisel, a physician and a Whig noted more for his political than his medical skills, as their special emissary to lobby for statehood. Brigham Young then arranged for the election of Democrat Almon W. Babbitt, an attorney and businessman who had previously lobbied for the Mormon Church, as the official delegate of the State of Deseret to Congress to join Bernhisel in lobbying for Utah's statehood.

The State of Deseret was the civil government of Utah for the next year while Congress decided what to do. It organized counties, granted rights to natural resources, regulated trade and commerce, established the Nauvoo Legion as an official state militia, passed an ordinance incorporating Salt Lake City, and in general fulfilled all the functions of a regular government, although Congress had not yet authorized it to do so.

This first effort at statehood failed. In September of 1850, after a long and bitter debate of nearly two years, Congress sought to diffuse the tensions resulting from the acquisition of Mexican lands by passing the Compromise of 1850. Under it, California was admitted to the Union as a free state, and Utah and New Mexico were organized as territories in which the local population would decide whether or not to allow slavery. In addition, the slave trade was prohibited in Washington, D.C., and a Fugitive Slave Law, much stronger than the previous one of 1793, was established for the return of runaway slaves to their masters. Two years later, in 1852, the Utah territorial legislature formally legalized slavery, although it had existed there since 1847, even before it was legally sanctioned. Exchanges and sales of black slaves, the use of blacks as payment of tithes to the Mormon Church, and general treatment of them as chattel continued until Congress abolished slavery in the territories a decade later. The law allowed the buying and selling of slaves of African descent and prohibited miscegenation. It required slaveowners to provide sufficient food, shelter, clothing, and recreation, as well as eighteen months of schooling to slaves between the ages of six and twenty, and specified that a slave was "to labor faithfully all reasonable hours, and do such service with fidelity as may be required by his or her master or mistress."[8]

In rejecting statehood, Congress also rejected the name "Deseret" because of the connotations it had with the Mormon Church's idea of the Kingdom of God. Congress chose the name "Utah" instead after the area's largest group of Native Americans, the Utes. The territory also was much smaller than the proposed state of Deseret, although it was still larger than the present state of Utah. It included all of present-day Utah, most of present-day Nevada, and what is now western Colorado. Over the next eighteen years those boundaries were reduced as the territories of Nevada, Colorado, and Wyoming were created, leaving Utah in 1868 with its present boundaries.

Utah's first petition for statehood was denied for several reasons. In the first place, concern about Mormons continued after their move to Utah, rather than abating as they had hoped. Second, Congress was reluctant to grant a single political entity, especially one that Mormons would dominate, the control of such a vast portion of the trans-Mississippi West. Utah also lacked the minimum sixty thousand eligible voters required for an area to be admitted as a state. Utah's population in 1850 was officially 11,380, excluding Native Americans. Finally, Utah's bid for statehood was caught up in the bitter debate over slavery. Northern congressmen wanted to prohibit slavery in all the land taken from Mexico, whereas Southerners wanted slavery to be protected there. Territorial status for Utah was part of an arrangement that was intended to help calm the situation, whereas statehood would have intensified the deep tensions that would soon lead to the Civil War.

President Millard Fillmore signed the Territorial Organic Act on September 9, 1850. He then appointed territorial officials. They included both Mormons and non-Mormons: Brigham Young became governor; Broughton D. Harris of Vermont was appointed territorial secretary; Seth M. Blair of Utah, territorial attorney; Joseph L. Heywood of Utah, marshal; Joseph Buffington of Pennsylvania, chief justice; and Zerubbabel Snow of Ohio and Perry E. Brocchus of Alabama, associate justices. After Buffington declined to serve, Lemuel G. Brandebury, also of Pennsylvania, replaced him as chief justice. Almost as soon as the non-Mormon territorial officials arrived in Utah, they found their influence was nearly negligible, and the situation did not change. Mormons "look to" Brigham Young, "and to *him alone*, for the *law* by which they are to be governed," said associate justice W. W. Drummond in his letter of resignation in 1857. "Therefore no law of Congress is by them considered binding in any manner."[9] Such feelings were common among non-Mormon officials during Utah's territorial period and helped generate a continuing conflict that would be a serious obstacle to statehood.

The Second Attempt at Statehood

Utah made a second attempt at becoming a state in 1856, when a constitutional convention comprised entirely of Mormons (18 percent of them Mormon "general authorities"—the highest ranking church officials) met in Salt Lake City from March 17 to March 27. There was "not much stir or excitement" when the election for delegates was held on February 18, because they all ran unopposed. Mormon leaders had either selected or spoken in support of them.[10] The constitution they drew up differed little from that of 1849. It was approved unanimously, as was a memorial to Congress asking that Utah be admitted into the Union again, as in 1849, as the State of Deseret. At an April 7 election, voters unanimously approved this constitution. They also approved sending Apostles John Taylor and George A. Smith to Washington to lobby along with territorial delegate John Bernhisel for its adoption.[11] They had every hope that their request for statehood might be accepted. After all, as historian Hubert Howe Bancroft said, "Their wars with the Indian tribes had been conducted successfully, and at their own expense; at their own expense also they had constructed public buildings, roads and bridges; they had conquered the desert, and amid its wastes had founded cities; their could be no doubt of their ability to maintain a state government."[12] Bernhisel and the others soon realized, however, that their statehood petition had virtually no chance of passing. Rather than waste their time, they decided not to present it for consideration.

The statehood petition had no chance because antagonism toward Mormons was so intense that the 1856 platform of the newly formed Republican Party denounced black slavery and polygamy as "the twin relics of barbarism" and promised to abolish each of them. Utah had both, and linking the two increased national attention on Utah and complicated its quest for statehood. In 1852, Utah had legalized slavery, and this action alone would have been reason enough for Congress to reject statehood. That same year Mormons had also publicly announced their adherence to the doctrine and practice of polygamy or "plural marriage," as they called it, although they had practiced it as an increasingly open secret since 1843. The practice outraged nineteenth-century Americans, and criticism was widespread and intense. Virtually all non-Mormons saw polygamy as a menace to everything Americans held sacred. Much of the criticism was lurid and sensational, but many critics were sincere reformers seeking to expose what they regarded as a great moral evil. For Mormons, on the other hand, polygamy was the ideal marriage system and a commandment from God. It was not just something they had chosen to do, but something God, in a revelation to Joseph Smith, had commanded them to do and, thus, was central to their religious practice. They held to it tenaciously and had no doubt as to its future. In contrast, Congress in general, and the Republican Party in particular, were furious at the thought that a slave territory whose people unapologetically practiced polygamy would seek admission to the Union.

In a larger sense, statehood in 1856 was a casualty of the alarm both the American people and their elected representatives felt about the kind of place Utah had become in its nearly ten years under Mormon control and the direction it was headed. Until 1870, Mormons were 98 percent of Utah's non–Native American population. Not only did they practice polygamy on an increasingly large scale as their population grew, but a close connection between church and state also continued after the initial period of a year or so of pure theocracy. In effect, the electoral process was seen as the equivalent of the Mormon church's practice of "sustaining" its leading authorities at "general conferences" each six months. Until 1870 neither local nor national political parties existed. Only one set of candidates appeared on the ballot. Church authorities often had nominated the candidates, and voting was limited to "yes" or "no." Territorial legislatures were composed entirely of Mormons. Typically no dissenting votes were cast during entire legislative sessions. Historians have characterized this situation as "the politics of unanimity." The explicit theory behind such political practices was that civil government was an arm of the church with specific functions to perform. The rights of voters were limited to consent. Political parties brought discord, self-interest, and corruption and were destructive of orderly government.

From the first, the Mormon Church took the lead in economic as well as political affairs, seeking to organize the economy so that all activities contributed to the goal of building the Kingdom. This economic role was as alarming to outsiders as polygamy and the near union of church and state. As J. Kenneth Davies notes, the goal was

> the establishment of a self-sufficient, highly diversified, centrally directed economy separate from that of the nation...not based on private ownership and direction but on a combination of private, state, and Church ownership—with Church direction. The distribution of the goods produced was to be more or less on the basis of equality and need.... Profits, if any, were to be used to build up the Kingdom, not to enhance personal worth.... There was to be no accommodation to the economic system of the world.[13]

Thus, for example, in 1849 the prices mill owners charged were made subject to the order of Mormon bishops. In 1850 the church established an extensive public works program to construct public and church buildings and to initiate enterprises not profitable for private enterprise to undertake. Beginning in 1859 church leaders discouraged the importation of luxury goods, including tea, coffee, tobacco, and liquor, and encouraged local production of all items. In 1864 the church fixed prices of agricultural products to prevent Mormon farmers from undercutting each other when they sold to mining and military camps. In 1866 church leaders called for a boycott of non-Mormon merchants, and two years later they formed Zion's Cooperative Mercantile Institution (ZCMI) as a way of lowering prices and driving non-Mormons out of business.

As Utah filmmaker Trent Harris says, Utah was settled by "a seriously radical bunch of people." And for statehood that radicalism was the problem. To the outside world Utah was deeply strange. It was seen as oppressive. More importantly it was viewed as threatening the foundations of American life—capitalist economic practices, democracy, and monogamy. No petition for statehood would be taken seriously until that situation changed.

The Third Attempt at Statehood

A third effort at statehood came during the early years of the Civil War. Mormons tended to see the Civil War as a sign that the collapse of the U.S.

government was imminent and that Christ would soon come. As part of their effort to prepare to govern themselves during Christ's millennial reign, they applied for statehood. The reasoning behind the quest for statehood is important. Mormons did not want statehood simply so they could have more control than they would have as a territory. It illustrates the deep religious motives at work in political affairs in Utah, about which non-Mormons, both inside and outside the territory, were so concerned. As historian Thomas G. Alexander says, Mormons saw the Civil War as

> the tribulation prior to Christ's second coming. They expected brother to rise against brother, state against state, religion against religion. In the last extremity, they thought Christ would reappear to rule the world and enthrone those Saints who had fled to Zion for refuge from a wicked world. Although they remained loyal to the Union, they believed that the nation would tear itself apart.[14]

Hoping that when the Union fell apart, Utah would be a sovereign state rather than a dependent territory, the Mormon hierarchy revived the Council of Fifty to direct the statehood effort. It arranged for elections to be held January 6, 1862, for delegates to a constitutional convention. As he often did, church president Brigham Young instructed local church leaders about the specific men to be nominated and elected as delegates to constitutional conventions. The all-Mormon convention met in Salt Lake City, January 22 and 23, 1862. With no dissenting votes, it drafted a new constitution and once again petitioned Congress for statehood as the proposed state of Deseret. The continued use of that name both signified the depth of Mormon attachment to the concept of the Kingdom of God and alarmed outsiders. William H. Hooper and George Q. Cannon were elected as delegates to present the petition to Congress and lobby for Utah's admission.[15]

Mormons expected that this time statehood would be granted. Although they realized that the American people were opposed to polygamy, they believed Americans would eventually accept their argument that, as a religious principle, polygamy was protected by the First Amendment, and they thought they saw signs that concern about it had lessened and was no longer so great as to prevent statehood. They also thought that with eleven states leaving the Union, Congress would welcome an addition to it. Brigham Young, in fact, initiated this third effort with a letter to Utah's territorial delegate to Congress, William H. Hooper, on December 27, 1860, just seven days after South Carolina had seceded.[16] And, while Congress considered their application, Mormon authorities, hoping to bolster their case, discussed publicly and privately whether or not to secede and join the Confederacy if statehood failed. They also made the argument that, ever since they had come to Utah, they had dealt with the Native Americans without much federal assistance. If Utah became a state, Brigham Young said, they would continue to ask for no help, for "the militia were ready and able, as they had ever been, to take care of them."[17] More fundamentally, they trusted that, with the millennium at hand, God would ensure statehood was achieved. They believed, as they said in their petition for statehood, that statehood was "their unquestioned right."

In the view of Mormon authorities, Congress's only function in admitting states was to decide whether a state had a republican form of government, whether the population was large enough to warrant statehood, and whether the people of the territory had approved admission. Because Utah met all of these qualifications, they said, Congress had no choice but to grant statehood. Thomas G. Alexander calls this point of view the theory of territorial, or popular, sovereignty. A number of Americans held to it in the nineteenth century, among them Michigan Senator Lewis Cass, the 1848 Democratic candidate for president. In his view, the U.S. Constitution limited the power of Congress "to the creation of proper governments for new countries, acquired or settled, and to the necessary provision for the eventual admission into the union, leaving in the meantime, to the people inhabiting them, to regulate their internal concerns in their own way."[18]

Congress did not agree, in general holding instead to a theory of "national supremacy" that allowed it much more discretion in considering petitions for statehood and an extensive role in regulating territorial affairs. Utah's 1862 bid for statehood was given no more serious consideration than was the 1856 effort, despite intensive lobbying by John Bernhisel, William H. Hooper, and Apostle George Q. Cannon. Alarm about Mormon practices was even greater than in 1856, and as Utah lobbied for statehood, the Republican-controlled Congress passed Vermont Congressman Justin Morrill's Anti-Bigamy Act. The act outlawed polygamy, thus fulfilling the Republicans' 1856 platform pledge to deal with both slavery and polygamy, levied penalties against anyone convicted of practicing plural marriage, disincorporated the Mormon Church, limited the value of real estate it could hold to $50,000, and authorized the federal government to confiscate any amount above that figure. Morrill had introduced a similar bill a number of times since 1858. None had previously gotten very far, but once the southern Democrats had withdrawn from Congress and Republicans were in control, it passed easily. Lincoln signed it into law on July 1, 1862. Although it was not immediately enforced, it was the first congressional action in what would be an extended anti-Mormon crusade.

As part of their bid for statehood, Mormons drafted a proposed constitution without waiting for congressional approval and elected officials for their proposed state as well as members of what they hoped would be the new state legislature. Governor-elect Brigham Young called the legislature into session in mid-April 1862. When statehood was denied, the legislature continued to meet regularly for eight more years, until 1870, as the General Assembly of the State of Deseret, which Mormons said would govern when Christ returned. Continuing such meetings was part of the Mormon Church's preparation for Christ's coming. Many of its members belonged to the Council of Fifty, and, because they were also members of the official territorial legislature, the decisions they made became law when they met as part of that body. Thus, from 1862 to 1870, there were two legislatures in Utah—the official territorial legislature, recognized by the federal government and part of the American political system, and an unofficial, "ghost" legislature that actually made the decisions which the official legislature merely formalized. Brigham Young explained this unusual procedure to the State of Deseret's legislature on January 19, 1863:

> We are called the State Legislature, but when the time comes we shall be called the Kingdom of God. Our Government is going to pieces and it will be like water that is spilt upon the ground.... But I do not want you to lose any part of this Government which you have organized. For the time will come when we will give laws to the nations of the earth.... We should get all things ready, and when the time comes, we should let the water on the wheel and start the machine in motion.[19]

In Charles S. Peterson's words, Mormons had in effect designed a "state-in-waiting," an early form of God's government, that was "a product of Mormon faith in the imminence of Christ's second coming and reflection of the Mormon yearning for self-government." Ever since their arrival in Utah in 1847, they had worked with a dual purpose: to function within the American nation while at the same time laying the foundations of their own emerging role in a new world system following Christ's return, which was soon at hand. They sought self-determination as they prepared for the millennium. The product of these goals had been, in the first place, the provisional State of Deseret that functioned from 1848 until 1851; then the territorial system beginning in 1851 when Brigham Young was governor; and finally the ghost State of Deseret in the 1860s. Peterson calls this millennialism "heaven-on-earth nationalism."[20]

The Fourth Attempt at Statehood

A fourth effort at statehood began in January 1872 when the Utah territorial legislature enacted a bill providing for a constitutional convention and appropriated $50,000 to finance it. Territorial Governor George Woods vetoed the bill, but the veto-proof Mormon legislature overrode him, and the convention met in Salt Lake City on February 19. The memorial it adopted called the territorial form of government a "colonial" system that was by its nature "inherently oppressive and anti-republican."[21] It is not clear why Mormons chose this time to try statehood again. There was no move in Congress in favor of it, and there was no particular reason to suppose it would be approved. In fact, given circumstances in Utah at the time, it was as certain to fail as ever.

Utah was entering a new period in its history. In some ways, it was a different place than it had been, but in other ways it was not, and, in any case, it was just as alarming as always to most Americans, and perhaps even more so. Although the population became less thoroughly Mormon as the Gentile population grew—by 1890, for example, Salt Lake City, which in 1870 was more than 90 percent Mormon, would be only 50 percent Mormon—antagonism between Mormons and non-Mormons increased. In a very real sense, the population was increasingly divided into two groups, those inside and those outside the Kingdom of God. This dichotomy was perhaps Utah's most striking feature in the last decades of the nineteenth century and remains a significant aspect of the state even today. Virtually every aspect of its life, including efforts at statehood, became entangled in that division, both reflecting it and becoming an occasion for its expression.

Two school systems existed. Most teachers and students in the public schools were Mormons; those in the growing number of private schools, many of them founded by Protestant churches that had come to Utah both to serve their members and to convert Mormons, were not. The emergence of fraternal organizations such as the Independent Order of Odd Fellows and the Ancient Order of United Workmen, coincided with the growth of the territory's non-Mormon population. Mormons were typically excluded from membership. Mormons and non-Mormons held their own separate celebrations of the Fourth of July and other national holidays. It would not be until July 1888 that Mormons and non-Mormons in Salt Lake City celebrated together. Distinct Mormon and non-Mormon residential neighborhoods developed. As the outside capitalistic world penetrated Utah, the territory became less self-sufficient and the economy more diversified. Non-Mormons were generally more comfortable with this diversification and more a part of it than were Mormons, who soon attempted to combat the intrusion by trying to re-establish their communitarian economic system, the United Order.

Political parties were finally organized, but they were not the national parties. In 1870 non-Mormons formed their own Liberal Party. In response the Mormon Church organized its People's Party. Both were disbanded in the early 1890s as part of the finally successful effort to gain statehood, but until then, for more than twenty years, elections in Utah were contests between Mormons and non-Mormons, with people essentially voting for or against the Mormon Church. Because they continued to constitute an overwhelming majority of the electorate, Mormons almost without exception were elected to office. Non-Mormons were not elected in Salt Lake City until 1890. The Mormon Church was open to the charge that it continued to dominate politics as thoroughly as it had previously in the absence of political parties, only now it did so through its own party.

Under these circumstances, the strategy of Mormon leaders to gain statehood was twofold. First, they sought to appear more conciliatory. Two years before the 1872 convention, they had quietly dropped the annual meetings of the legislature of the State of Deseret. For the first time, although Mormons were in the majority, the constitutional convention included non-Mormon delegates, a "safe though not ungenerous" representation, according to Robert J. Dwyer. In addition, a non-Mormon, General Eli M. Barnum, was chosen president of the convention, and non-Mormons were among the state officials that the convention proposed. Two non-Mormons, Thomas Fitch, who had ambitions to represent Utah in Congress if Utah became a state, and former Acting Governor Frank Fuller, as well as Mormon Apostle George Q. Cannon, were chosen to carry the statehood petition to Congress. Finally, the proposed constitution contained a provision obliquely inviting Congress to add a clause prohibiting polygamy, although if Congress did so, the people of Utah would have to approve the clause.[22]

The second piece of the Mormon Church leaders' strategy was to gain bipartisan support for statehood, courting the majority Republican Party while also seeking to cultivate the Democrats. They sought to persuade Republicans that after statehood Utah would be a Republican state. They also hinted that, out of gratitude, Mormons in surrounding states would vote Republican. As part of this effort, the Mormon hierarchy organized the first Republican group in Utah. It held a territorial convention in the spring of 1872 and sent a delegation of four Mormon general authorities to the national Republican convention in Philadelphia that summer. At the same time the territorial delegate to Congress and Mormon general authority George Q. Cannon privately reassured Democratic congressmen of Utah's future support once Congress granted statehood.

The effort failed for several reasons. First, the strategy of trying to convince each political party of Mormon support after statehood alienated both. It failed, in the second place, because national political leaders, as well as the American people as a whole, were opposed to granting statehood as long as Mormons continued to practice polygamy. It also failed because Utah was seen as a place where the Mormon Church dominated every aspect of life. Ordinary members placed such emphasis on "following council" in virtually all matters relating to their church-centered lives that they were in violation of the long-standing American principle of separation of church and state. As long as that was the case, statehood would not be granted, because granting statehood would mean giving more control to the Mormon Church. It was bad enough to have a territory with such predominant church influence, it was thought, but at least that influence was mitigated somewhat by the president of the United States' appointment of territorial officials.

This fourth petition for statehood aroused more opposition from non-Mormons within Utah than ever before. This opposition was a major factor in the denial of statehood this time and would continue to be so in the future as the non-Mormon population grew steadily. Opposition to statehood had always existed within Utah, of course, and the division was essentially along Mormon–non-Mormons lines. Mormon leaders had always initiated efforts at statehood. The opposition to it had always come from non-Mormons. And, as the non-Mormon population grew, particularly after 1870, so did opposition from a range of people, including members of the Liberal Party, Protestant ministers and members of their congregations, businessmen, federal officials, and members and supporters of the Anti-Polygamy Society. Statehood opponents were concerned about a number of issues: the establishment of a tax-supported public school system free of Mormon control, the abolition of plural marriage, the adoption of the secret ballot, the guarantee of separation of church and state, the growth of capitalistic economic institutions, and a denial of statehood for Utah as long as Mormons remained dominant. On this last issue, the opponents spoke out as never before. They held meetings throughout the territory, arguing that Utah was at odds with, and dangerous to, the larger society in a number of ways. They also argued, in a more narrow and self-interested way, that denying statehood helped reduce Mormon control and increased, or at least maintained and protected, their own position and influence.

The Liberal Party dispatched Robert R. Baskin and former Mormons Joseph R. Walker and Henry W. Lawrence to Washington to lobby against statehood. They carried with them an anti-statehood petition containing fifty-three pages of signatures, more than 2,700 in all. This petition stated that, because Mormons "believe in one supreme political as well as religious head," they were "antagonistic to the fundamental ideas of free government" and "incapable of comprehending, much less maintaining, a republican government."[23] The Liberal Party also sent a rival non-Mormon delegation to the national Republican convention in Philadelphia to oppose both statehood and the seating of the Mormon delegation.

The Fifth Attempt at Statehood

A fifth effort at statehood came ten years later, in 1882. It occurred in the midst of growing anti-Mormon sentiment soon after the passage of the Edmunds Act. Brigham Young had died five years earlier. Until his death he initiated and directed statehood efforts. Now George Q. Cannon, although not the church president, was the dominant member of the Mormon hierarchy, and he directed this campaign for statehood. In February 1882 the Utah legislature, following his lead, authorized another constitutional convention. It met from April 10 to April 27. All delegates were Mormons except for two members of the law firm the Mormon Church often hired. Before the opening of the convention, all of the delegates met with the Mormon Church's First Presidency and Apostles for advice and "counsel."

A significant change from previous constitutions was dropping the name "Deseret" —basically a synonym for the Kingdom of God and always proposed in the past for the new state—and adopting "Utah" instead. It also granted female suffrage and provided that the state's public school system would be free of sectarian influences. It adopted a new rhetorical stance that delegates hoped would be effective in countering impressions that Mormons were undemocratic, saying the proposed state would have a "republican form of government" under which citizens in Utah would enjoy the blessings of liberty the founders of the nation had sought to assure all citizens. Delegates approved the constitution unanimously. In mid-May it was submitted to voters, passing with 27,814 votes in favor and 498 opposed. The next month the convention reconvened and approved a memorial to Congress for statehood.

This bid for statehood found little support from either the president or the Congress. In his last State of the Union address in December 1880, President Hayes had addressed the "Mormon question." "Polygamy will not be abolished," he said, "if the enforcement of the law depends on those who practice and uphold the crime," and at a minimum he urged "the right to vote, hold office, and sit on juries in the Territory of Utah be confined to those who neither practice nor uphold polygamy." President Garfield had made similar proposals before his assassination in 1881, and his successor, Chester A. Arthur, argued that Mormon expansion beyond Utah's boundaries "imposes upon Congress and the Executive the duty of arraying against the barbarous system all the power which under the Constitution and the law they can wield for its destruction."[24]

Petitions on the "Mormon question" flooded the 1881–1882 session of Congress, when nearly two dozen bills and amendments were introduced. The proposal that became law was Vermont Senator George F. Edmunds's wide-ranging Edmunds Act. He was an influential senator genuinely interested in reform. During his long tenure in the Senate, he supported a number of important measures, including the Civil Rights Act of 1866, which was designed to protect the fragile rights of African Americans following the end of the Civil War; the Pendleton Act of 1883, which undertook civil service reform by requiring merit examinations for many federal offices; and the Interstate Commerce Act of 1887. As chairman of the Senate Judiciary Committee from 1872 to 1891, he was probably the true father of the Sherman Anti-Trust Act of 1890. He was also a vigorous supporter of any reform measure that curbed railroad abuses, and he genuinely thought polygamy was a form of tyranny.[25]

President Cleveland signed the Edmunds Act into law on March 22, 1882, several months before Utah forwarded its petition for statehood to Washington. The act outlawed "unlawful cohabitation," living together without a legal marriage, prescribing a maximum fine of $300 and imprisonment for up to six months for the offense. It allowed judges to exclude from serving on juries those who either practiced or believed in polygamy. It denied any polygamous man or any woman married to a polygamist the right to vote or hold elective or appointive office. It further declared all elective offices in Utah vacant and placed much of Utah's government in the hands of the Utah Commission, whose five members would be appointed by the president.[26]

Mormons hoped to soften the impact of the Edmunds Act by gaining statehood and thus attaining a greater influence over its implementation than they would as a territory. Having passed such a piece of legislation, however, Congress was in no mood to approve statehood. Rather, they were increasingly serious about forcing Utah to conform to national norms. So were the American people. After the Supreme Court found the Edmunds Act constitutional, federal authorities moved quickly to implement it, bringing enormous pressure on Mormons. Within a year the Utah Commission had excluded more than twelve thousand people from registering and voting. Because the Edmunds Act required them to give up a religious principle that they believed came from God, many Mormons decided to evade arrest by going into hiding, or "on the underground." Mormon president John Taylor set the example. On March 31, 1885, he gave what turned out to be the last public address of his life. After his speech, he disappeared from public view. He died, still in hiding, two and a half years later, two months after taking still another plural wife. Taylor's counselors followed his example. So did many others, and because they were often leading members of the community, involved in civic, economic, and political affairs, much of Utah was in disarray.

The Sixth Attempt at Statehood

Five years later Mormons petitioned for statehood for a sixth time. A constitutional convention of sixty-nine delegates met in Salt Lake City from June 30 to July 7, 1887. The delegates had been chosen at mass meetings of the Mormon Church's People's Party in twenty-two of Utah's twenty-four counties. The convention came at a time when anti-Mormonism had reached a fever pitch nationwide and followed the passage of the Edmunds-Tucker Act, which became law March 3, 1887. Sponsored by Senator Edmunds of Vermont and Representative J. Randolph Tucker of Virginia, this act put even more pressure on the Mormon Church than had the Edmunds Act five years earlier. It dissolved the corporation of the Mormon Church; provided for the confiscation of all church property in excess of $50,000; did away with the Nauvoo Legion (a territorial militia) and the Perpetual Emigrating Fund, which, which for more than thirty years had provided financial assistance to Mormon converts from other countries to emigrate to Utah; transferred control of public schools to a federal appointee; and abolished the right of all women, Mormon or non-Mormon, to vote.[27] By the following summer a government receiver had taken possession of $1 million worth of church property, the church's stock in a number of businesses, fifty thousand head of cattle, and $239,000 in cash.

In 1890 the U.S. Supreme Court found the Edmunds-Tucker Act constitutional, saying, in part,

> Looking at the case as the finding of the facts presents it, we have before us a contumacious organization, wielding by its resources an immense power in the Territory of Utah, and employing those resources and that power in constantly attempting to oppose, thwart, and subvert the legislation of Congress and the will of the government of the United States. Under these circumstances, we have no doubt of the power of the Congress to do as it did.... The tale is one of patience on the part of the American government and people, and of

contempt and resistance to law on the part of the Mormons. Whatever persecutions they may have suffered in the early part of their history in Missouri and Illinois, they have no excuse for their persistent defiance of law under the government of the United States.[28]

Mormon Church leaders applied for statehood under these circumstances as a way of minimizing the impact of the Edmunds Act and the Edmunds-Tucker Act. They thought they had an ally in Democratic President Cleveland, who seemed friendlier to them than his Republican predecessors had been, and this sixth effort was made in consultation with him and his advisors. For the first time, Utah's proposed constitution, drafted by U.S. Solicitor General George A. Jenks, included a clause prohibiting polygamy. It stated that, "Bigamy and polygamy being considered incompatible with a republican form of government, each of them is hereby forbidden and declared a misdemeanor." The proposed constitution also contained a provision, Article 5, Section 12, that, "There shall be no union of Church and State, nor shall any Church dominate the State."

Mormon Church leaders hoped that including these clauses would persuade Congress that as a state Utah would be free and democratic, conforming to American principles of government, but that the actual impact of the clauses would be minimal because Mormons, rather than hostile outsiders, would enforce them. They worked hard to see that key Mormon delegates to the constitutional convention supported the clause prohibiting polygamy. Once the constitution was written, they spoke in favor of it and urged local church leaders to encourage their members to vote for it when it was presented to them for ratification. In doing so, George Q. Cannon said, church leaders were engaged in "the most important political move since the church was organized." On August 1, 1887, voters approved the constitution by a vote of 13,195 to 502. It was submitted to Congress with a petition for statehood in December.

In connection with this sixth attempt at statehood, the Mormon Church launched its most elaborate and expensive lobbying and public relations effort ever. Its first presidency, Wilford Woodruff and his counselors, George Q. Cannon and Joseph F. Smith, led the campaign, directing a team that also included the church attorney, Franklin S. Richards, and Charles W. Penrose, editor of the church-owned *Deseret News*, both of whom were Democrats and People's Party leaders. Also on the team were Republicans Isaac Trumbo and Alexander Badlam, Jr., both prosperous non-Mormon California businessmen with Utah business and family connections. They also hired as lobbyists Republican attorney Jeremiah M. Wilson; former U.S. senator from Indiana, Joseph E. McDonald; and George Ticknor Curtis. Curtis was an attorney, a former Whig Massachusetts state legislator, and then a Democrat. He had been a defense attorney for Dred Scott, the slave who in 1857 sued for his freedom after his owner had taken him from slave territory into free territory.

The work of the team members was twofold. First, they sought to persuade influential newspapers across the country, including those in New York,

Philadelphia, Chicago, St. Louis, and San Francisco, to publish no negative stories about the Mormons. In 1887 church leaders authorized the payment of $144,000 to twelve papers if they would agree to that condition. Second, they tried harder than ever to woo prominent Republicans. Trumbo was particularly helpful in this regard and became the most important church lobbyist. He was connected with Republican Senator Leland Stanford of California and the Southern Pacific Railroad interests. The railroads were explicit about their interest in helping Utah gain statehood: they hoped that senators and other elected officials in Utah would support their economic interests in Utah and elsewhere in the United States. Trumbo also knew Judge Morris M. Estee, who had chaired the 1888 Republican national convention that nominated President Benjamin Harrison, and he gave access to the national Republican leadership: other California Republicans; James S. Clarkson of Iowa, chairman of the Republican National Committee; James G. Blaine, secretary of state in Benjamin Harrison's administration and former Republican presidential candidate; and Harrison himself. As a reward for his help, Trumbo hoped to become one of Utah's senators after statehood was granted.

The main obstacle Trumbo and the others faced was the unwillingness of Mormon leaders to do what was necessary to reduce the hostility they faced. The church had sympathizers in Congress and among the electorate, but not nearly enough. It still maintained its People's Party. Although it had recently disbanded the last of its United Order communities, it still held to the United Order as the ideal economic arrangement that God would eventually establish, and the United Order still played a huge role in the economy, seeking to organize society so that all activities contributed to the goal of building the Kingdom. The church's promises that statehood would enhance railroad and other economic developments in Utah were not persuasive. Even though the proposed constitution outlawed polygamy, it was only a misdemeanor, not a felony. Further, church leaders, after considerable discussion, had decided that they would continue to live with their plural wives and families. If Congress required otherwise, they would abandon their effort at statehood. Thus, because the majority of congressmen believed that Mormons were insincere in their protestations that Utah had changed, this effort at statehood met the same fate as its predecessors.

The Seventh and Final Attempt for Statehood

Utah's sixth bid for statehood officially ended on March 26, 1888, when the Senate Committee on Territories issued its report denying statehood. Even so, its seventh, and finally successful, effort began soon afterward. What made statehood possible at last was the decision of Mormon leaders, under enormous pressure, to bring the Mormon Church into the mainstream of American life. By the late 1880s, competing systems—the outside, gentile, and capitalistic worlds—had increasingly penetrated Utah, and finally, as a desperate act of self-preservation, Mormons stopped resisting them. When they did, statehood was granted. Until the late 1880s, Mormons were sure they could gain statehood without compromising what for them were fundamental, God-given principles and practices. For example, the Mormons believed that both polygamy and the United Order had been established in response to revelations from God. Finally it became clear that statehood was not possible without significant compromise on their part. Moreover, it was clear that, unless they compromised, their very existence was threatened. Thus, in the late 1880s, church authorities, after long and agonizing discussions, decided at last to undertake a process of rapprochement with the United States. They consciously embarked on what they hoped would be the road to prosperity and security: cooperation with the nation's dominant political and economic forces. From posing a radical challenge to the American way of life, the Mormon Church sought to be incorporated into it. After more than half a century of struggle to alter basic family, economic, and governmental structures, it gave in. Where the church once tried to change the world, now it was forced only to try to improve its position within it.

Accordingly, in September 1890 church president Wilford Woodruff, stating that he was "acting for the temporal salvation of the Church," issued a "Manifesto" proclaiming an end to the further performance of plural marriage.[29] As Jan Shipps says, this manifesto signaled the end of a world that not only tolerated, but celebrated polygamy. Nine months later, in June 1891, the church dissolved its People's Party and attempted to divide its members evenly between the Democratic and Republican parties. Eighteen months after that, following much debate occasioned by fear such measures were only temporary expedients designed to gain statehood for Utah and would be abandoned afterward, the Liberal Party also disbanded, and for the first time in its history Utah followed national party lines.

Of all the accommodations the church made, however, the most far-reaching was economic. Hostility existed toward the church not only because of plural marriage and its political practices and influence, but also because of its communitarianism, which was seen as drying up sources of income for speculative interests and interfering with the spread of capitalistic institutions. In the next several years the church made its peace with contemporary capitalism. It began a process of participation in, and accommodation to, the national economy. The results were so far-reaching that one might say the essence of its efforts to accommodate was to become capitalistic itself. The church no longer asked that its members "take counsel" about their economic affairs. It discontinued its cooperative enterprises. It sold most church-owned businesses to private individuals, many of them non-Mormon, eastern businessmen. Those it retained it operated as income-producing ventures rather than as shared community enterprises. Its Zion's Cooperative Mercantile Institution (ZCMI), for example, became just another company, with no social obligations, operating on the basis of profit, not social welfare. The group of Mormon businessmen who bought it no longer paid 10 percent of its profits to the church as a tithe, and non-Mormons were no longer prohibited from owning stock.

As part of its effort to assure the American people of its genuine commitment to economic transformation, the Mormon Church undertook a thoroughgoing and long-lasting critique of the socialist movement that had emerged in the United States in the late nineteenth century and would have a significant impact in the first decades of the twentieth century. For example, at its October 1906 General Conference, Charles W. Nibley asserted that in Utah, and among the Mormons, a feeling of safety, peace, and respect for law and order existed, so that "men who own railroads, mines, smelters, and other property of extensive and valuable character, feel, and know to a very considerable extent, that their interests are more secure here and better safeguarded in this company of Latter-day Saints than the same would be anywhere else in the world."[30]

The message Mormons sought to convey was that they were neither dangerous nor subversive, but rather were loyal, law-abiding Americans who posed no threat to the larger society. They were a conservative, prudent, patriotic, and, therefore, reliable people who would be staunch supporters of the existing economic and political system. Utah was and would remain a place where families, democratic institutions, and business interests and investments were safe.

THE CONSTITUTION AND PRESIDENTIAL ACTION

With these changes in both rhetoric and practice, statehood was possible, and events moved quickly. In the November 1892 election, Democrat Grover Cleveland defeated Republican Benjamin Harrison, and Democrats elected majorities in both houses of Congress. The next September Utah's newly elected Democratic delegate, Joseph L. Rawlins, introduced a bill for Utah's admission to the Union. It passed the House on December 13, 1893, with only five opposing votes. Senate passage stalled briefly out of concern over which political party the state's two new senators would likely belong to, but the bill passed the Senate on July 10, 1894, and Cleveland signed the Utah Enabling Act three days later.

In the November 1894 election, voters selected 107 delegates to the constitutional convention to be held the following March. Candidates ran by national party affiliation. Fifty-nine Republicans and forty-eight Democrats were elected. Mormons outnumbered non-Mormons seventy-nine to twenty-eight, a margin of nearly three to one. Mormon delegates included four general authorities, Republican John Henry Smith, and Democrats William B. Preston, Moses Thatcher, and Brigham H. Roberts, along with ten members of stake presidencies and fifteen members of bishoprics. Smith was elected president of the convention.

The convention met for almost two months, from March 4 to May 8, 1895, in the newly constructed City and County Building in Salt Lake City. In addition to providing offices for both city and county government, the building also housed the state legislature until the completion of the present state capitol in 1916. The constitution this convention wrote was twenty-eight printed pages in length and in most respects was similar to those of other states recently admitted to the Union, including Montana, South Dakota, North Dakota, and Washington in 1889 and Wyoming and Idaho in 1890. In two important respects, however, it was different. It contained a clause separating church and state much more explicitly than the U.S. Constitution's First Amendment or other state constitutions. It also prohibited polygamy. With regard to church and state, Article I, Section 4, declared:

> The State shall make no law respecting an establishment of religion or prohibiting the free exercise thereof; no religious test shall be required as a qualification for any office of public trust or for any vote at any election; nor shall any person be incompetent as a witness or juror on account of religious belief or the absence thereof. There shall be no union of church and State, nor shall any church dominate the State or interfere with its functions. No public money or property shall be appropriated for or applied to any religious worship, exercise or instruction, or for the support of any ecclesiastical establishment.

With respect to polygamy, Article 3 said, "Perfect toleration of religious sentiment is guaranteed. No inhabitant of this State shall ever be molested in person or property on account of his or her mode of religious worship; but polygamous or plural marriages are forever prohibited."

The hottest controversy was over female suffrage. On March 22 the convention's committee on elections and suffrage recommended the following clause be included in the new constitution: "The rights of citizens of the State of Utah to vote and hold office shall not be denied or abridged on account of sex. Both male and female citizens of this State shall equally enjoy all civil, political, and religious rights and privileges." A minority report opposed the inclusion of the clause, arguing that although women were as intelligent as men, they were ruled more by "their sympathies, impulses, and religious convictions" than were men. Further, it asserted, with female suffrage, Mormon women would vote as a block, thus continuing Mormon domination of political affairs in Utah. It also argued that the general population and the legislature should deal with the question of female suffrage after statehood, because it was a controversial issue nationwide, and its inclusion might endanger Congress's acceptance of the constitution.

The issue was debated for two weeks. Mormon Democrat Brigham H. Roberts was the main speaker against it. Women, he argued, did not need to vote because they already had a political voice through their husbands. Furthermore, their place was in the home where, as wives and mothers, they exercised their greatest influence, not in the voting booth. Also, Roberts said, only women of "low character" willing to "brave the ward politicians, wade through the smoke and cast their ballots" wanted to vote. "The refined wife and mother will not so much as put her foot in the filthy stream."

Those speaking in favor of women voting included Mormon Apostle Orson F. Whitney and Mormon Church attorney Franklin S. Richards. Female suffrage, Whitney said, was part of "the pageant of eternal progress; and those who will not join it must stand aside and see the great procession sweep on without them." Richards observed that he had never known a woman who felt complimented by the statement that she was "too good and pure to exercise the same rights and privileges as a man." In the end, on April 8, by a vote of 75-16, the convention followed Wyoming and Colorado in providing for female suffrage, which Utahans had enjoyed from 1870 until 1887, when the Edmunds Act had prohibited it.

Like many constitutions drafted during the period, Utah's contained a great deal of ordinary legislation. For example, it set salaries of the various state officials, at very low levels, rather than leaving such decision to the state legislature. It prohibited the state from lending its credit to businesses and provided for regulation of railroads, arbitration of labor disputes, and safety in mines. One clause set eight hours as a maximum day's work in underground mines and forbade women and children from working in them, although an amendment prohibiting employment of boys under the age of eighteen in "occupations dangerous to life and limb" was withdrawn in the face of a storm of protest.

Utah's male voters approved the constitution at an election on November 5, 1895, by a margin of more than four to one, 31,305 to 7,687, and also chose their first state officers. On January 4, 1896, President Grover Cleveland issued the proclamation of statehood.[31]

CONCLUSION

To become a state, Utah had to be "Americanized." Of course, this was true for every state—all of them had to be made part of the American state system. "Americanization" for Utah meant more than that, though. Utah had to be Americanized in specific ways that had not been true for other states. It had to give up the things that made it different, were seen as dangerous, and brought it into conflict with the larger society. It had to change, or at least begin to change, in significant ways. As long as Utah endorsed polygamy in a monogamous society, theocracy in a democratic society, and communitarianism in a capitalistic society, statehood would not be granted. Furthermore, Americans had to believe that the changes were real and permanent, not merely temporary expedients to gain statehood. Utah did not change completely before statehood, and it never would. Mormonism remained the state's most conspicuous feature and, more than anything else, set Utah apart from other states. Still, Utah increasingly relied on factors other than religion to dictate political, social, and economic preferences. The extent of those changes can be overstated. After statehood, the Mormon Church remained an enormous presence in Utah, and it still is, affecting everything from how people choose their friends to how they spend their leisure time, how they vote, whether or not they belong to a labor union, and whom they elect to public office. But other factors—including ethnicity, class, and gender—are important, too, as new groups have sought to establish their authority and make their place. According to Dale L. Morgan, the history of Utah is in part the story of the evolution of the Kingdom of God into another among the kingdoms of the world. That evolution made statehood possible.

NOTES

1. Leonard J. Arrington, *Great Basin Kingdom: An Economic History of the Latter-day Saints, 1830–1900* (Lincoln: University of Nebraska Press, 1958), p. 409.

2. Stow S. Persons, *American Minds, A History of Ideas* (Huntington, NY: Robert E. Krieger Publishing Co., 1975), p. 196.

3. Sermon of October 7, 1859, in *Journal of Discourses*, 26 vols. (Liverpool, England: Latter-day Saints Book Depot, 1854–1886), 7:280; available at http://journals.mormon-fundamentalism.org.

4. Revelation of March 1832 to Joseph Smith, in *Doctrine and Covenants* (Kirtland, Ohio, 1835), section 75, verse 1, p. 204.

5. The most important, and accessible, source for the Mormons' first years in Utah are the *Journal History of the Church of Jesus Christ of Latter-day Saints*, Church History Library of the Church of Jesus Christ of Latter-day Saints Church, Salt Lake City, Utah. It is essentially a massive scrapbook, of 750 volumes, including diaries, letters, reports, office journals, minutes, and newspaper clippings that, taken together, provide a nearly day-by-day account of Mormon history from 1830 to the present.

6. John A. Peterson, *Utah's Black Hawk War* (Salt Lake City: University of Utah Press, 1998), p. 103.

7. "Constitution of the State of Deseret," in Dale L. Morgan, *The State of Deseret* (Logan, UT: Utah State University Press, 1987), pp. 121–127.

8. *Acts, Resolutions, and Memorials, Passed By the First Annual, and Special Sessions, of the Legislative Assembly, of the Territory of Utah, Begun and Held at Great Salt Lake City on the 22nd Day of September, A.D. 1851* (Salt Lake City: Brigham Young, Printer, 1852), p. 93.

9. W. W. Drummond to Hon. Jeremiah S. Black, Attorney General of the United States, March 30, 1857, in U.S. House Executive Document no. 71, 35th Cong., 1st Sess.

10. Juanita Brooks, ed., *On the Mormon Frontier: The Diary of Hosea Stout, 1844–1861*, 2 vols. (Salt Lake City: University of Utah Press, 1964), 2:592.

11. The full text is in U.S. Senate Miscellaneous Documents, 35th Cong., 1st Sess., iii, no. 240.

12. Hubert H. Bancroft, *History of Utah* (San Francisco: The History Company, 1889), p. 484.

13. "The Accommodation of Mormonism and Politico-Economic Reality," *Dialogue: A Journal of Mormon Thought* 3 (Spring 1968): 42.

14. Thomas G. Alexander, *Utah, The Right Place: The Official Centennial History* (Layton, UT: Gibbs Smith, Publisher, 1995), p. 141.

15. For copies of the memorial and constitution, see U.S. House, Miscellaneous Documents, 37th Cong., 2d Sess., p. 78.

16. Brigham Young to William H. Hooper, December 27, 1860. Microfilm copy in Special Collections, Marriott Library, University of Utah.

17. Quoted in Bancroft, *History of Utah*, p. 605.

18. Lewis Cass to A. O. P. Nicholson, December 23, 1847, *Niles National Register*, January 8, 1848, pp. 293–194.

19. *Journal History*, January 19, 1863.

20. Charles S. Peterson, *Utah, A History* (New York: W.W. Norton and Co., 1977), pp. 78–87.

21. U.S. House Miscellaneous Documents 165(42-2), 1872, Serial 1526.

22. Ibid.

23. "Memorial of Citizens of Utah Against the Admission of that Territory as a State," U.S. House Miscellaneous Documents 208(42-2), 1872, Serial 1527.

24. James Richardson, comp., *A Compilation of the Messages and Papers of the Presidents, 1789–1897* (Washington, DC: Government Printing Office, 1898), 10:4558, 4601, 4644.

25. Howard R. Lamar, "Political Patterns in New Mexico and Utah Territories, 1850–1900," *Utah Historical Quarterly* 28 (Summer 1960): 384–385.

26. *Congressional Record*, 47th Cong., 1st Sess., pp. 1152–1153.

27. *Congressional Record*, 49th Cong., 2d Sess., pp. 581–597.

28. *Late Corporation v. United States*, 136 U.S. I (1890), 49–50.

29. The complete text is found at the end of every modern edition of the Mormon Church's *Doctrine and Covenants*.

30. *Church of Jesus Christ of Latter-day Saints, Conference Reports, October 1906* (Salt Lake City: Deseret News Press, 1906), p. 63.

31. *Official Report of the Proceedings and Debates of the Convention Assembled at Salt Lake City on the Fourth Day of March, 1895, to Adopt a Constitution for the State of Utah*, 2 vols. (Salt Lake City: Star Printing Co., 1898).

BIBLIOGRAPHY

Alexander, Thomas G. *Utah, The Right Place: The Official Centennial History*. Layton, UT: Gibbs Smith, Publisher, 1995.

Arrington, Leonard J. *Great Basin Kingdom: An Economic History of the Latter-day Saints, 1830–1900*. Lincoln: University of Nebraska Press, 1958.

Bancroft, Hubert H. *History of Utah*. San Francisco: The History Company, 1889.

Brooks, Juanita, ed. *On the Mormon Frontier: The Diary of Hosea Stout: 1844–1861*. Salt Lake City: University of Utah Press, 1964.

Davies, J. Kenneth. "The Accommodation of Mormonism and Politico-economic Reality." *Dialogue, A Journal of Mormon Thought* 3 (Spring 1968): 42–54.

Hansen, Klaus J. *Quest for Empire: The Political Kingdom of God and the Council of Fifty in Mormon History*. Lansing: Michigan State University Press, 1967.

Lamar, Howard R. "Political Patterns in New Mexico and Utah Territories, 1850–1900." *Utah Historical Quarterly* 28 (Summer 1960): 375–388.

———. *The Far Southwest, 1846–1912: A Territorial History*. New Haven, CT: Yale University Press, 1970.

Larson, Gustive O. *The "Americanization" of Utah for Statehood*. San Marino, CA: Huntington Library, 1971.

Lyman, E. Leo. *Political Deliverance: The Mormon Quest for Statehood*. Urbana and Chicago: University of Illinois Press, 1986.

Morgan, Dale L. *The State of Deseret*. Logan: Utah State University Press, 1987.

Persons, Stow S. *American Minds, A History of Ideas*. Huntington, NY: Robert E. Krieger Publishing Co., 1975.

Peterson, Charles S. *Utah, A History*. New York: W.W. Norton and Co., Inc., 1977.

Peterson, John A. *Utah's Black Hawk War*. Salt Lake City: University of Utah Press, 1998.

THE STATE OF VERMONT

Admitted to the Union as a State: March 4, 1791

Samuel B. Hand and H. Nicholas Muller III

INTRODUCTION

On January 10, 1791, more than a decade after Vermont had declared its independence, proclaimed a constitution, and organized a separate government, a special convention of Vermonters meeting in Bennington voted 105 to 4 to adopt the U.S. Constitution.[1] The legislature quickly confirmed the vote, clearing the way for Vermont to join the Union. Two leaders of the statehood movement, Nathaniel Chipman and Lewis R. Morris, hurried to Philadelphia to represent Vermont's interests in Congress. In early March 1791 Chipman reported to Governor Thomas Chittenden in a "hasty scrawl" that President Washington had signed the bill "admitting Vermont into the union as a state already formed & from the first rightfully possessed of Sovereignty independent of the union—this," he declared, "secures our property vested in former laws" of Vermont which asserted independence and, most importantly, authority over land titles.[2]

Statehood had not come easily. It followed decades of bitter controversy with New York, of political intrigue, and of boisterous posturing that occasionally led to violence. This decisive vote did not fully reflect the remaining pockets of opposition to joining the Union. At the Bennington convention Daniel Buck argued that "the advantage Vermont would receive from the Union would by no means be adequate to the sacrifices she must make" in giving up independence.[3] Ira Allen, who had played a major role in the Vermont independence movement as the principal means to secure land titles against New York claims, long opposed statehood, even if it would settle the issue of the titles. His brother Levi, who found statehood a "disagreeable" subject, wrote to

Vermont

Territorial Development:

- King George II declares the Connecticut River as the boundary between New York and New Hampshire in 1764
- Continental Congress approves Declaration of Independence from Great Britain, July 4, 1776
- Vermont declares itself an independent republic on January 15, 1777, but the Continental Congress refuses to recognize its claim
- The Republic of Vermont claims land laying east of the Hudson River, west of the Connecticut River, and north of the Massachusetts border, 1781
- The Continental Congress demands Vermont recede its claim, August 20, 1781
- Great Britain formally recognizes American independence through the Treaty of Paris, September 3, 1783
- The Republic of Vermont pays New York $30,000 in reparations for land taken, and New York recognizes Vermont's independence, October 7, 1790
- Vermont becomes the fourteenth state to join the Union, March 4, 1791

State Capitals:

- Montpelier, 1805–present

Origin of State Name: The French explorer Champlain named the Green Mountains "Verd Mont," or "green mountain," in 1647.

First Governor: Thomas Chittenden
Governmental Organization: Originally unicameral. The Vermont state legislature switched to a bicameral system in 1836.
Population at Statehood: 85,341 (1790 Census)
Geographical Size: 9,250 square miles

Ira from London emphatically expressing his "hope in the name of Common Sense, You have not, and in the name of Almighty <u>God</u>, you will not join Congress. Govr ____C [Chittenden], my deceased Brother [Ethan Allen], Yourself, Col. Lyon, Clark, Enos, Hitchcock, Spafford's, Coit, Ebenr [Allen] & c. &c. &c. all being fully to the Contrary when I left you."[4] But these older men, among the most prominent in the creation of Vermont independence, bearing the deep scars of decades of strife with New York, had yielded the center stage. Those who remained and attended the convention quietly acceded to the majority. By 1791 Ira Allen realistically swallowed the inevitable and voted with the huge majority at the Bennington convention. His action represented a major change in Vermont, from a stance of defiant independence in its fourteen years of standing alone to one, as Chipman told the convention, in which its "general interests will be the same as those of the union."[5] The contest for control of Vermont that led to its becoming the fourteenth state instead of making an accommodation with the British Empire or entering the Union as a northeastern appendage of New York began well before 1791. Earlier, Ethan Allen accurately reduced the necessity for Vermont independence and the contest with New York to the fundamental need to preserve title to land. As Vermont "could not trust New York who would have been rejoiced" had our lands "fallen into their hands; an object they have been pursuing for more than seven years past," it had to proclaim and establish its independence.[6] The struggle to secure titles to the land brought about the separation from New York and the creation of Vermont that eventually led to statehood.

THE COLONIAL ERA: YANKEES VERSUS YORKERS

Until General James Wolfe's victory at Quebec in 1759 and the fall of Montreal to the British the following spring ended the fighting phase of the French and Indian War, the region that became Vermont lay between the competing colonial empires of Great Britain and France. Before the Treaty of Paris in 1763 confirmed British hegemony, the limited settlements in the area generally formed near the protection of strongholds. In the 1740s some English colonists settled around Fort Dummer, the Massachusetts outpost in Dummerston north of its boundary on the west bank of the Connecticut River. By then the French had begun some small settlements of traders and families of the garrisons on Lake Champlain across from Fort St. Frederic at Crown Point and around Carillon, which the British captured and renamed Fort Ticonderoga in 1758. The defeat of the French and their Indian allies loosed an orgy of land speculation and opened the territory for settlement that commenced in earnest after 1760. Stimulated by the opening of the Crown Point Military Road across the Green Mountains, military land patents as a reward for veterans, and the familiarity with the territory New England militiamen had gained during the war, settlers flowed into Vermont.

Before the war, New Hampshire's acquisitive and aggressive governor, Benning Wentworth, had granted fifteen towns in Vermont. With the end of hostilities in 1760, Wentworth moved quickly to oblige the pent-up demand of speculators, land jobbers, and settlers and granted ninety-six more townships before his land operations in Vermont were closed in 1764 by a Royal Order citing Charles II's 1674 grant to the Duke of York making the Connecticut River New York's eastern boundary. The men who received Wentworth's largesse became proprietors, with the responsibility to survey and lay out parcels and to manage the town until sufficient settlement justified establishing local government. Most proprietors had little intention of living in Vermont. Some with large families would settle parcels on sons or use the parcels as a dowry for daughters, but many secured New Hampshire titles as a speculative venture, expecting to profit through sales to settlers and to other investors.

The early settlers in Vermont often flocked to live near others who had migrated from the same towns in the older colonies and with whom they had prior association. They formed clusters of groups with shared background, experiences and values, often with ties of kinship. New Light Congregationalists, dissenters from northwestern Connecticut towns in Litchfield County, came to Bennington and neighboring towns. Others migrated north to western Vermont through New York towns east of the Hudson River, where they had participated in the riots resisting the traditional New York leasehold-quit rent system of land tenure. A group of veterans of the French and Indian War returning overland to northern Massachusetts from Canada traveled through the Coos country of the upper Connecticut River. A few years later they began settlements there on Wentworth grants in Bradford and Newbury and across the river in Haverhill, New Hampshire, all named for their hometowns in the Merrimac River Valley.[7]

Ethan and Ira Allen, with several brothers and cousin Remember Baker, amassed holdings in the towns along the Winooski River, forming the Onion River Land Company in 1774. They sold land there to Thomas Chittenden, the one-eyed Revolutionary leader of Vermont who would serve as its first governor. Ira Allen frequently exchanged his surveying skills for land. With prices for the Wentworth grants depressed when the Royal Order of 1764 created reservations about the validity of the New Hampshire titles, the Onion River Land Company purchased tracts for bargain prices, often on credit, gambling that sales would carry their debt load.[8]

Speculators and settlers undeterred by the Royal Order continued to invest their capital and labor and stake their future on land with New Hampshire titles. They asserted that while the Royal Order established the New York boundary and its jurisdiction, it did not address the matter of the validity of the grants made prior to 1764. The Wentworth claimants and their allies made a strong case that the New Hampshire titles, as royal grants, superseded any later grants to the same land. New York took the opposite position and beginning in 1764 it intensified its activity in Vermont land.

Like Wentworth, the colonial governors and other top New York officials understood the potential of unsettled frontier to gain wealth and power. They regarded granting land as a perquisite of office, and with huge incentives to issue grants, these royal officials did not allow the opportunity to escape them. For each 1,000 acres that he granted, the governor pocketed a substantial fee of $31.25 (approximately £14). Six other royal officials, including Attorney General John Tabor Kempe, Deputy Secretary of the Council Goldsbrow Banyar, and Lieutenant Governor Cadwallader's son Alexander, as surveyor general, divided $59.00 (approximately £26.5) among themselves.[9]

After the Order in Council of 1764 halted Wentworth's operations, and the repeal of the Stamp Act in 1766, which added to the cost, removed serious impediments to grants, three royal governors of New York and Lieutenant Governor Cadwallader Colden (who held the reins of power as acting governor for three stints totaling nearly six years) made grants amounting to well over 2 million acres. In his first brief tenure as acting governor, Colden only granted 36,000 acres. His successor Sir Henry Moore confined his activity to 144,600 acres, perhaps inhibited by a Royal Order of 1767 that attempted to dampen the escalating uproar over Vermont by forbidding New York to issue grants that conflicted with the New Hampshire titles of actual settlers.

In 1766 Colden began his second term as acting governor, and he flagrantly disregarded the order to respect settlers' titles. He signed patents to nearly 560,000 acres, many of which overlapped the New Hampshire titles of settlers as well as those of speculators and absentee proprietors. In less than a year before Governor Tryon replaced him in 1771, Lord Dunmore made grants of over 460,000 acres, including a generous grant of 51,000 acres in Vermont to himself and several of his cronies. Tryon continued to exercise the royal prerogative, making grants of 485,000 acres, including a huge tract in Vermont to himself, and several other grants to henchmen who quickly conveyed title to Tryon. In turn, the avaricious governor rewarded them with appointments to office. In Vermont, Crean Brush participated in this transaction, receiving the offices of Court Reporter and Registrar of Probate in Cumberland County. Tryon, recalled to England from April 1774 through June of 1775, handed over the office to Colden, who proceeded to make grants of another 370,000 acres. Yorker Attorney General John Tabor Kemp, while collecting a fee of $7.50 for every 1,000 acres granted, also held title to many thousands of acres in Vermont. Justice Robert R. Livingston received grants of over 35,000 acres, and James Duane, a prominent attorney, owned about 75,000 acres in Vermont. In a decade, the Yorkers had issued title to over 1.1 million acres that conflicted with Wentworth's New Hampshire grants.[10]

Yorker governors and placemen also had other avenues by which to profit, including 300,000 acres in military patents, grants to "reduced officers" and discharged soldiers mustered out after the French and Indian War in amounts as little as 50 acres for privates to up 5,000 for generals. Speculators amassed large holdings in these patents, buying them for drinks and other trifles from soldiers embarking for England. The Yorker officials also offered to "confirm" New Hampshire titles by accepting fees to substitute New York titles for New Hampshire titles. Twenty-nine towns, mostly on the eastern side of the Green Mountains and along the Connecticut River, applied to Colden in 1765 to "confirm" their New Hampshire grants, a process that generally required them to sell land to raise money for the attendant fees. Nathaniel Chipman, who would lead the statehood movement in the late 1780s, concluded that New York "extorted large sums of money from the New Hampshire grantees and settlers for what they called a confirmation."[11] Nineteen towns received confirmatory titles. Another forty towns later sought confirming titles, and after Governor Tryon offered to confirm titles for half-fees, fifty-four Vermont towns, some with applications already pending or rejected, made application.[12] For speculators with huge holdings, like the Allens and their Onion River Land Company, the fees prohibited this avenue. Those who had previously defied New York authority in the land riots east of the Hudson River would not on principle accede to Yorker demands.

With New York's leading officials deeply involved in Vermont land speculation and amassing wealth in the process, the settlers with New Hampshire titles anticipated little success for establishing the validity of their claims in New York courts. The speculators had even less chance. The Yorkers confirmed these fears with their abrupt handling of the Ejectment Suits. Following several attempts of New York authorities to "eject" settlers with New Hampshire titles, in 1770 Ethan Allen, as the "Agent General for the Honorable Proprietors of the New Hampshire Grants," gathered evidence to pursue recognition of their titles in an Albany County court. The titleholders hired Connecticut attorney Jared Ingersoll and Peter Schuyler from New York to represent them. With James Duane, Judge Livingston (Duane's brother-in-law, who held title to 35,000 acres in Vermont), and other court officers personally interested in Vermont lands, the court summarily decided the question by ruling the New Hampshire titles inadmissible as evidence.[13]

With little expectation of relief from the Crown and no other alternative than to pay the fees and apply for a confirming title from New York, a strategy not available to speculators, a number of the New Hampshire titleholders resorted to open defiance of New York authority. This defiance spawned the birth of the Green Mountain Boys, with Ethan Allen at their head. This movement led haltingly to the declaration of Vermont independence. The open opposition to New York authority centered on the struggle for land, but for the Green Mountain Boys and their supporters, mostly from the western side of the mountains, the fight also became highly personal. The bombastic, shrill rhetoric that characterized Allen's outbursts—designed at once to win and hold supporters, frighten enemies, and bring attention to the plight of the New Hampshire titleholders—also reveals a deep antipathy for Yorker officials.

Allen's incendiary rhetoric did not sway New York's new governor, William Tryon, and after continued acts of defiance, in November 1771 the exasperated governor placed £20 rewards for the capture of Allen, his chief lieutenant Robert Cochran, and his cousin Remember Baker. The three Vermont "outlaws," in turn, issued a counterproclamation that declared, "Whereas James Duane and John Kempe of New York have by their menaces and threats disturbed the public peace and repose of the honest peasants of Bennington and the settlements to the northward," they would pay £15 for Duane and £10 for Kempe upon their delivery to the Catamount Tavern. This exchange carried overtones that went well beyond frontier humor. A subsequent nighttime effort of a New York sheriff and his posse to arrest Remember Baker and spirit him to jail in Albany ended in a bloody rescue that sorely exacerbated the personal grievances.[14]

In May 1772 the Yorker officials sought a truce that many of the settlers and the rank and file of Green Mountain Boys welcomed. Despite Ethan Allen's assuming their leadership, the vast majority of the Green Mountain Boys were hard-working, middle-class yeoman farmers striving to improve their economic status. Many identified with radical religious and political ideas. On their way from western Connecticut and Massachusetts, some had detoured through New York and taken part in the sometimes violent resistance to Yorker authority in Ancram, Claverack, and other towns east of the Hudson River.[15] The truce welcomed by many of the settlers did not provide recognition of the New Hampshire titles and threatened the speculators. Before the truce had much time to gain traction, it was shattered by Allen's rough treatment of Yorker surveyor William Cockburn and driving off of Yorkers attempting to settle in Panton. Allen loudly told one Yorker whom he chased out of Panton to return to New York and "complain to that damned scoundrel, your governor. God damn your governor, laws, king, council and assembly." Yorker Justice of the Peace John Munro lamented, "every person that pretends to be a Friend to this Government is in danger of both life and Property."[16]

Tryon received repeated shrill complaints from Yorker claimants and local officials, but without troops (which he had had in North Carolina, where he crushed another group of insurgent frontiersmen), he could do little but posture. Exasperated by the mounting tumult, in March 1774 he acceded to the request of an assembly committee led by Crean Brush and George Clinton, who would become the Revolutionary governor of New York, to issue a proclamation making the leaders of the Green Mountain Boys outlaws. The New York assembly passed an act that codified Tryon's proclamation, with a bounty of £100 for the apprehension of Allen and Baker and £50 for four lieutenants while sentencing all six to death if they did not surrender to New York authority within seventy days.[17] When news of this "Bloody Act" reached Vermont, a convention of west side settlers gathered in Manchester. This meeting reiterated claims to the validity of the New Hampshire titles and the iniquitous behavior of the Yorker government. The settlers asserted that they would "muster as good a regiment of marksmen and scalpers as America can afford." They promised to hold themselves ready at a "minutes warning" to defend their "proscribed friends and neighbors."[18] Thomas Rowley, a settler with a penchant for doggerel, penned a long poem that included the stanza of dubious rhyme: "We value not New York with all their powers/ For here we stay and work, the land is ours/ And as for great Duane, with all his wicked train/ They may eject again, we'll not resign." The derisive name-calling rested on the hearty and mutual dislike that transcended issues and any attempts to resolve them.[19]

The ruckus kicked up by the disruption of Yorker authority did not prevent settlers from pouring into Vermont. A 1771 New York census counted 4,746 people living east of the Green Mountains and 7,700 in the entire territory. By the middle of the decade, new settlers and growing families swelled the population to about 12,000, a 70 percent increase.[20] These residents demanded the rudimentary trappings of government: courts to "determine all suits, quarrels, controversies and differences," and the apparatus to enforce debts; punish crimes; sanction and record marriages, births, and deaths; keep the peace; lay out, build, and maintain roads; and assess and collect taxes. With each new settler the pressure increased to dampen the uproar and secure a stable, dependable environment.

As early as 1765, east side settlers, then nominally part of Albany County with its seat miles to the west across the mountains, petitioned New York to establish a new county so that they might have the institutions of the law and government more geographically accessible. To administer to the needs of the growing population along the Connecticut River, in 1768 the royal government of New York established Cumberland County running between the river and the spine of the Green Mountains north of the Massachusetts border, designating Westminster as the county seat. Two years later they carved Gloucester County out of the northern half of Cumberland, naming the unsettled New York township of Kingsbury (now Washington in Orange County) as the county seat. In 1772, in recognition of the impossibility of planting county government in an unsettled tract, the seat moved to Newbury. That same year, New York carved Charlotte County out of Albany County on the west side between the Green Mountains and the Adirondacks running north to Canada.[21]

The new counties brought bureaucratic infrastructure and a good deal of patronage. New York appointed the various officers of the county courts, sheriffs, justices of the peace, and county clerks. The "Freeholders and Inhabitants" of each township within a county could elect one supervisor, two assessors, two collectors, two overseers of the poor, surveyors and overseers of the highways, two fence viewers, and four constables. New York under the royal governor, followed by the New York Provincial Congress and Convention of the State of New York between April 1775 and August 1777 and after that under the New York State constitution, issued commissions to men to fill these various offices. In 1773 Cumberland County began to send representatives to the New York legislature, first as delegates to the colonial General Assembly and ending in the 1780s with members of the New York assembly and senate.[22]

By the 1770s the largest of the towns, predominantly on the east side, had stores, taverns, churches, and some schools, and they enjoyed the services of clergy, doctors, midwives, lawyers, and teachers. The maturing society gradually established an institutional infrastructure and transferred power from absentee proprietors to residents. The need for stability gradually eroded the support of the Green Mountain Boys, who cleverly turned to the rising tide of the American Revolution with its threats to the established order to keep the defiance to New York alive. In the spring of 1774, a group in Cumberland County angrily challenged the attempt of a local Yorker official to bury a request by Seth Lowe, Chairman of the Revolutionary New York City Committee of Correspondence, for support for the resistance to the Intolerable Acts and the patriots in Boston. Conventions gathered in Cumberland County in the fall of 1774 and the next spring and declared their support for the beleaguered people of Boston and their approbation for the work of the First Continental Congress. The legitimate, if harsh, efforts of the Yorker courts to enforce the payment of debts in specie-starved Cumberland County had already evoked discontent with the New York authority. The ideals of the American Revolution offered legitimacy to the resistance to constituted authority.[23]

The royal government of New York bucked strong cross-currents in Vermont. The gathering storm of the American Revolution buffeted Tryon's government, and the clumsy efforts of the Yorker courts to enforce the payment of farmers' debts in Cumberland County brought new recruits to the resistance to authority. Late in the winter of 1775, about forty farmers visited Thomas Chandler, chief justice of the (Cumberland) Court of Common Pleas, at his home. They left with a tepid promise to refrain from having armed officers at the court and to limit the docket of the March session to one murder case. With no hard money to meet their obligations, judgments against debtors led to the auction of their property at severely depressed prices. The farmers, fearing Chandler would renege on his promise not to try debtors, armed themselves with clubs and a few muskets and occupied the courthouse in Westminster the afternoon before the court's scheduled opening. Alarmed by the rumors that a mob would thwart the court's opening, Yorker Sheriff William Patterson organized an armed posse in Brattleboro. The posse trudged north to Westminster, where it found the courthouse occupied. After trading loud threats and insults with the farmers, Patterson and his men retired to Norton's tavern. Late that night the well-fortified posse returned and took possession of the courthouse after a bloody melee that left two of the farmers dead. Patterson jailed the rioters, and the court convened as scheduled the next morning.

Before the court could reconvene after a midday recess, several militia companies, including one from across the Connecticut River in New Hampshire, reversed the tide. They freed their neighbors and jailed Patterson, the posse, and the judges. With the situation already in control, Ethan Allen's lieutenant, Robert Cochran, at the head of forty armed and mounted Green Mountain Boys each sporting a green cockade of spruce, rode into Westminster. This action shrewdly linked dissidents on both sides of the Green Mountains and joined the force of the bloody court riot to the fight over land titles. Within a few days many Vermonters had bestowed on a debtors' riot the patriotic mantle of the "Westminster Massacre." The Yorker court in Cumberland County had convened for the last time.[24]

Events then moved rapidly. Within a few weeks in April 1775, almost simultaneously with Concord and Lexington, Tryon and his coterie fled to the safety of a British ship in New York harbor. The Revolutionary Provincial Congress and Convention of the State of New York assumed control of affairs and the conduct of the war there. Two years later New York established state government under a new constitution and elected as governor George Clinton, who as a member of the provincial assembly had urged naming Ethan Allen an outlaw. With Clinton, who served uninterrupted until 1795, at its head the New York government would not easily abate the hostility toward resistance in Vermont or the personal animus toward its leaders.[25]

INDEPENDENT VERMONT

As the New York revolutionaries pushed Tryon's royal government into the harbor, the fighting in Massachusetts at Lexington and Concord sparked the formal outbreak of Revolution. In May Ethan Allen and some eighty of his Green Mountain Boys stunned the British and also the Continental Congress with the bloodless capture of Fort Ticonderoga. The Revolution altered the environment. The Green Mountain Boys fought in the northern campaigns as a New York regiment commanded by Seth Warner, and the regiment along with Ethan Allen, at the direction of Congress, received pay from New York.

The wartime necessity to fight a common enemy did not resolve the long battle over land titles, nor did it diminish the genuine and deep personal animosity. With New York preoccupied by the war and New York City in British hands after August 1776, Vermonters made their own revolution within the Revolution and moved quickly to establish independence. A series of meetings, called conventions, begun in Dorset on the west side in January 1776, culminated with Vermont's assertion of independence as "New Connecticut" in January 1777. A subsequent convention gathered in Windsor in June 1777 renamed the state "Vermont," appointed a committee to draft a constitution, and adjourned until July 2. As the convention reassembled in Windsor to consider a draft constitution, General Burgoyne's legions of redcoats, Hessians, and Indians moving south up Lake Champlain approached Fort Ticonderoga and Mt. Independence across Lake Champlain. Settlers on the west side had begun to flee to the south to the protection of blockhouses and larger communities. The news of the military situation worsened as delegates began to deliberate on the draft constitution, and a providential thunderstorm checked the impulse to adjourn to protect their homes and families.

The preamble of the new Vermont constitution revealed the state's origins in the dispute with New York. After the obligatory denunciation of the "despotic dominion of the British Parliament," it catalogued the longstanding and continuing bitter dispute with New York. A succession of governors, it asserted, beginning with "Governor Colden," had "coveted" Vermont land and the New York legislature "ever have, and still continue to disown the good people of this State, in their landed property." After compiling the list of New York's transgressions, the preamble declared that "the representatives of the freemen of Vermont" had come together to exercise their innate right granted by the "Great Governor of the Universe" and by the "authority vested" by their constituents "to deliberately form for themselves...as they think best for governing their future society" a frame of government in the constitution of the State of Vermont.[26]

The Vermont constitution provided a counterpoint to the very conservative constitution adopted by New York that April. While it closely followed Pennsylvania's radical 1776 document, the new constitution also reflected some distinctive Vermont values and circumstances. It made Vermont the first state to abolish slavery and it granted universal manhood suffrage. It set up a unicameral legislature of one representative from each town while allowing a second for a period of seven years from towns with eighty taxable residents. This apportionment would give the west side, dominated by the remnants of the Green Mountain Boys and the faction that formed around the Allens and Thomas Chittenden, roughly equal representation with the more populous east side.

The constitution placed executive power in the hands of the governor and a "deputy" (lieutenant) governor with one-year terms. If no candidate for any statewide executive office received a majority, the constitution remanded the choice to the legislature. The constitution also established a twelve-member council elected at large annually. This council acted as both an executive branch cabinet and a quasi–upper house of the legislature, as the General Assembly had to submit legislation for its review.[27] In tacit recognition of the different political attitudes and environment on each side of the Green Mountains, the first election established the "Mountain Rule" that would persist well into the twentieth century. The governor and lieutenant governor would come from opposite sides of the mountains and the council membership would be divided nearly evenly between the east and west sides. In the three decades before Vermont selected a capital in 1807, the peripatetic legislature regularly rotated sessions between the east and the west sides of the Green Mountains.[28]

The constitutional convention at Windsor directed that elections take place in December 1777 and that the legislature convene in March 1778. The convention set up no ratification process, and the ruling Allen-Chittenden faction and other adherents of the new state wisely avoided a popular referendum. When in the summer of 1778 Cumberland County towns polled public opinion, large majorities in Hinsdale, Brattleboro, Guilford, Putney, and Westminster favored New York, while Weathersfield and Wilmington gave the new state slender margins of support. Ira Allen later wrote, "had the constitution been then submitted to the consideration of the people…it is very doubtful whether a majority would have confirmed it."[29]

The Council of Safety appointed to administer Vermont's affairs until the elections seamlessly assumed the reigns from the ad hoc council that had made many military and political decisions for the territory in the absence of effective New York authority. This informal council had frequently gathered in Chittenden's house in Arlington and later earned from historians the not entirely affectionate appellation of the Arlington Junto. Its members included Ira and Heman Allen, Chittenden, Moses Robinson, a Bennington associate, Nathan Clark, Jonas and Joseph Fay (sons of Stephen Fay, the proprietor of the Catamount Tavern, the informal headquarters of the Green Mountain Boys), and Chittenden's son-in-law Matthew Lyon. These men, who had all fought beside Ethan Allen and Seth Warner and had played leading roles in the movement that led to Vermont independence, made up a majority of the governing Council of Safety.[30]

The military exigencies created by Burgoyne's invasion rendered printing and promulgating the new constitution difficult. In December 1777, the Council of Safety convened a second convention in Windsor that approved delaying elections to early March of 1778, when the voters made Thomas Chittenden governor. They annually reelected him until his resignation shortly before his death in 1797, with the lone exception of 1789, when a scandal involving Ira Allen cut Chittenden's margin to a large plurality. In the absence of a majority of the popular vote, the legislature expressed "their gratitude and warmest thanks" for nearly a decade of Chittenden's service and elected Moses Robinson.[31] The first council confirmed the power of the Arlington Junto with the election of Ira Allen, Jonas Fay, and Moses Robinson, all members of the Council of Safety. Joseph Bowker, Timothy Brownson, and Jeremiah Clark, prominent west side leaders of the meetings that led to independence, also joined the council, which made Matthew Lyon its secretary. Most of the east side members had participated in one or more of the conventions that led to independence and the constitution. Until the mid-1790s, when the rancor of the national partisan strife reached Vermont, the roster of the council, following the Mountain Rule, remained very stable.[32]

With Burgoyne's stunning defeat at Saratoga in October 1777, the British and Indian military threat to the northern frontier, though never entirely absent, receded. This freed the new government of Vermont to focus on its agenda of securing land titles through twin activities: asserting and maintaining its authority in the face of overt resistance from pockets of residents who clearly preferred New York, and winning recognition of Vermont independence by Congress despite unrelenting New York opposition. The new government did not command the allegiance of all of its residents. A large meeting of New York supporters in Brattleboro in January 1778 alluded to "the pretended state of Vermont" and petitioned the New York legislature for protection. Governor Clinton responded with a proclamation that promised "the necessary measures for protecting the loyal inhabitants…residing in the counties of Albany, Charlotte, Cumberland, and Gloucester, in their persons and estates." It ordered that all who did not submit to Yorker authority to "yield that obedience and allegiance, which, by law and of right, they owe to this State." In the years ahead New York would regularly make bold statements in an effort to assert its authority and to stiffen the resolve of its supporters, but it never backed its increasingly hollow rhetoric with action.[33]

Had the Continental Congress, or after March 1781 the Congress established by the Articles of Confederation, recognized Vermont, it could have settled the dispute with New York and brought Vermont into the Confederation. Conversely, Governor Clinton thought that the Congress should settle the dispute in New York's favor and he pressed for "an explicit and unequivocal Declaration of the Sense of Congress" to recognize Vermont as part of New York State. Clinton and his ally James Duane, who held New York title to substantial acreage in Vermont and often represented New York in Congress, could never force a divided Congress to rule in favor of New York. Clinton knew that many residents in Vermont, especially in the east side towns, preferred New York authority, and he took seriously his oath to protect and defend New York and its citizens, including those in Vermont. Combined with his genuine dislike of the Vermont leaders, whom he thought had taken "ungenerous Advantage of our Situation" fighting the British, Clinton remained an obdurate and implacable foe of Vermont independence and statehood. Even those not inclined to harbor a grudge concluded "the Governor of New York and the authority of that Province, were guilty of the highest oppression and injustice toward the New Hampshire grantees."[34]

Along with New York resistance to recognition of Vermont, other issues also inhibited action by Congress, where both New Hampshire and Massachusetts maneuvered to promote their own remote claims. Vermont's entry into the Confederation would also threaten the uneasy balance among the New England middle and southern states. Though in agreeing to the Articles of Confederation states relinquished their claims to western lands, a number of them continued to squabble over conflicting grants, including a serious Massachusetts claim to vast tracts in western New York. Furthermore, explicit recognition of Vermont could establish the dangerous precedent that separatists within a state could legitimately break away.[35]

As the new government of Vermont looked to its interests in Congress, it also took immediate steps to defend itself against both the continuing British menace and enemies within the state. In 1778, with Seth Warner's regiment of Green Mountain Boys ordered to Albany, Vermont raised a battalion of militia under the command of Samuel Herrick. The militia proved more effective enforcing Vermont's policies within the state than combating British incursions. The Council of Safety had previously confiscated the personal property of Tories. The new Vermont assembly quickly moved to enact Ira Allen's scheme to give the governor and council the power to sequester the estates of "inimical persons" and, with the Banishment Act, the power to run people out of the state. Vermont ruthlessly exploited these powers to punish, intimidate, and remove its opponents. The program also raised sufficient funds that the cash-strapped state eager "to make the government popular" did not have to levy taxes until 1781. Many of the "inimical persons" were Yorkers, who in their complaints to Governor Clinton professed their allegiance to the United States. They believed their guilt lay in "acknowledging themselves to be subjects of the state of New York, and not recognizing the validity and existence of the State of Vermont."[36]

Commissioners of Sequestration, who initially included all of the council (and for a short time Ethan Allen, following his release after three years as a British prisoner), administered the program to great effect for the fledgling state. The commissioners came down hard on the absentee titleholders, especially Yorker beneficiaries of New York's colonial governors. Though they often proved lenient on Tories and Yorkers who in their view had "repented," they also settled old scores. The commissioners adjudicated cases of overlapping claims, consistently upholding the New Hampshire titles. In 1780 Chittenden attempted to end the title dispute summarily by proclaiming all New York titles null and void, but New York ignored the order and relinquished neither its claims nor its assertion of rights in Vermont.

The assembly also authorized the sale of the remaining "unappropriated" or ungranted land, generally in the northern part of the state, and it allowed the Commissioners of Sequestration to auction confiscated property. At these auctions the commissioners gave preference to veterans, new settlers, and members of the Continental Army in a transparent effort to secure the allegiance of the new population streaming into the state. They also employed land grants to curry the favor of the powerful. John and Abigail Adams, Generals James Sullivan, John Stark, and Oliver Wolcott, John Jay, John Paul Jones, Yale president Ezra Stiles, and other American notables found themselves the beneficial owners of tracts in Vermont. The assembly also responded favorably to hundreds of petitions from men eager to get a piece of the action and secure a grant, often as large as an entire township in this wholesale redistribution of land. The Allens ended up with thousands of acres of prime land.[37]

While Vermont led by the Allen-Chittenden faction imposed its authority, it had to remain constantly vigilant to thwart continuing threats from within the state and beyond. Strong internal opposition came from disgruntled New York adherents concentrated in Connecticut River towns, north of the Massachusetts line. Another serious challenge arose in some of the New Hampshire towns on the other side of the river. These towns maintained bitter grievances against the seaboard and Merrimac River towns that dominated the New Hampshire legislature and civil and military appointments and, the Connecticut River leaders believed, paid insufficient attention to building roads and defense against the marauding British and Indians. Led by Dartmouth College officers who had moved Eleazar Wheelock's Indian school to Hanover in 1769, the "College Party" found natural allies in Vermont's upper Connecticut River towns, whose residents, unlike their western Vermont counterparts, looked more to the coast than to Canada for a market and who harbored reservations about the motivations of the Allens and their colleagues. In 1778 sixteen New Hampshire towns secured the recognition of the Vermont legislature, which annexed the towns that came to be known as the "East Union." This at once threatened the Allen-Chittenden west side hegemony in the Vermont legislature and provoked the hostility of a New Hampshire government already scheming for control of eastern Vermont.[38]

In the February 1779 session of the Vermont legislature, Ira Allen skillfully maneuvered a vote to dissolve the East Union. He also helped secure an act to provide for the levy of recruits for the Vermont militia designed as much to smoke out those who would not support the state as to defend it. This law provided that for those who refused service under Vermont, the militia captain could hire replacements with funds raised from the public sale of goods and chattel of those who would not serve. A levy on cows owned by three men who declined their summons to join the Vermont militia provoked the armed resistance of about one hundred Yorker adherents in the southeast corner of Vermont. They boldly freed the bovine hostages at gunpoint, but they feared reprisal for their actions. These New York adherents petitioned Governor Clinton to ready the Albany militia for their defense. In response, Clinton advised "firmness and prudence, and in no instance to acknowledge the authority of Vermont," promising in case of trouble "instantly to issue orders to send the militia against the enemies of New York whoever they might happen to be." In a pattern that had become familiar, Clinton's advice amounted to empty promises.[39]

Vermont quickly responded by ordering Ethan Allen to raise a force, march to the Yorker enclave, and assert Vermont authority. Allen and the Vermont militia thoroughly intimidated the Yorkers and arrested forty of their most active members in a blustering action later dubbed the "Great Cow War." A Vermont court sitting in Westminster quickly tried, convicted, fined, and then released most of those arrested, and Governor Chittenden subsequently pardoned the rest. Ira Allen recalled that Vermont had deliberately tried to frighten the Yorkers, hoping "to make them our friends" in Vermont's "defiance to the old government of New York, with whom we have long contended for our properties."[40]

The East Union and these events caught Congress's attention and rekindled its sporadic interest in resolving the controversy. In May 1779 Congress appointed a committee of up to five members to go to "the New Hampshire Grants" to conduct an inquiry in order "to promote an amicable settlement" and to provide that "justice due to the states does not interfere with the justice which might be due to individuals." Governor Clinton opposed the mission, fearing "as an implied acknowledgement of their authority," it would stiffen the Vermont resolve.[41] Two of the committee, one short of a quorum, went to Vermont and met with Chittenden in June 1779. When they asked whether Vermont would submit to New York if Congress secured their land titles, Chittenden responded that Clinton would provide only responses "calculated to answer sinister purposes." To this statement that further revealed the continuing distrust and antipathy toward the Clinton and New York government, Chittenden added that Vermont would remain "as unwilling to be under the jurisdiction of New York" as he supposed America would be to "revert back to the power of Great Britain."[42] Citing the lack of a quorum, Congress took no action. Clinton understood that New York could not enforce its authority against "such a ferocious Sett of Men" and that congressional procrastination aided the Vermont rebels. When some of the New York Senate, recognizing that the two states would have to resolve the Vermont problem themselves, debated a bill to recognize Vermont and settle the matter, Clinton ironically contributed to the delay when he angrily prorogued the legislature bristling that ceding authority "woud [sic] have reflected lasting Ignominy & Disgrace upon the State & his Consideration alone ought to have forbid it."[43]

The efforts to establish independence assumed an added dimension in mid-1780 when the Vermont leadership opened negotiations with the British. Responding to an invitation to Ethan Allen from a Loyalist officer, the Arlington Junto, at first limiting knowledge to an inner eight, discussed becoming "a distinct colony under the crown on safe and honourable terms." Known as the "Haldimand Negotiations," the protracted discussions with representatives of General Frederick Haldimand, governor of Canada, occurred under the guise of a prisoner exchange. They revealed the depth of the resolve of the Allen-Chittenden faction to secure their independence and property. Led by Ira Allen and Jonas Fay, the Vermonters sought the immediate cessation of military activities on the northern frontier, recognition of Vermont self-rule, and land titles within the British Empire. They further sought opening of unlimited commerce over the Lake Champlain–Richelieu River route to the St. Lawrence River, the only practical outlet for the bulky forest and agricultural produce of the Champlain Valley, where the Allens had the vast majority of their holdings.

Fully appreciating the danger of the negotiations to Vermont's standing in Congress and at home where "nine-tenths" of Vermonters would regard them as treasonous, "the business," Ira Allen wrote, "was necessarily of a private nature." To cover themselves, the Arlington Junto also developed documents designed to represent the talks as a clever defensive ruse designed to achieve an armistice to forestall British military action. Rumors of the protracted negotiations began to circulate, causing an inquiry by the Vermont legislature. The British, never trusting the wily "Vermontese," sent clandestine representatives to observe the legislature in October 1781, at which Ira Allen had promised to introduce a proclamation from Haldimand inviting Vermont's return to the empire. Ethan Allen presented the suspicious and somewhat hostile Vermont legislature with an account of a cartel to return prisoners and went on to observe that he "discovered among the British officers a fervent wish for peace" and that "the English government was tired of war." As Ira Allen recalled of his own performance, both sides "seemed satisfied." Much to his amusement, he went on to ask rhetorically, "Is it not curious to see opposing parties perfectly satisfied with one statement, and each believing what they wished to believe, and thereby deceiving themselves."[44]

News of Washington's stunning victory at Yorktown ending the military phase of the American Revolution convinced the British and the Allens to call off the negotiations. Knowledge of them became widespread, however, when Clinton published documents that at once revealed their depth, damaged the tenuous Vermont position in Congress, and greatly angered George Washington, who had already begun to question the loyalty of Vermont. Added to the problem of the public disclosure of the Haldimand Negotiations, the sudden revival of the East Union compounded displeasure with Vermont. The coalition of disgruntled Yorkers in southeastern Vermont who recognized that New York could not protect them, inhabitants of New Hampshire's Connecticut River towns, and those across the river in Vermont who shared a similar character continued to want more direct control of their fortunes. A convention assembled in Charlestown, New Hampshire, and after failing to muster a majority to form their own state, voted to join Vermont. In April 1781 Vermont annexed thirty-four New Hampshire towns and, in recognition of the large addition of territory, established new county lines.[45]

At the same time settlers in New York towns north of Massachusetts and east of the Hudson River, who had received little response to their frequent petitions for defense and had disapproved of the treatment of their Vermont neighbors by New York, also discussed joining Vermont. Propelled by the fact that additional towns on the west side would offer a counterbalance in the legislature to the new towns to the east, Chittenden in June 1781 issued a proclamation announcing the West Union and the annexation of fifteen New York towns.[46]

The East and West Unions brought howls of complaint from New Hampshire, New York, and Congress and nearly led to an armed collision in the West Union. The appearance of about eighty New York militia near North Hoosic (then San Coick) confronted a force of Vermont militia across the Walloomsac River. When Chittenden sent reinforcements, Clinton could not answer in kind and the Yorkers prudently dispersed. In an effort to quell the rising din from the New Hampshire grants and test Vermont's loyalty, George Washington wrote to Thomas Chittenden in a letter dated January 1, 1782, suggesting that Vermont had legitimate claims to statehood. To secure their recognition, Washington wrote, "You have nothing to do but to withdraw" from the East and West Unions. Withdrawing, Washington suggested, would result in "acknowledgement of independence and sovereignty."[47]

On February 19, 1782, the report of a congressional committee confirmed that view. If Vermont would "relinquish" the unions within thirty days, the committee asserted, "their district should be acknowledged as a free and independent state and admitted into the union." In the meantime in Vermont, with the British threat removed and the anger caused by the growing revelations of the Haldimand Negotiations, the legislature in February 1782 proved less inclined to follow the Allen-Chittenden faction. It called for a review of Ira Allen's accounts as treasurer, dissolved the East and West Unions, and sent a delegation to tend to Vermont interests in Congress that included Paul Spooner and Isaac Tichenor, both opponents of the Allens.[48] Congress, as usual, could not gather enough votes to act on its committee's recommendations. The Vermont situation remained unresolved, but the political winds had begun to change.

THE PATH TO STATEHOOD

With each passing year Vermont independence became more secure. Thomas Jefferson noted that "the great difficulty arises with New York" and Congress only "interfered from time to time to prevent the two parties from coming to an open rupture." With the passage of time, he concluded, "New Yorkers have been familiarizing to the idea of separation."[49] Alexander Hamilton boosted the "familiarizing" in 1787 when he asked Yorkers rhetorically, "Are we now in a situation to undertake the reduction of Vermont?" as it had been "wisely inviting settlers by an exemption from taxes and availing themselves of discontents" from other states.[50]

Vermont policies and the postwar economic boom had exploded its population. From over 7,000 inhabitants in 1770, the population had grown fourfold by 1780 to about 30,000, and it more than doubled again to over 85,000 in 1791.[51] By the mid-1780s the great majority of Vermont residents had come to Vermont or been born after the dramatic actions in 1777 when the state declared its independence and drafted a constitution. They also had not experienced the prolonged hostilities with New York that led to separation. Most, like Isaac Tichenor, who came to Vermont during the war as a quartermaster in the Continental Army, felt none of the personal antipathy. They shared a sense of nationalism, and while they supported Vermont independence, they did so within the context of the United States. Gradually they became the leading force in the legislature in particular and Vermont political life in general.

The Treaty of Paris of 1783 that officially ended the Revolutionary War and placed Vermont within the boundary of the United States created no noticeable stir in the Green Mountains. In many ways Vermont acted much like the thirteen states that had formed the Confederation, though it did not bear some of their more onerous responsibilities like the federal war debt. In 1783 Vermont established a postal service between Bennington and Albany with the same postage rates and regulations as the United States. Vermont minted coins, as did Massachusetts, Connecticut, and Rhode Island. The legislature rejected a recommendation of the council that Vermont treat with foreign powers to legalize trade across the Canadian border. Canadian authorities, eager for the commerce, winked at the growing flood of produce flowing into Canada from the Champlain Valley. In 1787, Lord Dorchester, who had succeeded Haldimand as governor of Canada, issued a proclamation opening inland trade with the Champlain Valley.[52]

Vermont also worked cooperatively with neighboring states. Even though the scarcity of hard money to meet debts greatly troubled Vermont, provoking near riots in Rutland and Windsor counties, Vermonters did not go as far as Daniel Shays and his followers in Massachusetts and turn to open rebellion. Chittenden responded astutely by successfully proposing acts allowing payment of creditors in certain commodities to relieve debtors. Aware that some of the Shaysites had fled to Vermont, in response to a petition from Massachusetts Governor Bowdoin and a request from the assembly Chittenden issued a strongly worded petition that warned Vermonters not to harbor, entertain, or conceal the fugitives. Eventually Vermont authorities captured and delivered several of the rebels to Massachusetts, though Vermont allowed Shays himself to remain, impoverished but not arrested.[53]

The Vermont constitution provided for a Council of Censors, elected at large every seven years, to review the actions of the legislature and to recommend amendments to the constitution. When the first council convened in 1785, it seemed to anticipate statehood. It recommended the repeal of the most draconian acts of the legislature aimed at Yorkers "when the continuing existence of Vermont was in doubt." The censors reasoned that "those acts could afford our enemies the most solid argument they have yet offered against the reasonableness of existence as a sovereign state." They also suggested a constitutional amendment establishing a procedure to choose delegates to Congress.[54]

Though Vermont behaved like a state and had increasingly integrated its policies with the United States, achieving statehood still required overcoming forces in both New York and Vermont that harbored old, deep grudges and feared some of the potential consequences, as one old Vermonter later described, of putting Vermont's neck in the yoke of Union. Only an accommodation between Vermont and New York could overcome Congress's reluctance to act. New York's opposition to Vermont's statehood increasingly rested more on its stubborn recalcitrance, promoted by influential officials and speculators, often in the same person, than on sound economic reasoning or the possibility of actually asserting its alleged authority. These men, from an older generation of New York politicians and leaders, had taken advantage of their position to secure grants and had resisted Vermont from its beginnings. Their position mirrored apprehension in Vermont that statehood would give New York a legal advantage that would jeopardize speculators in New Hampshire titles and settler holdings. This fear, together with commercial interests that relied upon open trade with Canada and the St. Lawrence River system, guided the wary attitude of the Allen brothers, Chittenden, and their associates. Others, such as Alexander Hamilton in New York and Nathaniel Chipman and Stephen R. Bradley in Vermont—younger, better educated, and former Continental Army officers less burdened by pre-Revolutionary encumbrances—identified their interests with a strong national government.

VERMONT JOINS THE UNION

By the mid-1780s Alexander Hamilton had begun to urge Vermont statehood. An advocate of a stronger national government, Hamilton considered the new American nation "replete with difficulties and surrounded with danger." He regarded Vermont outside the Confederation a more serious threat to national security than did "many gentlemen equally solicitous for the public welfare" but with concerns about their New York titles or for setting a precedent dangerous to other states' claims. In April 1787, he succeeded in persuading the lower house in New York to recognize Vermont. The resolution failed in the senate, but proponents of statehood in Vermont took note of Hamilton's argument.

At the Annapolis convention in September 1786, convened to discuss reorganization of the Confederation, Hamilton drafted reports calling on all states to send commissioners to a convention in May 1787 in Philadelphia to discuss how "to render the constitution of the Federal government adequate to the exigencies of the Union." Congress waited until February 1787 to endorse the plan. In the meantime, seeking to remove impediments to national unity, Hamilton argued that "Vermont is in fact independent, but she is not confederated." New York, he pointed out, lacked the resources to compel submission and had "no rational prospect of success" with such a policy. Furthermore, he counseled, should Congress attempt to assist New York, Vermont might well obtain the assistance of Great Britain eager to enhance "the security of Canada and [the] preservation [of its] western posts." Since lessening Vermont's ties with Britain provided a strong reason to acknowledge Vermont's independence from New York, he insisted as a condition of recognition of its independence that Vermont join the Confederation.

Hamilton also addressed the issue of compensation to New York titleholders that would help neutralize their opposition, and he accurately professed recognition to be the "only" way in which they will "ever have an opportunity to validate their claims." Article 9 of the Articles of Confederation that designated Congress as "the last resort on appeal to all disputes and differences now existing or that hereafter may arise between two or more states" would, he reasoned, place the dispute in a federal setting where New York claimants would likely prevail.[55] This in turn would prejudice many Vermont titleholders against statehood and make it imperative that New York and Vermont reach an accommodation prior to the matter coming before Congress.

A few weeks later Hamilton went to Philadelphia as a New York delegate to the 1787 Constitutional Convention. Although not represented, Vermont's existence nonetheless colored some convention proceedings. Article 4, Section 3 of the proposed Constitution of the United States, with a perspective that included Vermont and Kentucky, provided that "no new State shall be formed or erected within the jurisdiction of any other State...without the Consent of the Legislatures of the States concerned as well as the Congress." The creation of a federal court system with jurisdiction over title disputes with

New York continued to concern Vermonters, since statehood might well enhance options for the New York titleholders while jeopardizing their interests.

On July 16, 1788, Virginia's action as the tenth state to ratify the Constitution positioned the new system to go into effect. In Vermont, proponents and opponents of statehood took note and went into action. Alarmed at the prospect of statehood, ironically on the same day Virginia ratified the Constitution and only a few months before his unexpected death, Ethan Allen wrote Lord Dorchester, governor general of Canada, aligning his interests with those of the Anti-Federalists. He proposed the reopening of negotiations with Great Britain and went so far as to ask for arms to help Vermont. Allen wrote of his concern that "the new government" might coerce Vermont into the federal Union. He and some other Vermonters firmly opposed confederation with the other American states because it could expose them to Britain's displeasure, which might go so far as to prohibit trade.[56] Dorchester apparently never replied. Well before the Vermont convention that ratified the U.S. Constitution, Ira Allen informed Levi of Ethan's death, confessing that despite their "wish for the most advantage in trade with Great Britain," he thought it impossible to stop the move toward statehood.[57]

Nathaniel Chipman, who saw things quite differently from the Allens, wrote Hamilton on July 14, 1788, echoing sentiments that the nation would derive "a considerable advantage" from Vermont's admission as a state. Chipman believed that if "certain obstacles be removed," Vermonters "might be induced almost unanimously" to throw in with the federal cause. Although Vermont hoped to avoid becoming a party to the national debt, the principal obstacle lay in the conflicting land claims. It was "for these reasons and I perceive no others, the governor and several gentlemen deeply interested in these land… have expressed themselves somewhat bitterly against the new federal plan of government." Chipman hoped that compensation to New York grantees could come from western lands. Some states had proposed amendments, ten of which were ultimately adopted and formed the Bill of Rights, and Chipman asked Hamilton whether "it might not be favorable for Vermont to make some of those amendments which have been proposed by several states, the basis of her admission?"[58]

Chipman's brother Daniel delivered the letter to Hamilton, then in conference with colleagues at New York's convention in Poughkeepsie to consider the ratification of the new Constitution. After consultation with his colleagues, who included General Philip Schuyler and Egbert Benson,[59] Hamilton replied and agreed that it would be "scarcely practicable for you to come into the union, unless you are secured from the claims under New York grants." He rejected the idea to compensate New York titleholders with western land, believing that the new government would need the territories' help to settle the war debt. Nonetheless, "the accession of Vermont to the confederacy is doubtless an object of great importance to the whole." One of the first issues facing the new Congress would be the admission of Kentucky, "for which the southern states will be anxious." Hence the "northern states will be glad to find a counterpoise in Vermont." As for the proposed amendments, Hamilton thought it "inadvisable to annex any other conditions to your ratification. For there are scarcely any of the amendments proposed that will not have a party opposed to it."[60]

While the Chipman-Hamilton exchange proposed no details of an immediate solution, the correspondence, which continued into early October, unleashed a series of events that brought New York and Vermont proponents of statehood together to work out a mutually satisfactory resolution of the claims dispute. John Kelly, a New York and Vermont land speculator accredited by Chipman as an intermediary who would keep in confidence anything Hamilton might suggest,[61] wrote Chittenden on August 23 suggesting that four New York "gentlemen of undoubted veracity and honor," identified as Hamilton, Dr. William Samuel Johnson, John Jay, and Samuel Latham Mitchell, "are desirous to know upon what conditions this State would come into the union." Their position in government "rendered a communication on their part improper," and so they requested Kelly to solicit the information. Colonel Hamilton "had no doubt of being at present able, with the assistance of his friends, to obtain such favorable terms for the Citizens of Vermont, as would effectively secure their property and relieve them from all Taxes from the War, if he could only be informed on what Terms Vermont would consent to come into the union."[62]

That October, shortly after the Vermont elections, but before the convening of the legislature, Johnson wrote to Chittenden of his pleasure "to find by Mr. Kelly upon his return from Vermont" that Chittenden and his council as well as other influential Vermonters were "well disposed towards the constitution of the United States and would, he thinks wish to come into the confederacy on terms which you conceive to be proper." As Hamilton had previously noted, in light of the Kentucky situation, they had reached "the favorable moment for effecting it upon the most advantageous terms for all concerned." The Yorkers also understood that the opportunity to assert authority in Vermont had passed, and that delay only diminished the values of their claims. As in Vermont, the generation most interested in the Vermont claims had died or lost power. Nearly 35 percent of the eventual compensation would go to Vermont's old nemeses Goldsbrow Banyar, William Cockburn, the heirs of James Duane, the executors of Cadwallader Colden, and heirs of Crean Brush. The moment had arrived, Johnson advised, for Vermont to call a convention to recognize the U.S. Constitution as "early as possible" and then "authorize such gentlemen as the state can place an entire confidence in to negotiate the particular terms of admission." The Vermont legislature responded positively and elected three delegates to Congress, instructing them to "use all diligence to remove every obstacle to the accession of this State to the Federal government."[63]

In February 1789 the New York assembly again acknowledged Vermont's independence, and again the senate rejected it. In July, however, John Jay (who had supplanted Hamilton as the New York leader of Vermont's cause) succeeded in having New York approve a six-man commission to negotiate conditions of agreement with Vermont.[64] Chittenden received notice of the commission appointments on October 7, 1789, but he had failed to secure a popular majority in the September gubernatorial election for his role in an Ira Allen land scandal. On October 9, the legislature chose Moses Robinson to succeed him. Apparently without enthusiasm, Chittenden officially forwarded the New York communication and the legislature subsequently elected a commission to deal with its New York counterpart.[65]

The commissioners began their deliberations in New York during January 1790. The sticking issue became whether Vermont should pay $30,000 or $20,000 to New York for that state to relinquish its land claims in Vermont. The Vermont commissioners acceded to a $30,000 settlement and also agreed upon a boundary separating the two states. In March the New York legislature formally approved the settlement. By October 1790 the Vermont voters had restored Chittenden to the governor's office, but events had proceeded too far to delay prompt action on statehood. The legislature that convened in October confirmed the terms set by the New York–Vermont commissioners, and on October 27 it authorized a convention of one representative from each Vermont town to "deliberate and agree to the constitution of the United States."

The convention called in Bennington on January 6, 1791, elected Chittenden president and Moses Robinson vice president, and deliberated for five days. Despite the overwhelming vote of 105 to 4 for adoption, the proceedings did not lack controversy and some who may have quietly opposed adoption resorted to delay rather than reveal their outright opposition. Procedure became a major concern. Opponents raised the issue of considering the Constitution paragraph by paragraph or whether it be "deemed best" to move directly to debate whether "it would be expedient or inexpedient for Vermont to enter the federal union."[66]

Chipman, the delegate from Rutland and Vermont's chief justice, delivered a long speech that temporarily mooted the procedural issue. He began his discourse on the "consequences…of our either continuing independent or our accession to the union," and then he addressed the "principles and tendency of the federal constitution." In his remarks he emphasized the concerns for security because of the precarious geography of the state. As an independent state "we must remain little, but united we become great." The second part of his oration provided an exegesis on the Constitution itself, after which the meeting adjourned the morning session.

When it reconvened that afternoon, the delegate from Woodstock, Benjamin Emmons, advanced a concern he shared with others that should a land case come to trial under the new Constitution, a federal court would not allow the treaty with New York to prevail, putting Vermont titles into jeopardy. He questioned whether New York "had in reality a right to cede to Vermont the property of individuals." Stephen R. Bradley and Israel Smith, lawyers and members of the commission that negotiated the treaty with New York, then "went into a lengthy and well arranged train of argument on the right of Newyork [*sic*] to proceed in the manner they had done." The issue remained in debate until the convention accepted Ira Allen's amendment to the ratification notice conditioning Vermont's adoption of Congress's approval of the treaty with New York.[67]

The delegates also debated whether Vermont should join the Union immediately or delay until a more propitious moment. The delegate from Norwich, Daniel Buck, the principal spokesman for delay, probably settled upon this tactic as the only feasible means to ward off statehood. In a lengthy presentation he stated his opposition to the motion for a paragraph-by-paragraph reading as foreclosing general discussion on the larger merits of the Constitution. After receiving assurances that the amendment would allow just such a general discussion, Buck revealed his reservations. Vermont was small, he asserted, with "the affairs of government managed…under the eye of the people" with a "uniformity of interest." Once Vermont joined the Union, "her interest must then bend to the interest of union." Furthermore, "all extensive governments had a natural tendency to destroy that equality among the people, which was necessary to keep one part of mankind from oppressing the other." As long as it remained "possible for [Vermont] to support her independence, it was her wisdom to remain independent." The time might come, he allowed, when union was advisable, but that time had not arrived.

Bradley, representing Westminster, leaped to the task of replying to Buck, pointing out that some of Buck's arguments against the immediate adoption of the Constitution would apply equally in the future. As a small independent state between the United States and the British in Canada, "Vermont stood totally incapable of supporting the rights of sovereignty, or protecting her own citizens from invasion." Israel Smith of Rupert and Samuel Hitchcock from Burlington, who had changed his posture since Levi Allen lumped him in with opponents, also assured Buck that the dangers from union did not compare to the dangers of independence. In response Buck accepted that the Constitution provided greater protections than he had initially believed, but he still thought it precipitous to "seek for union." Israel Smith then argued for immediate adoption, but he too, could not still the call for delay.

After Bradley offered the motion to choose a committee to draft a form of assent to the Constitution, Samuel Hitchcock seconded the motion and the debate resumed. Emmons reiterated his view that since the "matter under consideration [was] of the most serious consequences," the delegates should "proceed with the utmost consideration." As "the people are not yet clear in the idea of the propriety of entering the union at present," he wished to "adjourn the convention until some future day, perhaps the beginning of October next."

Emmons's suggestion outraged Chipman. He sarcastically retorted that as the town Emmons represented might lie "remote from every channel of intelligence, people may entertain groundless jealousies," but the freemen of Vermont at large clearly favored immediate ratification. Beriah Loomis, the delegate from Thetford, interjected that his sentiments coincided with Emmons's, and he reiterated the view that Vermont had "no reason for doing business in a hurry." He too would prefer delay to allow the people to become better acquainted with the Constitution. After supporting statements for immediate ratification by Bradley and Niles, the motion to choose a committee to draft a document asserting ratification passed overwhelmingly. The convention quickly approved the committee's draft with Ira Allen's amendment by a 105 to 4 vote, and every participant in the debate, including Emmons and Buck, signed the ratification notice. The four dissidents, silent throughout the debates, all represented eastern towns located in Windsor County towns harboring suspicion of the ruling faction.

On January 10, 1791, the same date the convention adjourned, the General Assembly convened. Both met in Bennington, and their memberships so substantially overlapped that in its first business the legislature adjourned to allow the convention to conclude its labors. Overlapping membership also complicated the transmission of the convention's ratification. Since Thomas Chittenden served both as governor and president of the convention and protocol dictated notice of ratification be presented to the governor, the convention's vice president, Moses Robinson, received the task. Once Robinson carried out the formality of the transmission, the General Assembly took up the business of implementing the "recommendatory resolution" of the convention. Meeting in grand committee, the legislature elected Nathaniel Chipman and Lewis Morris as commissioners to Congress to negotiate Vermont's admission into the Union, predicated on the "affirmation" by Congress of the October 1790 agreement with New York. The legislature also marked out the boundaries for two or three congressional districts, depending upon how Congress would determine the state's initial representation, and elected two U.S. senators. The assembly nominated Stephen Bradley and Noah Smith, and the council nominated Moses Robinson and Nathaniel Niles. The grand committee elected, prematurely as it proved, Robinson and Bradley.[68]

On February 9, shortly after Chipman and Morris reached Philadelphia, President George Washington officially informed Congress that Vermont and New York had agreed to Vermont becoming a state and that Vermont had ratified the U.S. Constitution. Although Kentucky's statehood petition predated Vermont's, and it had already begun its journey through Congress before Vermont held its constitutional convention, Vermont's admission held fewer impediments and achieved approval with greater dispatch. By February 18, 1791, Congress agreed to Vermont statehood as of March 4, and the following week assigned Vermont two seats in the House of Representatives until after "Congress shall be apportioned according to an actual enumeration of the inhabitants of the United States."[69] On March 2 Washington signed "An Act giving effect to the laws of the United States within the State of Vermont."[70] On March 4, 1791, Vermont became the first fully accredited member of the Union without an Atlantic port or having been one of the original thirteen colonies.

STATEHOOD

The celebrations that marked Vermont statehood began with raising the "federal standard" with fifteen stripes that also included one for Kentucky. The festivities included parades, cannon salutes, and interminable rounds of toasts hoisted at Williams's Inn in Rutland, which included one to "The state of Newyork," and another wishing for the blessing of "The conjugal union and rising generation." A "select" choir sang to the tune of "Washington's Birthday" a five-verse song composed for the occasion and closed the ceremony with a toast: "May Vermonters become as eminent in the arts of peace as they have been glorious in those of war."[71] The end to New York claims to Vermont titles, a fixed western boundary, a border with Canada, and a promise of greater security against British incursions provided substantial causes for rejoicing. But a few important details remained unattended.

In September, Vermonters elected Nathaniel Niles and Israel Smith to the Second Congress. When the legislature convened in January 1792, its first meeting since Vermont had joined the Union, Moses Robinson suggested that his and Stephen Bradley's election to the U.S. Senate in the previous session lacked validity as Vermont had not yet become a state. The legislature concurred and subsequently reelected both men. Most of the leading spokesmen for statehood received rewards. National appointments to statehood partisans included a federal judgeship to Nathaniel Chipman and appointment as U.S. marshal to Lewis Morris.

Few anticipated the hardships the purchase price for Vermont statehood would impose. Vermont bought its freedom from New York land claims for $30,000 owed to New York by June 1, 1794, and on November 3, 1791, the Vermont General Assembly passed "An Act For the Purpose of Raising Thirty Thousand Dollars" by imposing a statewide property tax of one half penny per acre.[72] Income from tax revenues, problematic in the best of times, proved even more elusive in the hard economic climate that accompanied statehood. Vermont failed to meet its payment deadline. New York agreed to extend the payment schedule, but not until 1799 could Governor Tichenor declare Vermont's debt paid. Ironically, Vermont sold some of the lands freed from New York claims for delinquent taxes to raise the money that released them. Another, and perhaps greater irony, preceded the final payment. In 1791 federal judge Nathaniel Chipman put an end to any remaining disputes over the New York land titles. Chipman, who had always tempered his eager solicitation of Vermont statehood with the belief that any claim suits held in federal courts would likely be settled in New York's favor, ruled that the details of a New York confirmation fee settlement had been validated by the "acceptance and acquiescence" of the New Hampshire proprietors. Though a technical decision that dealt directly with confirmatory patents, it effectively ended all disputes over New York land titles.[73] Thus ended quietly in a courtroom a quarter century of bitter struggle and the history of what some consider America's only true republic. Of all the states, Vermont "alone had truly created itself."[74]

NOTES

1. When the convention to draft a constitution for the new state met in Windsor in July 1777, it, for the first time, called itself "Vermont." The origin of the name remains the subject of a mild debate, but for purposes of simplification, this essay applies the name to the territory that became Vermont well before it became known as "Vermont."

2. E. P. Walton, ed., *Records of the Governor and Council of the State of Vermont*, 8 vols. (Montpelier, VT: Joseph Poland, 1873–1890), 3:486–487.

3. Ibid., 3:473.

4. Levi Allen to Henry Dundas, London, August 9, 1791, and Levi Allen to Nancy and Ira Allen, London, August 20, 1791, in John J. Duffy et. al., eds., *Ethan Allen and His Kin, Correspondence, 1772–1819* , 2 vols. (Hanover, NH and London: University Press of New England, 1998), 1:373–377.

5. Walton, ed., *Governor and Council*, 3:470. London, August 20, 1791.

6. J. Kevin Graffagnino, ed., *Ethan and Ira Allen: Collected Works*, 3 vols. (Benson, VT: Chalidze Press, 1992), 1:138–149.

7. Matthew Bushnell Jones, *Vermont in the Making, 1750–1777* (Cambridge, MA: Harvard University Press, 1939), chapter 2 and appendices A and G; Donald A. Smith, "Green Mountain Insurgency: Transformation of New York's Forty-four Year Land War," *Vermont History* 64 (4) (Fall 1996): 197–231; Allan S. Everest, *Moses Hazen and the Canadian Refugees in the American Revolution* (Syracuse, NY: Syracuse University Press, 1976), pp. 22–23; and Robert E. Shalhope, *Bennington and the Green Mountain Boys* (Baltimore, MD and London: Johns Hopkins University Press, 1996), chapter 1.

8. J. Kevin Graffignino, "'The Country My Soul Delighted In': The Onion River Land Company and the Vermont Frontier," *The New England Quarterly* 65 (1) (March 1992): 24–60.

9. Hiland Hall, "New York Land Grants in Vermont," *Collections of the Vermont Historical Society* 1 (1870): 145–159.

10. Ibid.; and Jones, *Vermont in the Making*, appendices H and L.

11. Jones, *Vermont in the Making*, appendix H; and Daniel Chipman, ed., *Reports of Cases Argued and Determined in the Supreme Court* (Middlebury, VT: D. Chipman & Son, 1824), p. 59.

12. Jones, *Vermont in the Making*, appendix L.

13. Charles A. Jellison, *Ethan Allen: Frontier Rebel* (Syracuse, NY: Syracuse University Press, 1969), pp. 26–34.

14. "Brief Narrative of the Proceedings of the Government of New York… " (1774); Graffagnino, *Collected Works*, pp. 32–33.

15. Smith, "Green Mountain Insurgency," pp. 197–231.

16. Jellison, *Ethan Allen*, p. 59; E. B. O'Callaghan, ed., *The Documentary History of the State of New York*, 4 vols. (Albany, NY: Charles Van Benthuysen, 1849–1851),

4:710–878 is replete with accounts by Yorker officials, settlers, and adherents of their mistreatment at the hands of the Green Mountain Boys.

17. O'Callaghan, *Documentary History*, 4:526; William Slade, Jr., *Vermont State Papers* (Middlebury, VT: J. H. Copeland, 1823), p. 42; and Hall, *History of Vermont, From Its Discovery to Its Admission Into the Union in 1971* (Albany, NY: Joel Munsell, 1868), pp. 179–182.

18. Hiland Hall, *History of Vermont*, p. 182.

19. Ibid., p. 185.

20. Jay Mack Holbrook, *Vermont 1771 Census* (Oxford, MA: Holbrook Research Institute, 1982), pp. ii–iii and Tables 6–11.

21. H. Nicholas Muller III, "Shifting Boundaries, and the Population of the 'Republic of Vermont,'" *Vermont History* 51 (3) (Summer 1983): 180–181.

22. Benjamin H. Hall, *History of Eastern Vermont* (New York: D. Appleton & Co., 1858), pp. 762–773, provides a full "List of the Civil and Military Officers of Cumberland and Gloucester Counties."

23. Ibid., pp. 202–205; and Walton, ed., *Governor and Council*, 1: appendix A.

24. Walton, ed., *Governor and Council*, 1:330–332; Hall, *Eastern Vermont*, pp. 2117–2141; and Jellison, *Ethan Allen*, pp. 98–99, provide basic documentation and interpretation in a crowded bibliography commenting on the Westminster Massacre.

25. John P. Kaminski, *George Clinton: Yeoman Politician of the New Republic* (Madison, WI: Madison House), p. 64.

26. Walton, ed., *Governor and Council*, 1:62–75.

27. The Vermont constitution of 1777 with its unique features has spawned scholarly interest and publication. Walton, ed., *Governor and Council*, 1:83–103 provides a solid introduction and the text. See also Gary J. Aichele, "Making the Vermont Constitution: 1777–1824," in *A More Perfect Union: Vermont Becomes a State, 1777–1816*, ed. Michael Sherman (Montpelier, VT: Vermont Historical Society, 1991), pp. 2–37; and John N. Shaeffer, "A Comparison of the First Constitutions of Vermont and Pennsylvania," *Vermont History* 34 (4) (Winter 1966): 34–35.

28. Lyman J. Gould and Samuel B. Hand, "A View from the Mountain: Perspectives of Vermont's Political Geography" in *In a State of Nature: Reading in Vermont History*, ed. H. Nicholas Muller III and Samuel B. Hand (Montpelier, VT: Vermont Historical Society, 1982), pp. 186–190.

29. Hall, *Eastern Vermont*, Appendix J; Nathaniel Hendricks, "A New Look at the Ratification of the Vermont Constitution of 1777," *Vermont History* 34 (Spring 1966): 136–140; and Ira Allen, *The Natural and Political History of the State of Vermont* (London: J. W. Myers, 1798), reprinted as *History of the State of Vermont* (Rutland, VT: Charles E. Tuttle Co., 1969), pp. 71–73.

30. Walton, ed., *Governor and Council*, 1:109. See ibid., pp. 107–229, for an introduction to the Council of Safety and its minutes and other records.

31. Ibid., 3:187.

32. H. Nicholas Muller III, "Early Vermont State Government: Oligarchy or Democracy?, 1778–1815," in Muller and Hand, eds., *State of Nature*, pp. 80–85.

33. Hall, *Eastern Vermont*, pp. 320–324.

34. Chipman, *Cases Argued and Determined*, p. 63.

35. For Congress and the "Vermont problem" see Winn L. Taplin, "The Vermont Problem in the Continental Congress and Interstate Relations, 1775–1787" (Ph.D. diss., University of Michigan, 1955).

36. See Sarah V. Kalinoski, "Sequestration, Confiscation, and the 'Tory' in the Vermont Revolution," *Vermont History* 45 (3) (Fall 1977): 236–246.

37. See Mary Greene Nye, ed., *Petitions for Grants of Land, 1778-181*, vol. 5, *State Papers of Vermont* (Montpelier, VT: State of Vermont, 1939).

38. Frank Smallwood, *Thomas Chittenden: Vermont's First Statesman* (Shelburne, VT: The New England Press, Inc., 1997), pp. 75–79, provides an excellent description of the machinations in the legislature that dissolved the first East Union.

39. Hall, *Eastern Vermont*, pp. 335–348, provides a full and convenient account.

40. Allen, *History of Vermont*, pp. 82–83.

41. Clinton to President (Congress) John Jay, June 7, 1779, quoted in Kaminski, *Clinton*, p. 68.

42. Chittenden to Dr. John Witherspoon and Col. Samuel J. Atlee, Members of Congress, June 24, 1779, in John A. Williams, ed., *The Public Papers of Governor Thomas Chittenden*, vol. 17, *State Papers of Vermont* (Montpelier, VT: State of Vermont, 1969), pp. 463–465.

43. Clinton to Gen. Alexander McDougall, April 6, 1781, quoted in Kaminski, *Clinton*, p. 73.

44. An extensive literature has developed around the Haldimand Negotiations. Ira Allen, *History of Vermont*, pp. 94–198, first stated the case that the dealings with the British represent a clever ploy to forestall British military action on the Vermont frontier and at the same time pressure Congress to recognize Vermont independence. Most other accounts followed Allen's position for about 150 years. Chilton Williamson, *Vermont in Quandary, 1763-1825* (Montpelier, VT: Vermont Historical Society, 1949), chapters 7 and 8, articulated the revisionist position that the negotiations had real substance as the Allen-Chittenden faction would have made an accommodation with the British Empire to secure their title to land and keep commerce through Canada open. The revisionist approach has become the most favored by modern scholars.

45. Walton, ed., *Governor and Council*, 3: appendix H; and Muller, "Shifting Boundaries," pp. 181–182.

46. Walton, ed., *Governor and Council*, 3: appendix H.

47. Washington to Chittenden, January 1, 1782, in *Public Papers of Thomas Chittenden*, pp. 573–575.

48. *Journals and Proceedings of the General Assembly of The State of Vermont*, vol. 3, part 2, *State Papers of Vermont*, pp. 4–93.

49. Jefferson to M. de Meusnier, January 24, 1786, quoted in Walton, ed., *Governor and Council*, 3:340.

50. Hamilton to the New York Assembly, March 14, 1787, in Harold C. Syrett, ed., *Papers of Alexander Hamilton, 1757-1804* (New York: Columbia University Press, 1962), 4:115–118.

51. Muller, "Shifting Boundaries," pp. 185–188.

52. Donald C. Creighton, *The Commercial Empire of the St. Lawrence, 1760-1850* (Toronto and New Haven, CT: Yale University Press, 1937), pp. 104–105.

53. Walton, ed., *Governor and Council*, 3:357–380, appendix F, "Vermont at the Period of Shays's Rebellion—1784 to 1787."

54. Paul S. Gillies and D. Gregory Sanford, eds., *Records of the Council of Censors of The State of Vermont* (Montpelier, VT: State of Vermont, 1991), pp. 19–83.

55. Hamilton to the New York Assembly, March 28, 1787, in Syrett, *Correspondence of Alexander Hamilton*, 4:125–141.

56. Ethan Allen to Guy Carleton (Lord Dorchester), July 16, 1788, Duffy, *Ethan Allen and His Kin*, pp. 273–275.

57. Ira Allen to Levi Allen, December 18, 1789, ibid., pp. 334–336.

58. Chipman to Hamilton, July 14, 1787, in Syrett, *Correspondence of Alexander Hamilton*, 5:161–162.

59. Benson was a prominent New York attorney and the grantee of several New York patents in Vermont. He attended the Annapolis convention and served as a member of the New York–Vermont commissions. He also served in Congress, founded the New York Historical Society, and served as a New York judge. Some authorities maintain that the town of Benson, Vermont, was named in his honor. General Schuyler also held New York patents on Vermont land.

60. Hamilton to Chipman, July 22, 1788, in Syrett, *Correspondence of Alexander Hamilton*, 5:186–187. Vermont restrained from acting on the amendments until January 1792, when it ratified all twelve that had been proposed.

61. Kelly had written Hamilton along with Chipman on July 14, 1787. Daniel Chipman delivered both letters to Hamilton, but Kelly's letter has been lost to posterity. Kelly, a New York attorney, speculated in both Vermont and New York titles. See Daniel Chipman, *The Life of Hon. Nathaniel Chipman, LL.D.* (Boston: Charles Little and James Brown, 1846), chapter 3.

62. Kelly to Chittenden, August 23, 1788, *The Public Papers of Thomas Chittenden*, pp. 693–694. William Blodgett wrote Chittenden on September 10, 1788, that "as to the public debt, should Congress claim our proportion, will estimate our numbers low and not insist on vouchers for all expenditures," ibid., p. 695.

63. Johnson to Chittenden, October 3, 1788, *Public Papers of Thomas Chittenden*, pp. 697–698. The delegates selected were Moses Robinson, Jonathan Arnold, and Ira Allen, who Isaac Tichenor later replaced. See *Journals and Proceedings of the General Assembly*, 3: part 4, p. 97.

64. Robert Yates, John Lansing, Gulian Verplanck, Simeon DeWitt, Egbert Benson, and Melancton Smith.

65. Isaac Tichenor, Steven Bradley, Nathaniel Chipman, Elijah Paine, Israel Smith, and Stephen Jacob.

66. Records of the convention are located in Walton, ed., *Governor and Council*, 3:467–481. No official record of the proceedings exists, and the editor of *Governor and Council* relied on reports published in the *Vermont Gazette*.

67. Although the convention report notes the adoption of Ira Allen's amendment, it does not reveal the precise nature of the amendment.

68. *Vermont Assembly Journal and Proceedings*, January 19, 1791, 3: part 4, pp. 246–247.

69. The act was entitled, "An Act regulating the number of Representatives to be chosen by the States of Kentucky and Vermont."

70. The March 2d act also provided for a state census to begin in April and be completed in five months. Vermont's congressional delegation remained at two until it was raised to four after the 1800 census.

71. Walton, ed., *Governor and Council*, 3:483–484.

72. *Laws of Vermont, 1791–1795*, pp. 49–52. The act exempted lands in public, pious, and charitable uses.

73. Chipman, *Cases Argued and Determined*, pp. 56–63, for *Paine and Morris v. Smead* (1791). See also Williamson, *Vermont in Quandary*, p. 191.

74. Peter Onuf, *The Origins of the Federal Republic* (Philadelphia: University of Pennsylvania Press, 1983), p. 145.

BIBLIOGRAPHY

Allen, Ira. *The Natural and Political History of the State of Vermont*. 1798. Reprint, Rutland, VT: Charles E. Tuttle Co., 1969.

Chipman, Daniel. *The Life of Hon. Nathaniel Chipman*. Boston: Little and Brown, 1846.

Duffy, John, Ralph Orth, J. Kevin Graffagnino, and Michael Bellesiles, eds. *Ethan Allen and His Kin: Correspondence, 1772–1819*. 2 vols. Hanover, NH: University Press of New England, 1998.

Graffagnino, J. Kevin, ed. *Ethan and Ira Allen: Collected Works*. 3 vols. Benson, VT: Chalidize Publications, 1992.

———. "'The Country My Soul Delighted In': The Onion River Land Company and the Vermont Frontier." *The New England Quarterly* 65 (1) (March 1992): 24–60.

Hall, Benjamin H. *History of Eastern Vermont*. New York: D. Appleton & Co., 1858.

Hall, Hiland. *The History of Vermont, from Its Discovery to Its Admission into the Union in 1991*. Albany, NY: Joel Munsell, 1868.

Jellison, Charles A. *Ethan Allen: Frontier Rebel*. Syracuse, NY: Syracuse University Press, 1969.

Jones, Matt Bushnell. *Vermont in the Making, 1750–1777*. Cambridge, MA: Harvard University Press, 1939.

Kalinoski, Sarah V. "Confiscation, and the 'Tory' in the Vermont Revolution." *Vermont History* 45 (4) (Fall 1977): 2236–2246.

Muller, H. Nicholas III. "Early Vermont State Government: Oligarchy or Democracy?, 1778–1815." In *A State of Nature: Reading in Vermont History*. Edited by H. Nicholas Muller III and Samuel B. Hand. Montpelier, VT: Vermont Historical Society, 1982, pp. 80–85.

———. "Shifting Boundaries, Elusive Settlers, and the Population of the 'Republic of Vermont.'" *Vermont History* 51 (3) (Summer 1983): 179–191.

———. "Freedom and Unity: Vermont's Search for Security of Property, Liberty, and Popular Government." In *The Bill of Rights and the States*. Edited by Patrick T. Conley and John P. Kaminski. 181–211. Madison, WI: Madison House, 1992.

Shalhope, Robert E. *Bennington and the Green Mountain Boys: The Emergence of Liberal Democracy in Vermont, 1760–1850*. Baltimore and London: The Johns Hopkins University Press, 1996.

Sherman, Michael, ed. *A More Perfect Union: Vermont Becomes a State, 1777–1816*. Montpelier, VT: Vermont Historical Society, 1991.

Smallwood, Frank. *Thomas Chittenden: Vermont's First Statesman*. Shelburne, VT: The New England Press, 1997.

Walton, E. P., ed. *Records of the Governor and Council of the State of Vermont*. 8 vols. Montpelier, VT: Joseph Poland, 1873–1880.

Williamson, Chilton. *Vermont in Quandary: 1736–1825*. Montpelier, VT: Vermont Historical Society, 1949.

Virginia

Territorial Development:

- Colony of Virginia established by the London Company, 1607
- Continental Congress approves Declaration of Independence from Great Britain, July 4, 1776
- Great Britain formally recognizes American independence through the Treaty of Paris, September 3, 1783
- Virginia becomes the tenth state to ratify the U.S. Constitution, June 25, 1788
- The state of Virginia is deprived of western Virginian land through the admission of the new state of West Virginia into the Union, June 20, 1863

Capitals Prior to Statehood:

- Jamestown, 1619–1699
- Williamsburg, 1699–1780
- Richmond, 1780–1788

State Capitals:

- Richmond, 1788–present

Origin of State Name: Virginia was named in 1584 in honor of Elizabeth, the "Virgin Queen" of England.

First Governor: Beverley Randolph
Governmental Organization: Bicameral
Population at Statehood: 747,550
Geographical Size: 39,594 square miles

THE COMMONWEALTH OF VIRGINIA

Ratified the Constitution of the United States: June 25, 1788

Adam R. Hornbuckle

INTRODUCTION

In June 1788, 170 Virginians gathered in Richmond, the state's capital, to ratify or reject the Constitution as the legal framework of the government of the United States. By ratifying the document, Virginia would become officially one of the United States of America. By rejecting it, Virginia would become a separate national and political entity. By the time Virginia held its constitutional convention, eight states had ratified the document, one short of the number required to make the Constitution official. In that sense alone, the decision pending in Richmond was a momentous one. On June 21, 1788, however, while Virginians deliberated the legitimacy of the document, New Hampshire became the ninth state to ratify the Constitution, thereby making it law. Yet New Hampshire's decision did not diminish the significance of Virginia's but gave it more importance. Acceptance or rejection of the document by the nation's largest and most populous state, which had produced George Washington, the Revolution's chief military leader, and Patrick Henry, the nation's most eloquent spokesman of liberty and individual rights, would certainly influence the decisions of the remaining states to approve the Constitution. The success or failure of the Constitution to permanently unite and preserve the Union permanently hinged arguably on the outcome of Virginia's decision.[1]

Although the politics of the delegates to the Virginia Constitutional Convention represented the spectrum of late eighteenth-century American political thought, the majority of them denounced the Constitution. Led by Patrick Henry, these assemblymen feared the power bestowed upon the federal government through the document. Despite the Constitution's carefully crafted separation of powers and checks and balances among the executive, legislative, and judicial branches, the Anti-Federalists, as they came be to known, maintained that the Constitution did little to nothing to protect and ensure the individual liberties fought for in the Revolution. For some Anti-Federalists, the issue was states' rights, as they refused to concede Virginia's political prerogative to a centralized federal government. The position embraced by the Anti-Federalists represented a radical political philosophy that entrusted government in the legislature, the branch of government most responsive to the electorate, rather than the executive and judiciary branches. Born out of the Enlightenment, this radical philosophy of government took root and flourished in Virginia's colonial experience and found its initial articulation in the state's first constitution and Declaration of Rights in 1776.[2]

The remaining delegates in Richmond supported ratification of the Constitution. These representatives believed in the need for a strong centralized federal government, led by a strong but independent executive branch to provide national unity and leadership. Unlike the Anti-Federalists, who believed in the need to entrust government in the common people represented and responsive to the legislative branch, the Federalists, as supporters of the Constitution came to be known, believed that government must be entrusted to elected office holders drawn from the educated, propertied elite. Virginia Federalists, led chiefly by James Madison, embraced a conservative political philosophy that had little confidence in the citizenry to govern. While the common man may be sincere in his political judgments, conservatives feared that he was prone to follow demagogues and, too often, acted short-sightedly without concern for the rights and welfare of others. While Federalists feared placing too much power of the citizenry, they also feared placing too much power in elected officials. For them, therefore, the Constitution with its mechanisms for distributing government across the legislative, executive, and judiciary branches ensured that no branch would supersede the other. This division of power provided by the Constitution would better serve the nation than would an all-powerful legislative branch.[3]

COLONIAL VIRGINIA

The origins of Virginia's opposition to the Constitution, or to the federal form of government proposed by it, may be traced back to the state's colonial era. During the colony's most formative years, from 1607 to 1700, Virginia developed a representative government responsive to the electorate, especially in matters concerning taxation. More importantly, the colony developed a strong sense of political autonomy during the seventeenth century, as England paid little attention to Virginia or the other colonies in the midst of its own political upheavals. Only when Britain attempted to reassert control over the colony, especially in the regulation and restriction of trade, did Virginians resent royal authority. The era also witnessed the rise of the southern agrarian culture, which in Virginia rested upon tobacco cultivation, available land, and an enslaved African labor force to maintain it.

In the late sixteenth century, most of the entire eastern seaboard of the United States, except for Spanish Florida, was known as Virginia. Sir Walter Raleigh, an adventurer and colonist, who envisioned English New World colonies as overseas trading posts, way stations for oversea voyages to China and India, and missions to spread Christianity, named the region Virginia after Queen Elizabeth I, the "virgin queen," of England. In 1584, Elizabeth authorized Raleigh to colonize Virginia and, in 1587, he dispatched 117 colonists, including 17 women and 9 children, to establish a colony. Situated on Roanoke Island, in what is now North Carolina, the colony vanished without a trace, after going unsupplied for nearly three years. After England's defeat of the Spanish Armada, a supply ship finally reached the deserted colony in 1590. The unexplained loss of the Roanoke colony thwarted English colonial aspirations for nearly two decades.[4]

England successfully established a permanent settlement, Jamestown, in Virginia in 1607. Named after King James I, the successor of Elizabeth, Jamestown resulted from joint-stock companies, such as London's Virginia Company, which publicly sold stock to finance colonization. In May 24, 1607, a Virginia Company expedition, commanded by Captain Christopher Newport, established the settlement on the banks of the James River. Within its first year, Jamestown nearly failed, as over two-thirds of the colonists died from malnutrition and disease. Unprepared to cope with the hardships of frontier life, most of the colonists were gentlemen unaccustomed and unwilling to perform the manual labor necessary for their existence. Most of them had come to Virginia expecting to make easy fortunes searching for gold and silver. In September 1608, Captain John Smith took command of the colony, imposed military discipline, and required the colonists to work. Smith governed Jamestown until 1609, when he returned to England for treatment of an injury. In Smith's absence, Jamestown succumbed to drought, Indian attacks, disease, and starvation, sinking to its lowest ebb during the winter of 1609–1610, a period known as "the starving time" to its survivors. Jamestown revived after the arrival of Governor Thomas West, in 1610, with fresh settlers and supplies.[5]

Jamestown's survival hinged on establishing peaceful relations with the region's indigenous population. Smith, whose military experience had introduced him to non-European populations, pursued a cordial interchange with Powhatan, the powerful chief of a confederacy of more than thirty tribes, trading knives and guns for surplus food. Peace between Jamestown and the Indians, however, hinged on the friendship between Smith and Pocahontas, Powhatan's daughter, who according to Smith saved his life during a dispute between him and her father. Pocahontas, who often warned Smith of her father's plans to attack Jamestown, married John Rolfe, a successful Jamestown tobacco planter, in 1614. Powhatan approved of the union between his daughter and Rolfe, and their marriage enhanced the peace between Jamestown and the Powhatan Confederacy. Peace lasted until 1622, when Opechancanough, Powhatan's brother and successor, launched several coordinated raids against the colonists along the James River. Opechancanough objected to Indian lands taken over for tobacco cultivation and Christian proselytizing by the colonists. The 1622 attacks resulted in the death of 347 colonists, nearly one-third of the population. In 1644 Opechancanough launched another attack, killing 500 colonists, but because the population of Virginia exceeded 8,000, this loss of life was not as devastating as that in 1622. After the death of Opechancanough following his capture by the colonists, the Indians accepted a treaty with the colony in 1646 that subordinated them to colonial authority.[6]

Jamestown's early economy depended on glass blowing, iron smelting, making potash, shipbuilding, and raising hogs. In 1611, John Rolfe introduced a South American variety of tobacco to Jamestown, which was not as harsh as the native types. The success and popularity of Rolfe's crop, especially in England, provided the financial foundation for Jamestown's survival, assuring the economic, political, and social viability of the Virginia colony. After shipping some of the crop to England in 1613, he and other planters exported 2,000 pounds to England in 1615. Tobacco shipments reached 40,000 pounds by 1620 and, by the end of the decade, exceeded 1.5 million pounds. Tobacco cultivation fueled the geographic expansion of the colony beyond Jamestown because the plant required fresh land. The Virginia Company promoted both tobacco cultivation and colonial migration through its headright policy in 1617, which promised a land grant of fifty acres to every new settler. The headright policy attracted hundreds of colonists to Virginia. By 1619 the population of Jamestown had reached a thousand. To encourage young men to make permanent homes in the colony, the Virginia Company sent a number of "young, handsome and honestly educated maids" to become the bachelors' wives. Just as the tobacco economy promoted family life in Virginia, it also contributed to the enslavement of Africans, who labored in the tobacco fields. Twenty Africans, the first of thousands brought to North America, arrived in Jamestown aboard a Dutch merchant ship in 1619.[7]

In that same year in which the first African slaves arrived in Virginia, the colony established the first representative legislative assembly in colonial America. Virginia had grown to eleven boroughs, with Jamestown serving as the capital. On July 30, 1619, two representatives, or burgesses, elected from each borough assembled in Jamestown. Known as the House of Burgesses, it served as a model for many of the elected lawmaking assemblies throughout the colonies and later, as new states took shape. While the approval of a great seal for the colony was its first act, the Burgesses later claimed the right to act on all tax laws. Although the House possessed total legislative authority, the governor and his council held the right to veto legislation. Conforming to English law, the House adopted the same procedures as in the English Parliament. In 1624, the year before his death, James revoked the Virginia Company's charter, declared Virginia a royal colony, appointed a royal governor, and dissolved the House of Burgesses. Virginians protested the abolition of their legislature and in 1629 reestablished the House of Burgesses. After 1629, the House gained significant governmental authority, as England under Charles I became preoccupied with domestic political struggles.[8]

From 1629 to 1660, England experienced significant political and social upheaval. During this period, Oliver Cromwell and his Puritan army defeated Charles I, dissolved the Crown and parliament, and established a strict religious fundamentalist Protectorate in England. Under Cromwell, the colonies flourished, especially in terms of immigration, as political and religious dissidents fleeing Puritan intolerance found refuge in the colonies. Virginia, in particular, became a haven for the cavaliers, supporters of the dispelled English crown. England under Cromwell exercised minimal governmental administrative control over the colonies, allowing them to develop political structures and practices of their own. In Virginia as well as in the other colonies, legislatures evolved into two houses. The House of Burgesses comprised the lower house of the legislature, while the governor's council comprised the upper house. Since the establishment of representative government in Virginia, members of the governor's council met jointly with the Burgesses to debate and vote on laws affecting the colony. As time passed, the fundamental differences between the two legislative bodies led them to separate into two distinct houses. Virginia recognized this legislative division as the General Assembly in 1663.[9]

The political autonomy enjoyed by Virginia ended with the fall of Cromwell's Protectorate and the restoration of the English Crown in 1660. Stuart kings, Charles II (1660–1685) and his brother James II (1685–1688), both concerned themselves with colonial administration more directly than any of their predecessors. Economic self-interest drove England's renewed attention to the colonies. The Stuarts wanted to ensure that colonial commerce would benefit England rather than compete with the mother country or aid other nations. Tobacco from Virginia, sugar from the West Indies, and slaves from Africa played into this mercantile global economy, which saw one nation's gain as another nation's loss. In this scheme, the colonies could supply England with valuable raw materials and they could serve as a market for the mother country's manufactured goods. England ensured this arrangement by a series of Navigation Acts, passed in 1660, 1663, and 1673. These laws ensured that only English and colonial merchants conducted colonial trade; that certain American products could be sold only to England; that all foreign goods destined for sale in the colonies had to be shipped through England and pay English import duties; and that the colonies could not produce or export items that competed with English products such as wool clothing, hats, and iron.[10]

The reinstitution of rigorous institutional control by England resulted in a clash between local autonomy and colonial administrative responsibility in Virginia. In 1660, Charles II appointed Sir William Berkeley as the royal governor. Berkeley had served in the position from 1642 to 1652 before stepping down during Cromwell's reign. During his first administration, Berkeley enjoyed favorable rapport with the colonists, but he angered them in his second administration by postponing elections in the House of Burgesses for more than a decade. More importantly, Berkeley promoted the rise of a Tidewater aristocracy to rule the colony by placing patriarchs of the region's wealthiest families in council positions. During his first tenure, Berkeley also encouraged westward expansion toward the Blue Ridge Mountains. During his absence more and more settlers migrated to the region and throughout the Piedmont, many in search of fresh land to plant tobacco. Although represented in the House of Burgesses, these frontier planters developed autonomous but viable government institutions to address local needs. Disagreement between frontier planters and local Indian tribes over land possession erupted into armed conflict in 1675 after the Indians allegedly killed a white servant. The planters sought colonial protection from the Indians, but Berkeley, who in his first term deployed British troops against eastern tribes, wanted to avoid war with the frontier tribes and refused to aid the frontier planters.[11]

Berkeley's failure to assist the frontier planters in their struggle against the Indians exacerbated other grievances they held against the Crown, such as the economic restrictions imposed by the Navigation Acts, depressed tobacco prices, over-taxation, and political exclusion. Nathaniel Bacon, an upper-house assemblyman and cousin by marriage to Berkeley, believed that "no Indian had any rights that an Englishman need respect." He sympathized with the planter's plight and organized and led an army of frontier planters in brutal assaults against the Indians in 1676. On July 30, 1676, Bacon delivered a "Declaration of the People" at Middle Plantation (now Williamsburg), claiming that he acted in behalf of the king against the failure of the governor to defend the colony from the Indian threat. Declared a traitor by Berkeley, Bacon turned his rebellion upon the Tidewater aristocracy, pillaging the estates of men loyal to the governor and enlisting servants and slaves in his fight. In September, Bacon drove Berkeley's forces out of Jamestown and ordered the capital burned to the ground, an act of defiance that many of his followers did not support. Bacon's Rebellion, as the event came to be known, ended with its leader's death from dysentery in October 1676. In retaliation to the revolt, the Crown sent troops to Virginia to quell further dissent and to extinguish lingering unrest between planters and Indians. In 1677, the year in which Berkeley returned to England in disgrace, the colony reached a treaty with the Indians, which opened much of the disputed land up to colonial settlement.[12]

In the decades following Bacon's Rebellion, the population of Virginia increased significantly, reaching 58,000, the most populous of the British North American colonies. With nearly the entire Tidewater populated by 1700, many of the new pioneers to Virginia moved westward, settling in the Piedmont, the Great Valley, and the Blue Ridge Mountains. Moreover, German and Scotch-Irish migration into the Great Valley from Pennsylvania added to the diversity of the colony. The westward expansion of Virginians, however, conflicted with the interests of the French, who occupied much of land west of the Blue Ridge, and the Indians, who were allied to the French economically. By 1754, the French had taken possession of the land at the confluence of the Allegheny, Monongahela, and Ohio rivers. Governor Robert Dinwiddie of Virginia dispatched a force of militiamen, led by George Washington, then a colonel, to engage the French. After a daylong battle, he surrendered to the French. Washington's capitulation marked the beginning of the French and Indian War, or the Seven Years' War, as it came to be known in Europe, in which Britain and France clashed over possession of North America. For two years, Britain and France waged an unofficial war against each other until declaring war in 1756. British military success remained low until William Pitt took command of both the military and diplomatic strategies of the war, culminating in a three-pronged attack in which France recapitulated Forts Louisbourg and Duquesne in 1759. The fall of Quebec that same year marked the defeat of France and, in 1763, as a result of the Treaty of Paris, France conceded all territory east of the Mississippi to Great Britain.[13]

INDEPENDENCE AND A STATE CONSTITUTION

After the French and Indian War, the British government sought again to tighten control over the colonies. Although the war had drained Britain's treasury, the Crown did not expect the colonists to help pay off the debt. However, it stationed troops in the colonies to defend the western frontier. Britain wanted the colonists to help pay for these troops and, from 1763 to 1775, Parliament passed a number of laws to increase income from the colonies. The first of these laws, the Sugar Act, placed a three-penny tax on each gallon of molasses entering the colonies from ports outside the British Empire. Although the British reduced the tax on molasses to a penny a gallon in 1766, the Parliament had enacted even more contentious laws in 1765, the Quartering Act and the Stamp Act. Intended to make the colonists pay part of the cost of stationing British troops in America, the Quartering Act ordered the colonies to furnish the soldiers with living quarters, fuel, candles, and cider or beer. The Stamp Act required the colonists to pay for stamps placed on newspapers, playing cards, diplomas, and various legal documents. While most colonies half-heartedly obeyed the Quartering Act, often providing fewer supplies than requested, they disobeyed the Stamp Act. The refusal of colonists to purchase the stamps resulted in riots, and merchants agreed not to order British goods until Parliament abolished the act.[14]

In opposing the Stamp Act, colonial legislatures argued that the right of taxation belonged only to the elected representatives of the people. One of the most ardent opponents of the Stamp Act was Patrick Henry, a successful self-taught lawyer from Hanover County, Virginia, who had just won election to the House of Burgesses in 1765.[15] A persuasive and passionate orator, he brought to the House a direct rather than deliberative debating style and a willingness to act forcefully. Denouncing the legality of the British Parliament to tax the colonies, Henry drafted seven "resolves" against the Stamp Act. In May 1765, he introduced his Stamp Act Resolves to the House, presenting only five of seven, holding back the most radical ones. The House adopted the first four resolves and on May 29, 1765, published them as the Virginia Resolves:

> Whereas the honorable House of Commons in England have late drawn into question how far the general assembly of this colony has power to enact laws for laying taxes and imposing duties payable to the pope of his majesty's most ancient colony—for settling and ascertaining the same to all future times, the House of Burgesses of this present general assembly have come to the several following resolutions:
>
> Resolved, That the first adventurers and settlers of this his majesty's colony and dominion of Virginia brought with them and transmitted to their prosperity and all others, his majesties subjects since inhabiting in this his majesty's colony, all the privileges and immunities that have at any time been held, enjoyed, and possessed by the people of Great Britain.
>
> Resolved, That by the two royal charters granted by King James the First, the colonists aforesaid are declared entitled to all privileges of faithful, liege, and natural born subjects, to all intents and purposes, as if they had been abiding and born within the realm of England.
>
> Resolved, That his majesty's liege people of this his most ancient colony have enjoyed the right being thus governed by their own assembly, in the article of taxes and internal police; and that the same have never been forfeited or any other way yielded up, but have been constantly recognized by the kind and people of Great Britain.
>
> Resolved therefore, That the general assembly of this colony have enjoyed the right being thus governed by their own assembly, together with his majesty or his substitute have in their representative capacity the only exclusive right and power to levy taxes and impositions on the inhabitants of this colony and that every attempt to vest such a power in any person or persons whatsoever other than the general assembly aforesaid is illegal, unconstitutional, and unjust, and has a manifest tendency to destroy British, as well as American freedom.[16]

As adopted by the House of Burgesses, Henry's resolves postulated indubitably that American colonists, especially Virginians, had not forfeited their rights as Englishmen, rights that had been theirs since the original settlement under James I in 1607. Acknowledging that consent to taxation was one of the most important rights, Henry argued that the colonies did not have to obey tax legislation imposed by a foreign legislature and that any opponent of that opinion was an enemy of the state. The fourth resolve, as adopted by the House, represented an amalgamation of the original language from Henry's fourth and fifth resolves. The fifth resolve proposed the radical notion, but one that had been in development since the early seventeen century, that only the House of Burgesses had the right to tax Virginians:

> Resolved therefore That the General Assembly of this colony have the only and sole exclusive right and power to lay taxes and impositions upon the inhabitants of this colony, and that every attempt to vest such power in any person or persons whatsoever other than the General Assembly aforesaid has a manifest tendency to destroy British as well as American freedom.[17]

Henry did not submit the most radical of the resolves, the sixth and seventh, to the House of Burgesses. The sixth reiterated the notion that the colonists, particularly Virginians, were not bound to obey "any law or ordinance whatever to impose taxation upon them other than the laws or ordinances of the General Assembly."[18] The seventh, perhaps the most revolutionary, maintained that "any person who shall, by speaking or writing, assert or maintain that any person or persons other than the General Assembly of this colony, have any right or power to impose or lay any taxation on the people here, shall be deemed any enemy of His Majesty's Colony."[19] Newspapers throughout the colonies printed versions of the Virginia Resolves with six or all seven resolutions, including the ones not passed, thereby establishing Henry as an uncompromising opponent of imperial policy not only in Virginia, but also throughout the British colonies.

In October 1765, representatives from the colonies gathered in New York for the Stamp Act Congress, from which they issued thirteen resolves. Although these Stamp Act Resolves echoed the themes inherent in the Virginia Stamp Act Resolves, the preamble to the document coming out of New York did not possess Henry's fire and passion for the right of the colonies themselves to decide their own laws, especially in regard to taxation. The preamble read as follows:

> The members of this Congress, sincerely devoted, with the warmest sentiments of affection and duty to His Majesty's Person and Government, inviolably attached to the present happy establishment of the Protestant succession, and with minds deeply impressed by a sense of the present and impending misfortunes of the British colonies on this continent; having considered as maturely as time will permit the circumstances of the said colonies, esteem it our indispensable duty to make the following declarations of our humble opinion, respecting the most essential rights and liberties Of the colonists, and of the grievances under which they labour, by reason of several late Acts of Parliament.[20]

In response to Stamp Act Resolves, Britain repealed the Stamp Act in 1766. According to historian Edmund S. Morgan, repeal of the Stamp Act alone may have been enough for the colonists, as they "would have been happy to settle down on this position and search no further. They wanted, as yet, no more freedom than they had enjoyed in the past. But they wanted no less, either, and were willing to fight for it."[21] In place of the Stamp Act, however, Parliament imposed new measures to collect colonial revenue. Charles Townshend, the Chancellor of the Exchequer, suggested placing duties on imported goods. Enacted in 1767, the Townshend Acts, as they came to be known, collected levies on glass, lead, paint, paper, and tea imported into the colonies, and established a customs agency in Boston, Massachusetts, to collect the monies efficiently. Although many colonists accepted Britain's right to regulate trade, they disagreed with the Townshend duties in principle, arguing that they were taxes in disguise. In 1769, George Mason of Fairfax County, Virginia, proposed the establishment of a nonimportation association of English and colonial merchants to force a repeal of the Townshend Acts. With the support of George Washington, the House of Burgesses adopted Mason's proposal. One of many formal protests against the Townshend Acts, Mason's nonimportation association encouraged the colonists to boycott British goods and pressured British merchants, hurt by the boycott, to lobby Parliament for repeal of the acts. In 1770, Parliament withdrew all the Townshend duties except the one on tea, which it kept in place to demonstrate its prerogative to tax the colonies.[22]

Colonial merchants avoided the Townshend duty on tea by smuggling tea in from the Netherlands. The smuggling financially damaged the East India Company, the chief source of tea for the colonies. The company sought help from Parliament, which in 1773 passed the Tea Act. This legislation permitted the East India Company to sell its tea below the price of smuggled tea. Lord North, who had become the king's chief minister in 1770, believed that the colonists would buy the cheaper British tea, thereby acknowledging Parliament's right to tax them. In the process, the colonists would lose their argument against taxation without representation. Samuel Adams, a Boston patriot, led the resistance to the Tea Act and, on the evening of December 16, 1773, Bostonians disguised as Indians raided British ships docked in Boston Harbor and dumped their cargoes of tea overboard. Enraged by the Boston Tea Party, the British Crown wanted to punish Boston as a warning to all colonists not to challenge British authority. In 1774, Parliament passed several laws that became known in America as the Intolerable Acts or the Coercive Acts. One law closed Boston Harbor and stated that it be reopened only after Bostonians paid for the tea and showed a proper respect for British authority. The House of Burgesses, in sympathy with the Boston colonists, made the day of the port closing a day of fasting and prayer. This action angered Lord Dunmore, the royal governor of Virginia, and he dissolved the House of Burgesses. Its members then met without official permission on August 1, 1774, in Williamsburg, as the First Virginia Convention.[23]

The passage of the Coercive Acts marked the rise of Thomas Jefferson, who had represented Albemarle County in the House of Burgesses since 1769 as a leader in colonial opposition against British parliamentary authority. A supporter of Patrick Henry, Jefferson drafted a resolution against the Coercive Acts in 1774. In a 7,000-word treatise, he argued that Parliament did not have legitimate legislative authority over the colonies because, historically, their own assemblies had governed them, a theme previously proposed by Henry in the Virginia Stamp Act Resolves. Drawing his argument from the venerable tradition of English constitutional law, Jefferson extended Henry's argument, maintaining that that the Americans possessed the natural right to govern themselves. In repudiating Parliament's authority, he left allegiance to a common king as the only bond of empire. Drafted at Monticello, his home in Albemarle, Jefferson forwarded the manuscript for adoption by the First Virginia Convention in August 1774 as instructions to the Virginia delegates to the anticipated Continental Congress. Most of the delegates to the Virginia Convention, however, considered his resolutions too bold, and held to the old position against Parliament, conceded its authority to regulate the trade of the empire, but not to levy taxes as a result of that regulation. Subsequently published without Jefferson's consent and without ascription of authorship, A *Summary View of the Rights of British America* demonstrated the young revolutionary's penchant for mingling legalism and rationalism in what would become the colonial argument for independence.[24]

On September 5, 1774, the First Continental Congress met in Philadelphia to plan common measures of resistance. All the colonies except Georgia sent representatives to the Congress. Virginia sent seven delegates to the Congress, one of whom, Peyton Randolph, served as the president of the Congress. The delegates agreed that the colonies could not be ruled by a Parliament in which they were not represented, and the most that Parliament could do was pass laws regulating the trade of the British Empire. Most colonists still wanted to remain members of the Empire, but they felt they owed allegiance only to the British Crown and not to Parliament. The delegates to the First Continental Congress hoped King George III and his ministers would free the colonies from the Intolerable Acts. In 1775, most colonists still did not favor declaring themselves independent of the British Crown, as such a declaration would cut the last bond linking the colonies to Great Britain.

The delegates to the Second Continental Congress, which assembled on May 10, 1775, continued to hope the king would help resolve the colonists' differences with Parliament. In July, the colonists sent a final petition to the Crown declaring their loyalty to the king and asking him to address their complaints, but the king ignored their request and declared the colonies to be in rebellion. Meanwhile, the Revolutionary War had begun in April 1775, when British troops clashed with colonial militia at Lexington, Massachusetts, and nearby Concord. As the fighting intensified, hopes of reconciliation with the British faded.

In April 1776 Virginians elected delegates to the state convention, which was planned to convene in June. By then, most of the leading Virginian politicians had accepted the inevitability of declaring independence from England. Fairfax County elected George Mason to attend the convention and, in preparing for the assembly, he studied various forms of government. Illness caused Mason to arrive in Williamsburg, the colonial capital and site of the convention, almost two weeks late, during which time the other delegates had voted unanimously for independence and created a committee to prepare a Declaration of Rights and a state constitution. Edmund Pendleton, the president of the convention, assigned Mason to the committee. He wrote the initial drafts for both the Declaration of Rights, which the convention unanimously adopted on June 12, 1776, and the first constitution of the Independent Commonwealth of Virginia, which the convention unanimously adopted on June 29, 1776.

A watershed document of the Revolutionary era, the Declaration of Rights laid out the basic principles of republican government, together with clauses affirming the right to jury trials in civil and criminal cases and a declaration in favor of religious toleration. The document possessed language that would echo throughout the Declaration of Independence, the U.S. Constitution, and the Bill of Rights. Consisting of sixteen "rights," the third described the responsibilities of government as providing for "the common benefit, protection, and security of the people, nation, or community." The best government, Mason continued, is that

> which is capable of producing the greatest degree of happiness and safety, and is most effectually secured against the danger of mal-administration;—and that, whenever any government shall be found inadequate or contrary to these purposes, a majority of the community hath an indubitable, unalienable, and indefeasible right, to reform, alter, or abolish it, in such manner as shall be judged most conducive to the publick weal.[25]

The convention adopted the Declaration of Rights on June 12, 1776, adding other guarantees of individual liberties, such as freedom of the press, protections against general warrants, and bans on excessive bail and cruel and unusual punishments. Despite revisions and amendments of the committee and Convention, many consider the Declaration of Rights as Mason's most influential and significant writing.

Building on themes expressed in the Declaration of Rights, Mason took the lead in drafting the first Virginia State Constitution, the first plan for an autonomous and independent government proposed by one of the British colonies. The document began as an indictment against King George III, charging him with imposing numerous laws and restrictions upon the colonists without their consent. In addition, Mason charged George III with promoting and maintaining slavery in Virginia by "prompting our Negroes to rise in Arms among us, those very negroes whom, by an inhuman use of his negative, he hath refused us permission to exclude by law." Moreover, he blamed poor relations with the Indians, a persistent theme in Virginia's history, on the Crown as well, noting that "by endeavouring to bring on the inhabitants of our Frontiers the merciless Indian savages whose known rule of Warfare is an undistinguished Destruction of all Ages, Sexes, and Conditions of Existance...."[26]

As a framework for state government, the Virginia constitution provided for the separation of the legislative, executive, and judicial branches of government and prohibited plural office holding. Fearing the abuse of power by the executive and judicial branches, Mason lodged the greatest share of power in the popularly elected lower house of the assembly. For example, to prevent future governors from abolishing the state legislature, as Lord Dunmore had done as recently as 1773, he wrote: "Either House of the General Assembly may adjourn themselves respectively: The Governour shall not prorogue or adjourn the Assembly during their setting, nor dissolve them at any time; but he shall, if necessary, Either by advice of the Council of State, or on application of a Majority of the House of Delegates, call them before the time to which they shall stand prorogued or adjourned."[27] The Virginia constitution became the model followed by the other colonies as they proclaimed autonomy and independence from the Crown.

On June 7, 1776, Richard Henry Lee of Virginia introduced a resolution to the Second Continental Congress stating that "these United Colonies are, and of right ought to be, free and independent States...." After several days of debate, the Congress appointed a committee to draft a Declaration of Independence. The committee appointed Thomas Jefferson to write the document, and he completed the work in about two weeks. Two other members, Benjamin Franklin of Pennsylvania and John Adams of Massachusetts, made a few minor changes. The committee submitted the proposed Declaration of Independence to the Continental Congress on July 2, 1776. Congress debated the treatise line by line for two and one-half days and speedily approved the philosophical preamble, but revised the body of the work, especially the extended indictment of George III. Jefferson thought the declaration lost more than it gained in the approval process, and some modern interpreters have sharply differentiated "Jefferson's Declaration of Independence" from the document adopted by Congress. At any rate, the Declaration was signed and presented to the colonies on July 4, 1776, marking the official independence of the colonies from Britain.

The Declaration of Independence bore unmistakably the stamp of Jefferson's genius. Written in bold yet elevated language, the Declaration read plainly and directly. Touched throughout with philosophy, it offered a solemn appeal to the reason of mankind. Although grounded in English law, Jefferson suppressed the recondite legalism of tradition to the revolutionary principles born of the Enlightenment. He encapsulated a cosmology, a political philosophy, and a national creed—for so it would become—in the celebrated second paragraph. The truths there declared to be "self-evident" were not new. Indeed, as Jefferson later said, his purpose was "not to find out new principles, or new arguments..., but to place before mankind the common sense of the subject."[28] For the first time in history these truths were laid at the foundation of a nation. Human equality, the natural rights of man, the sovereignty of the people—these principles endowed the American Revolution with high moral purpose and heralded the democratic future not just in America, but throughout the world.

In June 1776, the Second Continental Congress established a committee to draft articles of confederation to bind the colonies together in a single nation.

The committee, chaired by John Dickinson of Pennsylvania, completed the Articles of Confederation, which Congress approved on November 15, 1777. Congress sent the document to the states for ratification and, by July 9, 1778, eight states had signed the Articles. Maryland, the last state to sign, did so on March 1, 1781. Unlike many state constitutions, including Virginia's, which provided for the separation of powers among the executive, legislative, and judicial branches, as well as a bicameral legislature, the Articles granted only a unicameral Congress with no separate executive or judiciary. Representation in Congress was disproportionate, as the states could send up to seven delegates, with a minimum of two delegates to represent a state officially. Representatives to Congress would be elected annually according to a process determined by each state legislature. Moreover, each state had only one vote and a majority of nine votes was needed to pass legislation.[29]

The powers granted Congress in the Articles of Confederation reflected the colonists' affection for local legislative control and their fear of powerful central authority. Congress did not have the power to regulate foreign or interstate commerce, to levy or collect taxes, or to raise an army. It could only request the states to pay their share of federal expenses and supply soldiers for the Continental Army. Even before the adoption of the Articles, Congress observed most of the provisions by 1781, as the presence of British forces encouraged the states to meet their obligations to Congress. After peace returned, however, the Articles' inherent weakness became apparent and Congress attempted several times to strengthen them by amendment. The Articles granted Congress the power to declare war and peace, send and receive ambassadors, negotiate treaties, settle boundary disputes between states, regulate coinage, borrow money, manage Indian affairs, establish and regulate a post office, regulate an army and navy, and appoint admiralty courts.[30]

After multiple attempts to amend the Articles of Confederation failed, the Confederation Congress voted to abandon the Articles altogether and draft a new constitution. In May 1787, the Constitutional Convention convened in Philadelphia, Pennsylvania. James Madison, George Mason, Edmund Randolph, George Washington, and George Wythe represented Virginia. The Virginia delegates represented the philosophical positions popular in late eighteenth-century America. Mason, Randolph, and Wythe held to the radical political philosophy that placed the responsibility of government in the popularly elected legislature. The Virginia Declaration of Rights and the Virginia state constitution, both drafted by Mason, strongly reflected the radical political philosophy. Madison and Washington, on the other hand, represented the conservative political philosophy that recognized the need for a strong centralized federal authority to quell the tyranny of the majority. The Articles of Confederation, as a framework for government, acknowledged the need for centralized authority, but failed to provide the leadership required to unite a nation composed essentially of thirteen autonomous political entities.[31]

The conservative philosophy prevailed at the Constitutional Convention, as the document that emerged from the deliberations provided for a relatively powerful central authority to unite the individual states. The Constitution reflected the political viewpoint of James Madison more that any of the other fifty-five delegates. From the outset of the Convention, he argued early for a system of checks and balances.

> The great desideratum [desire] in Government is such a modification of the sovereignty as will render it sufficiently neutral between the different interests and factions, to control one part of the society from invading the rights of another, and at the same time sufficiently controlled itself, from setting up an interest adverse to that of the whole society.[32]

Madison believed that the government had to be constructed in such a way to avoid the pitfall of tyranny or fall wholly under the influence of a particular interest group. He favored a potentially large republic over a small one, because a large nation would include many different interest groups, none of which would be able to gain control of the government. Political stability, Madison maintained, would result from compromises among contending parties.

Madison's conception of national government was embodied in the so-called Virginia Plan, introduced on May 29 by his colleague Edmund Randolph. The plan provided for a two-house legislature with proportional representation in both houses, an executive and a judiciary, both of which the Confederation government lacked, and a congressional veto over state laws. It gave Congress the broad power to legislate "in all cases to which the separate states are incompetent." Had the Virginia Plan been adopted intact, it would have created a federal authority that reigned unchallenged with state power greatly diminished. The Convention, however, included many delegates, who, while recognizing the need for change, believed that the Virginians had gone too far in proposing national reform. After several weeks of debating the Virginia Plan, William Patterson of New Jersey presented an alternate scheme, dubbed the New Jersey Plan, which called simply for modifications to the Articles of Confederation. Asserting that the Articles provided the proper base for national government, the New Jersey delegate warned the remaining representatives that if they did not confine themselves to amending the Articles, their constituents would charge them with "usurpation." While most delegates rejected Patterson's narrow interpretation of the purpose of the Convention, they embraced some of his ideas, including the need to establish a bicameral national legislature, which agreed with the Virginia Plan.

The final product showed signs of its origins in the Virginia Plan, but compromises with other delegates had created a government less powerful at the national level than Madison and Randolph had imagined. Instead of giving Congress the nearly unlimited scope as proposed in the Virginia Plan, the delegates enumerated congressional powers and they provided for flexibility by granting all authority to carry out those powers. Discarding the legislative veto, the Convention implied a judicial veto instead. The Constitution plus national laws and treaties would constitute the "supreme law of the land; and judges in every state shall be bound thereby."[33] The key to the Constitution was the distribution of political authority, separation of powers among the executive, legislative, and judicial branches of the national government, and the division of powers between states and nation. The branches were balanced against one another, their powers deliberately entwined to prevent them from acting independently. The president was given a veto over congressional legislation, but his treaties and major appointments required approval by the Senate. Congress could impeach the president and the federal judges, but the courts had the final say on the interpretation of the Constitution. The system of checks and balances would make it difficult for the government to become tyrannical, as Madison had intended. At the same time, though, the elaborate system would sometimes prevent the government from acting quickly and decisively. Finally, the line between state and national powers was so ambiguously and vaguely drawn that the United States was to fight a civil war in the next century before the issue was resolved.[34]

On September 17, 1787, all but three of the forty-two delegates present at the final meeting of the Constitutional Convention signed the document. Virginians Edmund Randolph and George Mason declined to sign the Constitution. Their discontent became evident after the Convention agreed upon the Connecticut Compromise to settle the issue over determining how states would be represented in the national legislature. Randolph, in the Virginia Plan, proposed that congressional representation would be proportionate to the state's population. Delegates from smaller states, mainly Northerners, believed that the Virginia Plan favored the larger southern states, so they supported the New Jersey plan, which stipulated that all the states would have an equal number of representatives. The Connecticut Compromise provided for equal representation in the Senate, with representation in proportion to population in the House of Representatives. Randolph's proposal for a periodic census taken to determine state population for adjusting representation in the House led to a sectional debate over how slaves would be counted for representative purposes, which ended with the agreement that a slave would be counted as three-fifths of a free person. Believing that the Great Compromise favored the North, Mason "could neither vote for the system here, nor support it in [Virginia]" unless he could be guaranteed that the preponderance toward the North would change as population shifted.[35]

Not so much concerned about the northern attitude toward slavery, Mason's concern centered upon the familiar economic differences between the planting and commercial states, with the position of Virginia, and with the specter of minority control. In the Connecticut Compromise, he saw the weaknesses of Madison's systems of checks and balances. With the passage of the compromise between the densely and sparsely populated states, the South would be outnumbered slightly in the lower house and even more unfairly in the

Senate. Yet to preserve the Union, Mason accepted a temporary disadvantage in the lower house, knowing that the equality of voting in the Senate would prolong the northern domination of that branch. A periodic census, as Randolph proposed, the liberal admission of new states, and an exclusion of the Senate from the power of the purse comforted him as the minimal checks required in order to protect Virginia and the other planting states from the resulting risks to the essential interests, as well as to assure majority control.[36]

For Randolph, however, the minimal checks that comforted Mason were not enough to protect the economic interests of the South. Randolph's concern reflected the general fear of the southern delegates. Southerners wanted the Constitution to contain language requiring a two-thirds vote in Congress for the passage of commercial regulations; prohibition of a tax on exports; and a ban on any federal interference with the slave trade. Southern demands outraged Northerners, who believed that they had conceded too much already to the South. The sectional debate over commerce and trade, which persisted throughout, finally was resolved by the second famous compromise of the Convention. In exchange for New England's confirmation of the ban on export taxes and a temporary prohibition of restrictions on the slave trade, South Carolina voted to forgo the two-thirds on commerce. This agreement, combined with the Convention's alteration of the clauses concerning money bills, prompted Mason and Randolph not to sign the Constitution.[37]

For Mason, the compromise meant prolonging the slave trade, which he believed threatened the common interests and security of all states. The compromise furthermore diminished efforts of the Upper South to halt the slave trade as the Lower South was to continue to import new slaves and supply the West. Supporting the prohibition of a tax on exports, which seemed certain to be levied mainly on southern states, Mason bitterly condemned the other half of the convention's second compromise, protesting that the majority control of commerce would hold Southerners to the vagary of the eastern states. Randolph agreed, remarking that "There were features so odious in the Constitution as it now stands that he doubted whether he should be able to agree." Rejection of the two-thirds rule, he warned, "would complete the deformity of the system." Mason seconded this warning two days later, "declaring that he would sooner chop off his right hand than put it to the Constitution as it now stands."[38]

The conjunction of Mason and Randolph's sectional concern and their republican convictions added to their decisions not to sign the Constitution. Fearing the power of the executive branch, Mason urged the revival of a Privy Council as an additional check against the executive. He opposed extending extensive appointment powers to the president alone, as well as other links between the chief executive and the Senate. Mason especially disapproved of the Senate, feeling that the lengthy terms would make senators relatively independent of the people. Randolph also objected to the powerful executive, a misapportioned Senate, and granting powers to a congressional majority that could be manipulated to the disadvantage of the planting states.[39]

In the end, the Convention tried to reconcile the objections of the dissenting Virginians. It decided that all money bills must originate in the House of Representatives. The Convention ruled that two-thirds of the Congress, rather than three-fourths, would be enough to override a presidential veto. It transferred from the Senate to the House the power to select the president whenever an electoral majority should fail to appear. Still, the delegates would not reinstitute the two-thirds rule on navigation laws or listen seriously to Mason's arguments that two-thirds should be necessary to adopt commercial regulations until 1808. The Constitution delegations also rebuffed and unanimously declined to add a bill of rights.[40]

RATIFICATION OF THE CONSTITUTION

As a prologue to the ratification contest in Virginia, the actions of the state's delegates at the Constitutional Convention suggested that the process in Virginia would be close and hard fought. Powerful men, many who had stood solidly together through the Revolution, now stood opposed on the issue of nationhood. George Washington, commander of the Continental Army and president of the Constitutional Convention, favored the Constitution for its mechanisms to unify the states. James Madison, the principle author of the Constitution, supported its ratification for its nationalist and conservative bent. Edmund Randolph, who did not sign the Constitution in Philadelphia, agreed with its thrust toward national unity, but agonized over its conservative structure. Richard Henry Lee, who held to radical political philosophy, opposed the Constitution's federalism in favor of local government, in which for him sat individual freedom and liberty. Similarly, George Mason, who refused to sign the Constitution as well, distrusted the conservatism of the document in favor of the radical concept of good government. Patrick Henry opposed the Constitution simply because his loyalty was first and foremost to Virginia.[41]

Political parties, as we know them today, did not exist in late eighteenth-century America. Politicians adhered to various political philosophies, the most common being the radical or the conservative philosophies, which, respectively, favored local or national political structures. Political parties, however, emerged from these philosophical positions, coalescing around those supporting ratification of the Constitution and those opposing it. Those favoring ratification took the name Federalists, while those opposing it became known as Anti-Federalists. The Federalists were divided into two factions. Washington and Madison led a faction that favored both the Constitution's nationalism and conservatism. A second group, led by Edmund Pendleton, disapproved of the Constitution's conservative structure, but supported its goal of unifying the states. Between the Federalists and the Anti-Federalists stood Edmund Randolph, governor of

Virginia, who privately confided to Madison after the Convention that he had doubts about his refusal to sign the Constitution. He was convinced, however, that the way to prevent the document's outright rejection was to advocate the cause of prior amendments, particularly a bill of rights.[42]

As Virginia's leading Federalists, Washington and Madison recognized the need to develop and implement a strategy to unify Virginians sympathetic to the Constitution. They knew that successful ratification of the Constitution depended upon votes of men such as Pendleton and Randolph, who, despite having reservations over the document's conservatism, supported it in spirit. This strategy aimed to shift the debate from the merits of the Constitution to the issue of union or disunion. Washington believed that the only real choice in the debate was "the Constitution or disunion." "There is no alternative," he maintained, "between the adoption of the Constitution and anarchy." If those sympathetic to the Constitution could be made to understand that choice, then ratification could be successful. Washington urged the prior amendment faction, led by Randolph, to clear the way for "amendments in a peaceable manner, without tumult or disorder."[43] Sharing Washington's views, Madison summed the ratification contest up in these words: "I have for some time been persuaded that the question on which the proposed Constitution must turn, is the simple one whether the Union shall or shall not be continued. There is in my opinion no middle ground to be taken."[44]

Anti-Federalist motives to defeat the Constitution were as complex as those of the Federalists to confirm it. Just as varying adherence to conservatism and nationalism cleaved Federalists into factions, diverging loyalties to radicalism and fear of federalism subdivided the Anti-Federalists. Patrick Henry, author of the Virginia Stamp Act Resolves, led the largest group of Virginia Anti-Federalists, the Virginia First faction, who would not consent to the subordination of Virginia's interests to national interests. They feared that the Constitution would remove significant decision-making power from the hands of Virginians and force them to contend as a minority in a larger national arena. Henry's followers, observed one Federalist, were "opposed to any system, was it even sent from heaven, which tends to confirm the union of the states."[45] Fearing something more sinister, Madison wrote of Henry, "I have for some time considered him as driving at a Southern Confederacy."[46]

George Mason was the best known of the extremely radical faction of the Anti-Federalists. Whereas Henry's loyalty was to Virginia, Mason's was to the philosophical principles of revolutionary egalitarian radicalism, the same principles he extolled in the Virginia Declaration of Rights and state constitution. Although Mason considered the Constitution a threat to southern sectional and economic interests, he did not consider it a threat to Virginia sovereignty. His main concern, however, was the document's lack of a bill of rights to protect individual liberty. Before the close of the Constitutional Convention, Mason drafted and circulated his *Objections*, which opened with the statement: "There is no declaration of rights."[47] For the author of the

Virginia Declaration of Rights, to propose a Constitution without a bill of rights was an open invitation for a tyrant. Richard Henry Lee, with whom Mason corresponded throughout the Convention, operated from premises similar to Mason's. Lee predicted that the adoption of the Constitution, "in its present state, unamended, will put civil liberty and the happiness of the people at the mercy of rulers who may possess the great unguarded powers given."[48]

Whereas the Federalists pursued a strategy of union versus disunion, the Anti-Federalists emphasized the lack of a bill of rights and the need for such amendments prior to ratification. Oddly enough, the chief instigator of this tactic was Patrick Henry, who understood that if the ratification issue remained a simple choice between approval or rejection of the Constitution, a majority of Virginians might be swayed to approve from fear of disunion. He believed that if the issue could be shifted to a choice between approving with all its defects, or amending the defects to make a better contract, the same majority would support the idea of amendments. On that ground, the Anti-Federalists would hold the upper hand, having persuaded the populace that amendments would not only protect individual rights, but also return all sovereignty to the state governments, the ultimate goal of Henry's Virginia First faction. Henry spoke with the same conviction for amending the Constitution that he did for independence and liberty decades earlier, persuading each listener to conceive of the Constitution as being personally amended for him. Vague on the issues, however, one Federalist observer noted that Henry had not "specified the amendments he would have in the project."[49] George Nicholas of Albemarle County, a long time student of Virginia politics, noted that "Mr. Henry is now almost avowed an enemy to the union, and therefore will oppose every plan that would cement it."[50]

In March 1788, Virginia held elections for delegates to the ratification convention scheduled to be held in Richmond in June. A total of 170 delegates would be elected from across the state, two delegates representing each of Virginia's eighty-four counties. One delegate would represent the boroughs of Norfolk and Williamsburg each. Despite the distances required by some citizens to travel to the single polling location in each county, voter turnout was exceptional, upon which James Monroe, the successful candidate from Spotsylvania County, noted to Thomas Jefferson that "the people seem much agitated with this subject in every part of the state."[51] In fact, Virginians seemed to be evenly divided over the issue of ratification, although both sides seemed to exude much confidence and energy during the elections. "Virginia," noted a French observer, "is the only state in which the parties pro & con seem to run very high."[52] Federalist and Anti-Federalist sentiments so divided the state that Spotsylvanian John Dawson observed that the final "outcome would hinge on a factor beyond the control of Virginians." If nine states had ratified the Constitution before Virginia made its decision in June, then the Old Dominion would acquiesce, join the Union, or renounce the document, becoming an independent political entity.[53]

Patrick Henry, George Mason, James Madison, and Edmund Randolph won election as delegates to the ratification convention. Henry easily won the contest to represent Prince Edward County. The citizens of Stafford County invited Mason to represent them because Fairfax, his home county, was decidedly a Federalist stronghold. Madison initially announced that he did not intend to stand for election, but several friends from Orange County informed him that the election of a Federalist to represent the county hinged entirely on his candidacy and his presence on election day. "Only you, they cautioned him, will be able to silence the disaffected" and sway those "who are wavering on the Constitution."[54] Madison reached Orange "to find the County filled with the most absurd and groundless prejudices against the federal Constitution."[55] He felt compelled for the first time in his political career to mount the rostrum and harangue the election crowd. The election then produced a majority of nearly 4 to 1 in the Federalist's favor. The turnabout, he admitted, hinged on his presence.[56]

By mid-April, 1788, Virginians cast their final votes for delegates to the ratification convention. Voting patterns revealed that Federalists won the Tidewater, Northern Neck, Great Valley, and Allegheny regions overwhelmingly. Anti-Federalists captured the region on the south side of the James River, the Southwest, and Kentucky. The Piedmont north of the James resembled a checkerboard of Federalist and Anti-Federalist delegates. Although the division of the state appeared to be north against south, a number of counties in the northern Piedmont had elected Anti-Federalists and some of the Tidewater counties in Southside had chosen Federalists. A closer look at this region revealed a pattern resembling two interlocked crescents. One, beginning at Norfolk arching up to the headwaters of the Potomac, was Federalist. The other, beginning along the middle of the James River, sweeping south and west until it reached the lower Ohio and Mississippi, was Anti-Federalist. Edward Carrington described the delegation as containing "many obscure characters," predicting that a few men of "popular talents" would dominate the Convention and the rest would "act from the influence of a few."[57]

On the eve of the convention, the Anti-Federalist tactic of demanding amendments seemed to be successful as the talk around the state echoed that issue. As a burgeoning political party, however, its internal views of amendments left members deeply divided. The deepest division lay between the Henry Virginia First faction, which planned to use prior amendments as a way to gut the Constitution, and the Mason-Lee faction, which sought to protect individual rights. The Federalists, led by Madison and Washington, opposed prior amendments as unnecessary for the protection of individual rights and because they would lead to disunion not union. In the middle stood Randolph, who, despite not signing the Constitution originally in Philadelphia, proposed prior amendments as a vehicle toward preserving the union of states. In fact, in the time since the Constitutional Convention, he had persuaded Mason and Lee to at least consider the case for union more than their fear of national government. Henry, on the other hand, would consider no such compromise. It was Virginia first or nothing at all![58]

Agricultural interests, more than any other factor, bound most of the 170 delegates together in Richmond on June 2, 1788, for the constitutional convention. A closer examination of their agrarian means, however, reveals how their interests varied regionally through the Tidewater, Southside, Northern Neck, Piedmont, and Trans-Mountain regions. Following the analytical model set pioneered by economic historian Charles Beard in 1913, Forrest McDonald and Jackson T. Main have evaluated the property assets of Federalists and Anti-Federalists and concluded that despite regional differences, they were virtually alike. Although the delegates' wealth was concentrated in land, homes, farm buildings, and slaves, not all delegates were equally wealthy. McDonald identified 67 delegates owning over 1,000 acres of land, of which 36 were Federalist and 31 were Anti-Federalist. Of slaveholding delegates, 41 owned more than 50, of whom 26 were Federalists. Ownership of slaves, however, was not a significant variable in determining support for the Constitution, as most of the small farmers who owned none or very few slaves voted for ratification.[59]

The delegates in Richmond represented a broad cast of occupations and military experience. Although the majority of the delegates were lawyers, farmers, or planters, nine worked as merchants, eleven as physicians, and three as clergymen. Merchants, physicians, and clergymen were evenly divided over ratification. While the lawyers claimed affiliation with Federalism more than Anti-Federalism, farmers and the planters, who composed two-thirds of the delegates, evenly split between the parties, as 64 favored and 60 opposed the Constitution. Of the 170 delegates, 128 had held an officer's commission at some time during the Revolutionary War; 81 had served in the Continental forces and 47 in the state militia. Delegates with military experience split evenly on the merits of the Constitution. Property, slaves, occupation, and military experience were not going to determine the outcome in Virginia.[60]

What would determine the decision in Virginia would be the persuasive oratorical skills of Patrick Henry and James Madison, the chief spokesmen, respectively, for the Anti-Federalist and Federalist causes. As a study in contrasts, Henry was emotive, flamboyant, yet captivating, as he possessed the ability to bring about "a perfect stillness throughout the House and in the galleries." On the other hand, Madison's presentation manner was quiet, sometimes barely audible, relying on the coldly logical. Henry would speak long and often during the convention; his speeches alone constituted a fourth of all deliberations. At one point, Randolph admonished the convention for tolerating Henry's prolonged, rambling orations, saying "it will take us six months to decide this question." Rebuttal then became Madison's responsibility as the chief spokesman for the Federalists. His style contrasted markedly to Henry's dramatic orations. Madison would rise and quietly expose the flaws in Henry's reasoning, the inappropriate use of historical examples, and the distortions inherent in his interpretation of the language of the Constitution.[61]

An example of the exchange between Henry and Madison was one on the powers of the president and the executive branch. The Anti-Federalists maintained it was despotism in disguise:

> There is to be a great and mighty President, with very extensive powers—the powers of a King. He is to be supported in extravagant magnificence; so that the whole of our property may be taken by this American government, by laying what taxes they please, and suspending our laws at their pleasure.[62]

Henry attacked the "American chief" as a man of "ambition and ability," who would be easily directed toward absolutism. Placing the nation's military under the command of the president would permit the executive branch "to execute the execrable commands of tyranny."[63] As these statements illustrate, Henry's purpose was to insight and instill fear of Federalism in the minds of the delegates.

In response to Henry's unsupported fears, Madison pointed to historical examples to assure the convention that tyranny was a gradual and incipient process rather than one immediately imposed by individual ambition:

> Since the general civilization of mankind, I believe there are more instances of the abridgement of the freedom of the people by gradual and silent encroachments of those in power, than by violent and sudden usurpations; but, on a candid examination of history, we shall find that turbulence, violence, and abuse of power, by the majority trampling on the rights of the minority, have produced factions and commotions, which, in republics, have, more frequently than any other cause, produced despotism.[64]

Before the vote to ratify the Constitution on June 25, 1788, the convention voted on Henry's resolution that a bill of rights and amendments "ought to be referred by this Convention to the other states in this American confederacy for their consideration."[65] Although the Anti-Federalists took an impressive 25 to 12 lead early, the Federalists closed the gap, and tied the votes at 60. At that point, the Federalists pulled away, defeating Henry's motion by a margin of 88 to 80. As a prelude to the ratification, the outcome of this poll revealed the effectiveness of Henry's arguments on the swing votes of the Upper Ohio River Valley. The first clue to the region came when Greenbrier voted Federalist. Harrison County then voted Federalist as well. Montgomery, which stretched to the North Carolina border, voted with the Anti-Federalists. Jefferson, a Kentucky county on the Ohio River, also voted no. By claiming six of the eight coveted Ohio River delegates, Federalists had extinguished the fire of Henry's oratory.[66]

After the vote on Henry's motion for a bill of rights and amendments, Edmund Pendelton, president of the convention, called the roll on the motion to approve ratification. All of those who, with Madison and Randolph, had voted no on Henry's resolution now voted yes for ratification. David Patteson of Chesterfield County, who voted against Henry, however, voted no against ratifying the Constitution, the only delegate to reverse his vote in that direction. Otherwise the pro-ratification side picked up two additional "aye" ballots from the pro-Henry bill of rights and amendments faction. Virginia, thereby, ratified the Constitution by the final vote 89 to 79. The vote was a triumph for Madison, the Father of the Constitution, who had been present at its conception and birth in Philadelphia, and now at its adoption in Richmond.[67]

Virginia's decision to ratify the Constitution cemented the nation. While the new government could function without a full complement of thirteen states, as it would operate for over a year without North Carolina and Rhode Island, the United States could have hardly survived without Virginia or New York.[68] Without these states, the nation would have been subdivided into three regions, each smaller than its foreign neighbors, at home and abroad. New England would have been isolated from New Jersey, and Delaware and Pennsylvania left alone by New York. Those states would have been isolated from South Carolina and Georgia by Virginia and North Carolina. A United States divided and weakened in such a manner could have not dealt successfully with the troublesome decade ahead. The first nine states to ratify were the weakest. They could not have managed as a nation alone. While they needed either New York or Virginia, they needed Virginia more, especially to get George Washington, the only man all agreed could be safely entrusted with the powers of the executive branch, to serve as the nation's first president.[69]

After holding elections in late 1788 and early 1789, the new nation formally began operation in March 1789. The nation elected Washington as its first chief executive. Virginia elected Madison to the House of Representatives. Disgruntled Anti-Federalists Lee, Mason, and Henry promoted the need for a second Constitutional Convention to inspire a radical alteration in the Constitution. But Madison successfully undermined the second convention movement by guiding a set of Constitutional amendments through Congress, which left the powers and functions of the new government alone, but satisfied the incessant demands for a federal bill of rights. Ten amendments, the Bill of Rights, as they are known, were approved on December 15, 1791. The first eight amendments contain the fundamental rights and freedoms of every citizen. The ninth amendment forbids the government to limit freedoms and rights that are not listed in the Constitution. The tenth amendment limits the powers of the federal government to those that are granted to it in the Constitution. With the passage of the Bill of Rights, the second convention movement died.[70]

CONCLUSION

During the state ratification convention, Patrick Henry remarked of the government proposed in the Constitution that it "is not a Virginian, but an American government."[71] While this statement is not surprising coming from the leader of the Virginia First faction of the Anti-Federalists, it is rather ironic in that the "American government" Henry so despised had its origins in the colonial and political development of Virginia more than in any of the other former British colonies. While his radical discourse on individual rights, liberty, and local autonomy was as important in the post-Revolutionary era as it was when he presented his Stamp Act Resolves, it did not meet the needs of a young nation requiring the tempered discipline to grow and mature. Madison, no less a proponent of the liberties embraced by Henry, realized through his study of past republics that liberties won in the Revolution could only be preserved through a strong, but balanced national government.

NOTES

1. See Michael Allen Gillespie and Michael Lienesch, eds., *Ratifying the Constitution* (Lawrence: University of Kansas Press, 1989), pp. 13–14; and Alan V. Briceland, *1788: The Year of Decision: Virginia's Ratification of the United States Constitution* (Richmond, VA: Virginia Department of Education, 1989).

2. See Briceland, *Year of Decision*; and Jackson Turner Main, *The Antifederalists: Critics of the Constitution, 1781–1788* (Chapel Hill: University of North Carolina Press, 1961).

3. See Briceland, *Year of Decision*.

4. Edmund S. Morgan, *American Slavery–American Freedom: The Ordeal of Colonial Virginia* (New York and London: W.W. Norton and Company, 1975), pp. 25–43.

5. See Alden T. Vaughan, *American Genesis: Captain John Smith and the Founding of Virginia*, ed. Oscar Handlin (Boston: Little, Brown, 1975).

6. Morgan, *American Slavery–American Freedom*, pp. 97–100.

7. Ibid., pp. 90–109.

8. Ibid., pp. 96–103.

9. Ibid.

10. Ibid., pp. 153–157.

11. Ibid., pp. 250–258.

12. Ibid., pp. 254–270; see Wilcomb E. Washburn, *The Governor and the Rebel: A History of Bacon's Rebellion in Virginia* (Chapel Hill: Published for the Institute of Early American History and Culture at Williamsburg by the University of North Carolina Press, 1957).

13. See James Titus, *The Old Dominion at War: Society, Politics, and Warfare in Late Colonial Virginia* (Columbia, SC: University of South Carolina Press, 1991).

14. Morgan, *The Birth of the Republic: 1763–1789*, 3rd ed. (Chicago: University of Chicago Press, 1992), pp. 15–28.

15. Norine Dickson Campbell, *Patrick Henry: Patriot and Statesman* (New York: Devon-Adair, 1969).

16. Patrick Henry, "*Virginia Resolves on the Stamp Act*," 30 May 1765, http://www.constitution.org/.

17. Ibid.

18. Ibid.

19. Ibid.

20. "The Stamp Act Resolves," October 19, 1765, *U.S. Historical Documents Archive: A Reference For the People*, http://www.ushda.org/stamp.shtml.

21. Morgan, *The Birth of the Republic*, p. 28.

22. Ibid., pp. 34–41, 45, 49–50.

23. Ibid.

24. See Dumas Malone, *Jefferson and the Rights of Man* (Boston: Little, Brown, 1951).

25. "Virginia Declaration of Rights," June 12, 1776, *The Founders Constitution: Fundamental Documents*, http://press-pubs.uchicago.edu/founders/documents//v1ch1s3.html.

26. "Virginia Constitution," June 29, 1776, *The Founders Constitution: Fundamental Documents*, http://press-pubs.uchicgao.edu/founders/documents/v1ch1s4.html.

27. Ibid.

28. "Declaration of Independence," July 4, 1776, *The Founders Constitution: Fundamental Documents*, http://press-pubs.uchicago.edu/founders/documents/v1ch1s5.html.

29. Morgan, *Birth of the Republic*, pp. 113–128.

30. "Declaration of Independence," July 4, 1776, *The Founders Constitution: Fundamental Documents*.

31. Briceland, *Year of Decision*, pp. 8–9.

32. Quoted in Mary Beth Norton et al., *A People and A Nation: A History of the United States* (Boston, MA: Houghton Mifflin Company, 1982), 1:158.

33. "Constitution," September 17, 1787, *The Founders Constitution: Fundamental Documents*, http://press-pubs.uchicago.edu/founders/documents/v1ch2s5.html.

34. Norton et al., *A People and A Nation*, p. 160.

35. Max Farrand, ed., *The Records of the Federal Convention of 1787*, 4 vols. (New Haven: Yale University Press, 1966), 1:578–579.

36. Lance Banning, "Virginia: Sectionalism and the General Good," in Gillespie and Lienesch, *Ratifying the Constitution*, pp. 268–269.

37. Ibid., p. 270.

38. Farrand, *Records of the Federal Convention*, 4:56–57.

39. Banning, "Virginia," p. 271.

40. Ibid., pp. 271–272.

41. Briceland, *Year of Decision*, pp. 8–9.

42. Ibid., p. 10.

43. George Washington to Charles Carter, December 14, 1787, in Campbell, *Patrick Henry: Patriot and Statesman*, p. 328.

44. James Madison to Edmund Pendleton, February 21, 1788, in Robert A. Rutland, ed., *The Papers of James Madison*, 15 vols. (Charlottesville: University of Virginia Press, 1962–1985), 10:532.

45. Henry Lee to James Madison, December 20, 1788, Ibid., 10:339.

46. James Madison to Edmund Randolph, January 10, 1788, Ibid., 10:355.

47. George Mason, "Objections," in *Pamphlets on the Constitution of the United States*, ed. Paul L. Ford (1888; reprint, New York, 1968), p. 329.

48. Richard Henry Lee to George Mason, October 1, 1787, in Rutland, ed., *The Papers of George Mason, 1725–1792*, 3 vols. (Chapel Hill: University of North Carolina Press, 1970), 3:441.

49. Edward Carrington to James Madison, February 10, 1788, in Rutland, *Madison Papers*, 10:383.

50. George Nicholas to James Madison, April 5, 1788, Ibid., 11:9.

51. James Monroe to Thomas Jefferson, April 16, 1788, in Julian P. Boyd, ed., *The Papers of Thomas Jefferson*, 18 vols. (Princeton: Princeton University Press, 1950–1974), 12:49.

52. St. John Crevecour to William Short, February 20, 1788, quoted in Rutland, *The Ordeal of the Constitution: The Anti-Federalists and the Ratification Struggle of 1787–1788* (Chicago: University of Chicago Press, 1968), p. 190.

53. Briceland, *Year of Decision*, p. 18.

54. William Moore to James Madison, February 1, 1788, in Rutland, ed., *Madison Papers*, 10:454.

55. James Madison to Eliza House Trist, March 25, 1788, Ibid., 11:5.

56. Briceland, *Year of Decision*, pp. 18–19.

57. Edward Carrington to Thomas Jefferson, April 24, 1788, in Boyd, ed., *Jefferson Papers*, 13:16–17.

58. Briceland, *Year of Decision*, p. 23.

59. See Charles Beard, *An Economic Interpretation of the Constitution of the United States* (New York: Macmillan, 1913); Forrest McDonald, *We The People: Economic Origins of the Constitution* (Chicago: University of Chicago Press, 1958); Jackson T. Main, *The Anti-Federalists: Critics of the Constitution, 1781–1788* (Chapel Hill: University of North Carolina Press, 1961).

60. See McDonald, *We The People*; and Main, *The Anti-Federalists*.

61. Briceland, *Year of Decision*, p. 26.

62. Jonathan Elliot, ed., *The Debates of Several State Conventions on the Adoption of the Federal Constitution*, 5 vols. (Washington, DC, 1936), 5:56.

63. Ibid., 5:51.

64. Ibid., 5:87.

65. Ibid., 5:70.

66. Briceland, *Year of Decision*, pp. 38–39.

67. Ibid., p. 39.

68. New York ratified the Constitution on June 26, 1788.

69. Briceland, *Year of Decision*, p. 40.

70. Ibid., p. 41.

71. Elliot, *Debates*, 5:55.

BIBLIOGRAPHY

Banning, Lance. "Virginia: Sectionalism and the General Good." In *Ratifying the Constitution*. Edited by Michael Allen Gillespie and Michael Lienesch, 261–299. Lawrence: University of Kansas Press, 1989.

Beeman, Richard R. *The Old Dominion and the New Nation, 1780–1783*. Lexington: University of Kentucky Press, 1972.

Boyd, Steven R. *The Politics of Opposition: Antifederalists and the Acceptance of the Constitution*. Millwood, NY: KTO Press, 1979.

Briceland, Alan V. *1788: The Year of Decision: Virginia's Ratification of the United States Constitution*. Richmond: Virginia Department of Education, 1989.

Campbell, Norine Dickson. *Patrick Henry: Patriot and Statesman*. New York: Devon-Adair, 1969.

Main, Jackson Turner. *The Antifederalists: Critics of the Constitution, 1781–1788.* Chapel Hill: University of North Carolina Press, 1961.

Miller, Helen Hill. *George Mason: Gentleman Revolutionary.* Chapel Hill: University of North Carolina Press, 1975.

Morgan, Edmund S. *American Slavery–American Freedom: The Ordeal of Colonial Virginia.* New York and London: W. W. Norton and Company, 1975.

———. *The Birth of the Republic, 1763–89.* 3rd ed. Chicago and London: University of Chicago Press, 1992.

———. "The Virginia Federalists." *Journal of Southern History* 34 (November 1967): 486–517.

———, and Gordon DenBoer. "The Evolution of Political Parties in Virginia, 1782–1800." *Journal of American History* 60 (1974): 961–984.

Risjord, Norman K. *Chesapeake Politics, 1781–1800.* New York: Columbia University Press, 1978.

Rutland, Robert A. *George Mason, Reluctant Statesman.* Williamsburg, VA: Colonial Williamsburg; distributed by Holt, Rinehart & Winston, New York, 1961.

Titus, James. *The Old Dominion at War: Society, Politics, and Warfare in Late Colonial Virginia.* Columbia: University of South Carolina Press, 1991.

Vaughan, Alden T. *American Genesis: Captain John Smith and the Founding of Virginia.* Edited by Oscar Handlin. Boston: Little, Brown, 1975.

Washburn, Wilcomb E. *The Governor and the Rebel: A History of Bacon's Rebellion in Virginia.* Chapel Hill: Published for the Institute of Early American History and Culture at Williamsburg by the University of North Carolina Press, 1957.

THE STATE OF WASHINGTON

Admitted to the Union as a State:
November 11, 1889

Robert E. Ficken

INTRODUCTION

Washington Territory was created out of Oregon Territory in March 1853 and officially expired after a political life of thirty-six years. The state of Washington was admitted to the Union as the forty-second state in November 1889. During those thirty-six years, Washington Territory was transformed in nearly every respect. When the first territorial governor, Isaac Stevens, came into office, territorial land was claimed by the Indians living there, and their claims were acknowledged by the federal government. Stevens made treaties with the tribes that removed them to reservations in return for their land claims. Settlers who then poured into the territory served to accelerate the sectional differences between western timber and eastern agricultural interests. The Cascade Mountains naturally divided the territory into differing geographical areas and hampered communication, transportation, and political administration. Neither easterners nor westerners benefited from their mutual labors and production. The creation of Idaho Territory in 1863, which took all of Idaho and western portions of Montana and Wyoming away, did not solve any of these problems. The failed attempt at statehood in 1878 reflected the hardiness of sectional politics. As the redefined territory boomed, an economic downturn in the mid-1880s gave birth to anti-Chinese nativism in spite of the long presence of Chinese in the territory. With improved economic conditions and the uniting of east and west by the Northern Pacific Railroad in 1887, however, a sense of unity was created in anticipation of statehood for Washington.

In spite of the transformations that eventually united the citizens of Washington Territory into a workable political entity, thirty-six years was a

Washington

Territorial Development:

- The United States and Great Britain sign a temporary treaty for joint tenancy of the Oregon Country, October 20, 1818
- The United States obtains formal title to all land in the Oregon Territory south of the 49th parallel from Great Britain through the Oregon Treaty, June 15, 1846
- Washington organized as a U.S. territory, March 2, 1853
- Washington admitted into the Union as the forty-second state, November 11, 1889

Territorial Capitals:

- Olympia, 1853–1889

State Capitals:

- Olympia, 1889–present

Origin of State Name: Washington was named in honor of George Washington.

First Governor: Elisha P. Ferry
Governmental Organization: Bicameral
Population at Statehood: 349,390
Geographical Size: 66,544 square miles

long time to live under a territorial government that was largely powerless and often corrupt. Early on, politically aware Washington inhabitants complained of living under the oldest territorial government in the country. The complaints endured, expressed on a regular basis by offended and apparently second-class citizens. "We have already passed nearly 23 years in a state of…vassalage," the Seattle *Weekly Intelligencer* pointed out in 1875, "and to continue so much longer would naturally suggest a suspicion in the minds of people that we were destined always to continue so." Writing in 1878 from east of the Cascade Range, a journalist archly observed that the residents of Washington "ought to have realized all the advantages under a Territorial form of government by this time if any exists."[1]

TERRITORIAL DEVELOPMENT

Readily accessible timber resources that could be shipped from natural harbors spurred the growth of North Oregon Territory. With economic development, however, came political frustration and the demand for a government attuned to local issues. Splitting Columbia Territory from the immense Oregon Territory, many settlers believed, was the obvious solution.

Accounts of "splendid prairies, surrounded with the finest of fir, pine and cedar" and of "water power well calculated to propel any kind of machinery" attracted the first American immigrants to Puget Sound in late 1845. The early settlers who founded New Market, renamed Tumwater, and then Olympia at Tidewater were dependent, much to their chagrin, upon assistance from the Hudson's Bay Company at nearby Fort Nisqually. Americans were not enthusiastic about dealing with the British Hudson's Bay Company, whose representatives had administered the territory since the late eighteenth century, protecting its fur trading enterprise through a system of forts at Nisqually, Walla Walla, Boise, Vancouver, and other locations. Two factors eventually produced a boom in North Oregon, the common contemporary name for the region beyond the Columbia River. Gold was discovered in the Sierra Nevada of California, sparking a frenzied demand for lumber in San Francisco and its tributary mining country. And Puget Sound, as local boosters never tired of asserting, was both "unrivaled by any other sheet of water of equal size" and "skirted on either side, throughout its length and breadth, with…valuable timbered land, all…of easy access to the shore."[2]

Bolstered by the California lumber trade and by secondary markets in Hawaii and around the Pacific Rim, Puget Sound was a prospering offshoot of Oregon Territory by 1853. By one conservative accounting, fifty vessels visited that year, loading timber for sale in San Francisco.[3] Olympia, recently made the port-of-entry for North Oregon, was far and away the leading settlement, casting more votes in territorial elections that the rest of the sound combined.[4] Close to Fort Nisqually, Steilacoom mounted a feeble challenge to Olympia.

To the north, Seattle, focused economically upon Henry Yesler's new steam-powered sawmill, was better equipped for the task of long-term commercial growth. Along the western shore of Puget Sound, the first of the great Yankee lumbering ports—Ludlow, Gamble, and Madison—commenced business in 1853.

Economic growth produced, in addition to profit, wholesale dissatisfaction regarding the isolated and powerless position of Puget Sound. "Neither time nor room," claimed the Olympia *Columbian*, the region's first newspaper, "would answer our purpose, in one article, to set forth all the grievances which northern Oregon has been compelled quietly to submit to." Aside from organizing counties north of the Columbia, territorial legislators appeared intent upon thwarting the ambitions of persons residing in the new settlements. Roads were nonexistent, protection against the Indians denied, and federal money expended only in the Willamette Valley. Such, in any event, were the charges levied by unhappy settlers. The likelihood of any change for the better, moreover, was virtually nil. "So long," the *Columbian* asserted in November 1852, "as we are content to be dependent upon the legislative assembly of Oregon for the passage of wholesome laws...or provision for improvements within or limits, so long will we be obliged to content ourselves without either."[5]

Concerted action had already taken place to appeal to Congress for a division of the territory that would end North Oregon's isolation. Meeting in August 1851 at Warbassport on the Cowlitz River, the traditional route of travel between southern and northern Oregon, twenty-four delegates called for the creation of Columbia Territory. Possibly misunderstanding the poorly drafted petition, much of which dealt with complaints against the Hudson's Bay Company, Congress ignored the Warbassport memorial.

A new territorial convention, carefully planned in advance to produce a definitive result, met at Monticello, near the mouth of the Cowlitz, on November 25, 1852. The forty-four delegates in attendance agreed with keynote speaker Quincy Brooks that the only relevant questions were "when shall the division be made, and...how shall the dividing line run?" Both queries, Brooks responded on behalf of his listeners, had obvious answers: "our wants demand the immediate organization of the 'Territory of Columbia,' and...the Columbia River should be the southern and eastern boundary line." Although ignorant of conditions beyond the Cascades, the delegates insisted that their proposed commonwealth contained sufficient natural resources to support a population "at least so large as any State in the Union possessing an equal extent of territory."[6] Deliberately optimistic in their public pronouncements, Columbia Territory's friends privately cautioned one another to be patient, as no response to the Monticello memorial, positive or negative, could be expected from Congress until at least 1854. The one-day meeting adjourned with plans to reconvene in May 1853.

THE DIVISION OF OREGON TERRITORY AND
THE CREATION OF WASHINGTON TERRITORY

To widespread astonishment, Congress acted on dividing the enormous Oregon Territory, but it named the new territory Washington rather than Columbia. The mass of this territory did nothing to settle sectional conflict, make Washington more easily governed, or liberate it from the influence of Oregon. Sentiment south, rather than north, of the Columbia River proved decisive in the outcome. Contemporary observers considered Oregon Territory, embracing the later states of Oregon, Washington, and Idaho, as well as western Montana, as simply too enormous an entity for admission to the Union. Congressional delegate Joseph Lane, hero of the Mexican War and ambitious leader of Oregon's Democratic Party, agreed with this assessment. Intent upon becoming a U.S. senator at the earliest possible date, Lane sacrificed North Oregon and considerable acreage east of the Cascades on behalf of a politically necessary reduction.

Legislation creating Columbia Territory, introduced by Lane in December 1852, was already under consideration by the time the Monticello petition arrived in the nation's capital. "Oregon is too large for one...State," Lane noted in explaining his action to supporters in the Willamette Valley. Although the north-of-the-Columbia document was cited in debate, the Oregon legislature's pro-division memorial, asserting that the two sections were "in a great degree distinct communities, with different interests," provided Lane with vital support.[7] Discussing the proposal, house members decided that the name should be changed to Washington, thereby avoiding confusion with the District of Columbia. The reasoning defied comprehension, Washington being obviously no improvement in this respect, but the honor extended to the first president of the United States enhanced the prospects for approval.

Shrewdly amended in the interest of maximum support, Joseph Lane's handiwork passed the House of Representatives on February 8, 1853. "The most striking feature of the Bill," the Olympia *Columbian* observed in reporting the unexpected news five weeks later, "is the name which is given to our Territory." Patriotic considerations aside, Washington "met with some distaste among many of our citizens" and became, in fact, a long-term source of settler irritation over outsider interference in local affairs.[8] A separate territory north of the river, however, was far better than no division at all, regardless of the nomenclature. Puget Sound residents therefore waited anxiously for favorable senatorial action in the final days of the congressional session. The Senate approved creation of Washington Territory on March 2, a day prior to adjournment. President Millard Fillmore, at the end of his term in the executive mansion, immediately signed the act of Congress.

Washington Territory had both a different name and substantially larger limits than anticipated by the delegates to the Warbassport and Monticello conventions. Instead of following the Columbia upstream to the English possessions east of the Cascades, the original boundary left the river at the 46th parallel, running direct to the Rocky Mountains. Upon Oregon's admission to statehood in 1859, the territorial bounds were extended to embrace all of Idaho, plus Montana and Wyoming west of the Continental Divide. A vast land, from fog-enshrouded ocean beaches to the granite peaks of the Rockies, fell within the political limits. In terms of actual American occupation, though, Washington was relatively constricted. A careful federal census tallied 3,965 non-Indian inhabitants as of late 1853.[9] No bona fide settler lived beyond the mountains, an inhospitable region best left, in the opinion of most contemporary students, in the exclusive possession of the resident tribes. West of the Cascades, settlement was concentrated on major waterways, Puget Sound, and the Columbia River. On the coast, Shoalwater Bay was enlivened by the activities of oyster harvesters eager to exploit tide flat shellfish beds for the California market. From Grays Harbor around Cape Flattery to near Port Townsend, government agents failed to note the presence of a single white man, woman, or child.

The territorial borders made sense only in light of Oregon's eagerness to shed excess political acreage in the interest of becoming a state. Adding to the sense of Washington's fundamental unreality, Oregonians intended to secure and maintain effectual control of the interior Pacific Northwest. Like water flowing downhill in accordance with the physical laws of gravity, communication and trade followed the Columbia River, making eastern Washington a dependency of Portland. Merchants of the Willamette Valley metropolis introduced steamboat service on the lower and middle rivers, built a portage railroad between the Cascades and The Dalles, and campaigned for federal navigation improvements. Efforts on Puget Sound to circumvent Oregon by opening a direct route across the Cascades were frequent, fervent, and invariably unsuccessful. Completed in 1853 under the nominal supervision of Captain George McClellan, the Naches Pass wagon road connected Fort Walla Walla with Steilacoom on Tidewater. Although forty-six settlers with eleven wagons and sixty-two head of cattle crossed to the sound that year, Indian troubles thereafter closed the pass and left Portland in charge beyond the mountains.

Learning of Washington Territory's creation on April 25, the citizens of Olympia, the obvious choice for capital, fired a ragged hundred-gun salute from the locally available assortment of muskets, rifles, and pistols. The celebration was marred by confusion, economic uncertainty, and fear that the region had exchanged "our poor dependency upon the cold charities of Oregon" for direct subservience to a distant federal government. Colonial methods appropriate for impoverished or remote societies, the *Columbian* pointed out, were "wholly foreign...to the wants, the absolute necessities, of a people whose home is upon the...shores of a vast ocean, whitened with the sails of the richest... traffic known to the commercial world." Self-interest, in the *Columbian*'s view, required that "every trace of proconsularity" be quickly "eradicated" and that "the closest approximation to the sovereignty of a State" be attained at the earliest opportunity. With its readers, Olympia's newspaper awaited the arrival of Washington's first governor in the manner of "a bride who looks anxiously for the coming of the groom." Already, however, a struggle between localized and outside control—the driving force in the political life of the western territories—portended a difficult and problematic betrothal.[10]

GOVERNOR ISAAC STEVENS AND THE REMOVAL OF INDIANS TO RESERVATIONS

Isaac Ingalls Stevens, Washington Territory's first governor, was an able, energetic, and exceedingly controversial figure. In the course of one term, he resettled the native population in reservations and ended Indian hostilities in the territory. Thirty-five years of age, the Massachusetts-born Stevens graduated first in the West Point class of 1839, served with distinction in the Mexican War, and secured a coveted posting with the Coast Survey in the nation's capital. Resigning his major's commission and thereby exchanging a promising military career for the peculiar hazards of civilian partisan combat, he accepted the territorial governorship from Franklin Pierce, his fellow New England Democrat elected president in 1852. Finally reaching Olympia in late November 1853, having surveyed the proposed northern transcontinental railroad line on the way west, Stevens formally organized Washington's government and scheduled the first elections. The governor impressed local observers as a man of superior intellect and forceful personality in spite of his backwoodsman attire and apparent predilection for strong drink. Stevens in Washington and Joseph Lane in Oregon shared an interest in the rapid achievement of statehood and the personal political advancement that would come with it.

Stevens also served as superintendent of Indian affairs. In this capacity he faced an immediate and defining problem. The native tribes and bands retained legal possession of every acre of land in Washington Territory. The peculiar root of this troublesome circumstance lay in the fact that the overland trail had been opened in 1842, four years prior to the assertion of American sovereignty over the Pacific Northwest south of the 49th parallel and six years in advance of the creation of Oregon Territory. According to the experienced army officer Benjamin Alvord, "the whole early settlement of this Country...was in utter neglect of the Indian title."[11] The Oregon Donation Act of 1850 compounded the problem by affirming the existing informal claims and allowing qualified male immigrants to freely take 320 acres if single and double the acreage if married. Under these terms, settlers claimed extensive tracts that by government acknowledgment belonged to the Indians. Discovering a crisis in the making, Governor Stevens reported that "the lands of all the Indians... [are] becoming settled by the whites so fast that within another year there will not be a valley...but that will be taken by the whites, and...the Indians... driven from their homes."[12]

From personal observation and semi-informed sources, Stevens calculated "the whole number of Indians in Washington Territory" as precisely 14,059 men, women, and children, or four times the settler population.[13] Half resided west of the Cascades and were "rather disposed to be saucy" when inebriated, agent Michael Simmons advised, "twitting the whites with having *stolen* their land without any intention of ever paying for it."[14] No responsible civil or military official, however, expected real trouble on the part of villagers who were divided into numerous small tribes and bands, poorly armed and inclined, when not provoked, toward peaceful pursuits. East of the mountains, in contrast, the Indians, including the Yakama, the Cayuse, the Walla Walla, and the Nez Perce, were well mounted, outfitted with guns, and both ready and able to resist encroachment. Ignoring an army prohibition against claim taking, immigrants intended to take land up the Columbia from The Dalles. Contributing to the unrest, Governor Stevens demanded as an inducement to settlement that the General Land Office extend its surveys to the territorial interior.

Congress authorized treaties to be made with the Indians to resolve disputes over land and resources in the Washington and Oregon territories in August 1854. After an absence of nine months spent retrieving his family from the Atlantic coast, Governor Stevens determined in December upon an ambitious program designed to extinguish the native title to "every acre of land in the Territory" prior to the arrival of the seasonal wagon trains in the fall of 1855.[15] Working from copies of the so-called "Omaha treaties," the governor and his advisers drafted a standard locally applicable document providing for cessions of land, the creation of reservations, the provision of educational and other forms of assistance, and eventual allotment of land in severalty. On his own initiative, Stevens added a provision that permitted Indians and territorial citizens to fish at their usual places. Although this provision would later cause controversy, common sense seemed to demand that the Indians be able to feed themselves.

Between Christmas Day and the end of January 1855, Stevens concluded the treaties of Medicine Creek, Point Elliott, Point No Point, and Neah Bay, establishing nine tidewater reservations from Cape Flattery to Squaxin Island on southern Puget Sound. In May and June, the governor and his Oregon superintendency counterpart, Joel Palmer, conferred with five thousand Indians in the Walla Walla Valley. The proceedings were contentious and prolonged, filled with emotional oratory, and often interrupted by rainstorms. Skilled and, when necessary, cynical in the arts of manipulation, Stevens utilized confidential meetings with individual native leaders to somehow secure formal agreement to the Walla Walla treaties. The documents created the Yakama Reservation east of the Cascades, the vast Nez Perce Reservation in southeastern Washington and northeastern Oregon, and the Umatilla Reservation, entirely within Oregon Territory.[16]

Escorted by Nez Perce warriors, Stevens rode east to treat with the Flatheads and the Blackfoot, oblivious of the ill will left behind. On Puget Sound, Indians residing on the upper stretches of rivers flowing into the great waterway opposed relocation to the tide front reservations. The governor's subordinates in Olympia ignored the rumors of native disaffection received from remote settlers. In eastern Washington, meanwhile, many of the signatories to the Walla Walla treaties bitterly regretted their acceptance of the government's terms. "It is pretty evident," Joel Palmer reported of the Yakamas in particular, "that the signing of the Treaty was adverse to the will of the nation." Although the agreements took effect only upon Senate ratification, the Olympia *Pioneer and Democrat*, editorial voice of the Stevens Democratic organization, irresponsibly announced in late June that "the land ceded is now open for settlement."[17] Fifty homesteaders soon occupied claims in the Walla Walla Valley, placing, noted Palmer, "an additional argument in the mouthes of the opposees of the treaty."[18] The mid-July discovery of gold in northeast Washington sent hundreds of unwary and uncouth miners into the Indian country in a final disturbing development that provoked episodes of assault, theft, and alleged murder.

INDIAN HOSTILITIES

Soon after departing on the long journey home from the upper Missouri River, the scene of the last of his treaty councils, Governor Stevens received express messages detailing the outbreak of war on both sides of the Cascades. On September 23, 1855, angry Yakamas murdered Indian agent Andrew Bolon. A small regular army force dispatched from Fort Dalles to investigate the killing was forced to retreat after suffering five fatalities. In late October, Puget Sound Indians killed eight whites in the valley of the White River. Horrified by this "massacre," settlers from Olympia on the south to Port Townsend and Bellingham Bay on the north took shelter in hastily constructed blockhouses.

On either side of the mountains, the conflicts were sordid, albeit limited, affairs. Seven hundred regulars and Oregon volunteers marched against the Yakamas in October and November. The Indians retreated ahead of the column, however, and the expedition returned after sacking the Catholic Ahtanum mission and posting a note addressing Kamiakin, the principal native leader, as an "S.O.B."[19] Unbloodied by this exploit, the Oregonians invaded the Walla Walla Valley in December, attacking the previously neutral local Indians and murdering the well-known Walla Walla, Peopeo Moxmox. West of the Cascades, two hundred warriors confronted the army, territorial recruits, and a hundred Indian allies in the occasional rain-spattered skirmish, including the farcical daylong exchange of aimless gunfire known to popular history as the "Battle of Seattle." Relocated to temporary reservations for the duration of the hostilities, the overwhelming majority of the Puget Sound native population sat out the war.

Fighting of sorts resumed in the spring, with timely, though far from definitive, results. Flushed out by Colonel Silas Casey's carefully orchestrated approach, the hostile Puget Sound Indians attacked along the White River on the first and again on the tenth of March. Driven off on both occasions, they crossed the mountains to sanctuary with the interior tribes. In April, Colonel George Wright marched to the Yakima Valley, went into camp on one bank of the swollen Naches River and commenced talks with the Indians, ensconced on the opposite shore. Despite provocative interference on the part of Governor Stevens, who insisted that the tribes must be defeated on the battlefield, Wright managed by late September 1856 to pacify both the Yakamas and the Walla Wallas in close to bloodless fashion.

Washington's two-front Indian war sputtered to inconclusive resolution, to the dissatisfaction of settlers and their political representatives. On the south, emotional disagreement over territorial policies resulted in the declaration of martial law in Pierce and Thurston counties. Whites took revenge upon Indians as opportunity offered, including one episode in which supposedly unknown persons murdered a native leader being held under guard in the governor's Olympia office. Stevens himself managed the prosecution of Leschi, his most prominent antagonist, resulting after prolonged wrangling in and out of court, in the tragic execution of the Nisqually. As for the situation east of the Cascades, the governor was "mortified" by Wright's failure to fight and by the continued military ban on settlement in the region. Stevens devoted considerable time to pressing the War Department for punishment of individuals deemed responsible for the Bolon murder and other transgressions after he was elected the congressional delegate in 1857. A victory of sorts for his position came in 1858 when renewed conflict in eastern Washington, featuring a brutal army campaign, resulted in repeal of the anti-settler prohibition and ratification of the treaties concluded in 1855.

Formal Indian-white warfare within the boundaries of Washington ended with the 1858 battles between regulars and interior tribes. The subsequent struggles of the Pacific Northwest—the Paiute troubles of the 1860s, the Modoc conflict of 1873, and the Nez Perce and Bannock wars of 1877 and 1878—took place outside the territorial limits. These distant events nonetheless produced considerable consternation among settlers. Urban residents and homesteaders alike worried that local tribes would be inspired, by example, to open hostilities. Widely believed accounts reported that confidential agents of the Nez Perce purchased guns and ammunition from Puget Sound merchants and plotted among the tidewater villagers.[20] Far out at Cape Flattery, the Indian agent claimed that the whale-hunting Makahs were ready to paddle off to the assistance of Nez Perce Chief Joseph.[21]

Balancing such ludicrous expressions of hysteria, Indians, who as late as 1870 were still two of every five inhabitants, for many years held a vital place in territorial economic and social life. Tidewater natives supplied the demand for salmon and shellfish, worked in the coalmines, and loaded timber at the sawmills. Interior tribes people traded ponies, buffalo robes, and produce, and took part in horse races and other community festivities. "There is not a day passes," a local observer noted, "that you cannot see a large number of Indians in…Lewiston, Walla Walla, Wallula and Umatilla, purchasing anything and everything they may take a fancy to, and have the means to barter for, or purchase with cash."[22] Out of business necessity, settlers mastered the Chinook trade jargon, utilizing the rude dictionaries published in newspapers. For much of the period, the federal courts recognized the existence of an aboriginal justice system, relying upon traditional cultural precepts for resolution of intra-Indian disputes.

THE POLITICS AND PATRONAGE
OF TERRITORIAL GOVERNMENT

Isaac Stevens served a single term as governor and was elected twice to Congress before returning to the army and eventual Civil War martyrdom. He was far and away the great political figure of territorial Washington. Yet in spite of a momentous beginning, territorial government quickly devolved into fraudulence and inefficiency that earned it the scorn of the citizenry. Subsequent occupants of the gubernatorial chair, not to mention the holders of other offices, failed to measure up to "the skillful and energetic engineer, the wise ruler, the great captain, [and] the honorable man" celebrated by an Olympia monument erected in 1868.[23] His power and patronage, however, came from a combination of inordinate personal ambition and the jobs and contracts belonging to the Indian superintendency. Rather than a representative individual or model for his successors, Stevens was an atypically strong operative in an inherently weak and insignificant political system.

Close to five hundred persons, local postmasters included, eventually labored on the federal payroll in Washington Territory. Enshrined since the age of Jackson, near-immortal appointive dictates subjected all, from the governor to the lowliest employee on the most forgotten reservation, to removal upon a change of presidential administration. Washington had a single nonvoting congressional delegate and cast no electoral votes, so the likelihood of a local resident being appointed to a major position was minimal. Instead, outsiders, from states where patronage might truly reward past loyalty and influence future partisan contests, filled the best offices.

The second and third occupants of the executive position, Fayette McMullin and Richard Gholson, were, respectively, pro-slavery Virginia and Kentucky politicians who returned to the South to fight for the Confederacy. Under Lincoln and Grant, Illinois residents William Pickering, Edward Salomon, and Elisha Ferry secured appointment. Salomon, who admitted to complete ignorance of Washington's location and resources, had the additional qualification of prominent status in Chicago's German and Jewish communities. William Newell obtained the governorship as a sort of consolation prize after losing the New Jersey statehouse to George McClellan in 1880. Watson Squire, a wealthy New York investor who had recently relocated to Seattle, was appointed in 1884 on the basis of a strong recommendation from his home state

Republican organization. Eugene Semple, a Vancouver sawmill owner, was considered an Oregonian by his constituents on account of a long career in business and partisan affairs south of the Columbia. Appointed on the eve of statehood in 1889, Miles Moore was the first genuine resident of the territory to hold the governorship.

Stevens again providing the exception to the rule, the governor lacked significant political power. The three other officials of the territorial executive branch—the secretary, the U.S. attorney, and the federal marshal—were independent presidential appointees. Until 1864, the governor lacked authority to veto acts of the assembly and was therefore effectively powerless against local legislative initiatives. In 1874, Congress placed a number of offices previously filled by legislative election, including auditor, treasurer, and university board of regents, under the direct control of the territorial chief executive. Finally reckoned a potent political factor, the governor thereafter dispensed, at most, three dozen jobs.

Politicians interested in securing wealth from public employment preferred other appointive opportunities. The Indian superintendency, which disposed of federal funds and contracts, offered patronage and influence. The customs collectorship offered funds from duties and seized illegal goods. Land office employees regularly and illegally loaned out the public deposits, charging high rates of interest to short-term borrowers. Governor Edward Salomon was dismissed for cause in 1871 when an inspector discovered his involvement in the fraudulent use of land office funds. By one method or another, contractors rewarded the surveyor general for granting work on favorable terms.

Regardless of partisan affiliation or personal philosophy, settlers tended to view politics and politicians with contempt. Federal officials came from far away and they were selected for reasons that had little or nothing to do with the everyday concerns of Washington residents. Worse, they were often bumbling incompetents. Popular disregard was also evident in localized democratic affairs. The normal turnout in territorial elections was thought to be "not more than one-third of the voters."[24] The most prestigious elected officer, the delegate to Congress, had no vote and modest influence in the nation's capital, justifying the lack of constituent interest. Even the well-connected Isaac Stevens failed to accomplish much of import beyond ratification of the Indian treaties during his two terms as the territory's representative in Congress.

There was little reason, moreover, for the public to care about the territorial assembly, composed of the house of representatives and the council. Critics maintained that the territorial legislature simply did not have the political power of a state legislature. In response to a legislative memorial asserting that the originally mandated annual meetings were unnecessary, given the lack of political business, Congress in 1865 provided for biennial sessions limited to forty days. Before as well as subsequent to this action, members were severely restricted in their freedom to make laws. Because the federal funds supplied to Olympia did not belong solely to the territory, according to the U.S. Treasury

Department, binding legislation could be made only in connection with acts of Congress. Meetings of the house and the council therefore focused on the granting of divorces to politically influential petitioners—including, on one memorable occasion, Governor Fayette McMullin—and on the "picking… to pieces and putting…together again" of existing statutes.[25]

Local government was the one area of genuine political concern for the average citizen, since territorial taxes were assessed and collected at the county level. Here, too, the system operated in an inefficient manner. A single rate of taxation, four mills per dollar of valuation, prevailed across the territory, but the actual amount paid varied widely, depending upon the values set by each auditor. Assessments varied from county to county. Absentee property owners paid more than genuine inhabitants and the politically influential less than the regular settler. The lack of a method to equalize assessments may have cost the territory a third of its potential annual revenue. Sloppy bookkeeping and casual methods of delivery to Olympia encouraged the theft or inadvertent loss of an undetermined amount of money.

TIMBER, AGRICULTURE, AND DIVIDED INTERESTS

The Cascade Mountains divide Washington into prairie and timber regions. Propelled by the discovery of gold and good soil and water, the prairie began to develop rapidly. Wheat became the cash crop and Walla Walla became the hub for inland transportation. The need for east-west communication and transportation became ever more necessary, if Washington Territory were to become a viable political entity. The call went out to divide the territory again. Local residents, of course, well understood the peculiar geographic division of their territorial home as well as the appropriate opportunities for profit on one side or the other of the Cascades. Puget Sound offered endless forest and a hazard-free inland sea.

Patterns of exploitation already established by 1853 remained in effect for a quarter century. The San Francisco–owned sawmills produced most of Washington's lumber, shipping three-fourths of their cut to California and the remainder to foreign ports. By substantial margins, territorial manufacturers were larger, better financed, and more export oriented than competitors south of the Columbia. Although the companies purchased land whenever possible, most preferred to operate on the public domain, logging free of charge or through such legal subterfuges as the payment of stumpage money. Timber worth $40 million was stolen in western Washington during the 1860s alone.

Fundamental change was more in evidence east, than west, of the mountains. Ratification of the Stevens treaties with the Indians in early 1859 sent white land seekers into the interior Northwest. Within a year, large herds of cattle roamed the range, and Walla Walla, originally a few log shanties adjacent to an army post, had become a promising settlement of fifty frame buildings.

The discovery of gold on the Nez Perce reservation in late 1860 produced a stampede the following spring of thousands of prospectors to the Clearwater River and other points in northern Idaho. Walla Walla, the major inland point of distribution for goods needed in the diggings, prospered immediately as the "Sacramento of the Upper Columbia." No later than 1863, the remote community was the largest and wealthiest urban area in the territory. A commercial artery flowing in gold, the Columbia River tied eastern Washington to Portland as never before, the Oregon Steam Navigation Company securing and maintaining a transportation monopoly.

Walla Walla soon became far more than a trans-shipment center for the mining regions of Idaho and Montana. Water and the best soil yet encountered east of the Cascades accounted for the exceptional fecundity of the greater valley west and north of the town. All but five thousand of the thirty thousand cattle in the vicinity perished in the harsh winter of 1862, stimulating a shift from grazing to farming. By 1864, four thousand acres were planted in wheat, "the only grain crop," according to a local newspaper, "that finds a ready cash market at a remunerating price."[26] The inability of valley flouring mills to keep pace with a rate of production approaching, and then exceeding, a half million bushels annually was the only negative aspect of the upsurge. Downriver grain shipments to Portland, meanwhile, mounted at an equivalent rate. Wheat, not gold, was the enduring Walla Walla mainstay.

Settlers intent upon claiming new grain acreage moved north toward, and eventually across, the Snake River. Ranging east from the Mullan Road to the Idaho line, the Palouse quickly attained fame as a beautiful and fertile country of undulating hills covered with grass. In what amounted, at the outset, to a slow extension of the Walla Walla settlement impulse, homesteaders took land along the initial tier of westward-flowing Palouse River tributaries. By 1871, two hundred Americans resided in the Union Flat subregion. Although navigation hazards on the Snake interfered with access to markets, early per acre yields equaled those of established eastern Washington farms.

Reflecting the rapid pace of settlement, wheat and flour shipments out of the Columbia River mounted from $593,000 in 1869 to over $4 million in 1874.[27] In earlier times, the territory amounted, as far as actual pioneers were concerned, to little more than the region west of the Cascades. Recent developments altered a bygone equation, shifting the focus to eastern Washington. Two-fifths of the non-Indian population resided east of the mountains by the late 1870s, compared to less than a third on Puget Sound. The eastside had the three most-heavily populated counties and five of the top seven. Urbanization was more pronounced on the sound, but the interior claimed four of the nine largest towns.

Divisions of geography and commercial orientation made Washington a fundamentally unstable territory. West of the high mountains, the weather was inclement and the lumber manufacturing economy dominated by San Francisco. The eastside featured an arid, or at least semi-arid, climate and a wheat-growing society linked by river navigation to Portland. The commonwealth was being drawn by contrasting trends of development, which was a discouraging prospect to early statehood advocates. The complete lack of direct year-round communication over the Cascades remained a defining obstacle to unification of interests. To reach the Walla Walla Valley treaty ground in 1853, Isaac Stevens took a necessarily roundabout route, down the Cowlitz River to the Columbia, then up the latter stream to The Dalles. Three decades later, Eugene Semple, the next-to-last governor, reported that he must leave the territory when traveling between western and eastern Washington, a detour by way of Oregon being the only means of reaching Walla Walla City or Spokane from Olympia.[28]

Major alteration of regional political boundaries seemed to be a likely outcome of the interior boom for many years. "The time has come," a San Francisco newspaper stated in the spring of 1862, "when...Washington Territory should be divided, and a new territory organized out of the district east of the Cascade Mountains." As presently constituted, after all, Washington was larger than California, twice the size of New England, and split into "two districts which are entirely dissimilar in all their resources and wants."[29] Directly on the scene, the pro-division *Walla Walla Statesman* asserted in a series of commentaries that westside officials had "humbugged and victimized" eastern Washington to such an extent that the outraged settlers opposed "any further affiliation with... clam-eating politicians." In the face of ongoing west-to-east demographic change, Puget Sound opposed meaningful reapportionment of the legislature. Tidewater interests also thwarted creation of a second judicial circuit beyond the Cascades, forcing judges to travel hundreds of miles a quarter by all available means of transportation.

Idaho Territory was carved out of Washington Territory in 1863 as a result of the Nez Perce and related gold rushes, thus leaving Washington with its modern day boundaries. This failed, however, to mollify supporters of division. The early transfer of the territorial capital from Lewiston to Boise reinforced a natural community of interests between northern Idaho and eastern Washington. Panhandle residents with business to conduct in Boise had to negotiate a difficult mountain trail, the closest thing to a direct means of communication. Since interior Washington was just as remote with respect to Olympia, a union of the two unhappy sections appeared to be a common sense response to prevailing geographical shortcomings. First proposed in 1864, realignment drew widespread support from all factions and interests.

THE FAILED ATTEMPT AT STATEHOOD

A long delay in completing a railroad and the widespread conviction that statehood was unlikely exacerbated traditional sectional rivalries during the 1870s. Republicans and Democrats alike east of the Cascades advocated the annexation of northern Idaho and the creation of a new territory in the interior Northwest. Separatists maintained that geographical barriers made trips to Olympia or Boise nearly impossible. Given prevailing trends in population and economic growth, Puget Sounders confronted unacceptable prospects. At best, they would have permanent minority status in an enlarged Washington and at worst, an untenable rump existence leading to eventual reunion with Oregon. Taking advantage of their control of the legislature, now badly out of demographic alignment, westside leaders moved to preempt disunion by securing admission to the Union.

Fifteen constitutional convention delegates and then a sixteenth representing northern Idaho were chosen by a largely indifferent electorate in April 1878. Meeting in Walla Walla from mid-June through late July, the would-be founders of a new state produced a densely worded document containing, when reduced to the essentials, three provisions of paramount interest. One, designed to appeal to residents of the interior, annexed the Idaho panhandle. The other two points preserved the political power of western Washington even in an enlarged commonwealth. Olympia could be displaced as capital only in the very unlikely event of an alternative site receiving a majority of all the votes cast in a statewide referendum. Built into the constitutional framework, an apportionment of legislative seats favorable to the westside was virtually immune to challenge.

Washington voters approved the constitution and statehood at the November 1878 election by an apparent two-to-one margin. Properly understood, however, the electorate rendered only a narrow and sectionally based verdict. Individuals wrote "for" or "against" on their ballots, with a majority of the total vote cast for congressional delegate required to pass the constitution. Favorable tallies alone truly counted, so there was a large fall-off in participation in areas opposed to statehood. One-fourth of the congressional voters registered no opinion, pro or con, and the document was actually endorsed by only 51 percent of the electors. Outside new immigrant- and wheat-prosperous Whitman County, two-thirds of the eastern Washington voting population rejected statehood, either directly or by declining to proclaim a preference. On Puget Sound, in contrast, two of every three persons casting a ballot for Congress expressly supported the constitution. Although the territory's representative regularly and vainly introduced legislation for admission, traditional points of contention produced a clear division of opinion on the question of Washington's admission to statehood.

THE NORTHERN PACIFIC UNIFIES THE TERRITORY

East- and westsiders alike agreed that construction of a railroad across the Cascades was the only means of preventing disunion. A railroad uniting east and west would also bring economic benefits to both sides. Wood, coal, and lumber would become available in eastern Washington and western Washington's agricultural products would become available in the east, all at cheaper prices. Breaking Portland's regional transportation monopoly would result in reduced freight rates. Of equal significance, at least for those persons opposed to territorial division, a direct linkage between Puget Sound and the Columbia Basin would unite Washington into a workable political and commercial entity.

The Northern Pacific Railroad was organized by act of Congress in 1864 and became, through years of delay and frustration, the ultimate agent of Washington statehood. The Northern Pacific eventually secured title to over 7 million acres or a fifth of the territory. Despite some grousing over the size of the federal land grant, Puget Sounders in particular greeted the firm as the manifestation of a long-sought transcontinental dream. Although the company shifted the destination of its originally conceived Snake River-to-the-sea mainline from the sound to Portland, settlers remained convinced that they would be the ultimate beneficiaries of construction. The change, most observers agreed, was only temporary, designed to reduce costs through short-term reliance upon the facilities of the Oregon Steam Navigation Company. The Northern Pacific remained committed to a crossing of the Cascades when fiscally practicable, and, in the meantime, moved ahead with plans for a branch line from the lower Columbia to one of the tidewater ports.

Knowing full well that selection of the Puget Sound terminal was worth many millions to the Northern Pacific, railroad officials declined to make an early selection of the favored spot. This kicked off rivalries among those towns that hoped to be chosen. From Olympia north to Bellingham Bay near the Canadian border, urban boosters proffered incentives of land and cash to the railroad. Corrupt federal officials plotted to remove waterfront acreage from the Nisqually and the Puyallup Indian reservations, so that the Northern Pacific might be attracted to those previously unexploited places.

Railroad engineers determined that Seattle and Whatcom, the principal settlement on Bellingham Bay, were the superior points. Influential persons connected with the Oregon Steam Navigation Company (O.S.N.), however, favored Commencement Bay, a deepwater port featuring high bluffs and vast tide flats, as the site most easily controlled from Portland. John C. Ainsworth, president of the O.S.N. and western managing director for the Northern Pacific, personally selected Tacoma as the terminus in the summer of 1873. A "ring" of railroad stockholders organized by the aggressive and versatile Ainsworth secured much of the land and most of the valuable resources in and near the new boomtown. Completed in mid-December, the so-called Puget Sound branch linked Tacoma with the Columbia River. By then, unfortunately, the Panic of 1873 had bankrupted the Northern Pacific, halting further rail construction in Washington Territory.

Work finally resumed in 1879 under reorganized and reformed management. The Pend Oreille division proceeded on a northeasterly line, from the mouth of the Snake River along the flank of the Palouse to Spokane Falls and beyond into northern Idaho. Preempting plans to also build across the Cascades to Puget Sound, Henry Villard of the Oregon Railway & Navigation Company, successor to the old Ainsworth steamboat concern, secured control of the Northern Pacific in 1881. In alliance, the two firms laid rails down the Columbia to Portland, producing a shift in regional transportation from navigation to reliance upon the land. With this accomplished, Villard believed that Portland would be the transportation hub of the Northwest. Villard was, however, over-extended and caught up in a maze of interlocking construction and development projects. He was driven from power in January 1884 and supplanted by Northern Pacific stockholders with primary investments in Tacoma, not Portland. This meant that the railroad would finally go through the Cascades. Accordingly, work began in earnest east of the Cascades in 1884 as construction crews pushed the mainline up the Yakima Valley toward Stampede Pass. On July 3, 1887, the first Northern Pacific train from the east arrived in Tacoma via the briefly famous Switchback, a deftly engineered means of temporarily crossing the summit. The tunnel itself, at ten thousand feet the second longest yet bored in the United States, opened the following May. At last completed to its tidewater terminus, the Northern Pacific significantly reduced travel time, directly linked eastern and western Washington, and initiated a shift in commercial predominance from Portland to the great estuary of the north. The roundtrip from Yakima to Puget Sound was cut from 466 miles to 169 miles.

Things changed rapidly as a result of the resuscitation of the Northern Pacific. Railroad publicity, cheap rates of transportation west, and favorable land prices accelerated the pace of settlement long before completion of the mainline across the Cascades to Commencement Bay. Washington's population tripled between 1877 and 1883. Eclipsing Walla Walla, Seattle, Tacoma, and Spokane Falls, the latter a new community ideally located to exploit the Palouse and the Coeur d'Alenes east of the Idaho line, surged to the lead among cities. The value of taxable property in the territory more than doubled between 1877 and 1884. Mining, centered on a large coalfield in the vicinity of Lake Washington, expanded to rival timber manufacturing as an industrial activity. Coal shipments, most to San Francisco, tripled in tonnage from 1875 to 1883. Sawmill production, meanwhile, surged thanks in large part to an infusion of capital from the forest-depleted Great Lakes. By 1889, Washington ranked fifth among the nation's lumber-producing states and territories. With its growing network of feeders, the Northern Pacific stitched the territory together, making it a viable entity politically and economically, and opening the door to statehood.

THE ANTI-CHINESE CAMPAIGN

Some developments, to be sure, were controversial in nature, producing agitation rather than celebration. The Chinese, in particular, had been a regular presence in the territory since the mid-1860s, to the periodic chagrin of their American neighbors. The legislature imposed a special tax on Asian residents in 1864. Outbreaks of pestilence in Olympia in 1869 and of smallpox in Walla Walla in 1871 were blamed upon the supposedly lax sanitary habits of the "moon-eyed heathen."[30] Indians learned that they could freely attack Chinese miners, since the local authorities refused to take action in such cases. The "Chinese labor question" was a regular subject of public debate and newspaper editorial columns.

A sharp, though brief, economic downturn in the summer and fall of 1885 made the Chinese presence the topic of local concern. Growing fast in the mills and the mines, the Knights of Labor blamed prevailing wage reductions and unemployment on low-cost Asian competition for jobs, an argument that was both effective and an accurate depiction of employer practices. On the night of September 7, a party of white hop ranchers and displaced Indian pickers attacked a camp of recently hired Chinese hands in the Issaquah Valley, east of Seattle, murdering three men in cold blood and causing the remainder to flee in terror. Later in the month, unidentified persons burned Chinese-occupied cabins at a nearby coal mine. A carefully orchestrated roundup engineered by municipal officials drove all 197 Asian residents out of Tacoma on November 3. After weeks of tension, the forces of bigotry struck in Seattle on February 7, 1886. A substantial portion of the Chinese population, 196 persons by authoritative count, departed by steamer, but 185 individuals placed themselves under the protection of a previously organized Home Guard. Governor Watson Squire declared martial law, called out the territorial militia and secured the assignment of federal troops to Seattle.

Firm resolve, motivated in part by decency and in part by self-interest, exercised by "law abiding citizens" prevented similar outbreaks in other Washington towns. As employers feared, however, the anti-Chinese campaign was merely the first stroke in a sustained effort to secure higher wages. The lumber industry was soon forced to reduce the standard mill shift from twelve to ten hours, with no reduction in daily pay. The coalmines near Seattle and at Roslyn on the far side of Snoqualmie Pass were disrupted by Knights of Labor action in 1888 and 1889. The sense of euphoria created by approaching statehood, therefore, was balanced by a social unrest and uncertainty regarding the present and the future.

THE CONSTITUTIONAL CONVENTION

Ready for statehood from the early 1880s on by reason of population, economic growth, and a newly united polity, Washington was frustrated by delays of a partisan nature. The territory was overwhelmingly Republican, but for years one or another house of Congress, and since the election of 1884 the presidency as well, was in Democratic control. The party of the Old South and the big cities was unlikely to accept the creation of new states sure to increase the congressional representation and the electoral votes of its rival. Virtually impossible to breach in the past, the political obstruction suddenly crumbled with the national Republican victory in 1888. Expecting Benjamin Harrison to call a special session of Congress upon his inauguration as president in March 1889, Washingtonians convened a special statehood conference in early January. Intent upon securing at least some credit for an inevitable development, the outgoing Democrats unexpectedly approved "omnibus" legislation admitting North and South Dakota, Montana, and Washington. Signed by President Grover Cleveland on Washington's Birthday, the measure provided for the election of delegates in May, a constitutional convention in July, and an October 1 vote on both the constitution and the principal state government offices.

Genuine territory-wide approval was far more likely in 1889 than it had been in 1878. Under the act of Congress, the governor and the chief judge of the Supreme Court divided the territory into twenty-five districts of roughly equal population. Only two of the three delegates allowed from each district could be from the same party. The Republicans thereby secured control of the proceedings, but the Democrats were guaranteed a significant minority position. The mid-May election produced anticipated results. Republican candidates won forty-five of the seventy-five seats. The victors tended to be politically experienced and relatively youthful professionally trained persons. Twenty-one were practicing attorneys and eighteen had served in the territorial assembly. One, William Prosser, was a former member of Congress from his home state of Tennessee.

A month and a half intervened between the election and the convention, allowing ample time for initial debate on contentious issues. Washington, for instance, would inherit a vast landed empire upon its admission to the Union. In addition to sections 16 and 36 in every surveyed township that were donated for the support of education, the federal government granted specified tracts to finance construction of a capitol and other public buildings. The total, according to one newspaper estimate, "well nigh reaches two millions of acres, and all...rapidly appreciating in value." Some observers wanted to sell the acreage as rapidly as possible, stimulating settlement and underwriting a "permanent" school endowment. Others favored the alternative of leasing the land, protecting "the inheritance of the children" from "the vandalism of grasping corporations" and preserving for the state the increasing valuation of its lands.[31]

Opinion was even more divided over the disposition of tidelands. The export-oriented Puget Sound economy had always impinged upon such tracts, since ships could be loaded and unloaded only at wharves extending out from the shore to deep water. The federal government retained title below the line of mean high tide, but private upland owners claimed the right, under riparian doctrine, to build adjacent docks and other improvements. First-comer shoreline claimants denied later arrivals access to the waterfront. Denounced by the former as squatters, the latter supposedly considered the flats "legitimate plunder" for trespassers. Public port advocates insisted that tidal sections be turned over to municipal control, so that development work might proceed according to rational planning. In spite of the contention that people on the far side of the Cascades knew "little, if anything" about such salty matters, eastsiders also insisted upon a voice in the disposition of the tidelands, because of the inevitable impact upon the means of exporting wheat.

Conflicting claims, all parties agreed, ought to be resolved at the convention. Between existing federal law and the long-established "equal footing" doctrine, under which new states possessed the same rights as the old states, no one doubted that title passed to Washington upon admission. The debate focused on the next step. Waterfront interests wanted the constitution to expressly grant "owners of fast shore land" the right to purchase tidal acreage "in front of their holdings." Squatters demanded that "a rude awakening" be administered riparian claimants. A third position, well represented among the convention delegates, advocated permanent state ownership.[32]

Meeting in Olympia on July 4, delegates, lobbyists, and reporters exposed themselves to various discomforts. Also meeting in the capital city, a territorial teachers' institute placed a premium upon accommodations and restaurant meals. Temperatures soared daily to ninety degrees and above, and smoke from forest fires permeated the atmosphere out-of-doors and inside the small chamber normally used by the legislature. Sundays and the occasional Monday excepted, the convention sat until August 23, exceeding its congressionally authorized budget by 50 percent. Early public complaint that oratory-minded members were wasting time and money in pontification upon pet nostrums resulted in a decision to conduct business in closed-door meetings of the two dozen standing committees.

Several potentially divisive issues were disposed of behind the scenes. The appropriate committees respectfully received woman suffrage and prohibition petitions before consigning resolution to separate October votes of the general electorate. The state capital question was handled in similar fashion, Olympia being designated the "temporary" seat of government until such time as a majority of all the votes cast in a statewide election favored relocation to a new site. Other matters were dispatched with a minimum of public rancor. The judiciary article, providing for a five-person supreme court and continuous session county superior courts, was generally considered a much-needed advance in the means of conducting legal business. Establishing a house of seventy and a senate of thirty-five members, Article 2, Section 2, addressed fears that a small legislature would be prone to corruption by special interests.[33]

On a more controversial note, the convention rejected a committee report recommending inclusion of a railroad commission in the constitution. The final document retained the strong anti-corporate language favored by critics of the rail lines—"monopolies and trusts," for instance, "shall never be allowed"—but left the actual means of regulating business to the legislature.

Article 16 authorized the sale of state lands at auction. No more than a quarter of the total acreage, however, could be sold prior to January 1895, and no more than half before January 1905. Unhappy territorial experience with railroad construction subsidies made local government debt a controversial issue. After much discord, a compromise constitutional provision allowed cities and counties to incur debt, with three-fifths voter approval, only up to 5 percent of total assessed property valuation.

Tidelands provided, as expected, the principal point of contention. Concluding, on the eve of the convention that their original goal, explicit recognition of the right to purchase tidal tracts, was beyond reach, shoreline interests pursued a revised agenda. The fallback position was simply to defer the issue to a new legislature. Cyrus Walker, the territory's most influential lumberman, personally distributed $5,000 among susceptible delegates. Devised in committee on behalf of waterfront corporations, the appropriate terms were accepted in one of the final floor votes on the draft constitution. Under Article 17, the state of Washington asserted "ownership to the beds and shores of all navigable waters...up to and including the line of ordinary high tide." Article 15 provided for the appointment of a commission "to locate and establish harbor lines in the navigable waters." Declaring that the legislative branch "shall provide laws for the leasing" of tracts between the lines so designated and high tide mark, the second section supplied the mechanism by which private industry expected to maintain effectual control of the shorefront.

The constitution was signed by weary delegates in late August and generally considered a "tolerably liberal," if far from perfect, document. Many Washington residents complained of the lack of a railroad commission and of the failure to resolve the tideland controversy. No major voice of influence, however, called for rejection at the polls. Majority Republicans were unwilling to deny installation of their heavily favored slate of state office candidates by voting against the constitution. Congress, moreover, had mandated that the convention reconvene in the event of defeat. "While there are several things in the Constitution which should be out, and several things out which should be in," one observer noted of this practical consideration, "we deem it better to adopt it...than to defeat it and run the chance of having a better one formed by the men who constructed the present one."[34]

Virtually every commentator on Washington political affairs agreed that the constitution would pass. Except for occasional Republican accusations that the Democrats opposed statehood, the constitution was rarely mentioned during a campaign that focused on such genuinely divisive issues as prohibition and woman suffrage. In particular, the contest for state capital, with Yakima and Ellensburg mounting heavily publicized challenges to Olympia, attracted far more attention.

Downed telegraph wires from a series of storms sweeping the territory in its final days of legal existence delayed the counting of votes. Released after two weeks of impatient expectation, the official tally recorded victory for the constitution by a nearly four-to-one margin. Only four of the thirty-four counties, including Walla Walla, the traditional center of sentiment for territorial division, cast negative majorities. Statehood drew the heaviest support in Washington's most economically dynamic locales. Seattle, Tacoma, and Spokane endorsed admission by overwhelming rates of approval. Elisha Ferry, meanwhile, was easily elected governor and his party secured sufficiently one-sided control of the legislature as to make the new state virtually a Republican satrapy. Woman suffrage and prohibition went down by respective negative ratios of two to one and three to two. Although Olympia finished first in the race for capital, with just over 25,000 votes, the combined east-of-the-mountains 28,000 figure for Yakima and Olympia reflected the persistence of regional loyalties and suggested that, if one or the other had dropped out, the seat of government would have been relocated to the far side of the Cascades.

STATEHOOD ACHIEVED

Overnight squalls gave way to bright late fall sunshine as the government of the nation's forty-second state was formally installed on November 18, 1889. The Republican legislature commenced business that morning and, at three quarters of the hour past noon, Elisha Ferry took the gubernatorial oath. Until quite recent times, the dream had been little more than a fantasy, a vision compromised by geographical disunity and divergent economies. Since 1880, though, Washington's population had increased by an astounding 356 percent, from 75,000 to 357,000. Reversing the trends of previous decades, a shift from eastside to westside dominance and from country to urban life was substantially underway. Seattle, Tacoma, and Spokane became, and remained, the focal points of old territory and new state. The Northern Pacific Railroad, stimulating immigration and enabling the exchange of goods and services, transformed Washington from a dysfunctional entity to a working political and economic commonwealth.

NOTES

1. Seattle *Weekly Intelligencer*, November 27, 1875; Dayton *Columbia Chronicle*, September 7, 1878.
2. Oregon City *Oregon Spectator*, February 19, 1846, September 5, 1850; Portland *Oregonian*, July 17, 1852.
3. Isaac N. Ebey to W. S. Ebey, September 28, 1853, Winfield S. Ebey Papers, University of Washington Library.
4. Michael T. Simmons to Joseph Lane, June 22, 1852, Joseph Lane Papers, Oregon Historical Society.
5. Olympia *Columbian*, October 23, November 13, 1852.
6. Ibid., November 20; December 4, 11, 1852.

7. Ibid., March 12, April 9, February 2, 1853.

8. Ibid., April 16, 1853.

9. Olympia *Washington Pioneer*, December 17, 1853.

10. Olympia *Columbian*, September 24, October 15, April 30, May 7, October 22, 1853; Kenneth N. Owens, "Pattern and Structure in Washington Territorial Politics," *Western Historical Quarterly* 1 (October 1970): 375–377.

11. Benjamin Alvord to John J. McGilvra, October 8, 1862, John J. McGilvra Papers, University of Washington Library.

12. Isaac I. Stevens to George W. Manypenny, December 26, 29, 1853, Records of the Washington Superintendency of Indian Affairs, 1853–1874, M5, National Archives; September 16, 1854, in *Annual Report of the Commissioner of Indian Affairs, 1854*, p. 457.

13. Stevens to Manypenny, September 16, 1854, in *Annual Report of the Commissioner of Indian Affairs, 1854*, pp. 457–460.

14. Simmons to Stevens, July 1, 1854, Records of the Washington Superintendency of Indian Affairs.

15. Stevens to Manypenny, December 21, 1854; May 1, 1855.

16. Kent D. Richards, *Isaac I. Stevens: Young Man in a Hurry* (Provo: Brigham Young University Press, 1979), pp. 199–207, 215–226.

17. Olympia *Pioneer and Democrat*, June 29, 1855.

18. Palmer to Manypenny, October 9, 25, 1855, Records of the Oregon Superintendency of Indian Affairs.

19. Journal, November 6–13, 15, 1855, Granville O. Haller Papers, University of Washington Library; William N. Bischoff, S.J., "The Yakima Campaign of 1856," *Mid-America* 31 (July 1949): 167–168.

20. Olympia *Puget Sound Weekly Courier*, June 29, 1877; Seattle *Weekly Intelligencer*, June 23, 1877; *Tacoma Herald*, July 14, 21; August 18, 1877; Olympia *Washington Standard*, June 30, July 14, 1877.

21. C. A. Huntington to J. Q. Smith, July 14, 1877, Correspondence of the Office of Indian Affairs.

22. *Walla Walla Statesman*, July 5, September 6, 1867; *Walla Walla Union*, August 16, 1873.

23. Port Townsend *Weekly Message*, January 30, 1868.

24. Olympia *Puget Sound Weekly Courier*, April 19, 1878.

25. Olympia *Washington Standard*, December 22, 1860; Seattle *Weekly Intelligencer*, September 25, 1875.

26. *Walla Walla Statesman*, January 10, 25, February 8, 22, 1862; February 17, November 10, 1865; Meinig, *Great Columbia Plain*, pp. 223–225.

27. Astoria *Weekly Astorian*, January 1, 1876.

28. Eugene Semple to First Auditor of the Treasury, November 28, 1888, Semple Papers.

29. Olympia *Washington Standard*, March 15, 1862, reprinting from San Francisco *Alta California*; Portland *Oregonian*, June 7, 1862.

30. Olympia *Washington Standard*, July 24, 1869; Seattle *Weekly Intelligencer*, September 11, 1871; Colfax *Palouse Gazette*, April 20, 1878.

31. *Tacoma Daily Ledger*, March 27, May 3, 10, 14, 1889; *Seattle Post-Intelligencer*, March 8, 12, May 21, June 2, 1889; Olympia *Washington Standard*, June 28, 1889;

Spokane Falls Review, May 18, 1889; *Seattle Times*, July 16, 1889; Port Townsend *Puget Sound Weekly Argus*, May 23, 1889.

32. Howard to Smith, June 23, 1884, June 4, October 5, 1888, February 13, 1889; to C. A. Dolph, May 9, 1889, Oregon Improvement Company Records; *Tacoma Daily Ledger*, March 6, 27, April 25, 1889; *Tacoma News*, April 6, 13, 25, June 22, July 11, 1889; *Seattle Post-Intelligencer*, May 5, 21, 1889.

33. Discussion and quotations of constitutional provisions from *Journal of the Constitutional Convention*.

34. *Walla Walla Union*, September 28, 1889; *Seattle Post-Intelligencer*, August 23, 1889; *Spokane Falls Review*, August 27, 1889; *Tacoma Daily Ledger*, August 12, 24, 1889.

BIBLIOGRAPHY

Avery, Mary W. *Washington: A History of the Evergreen State*. Seattle: University of Washington Press, 1965.

Beckett, Paul L. *From Wilderness to Enabling Act: Evolution of the State of Washington*. Pullman: Washington State University, 1968.

Ficken, Robert E., and Charles P. LeWarne. *Washington: A Centennial History*. Seattle: University of Washington Press, 1988.

LeWarne, Charles P. *Washington State*. Seattle: University of Washington Press, 1986.

Meany, Edmond S. *History of the State of Washington*. New York: Macmillan, 1924.

Snowden, Clinton A. *History of Washington; The Rise and Progress of an American State*. 4 vols. New York: Century History Company, 1909.

White, Sid, and S. E. Solberg, eds. *Peoples of Washington: Perspectives on Cultural Diversity*. Pullman: Washington State University, 1989.

West Virginia

Territorial Development:

- Virginia secedes from the Union on April 17, 1861
- Citizens in the western region of Virginia form the Restored Government, and declare allegiance to the Union, June 11–25, 1861
- The United States recognizes western Virginia's Restored Government as the state of Virginia's legitimate governing body when western Virginian representatives fill all seats vacated by the former state of Virginia in Congress, summer 1861
- West Virginia admitted into the Union as the thirty-fifth state, June 30, 1863

Capitals prior to Statehood:

- Jamestown, 1619–1699
- Williamsburg, 1699–1780
- Richmond, 1780–1861
- Wheeling acted as the seat of the Restored Government from 1861–1863

State Capitals:

- Wheeling, 1863–1870
- Charleston, 1870–1875
- Wheeling, 1875–1885
- Charleston, 1885–present

Origin of State Name: Like Virginia, West Virginia was named in 1584 in honor of Elizabeth, the "Virgin Queen" of England.

First Governor: Arthur I. Boreman
Governmental Organization: Bicameral
Population at Statehood: 442,014 (figure taken from the 1870 Census)
Geographical Size: 24,078 square miles

THE STATE OF WEST VIRGINIA

Admitted to the Union as a State: June 30, 1863

Frankie Hutton

INTRODUCTION

West Virginia's admission to the Union is a story of sectional rivalry, rebellion, war, and legal maneuvers in the setting of a divided nation. The western counties of Virginia had long been alienated from the government of Virginia, which favored wealthy slaveholders in its taxation policies and in representation in government. When Virginia seceded from the Union in April 1861, westerners and others found the opportunity to secede from old Virginia.

After abundant debate and contentious procedural discussion, leaders mostly from the western and northwestern counties remaining loyal to the Union forged a new Restored Government of Virginia as of August 1861. The new state of West Virginia was engineered out of the new Restored Government, although some citizens of the region remained secession-minded and joined the Confederate Army to fight against the Union. With support and protection during the process by the federal government, West Virginia was approved for statehood by Congress and President Abraham Lincoln in December 1862. The proclamation was to "be in force from and after sixty days."[1] West Virginia's statehood saga, however, does not end there. After the Civil War ended, Renewed Virginia contested West Virginia's legality twice in a case that went all the way to the U.S. Supreme Court and was not settled until 1871.

WESTERN VIRGINIA BEFORE STATEHOOD

The fact that poorer western Virginia was once part of one of the largest, most powerful of the original British colonies and that a conflicted clump of counties broke away during the Civil War to form another state is a unique story in statehood history. During the colonial period, the term "western Virginia" actually referred to the region in the westernmost portion of the colony of Virginia. As the colony grew up to be relatively wealthy, aristocratic, and of inestimable influence in national politics, its western outer reaches lagged behind economically and politically.

During the pre–Revolutionary War era, Virginia was under the authority of the British Royal Governor Lord John Murray Dunmore. As early as 1770 the western outer reaches of Virginia came to the attention of George Washington, who went there in search of land. As a young military officer he voiced strong opinions against the British royal governor in charge of the Virginia colony. In a word, Washington thought Dunmore was "dangerous." Because Governor Dunmore had not hesitated to advocate arming and using loyalist slaves as soldiers in service with the British during the Revolutionary War, Washington opined in 1775 that "if that man Dunmore is not crushed before the Spring, he will become the most dangerous man in America."[2]

Dangerous or not, Dunmore led the most influential and powerful of all the original British colonies. During his reign a portion of the colony, the entire territory west of the Blue Ridge Mountains, was referred to as "transmountain Virginia" or simply "western Virginia." Later, when this territory practically forced itself to become a state, it comprised about two-thirds of the original territory west of the Blue Ridge Mountains in the center of Appalachia, embracing not only the Blue Ridge Mountains, but also the Allegheny mountain ranges. The region known as Appalachia stretches from northwestern New York State into northern Alabama. The entire region has been notoriously rich in culture and lore and, like West Virginia, economically poor.

Historian John Alexander Williams has called the battle of Point Pleasant or Dunmore's War the "climactic event" in the history of colonial western Virginia.[3] It was at Point Pleasant during the Revolutionary War era that an army of 1,100 western Virginia militiamen fought tribes of Ohio Indians over land rights. As Williams explains the intricate history surrounding the early quest for land in the region, George Washington comes to light as one of the first bigwigs to come to western Virginia on behalf of a "syndicate" of veteran military officers. These former military leaders favored large parcels and held warrants for "free land by virtue of their service in the French and Indian War."

Whereas the land quest dictated western Virginia's early history, the difference in the composition and use of the terrain in the east as opposed to the west dictated the political and economic divide between the two regions. The divide had been noted earlier, but was particularly apparent just after the mid-seventeenth century. One historian has noted that "the combination of exploitative landholders with landless ex-servants created a menace to social stability and nearly tore the colony [Virginia] apart in Bacon's Rebellion."[4]

The story of that rebellion bears summary here to illuminate the root of the divide in early Virginia.

In essence, western settlers, representing the former indentured servant class, revolted in 1675 against eastern aristocratic landowners in an event that has come to signal a turning point in the history of slavery in Virginia. Led by Nathaniel Bacon, a wealthy young western landowner who had problems with the Susquehannock people as much as with the eastern stronghold in power in the colony, the revolt practically destroyed Jamestown, the colonial capital. The revolt revealed in the long run that former indentured servants, mostly white men, were not a reliable source of labor for the colony. Chattel slavery, growing steadily in the colony by the end of the seventeenth century, turned out to be much more reliable and lucrative. Thus, the eastern portion of the colony developed around a rich, agriculturally based economy tied chiefly to tobacco, the planting, cultivation, and harvesting of which was labor intensive. In time, the region relied heavily on slave labor in support chiefly of the tobacco crop and impressive, large plantations that gave birth to, at least initially, a successful impressive tobacco-based economy. The presence of a growing number of black slaves skewed the political landscape and the balance of power to the land and slaveowners in the eastern corridor of Virginia, although the number of white settlers—frontiersmen, yeoman farmers, and the like—grew steadily in the backcountry, western region.

The political clout of Virginia in America's pre- and post-Revolutionary history is legendary. A significant number of the new nation's "founding fathers" and forgers of the U.S. Constitution hailed from Virginia, including George Washington, James Madison, James Monroe, Thomas Jefferson, and Edmund Randolph. Madison, born in Port Conway, Virginia, helped to draft the state's constitution and was the brain behind the much-debated Virginia plan of national government. He was also a leader in proposing that the Articles of Confederation should be scrapped in favor of a stronger central or federal government. It was not by chance that Madison and other Virginians in 1785–1786 also provided the leadership for a commercial conference held at Annapolis to iron out uniform commercial regulations, duties, and currency laws in the new nation.

Virginia's leaders were also important brokers in the U.S. Constitution's great compromise between the North and the South over the issue of slavery. Madison reasoned on behalf of all southern big plantation owners that although slavery was an evil, "dismemberment of the union would be worse." It was exceedingly clear from the beginning, then, that Virginia and the other southern colonies had no plans to give up slavery. In fact, when the Virginia state constitution was adopted in 1776, it clearly discriminated against small landowners in favor of those white men in the east who owned land in excess of twenty-five acres. The western counties or backcountry of the colony relied much less on slaves. Between the Blue Ridge and the Allegheny mountains settled mostly poor immigrant Germans, Scotch-Irish, and eastern-minded, landowning Anglo settlers. Completely west of the Alleghenies were mostly German and northern immigrants who were not sympathetic to slavery. The men residing in this portion of the state continued an unrelenting quest for real democracy—that is, they wanted one man, one vote, and better representation in the state's government. To no avail, delegates from this region attempted to make their voices heard throughout the history of the colony and particularly in a series of documented westward conventions held in Staunton in 1816 and 1825.

Year after year and decade after decade up to the Civil War, the eastern-dominated General Assembly denied the faster growing white male population in the west the democratic process westerners thought to be fair and reasonable. For instance, little was accomplished for the west at the 1829–1830 constitutional convention held at Richmond, except that the state was divided into four distinct districts: Tidewater, Piedmont, the Valley, and Trans-Allegheny. By the time it was granted, the reapportionment of the senate did provide better representation from western counties, but it was not enough to placate those counties that had been accustomed to short shrift. Nor did the constitutional convention provide what the western counties wanted most: one man, one vote.

The counties in the Trans-Allegheny district also needed and wanted improved transportation routes, roads and canals, essential to improve the economic outlook of the region and to connect to the rest of the state. Some of the needs of the west were appeased, but generally the landed gentry preserved its lifestyle and political edge. The white males most often appointed, not elected, as political leaders sought to protect the "peculiar" institution of slavery as it ripened in the mid-eighteenth century, at first to provide the labor needed to fashion a superior economy and lifestyle. Later, slaves were also important for breeding and lucrative trade to maintain its lifestyle since "Virginia was living on its slave-capital: blacks formed 50 percent of the Virginia population in 1782, but only 37 percent in 1860—it was selling its blacks to the Deep South" according to historian Paul Johnson. By the 1860s Virginia was concentrating on breeding a "specially hardy type of Negro."[5]

Eastern Virginia's plantation-owning aristocracy carefully engineered the political scene in the state and even nationwide to its favor. In this way, the Virginia colony and later the state, like South Carolina, was inherently antidemocratic in its political practices. Moreover, settlers in the western portion of the colony remained relatively isolated and for many years were hampered in their attempts to secure approval for basic democratic rights. To the increasing gall and dismay of those in the western counties, the hegemony of landowning white males in the east continued to dominate the political and economic scene in Virginia for nearly two centuries. Because of the lack of concord, as early as 1829 there were calls from the west to split the state. In fact, the situation worsened until the time of the Civil War. Numerous attempts were made to find solutions to the transportation problem of the western region and to adjust voting inequities. Apparently, none of the proposed solutions was sincere and significant enough to placate the western portion of the state. A strong sectional divide in the state and nationally was simply inevitable, especially as a result of the doings and destinies of remarkably bold characters. It could be reasoned, for instance, that Nat Turner's 1831 slave revolt in Southampton, Virginia, opened the trap door to a series of other troubling, sometimes violent events that impacted the South and the entire nation. Turner's revolt reverberated far and wide and fed the worst fears of those who dealt in the peculiar institution of slavery. They naturally became more fearful and more restrictive with every rumor of conspiracy or actual revolt.

During the turbulent 1850s there occurred more troubling, sometimes violent events, including the battles fought in "Bleeding Kansas" over the issue of the expansion of slavery. In 1854 Massachusetts abolitionist Eli Thayer organized an aid society to provide enough funds to flood Kansas with anti-slavery forces that would "save" the region from slavery. Roughly two thousand armed settlers went there to live and to ensure that the region would grow up without the ill of slavery. Pro-slavery Southerners had other notions, as they also encouraged settlement in the area and came armed to manipulate Kansas politically toward slavery. The battles that ensued were violent and severe enough that Kansas was said to be "bleeding." Also having a tremendous impact on the tense national political landscape, the U.S. Supreme Court's decision against Dred Scott in 1857 and John Brown's failed 1859 raid at the Harper's Ferry federal arsenal signaled that no reconciliation was likely between the North and the South. Brown became the ultimate martyr for the abolitionists. His hanging had the impact of causing abolitionists and pro-slavery sympathizers mostly in the South to become even more vehement in their postures.

By the eve of the Civil War, sectional differences gurgled to the surface in Virginia just as they had become intolerable nationally. Given her size and influence, it was not surprising that Virginia was the scene of two of the most poignant slavery-connected events in the history of the nineteenth-century South: Nat Turner's revolt in 1831 and the hanging of John Brown in 1859. These events did not deter Virginia from slavery. It was too late and Virginia was too much attached to a major economic investment. The investment was locked in tandem with the lifestyle and preferences of the landed gentry.

THE CIVIL WAR AND STATEHOOD

As a result of sectional differences over issues very similar to those brewing in Virginia, the two major regions of the nation were in a political dead heat by 1860 when Abraham Lincoln was elected to the U.S. presidency. Lincoln had run on the newly formed Republican Party ticket and, despite his attempts to moderate the view, he and the party were perceived to be controlled by the abolitionists. Lincoln's election practically ensured that the already recalcitrant slaveholding South would leave the Union. When the Civil War came, it did so with such a vengeance that no compromise between the North and the South was possible. Likewise, western Virginia counties began their agonistic split from the paternalistic eastern portion of the state. When John S. Carlile, an ardent unionist and spokesman for western Virginia delegates, spoke at the Richmond convention, he denounced secession and concluded that "with the dissolution of this Union, I hesitate not to say, the sun of our liberties will have set forever."[6] Carlile was right. After the Richmond meeting there would be no reconciliation of eastern and western Virginia. From that point on, West Virginia's statehood quest became somewhat complex, the actual process of which was a checkered story that follows the fault line of the Civil War and continues for almost a decade beyond.

Virginia was not in the first batch of six states to leave the Union, but soon after it did, hell seemed to break loose. South Carolina, a hotbed where issues connected to slavery were concerned, was the first to secede in 1860. It was followed quickly by Mississippi, Alabama, Florida, Louisiana, and Georgia to form the Confederate States of America. Foremost in the constitution of the new Confederate government headed by Jefferson Davis, a Kentucky-born, large plantation owner in Mississippi, was protection for the institution of slavery. Davis well understood the institution, for he was a rich planter or "cotton nabob" who had a vested interest in protecting his own slave property. Shortly after the Civil War began at Fort Sumter in coastal South Carolina in January 1861, a convention of men meeting at Richmond on April 17 voted 88 to 55 that Virginia should also leave the Union. Ratification of Virginia's bold secession ordinance by voters did not take place immediately, but authorities at Richmond still began the call for troops. Although Virginia was not in the first wave to secede, her moves were swift and decisive when she did join other southern states leaving the Union: North Carolina, Tennessee, and Arkansas. Even the wording of the Ordinance of Secession was not minced regarding the fact that protection of Virginia's right to slavery was the essential issue. The ordinance declared boldly that Virginia was injured and oppressed and therefore "in the full possession and exercise of all the rights of sovereignty which belong to a free and independent State." The federal government had "perverted" its powers according to the ordinance, "not only to the injury of the people of Virginia, but to the opposition of the Southern slaveholding States." Like other southern states, Virginia simply wanted to be left alone to call its own shots—to exercise its state's rights—especially regarding the issue of slavery, which constituted a major economic investment.

In short order after the Ordinance of Secession, the Harper's Ferry arsenal and the Norfolk navy yard were seized from the federal government by Virginia Confederate forces. Citizens of eastern Virginia did indeed ratify the ordinance on May 23, and after that there was absolutely no turning back. Emboldening the first group of states that had already seceded, Virginia played no small role in the Confederacy nor in the forty-eight-month-long horrific Civil War that ensued. Effectively two separate nations came to a violent, tragic, bloody confrontation, each charging that the other had caused the breakup of the Union. After Virginia voters ratified the secession ordinance, President Lincoln gave the order to advance federal troops from Ohio commanded by Major-General George B. McClellan, who crossed into western Virginia several days later. The general aim was to get control of the Virginia Central Railroad and all the lines operating east of White Sulphur Springs in what is now West Virginia. This feat would provide a direct link to the Confederate capital, Richmond.

The first battle after Ft. Sumter, fought at Philippi (West Virginia), was small in the scheme of the war, but significant as a propaganda victory for the Union. Confederates were defeated there, and Union troops gained control of Monongahela Valley and important railroads in the region. By the end of 1861, Union troops were credited with freeing antisecession mountain residents in West Virginia. Adding to the irony of the history of the region, two former Virginia governors, both Confederates, both army generals, and former political enemies were at White Sulphur Springs during the summer of 1861 locked in discussions about military strategies and tactics. Generals John Floyd and Henry Wise were said to have bickered for "days and weeks" amid the "oaks, cottages and porches of the South's premiere resort," the Old White Hotel.[7] General Robert E. Lee was ordered to the area and arrived to find "chaos, sickness, rain and more rain." Meanwhile, the lovely hotel-resort, now known as "Greenbrier," was used as a hospital for the Confederacy until 1863.

After Virginia's bold Ordinance of Secession, the *Wheeling Intelligencer* noted on April 25, 1861, that about 1,000 to 1,200 enthusiastic citizens of Harrison County assembled at the Court House in what has come to be known as the Clarksburg convention. At the Clarksburg meeting delegates declared that Virginia had no official Ordinance of Secession because essentially the process had not been democratic. The citizens assembled at Clarksburg also declared that they were very much still in allegiance to the federal government and felt the need to "look to and provide for" their "own safety."

The Clarksburg meeting was to be followed by a series of meetings at Wheeling, the first of which was to organize opposition to secession. Divided about procedures, some preferring moderation, some not, the delegates struggled to find their way. Right from the start, the legitimacy of delegates attending became an issue at the first Wheeling convention. General John Jay Jackson of Wood County moved that "any gentleman who is present from any county in Northwestern Virginia" should be received as a delegate at the convention.[8] Democrat John S. Carlile was also a delegate to the Wheeling meetings and had in fact been a pro-Union leader at the Richmond secession meeting. He also advocated against Virginia's breakaway politics. Carlile was apparently so detested by other Democrat-secessionists that his life was threatened. One eyewitness in attendance at the Richmond meeting, William Henry Edwards of Kanawha County, described Carlile as "bright and able" but "very obnoxious to the secessionists."[9] Nevertheless he would continue to play a key role in West Virginia's statehood throughout the process.

At this juncture Carlile was concerned about the status of the delegates. He wanted them all to be official representatives to the convention. To this, General Jackson responded that it would be too difficult to tell who the real delegates were. He seemed to think that if a man did not mind taking on the responsibility of being a delegate, he should be accepted. And so the discussions went, often bogged down in diatribe, until John Burdett of Taylor reminded those attending that time was of the essence. Burdett did not favor more talk at the convention; he wanted action through "stern deliberation, and a resolve to do what is right to defend and protect ourselves." Carlile was not nitpicking; for him there seemed to be a larger gut issue, so to speak. He did not want to see Virginia divided, period. Carlile apparently wanted the middle ground—that is, no talk of secession from Virginia and no interference in the state's affairs from Washington.

Some of the men connected with the secession process had no doubt been posturing. If Virginia, the most powerful of the southern states, threatened to leave the Union, then the president, meddlesome Republicans, and those likeminded would back off and leave the South to run its own affairs. The thinking was that "if Virginia cast her lot with the southern states, it would make for peace" not war.[10] But the secession ordinance had taken place, so the only strategy Carlile could assume after that was to charge that it was illegal. And so it had been illegal, but Virginia had broken away to the Confederacy, the war had begun, and there was nothing that Carlile could do to reverse the process. To the consternation of some of his pro-Union peers, Carlile voiced his view in meetings around western counties that Virginia's secession was illegal. By the time he reached Lewis County, he was threatened with hanging for treason. Perhaps in naivete or in stubbornness, as the war loomed, Carlile pressed two points: first, that the delegates should be legal; and second, that the convention at Wheeling should repudiate "monstrous usurpations" and show its loyalty to both Virginia and to the Union.

The second Wheeling convention met first on June 13, 1861, to pursue the urgent business of forming a new government of Virginia. The first clause of Article 4, Section 3, of the U.S. Constitution clearly forbids the division of a state without its own consent.

> New states may be admitted by the Congress into this Union; but no new State shall be formed or erected within the Jurisdiction of any other State; nor any State be formed by the Junction of two or more States, or Parts of States, without the Consent of the Legislatures of the States concerned....

With this in mind, while Union troops held the advantage in the area around Randolph County, delegates from forty-six western counties met at

Wheeling on June 11, 1861, supposedly to address the constitutional require-ment that West Virginia should have the approval of Virginia. Technically, however, the consent requirement was never properly addressed because those delegates, representing only some of the western and northwestern counties, could not by law legislate and make decisions as if they represented the entire state. The men meeting at Wheeling, in the upper northwestern corner of Virginia near Ohio, did not have the support of the eastern portion of the state nor did they have the support of Confederates in their own boundaries, but the delegates drew up a state constitution anyway. The constitution they drafted was ratified in an election open only to those willing to take an oath to the United States.

An oddity in itself, the second convention opened with one hundred dele-gates attending from thirty-four counties. Some of the delegates were former members of the Virginia assembly and a few were military authorities. Ap-parently, some of the western counties were not represented, although this second Wheeling convention appointed itself the official, legitimate govern-ment of Virginia. As a precursor to congressional approval for the new state of West Virginia, the Restored or Reorganized Government of Virginia was set up at Wheeling during this second Wheeling convention and, at least in the mind of President Lincoln, began to function as the official government. Constituting a "first" in American statehood history, both Virginia govern-ments collected taxes and had authority in their designated jurisdictions. The irony here is that the old State of Virginia government had seceded in April of 1861, but in numerous ways, such as tax collection, it rivaled the Restored Government. At least some of the citizens in both regions must have been confused by the political mess, but 30,000 of the white male population appar-ently knew enough to take sides by enlisting to fight with either the Union or with the Confederacy.

Meanwhile delegates at Wheeling, representing the Restored Government, elected a new governor, Francis H. Pierpoint. They also elected John Carlile and Waitman T. Willey as U.S. senators and Jacob Blair, William G. Brown, and Kellian V. Whaley as members of the House representing pro-Union Virginia. Amid differences that would later come to a boiling point, these legislators generally continued the strategic planning and politicking necessary to move the statehood process forward. While the delegates at Wheeling worked to ready western counties for statehood, Union troops were made available to guard the polls as thirty-nine counties voted for restoration of Virginia.

The western region's pro-South sympathizers from within made their voic-es heard too, mostly by enlisting to fight. Perhaps no Confederate-minded western Virginian better symbolized the pulse of the Old South than Thomas Jonathan Jackson or General "Stonewall" Jackson who, ironically, was born in 1824 at Clarksburg in Harrison County, the seat of significant initial pro-Union activity. Jackson's birthplace did not hint at his choice of political alignment. Jackson had resigned from the army in 1852, but at the start of the Civil War, he joined the Confederate Army from Virginia Military Institute, where he was teaching artillery tactics and philosophy. He eventually became one of the Confederate Army's most important, high-ranking, and legendary officers. A graduate of West Point, the U.S. Military Academy, Jackson was devoutly religious and said to be a brilliant military strategist who and earned the nickname "Stonewall" as a result of his cool during the tumult of battle. His diversionary tactics and maneuvers during the Shenandoah Valley campaign have been well recorded. The valley was important in Civil War history because it provided a railroad corridor for moving troops and supplies. Wounded by friendly fire at Chancellorsville, Jackson died of pneumonia on May 10, 1863, and was buried at Richmond, the Confederate capital, just prior to West Virginia's official statehood.

Symbolic of the pro-Union resolve from the western region was Major-General Jesse L. Reno, a native of Wheeling in Ohio County. Reno is said to be West Virginia's most "distinguished son" who fought for the Union. He too was a graduate of the Military Academy at West Point, and was an accomplished army officer in numerous battles in Mexico in the late 1840s. Whereas Stonewall Jackson was a distinguished professor at the Virginia Military Academy (VMI), Reno taught mathematics at West Point. A triple irony links Jackson and Reno. The first is that they were both educators and probably two of the greatest military minds of nineteenth-century West Virginia's Civil War history, and, of course, both were natives of strongholds of pro-Union sentiment, Wheeling and Clarksburg. From the same region of western Virginia, they were both high-ranking officers killed before the statehood question was settled.

Wheeling, it should be remembered, was the site of numerous meetings, fourteen in all, connected with West Virginia's statehood. On October 4, 1861, the work of the Wheeling delegates culminated into an "Ordinance to Provide for the Formation of a New State out of a Portion of the Territory of this state," which was put to vote in western Virginia. Returns showed that 18,408 votes favored the new state and 781 were against.

THE CONSTITUTIONAL CONVENTION

Delegates assembled in Wheeling from November 26, 1861, until February 20, 1863, to produce a constitution for the proposed new state of Kanawha. While much time was taken by squabbling over delegates' credentials and confusion about what the boundaries of the state should be, as well as by the usual job of constitution building, the debates about the name of the new state and how it would handle the slavery issue exposed the true feelings and beliefs that lay behind the movement for statehood.

One of the first matters of debate among this delegation of mostly native Virginian lawyers, farmers, physicians, ministers, and merchants was the name of the state itself. While the voters had approved the ordinance with the name of Kanawha stipulated as a compromise, feelings remained strong among some delegates that naming the new state after the Kanawha rivers would leave it without a clear identity to the world. Making Virginia part of the name of the future state would give it place, gravity, and historical meaning. On the other hand, ridding the new state of any reference to its past connection to the dreaded state of Virginia was deemed by some to be vital to the state's new identity. This debate was emblematic of the strong divisions that characterized the political realities of the times.

Harmon Sinsel of Taylor Country was the first to rise in objection to the name Kanawha by moving that it be stricken:

> Mr. President, one reason I have for striking it out is that I am a Virginian; I was born and raised in Virginia, and I have ever been proud of the name. I admit that Virginians have done wrong—that many of them in this rebellion have disgraced themselves; but that has not weaned me from the name. When we look back into history and see the origin of the name—Virginia, from the Virgin Queen—the queen who swayed the scepter of England with so much glory and renown—we might almost go back a little further to Virginia, the Virgin. It always makes me think of the Virgin Mary, the mother of our blessed Redeemer. It is a name that I almost revere; and I am utterly opposed to leaving it out and substituting the name "Kanawha" in its stead.

James Henry Brown, a lawyer from Kanawha Country, not surprisingly disagreed:

> It has been said by gentlemen that they cherish the name of Virginia, from the source, from the Virgin Queen after whom it was named, but, sir, when this was mentioned, I confess my mind reverted to the fact that that virgin was not above suspicion (laughter) that the history that tells the truth tells of dalliances not to the credit of that virgin, and we need seek no honor or pleasure in the recollection. I only regret that our old mother state has been caught in dalliance from which we are trying to rid ourselves by a division of our territory.

John Powell, a minister from Harrison Country, said that his constituents had wanted the name of the new state to be Western Virginia. Thomas Trainer, a minister from Marshall County allowed that

> I have no particular objections to the word "Kanawha." They have a very beautiful river down there, a very beautiful valley, and I suppose they are very clever people; but I think, sir, we may get a more proper name for this new State than Kanawha. I think that we can find a name that will identify us so that everybody will know who we are and where we are and the material out of which we are made.

Edward Mahon, a farmer from Jackson County, said that he preferred the names "Western Virginia, or New Virginia, or some other name." His constituents "had great objections" to the name of Kanawha. Daniel Lamb, a cashier from Ohio County, took the resolute position that "if Kanawha is stricken out, I do not want to see anything that has Virginia to it inserted in the blank." Lamb spoke for those who could no longer tolerate Virginia's "oppression" or denial of "our proper share in the representation a government of the State," the very things that generated the call for separation.

> What has been the policy of Virginia throughout? Are we going to keep that policy along with the name, when we come here for the very purpose of revolutionizing that policy in every respect almost in which it is impossible for us to do so? Are we still to retain the name? Are we to change everything in Virginia but the name? Shall we make a change in everything—in all the essentials—and yet stick upon this slight matter? Shall we proclaim in the very act which this Convention is now about to adopt that we feel grateful for the favor of the State of Virginia as heretofore bestowed upon us? No, gentlemen, no! I want to cut loose from these recollections. I want to have a new State, not merely in substance, but even in name. A resident of the state as I have been more than thirty years, I have no hesitation in proclaiming to this Convention and my constituents that there is nothing in the conduct of the State of Virginia to the people of western Virginia that entitles her or the name to our attachment.

In spite of high-minded rhetoric and deeply felt convictions on both sides, the final vote on the name of the new state was lopsided. West Virginia was the choice of thirty delegates. Only nine delegates wanted to keep the name Kanawha. The names Western Virginia, Allegheny, and Augusta received a total of five votes.

The constitutional convention delegates had sought to avoid the issue of slavery as much as possible. Slavery was viewed by most practical politicians as a no-win issue that led to predictable speechifying rather than resolution. When Congress imposed the constitutional requirement of gradual emancipation as a condition for statehood, a discussion of slavery could no longer be avoided. Senator Willey addressed the convention. He told the delegates that he had no intention of discussing the morality of slavery and in fact, it was unimaginable that slavery could exist in West Virginia, a land sandwiched between the free states of Pennsylvania and Ohio. Indeed, there were so few slaves that their emancipation was a matter of small importance. Willey argued that the evidence was clear: states in which there was free labor had faster population growth and stronger economic development. Giving birth to the new state encumbered by slavery would hinder its growth and development. Perhaps even more importantly, from a practical political point of view, Congress had the right and the power to determine the qualifications for any new state to enter the Union. If the delegates, who had labored over a year on a constitution, wanted statehood without delay, they needed to accept the amendments made by Congress to that constitution.

The debate formed around a resolution introduced by one of the delegates and amended by another that the owners of slaves emancipated under the provisions of the constitution should be "constitutionally and legally entitled to recover the actual value of such slaves at the time of emancipation, if they have not forfeited that right by disloyal acts." Lewis Ruffner, a salt manufacturer from Kanawha County, was dismayed that the compromise on slavery—to let future legislatures deal with it—agreed to earlier by the convention and voted on by the people was subverted by Congress. It was understood, he claimed, "on all hands that in our good time we would adopt the system of emancipation." He went on:

> I know sir, it is a very ungracious matter for a man who is a slave holder in these times of madness on that question to say anything about a just protection of the rights of a slave holder; but, sir, this madness will pass away and justice will have to be done sooner or later to all classes of our community if we expect to maintain in its integrity the principles of our Constitution. I look upon this stand taken by the members opposing this proposition as abolition in its sentiment. No class in the community except abolitionists outright ask for the abolition of slavery without compensation....

Moses Tichenell, a minister from Marion County, rose to call Ruffner to order, remarking that "I deem it a slander on me to call me an abolitionist."

The 1860 U.S. Census had counted 12,600 slaves in the counties that were to make up the state of West Virginia. The delegates had determined that 1,500 slaves would remain to be paid for when the congressional formula had worked its way out. At $300 each, considered a high price by some, the compensation package would come to $450,000. Some delegates thought that amount a small price to pay to finally get rid of slavery, but the federal government, since it mandated the emancipation formula, should pay the money to make it happen. John Boggs, a farmer from Pendleton County, expecting to find harmony at the convention, was disappointed at the state of dissension. He had a different view of the matter.

> The negro question, that is the thing that drove us off from eastern Virginia, because we were in bondage by the negro. Our foes there owned them and we wished to be free, and therefore we clung to that thing called the new State. We did it under arms, because what voting we do we are compelled to do in that way. It does appear to me at least the money spent in arguing this negro question, if it had been appropriated to the defense of the frontier, it would have done more good than all your arguments.

To many delegates, lawyer Richard Lauck among them, the slavery issue was a simple property issue. "The man that owns a servant, it is his property, just as his house, or ox, or anything else." The constitution protects all property. Lauck refused to place one species of property above another and was, therefore, against a specific compensation resolution. "Why should negro property override everything else?" he asked. "That is what has brought on this rebellion." Lauck saw the "old fogyism" of eastern Virginia, which had been the source of complaint and oppression, rising up in the new state. William Stevenson, a farmer from Wood County, figured that there were only 200 loyal slaveholders in the entire new state, and he was outraged at the prospect of even mentioning compensation for emancipated slaves. He feared that the public reaction would do harm to the nascent state, given the fact that Virginia had taxed "everything the non-slaveholder had down to the smallest articles...on their full cash value, while a slave worth $1,500 to $2,000, under the same kind of legislation could not be taxed more than $300 worth of real estate." Publicly bringing up a history of taxation discrimination against non-slaveholders would be unwise.

Dr. Samuel Griffith, who considered the epithet abolitionist "no stigma," told his fellow delegates that he had talked to people in Wheeling and they would vote two to one against the new state if it contained a provision to compensate slaveholders. He said that all of the people of Wheeling he talked with "will never consent to the principle of paying rich aristocrats. Slaveholders, who have ruled everything from the commencement of the government until now; have broken up the government for their negroes, a species of property that never did them any good; they will not do it."

In the end, the argument that statehood would be held up if the convention did not act positively on the congressional amendment won the day. The constitution would have no special provision for the compensation of slaveholders whose slaves were freed, and West Virginia would enter the Union constitutionally committed to the gradual emancipation of the slaves within its borders.

THE CONSTITUTION OF 1863

Some delegates may have had a sentimental attachment to the name Virginia, but there was no attachment to what was viewed as Virginia's discriminatory taxation and representation policies. All the delegates wanted to create a new order of government, based on a structure of counties and townships working in harmony with each other. They tried to avoid the contentious slavery issue, just as the Founding Fathers of the United States had, but Congress would not let them do it.

The first article of the constitution contained acknowledgement of West Virginia's confused boundary situation as well as a commitment to put to rest the long-held complaint about representation. Forty-four former counties of Virginia were made part of the new state. Seven more counties, pending their approval of the constitution, may be added later. West Virginia also claimed for itself "so much of the bed, banks, and shores of the Ohio river as appertained to the State of Virginia." Section 6 states clearly that "every citizen shall be entitled to equal representation in the Government, and in all apportionments of representation, equality of numbers of those entitled thereto shall as far as possible, be preserved."

The second article of the constitution laid out a familiar bill of rights in ten sections. Article 3 gave white male citizens who had been residents of the state for one year and residents of the county in which they were voting for thirty days the right to vote. Minors, paupers, and those convicted of treason, of a felony, or bribery in an election were specially excluded. Impeachment for "maladministration, corruption, incompetence, neglect of duty, or any high crime or misdemeanor was permitted. But anyone engaged in dueling could not hold any "office of honor, trust or profit under this State."

Article 4 set out the legislature, which was composed of a senate and a house of delegates. There were to be eighteen senators and forty-seven delegates, those numbers to be increased if and as additional counties came into the state. The senators, serving two-year terms, were to be elected from a minimum of nine senatorial districts, which were to be "equal, as nearly as practicable, in white population, according to the United States census." Delegates, serving one-year terms, were to be elected from delegate districts in a somewhat complicated formula that permitted for the representation of all the counties. The legislature was to meet "once every year, and not oftener, unless convened by the Governor." Wheeling was made the capital until a permanent seat of government was established by law. Senators and delegates were to receive not more than $3.00 a day when in session, and a session was not to exceed forty-five days unless there were special circumstances. Travel expenses were to be reimbursed at the rate of ten cents per mile.

Executive power was vested in a governor by Article 5. The governor was to be paid $2,000 per year and serve a two-year term. He also had to live in the capital. This article also called for the election of a secretary of state, a treasurer, and an auditor at the same time gubernatorial elections were held. Interestingly, the auditor's annual salary of $1,500 per year was set at $100 more than the salary of the treasurer. Article 6 vested judicial power in a Supreme Court of Appeals and nine Circuit Courts. The three Supreme Court judges were to be elected statewide and hold office for terms of twelve years. Circuit Court judges were to be elected by the voters in the circuits and hold office for terms of six years. Circuit Court was expected to be held at least four times a year in each county. Section 16 called for the election of an attorney general at the same time governors were elected.

Article 7 set up structures for county and township governance. Each county was to be divided "into not less than three, nor more than ten townships, laid off as compactly as practicable, with reference to natural boundaries, and containing, as nearly as practicable, an equal number of white population, but not less than four hundred." The voters of each township were to elect a supervisor, a clerk, and a surveyor of roads for each precinct in the township. The supervisors chosen in the townships then constitute a board that can enact ordinances and be sued. The supervisors of the county were to be responsible for administering all "internal affairs and fiscal concerns" of their county. Provisions were also made for every county to elect a sheriff, a prosecuting attorney, a surveyor of lands, a recorder, and at least one assessor.

Taxation and finance were covered in the eighth article. Real and personal property was to be taxed in proportion to its value and uniformly throughout the state. Provisions were made for a $1.00 per capita tax on all white males twenty-one years of age and older and an annual tax to defray government expenses. Debt could be contracted by the state only "to meet casual deficits in the revenue, to redeem previous liability of the State, to suppress insurrection, repel invasion, or defend the State in time of War." The new state further agreed to assume "an equitable proportion of the public debt of the Commonwealth of Virginia" prior to January 1, 1861, and provide a sinking fund to liquidate that debt. Article 9 dealt with provisions for forfeited and unappropriated lands. Article 10 established a school fund, the interest from which was to be applied annually "to the support of free schools throughout the State."

Article 11 covered miscellaneous items. Lotteries were outlawed, but the regulation or prohibition of the sale of intoxicating liquors by future legislatures was permitted. Churches and religious organizations could not be chartered through incorporation by the state. Congressional districts were provided for the election of congressmen and common law and such laws of Virginia "not repugnant to" the new state's constitution were left in force until revised by future legislatures. Section 7, however, was the most controversial and certainly the most curious given that the country was deep into a civil war caused ostensibly by the slavery issue. Originally, this section had stated that "no slave shall be brought, or free person of color be permitted to come into this State for permanent residence." The Willey Amendment revised this to read: "The children of slaves born within the limits of this State after the 4th of July, 1863, shall be free, and no slave shall be permitted to come into the state for permanent residence therein." This amendment, in acknowledgment of congressional pressure, would be changed further by Congress before West Virginia would be accepted into the Union.

FEDERAL APPROVAL OF STATEHOOD

The General Assembly of the Restored Government of Virginia had met in Wheeling in May 1862 and passed an act for the formation of a new state within the jurisdiction of Virginia. This act helped to legitimize the work of the convention by fulfilling a constitutional mandate. Commissioners were appointed to bring the question before the U.S. Congress in what was then called "Washington City." The matter was immediately referred to the Committee on Territories as Senate Bill No. 365.

While the U.S. Senate began the actual debate on West Virginia statehood in June 1862, the Civil War carried on with devastating effect. Just the month before, the *Virginia* and the *Monitor* shelled each other for hours, and Union General McClellan transported his troops by ship to Norfolk in an effort to get at the Confederate capital, Richmond. Following that, in what has come to be known as the Peninsula Campaign, McClellan cautiously moved up Virginia's coastal waterways toward the Confederate capital to attack Confederate troops in Richmond by surprise. Joseph E. Johnson, commander of the Confederate Army of Northern Virginia, retreated at first, then wheeled around in a surprise attack that ended indecisively. By the end of 1862 the battle at Antietam Creek in Maryland, said to be the bloodiest day of the war, had made it clear that there was no hope for a swift end to the war. Massive desertions and heavy casualties were the norm following Antietam, where 5,000 died and 19,000 were wounded. The overall statistics of the war are as overwhelming now as they were staggeringly sad news at the time: more than 620,000 men dead, 360,000 Union and 260,000 Confederate. Another 275,000 Union and 190,000 Confederate troops were wounded.

The Senate debate on West Virginia's fate waged on through the summer of 1862, being taken up on June 23, 26, 27 and again in July on the 1st, 7th, and finally on the 14th almost as if there was no war at hand. The bill to admit West Virginia to statehood passed with twenty-five yeas and eleven nays on July 14. Still at issue was an amendment proposed by Massachusetts Senator Sumner to strike out words in lines sixteen and seventeen: "the children of all slaves born within the limits of said State shall be free," and insert "Within the limits of said State there shall be neither slavery nor involuntary servitude, otherwise than in punishment of crime whereof the party shall be duly convicted." To no avail, Sumner reiterated that he wished to see no form of slavery in the new state of West Virginia.

> [W]e all know that it takes but very little slavery to make a slave state with all the virus of slavery. Now, by my vote no new state shall come into this Union, and Senators into this body with this virus. Enough have our public affairs been disturbed, and enough has the Constitution been poisoned. The time has come for the medicine.

The debate dragged on and was interrupted on several occasions so that votes could be taken on other pressing Senate bills. Efforts to fine-tune the bill regarding the issue of slavery continued. Were the people of the new state to decide the issue of slavery for themselves? Was gradual emancipation better for the new state than "exceedingly harsh" or "abrupt" emancipation? What was to become of older slaves who had been with their families for a long while, a group Senator Benjamin Wade of Ohio referred to as "residuum?" Senator Wade insisted that the bill to admit West Virginia needed to be "smoothed down, softened and rendered harmonious" to be accepted by the Senate.

The U.S. Senate debate on the proposed new state's fate was arduous and ironic. More than any other issue, slavery slowed the process of statehood for

West Virginia. It was not surprising that Senator Sumner, an avowed abolitionist, radical Republican, and a member of the U.S. Senate's Committee on Territories, continued to play a leading role in the West Virginia statehood debate. Sumner had done more than distinguish himself in the U.S. Senate and in the anti-slavery fight. He had become a martyr for the abolitionist cause as a result of being beaten nearly to death by a pro-slavery South Carolina senator. In 1856 Sumner was violently and brutally attacked by the nephew of South Carolina Senator Andrew Butler following an insulting speech against pro-slavery advocates and Senator Butler. Butler had been singled out in Sumner's tirade and although the South Carolina senator was absent, his nephew Preston Brooks accosted and struck Sumner repeatedly with a walking cane until he was practically unconscious. Brooks was censured in the Senate for his behavior, but he was hardly praised in his home state for the atrocious attack on Sumner. He was also easily reelected in South Carolina. Sumner went back to Massachusetts for a lengthy recuperative period. He too was reelected and played the role of conscience when the slavery issue was concerned in the West Virginia statehood debate. Ironically, if not surprisingly, slavery was an impeding issue in West Virginia statehood, even in the middle of the Civil War.

The beating endured by Senator Sumner clearly did not deter his anti-slavery fight. By 1862 he was back, unrelenting, on the Senate floor making trouble for those who wanted to slip West Virginia into statehood with a clause that would have provided for gradual emancipation of slavery. Senator Wade introduced the Senate debate on West Virginia statehood on June 26, 1862, with the proviso that "from and after the 4th day of July 1863, the children of all slaves born within the limits of the state shall be free." Senator Sumner countered with his own amendment to the bill. He found the provision regarding slavery objectionable, reasoning that as "short as life may be it is too long for slavery...."

Restored Virginia Government Senator John Carlile of Harrison County was also a member of the Committee on Territories in the U.S. Senate, but seemingly more than any other senator he retarded the process. It should be remembered that Carlile had led the pro-Union walkout of delegates from the secession convention at Richmond in 1861. While he managed to be part of the statehood process from beginning to end, here now on the Senate floor in July 1862 Carlile managed rather eloquently to be a thorn in the side of Senator Sumner and others, including his nemesis of sorts, Senator W. T. Willey of Monongalia. Carlile, who seemed at times to be operating on principle, was determined not to make any change in "organic laws," as he put it, until the proposed change was "first submitted to the people of the State, and by them ratified and adopted." Although pro-Union and pro-admission of the new state of West Virginia, he remained adamant that the people in the western counties and only those citizens should decide the key issues of statehood, especially slavery.

Carlile reminded fellow legislators that there was something strangely inequitable about the voting process that had occurred in western Virginia. Even now, months after the Wheeling conventions, Carlile was a stickler for procedure. He did not like the idea that a new state would be admitted to the Union when so few people had participated in the process. By his estimation, only 19,000 western Virginia citizens had voted for the new state in comparison to 47,000 who had voted in the last presidential election. According to Carlile "a majority of the voting population within the boundaries of this proposed new state have never assented even to the constitution that is now before you by a direct vote at the polls." He refused to yield the opinion that the new state should decide the issue of slavery in an election, maintaining "I propose to admit her [West Virginia] with the Constitution she has formed for her own government. I am in favor of her admission without conditions upon the precise terms that she asks."

Carlile did not want Congress to tamper with the small number of slaves left in what was soon to be West Virginia. He did not seem to think that the institution was ordained by God, as a few of his fellow senators did; at issue for Carlile was simply that West Virginians should decide for themselves what to do about slavery. The bill to admit West Virginia as proposed by Carlile was never approved. And yet, records of the Senate debate reveal that Carlile continued on in a voluminous mini-filibuster about the need for western Virginia's citizens to decide the issue of slavery. At one point during the deliberations, making his repudiation of Virginia Governor John Letcher and the matter of West Virginia statehood clear, Carlile quoted a long passage from the *National Intelligencer* that had earlier quoted him:

> Let us pursue the policy laid down in the declaration, and let us repudiate Letcher and his transfer; let us assemble a Legislature here of our own, sworn to support, not the southern confederacy constitution, but that which Washington and Madison formed, the Constitution of our fathers, under which we have grown and prospered as never people grew and prospered before.[11]

Despite Carlile's insistence, the Senate did not approve West Virginia's admission when and as he wished. Instead, an amendment offered by Senator Willey pressed concern for slaves in the western counties that were contiguous to Kentucky. It was Waitman Willey's sense that these slaves would be quietly, as he put it "silently" transferred further south, in light of the secession sentiment yet in that region. According to Willey, since the war began there were no more than eight thousand slaves in the proposed state of West Virginia, and they would be best served by gradual emancipation, rather than by the owners selling them farther south. Willey reasoned well that West Virginia was not suited for slavery anyway: "The Slave cannot live there; he cannot exist there; and Eastern Virginia can find argument against me to say I am not true to her interests when I vote in favor of gradual emancipation...."

The debate went on until a compromise was reached between the amendments to the bill proposed by Willey and Senator Wade of Ohio. Senator Willey's proposal permitted the ownership of slaves under the age of twenty-one, while Senator Wade offered that all slaves over twenty-one would be free and younger slaves would receive their freedom at age twenty-one. Haggling over the issue of slavery in the new state went on for weeks. Initially the Senate rejected the statehood bill proposed by Carlile and on July 14, 1862, approved the proposal containing the Willey Amendment. The House of Representatives passed the act on December 10, 1862, and on December 31, President Lincoln signed the bill into law that admitted West Virginia as a new state without abolishing slavery. Handwritten, the enactment document signed by the president was formally titled "An Act For the Admission of the State of West Virginia into the Union and for other Purposes" and it made mention of the delegates who had assembled at Wheeling "for the formation of a new State within the jurisdiction of the said State of Virginia." The president elected to take the whole process of the Wheeling conventions to have been legal and appropriate to the constitutional mandate. In 1863, Berkeley and Jefferson counties, bordered by Maryland and Virginia in what is commonly known as the "eastern gateway" portion of the state, also became part of West Virginia. This addition would be contested later when West Virginia underwent still another hurdle in its statehood history.

The first official year of West Virginia's statehood, 1863, was the violent midpoint of the Civil War, and the nation was in political turmoil. Citizens not even enlisted in the military rampaged. In March of that year a Conscription Act passed by Congress had the effect of declaring all single men between the ages of 20 and 45 and all married men between 20 and 35 eligible for service. Thereafter, draftees were selected by lottery, but the affluent could purchase exemption by paying a $300 fee. The Confederate states had a much-contested draft too. Its Twenty Negro Law provided an exemption for owners of twenty or more slaves, although the law was modified such that planters were required to pay $500 for an exemption. Both conscription laws caused problems, but in New York, demonstrators took to the streets in three days of rioting and destruction. The Colored Orphan Asylum was destroyed and six blacks were killed. Free blacks were now permitted to enlist, to the dismay and resentment of Confederate soldiers, who refused to take black prisoners. By mid-year, the Battle of Chancellorsville had been fought and finished with roughly 1,600 losses on both sides. The Battle of Gettysburg followed from the 1st through the 3rd of July 1863, just days before the U.S. Senate finished its debate on West Virginia's statehood.

Arthur I. Boreman of Wood County became the first unopposed governor of the new state of West Virginia in 1863. Strangely enough, the Restored Government under Governor Francis Pierpont continued too, and in 1865 challenged the legality of West Virginia statehood. Meanwhile, there also existed the Virginia that had broken away to join the Confederate States of

America. That government ended on May 25, 1865, when the Reorganized Government left Alexandria for Richmond to take over the government of Virginia alone.

THE LEGAL CHALLENGE TO STATEHOOD

After the Civil War ended, the Confederate State of Virginia was defunct. Nevertheless, the General Assembly of the government that had declared itself "Restored" and "Reorganized" during the war tried to get the western counties that comprised West Virginia back to Virginia. In late December 1865, the Virginia General Assembly repealed the act of 1863 that had set wheels in motion for West Virginia statehood. In a move that was again destined to ensure its singularity in statehood history, Virginia brought a suit that would effectively dissolve West Virginia. In 1866, to no avail, Virginia, amid all of the desolation and destruction of the Civil War, approached the U.S. Supreme Court in an attempt to regain jurisdiction over what that state still considered to be its western counties. At that time, according to a transcript of the case, Virginia relied almost solely on the "Federal Constitution" defense which ordains that "no State shall, without the assent of Congress, enter into any agreement or compact with [78 U.S. 39, 51] any other State..." especially when controversies existed between the two. Supported by the president, the Senate had debated the matter of West Virginia statehood well. There was little question in the mind of West Virginia that the Supreme Court would decide in her favor.

After the Constitution defense did not work, Virginia yet again tried to regain West Virginia in 1871. The second time, Virginia's legal case was built around the fact that no proper vote had been taken by the people to bring the counties of Berkeley, Jefferson, and Frederick into West Virginia when those counties were admitted in 1863. It was not until 1871 that the Supreme Court ruled, although not unanimously, to let West Virginia statehood stand as it was. The voting justices showed remarkable sensitivity for the fact that the nation's only Civil War–born state had been an oddity from the start. Moreover, regarding the particular counties in question, the Court understood that no proper vote had been taken from those areas and reasoned that "... probably none could be taken under any but a hostile government." As with practically everything concerning West Virginia's statehood process, the U.S. Supreme Court's decision appears to have been laborious. On the one hand, justices considering the case apparently did not want to negate the earlier decision of Congress that admitted West Virginia. On the other hand, the justices made it clear that they were aware that some of the western counties indeed had not voted appropriately. Of the delegates who did vote, some had been self-appointed rather than elected, or possessed dubious delegate status. Not surprisingly, the majority of justices were satisfied that both Virginia—that portion represented by the western delegates—and the U.S. Congress had given West Virginia all of the appropriate consideration that needed to be given for its statehood:

> It is, therefore an inference clear and satisfactory that Congress...intended to consent to the admission of the State with the contingent boundaries provided for in its constitution and in the state of Virginia, which prayed for its admission on those terms, and that in so doing it necessarily consented to the agreement of those States on that subject.... There was then a valid agreement between the two States consented to by Congress.[12]

Statehood was acted on by Congress in 1863 and underscored by the Supreme Court's majority ruling in 1871. By the time of the Court's decision, West Virginia had been confident enough in her status to have an official seal for eight years. The Great Seal of West Virginia was designed by Joseph H. Diss Debar of Doddridge County and bears the legend of the state and the motto "Montani Semper Liberi" ("Mountaineers Are Always Free"). Approved by the legislature on September 26, 1863, about three months after Congress granted statehood, the seal represents West Virginia's ethos, resources, and immense pride. Almost one hundred years later, the official state colors, old gold and blue, were adopted by the legislature in March 1963.

CONCLUSION

West Virginia was a known entity long before the Civil War and its battle for statehood. It was a center for coal mining as well salt and iron production. Wheeling had already become an industrial center. Perhaps more than any other single American, John Brown in 1859 brought attention to Harper's Ferry in soon-to-be West Virginia, when he failed in an attempt to help slaves by raiding the federal arsenal there. Before Brown's coming to Harper's Ferry to pursue the raid that would lead to his hanging and subsequent martyrdom, the area was relatively unknown by the average American citizen. Located reasonably close to the nation's capital, it was, however, known to the federal government as a manufacturing and storage area for weapons. Craftsmen at Harper's Ferry made individually distinctive muskets and rifles. As a result of the U.S. Army's decision to adopt the Hall Rifle in 1819, inventor John H. Hall, a native-born New Englander, was enticed by the federal government to begin a weapons factory at Harper's Ferry.[13] He did so, and introduced the principle of interchangeable parts there between 1824 and 1840.

Still, the process by which West Virginia was admitted to the Union was unusual and paradoxical, not only because it took place during the Civil War and emanated from counties that were themselves divided or because Virginia sued in an attempt to regain the counties that made up West Virginia. The biggest paradox lies deeper in West Virginia's experience. Virginia's eastern landholding elite were a predominant force in the politics and economics of that state and in building the nation through the U.S. Constitution. In the orchestration of these broad powers, representatives of the western counties were largely excluded. In a touch of fate, Virginia turned on itself through the formation of West Virginia. In the fluke of becoming a state, West Virginia challenged everything old elite eastern Virginia stood for, including a clause in the U.S. Constitution that forbade the formation of a new state without its consent—a clause that Virginia's early eastern leaders no doubt had been instrumental in forging.

NOTES

1. Interestingly, the date of Lincoln's signature varies and at least two proclamations exist. One is dated April 1862, and the other December 31, 1862.

2. Quoted in Darlene Hine et al., *The African-American Odyssey*, 2nd ed., Combined Volume (Upper Saddle River, NJ: Prentice Hall, 2002), p. 84.

3. John Alexander Williams, *West Virginia: A History* (Morgantown: West Virginia University Press, 2001), pp. 3–5.

4. See John Murrin's essay "Political Development" in *Colonial British America: Essays in the New History of the Early Modern Era*, ed. Jack Greene and J. R. Pole (Baltimore: Johns Hopkins University Press, 1984), p. 421.

5. Paul Johnson, *A History of the American People* (New York: HarperCollins Publishers, 1997), p. 461.

6. This excerpt from Carlile's speech was quoted in *West Virginia: The Centennial of Statehood 1863–1963: An Exhibition in the Library of Congress*, Washington, DC December 12, 1963 to December 11, 1964, p. 9.

7. Robert S. Conte, *The History of the Greenbrier: America's Resort*, rev. ed. (Charleston, WV: Pictorial Histories, 1998), pp. 59–60.

8. West Virginia Division of Culture and History, "A State of Convenience; The Creation of West Virginia. An Online Exhibit," www.wvculture.org. This website is an extraordinary resource for primary documentation on West Virginia's creation that includes proceeding and debates of constitutional conventions, U.S. Senate debate on West Virginia's admission to the Union, the 1863 West Virginia constitution, as well as many other resources. This online resource has been used extensively throughout this essay and all quotations not otherwise noted have been taken from it. Also of interest is *Acts of the General Assembly, Passed at the Extra Session*, City of Wheeling, May 6, 1862.

9. See William H. Edwards's eyewitness account of the Richmond convention in "A Bit of History," *The West Virginia Historical Magazine Quarterly* (July 1902). (Edwards was a native of Coalburg, Kanawha County, and had been a naturalist and explorer who led an expedition to the Amazon in 1846.)

10. Edwards's account in *West Virginia Historical Magazine Quarterly*, 1902.

11. Quoted from the *National Intelligencer*, June 22, 1861, in the *Proceedings of the United States Senate Debate on West Virginia Statehood*, July 14, 1862.

12. U.S. Supreme Court, *State of Virginia v. State of West Virginia*, 78 U.S. 39 (1870).

13. John Alexander Williams, *West Virginia: A History for Beginners* (Martinsburg, WV: Appalachian Editions, 1997), pp. 122–123.

BIBLIOGRAPHY

Callahan, James M. *History of West Virginia, Old and New.* 3 vols. Chicago: American Historical Society, 1923.

Hall, Granville D. *The Rending of Virginia: A History.* Knoxville: University of Tennessee Press, 2000.

Rice, Otis K. *West Virginia, a History.* Lexington: University of Kentucky, 1985.

West Virginia: The Centennial of Statehood 1863–1963: An Exhibition in the Library of Congress. Washington, DC, December 12, 1963 to December 11, 1964.

Williams, John Alexander. *West Virginia: A History for Beginners.* Martinsburg, WV: Appalachian Editions, 1997.

———. *West Virginia: A History.* Morgantown: West Virginia University Press, 2001.

THE STATE OF WISCONSIN

Admitted to the Union as a State:
May 29, 1848

Jonathan Kasparek

INTRODUCTION

With the admission of Iowa to the Union in 1846, congressional leaders looked forward to quick statehood for the Territory of Wisconsin. After Iowa, the Union consisted of fifteen slave states and fourteen free states; one additional free state was required to restore balance, a principle that had become central to American politics, to the U.S. Senate. Northern leaders were particularly anxious to redress the balance; between the admission of the free states of Maine in 1820 and Iowa in 1846, only one free state, Michigan, had joined the Union in 1837, but four slave states had joined: Missouri in 1821, Arkansas in 1836, Texas in 1845, and Florida in 1845. Moreover, Texas's large area raised the possibility of its division into multiple slave states, a fact that alarmed Free-Soilers and abolitionists in the North. Some in Wisconsin hoped the need for another free state might encourage Congress to provide special benefits as further inducements, as the editor of the *Mineral Point Democrat* noted.[1] Iowa statehood also marked the first trans-Appalachian free state to join the Union without the tutelage imposed by the Northwest Ordinance of 1787, which prohibited slavery in the territory north of the Ohio River. Wisconsin was the last state to be carved out of the Old Northwest and the last, with the exception of the Civil War secession of West Virginia, to be formed east of the Mississippi River. The provisions of the Northwest Ordinance were a bone of contention among state leaders, who believed that Wisconsin's birthright had been infringed upon by earlier states, and among members of Congress, who were anxious to assert their prerogatives over the nearly sixty-year-old document. This disagreement over the ordinance delayed Wisconsin

Wisconsin

Territorial Development:

- The United States obtains future territory of Wisconsin from France through the Treaty of Paris, September 3, 1783
- The United States passes the Northwest Ordinance: territorial claims inherited from colonial charters ceded to the public domain, July 13, 1787
- Future Territory of Wisconsin organized as part of the Northwest Territory, July 13, 1787
- Reorganized as part of the Indiana Territory, 1800–1805
- Reorganized as part of the Michigan Territory, 1805–1809
- Reorganized as part of the Illinois Territory, 1809–1818
- Reorganized as part of the Michigan Territory, 1818–1836
- Reorganized as part of the Wisconsin Territory, July 4, 1836
- Wisconsin admitted into the Union as the thirtieth state, May 29, 1848

Territorial Capitals:

- Belmont, 1836
- Burlington, now part of Iowa, 1836–1838
- Madison, 1838–1848

State Capitals:

- Madison, 1848–present

Origin of State Name: "Wisconsin" means "grassy place" in Chippewa. This name was given to the Wisconsin River, after which the state was named.

First Governor: Nelson Dewey
Governmental Organization: Bicameral
Population at Statehood: 305,391
Geographical Size: 54,310 square miles

statehood as did conflicts among political reformers and conservatives, both of whom wanted to assert political dominance over the constitution. In the end, political compromise resolved the political dispute and generous grants from Congress smoothed over a prolonged and often difficult transition from territory to state.

CREATION OF WISCONSIN TERRITORY

Congress created Wisconsin Territory in 1836 after the administration of the area between the Mississippi River and Lake Michigan had already passed from the Territories of Indiana (1800–1805) to Michigan (1805–1809) to Illinois (1809–1818) and Michigan (1818–1836). While administered from distant Detroit, the area was a virtually autonomous district, still largely inhabited by Native American tribes. Euro-American settlement was concentrated in three areas. A lead mining district straddled the Illinois border just east of the Mississippi River. Another sizable settlement existed near present-day Green Bay, where John Jacob Astor had established a major fur-trading post and where the U.S. Army maintained Fort Howard. Beginning in the 1820s, a third population center based on lake trade began developing along the Lake Michigan coast at present-day Milwaukee. Since the late 1820s, some of the inhabitants of western Michigan had agitated Congress for its own civil government, and in 1828 a bill to divide Michigan Territory and create the "Territory of Huron" was introduced in the House of Representatives, but abandoned during the hectic final days of the John Quincy Adams administration. In 1832, a similar bill died in the House, overshadowed by the tumult surrounding the issue of Michigan statehood and its disputed border with Ohio.[2]

By 1836, with Michigan statehood apparently imminent, its inhabitants west of Lake Michigan again considered their future. Eager for the economic development of the area and tired of Detroit's neglect, they urged Congress to take action. On January 7, 1836, Michigan territorial delegate George W. Jones presented Congress a memorial requesting the formation of a territorial government for what was by then generally known as "Wisconsin" after the area's principal tributary to the Mississippi River, although various spellings (Ouisconson, Wiskonsan, Wisconsan) continued to appear. On January 21, John M. Clayton of Delaware introduced a bill in the Senate to create Wisconsin Territory. In the Senate, action was swift. The bill was referred quickly to Clayton's own Judiciary Committee, which reported it back to the floor on March 28. The Senate passed it the next day. In the House, however, sectional and political rivalries threatened to scuttle the bill. The Northwest Ordinance of 1787 directed that Congress should divide the territory north of the Ohio River into no more than five states and that the southern boundary of the northern two states would be an east-west line drawn from the southernmost point of Lake Michigan. This provision had already been violated with the admission of Ohio, which included a strip of land that was intended for Michigan under the ordinance's provisions. The disputed boundary had produced not only bickering, but also fighting among residents around Toledo. The boundaries of Indiana and Illinois similarly violated this provision. Representative William L. May of Illinois was well aware of the controversy and wanted to be certain that his state's boundaries were not threatened. Defending the sixty-mile strip of northern Illinois from the territorial assertions of Wisconsin's leaders, May secured a provision affirming Illinois's northern boundary. Other House amendments addressed financial considerations. The appropriation for constructing the territorial capitol was changed from 10,000 acres of public land to $20,000, and the governor's salary was reduced from $3,500 to $2,500. Congress passed the amended bill on April 20 with its provisions to take effect July 3, establishing a vast new territory that extended west to the Missouri River and south to the Missouri border.[3]

The Wisconsin Organic Act served as the territory's constitution and established the most liberal framework of government yet seen in an American territory. The Northwest Ordinance originally mandated an initial "district" phase of government under which the territory was governed by an appointed governor and justices who together acted as a territorial legislature, but Congress omitted this phase altogether and instead outlined the more familiar tripartite government. The executive branch consisted of a governor, also acting as superintendent of Indian affairs and commander-in-chief of the militia, appointed by the president for three years and a secretary, attorney, and marshal, all appointed for four years. The bicameral legislature, uncommon in territories prior to this, consisted of a council of thirteen members elected for four years and a house of representatives of twenty-six members elected for two years. The legislature was to meet annually for no more than seventy-five days and Congress reserved the right to veto its acts. Members of the legislature were elected directly by the people. Under earlier territorial governments, the president appointed legislators from a list of nominees approved by a popular vote. The judicial branch consisted of three circuit judges appointed by the president who met periodically as a supreme court to hear appeals from their own decisions. The act also allowed a broad franchise. There was no property requirement and all free white males over age twenty-one could vote. Some local officers were elective, as was the delegate to Congress. Congress gave the territory a firm grounding in legal affairs by establishing the Laws of Michigan Territory as the territorial statutes. In 1839, Congress furthered the democratic nature of the government by granting the right of the legislature to override the governor's veto. In 1843, changes to the Organic Act reduced the terms of office to two years for members of the council and to one year for members of the house and provided for popular election of justices of the peace, sheriffs, and county surveyors. Elections thereby became an annual event in the political life of the state. In 1844, Congress allowed territorial legislatures to apportion themselves and provided for the election of militia officers.[4]

President Andrew Jackson signed the bill immediately, and within a week forwarded to the Senate a list of territorial officers. Delegate George W. Jones had urged the president to appoint those already inhabiting the territory to its offices rather than using the posts as patronage for eastern supporters. Jackson apparently agreed with Jones and to nobody's surprise appointed Jones's close associate General Henry Dodge governor.[5] A military hero and leader among the settlers in the lead district and a loyal Democrat as well, Dodge was extremely popular both among his constituents and with the national government, although his habit of wearing pistols in his belt at formal occasions alarmed some of the territory's more refined inhabitants. The Senate confirmed his appointment at once.

Dodge was a fitting choice for governor. Born in 1786 in Vincennes, Indiana, he had lived in Kentucky and Missouri. His father was a wealthy planter and merchant, and Dodge moved to the lead region in 1827 to expand his father's trade along the Mississippi River. He quickly established himself as the leading figure in the area and led the militia in skirmishes with tribes and negotiated land cessions by the Ho-Chunk. His reputation as an "Indian Fighter" remained intact during his tenure as governor due in part to his frequent concern over the removal of Indians and the threat they posed to white settlers. The Black Hawk War of 1832 made him a military hero and in 1836 he had just returned from military expeditions of exploration in the West. He would go on to a career as governor, delegate to Congress, and U.S. senator.[6] Filling out the rest of the territorial offices were John S. Horner as secretary, the same office he currently held in Michigan Territory, and W. W. Chapman and Francis Gehon (both from western portion of the territory) as attorney and marshal, respectively. Jackson also appointed three judges for the territory, Charles Dunn of Illinois, David Irvin of Wisconsin, and William C. Fazer of Pennsylvania. Elections were held in October, and legislators gathered on October 26.[7]

TERRITORIAL DEVELOPMENT

One of Dodge's first acts as governor was to direct sheriffs to undertake a census of the territory for apportionment to the first legislature. The census revealed a total population of 21,213, roughly half on each side of the Mississippi. On the eastern side of the river, the lead region, including settlements at Mineral Point, Cassville, and Belmont, contained the largest number of people, just over 5,000. Along Lake Michigan, approximately 2,700 lived near the mouth of Fox River in the northeast at present-day Green Bay, and another 2,800 lived near the mouth of the Milwaukee River. Wisconsin was thus split between the mining economy of the southwest and the developing commercial ports of the lakeshore. The characters of these two populations were decidedly different. The lead region tended to be a "floating population" of migrant workers from the south, while beginning in 1837 the eastern portion of the state tended to be settled by homesteaders from New England and New York.[8]

The first territorial election was dominated by personalities rather than by party or platform. The counties sent men of local prominence to the first meeting of the legislature in Belmont, the location specified by Dodge, on October 25. Not surprisingly, delegate George W. Jones of the lead region won the only territory-wide election as delegate to Congress, a fitting reward for his key role in establishing the territory. Dodge outlined the legislature's tasks on October 26. He urged the body to memorialize Congress for a new pre-emption law that would allow squatters to legally claim land on which they had lived before it was opened for general sale. He also called for internal improvements such as lighthouses and harbors on Lake Michigan, improvements to the Mississippi and Rock rivers, and a survey of the Fox and Wisconsin rivers. Dodge's emphasis was on economic and commercial development, a territory tied together by water to export its resources. Other tasks included organizing territorial courts, establishing counties and county seats, and charting a few banks and other corporations.[9]

County offices and county seats provided the opportunity for political patronage, but the biggest prize was the location of the permanent capital, a matter that Governor Dodge left to the legislature. As members championed a variety of sites around the territory, the decision quickly became a contentious and divisive issue. Into this confusion came James Duane Doty, who would become Governor Dodge's chief rival and around whom political factions would coalesce. Doty was born in Salem, New York, in 1799 and moved to Detroit in 1818. The charming and intelligent young Yankee was quickly admitted to the bar and became a major figure in the administration of Governor Lewis Cass. Doty in fact accompanied Cass in his four-month canoe expedition around the western half of the territory. His familiarity with the region resulted in his appointment as "additional judge" for the western district of Michigan and his settlement near Fort Howard on Green Bay. In 1832 he turned to land speculation and became the leading land speculator in the territory, commissioned to lay out roads between Fort Howard and Chicago and between Fort Howard and Fort Crawford. By the time the first territorial legislature met in 1836, Doty knew the area better than anyone else, and he was prepared to make a fortune in its development.[10]

Doty had platted and developed several town sites, but none was more dramatic than Madison, located on an isthmus between two lakes halfway between the Mississippi River and Lake Michigan. Those who were not convinced by the geographic compromise or by the grandiose plat were convinced by generous gifts of city lots. Madison was designated the permanent capital, with Burlington (now in Iowa) as a two-year temporary capital. The legislature later appointed Doty one of three commissioners entrusted with the erection of public buildings in the capital city. Dodge was appalled at the political maneuvering and regretted that Congress had not specified the capital, noting to Jones that he believed it "is to be a bone of Contention for years[.] Speculation and a thirst for gain appears to swallow up and runs everything here[.] Patriotism and duty is apparently lost sight of...." Nonetheless, he stood by his decision and refused to veto the measure.[11]

One of the most pressing issues was the process of extinguishing Indian title to territorial land and opening it to settlement. Throughout the early years in the territory, the settlers eagerly petitioned Congress for a pre-emption law and for laws securing mineral rights to their land. A precursor to settlement and development was the purchase of land from its original inhabitants and the most important duties of the governor in preparation for settlement and eventual statehood were the negotiations of land cessions with the Indian tribes. Wisconsin Territory was home to a large number of native peoples, both indigenous inhabitants and refugees from the east. The largest portions of land were owned by the Ojibwa in the north and west, the Menominee in the east, and the Ho-Chunk in the south, although the scattered patterns of settlement and the presence of recent arrivals made the process of negotiations complicated and often necessitated multiple land cessions. The three principal tribes living in the territory were both agriculturalists and hunter-gatherers. The Menominee lived in numerous villages and practiced small-scale farming and gardening as well as harvesting wild rice. The Ojibwa, too, planted crops, but broke into smaller bands during the winter months to hunt deer and other game. The Ho-Chunk also had several sizable settlements in the south-central part of the territory. The fur trade and the introduction of European trade goods dramatically altered the tribes' economies and made them much more dependent on trade with white settlers as well as increasing intertribal competition over land and resources. The process of negotiating land cession had begun in 1804 when the Sauk and Fox signed treaties ceding much of the lead region, although some bands disputed the authority of negotiations. By 1836, the Menominee had ceded all their territory along Lake Michigan and Green Bay. Bands of Ojibwa, Ottawa, and Potawotami had ceded their lands in the southeast and the Ho-Chunks had ceded their remaining lands south of the Fox River.[12]

The task facing Governor Dodge and his successors was the obtaining of title to almost all land northwest of the Fox-Wisconsin waterway. On September 3, 1836, Dodge negotiated a treaty with the Menominee whereby the tribe agreed to sell over 4 million acres for cash payments, provisions, and annuities totaling approximately $700,000. The Santee Lakota sold their remaining land east of the Mississippi in 1837. The Ho-Chunk signed a treaty in Washington agreeing to give up their land north of the Wisconsin River, although their continued presence vexed settlers for years. The Ho-Chunk refused to move west of the Mississippi supposedly because they feared attack by the Sauk and Fox, which had already relocated, and they returned continually to their old grounds. Dodge's determination to remove them became a recurring theme in his administration. He had little sympathy for them. "The Indians," he noted, "must see and feel, if necessary, the power of the Government to enforce a strict observance of Treaties...."[13] Many viewed the removal of the Ho-Chunk as an eventual necessity, but Dodge also perceived the tribes as an immediate threat. In 1837, he recommended that the legislature establish more militia units to deal with potential attacks: "...such is the restless disposition of all Indians that it is difficult to determine when they will commence their attack on our frontier inhabitants."[14] For the next three years, Dodge would continue to draw attention to the remaining Ho-Chunks, and called for rapid removal and annuity payments to protect settlers.

Also in 1837, bands of Ojibwa meeting with Dodge at Fort Snelling gave up a vast swath of land extending from the Wisconsin River to the St. Croix River in exchange for payments, supplies, and annuities totaling approximately $850,000. The federal government thus gained access to one of the largest stands of white pine on the continent easily accessed by the Chippewa, St. Croix, and Black rivers. In 1842, bands of Lake Superior Ojibwa likewise ceded their land after reports of large deposits of copper piqued developers' interests. Although far removed from the areas of American settlement, the Ojibwa lands were recognized as early as the 1830s as a tremendous source of wealth. Altogether in 1837, one-half of the area that would become the state of Wisconsin changed legal ownership. By the end of the territorial period, sawmills and lumbering operations began appearing along the St. Croix and Chippewa rivers. The last cession was a tract of land just north of the Fox-Wisconsin portage by the Menominee. The establishment of reservations began in 1838 with, ironically, a band of Oneida from New York who received a parcel of land near Green Bay. Reservations for native Wisconsin tribes waited until after statehood, when the pressure of white settlement and the continued tribal presence forced the issue.[15]

POLITICAL DEVELOPMENT

In its early years as a territory, Wisconsin's political life centered more around personality and local issues rather than party. By the time of statehood, the territory had developed a two-party system dominated by Democrats. Early on, Dodge and Jones were able to arrange important positions for their allies, but Democratic unity often failed in popular elections. In 1838, Congress divided the territory at the Mississippi to create Iowa Territory, thus necessitating a new census, apportionment, and elections. Dodge easily secured appointment for Moses Strong of Mineral Point as attorney. In a three-way race for territorial delegate, however, James Doty had the solid support of the eastern counties and received 1,758 votes. Two candidates from the west, incumbent Jones and Thomas Burnett of Prairie du Chien, split 2,094 votes, indicating that population and political clout still rested with the more populous lead district, but nonetheless leaving the election to Doty.

Two factions thus emerged, led by Dodge and Doty. The next year, two political conventions met to nominate candidates. A "Territorial Convention" met on June 18 and, packed with supporters of Doty, endorsed him for another term in Congress; the next day, a "Democratic Convention" met, firmly declared its allegiance to the national party, and promoted Milwaukee banker and railroad developer Byron Kilbourn for Congress. Already being pushed into the arms of opposition Whigs, Doty won a bare majority in another three-way race for delegate.[16] Factionalism bedeviled Democrats, who could rarely remain unified and kept party politics in the territory somewhat competitive, allowing the Whigs some power in the legislature and later in the constitutional conventions.

The animosity between Doty and Dodge played well into a nascent Whig Party. In 1839, Doty tried to convince President Van Buren not to reappoint Dodge to a second term as governor, suggesting him to be a danger to the territory. "He is more likely," Doty charged, "to embroil the citizens of the frontier in difficulties with the savages by adopting violent measures, than to pursue those of a peaceable character." Doty remained suspicious of Dodge and questioned his fitness to be governor of a civilized territory. Although he was unsuccessful in arranging Dodge's removal, Doty did manage to secure passage of a federal law placing limitations on the veto powers of territorial governors. During the pivotal 1840 presidential campaign, Doty circulated a letter modeled on the Declaration of Independence alleging a variety of grievances the territory had suffered at the hands of a Democratic president and governor. This "Voice of an Injured Territory" contributed to the election of General William Henry Harrison, a development that had significant implications for Wisconsin. After Harrison's death in April 1841, President Tyler removed all territorial officials and replaced Governor Dodge with Doty. This action inspired Doty loyalists to formally organize a Whig convention to nominate candidates, and shook Democrats from their complacency. Dodge loyalists responded by holding a Democratic convention, which nominated its leader for delegate to Congress. Dodge easily defeated the Whig candidate and he and his supporters planned to make Doty a heavy burden for President Tyler. Dodge allies pressed hard against Doty by filing suit against him for misuse of the congressional funds for building the capitol and his involvement in two failed banks. Moses Strong even charged that Doty's claims in Madison—including those he donated to the territory—were fraudulent. Democratic strength continued to lie in the lead region and increasingly in the northeast, while Whigs consolidated their strength in the central farming counties of Dane, Sauk, and Rock.[17]

A conflict between Doty and the Democratic-dominated legislature was almost inevitable. During the 1841–1842 legislative session, Doty vetoed several bills and refused the council's request for a list of names of those territorial officials whom Doty had replaced. Open conflict came on December 5, 1842, when the governor refused to acknowledge the legislature's authority to meet, citing the fact that it had already exceeded the congressional appropriation.

In response, Democratic members of the legislature urged President Tyler to remove the governor, citing "dereliction of duty" and his role in the capitol construction scandal. Doty did not conduct any business with legislators until after he called a special session that met in March 1843. The feud ranged from the momentous to the petty. The legislature refused to take action on Doty's statehood referendum, and the Doty-appointed state librarian refused to serve the members of the legislature. For the next two years, the struggle between the branches continued, delaying any significant action on statehood until the end of Doty's term. Sensing that his reappointment was unlikely, Doty informed President Tyler that he no longer desired the governorship and hoped for quieter times. In Doty's place, the president appointed New York Senator Nathaniel Tallmadge in 1844. Tallmadge, a close political ally of Doty who had invested heavily in territorial lands, conducted harmonious relations with the legislature, but the agitation for statehood virtually ceased. Tallmadge's term was short, since President Polk appointed Dodge governor in 1845.[18]

BANKING AND ECONOMIC DEVELOPMENT

Aside from the removal of Native Americans and the sale of federal land, no other issue provoked as much discussion as the banks. The chaotic banking situation in the territory had its roots in national politics years earlier. In 1833, President Andrew Jackson withdrew federal funds deposited in the Second Bank of the United States in Philadelphia and the bank in turn contracted its operations. As a result, numerous small, undercapitalized banks sprang up, especially in the West, fueled by the land speculation frenzy. Jackson's 1836 "Specie Circular," directing that land had to be purchased from the government in gold or silver coin, and the subsequent failure of several New York banks in 1837, produced a severe depression. Banks across the nation suspended specie payments or failed altogether.

The crisis badly affected the four banks of issue in Wisconsin. The Bank of Wisconsin in Green Bay had been chartered by the Michigan territorial legislature in 1835. The Wisconsin legislature chartered three banks in 1836: The Bank of Milwaukee, the Miners' Bank of Dubuque, and The Bank of Mineral Point. In 1837, all of these suspended specie payment and wild rumors began circulating about missing deposits, larcenous clerks, and other financial misdeeds. The legislature launched several investigations. By 1841, it revoked the charters of the Green Bay, Milwaukee, and Mineral Point (Dubuque was by then part of Iowa Territory). The territory was plagued with a shortage of paper money and made do with devalued eastern currency and foreign coin. A five-franc coin was valued at ninety-five cents; a British gold sovereign at $4.90. The nearest thing to an actual bank in the territory was the Wisconsin Marine and Fire Insurance Company, chartered in 1839 with the authority to insure buildings, receive deposits, and loan money. Managed by the canny Alexander Mitchell and George Smith, the bank issued "notes of deposit" that circulated freely and served as de facto currency. Although the notes were essentially sound, the legislature initiated an investigation to determine whether the company was operating in violation of its charter. In 1846, the legislature repealed its charter, ending the only stable paper currency in Wisconsin.[19]

Of critical importance was the construction of infrastructure, both for administrative reasons and for economic development. Congress directed the construction of a military road from Fort Howard at Green Bay to Fort Winnebago at the Fox/Wisconsin portage to Fort Crawford at Prairie du Chien between 1832 and 1837. East-west roads connecting Lake Michigan to the Mississippi River began in 1838. By 1848, about 250 roads served settlers and traders as well as providing routes for the mail. Stagecoaches were common as early as 1841. Plank roads and railroads were much discussed and promoted, but did not become a significant factor until after statehood. Canals offered solutions to slow travel as well as profits for investors. A short canal connecting the Fox and Wisconsin rivers began in 1848, but the grander scheme connecting the Rock River with Lake Michigan was never completed, despite support from federal land grants and funds. By statehood, the canal fad had given way to the more practical and promising railroad.[20]

The frontier economy was, not surprisingly, based largely on the extraction of natural resources. Fur trading posts dotted the shores of Lake Superior and Lake Michigan, providing the sites for many future cities and towns. In the southwest, lead extraction and smelting supported communities such as Mineral Point, Platteville, and Dodgeville, with Prairie du Chien on the Mississippi River a major entrepôt. By statehood in 1848, lumbering began to develop along the Chippewa and Black rivers, foreshadowing the great lumber boom that was to occur later in the century. In the southeast and south-central portions of the state, small farms took advantage of the fertile prairie and oak openings. By 1848 subsistence farming was gradually giving way to a market-based economy, with wheat as the main cash crop. The growing metropolis of the territory, Milwaukee, began to develop industry in the 1840s to complement its trade, particularly those industries that complemented the resources of the territory. Tanning, brewing, and farm implements were particularly important.[21]

The population of Wisconsin increased dramatically between its formation and statehood. The census of 1850 reveals this remarkable growth. Milwaukee, barely a village of 1,700 people in 1840, was by mid-century a city of over twenty thousand. The state as a whole contained 305,000 people. Almost a third of the population was from New England and the Middle Atlantic states, a migration greatly facilitated by the Erie Canal. The Yankees, eager to develop the resources of the territory, dominated the economic and political life of the state. Smaller numbers were born in Wisconsin (63,000) or other Great

Lakes states (21,400). Only about 5,400 had migrated from the South. About 110,000 of those living in Wisconsin in 1850 were foreign born. During the territorial period, the area attracted about 38,000 Germans, 21,000 Irish, and 28,000 British immigrants (including those from Wales, Scotland, and Cornwall) as well as about 9,000 Scandinavians. The Germans and others from continental Europe emigrated for economic reasons and were usually small farmers or artisans in search of a more lucrative home. The newly opened farming areas particularly attracted large numbers of Norwegians, who found the geography and climate similar to their homeland. Norwegians, as well as Swiss, Dutch, and Cornish settlers, formed rural ethnic islands that perpetuated their language and customs. The Germans and the Irish more than other ethnic groups tended to settle in cities and towns, and were most quickly assimilated into the Yankee-dominated culture. The Germans quickly became prominent in political efforts and the later formation of the Republican Party.

TOWARD STATEHOOD

As early as 1838, there was significant discussion about statehood. Immediately after Iowa Territory was formed, Governor Dodge recommended a referendum on statehood. That same year, a petition signed by seven prominent citizens arrived in Congress requesting the passage of an Enabling Act. The boundary issues continued to be a problem, however, and when the legislature authorized a canvass for or against statehood at the next election, it included those inhabitants of northern Illinois. Although some residents of northern Illinois met and adopted resolutions in support of a revised boundary placing them in Wisconsin, there appeared little sympathy for either statehood or revised boundaries in the territory itself. The vote was almost unanimous against statehood.[22]

After becoming governor in 1841, Doty viewed his central duty as promoting statehood. In his December 1841 message to the legislature, he came out strongly for statehood as well as promoting traditional Whig policies of a central bank and tight-money policy. By this time, the population was around 50,000 and more recent arrivals from the east pushed territorial sentiment toward statehood. Doty was especially aggressive in procuring the lost territory for the "fifth state." When the governor of Illinois began selecting land grants from the federal government, Doty sent him a belligerent letter protesting the selection of these sections in the disputed territory.[23] The council again proposed a referendum on statehood that would include residents of northern Illinois. Indeed, some popular meetings and rallies in Illinois called for union with the new state of Wisconsin, and in March 1843 Doty issued a proclamation calling for such a referendum. The results were disappointing to him and his followers. Only nine of twenty counties delivered returns, with 619 for statehood and 1,843 against.[24]

Soon Doty became more strident, outlining in December 1843 his legal arguments for a strict interpretation of the Northwest Ordinance. "A state out of the union," he told the legislature, "has as good a right to her established boundaries as a state in it." Doty maintained that the inhabitants of the "fifth state" could not legally be denied the territorial and political rights granted by the Northwest Ordinance, and he virtually threatened to form an independent republic if Congress denied those rights. Despite the tempestuous political scene, a legislative committee supported Doty's assertions, reporting that the territorial integrity of Wisconsin had been infringed upon by Illinois and Michigan statehood and by the Webster-Ashburton Treaty that established the boundary between the United States and Canada.[25] Doty's position seemed to have support south of the disputed border as well. In January, Doty received a letter from "the inhabitants of that part of the fifth of the North Western states now under the jurisdiction of the state of Illinois" asking to participate in Wisconsin's efforts toward the formation of a state government.[26] Even Doty's enemies in the legislature were willing to assert Wisconsin's rights bluntly. In February 1846, the legislature wrote Congress claiming over 8,000 square miles in northern Illinois, all of the land west of Lake Michigan and the St. Mary's River, and all of the land north of Lake Superior ceded by Great Britain under the terms of the Webster-Ashburton Treaty. "Wisconsin though yet in her minority," the memorial read, "regards her rights of boundary as sacred and feels as sensibly any invasion of those rights as if she possessed the power and influence of an Empire." As sensibly as the territory might feel about those rights, the memorial did offer compromise if Congress would provide monetary compensation for the lost territory. All the bluster came to naught. The 1844 referendum was solidly against statehood.[27]

Those who opposed statehood based their arguments primarily on financial reasons. Rather than state and federal taxes, an annual appropriation from Congress paid the territory's expenses. Yet by the 1840s, even this argument was wearing thin. In December 1841, Congress passed legislation restricting territorial appropriations and forbidding expenditures beyond prior funding to end the usual custom of territorial legislatures appropriating sums and assuming that Congress would eventually provide the funds. Although appropriations for internal improvements continued to be made, including $30,000 for a harbor at the mouth of the Milwaukee River in 1843 and a further $45,000 for harbors at Milwaukee, Racine, and Southport in 1844, the Democratic administration of James K. Polk essentially ended these. In 1845, Congress appropriated only $13,700, half as much as normal, and nothing for harbors.[28]

By 1846, the population had grown to 155,000 and the mood had swung decisively toward statehood. In early 1844, the ever-perceptive Moses Strong wrote Dodge that although he opposed statehood he favored letting the people vote on the matter: "The current public opinion is shifting that way very rapidly—the people are getting tired of the general Government and its officers."[29] For the next few years, as population increased and funds from Congress slowed, sentiment did indeed shift in the direction Strong believed. On New Year's Day 1846, the *Madison Express* opined that since the 1843 referendum that rejected statehood, "a great change has taken place in our circumstances, and with the change, a complete revolution in public sentiment." Wisconsin was not the remote frontier it was in 1836, and the romantic image of the pioneer establishing a home in the wilderness was giving way to the realization that collective action was needed for development. Such action could only come with the relative autonomy of statehood. Dodge echoed these sentiments in his address to the legislature by again calling for a referendum on statehood.[30] A few months earlier, the *Mineral Point Democrat* had come out strongly for statehood, bemoaning the fact that an area with a population of over 100,000 had no voice in Congress and shrewdly pointing out that since Wisconsin was needed for the sectional balance between slave and free states, Congress might provide some generous inducements for statehood. Congress did indeed promise rewards for quick approval of statehood. The legislature's joint committee on state government reported that Congress would grant the state upon entering the union 500,000 acres, section 16 acres of every town for school purposes, 72 sections for the establishment of a university, 10 sections for government buildings, and 5 percent of all land sales for use in building roads and canals. In addition to the financial benefits of statehood, the rapidly growing population expressed the desire to elect its own governor and delegation to Congress.

It rankled many that a population of such size should have no vote in national affairs. In the House, one member declared that the vast natural resources of the state could be exploited and internal improvements made only under a state government without the supervision of Congress. In January, the legislature called for a vote on statehood, the first time the issue had been put to the voters independently and not during an election. The governor was directed to take a census and apportion delegates to a convention to draft a constitution. In April, the referendum was 6-1 in favor of statehood. Governor Dodge quickly issued proclamations apportioning 125 delegates and calling for election of a constitutional convention.[31]

Congress moved quickly as well. On January 13, Delegate Morgan Martin introduced a bill enabling the territory to form a state government. The House of Representatives passed the bill on June 9, but the boundary issue again raised problems. The day after the bill was first passed, Representative John A. Rockwell moved reconsideration, since the bill as passed allowed the convention to set the northwestern boundary. Although the House was willing to provide ample boundaries, a new state swallowing up the residue of the Northwest Territory was far too large. Congress once more asserted its prerogatives over the strict specifications of the Northwest Ordinance. The boundary provision was revised and the bill passed on June 11. On August 6, the Senate passed the bill and President Polk signed it. The Enabling Act set the boundaries of the new state, authorized the formation of a state government, and donated public land for schools, public buildings, and a university, and a further 5 percent of all net proceeds of public land sales. The remaining portions of the Northwest Territory west of the Mississippi and St. Croix rivers would eventually become part of the new territory of Minnesota, a "sixth state" never envisioned by the framers of the Northwest Ordinance.[32]

THE CONSTITUTION OF 1846

The convention that gathered on October 5, 1846, was made up of some of the leading figures of the territory. Moses Strong of Mineral Point, former territorial attorney and Dodge intimate, was allied with Edward G. Ryan of Racine, the future chief justice. Marshall Strong also represented Racine and was one of the convention's most conservative members. The Whigs were led by John H. Tweedy of Milwaukee. The liberal Democrats' leading figure was future governor Alexander Randall of Waukesha, who promoted the cause of black suffrage. Also present was James Doty, quietly working with moderates of both parties. Of the 125 delegates, 98 were from New England, New York, or the Middle Atlantic states; 13 were foreign born (7 Irish, 3 English, and 3 German). The convention was also young: 94 delegates were between the ages of 30 and 50.[33]

The convention had a sizable Democratic majority of 103 members, but the Whigs maintained a unified minority led by former governor Doty. Democratic unity was absent from the start, however, as party members were divided between reformers and conservatives, those who favored hard money and those who favored soft money, and those from commercial areas and those from agricultural and mining areas. The proceedings got off to a rough start almost from the beginning as long-simmering issues that had vexed the territory for years suddenly came to open discussion. Those in attendance spoke freely and at length on all subjects, frequently rising to correct newspaper accounts of their past statements. At times the debate became highly personalized as old rivals debated the greatest issues of the day. The actual writing of the constitution was divided among twenty-two committees, but no schedule was established, resulting in an ad hoc calendar with an often confusing order of procedure.[34]

The first major issue to come to the floor of the convention was banking. On October 9, Edward Ryan, chair of the committee on banking, delivered his report, which called for an absolute ban on banks of issue and the prohibition of corporations from acting as such. Hard-money Democrats such as Ryan were determined to prevent the misuse of banknotes that had plagued the territory. The latter provision was a deliberate slap at "Mitchell's Bank," the Wisconsin Marine and Fire Insurance Company, which issued "notes of deposit" that acted as de facto paper money. The article as reported also imposed steep fines and sentences, ranging from $500 to $10,000 and three months to five years for issuing, receiving, or even using banknotes.[35]

Few opposed the prohibition of banknotes, but some objected to the restriction placed on the legislature and many opposed the inclusion of penalties in the constitution. William Smith of Mineral Point complained that to "enact a penal code was the legitimate business of a legislature." Ryan retorted that he feared a "soft" legislature and that the convention needed to "place the penalty where the 'softs' cannot reach it." Moses Gibson of Fond du Lac delivered a minority report on October 12, objecting to content and to how the report was written. He claimed that Ryan had written the entire article himself without consulting other members of the committee until the morning he introduced it. After much discussion and amendment, the article passed on October 20. In its final form, the article prohibited the incorporation of a bank or the establishment of a branch from another state. Banknotes of less than $10 could not circulate after 1847. Banknotes of less than $20 could not circulate after 1849. Rather than outlining penalties, the article directed the legislature to do so.[36]

Equally divisive was the article on suffrage, also introduced on October 9 by Moses Strong. Strong's article gave the franchise to every white male citizen at least 21 years old and to non-citizens who had filed a declaration of intent to become citizens. Electors had to have resided in the state for at least six months. The article also specified that elections were to be held *viva voce*. This last provision was challenged first. On October 20 Ryan proposed an amendment specifying paper ballots, which was adopted. One delegate opposed to *viva voce* voting told the convention that he "had seen the evil consequences arising from the system…where men would be fearful of voting as their conscience would dictate…." Some debate ensued on the generous provision for foreign voting, the foreign born of the convention ably defending the rights of immigrants. The residency requirement was eventually extended to one year. Abolitionists petitioned the convention to strike the word "white" from the article. The census of 1840 revealed that 185 free blacks and 11 slaves resided in the territory despite the anti-slavery provisions of the Northwest Ordinance. Slaves were brought to the territory by Southerners, including Governor Dodge, who freed his five slaves in 1838. David Giddings of Sheboygan proposed just such an amendment. Moses Strong and Ryan were both violently opposed to black suffrage, Ryan predicting that the state would be "overrun with runaway slaves" should it pass. Moses Strong came out in "violent" opposition to suffrage. He predicted that if the clause were inserted into the constitution, the document "would not receive fifty votes west of the Rock River; the people would deem it an infringement upon their natural rights thus to place upon an equality with the colored race."

Strong's reference to the Rock River was a slap at the delegates from Waukesha County, where abolitionist sentiment was strongest and where the *American Freeman* was published. Another delegate responded that, "it is true that the negro is not a white man, nor can we make him such but it is nevertheless true that he is here among us…he knows no other country or government, is protected by our laws, and made subject to them." Moderates sympathetic to "philanthropic feelings" countered that such an unpopular provision was a legislative matter and should not be included in the constitution. Eventually the convention voted 53-46 to submit a separate referendum to the people on the question of black suffrage at the same time as the constitution. The editor of the *American Freeman* was outraged at how the article on suffrage contradicted the Bill of Rights, which declared all men were born free and independent, and foreshadowed the tone of the debate over the constitution. "Let every Liberty man," the paper stridently declared on November 24, "that hates oppression and is opposed to seeing his adopted land disgraced by the adoption of a constitution that is to govern a great and growing people reject any and every one that…offers such insult and injustice to the colored man."[37]

One of the longest and most complicated discussions involved the makeup of the supreme court. On October 27, the committee on the judiciary delivered a report providing for a supreme court of three elected justices and a separate circuit court system. Conservatives reacted in horror at the thought of an elected judicial branch. Former territorial attorney Henry S. Baird of Green Bay thought the elective system too untried. He feared that the voters would not be informed enough and that judicial elections would become corrupted by party politics. The Democrats held together and the supreme court remained elective. Democrats, however, were divided over whether the supreme court should be comprised of separate justices or should be comprised of the circuit judges (the *nisi prius* system). Ryan championed the *nisi prius* system, arguing that trial court experience was necessary for an appellate court. Others thought it improper for judges to be sitting on their own appeals. The end result was something of a compromise. After four days of discussion, the article established the *nisi prius* system for five years, after which the legislature could change it.[38]

The committee on boundaries, chaired by James Doty, delivered its report on October 29. Not surprisingly, the actual article, which consented to the boundaries laid out in the Enabling Act, was prefaced with a long diatribe on the injuries suffered by the state from the federal government, Illinois, and Michigan. That Doty himself seemed to give up his long attempts to secure more generous boundaries at first seemed to settle the matter, but William Holcombe, the delegate from St. Croix County in the northwest, proposed a new boundary much farther to the east that would have excised about a third of the present state and cut off the new state from Lake Superior entirely. He argued that the settlements around the St. Croix River would have too much common interest to be divided between two states. He also suggested that it was too distant to be properly administered from Madison and that its interests were too different from the rest of the territory. In this manner Wisconsin could be admitted while leaving enough territory for another state. Holcombe probably also envisioned a grand political future in the new state formed from the leftover portion of Wisconsin that would embrace the entire eastern portion of Lake Superior. As unconcerned as they were with the northwest, however, the delegates had no interest in cutting the territory in half. A compromise was reached whereby the northwest boundary was set about fifteen miles east of the St. Croix River. Wisconsin was thus reduced further in size and the dreams of recovering the lost territory from its fellow states finally abandoned.[39]

The reforming zeal of the radical Democrats produced the most controversial section of the new constitution. Article 14 contained two sections: the first asserted the right of women to own property independent of their husbands, and the second exempted forty-acre homesteads from forced sale for debt. The exemption clause first appeared as part of the bill of rights, reported from committee on October 28. The provisions were referred to the committee on miscellaneous provisions, which reported the article on November 25. Rhetoric on both issues quickly became inflamed on both sides. Proponents of exemption declared seizure of the home for debts a barbaric relic and urged the convention to protect the sanctity of the home and family. Horace Patch of Dodge County offered perhaps the most eloquent defense of the homestead exemption. On December 4 he appealed to his fellow delegates' republican principles: "While I would extend an arm of the law to the creditor for the protection of his property, and assert his rights, I would not beggar the debtor nor erect over him a petty monarchy (in the shape of a creditor) to trample upon him with impunity." Marshall Strong argued that the convention should leave such "experimentation" to the legislature and pointed out that homestead exemption could provide a loophole for wealthy scoundrels to avoid paying their debts. At times his predictions become comical as he depicted the complete breakdown of law and order caused by the exemption. "The passage of this article," he promised, "would lead directly to the greatest frauds, and a consequence would be to bring the knaves of the world among us, and would induce men to seek redress by private punishments."

Ryan was particularly opposed to the provision asserting married women's property rights, which he decried as contrary to the customs of society and the dictates of the Bible. He predicted that such a provision would "lead the wife to become a speculator, and to engage in all the turmoil and bustle of life...and thereby destroy her character [as] a wife." He also suggested that it would provide ample opportunity for husbands to "cover up their frauds." Both Ryan and Strong were conservatives at heart despite belonging to different parties. Their sympathies lay with the propertied and professional classes. Nor had they engaged in the speculation that gripped the West and so assumed that the motives of their adversaries were impure. Their motivations seem to have come from old-fashioned notions of a woman's place and the desire to protect the inherently naïve and helpless woman from the predatory and unscrupulous frontier speculator. David Noggle of Beloit championed the article and fended off charges that both the exemption and women's property rights would somehow open the future state to frauds beyond measure. He assured its passage by turning Ryan's and Strong's arguments against them. Surely, he reasoned, if wives could be trusted with maintaining homes and raising children, they would not be nearly so susceptible to fraud and could manage their own property. Ryan and Strong, he remarked, "tell us that the gentle, fair sex are so destitute of virtue and integrity that they will sell their peace for pence… that the intelligence, integrity, virtue, and excellence of your mothers, your wives, and your daughters depend wholly upon legislative action." Immediately after Noggle's speech, the article passed 61-34, although the homestead exemption was limited to forty acres and $1,000.[40]

The exemption article was one of the last approved by the convention and it, as well as the mocking and able arguments made against his speeches, so enraged Marshall Strong that he resigned from the convention and immediately began planning a campaign to defeat the proposed constitution. The convention adjourned on December 16 with storm clouds on the horizon. Within a month, strong opposition to the proposed constitution developed, led by Marshall Strong in the council. Opposition included both Democrats and Whigs, and swirled around three major points. Whigs, particularly those from Milwaukee County, the domain of the Wisconsin Marine and Fire Insurance Company, opposed the absolute prohibition on banking, believing it would retard prosperity. The Milwaukee *Sentinel and Gazette* printed editorials in favor of banking and insisted that a large money supply would increase wages and the prices farmers received for their produce.[41]

Radical Democrats attacked the suffrage article. The Madison *Wisconsin Argus* criticized the "unnecessary delay" presented by the one-year residency requirement. Abolitionist groups attacked the exclusion of African Americans from the article. The *Madison Express* challenged Ryan's assertion that "every negro was a thief, and every woman worse" by calling attention to the educated and prosperous African American population of New York. Ryan's comments on women indicated the tone of the debate over the married women's property rights and the exemption article. Opponents predicted the downfall of the family and society if it passed, and pointed to the opportunities both presented for fraud. Despite its support for black suffrage, the *Madison Express* opposed the exemption article, arguing that it "established different interests between the husband and the wife" and suggested that "the rich swindler" could exempt a fortune on a forty-acre homestead. The Milwaukee *Courier* sarcastically wondered why women could not be trusted with their own property if they were already entrusted with their husbands' property and children. "Is woman," the editor asked on February 24, 1847, in response to one of Marshall Strong's speeches opposing the constitution, "naturally bad, dissolute, corrupt…? People of Wisconsin, is this your estimate of her character? Will you sanction this foul slander upon your wives, sisters, and daughters by rejecting this constitution?"[42]

Members of the legislature perceived the possibility of defeat, and a bill was introduced in the council providing for a second convention should the constitution fail. Its supporters argued that if Congress passed a statehood bill and the constitution failed, there would be no congressional appropriation to fund the territory and statehood could be delayed another two years. Democrats reacted angrily and charged that the bill was a Whig plot to scuttle the constitution because it contained too many reforms. Marshall Strong made good on his promise to work toward the constitution's defeat. He suggested a new and smaller convention to amend the constitution, but not before going on a lengthy tirade against the current version, particularly the women's property provision, and predicting a host of legal problems that would result.[43]

Leading up to the vote on April 6, 1847, the public debated the merits of the constitution. Public rallies and speeches generated a great deal of excitement, and leaders such as Moses Strong and Ryan traveled the territory to promote ratification. Every local newspaper offered its opinion on every provision. The vote was decisive: 14,119 for adoption and 20,233 against. Only seven counties—Brown, Manitowoc, Iowa, LaFayette, Richland, St. Croix, and Washington—returned a favorable vote. Black suffrage was even more decisive: 15,415 of 22,279 votes cast opposed extending the franchise to free blacks. The referendum passed in eight counties—Dodge, Fond du Lac, Jefferson, Marquette, Racine, Walworth, Waukesha, and Winnebago—interestingly none of which approved the constitution itself.[44] The issue was not any fundamental defect in the framework itself, but in the several reform propositions contained therein, denounced by opponents as "new, untried and unsound principles." The Wisconsin *Argus* blamed the Democrats who promoted the measures. The constitution was, the editor wrote, "blotted and marred by these unsound and pernicious principles, got up and crowded into the document for the special glorification of a few soulless, brainless demagogues and renegades." The Milwaukee *Courier*, itself a proponent of many of the reforms, bluntly declared that the defeat of the constitution was a victory for the money power. The defeat of the first constitution had at least one fortunate effect. Congress had assented to the altered boundaries that cut off the St. Croix River, contingent on the ratification of the constitution. When the constitution failed, the boundaries of the future sate reverted to those outlined in the Enabling Act.[45]

THE SECOND CONSTITUTION

Despite the clear mandate for statehood, with the legislature adjourned it appeared that drafting a new constitution and applying for statehood would have to wait. Wisconsin residents of both parties, however, were eager to participate in the presidential election of 1848, and much public debate ensued as to what steps should be taken next and what form the next constitution should take. Many hoped for a mere revision of the rejected document, free of the reforms and theories that bedeviled the previous convention. The Southport *Telegraph* noted that people were generally satisfied except for the banking and exemption articles. The Watertown *Rock River Pilot* hoped that the revised constitution would be free of "legislative provisions" and "new theories." The Lancaster *Wisconsin Herald* was more blunt and called for a convention to "lop off the innovations and rid it of all 'progressive' features." Democrats recognized that internal differences had played a large part in the rejection of the constitution and hoped that party harmony would prevail.[46]

On September 27, 1847, Governor Dodge called a special session of the legislature to convene on October 18. Addressing the council and the house, Dodge indicated the urgency in quickly forming a state government. The financial benefits of statehood greatly surpassed current congressional appropriations and the population already exceeded those of all other western states at the time of admission. Also pressing was the balance in the U.S. Senate between free and slave states. Early the next year, the Watertown *Rock River Pilot* hoped for statehood because "it is very apparent that the political power and influence of the great Northwest will be augmented in the United States Senate, where such influence is much needed...." After Dodge's message, events moved quickly. Within ten days, the legislature passed an act calling for a convention to meet on December 15, 1847. The act apportioned sixty-nine delegates, with the election to be held on November 5.[47]

The resulting convention consisted of forty-one Democrats, twenty-five Whigs, and three Independents, with only six members returning from the previous convention, including Ryan, both Strongs, and Alexander Randall, whose personalities had so overwhelmed the previous convention. Fifty-one delegates were from New England and New York, and the convention was even younger than its predecessor. Only two delegates were fifty or older, and twelve were younger than thirty.[48] The convention organized itself much more effectively than its predecessor and appointed only six committees: general provisions; executive, legislative, and administrative; judiciary; education and school funds; banks and incorporations; and schedule and miscellaneous provisions. Much of the basic framework of the previous constitution was retained, although there was some debate over the terms of office and salaries of state officials. The committee on banking delivered its report on December 23, proposing an article that prohibited the legislature from chartering banks unless specifically approved by the vote of the people. The suffrage article was introduced the next day and enfranchised free white male citizens 21 and older and non-citizens who filed first papers. It also allowed the legislature to enfranchise "persons not herein enumerated," if approved by a popular vote—an opening for black suffrage. An elective judiciary was retained as was the *nisi prius* system until the legislature otherwise provided. Debate was cordial, often restrained, and articles were usually passed with only minor amendment. The most discussed proposal was the exemption article, which continued to provoke strong feelings on both sides of the issue, but after much debate, the article passed by two votes. The provision for separate property rights for married women was quietly dropped.[49]

After completing its work in a speedy six weeks, the convention adjourned after framing the final article as an ambitious schedule. The schedule called for a referendum on the second Monday in March, election of state officials on the second Monday in May, and the state legislature to convene on the first Monday of June. If public debate was less heated in the early months of 1848 than it was a year previously, it was because the new constitution met with almost universal acclaim. It was generally seen that partisanship had not affected the new constitution as much as it had the first, and the result was a more moderate document, closer to the wishes of the people. Across the territory, editors and citizens alike hailed the new document, perhaps relieved that the second convention had been so much less rancorous. The editor of the Potosi *Republican* believed the constitution broadly reflected the wishes of the people. "We cannot conceive of a better reason for giving it our hearty support—which we shall give in the confident hope of its adoption." The Prairie du Chien *Patriot* rejoiced that the "obnoxious" provisions had been jettisoned and a document more in accord with the wishes of the people had been written. Only the Waukesha *American Freeman* stridently denounced the new constitution because it restricted suffrage to white men—the same reason it had opposed the first constitution. The editor urged rejection of the "mongrel, God-dishonoring, liberty-hating, man-crushing document." The public confidence was well placed. On March 13, 1848, voters approved the constitution by a vote of 16,797–6,383.[50]

Once the constitution was approved by voters, Congress also acted with dispatch. On May 9, the House of Representatives debated the Admission Act. Representative Robert Smith of Illinois introduced an amendment to set the northwest boundary so far east of the St. Croix River as to remove approximately one-third of the northwestern part of the state. His amendment was met with fierce resistance and the House confirmed the same boundaries it had outlined in the 1846 Enabling Act, passing the act on May 11. The twelve-year saga of boundaries had at last come to an end, and despite the provisions of the Northwest Ordinance calling for "no more than five states," a sizable chunk of territory remained unorganized until it became part of Minnesota Territory in 1849. The Senate passed the bill eight days later and on May 29, President Polk signed the bill into law making Wisconsin the thirtieth state.[51]

Despite Congress's speedy approval of the Admission Act, the people of Wisconsin had already gone ahead with the election of state officers in early May. Democrat Nelson Dewey of Grant County easily defeated the Whig candidate, delegate John Tweedy. Democrats also swept the other state offices and sent two more, Mason Darling of Fond du Lac and William Lynde of Milwaukee, to Congress. Democrats also controlled both houses of the legislature, which met on June 8 and elected Henry Dodge and Isaac Walker of Milwaukee to the U.S. Senate. It was a fitting acknowledgment for Dodge, who had been such an important figure in the early and the late days of the territory to take his seat in the Senate on behalf of his people.[52]

CONCLUSION

Much had changed in Wisconsin in the twelve years between the creation of the territory in 1836 and statehood in 1848. Congress reduced the vast territory extending from Lake Michigan to the Missouri River to an average-sized state, thereby thwarting the imperialistic hopes of those who sought to recover lost territory from Illinois and Michigan and those who dreamed of creating another state in the timber-rich northwest. The population soared from less than 12,000 to almost 300,000, settling on land only recently acquired from the native tribes. European immigration laid the groundwork for a multi-ethnic and religiously complex state in which cultural and linguistic customs survived well into the twentieth century. Within ten years, the growing population recognized the benefits of statehood in a time of decreasing congressional appropriations. Politically, the state had matured as well. The stormy personal feuds that dominated the early years of the territory gave way to organized political parties that espoused clear ideas and positions. In many ways, the political development of the state hindered its admission to statehood as conservatives and radicals aired their differences in the first constitutional convention, each trying to stamp their views on the new state. The people were fundamentally conservative and unwilling to incorporate "experiments" like black suffrage, homestead exemptions, and married women's property rights in their constitution. The second convention was composed of cooler heads who produced a more restrained and ultimately acceptable document. Although amended from time to time since its adoption in 1848, it is the same constitution that remains in effect today.

The admission of Wisconsin to statehood in 1848 coincided with the beginning of a new era in American history. The recent war with Mexico increasingly pushed the issue of slavery to the forefront of politics, and Wisconsin residents quickly asserted themselves in the debate. Within just a few years of statehood, the same forces that proposed black suffrage in 1846 would develop into a powerful abolitionist force. Citizens and the state supreme court would also defy the federal government over the Fugitive Slave Act. The territorial development of the United States took a dramatic turn as well. One of the state officers elected in 1848 was Treasurer Jairus Fairchild, a recent arrival from Ohio. Within a year after seeing his adopted home join the Union, Fairchild watched in tears as his son Lucius mounted a black pony and left the state capital for California, where he dreamed of making a fortune in the gold rush.[53] Territorial development leapfrogged across half a continent, leaving behind the prairies and lead mines of southern Wisconsin and instead embracing the gold fields of northern California.

NOTES

1. *Mineral Point Democrat*, October 22, 1845, in Milo M. Quaife, ed., *The Movement for Statehood* (Madison: State Historical Society of Wisconsin, 1918), p. 361.

2. Moses M. Strong, *History of the Territory of Wisconsin, From 1836 to 1848* (Madison: 1885), pp. 187–188; Alice E. Smith, *The History of Wisconsin: From Exploration to Statehood* (Madison: State Historical Society of Wisconsin, 1973), pp. 226–229.

3. "An Act Establishing the Territory of Wisconsin," in *Territorial Papers of the United States*, ed. John Porter Bloom, vol. 27 (Washington: National Archives, 1969), pp. 41–52 (henceforth cited as TPUS); Strong, *Territory of Wisconsin*, pp. 207–210. The debates in Congress can be followed in the *Congressional Globe*, 24th Cong., 1st Sess., pp. 83, 124, 147, 159, 277–278, 289, 293–294, 296, 312.

4. Smith, *Exploration to Statehood*, pp. 243–249, 347–348.

5. Jones to Andrew Jackson, April 13, 1836, in Bloom, ed., TPUS, 27:37.

6. For biographical information on Henry Dodge, see James I. Clark, *Henry Dodge: Frontiersman* (Madison: State Historical Society of Wisconsin, 1957).

7. Proclamation of Governor Henry Dodge, October 25, 1836, in Bloom, ed., TPUS, 27:88–89.

8. Proclamation and census returns in Bloom, ed., TPUS, 27:84.

9. Dodge's message of October 26 is in Bloom, ed., TPUS, 27:89–95.

10. For James Duane Doty, see Alice E. Smith, *James Duane Doty: Frontier Promoter* (Madison: State Historical Society of Wisconsin, 1954).

11. Smith, *James Duane Doty*, pp. 192–208; "Resolution by the Legislative Assembly," December 6, 1836, in Bloom, ed. TPUS, 27:698; Dodge to Jones, November 16, 1836, in Bloom, ed., TPUS, 27:670–671.

12. Elbert Herring, the commissioner of Indian affairs, described the existing situation to Dodge in a letter dated June 22, 1836, in Bloom, ed., TPUS, 27:63–76. The cessions of Indian lands is discussed most thoroughly in Nancy O. Lurie, *Wisconsin Indians*, rev. and exp. ed. (Madison: Wisconsin Historical Society, 2002), pp. 5–23.

13. Dodge to Harris, December 28, 1836, in Bloom, ed., TPUS, 27:698–699.

14. "Message to the legislature," November 6, 1837, in Bloom, ed., TPUS, 27:137.

15. Smith, *Exploration to Statehood*, pp. 143–149.

16. Smith, *James Duane Doty*, pp. 238–242.

17. Doty to President Van Buren, February 1, 1839, in Bloom, ed., TPUS, 27:1164–1166; Strong, *Territory of Wisconsin*, pp. 321–323.

18. Smith, *James Duane Doty*, pp. 265–285, 295–296.

19. The best discussion on banks and banking is Alice E. Smith, *From Exploration to Statehood*, pp. 273–306. For the Wisconsin Marine and Fire Insurance Company, see Alice E. Smith, *George Smith's Money: A Scottish Investor in America* (Madison, State Historical Society of Wisconsin, 1966).

20. Smith, *From Exploration to Statehood*, pp. 436–444.

21. Smith, *From Exploration to Statehood*, pp. 436–463, 499–545.

22. Henry Dodge, "Message to the Legislature," November 27, 1838 (p. 166) and "Memorial to Congress by Citizens of the Territory," April 12, 1838 (pp. 88–89), both in Bloom, ed., TPUS, vol. 27.

23. James Doty to Thomas Carlin, June 28, 1842, in Bloom, ed., TPUS, 27:358–359.

24. James Doty, "Message to the Legislature," March 6, 1843, in Bloom, ed., TPUS, 27:371; Strong, *Territory of Wisconsin*, pp. 360–364.

25. Strong, *Territory of Wisconsin*, pp. 423–437.

26. Doty to House of Representatives, January 12, 1844, in Bloom, ed., TPUS, 27:431–432.

27. "Address to Congress By the Territorial Assembly," February 27, 1844, in Bloom, ed., 28:652–655.

28. Strong, *Territory of Wisconsin*, pp. 386, 421.

29. Moses Strong to Henry Dodge, February 5, 1844, in Bloom, ed., TPUS, 27:633.

30. Madison *Express*, January 1, 1846, in Quaife, *Movement for Statehood*, p. 143; Henry Dodge, "Message to the Legislature" January 6, 1846, in Bloom, ed., TPUS, 27:441.

31. "Report of Select Joint Committee on State Government," pp. 60–69; "Remarks of Rep. Croswell," January 8, 1846, pp. 73–82; and "An Act in Relation to the Formation of a State Government in Wisconsin," pp. 117–124, all in Quaife, *Movement Toward Statehood*.

32. "Proceedings in Congress," in Quaife, *Movement Toward Statehood*, pp. 128–136. The act is in *U.S. Statutes at Large*, IX, 56-58 and is reprinted in Quaife, *Movement Toward Statehood*, pp. 136–140.

33. Brief biographies of the delegates are found in Milo M. Quaife, *The Convention of 1846* (Madison: State Historical Society of Wisconsin, 1919), pp. 756–800.

34. The convention kept no record of debates in its journal, but newspapers printed them in detail. These reports were used to compile a thorough record published in Quaife, *Convention of 1846*.

35. Ibid., pp. 70–71.

36. Ibid., pp. 84–85, 91–92, 204, 744–745.

37. Ibid., pp. 75, 205–206, 210, 221–222, 230–235, 240, 275–298; Strong, *Territory of Wisconsin*, pp. 521–522.

38. Quaife, *Convention of 1846*, pp. 286–296, 526–537, 585–503, 611, 739–743; Smith, *Exploration to Statehood*, pp. 636–657.

39. Quaife, *Convention of 1846*, pp. 311–320, 560–569, 582–583, 670–673, 701–702.

40. Ibid., pp. 303, 539–540, 631–636, 647–670.

41. Milwaukee *Sentinel and Gazette*, October 17 and 26, 1847, in Quaife, *The Struggle Over Ratification, 1846–1847* (Madison: State Historical Society of Wisconsin, 1920), pp. 177–179 and 183–184.

42. Madison *Wisconsin Argus*, November 3, 1847, pp. 151–155; Madison *Express*, November 10, 1847; Madison *Express*, December 8, 1846; and Milwaukee *Courier*, February 24, 1847, all in Quaife, *Struggle Over Ratification*, pp. 174–175 and 564–587.

43. *Council Journal*, 1847, pp. 99–101; *House Journal*, 1847, pp. 214–217. Strong's remarks are in Quaife, *Struggle Over Ratification*, pp. 235–262.

44. Proclamation of Governor Dodge, May 10, 1847, in TPUS, 27:505. Official returns by county are reprinted in Quaife, *Struggle Over Ratification*, p. 697.

45. Madison *Wisconsin Argus*, April 13, 1847; and Milwaukee *Courier*, April 14, 1847, both in Quaife, *Struggle Over Ratification*, pp. 344–345, 612–614; Strong, *Territory of Wisconsin*, pp. 550–557.

46. Southport *Telegraph*, November 3 and 17, 1847; Watertown *Rock River Pilot*, November 3, 1847; and Lancaster *Wisconsin Herald*, April 17, 1847, all in Quaife, *Attainment of Statehood*, pp. 55–58, 74–76, 104.

47. Proclamation of Governor Dodge, September 27, 1847, in TPUS, 27:547–548; "Governor Dodge's Message on Statehood [October 18, 1847]," in *The Attainment of Statehood*, ed. Milo M. Quaife (Madison: State Historical Society of Wisconsin, 1928), pp. 2–3; *Laws of Wisconsin Territory*, special session 1847, pp. 3–11, reprinted in Quaife, *Attainment of Statehood*, pp. 4–10; Watertown *Rock River Pilot*, February 9, 1848, in Quaife, *Attainment of Statehood*, pp. 88–89.

48. Biographical information on the delegates is in Quaife, *Attainment of Statehood*, pp. 900–931.

49. The journal of debate is in Quaife, *Attainment of Statehood*, pp. 173–883.

50. Potosi *Republican*, February 10, 1848; Prairie du Chien *Patriot*, February 15, 1848; and Waukesha *American Freeman*, February 9 and 23, 1848; all in Quaife, *Attainment of Statehood*, pp. 91–114; Strong, *Territory of Wisconsin*, pp. 564–576.

51. Congressional proceedings are reprinted in Quaife, *Attainment of Statehood*, pp. 119–172.

52. Smith, *Exploration to Statehood*, pp. 679–680.

53. Sam Ross, *The Empty Sleeve: A Biography of Lucius Fairchild* (Madison: State Historical Society of Wisconsin for the Wisconsin Civil War Centennial Commission, 1964), pp. 5–6.

BIBLIOGRAPHY

Bloom, John Porter, ed. *Territorial Papers of the United States*. Vols. 27, 28. Washington, DC: Government Printing Office, 1969.

Quaife, Milo M., ed. *The Movement For Statehood: 1845–46*. Madison: State Historical Society of Wisconsin, 1918.

———. *The Convention of 1846*. Madison: State Historical Society of Wisconsin, 1919.

———. *The Struggle Over Ratification: 1846–1847*. Madison: State Historical Society of Wisconsin, 1920.

———. *The Attainment of Statehood*. Madison: State Historical Society of Wisconsin, 1928.

Smith, Alice E. *James Duane Doty: Frontier Promoter*. Madison: State Historical Society, 1954.

———. *The History of Wisconsin: From Exploration to Statehood*. Madison: State Historical Society of Wisconsin, 1973.

Strong, Moses M. *History of the Territory of Wisconsin From 1836 to 1848*. Madison: Democrat Printing Co., 1885.

Wyman, Mark. *The Wisconsin Frontier*. Bloomington: University of Indiana Press, 1998.

THE STATE OF WYOMING

Admitted to the Union as a State: July 10, 1890

Phil Roberts

INTRODUCTION

Wyoming, the forty-fourth state admitted to the Union, was the last of the western states admitted in the flurry of new states brought to statehood in 1889–1890. Like the earlier western states of Idaho, North Dakota, South Dakota, Montana, and Washington, Wyoming's admission came as a result of the territory's record of support for Republicans. When the presidency and both houses of Congress returned to Republican hands as a result of the 1888 election, Wyoming was well positioned for admission, despite two serious handicaps—the most serious, a perceived population deficit and, less worrisome, the inclusion of women's suffrage in the original laws of the territory. Both would become issues in Congress during the debates over statehood, but primarily by those who were opponents of statehood on political grounds.

Wyoming was unique among western states for seeking admission even before Congress gave the territory the authority through passage of an Enabling Act. Territorial Governor Francis E. Warren, anxious for statehood, moved forward as though the enabling legislation had passed. With the assistance of his political ally, Joseph M. Carey, who was Wyoming's territorial delegate, Warren gained sufficient support from the commissioners of seven of the ten counties to call a constitutional convention.

On July 8, 1889, fifty-five delegates were elected to the convention that was to be held in Cheyenne in September. Even though women had full rights in Wyoming and had voted in every election after the initial election for territorial legislatures, not one woman was elected a delegate to the constitutional convention. No women had served in the territorial legislature, but numerous

Wyoming

Territorial Development:

- The United States obtains future territory of Wyoming from France through the Louisiana Purchase, April 30, 1803
- The United States and Great Britain sign a temporary treaty for joint tenancy of the Oregon Country, October 20, 1818
- The United States obtains more land containing future territory of Wyoming through the annexation of Texas, December 29, 1845
- The United States obtains formal title to all land in the Oregon territory south of the 49th parallel from Great Britain through the Oregon Treaty, June 15, 1846
- The United States obtains more land containing future territory of Wyoming from Mexico through the Treaty of Guadalupe Hidalgo, February 2, 1848
- Wyoming becomes a U.S. territory, March 19, 1869
- Wyoming admitted into the Union as the forty-fourth state, July 10, 1890

Territorial Capitals:

- Cheyenne, 1869–1890

State Capitals:

- Cheyenne, 1890–present

Origin of State Name: The name Wyoming results from the two Delaware words "mecheweamiing," which mean, "at the big flats."

First Governor: Francis E. Warren
Governmental Organization: Bicameral
Population at Statehood: 60,705
Geographical Size: 97,100 square miles

women held county offices, principally county superintendent of schools and also justices of the peace.

After twenty-five days of deliberations, the forty-eight delegates who attended the convention submitted the constitution for voter approval. The constitution was adopted overwhelmingly. As T. A. Larson observed, both political parties favored statehood although Democrats preferred statehood without its coming under the leadership of Warren and Carey, two Republicans.

TERRITORIAL ORIGINS

"For the first time in the history of our country, the organization of a territorial government was rendered necessary by the building of a railroad," John A. Campbell, Wyoming's first territorial governor, observed in his first inaugural address in 1869.[1] While it was true that the territory finally had sufficient (albeit transient) population once the transcontinental railroad was built through what became its southern part, there had been attempts to establish it as a separate territory since January 1865. During the pre-territorial period, an estimated 350,000 people crossed what is now Wyoming, en route to Oregon, Utah, and California. Like the estimated 3,000 fur trappers who ranged throughout the area in the 1820s and 1830s, few travelers west elected to stay. The first permanent white settlement, Fort Laramie, began as a fur trading post in 1834, but became a U.S. Army post in 1849 to protect trail travelers.

Various parts of the land area now encompassing Wyoming had been governed by a half dozen foreign countries and an equal number of territorial governments. Part of Wyoming came to the United States with the Louisiana Purchase, and another part with the Oregon cession. A substantial portion of southwestern Wyoming was part of Mexico, ceded to the United States after the Mexican War. One sliver of south-central Wyoming had even been part of the Republic of Texas, although the area had no Euro-American population at the time. When American control was established over what was to become Wyoming, the few Euro-Americans residing in the eastern and southeastern parts of the territory came under the governance of the Territory of Louisiana (1805–1812), Territory of Missouri (1812–1820), Nebraska Territory (1854–1863), Dakota Territory (1861–1863 and 1864–1868), and Idaho Territory (1863–1864). The few individuals living in what is now western Wyoming came under the governments of Oregon Territory (1846–1858), Washington Territory (1859–1863), Idaho Territory (1863–1868), and a smaller southwestern portion under Utah Territory (1850–1861).[2]

When Rep. James Ashley of Ohio introduced the first bill to create a Wyoming territory on January 5, 1865, it included the present panhandle of Nebraska and the Black Hills of South Dakota, but excluded the parts later taken from Utah and Idaho in the west. The Ashley bill died in committee, but similar bills were introduced in 1866 and 1867 by Rep. William Lawrence, also from Ohio. The Lawrence bills referred to the territory as "Lincoln," in honor of the recently assassinated president. It was Ashley who named "Wyoming," a word having no connection to the territory, but a Delaware Indian term for "on the broad plain," applied to a valley in Pennsylvania from which Ashley had come.

Both Lawrence bills also failed to pass, and in January 1868 Ashley resubmitted his "Wyoming" bill. Again, it failed, but a similar measure introduced in the U.S. Senate by Senator Richard Yates of Illinois did gain congressional approval. The apparent impetus for Yates's bill came from an unlikely source—the governor and territorial legislature of Dakota Territory, the government supposedly presiding over the sparsely populated area. This western county of Dakota (designated Laramie County) had difficulties sending territorial legislators to the capital at Yankton.[3]

Officials of Dakota knew virtually nothing of the needs of the population in the far-flung reaches of the territory's western edge. Consequently, in December 1867, Territorial Governor A. J. Faulk told the Dakota territorial legislature that he saw no reason why that western county ought to stay in their territory. (Larson estimated the Euro-American population at the time at about 1,500, mostly soldiers at Forts Laramie, Sanders, Phil Kearny, Reno, and Bridger.) The Dakota legislature passed a memorial to Congress urging that the area be made a separate territory. Rarely has a government been so eager to rid itself of part of its territory.

Meanwhile, the population, mostly temporary, increased dramatically during the summer of 1867 when the railroad's end of tracks entered what would become Wyoming. The new "residents" of the "hell-on-wheels" construction towns popping up at the end of tracks and along the route of the Union Pacific transcontinental railroad, along with the miners living in the boomtown of South Pass City, represented most of the area's population.

At the same time, residents of Dakota's "western county" sent two lobbyists to Washington to seek territorial status. One, Dr. Hiram Latham, was the Surgeon for the Union Pacific Railroad and probably represented the railroad's interests as much as the new residents of the area. The railroad sought settlers to purchase its huge tracts from the land grant as well as to utilize the rails for shipping and travel. Latham distributed a brochure to the members of Congress asserting that the territory was already home to more than 35,000 Americans and promised 60,000 within a year. (These figures were greatly inflated and the population question would continue to challenge Wyoming promoters for the next quarter century.) With support from friends of the Union Pacific Railroad, Congress created the territory. The Senate passed the territorial bill by a comfortable margin and it went to the House, where it passed by a vote of 106-54.[4]

TERRITORIAL GOVERNMENT

When Congress passed the act creating Wyoming Territory and President Andrew Johnson signed the bill, friction between the two branches of government was mounting over Johnson's reconstruction programs and his perceived efforts to subvert the congressional will. The president, already close to impeachment, appointed a slate of territorial officers, but Congress refused to confirm his nominees. Consequently, the territory was created as impeachment of Johnson was moving forward, but it was not organized until the following year when President U. S. Grant submitted a slate of territorial appointees that gained congressional approval.

The new president's choice for territorial governor, approved barely a month after Grant's inauguration, was a thirty-four-year-old former Union Army brigadier general from Ohio, John A. Campbell. The territorial secretary, two years younger than Campbell, was Edward M. Lee, also a Union army officer in the Civil War who had served a single term in the Connecticut legislature prior to his appointment. The territorial attorney was Delaware-born Joseph M. Carey, who was to become prominent in Wyoming politics for the next half-century and a key figure in the successful effort to gain statehood.

Campbell arrived in Cheyenne and designated it Wyoming's "temporary capital," a status it still constitutionally retains, in the summer of 1869. He called for elections to the territorial legislature to convene in Cheyenne in mid-October. Nine men, all Democrats, were elected to the council. All twelve members of the lower house were also Democrats.

William Bright, a Virginia native and Democrat who had served as a Civil War Union officer, was elected president of the council (upper house). A saloonkeeper in South Pass City, he left the chair as presiding officer to introduce a bill providing for women's suffrage. The bill passed the council by a vote of 6-2 with one member absent. Despite vocal opposition, the bill passed the house by a vote of 7-4 and went to Governor Campbell for his signature. On December 10, 1869, Campbell signed the Suffrage Bill, making Wyoming the first government in the country to give women the right to vote.

The bill's passage brought significant national attention to the new territory. Throughout the state's history, the measure remained a source of state pride. In the 1930s, the legislature designated Wyoming's nickname, "the Equality State," and set December 10 as "Wyoming Day," in honor of the Suffrage Bill's passage and signing.

Details of the bill's passage remain controversial to the present. The record indicates that Governor Campbell and Secretary Lee both favored the measure from the beginning. Numerous national suffrage speakers appeared in the territory during the legislature's deliberations, arguing for a suffrage bill. Bright's wife Julia is known to have been involved in the suffrage movement prior to their moving to South Pass City. The circumstances of the passage, however, have led commentators to ascribe various reasons for why the brand new territory would pass such a landmark act. Was the measure passed simply as a means of gaining national advertising for the new territory? Was it passed as a joke, as one legislator asserted many years later? Was it passed by the Democratic legislature as a means to try to embarrass Republican Governor Campbell? Was it a "protest" against the granting of the franchise to former slaves? After reading the record, contemporary newspaper accounts, and memoirs of participants, it seems likely that the measure passed because of the accidental convergence of Campbell, Lee, Bright, and others who believed in suffrage as a matter of principle.

Two months after passage of the Suffrage Bill, three women were commissioned justices of the peace. Only one, Esther Hobart Morris, a New York–born South Pass City housewife, is known to have served. Morris, the first woman in America to serve as a judge, held the office for eight and a half months, hearing only two dozen cases. Nonetheless, her judging abilities were nationally celebrated by suffrage groups as demonstrating that women were capable of serving in judicial offices. Morris's service as the first woman judge is commemorated by Wyoming with one of the two statues in Statuary Hall in the U.S. Capitol. The statue has under it the legend "Mother of Woman Suffrage," an inaccurate reference to the story that is still embraced by some historians.

In March and April of 1870, women served on juries in at least two courts in Wyoming. The first was in Laramie where the judge allowed for women to be empanelled for a district court jury. The second was a few weeks later in Cheyenne. The women jurors were viewed as a novelty by the national press, and many newspapers featured the inaccurate artist depictions of women sitting in the jury box suckling children and darning socks. Women on juries did not, however, become common in Wyoming. The next year, the Supreme Court ruled that suffrage did not automatically mean that women could serve as jurors, and no other women served on juries during the territorial period.

In September 1870, women turned out to vote in Wyoming for the first time. The results were carefully observed and most concluded that the impact of the "women's vote" was to increase the aggregate number of voters, but not to change the outcome of any election. A few saloonkeepers feared that women had a higher propensity to support temperance. In the 1871 legislature, opponents of suffrage came within one vote of reversing the experiment. Governor Campbell vetoed the bill passed by both houses that would have repealed suffrage. In an override effort in the legislature, the governor's veto was sustained by just one vote. The Suffrage Bill was not challenged again in the territorial period, but the issue became important in the constitutional convention.

TERRITORIAL INDUSTRY AND GOVERNMENT

Throughout the territorial period, Wyoming's economy was dependent on the federal government and on three industries: transportation (the main line of the Union Pacific Railroad crossed the state), coal mining (again, most mines were operated by the Union Pacific's wholly owned coal mining subsidiary), and cattle ranching. The territorial legislature usually reflected a balance between Union Pacific representatives and legislators with a ranching background. The railroad, with its huge land grant from the federal government—odd-numbered sections running for twenty miles either side of the tracks across southern Wyoming—was the largest private landowner in the territory. Cattle ranchers, utilizing the federally owned public lands mostly north of the railroad, practiced open range ranching. Common practice was to establish a "home place" on a 160-acre tract, but run thousands of cattle on the federally owned land in the vicinity and use the water without having to pay for any of it, not even property taxes. In 1872, the Congress designated the northwest corner of Wyoming, Yellowstone, as the nation's first national park. Patrolled initially by the army, the park lacked convenient road or rail connections to the main population centers of the territory.

The Department of the Army retained key military posts in Wyoming throughout the period to protect residents and the railroad from possible native threats. In the years immediately before the territory was created, the army was called upon to protect miners en route to Montana on the Bozeman Trail through north-central Wyoming. The most serious confrontations with Indians came in the battles against the Sioux in the Powder River country of what is now northeastern Wyoming. After one bloody incident cost the army its greatest loss of life in the West before the Custer affair, the federal government closed Fort Phil Kearny, withdrew from the land, and gained assurances from the tribes occupying the area that, if they were left to roam the Powder River country, they would not interfere with railroad construction about to begin farther south. After the Little Bighorn Battle in Montana in 1876, the Sioux were consigned to reservations in neighboring South Dakota. Their Wyoming lands, confirmed by three Fort Laramie treaties in 1851, 1866, and 1868, were opened to cattle ranching in the late 1870s.

The Wind River Indian Reservation, originally established as the "Shoshone Indian Reservation," was the only reservation in Wyoming.[5] The territory was the native home of the Shoshone tribe, led for most of the century by Chief Washakie. In two treaties with the federal government, the Fort Bridger treaties of 1863 and 1868, the tribe's reservation encompassed some of their ancestral lands in what was to become west-central Wyoming. Unlike the Sioux and the Arapahoe, who occupied other parts of Wyoming in the pre-territorial period, the Shoshones never went to war against the United States, mostly because Washakie wisely understood the differential in power between the army and his people. He concluded that cooperation would be as desirable for his people in the long run as open confrontation.

The federal government placed northern Arapahoes on the reservation in 1878, asserting that the move was only temporary. Chief Washakie reluctantly accepted the "guests." Throughout the next half-century, the "temporary" arrangement persisted even though the federal government broke its promise to create a separate reservation for the northern Arapahoes. Finally, when both tribes were experiencing the hardships brought on by the Great Depression, the federal government worked out an agreement granting the Arapahoes "permanent" status on the reservation. The Shoshones were paid a modest sum, as were the Arapahoes, to buy land adjacent to reservation lands, part of which became today's "Arapahoe Ranch." While tensions between the two tribes have eased in recent years, the two tribes continue an uneasy joint supervision over the reservation.

The federal government also retained ownership over vast tracts of forested lands in northwestern Wyoming. National forests were designated in the 1890s, but except for the Public Land Office, government land-owning agencies were not a factor in pre-statehood Wyoming. Except for the 4 million acres of Wyoming owned by the Union Pacific, the territory had few private landowners. At the time of statehood, more than 75 percent of the land area of Wyoming was federally owned. Federal lands constituted nearly 50 percent of the land area in 2003.

In the late nineteenth century, vast stretches of Wyoming were federal lands open to entry for homesteads, but the quality of the soil, aridity, high elevations, and relatively short growing seasons discouraged crop agriculture in most of the state. The gold mining town of South Pass City reached its zenith just as the territory was established, declining rapidly as prospects for a major gold strike dimmed in the 1870s.

Unlike the neighboring territories of Montana, Idaho, South Dakota, and Colorado, metal mining never was important in the territory. Until widespread irrigation in the early twentieth century, crop agriculture was equally limited. As a result, Wyoming politics experienced little of populist agitation and population growth was steady, but slow in the territorial period.

In the twenty-five years as a territory, just one local man, Francis E. Warren, was appointed territorial governor. The rest were political allies of the various presidents. One, Thomas Moonlight, had lived in Wyoming during his military career, serving as commanding officer of Fort Laramie. The others, however, had little familiarity with the territory. This is not to say that they were either corrupt or incompetent. None was justifiably accused of either flaw. One, the third man to occupy the office, was particularly talented. John Hoyt, unusually well educated for the time, held a medical degree and a law degree. During his term as territorial governor (1878–1882), he organized an "academy of science" and advocated establishment of a state university. After leaving office, he remained in Wyoming and in 1887 was appointed the first president of the University of Wyoming. Elected a delegate to the constitutional convention in 1889 while serving as University of Wyoming president, he was influential in drafting the education articles in the constitution, including one asserting that tuition for higher education in Wyoming "shall be as nearly free as possible."[6]

The sixth territorial governor, Francis E. Warren, was the first resident chosen to that post. (His predecessor, E. S. N. Morgan, the fifth governor, was not formally appointed, but acted in that capacity following the death of Governor William Hale in 1885. Morgan remained in Wyoming and, like the third governor of the territory, John Hoyt, served in the constitutional convention.) During this brief term, Warren became involved in what was known as the Rock Springs massacre. Miners employed by the Union Pacific coal company resisted company efforts to replace them with cheaper Asian miners. The efforts came to a head in September 1885, when a confrontation inside a mine between whites and Chinese miners caused the company to close down the entire operation for the rest of the day. The saloons of Rock Springs opened early and by late afternoon, a group of miners (ironically all immigrants themselves) led a mob into "China town," where they killed an estimated twenty-eight Chinese miners and drove the rest from town. Warren requested army troops from Fort D. A. Russell, and they were sent to the scene to "establish order" and, incidentally, to protect Union Pacific property. While he lost support from miners who accused him of being sympathetic to "the Chinamen," Warren gained strong backing from the Union Pacific. Even though most Republican territorial governors were immediately replaced on Democrat Grover Cleveland's inauguration, Warren was retained until November 1886, largely on the strength of how he dealt with the Rock Springs issue.

Meanwhile, Joseph M. Carey, who came to Wyoming as Grant's appointee for territorial attorney, served as one of the three territorial justices and, later, was elected to the Congress as Wyoming's territorial delegate. His good friend, Massachusetts-born Warren, who had come to Wyoming to enter the mercantile business in the early 1870s after compiling a distinguished record in the Civil War, entered politics as mayor of Cheyenne. After service as territorial treasurer, like Carey, Warren entered the livestock business. By the year of Wyoming statehood, Warren and Carey were regarded as the wealthiest men in the territory, both fortunes stemming primarily from the cattle business.

The Union Pacific's control over the territorial legislatures was shared with the livestock ranchers, the most prominent having joined together to form the Wyoming Stockgrowers Association. Most of the good grazing lands were remote from the Union Pacific line. Except for the issue of responsibility for wandering cattle killed on train tracks, few issues brought direct conflict between the two powerful forces in the territorial period. Taxation issues brought confrontations between the two industries in later years.

In the early 1880s, the Stockgrowers Association wielded sufficient influence to have most governmental functions involving livestock, such as branding laws, roundup rules, and inspections, granted to its officers. In the 1880s, pressures mounted on the open range from "newcomers" as well as from small ranchers who utilized homestead laws to carve out sections of the public domain, sometimes in prime open range pasture. Prices for livestock started falling in the early 1880s as more and more ranchers entered what James Brisbin, author of an 1881 promotional book on the open range cattle industry, had called and titled his book *The Beef Bonanza*.

The entire industry in Wyoming met calamity in 1886–1887. The rangelands already were heavily overgrazed by the million or more cattle in the territory in 1886. That year an extremely dry summer was followed by an unusually cold and snowy winter. After a succession of storms swept over the territory weekly from early November to late April, the industry was left in shambles. Many absentee-owned open-range operations folded. Others, like the ranches owned by Carey and Warren, managed to pull through, but not without heavy losses. Many cowboys, once employed year-round by the large open-range operators, lost their jobs. Not educated or experienced in any other line of work, a number of cowboys opted to enter the ranching business themselves, taking up small homesteads throughout "cattle country" to raise their own herds. The larger, more established ranchers viewed these newer competitors with even greater anxiety, assuming that many intended to succeed through rustling from their former employers. The Wyoming Stockgrowers Association members established strict membership rules in an effort to squeeze out those who were viewed as "interlopers."

Incidents between the two groups accelerated in the years immediately after statehood, culminating in the so-called Johnson County War of 1892.[7] The association (or, at least, some of its most powerful members) hired a private army to go to Johnson County supposedly to "dispose" of rustlers and their sympathizers, including the county sheriff and commissioners. Ironically, three of the participants had been delegates to the constitutional convention and the private army directly violated one article specifically prohibiting such private forces. While evidence of their involvement is circumstantial, Warren and Carey supported the big, established cattle operators in their "invasion" of a northern Wyoming county where the newer stockmen had the temerity to establish their own association and set their own livestock rules. But in the late 1880s, this divisive incident was far in the future.

After the 1888 general election, Warren was reappointed to the territorial governorship after being out of office for nearly three years. Carey was elected to Congress for another term as delegate.

DEBATES OVER STATEHOOD

Statehood had proponents in Wyoming as early as 1869, soon after the territory was established. Realistically, however, the disappointingly slow population growth was seen as hindering statehood efforts. In the late 1880s, statehood efforts enjoyed broad bipartisan support. Territorial Governor Thomas Moonlight, a Democrat who had supported statehood when Cleveland was president but opposed it after Harrison's election in November 1888, reported to the secretary of the interior in December 1888 that Wyoming had no more than 55,500 people. (As later census figures revealed, his estimate was surprisingly accurate.) His statement was met with derision by both Democrats and Republicans.[8] Statehood was not a party issue, even though there were isolated individuals like Moonlight who opposed it. Most Democrats and nearly every Republican seemed to favor removal from territorial status in the late 1880s. The benefits of not having to pay for the salaries of territorial officers were offset primarily by Congress' control over land and water questions. With the small state population, mostly living on ranches and in small towns, the major employers were the railroads and the coal mines. By 1890, the Union Pacific had been joined by the Chicago, Burlington and Quincy, and the Chicago and Northwestern, and the railroads owned most of the coal mines. None of the promised industrial developments brought success, and few of them employed significant numbers of people. The population remained small and scattered over the 98,000 square miles of the territory.

Population, according to most observers, might have been the Achilles heel for statehood. Carey and other statehood proponents argued that while the Northwest Ordinance designated 60,000 people as the threshold for admission, it was not unprecedented for smaller states to be granted statehood. Warren, Carey, and the others knew, however, that the issue could be fatal. When Congress did not act on Carey's proposal for enabling legislation in 1889, presumably because of questions of population, Warren ignored the congressional omission and set a date for the election of delegates to the constitutional convention anyway. The election was called for July 8, 1889.

THE CONSTITUTIONAL CONVENTION

Of the fifty-five elected members, forty-nine of them assembled in September 1889 in Cheyenne to draft the constitution.[9] Four of the forty-nine did not sign the constitution and attended only occasionally. Of those elected, thirty-six were Republicans and nineteen were Democrats. Of those who did not participate, five were Republicans and one was a Democrat.[10]

On the first day, the convention delegates voted to create seventeen committees, each responsible for a particular subject. For example, one was a committee of five "to be known as the committee on the preamble and the declaration of rights and executive." Another committee reflected the state's economic interests: the "committee of seven to be known as the committee on agriculture, manufactures, commerce, live stock interests and labor."[11]

Knowing that they had twenty-five days to debate and draft the document, the delegates borrowed articles from many other constitutions.[12] In essence, the constitution was a "scissors-and-paste" recapitulation of sections pulled from many other states except in two major areas: water and irrigation, and women's rights.

As the convention got underway, the committees began deliberations on the main provisions. In terms of governmental structure, the delegates reflected the nineteenth-century distrust of legislative power. This view is particularly apparent as to fiscal matters, but many of the thirty-seven sections in the Declaration of Rights article place limits on legislative power.

Likewise, the constitution explicitly states that the "executive power" of the state "shall be vested" in the governor and he "shall take care that the law be faithfully executed." These seemingly broad powers, however, were substantially limited. Most notable was the creation of numerous boards to administer many of the important state functions. The boards were made up of the governor acting with the other four statewide elected officials. The constitution also provided for appointments to various other boards to be made for terms longer than that of the governor. For example, University of Wyoming trustees are appointed for six-year terms. The constitution allowed for the various boards and commissions to govern specific state agencies and even appoint the directors, taking that appointment power out of the governor's hands. (This existed for more than a century until government reorganization in the 1990s made many of these formerly governing boards advisory only.)

The constitution provided for a four-year term for the governor, with no restrictions on the number of terms an individual could serve. The legislature would need a two-thirds vote to override a gubernatorial veto. During the sixteenth day, delegate A. C. Campbell introduced an amendment attempting to make it a simple majority, but his proposal failed.[13]

Some of the main debates concerned how counties should be organized and what the minimum population and assessed valuation should be to establish new counties. Some delegates argued that the constitution ought to make it easy to create new counties so that people would not have to travel great distances to transact business at county seats. Others, however, saw a danger in allowing new county formation. It could drain off essential resources from older, established counties. The compromise was a provision for a relatively low threshold for county formation, but with the requirement that the county from which the new one was carved would have to meet a specific threshold for assessed valuation, with sufficient financial resources to continue functioning.

Debates over county business continued throughout the session. On the very eve of adjournment, the question of how to determine salaries paid to county officers consumed most of the session. Some delegates believed county officials would be more diligent if their pay was gained from a percentage of tax collected, from fees, or other similar measure. The majority, however, favored salaries set by the legislature.[14]

In deliberations over the judicial article, the delegates debated whether or not to have a supreme court separate from district courts. The three territorial justices "rode circuit" sitting as trial judges and returning for appellate hearings as the supreme court. Many delegates, particularly non-lawyers, believed making two separate courts would be wasteful. In the opinion of several delegates, the district judges would conduct most of the work while the supreme court justices would be left with little to do. Lawyers, however, favored separate courts and managed to defeat an effort to retain the territorial system, but barely by a 21-17 vote. Judges at all levels were to be elected to their offices. This practice remained in force until a 1972 constitutional amendment adopted the "Missouri plan" of judicial selection, whereby a judicial nominating committee accepts applications from lawyers admitted to practice in Wyoming who have an interest in serving as a judge, selects three names, and forwards them to the governor. The governor then selects one of them to serve on the court until the next general election. At that time, the judge's name appears on the ballot with voters given the option of voting to "retain" or to "not retain" the judge for the entire term.[15]

Legislative apportionment consumed substantial delegate debate. Delegates from the older established counties, the southern tier of counties stretching along the main line of the Union Pacific Railroad, fought efforts by delegates from the smaller northern counties to follow a "federal plan" for senate membership, by which each county would be given an equal number of senators. Delegates from the "Union Pacific" (southern Wyoming) counties, led by Charles Potter and E. S. N. Morgan, both from Cheyenne, argued that the federal analogy was flawed. Counties have no independence. They are creations of the state, not at all like the states' relationship to the federal government. George Baxter, also from Cheyenne, pointed out that it would be as unfair to give each county a senator as it would be to demand that each county give the same contribution to the state's general fund. If delegates from the southern counties had been uniformly in agreement, the issue would have been settled very quickly. However, former territorial governor John Hoyt and M. C. Brown, the president of the constitutional convention, broke with their southern colleagues. Both argued that a smaller senate, constructed along federal lines, could serve as a check on the popular will in the lower house. In describing the federal plan for senate representation, Brown, a Republican lawyer who had served as Laramie's first mayor, called it "the happiest compromise that ever came to man."

The disagreements came with apportionment in the senate. All along, the delegates opted for apportionment in the house to be based on population. Elections were to be at-large in each county. Even the least populated county, therefore, would have at least one representative. (Not until the legislative reapportionment after the 1990 census and a legal challenge were legislators in Wyoming elected from single-member districts.) On the nineteenth day of deliberations, the convention rejected the federal analogy by allocating more than one senator to more populous counties. The delegates, however, gave a sop to several northern counties in the form of one additional house member each. While the more populous counties gained greater representation in the senate, arguably, a modified "federal" plan still prevailed because one senator was granted to each county—even to the least populated one.[16]

The delegates seemed comfortable with retaining women's suffrage by incorporating it into a provision of the constitution. One delegate reported that the courts in Washington Territory had found against women's suffrage because the definition was not clear as to who were "citizens." The Wyoming provision flatly stated that equality would exist without reference to gender. For the majority of delegates, more specific language was not needed.[17] The delegates did argue, however, about including literacy as a requirement for voting.[18] One member argued that if a voter had to read to vote, newcomers would have the franchise while old established ranchers, many of whom were war veterans who had been voting for many years, would be stripped of their voting rights. The entire article, incorporating equal rights and the much more debated requirement for literacy, passed by a vote of 30-12.[19] Only one delegate, Louis J. Palmer, an Illinois-born lawyer and Democrat from Sweetwater County, flatly stated opposition to women's suffrage.[20]

Even though women could vote and exercise all legal rights in Wyoming under the proposed constitution, they were barred from mining coal. Delegate Preston believed that restricting boys under the age of fourteen and women from coal mining ought to be the prerogative of the legislature: "...as this convention has delegated to women the right to vote, she ought to have the right to dig coal if she wants to," he said.[21] A motion to strike the prohibition failed. Later, at the very end of the deliberations, Nickerson brought the matter up again, arguing that it would be too restrictive. Sutherland responded that he had seen women working in the mines in Pennsylvania and "I hope we shall never see that in Wyoming."[22] Despite Nickerson's last-minute efforts, the article barring women from coal mining remained in the article on mining. Women were constitutionally barred from coal mining until 1978.

Convention President M. C. Brown introduced an article that would have established a "coal tonnage" tax. Brown pointed out that the coal industry was making substantial profits as the companies, primary the Union Pacific Coal Company, removed more and more coal from the territory. Little of mined coal was used within the borders of Wyoming. Brown argued that the state would be financially sound for years to come if a modest tax were assessed against every ton of coal shipped out of Wyoming. "Can they afford to pay out of that 75 cents (of clean profit) two and a half cents per ton?" he asked. Without such a tax, "our new state shall be depleted of its wealth in coal, the coal taken and carried to other states and territories around us, to be used for their purposes, and she get no benefit...."[23] The measure passed initially during an afternoon session on the twentieth day of the convention, but that evening, the delegates reconsidered their earlier action after hearing the impassioned arguments of C. D. Clark, a delegate from Uinta County who, at the time he was elected a delegate, was working as the Union Pacific Railroad's legal counsel in that area. The Uinta delegate/railroad lawyer questioned what would happen if the state were to have revenues from every ton of coal mined. He argued that the result would be waste, inefficiency, and corruption. It would be preferable, he argued, to keep government lean and honest. This could only be done, he asserted, if the tax on coal were not made part of the constitution. (Wyoming finally adopted a similar "severance tax" on coal in 1969, after efforts for such a tax continued to be defeated through the lobbying efforts of the railroad and mining companies.)

While taxation of coal would have forever changed state funding, Wyoming's Article 8, involving water and irrigation, was revolutionary in its approach to water control, use, and allocation. The constitution set up a complete system of water allocation, unique among states to that time, but it also established the principle of state ownership of the resource.

The state could intervene on water issues because of the declaration that the state owned all waters within its borders. Further, the article established a state engineer's office and board of control so that the state's interests in water would be protected. It also set forth the principle that "beneficial use" determined the better right and no appropriation could be denied unless "demanded by the public interest." As several scholars have pointed out, the most important figure in drafting the water and irrigation article was Dr. Elwood Mead, the territorial engineer with substantial experience in administering the territorial water laws as well as the laws in Colorado. Frustrated by endless court adjudications of water rights in Colorado, Mead advocated removing such controversies to a group of individuals having substantial expertise in the subject, namely, a state engineer and a board of control.

Water and irrigation issues attracted substantial convention attention. The importance is shown from the lengthy debates over questions of water and irrigation. Even more indicative was the mid-convention adjournment for an entire afternoon so that delegates could meet with the visiting U.S. Senate Committee on Arid Lands. At the beginning of the afternoon session on the fourteenth day of the convention, the delegates voted 13-10 to adjourn for the remainder of the day.[24] This action was unprecedented. At no other time did the convention adjourn for an entire half-day. As another example of the importance the delegates placed in the water questions, the entire morning session of the eighteenth day involved a lengthy debate over the definition of "appropriation."[25]

J. A. Johnston, a Laramie County farmer, and Charles H. Burritt, a Johnson County lawyer, were the two delegates credited with the water article. Territorial Engineer Dr. Elwood Mead, who was not a convention delegate, also figured prominently in the discussions. Nonetheless, he advocated adoption of the prior appropriation doctrine already in operation, to some extent, in California and in Colorado, where he once had served as assistant water engineer. During his term as territorial engineer, he traveled throughout the territory urging support for his system as a means of fair allocation for everyone. Asbury B. Conaway, a former territorial court justice but serving as a delegate from Sweetwater County, questioned if the Mead-inspired article changed the common law rule about riparian rights to water.[26] Johnston and Potter said it did.[27] The rest of the delegates approved.

While prior appropriation and administrative control by experts seemed reasonable, more revolutionary was state ownership of all waters within the boundaries of the state.[28] Some commentators believe declaration of state ownership simply confirmed that "cattle kings" who would control state government also would also control state water allocations.[29] This interpretation, however, does not account for an interesting exchange among delegates early in the water debate. M. C. Brown pointed out that without state declaration of ownership, prior appropriators would not be subject to the constitution. "It would be utterly impossible for the legislature, or any power of the state, to control, regulate, or in any manner interfere with its use." He concluded thusly: "It is only by the declaration that we are to be the absolute owners of all the water that we may be enabled to control unreservedly the uses to which it may be put."[30]

Later, Sheridan County Democrat Henry A. Coffeen questioned if the water appropriation was a move to enrich corporations. Charles Burritt took issue with the insinuation. Such a connection "exists only in the very fertile imagination of the gentleman from Sheridan."[31]

Contrary to Coffeen's suspicions, historian Don Pisani argues that the lack of big mining interests, the relatively ample supply of unappropriated water, and the absence of large groups of farmers made the Wyoming article possible.[32] Other historians argue that the water article came from the "cattle kings"— who were early arrivals and the earliest users of water. They were confident such prior appropriation would ratify their holdings. At the same time, state ownership of the water would not be harmful because they were confident in their control over state government.[33] Further, these interpretations do not account for the concern delegates had over city rights to water. Surely any "cattle king" would be expected to worry about appropriations by urban entities. Delegates debated whether or not municipalities should have the power to appropriate water.[34] The cities were given that power.

Elwood Mead was crucial to the debate and to the eventual adoption of the water and irrigation article. Delegates drew from his experience with water and his persuasive abilities to argue for a predictable, expert-driven means of determining rights. As Mead biographer James Kluger points out, Mead's ideas about water spread worldwide, and the Wyoming convention gave him his first opportunity to articulate his water vision.[35] Just as in the case of women's suffrage in the first territorial legislature, men of like minds about water as a key to development, in the form of key delegates like Johnston and Burritt and even Warren and Carey, who were not delegates, were making a revolutionary decision about water use and allocation. Mead had his plan and the receptive "audience" in the form of delegates, anxious to bring development to the new state as well as predictability in resource allocation. The delegates remained consistent in this debate about making certain that control would not be entirely in the hands of a few big corporations. Mead's proposals, incorporated into the water article, ensured that a few big corporations would not hold the rest of Wyoming captive through control of water. After all, in the territorial days, the railroads controlled far more land than any other private landowner and, with it, the waters on it.

Throughout the wide-ranging convention discussions on the state's owner-ship of water, no mention was made of the rights of the earliest water users, the Indians. Following congressional passage of the Dawes Act, which authorized the breakup of tribal lands into individual allotments, the Shoshone reservation diminished in size. In the early 1900s, federal authorities opened a substantial parcel to white settlement. Water from the Wind River would be used for federal irrigation projects on what had been Indian lands. In the 1970s, disputes over the waters of the Wind River pitted the Indians against downstream water users who claimed they were "senior appropriators" as recognized by the State of Wyoming. The state claimed that under its constitution, all water in the state came under its control. The state claimed that the Indians, even if they had treaty rights to the water under the so-called Winters doctrine, had neither filed nor followed proper state provisions for claiming a senior appropriation in Wyoming. The federal courts appointed a special master who sorted out the thorny water rights issues, allocating most of the Wind River flow to the tribes under provisions of federal reserved water rights. But even beyond natural resource issues and except for the references to exemption from taxation and voting, delegates made no other mention of the presence of native people within the state's borders.

Except for their reversal on the coal tonnage tax, the delegates displayed independence from the Union Pacific by passing several provisions control-ling the way it did business. One provision barred the railroad from bypassing an established community to set up a depot nearby. "No railroad company shall construct or operate a railroad within four miles of any existing town or city without providing a suitable depot or shipping place at the nearest practicable point for the convenience of said town or city, and stopping all trains doing local business at said stopping place."[36] Another provision declared railroads common carriers and required them to "deal impartially with the public, and shall make no unjust discrimination or unreasonable charges for the services rendered."[37] The delegates extensively debated how the master-servant rule would be applied in Wyoming so that employees would not be barred from collecting for damages resulting from the negligence of another employee. Many delegates pointed out that the other corporations existed beyond the Union Pacific.[38] Nonetheless, most knew that when provisions were being offered to curb corporate power, the railroad stood the most to lose.

The convention passed a section restricting the legislature from providing any form of financial aid for railroad construction. "The legislature shall have no power to pass any law authorizing the state or any county in the state to contract any debt or obligation in the construction of any railroad, or give or loan its credit to or in aid of the construction of the same."[39] The delegates also debated a proposal that would restrict corporations to one line of business. Adopted by the convention, Article 10, Section 6 was amended in 1960 to loosen the requirement.

"Chinese labor" was debated extensively. The issue was whether or not the constitution ought to ban use of Chinese labor on public works projects. It was introduced by Thomas R. Reid, a Democrat and Union Pacific railway worker from Cheyenne, a native of England who had immigrated to Wyoming as a young man from Australia.[40] Some viewed it as a dig at Warren for his actions four years earlier against the rioting miners at Rock Springs. The measure passed. It demonstrated discrimination against Chinese labor de facto: "No person not a citizen of the United States or who has not declared his intention to become such, shall be employed upon or in connection with any state, county or municipal works or employment."[41] Ultimately even this measure passed with bipartisan support.

On another labor-related issue, the constitution instituted the eight-hour day for miners.[42] The strongest proponent was John L. Russell, a Democrat and delegate from Uinta County. Another section forbade the importation of "private armies" into the state. The measure was meant to restrict such operations as the Union Pacific from importing Pinkerton agents to break labor strikes. The measure passed.

The convention showed skepticism of corporations, but also of organized religion. It also insisted on separation of church and state. Article 3, Section 36, asserts that: "No appropriation shall be made for charitable, industrial, educational or benevolent purposes to any person, corporation or community not under the absolute control of the state, nor to any denominational or sectarian institution or association." A similar provision in the Declaration of Rights states it even more clearly: "No money of the state shall ever be given or appropriated to any sectarian or religious society or institution."[43] During the course of debate over requiring an oath for jurors, delegates made it clear that "belief or non-belief in God" ought to be no bar to service.[44] The measures had near-unanimous and bipartisan support.

Republicans held a significant majority in the convention, but in terms of party loyalties, the convention did not divide along partisan lines. Delegate Carey noted this fact in his speech to the Congress advocating admission in February 1890, and the fact is fairly clear from reading the proceedings of the convention. The body did seem to have a fair share of "progressives" and reformers. Along with Brown's efforts at taxation of coal, several other "reform" measures were proposed. For example, delegate and University of Wyoming President Hoyt offered a section that would create a civil service for state employees, but his recommendation was defeated by a substantial margin (21-11).[45] C. D. Clark, who had eloquently opposed the coal tonnage tax, also led opposition to the reform measure. Brown, Hoyt, and Clark were all Republicans.

More significant than political party affiliations were sectional differences. Debates over legislative apportionment consumed substantial convention time. So did other issues that were sectionally divisive, mostly between the earlier-populated southern counties and the newly developing ones in the north.

These divisions were illustrated once again on the question of location of state institutions. Delegates from the longer-settled southern counties wanted the convention to ratify the territorial legislatures' designated locations of the already existing capital (Cheyenne), state "insane asylum" (Evanston), university (Laramie), and prison (Rawlins). Northern delegates, believing their region was about to experience huge spurts in population and, thus, ought to have an opportunity to gain these lucrative state facilities, disagreed. The convention struck a compromise. At an election to be held "no sooner than 10 years" after the passage of the constitution, voters would decide the "permanent" locations of state institutions.[46] During the interim, the institutions would be "temporarily" housed in the communities previously designated by the territorial legislatures.[47]

In 1904, the election for the permanent locations finally was held. Laramie was the sole candidate for the university; Evanston, the state hospital; Rawlins, the state penitentiary. Cheyenne, however, was challenged by several cities for the capital. The most serious competitor was the relatively "new" town of Casper, founded in 1888 as a wool shipping point, but soon after, the center for oil exploration and development. It had the advantage of central location. Cheyenne, in the extreme southeast corner of Wyoming, was a mere nine miles from the Colorado border and barely fifty miles from Nebraska. Another centrally located community, Lander, got into the contest. A promoter from southern Wyoming advocated placing the capital at the "geographic center" of Wyoming along Muskrat Creek. He proposed naming the new capital "Muskrat." His proposal gained little support. As one person ignorant of the muskrat genus observed, "How many state capitals are named for rodents?" The election result gave Cheyenne more than 40 percent of the vote, but not the required 50 percent plus one, as designated in the constitution for permanent location. Consequently, Cheyenne remains, at least constitutionally, the "temporary" capital of the state.

The delegates never seriously questioned the ordinance, included in the constitution, stating that: "The people inhabiting this state do agree and declare that they forever disclaim all right and title to the unappropriated public lands lying within the boundaries thereof...." Yet, totally disregarding the language in the constitution, "sagebrush rebels" over the years have persisted in demanding that the federal government "return" all federal lands to the state.[48]

The delegates debated numerous education issues. Most significant was how state lands, held in trust for the benefit of the schools, would be sold or leased. Any sale had to be made at or above appraisal. All revenues from sale or rent of these lands went into a permanent school fund for the exclusive support of public schools.[49] Delegates endorsed a provision barring the state superintendent or the legislature from choosing textbooks for use in schools. The section became part of the constitution with just one comment explaining the rationale: "I venture to say there is no more corruption than that which is caused where the prescribing of textbooks is left to the legislature."[50]

In what would be a precursor to education funding questions for the next century and beyond, the constitutional convention debated how funding for schools could bring fairness to both small schools and large. With the details left to the legislature, the convention concluded that after a threshold amount was allocated to each school, regardless of enrollment, the average class attendance would be used for determining allocation of additional funds. Details were left to the legislature.[51] A provision authorizing a state tax for support of public schools became a part of the Wyoming constitution in 1948 and amended in 1982.[52] A series of Wyoming Supreme Court decisions, handed down in the last ten years, demanded equity in education funding throughout the state. Consequently, education funding issues dominated legislative sessions in the late 1990s and early 2000s.

The constitutional convention placed three sections in the general article on education establishing a state university. Declaring that it be governed by a board, higher education provisions also reaffirmed equality. "The university shall be equally open to students of both sexes, irrespective of race or color...." The constitution stated that higher education would receive adequate state funding either from land grants or other sources "in order that the instruction furnished may be as nearly free as possible."[53]

Once the issue of location of institutions was settled, the delegate committees' reports concluded, and the language perfected, the delegates looked toward adjournment. Before that, however, came a discussion about admission tactics. One member, Hubert Tschemacher, proposed that they not submit the constitution to popular vote until after Congress passed enabling legislation. M. C. Brown disagreed. "Senator Stewart, when here the other day, said that if we would prepare our constitution, submit it to the people, have it ratified, and then come down to Washington and say Wyoming wants to be a state, and we will be a state."[54]

On the twenty-fifth day of the convention, the delegates voted on adoption of the entire document. The resolution passed 37-0. Later in the day, forty-five of the fifty-five elected delegates signed the constitution and adjourned, as they sent it to the voters for their approval. Governor Warren called a special election for November 5, 1889. The vote count in the election was the source of problems for Warren, Carey, and congressional supporters of Wyoming statehood. The constitution passed overwhelmingly by a vote of 6,272 in favor to 1,903 against. But the problem was not the margin; it was the total number of voters.

WYOMING STATEHOOD IN THE CONGRESS

On March 26, 1890, Territorial Delegate Joseph M. Carey introduced a bill calling for statehood for Wyoming. This was not the first proposal for Wyoming statehood, however. Carey introduced the first statehood bill on February 27, 1888, but H.R. 7780 was not reported out of committee. Senator Henry M.

Teller introduced a second statehood bill on March 19, 1888, S.F. 2445. After languishing in committee for more than a year, Senator Orville H. Platt of Connecticut attached the Senate Committee on Territories Report 2695 to the Teller bill, but Congress adjourned five days later without considering the measure.[55] Another house bill, H.R. 3830, would have included Wyoming with admission of three other states—Arizona, New Mexico, and Idaho—it, too, failed. Representative Isaac S. Struble, an Iowa Republican, introduced a statehood bill for Wyoming on January 13, 1890, but it did not get out of committee.[56]

In the months prior to the special election on the constitution, delegate Carey had been telling colleagues that Wyoming's true population was far in excess of the 60,000 normally considered the threshold for statehood. At one point, he was quoted as estimating the population at 125,000! He was embarrassed to explain that if the population was so great, why did so few people vote in the special election? When he took to the floor to advocate passage of H.R. 982, the Wyoming Statehood Bill, he began by discussing the vast expanses of land, their fertility, and the glittering potential the new state promised. After describing the various industries, mining, and the educational system, he addressed the "Questions of Population."

"In estimating population there is always a latitude for important differences of opinion," Carey began. Having "made some comparisons" and "following all precedents heretofore established," Carey argued that "Wyoming is entitled to admission at this time." He then compared the estimates for ten states admitted over the years, seven of the ten with an estimated population well below 60,000. "Nearly every State doubled it population in five years after admission," Carey said. He promised that Wyoming would have similar stellar growth because "with booms and immigration societies, the territory has steadily increased each year since organization in population and wealth." He then explained the problem with the small election turnout. "The population can not be properly based on the vote. There is but little of politics in Wyoming. Every year is an off year. The vote this year will be 23,000 in round numbers. If State government is given the people, it will be from 25,000 to 28,000—note my prediction." He then pointed out how difficult a "true census" was in a territory of some 100,000 square miles. "To get a full vote or a full census is an impossibility," he concluded. He then turned to a discussion of finances and the economy. Representative Baker interrupted Carey to ask again about the population. Carey, this time, responded with a lengthy argument that the commonly accepted 60,000 threshold was, in fact, not recognized as critical. He quoted a number of past members of Congress on this question.[57]

Curiously, Carey made no mention in his speech of the women's suffrage article, one that some delegates believed might have been harmful to gaining statehood. Nonetheless, numerous members of the House, mostly Democrats, rose to oppose admission of Wyoming, which was known to be leaning Republican. As T. A. Larson observed, the Democrats could hardly argue against admission based on party affiliation—the Republicans controlled the House—but they could argue against statehood for a Republican territory by attacking women suffrage. Despite persistent objections to Wyoming's Article 6 that granted women equal rights, the statehood bill finally passed the House of Representatives by a close vote of 139-127.

Warren and Carey both assured Wyomingites that the bill would pass the Senate within ten days. Passage did not come nearly that quickly, however. Several prominent Democrats in the Senate continued to question both the territory's population and the woman suffrage provision. Three months after House passage, the Wyoming Statehood Bill finally passed the Senate, but by a more comfortable 29-18 margin. President Harrison signed the Statehood Bill on July 10, 1890, making Wyoming the forty-fourth state admitted to the Union.[58]

STATEHOOD PERSONALITIES: THEIR LATER CAREERS

Soon after statehood, the first Wyoming State legislature sent forty-five-year-old Joseph M. Carey to the U.S. Senate. Governor Warren, age forty-six, finished his term as territorial governor only to win election as the first state governor handily over his Democratic opponent. The constitutional convention delegate from Uinta County, C. D. Clark, who successfully argued against the coal tonnage tax in the convention, won election to the U.S. House of Representatives as Wyoming's only representative. Two and a half months later, Warren gave up his governor's seat to accept the legislature's election to the U.S. Senate. Except for a two-year period, he remained in that chamber, and as a power in state politics, until his death in 1929. As chairman of the Senate Armed Services and Appropriations committees, he was important to the career of his son-in-law, John J. Pershing, as well as to the continued federal presence at Fort Russell near his hometown of Cheyenne. After Warren's death, the fort was renamed in his honor. Today, it is Warren Air Force Base.

Carey's influence in the statehood drive was considerable.[59] In 1894, he and Warren, both Republicans, began a quarter-century feud when Warren successfully pushed his old friend out of the Senate. "Wyoming will accept only one Cheyenne man in the Senate so that will be me," Warren was quoted as telling friends before the *coup d'etat*. Warren joined C. D. Clark in the Senate while Carey, blindsided by Warren's treachery, nursed a grudge until 1910 when he managed to gain the Democratic nomination for governor, beat the Warren candidate, and served for one term. His political career ended, however, when he backed his old friend Theodore Roosevelt in the three-way presidential race of 1912. Democrats turned on him; Republicans, still controlled by the "Warren machine," repudiated him. He died in 1923, five years after the "Warren machine" ended the feud by nominating his son, Robert Carey, for the governorship.

M. C. Brown, the president of the constitutional convention who introduced the coal tonnage measure, later moved to Alaska to serve as a federal judge. Implicated in improprieties there during the gold rush, he resigned his judgeship, returned to Laramie to practice law, and died in relative obscurity in 1928.

Hoyt, the University of Wyoming resident who was elected a delegate and who drafted much of the education article, returned to the university after statehood. Soon after, however, he was fired by the trustees over disagreements with administrative control. He moved to Washington, D.C., tried unsuccessfully to interest Congress in creating a national university, and served for a time as an ambassador.

Delegate Charles Potter, active in many of the convention debates, was elected to the Wyoming Supreme Court. Richard Scott, after service on the state district court bench, became a supreme court justice too. So did delegate Jesse Knight. John A. Riner, who, like Potter, came from Cheyenne, was appointed to the federal bench, where he served for the next three decades as Wyoming's first U.S. district judge.

Delegates W. C. Irvine, H. C. Teschemacher, and Charles Burritt were implicated on the side of the "invaders" in the Johnson County War. C. D. Clark was later elected to the U.S. Senate, and Henry Coffeen to the U.S. House of Representatives.

Two delegates, Charles Burdick and William Chaplin, were later elected secretary of state. Delegate DeForest Richards was serving as Wyoming governor at the time of his death in 1902.

STATEHOOD: THE AFTERMATH

When the 1890 census figures for Wyoming finally became available nearly two years after statehood, the result showed how close the territory had been to the 60,000 "threshold." The census recorded 62,555 people in Wyoming, according to the official government count made in April 1890—two months after Carey's speech in the House. The question of population remained a significant one for Wyoming. Since statehood, Wyoming has been close to last in population (only Nevada was smaller in the early twentieth century; only Alaska, for one census in the middle of the century). Throughout the years since statehood, government officials almost uniformly have advocated for economic diversification to increase the state's population base and diminish the state's dependence on agriculture and natural resources. In the late twentieth century, many residents of the state were comfortable with the small population and opposed promotional drives except for attracting tourists for temporary stays.

The industries prominently represented in the constitutional convention remain important to the Wyoming economy today. Wyoming leads the nation in coal production and has led every year since 1988. Tourism, anchored by Yellowstone and Grand Teton national parks, is central to the economy of many of the state's towns. The federal government still owns nearly 50 percent of the land area of Wyoming, much of it administered by the Bureau of Land Management. Agriculture has lost considerable economic importance during the past century. Nonetheless, cattle ranching remains symbolically important to residents of the "Cowboy State." The reputation as the "Equality State," gained from being first to give women the right to vote, was bolstered in 1894 with the election of the first woman in America to a statewide office. Estelle Reel was elected state superintendent of public instruction. And in 1924 Nellie Tayloe Ross was elected the first woman governor of any state.

The national influence exercised in Congress by Warren and Carey in the early years of statehood has rarely been equaled since. The Wyoming constitution, amended some seventy times since its adoption, remains generally similar to the document drafted in 1889. It is the eleventh longest of any state constitution. Major amendments have been made to articles on judicial selection and on public finance. An amendment was passed in 1974 making it difficult to adopt a state income tax, and Wyoming remains one of seven states without an income tax. The first sales tax was authorized in 1935.

Through the years, the question of executive power has been raised by a number of governors. Amendments have made it easier for governors to administer departments and hire and fire their directors. While gubernatorial power increased with government reorganization in the 1990s, the constitution continues to dilute the power of the chief executive by providing for such entities as a state land board made up of the governor and the other four statewide elected officials.

Frequent amendments to the Wyoming constitution have been made and even more have been proposed. To pass, an amendment must have two-thirds vote of each house and then a vote of the majority plus one of all voters casting ballots in the election.[60] Since its adoption in 1889 and Wyoming statehood the following year, there has been no call for a second constitutional convention to replace the current version. Wyoming's constitution, the eleventh longest among the states, retains the outlines drawn for it by the drafters in 1889 and accepted by Congress in 1890 as Wyoming became the forty-fourth state.

SUMMARY

Wyoming statehood came less than twenty-five years after the creation of Wyoming Territory. The first territorial legislature authorized women's suffrage, making the territory the first in the nation to give women the right to vote and equal political and legal rights. Ironically, no women were elected to territorial legislative offices and no women were elected to the constitutional convention, held in September 1889. The convention met for just twenty-five days. Consequently, many articles were borrowed from constitutions of existing states. Few articles were unique to the Wyoming document. Individual to the Wyoming constitution were: the article and sections giving women equal rights and the article on water and irrigation. The constitution affirmed state ownership of water and established a means of government regulation as well as priority of use. Little partisanship existed in the deliberations and on the statehood question. The delegates divided, however, along sectional lines with delegates from the later-developing northern parts of Wyoming often in opposition to those from the counties in the southern part of the territory, which were formed soon after the transcontinental railroad was built. Contentious issues in the constitutional convention included location of state institutions, legislative apportionments, and efforts to tax and to control actions of corporations, particularly the Union Pacific Railroad. Delegates generally agreed on questions of land policy and water use. Partisan issues were important to admission, however, with Republicans in the U.S. Congress favoring admission while many Democrats were opposed. Opponents resorted to questioning the level of population. Wyoming, at the time of statehood, had a population just barely above 60,000, generally agreed to be a threshold for admission. Through the efforts of Territorial Governor Francis E. Warren and Delegate to Congress Joseph M. Carey, Wyoming gained admission as the forty-fourth state, the last of the group of western states admitted in 1889–1890.

NOTES

1. Campbell's address, the territorial legislative records, and the committee reports from the constitutional convention are all held in the collections of the Wyoming State Archives, State Parks and Cultural Resources Dept., Cheyenne.

2. Maps showing these demarcations are in: Marie Erwin, *Wyoming Blue Book I*, Virginia Trenholm, ed. (Cheyenne: Wyoming State Archives and Historical Dept., 1974), pp. 37–50.

3. The best source for the territorial issues is T. A. Larson, *History of Wyoming* (Lincoln: University of Nebraska Press, 1965, 1978).

4. Larson, pp. 68–69.

5. For a recent account of the controversy, see Geoff O'Gara, *What You See in Clear Water: Life on the Wind River Reservation* (New York: A. A. Knopf, 2000). Shoshone chief Washakie, the leader of his tribe for more than a half century, is the second Wyomingite honored with a statue in Statuary Hall.

6. For a brief biography of Hoyt, see Erwin, *Wyoming Blue Book*, pp. 92–93.

7. A number of authors have examined the political underpinnings of the Johnson County Invasion. One of the most even-handed remains: Helena Huntington Smith, *War on Powder River* (Lincoln: University of Nebraska Press, 1966).

8. For Moonlight's stormy term as territorial governor, see W. Turrentine Jackson, "Administration of Thomas Moonlight," *Annals of Wyoming* 18 (July 1946): 139–162. For an overview of politics of the period, see Lewis L. Gould, *Wyoming: A Political History, 1868–1896* (New Haven: Yale University Press, 1968).

9. Biographical sketches of all delegates, with accompanying photographic portraits, can be found in Erwin, *Wyoming Blue Book*, pp. 541–557.

10. Erwin, *Wyoming Blue Book*, p. 541.

11. The account of the deliberations of the constitutional convention is drawn almost entirely from the printed proceedings: *Journal and Debates of the Constitutional Convention of the State of Wyoming* (Cheyenne: Daily Sun, Book and Job Printing, 1893). References to specific articles passed by the convention are from the convention files, held in the Wyoming State Archives, Cheyenne.

12. For the origins of many of the articles, see Robert Keiter, *The Wyoming State Constitution: A Reference Guide* (Westport, CT: Greenwood Press, 1993). For excellent insights on the constitutional convention issues, see Gordon M. Bakken, *Rocky Mountain Constitution Making, 1850–1912* (Westport, CT: Greenwood Press, 1986).

13. *Debates*, p. 461.

14. Ibid., pp. 801–819; *Wyoming Constitution*, Art. 14, Sec. 1.

15. *Wyoming Constitution*, Art. 5.

16. *Debates*, pp. 570–576. For a recent description of the districting debate, see Matilda Hansen, *Clear Use of Power: A Slice of Wyoming Political History* (Laramie: Commentary Press, 2003).

17. *Debates*, pp. 366–367.

18. Ibid., pp. 370–378, 383–401, 428–443.

19. Ibid., p. 443.

20. Ibid., p. 442.

21. Ibid., p. 765.

22. *Debates*, p. 793.

23. For the Brown discussion on the proposal, see *Debates*, pp. 640–641.

24. *Debates*, p. 380.

25. Ibid., pp. 496–512.

26. Ibid., pp. 291–292.

27. Ibid., p. 292.

28. For the extended debates over the water question, see, for example, *Proceedings and Debates*, pp. 289–297.

29. Andrew P. Morriss, "Wyoming Constitution, Article VIII," in *Law in the Western United States*, ed. Gordon Bakken (Norman: University of Oklahoma Press, 2000), pp. 168–169.

30. *Debates*, p. 289.

31. *Debates*, p. 535. The section was adopted by a vote of 35-2 with 12 absent. *Debates*, p. 537.

32. Don Pisani, "Enterprise and Equity: A Critique of Western Water Law in the Nineteenth Century," *Western Historical Quarterly* 18 (1987): 15–37.

33. Morriss, pp. 168–169.

34. *Debates*, pp. 259 et seq.

35. James Kluger, *Turning on Water with a Shovel* (Albuquerque: University of New Mexico Press, 1992).

36. *Wyoming Constitution*, Art. 10, Sec. 19.

37. Ibid., p. 581.

38. See, for instance, Harvey comments, *Debates*, pp. 453–454.

39. *Wyoming Constitution*, Art. 3, Sec. 39.

40. *Debates*, p. 276. For Reid's biography, see Erwin, *Wyoming Blue Book*, p. 554.

41. See Article XIX, Labor on Public Works, Sec. 1, in the original constitution.

42. For the spirited debate on this question, see *Debates*, pp. 607–611.

43. *Wyoming Constitution*, Art. 1, Sec. 19.

44. *Debates*, p. 727.

45. *Debates*, pp. 833–837.

46. Ibid., pp. 539–576.

47. For final resolution of the issue, see *Proceedings and Debates*, p. 775.

48. *Wyoming Constitution*, Art. 21, Sec. 26.

49. *Wyoming Constitution*, Art. 7.

50. Charles Potter comments, *Proceedings and Debates*, p. 737; *Wyoming Constitution*, Art. 7, Sec. 11.

51. *Debates*, pp. 734–736.

52. *Wyoming Constitution*, Art. 15, Sec. 15.

53. *Wyoming Constitution*, Art. 15, Sec. 16.

54. *Proceedings and Debates*, 779.

55. See Cong. Docs., serial 2619, S. Rept. No. 2695.

56. *Congressional Record*, 21, p. 523.

57. Carey's remarks were made during deliberations over the Statehood Bill, H.R. 982, on March 26, 1890, and published in the *Congressional Record*, 21, pp. 2672–2683. Carey introduced H.R. 982 on Dec. 18, 1889. See *Congressional Record*, 21, p. 261.

58. For final passage in the House on March 26, 1890, see *Congressional Record*, 21, p. 2712; for passage in the Senate on June 27, 1890, *Congressional Record*, 21, p. 6589.

59. No definitive biography exists on Carey. While some of his papers are held in the collections of the Wyoming State Archives, he apparently had many of them destroyed prior to his death.

60. *Wyoming Constitution*, Art. 20.

BIBLIOGRAPHY

Bakken, Gordon M. *Rocky Mountain Constitution Making, 1850–1912* . Westport, CT: Greenwood Press, 1986.

Brown, M. C. "Constitution Making." *Proceedings and Collections of the Wyoming State Historical Department*, 1919–1920, pp. 96–108.

Erwin, Marie. *Wyoming Blue Book I*. Edited by Virginia Trenholm. Cheyenne: Wyoming State Archives and Historical Department, 1974.

Gould, Lewis L. *Wyoming: A Political History, 1868–1896* . New Haven, CT: Yale University Press, 1968.

Hansen, Matilda. *Clear Use of Power: A Slice of Wyoming Political History*. Laramie, WY: Commentary Press, 2003.

Jackson, W. Turrentine. "Administration of Thomas Moonlight." *Annals of Wyoming* 18 (July 1946): 139–162.

Journal and Debates of the Constitutional Convention of the State of Wyoming. Cheyenne: Daily Sun, Book and Job Printing, 1893.

Keiter, Robert. *The Wyoming State Constitution: A Reference Guide.* Westport, CT: Greenwood Press, 1993.

Kluger, James. *Turning on Water with a Shovel.* Albuquerque: University of New Mexico Press, 1992.

Lamar, Howard R. *Dakota Territory, 1861–1889: A Study of Frontier Politics*. New Haven, CT: Yale University Press, 1956.

Larson, T. A. *History of Wyoming.* Lincoln: University of Nebraska Press, 1965, 1978.

———. *Wyoming: A History.* New York: W. W. Norton, 1977.

Morriss, Andrew P. "Wyoming Constitution, Article VIII." In *Law in the Western United States.* Edited by Gordon Bakken. Norman: University of Oklahoma Press, 2000, pp. 168–169.

O'Gara, Geoff. *What You See in Clear Water: Life on the Wind River Reservation.* New York: Alfred A. Knopf, 2000.

Peters, Betsy Ross. "Joseph M. Carey and the Progressive Movement in Wyoming." Unpublished Ph.D. diss., University of Wyoming, 1971.

Peterson, H. J. "The Constitutional Convention of Wyoming." Unpublished M.A. thesis, University of Wyoming, 1956.

Pisani, Don. "Enterprise and Equity: A Critique of Western Water Law in the Nineteenth Century." *Western Historical Quarterly* 18 (1987): 15–37.

Pomeroy, Earl S. *The Territories and the United States, 1861–1890*. Philadelphia: University of Pennsylvania Press, 1947.

Prien, R. K. "The Background of the Wyoming Constitution." Unpublished M.A. thesis, University of Wyoming, 1956.

Report of Territorial Gov. Francis E. Warren to the Secretary of the Interior, Oct. 15, 1889, House Executive Documents, 51 Cong., 1st Sess., 1889–1890, Vol. XIII (Serial 2726), pp. 561–705.

Smith, Helena Huntington. *War on Powder River.* Lincoln: University of Nebraska Press, 1966.

Warren, Francis E. *Letterbooks.* Laramie: American Heritage Center, University of Wyoming.

Appendix I: Quick Reference List of States in Order of Admission

State	Admission Date
1. Delaware	December 7, 1787
2. Pennsylvania	December 12, 1787
3. New Jersey	December 18, 1787
4. Georgia	January 2, 1788
5. Connecticut	January 9, 1788
6. Massachusetts	February 6, 1788
7. Maryland	April 28, 1788
8. South Carolina	May 23, 1788
9. New Hampshire	June 21, 1788
10. Virginia	June 25, 1788
11. New York	July 26, 1788
12. North Carolina	November 21, 1789
13. Rhode Island	May 29, 1790
14. Vermont	March 4,1791
15. Kentucky	June 1, 1792
16. Tennessee	June 1, 1796
17. Ohio	March 1, 1803
18. Louisiana	April 30, 1812
19. Indiana	December 11, 1816
20. Mississippi	December 10, 1817
21. Illinois	December 3, 1818
22. Alabama	December 14, 1819
23. Maine	March 15, 1820
24. Missouri	August 10, 1821
25. Arkansas	June 15, 1836

26.	Michigan	January 26, 1837
27.	Florida	March 3, 1845
28.	Texas	December 29, 1845
29.	Iowa	December 28, 1846
30.	Wisconsin	May 29, 1848
31.	California	September 9, 1850
32.	Minnesota	May 11, 1858
33.	Oregon	February 14, 1859
34.	Kansas	January 29, 1861
35.	West Virginia	June 30, 1863
36.	Nevada	October 31, 1864
37.	Nebraska	March 1, 1867
38.	Colorado	August 1, 1876
39.	North Dakota	November 2, 1889
40.	South Dakota	November 2, 1889
41.	Montana	November 8, 1889
42.	Washington	November 11, 1889
43.	Idaho	July 3, 1890
44.	Wyoming	July 10, 1890
45.	Utah	January 4, 1896
46.	Oklahoma	November 16, 1907
47.	New Mexico	January 6, 1912
48.	Arizona	February 14, 1912
49.	Alaska	January 3, 1959
50.	Hawaii	August 21, 1959

Appendix II: Quick Reference List of State Admission Dates Alphabetically

State	Admission Date
Alabama	December 14, 1819
Alaska	January 3, 1959
Arizona	February 14, 1912
Arkansas	June 15, 1836
California	September 9, 1850
Colorado	August 1, 1876
Connecticut	January 9, 1788
Delaware	December 7, 1787
Florida	March 3, 1845
Georgia	January 2, 1788
Hawaii	August 21, 1959
Idaho	July 3, 1890
Illinois	December 3, 1818
Indiana	December 11, 1816
Iowa	December 28, 1846
Kansas	January 29, 1861
Kentucky	June 1, 1792
Louisiana	April 30, 1812
Maine	March 15, 1820
Maryland	April 28, 1788
Massachusetts	February 6, 1788
Michigan	January 26, 1837
Minnesota	May 11, 1858
Mississippi	December 10, 1817
Missouri	August 10, 1821

Montana	November 8, 1889
Nebraska	March 1, 1867
Nevada	October 31, 1864
New Hampshire	June 21, 1788
New Jersey	December 18, 1787
New Mexico	January 6, 1912
New York	July 26, 1788
North Carolina	November 21, 1789
North Dakota	November 2, 1889
Ohio	March 1, 1803
Oklahoma	November 16, 1907
Oregon	February 14, 1859
Pennsylvania	December 12, 1787
Rhode Island	May 29, 1790
South Carolina	May 23, 1788
South Dakota	November 2, 1889
Tennessee	June 1, 1796
Texas	December 29, 1845
Utah	January 4, 1896
Vermont	March 4, 1791
Virginia	June 25, 1788
Washington	November 11, 1889
West Virginia	June 30, 1863
Wisconsin	May 29, 1848
Wyoming	July 10, 1890

Index

About the Editor and the Contributors

BENJAMIN F. SHEARER is retired Vice President of Student Affairs at Neumann College. Along with Barbara Shearer he is co-author of *State Names, Seals, Flags, and Symbols*, third edition (Greenwood Press, 2002), *Notable Women in the Physical Sciences* (Greenwood Press, 1997), and *Notable Women in the Life Sciences* (Greenwood Press, 1996), among others.

VALERIE L. ADAMS, Ph.D., is Assistant Professor of History at Embry-Riddle Aeronautical University in Prescott, Arizona. Her main interests are in twentieth-century American history and diplomatic history. She is the author of several pieces on the Cold War and on science and technology.

KATHERINE G. AIKEN is Professor of History at the University of Idaho and Chair of the History Department. She received her Ph.D. from Washington State University. Her areas of specialization are twentieth-century United States, social and cultural history, and women and labor.

J. CHRIS ARNDT received a Ph.D. in history from Florida State University in 1987. A Professor of History at James Madison University in Harrisonburg, Virginia, he is the author/editor of several works, including *"So You Want to Be a Historian": A Guide to Historical Methods* (forthcoming) and *Voices of the American Past: Documents in U.S. History* (with Raymond Hyser). He is currently completing a book-length manuscript, "States Once 'Free and Independent' Are Dwindling to Mere Provinces": Maine, State's Rights, and the Northeastern Boundary Controversy, 1820–1842.

STEPHEN ASPERHEIM is Assistant Professor of History at Savannah State University in Savannah, Georgia.

WILLIAM D. BAKER holds a Ph.D. in political science from the University of Alabama and teaches American government and American studies in the

Department of Humanities at the Arkansas School for Mathematics, Sciences, and the Arts in Hot Springs. He is the author of several publications on political behavior, the American presidency, and American political history.

J. D. BOWERS is Assistant Professor of History at Northern Illinois University, where he focuses on public history and Pacific Island history. He is currently at work on a project titled *Living in a Sovereign Land: Hawaiian History and Culture in the Twentieth Century*, which investigates the birth and development of Native Hawaiian sovereignty and its cultural intersections with state politics, music, ecology, federal government policy, tourism, and historical memory.

JEFFREY D. CARLISLE received his Ph.D. in history from the University of North Texas in 2001. He is currently a Lecturer at the University of North Texas in Denton. He has contributed a number of entries on Native American topics for *The New Handbook of Texas* and other reference works. He is now researching the Apache Indians in Texas.

PETER E. CARR is an archaeologist, historian, author, and lecturer. His varied interests have led him to be involved in writing about history, archaeology, political commentary, and family history. He has been the publisher and editor of the *Caribbean Historical & Genealogical Journal* since its inception in 1993.

MARK R. CHEATHEM, a native Tennessean, received his Ph.D. from Mississippi State University in 2002. His major fields of research are the Jacksonian and Civil War periods. He is currently revising his dissertation, a biography of Tennessee politician Andrew Jackson Donelson, for publication. Cheathem is also the co-listed editor and book review editor for H-Tennessee, an Internet discussion network devoted to Tennessee history and culture, http://www2.h-net.msu.edu/~tenn/.

DAVID B. DANBOM is Professor of History at North Dakota State University.

HARRIET E. AMOS DOSS, Ph.D., is Associate Professor of History at the University of Alabama—Birmingham. Her research interests include race relations in religious matters during Reconstruction in Alabama and Mississippi as well as frontier Alabama.

MARK R. ELLIS is Assistant Professor of History at the University of Nebraska at Kearney. He teaches courses on the history of Nebraska, the Great Plains, and Plains Indians. His publications relating to early Nebraska statehood include "Reservation Akicitas: The Pine Ridge Indian Police," published by *South Dakota History*, and "Pioneer Legal Communities in Nebraska's Platte Valley," published by *Nebraska History*.

WILLIAM M. FERRARO, Ph.D., is a documentary editor with the Ulysses S. Grant Association, Southern Illinois University, Carbondale. Since completing his dissertation at Brown University on town meeting government in

Rhode Island between the seventeenth and twentieth centuries, his research and publications have centered on the political and social history of the nineteenth century, with a particular focus on the lives and family of John and William Tecumseh Sherman.

ROBERT E. FICKEN is a distinguished historian of the Northwest. The author of several books on Washington history, he has been the recipient of the Charles M. Gates Memorial Award from the Washington State Historical Society.

ANDREW K. FRANK is Assistant Professor of History at Florida Atlantic University. He has published several books and articles, including *The Routledge Historical Atlas of the American South*. He is currently working on *Creeks and Southerners: Biculturalism on the Early American Frontier*, an exploration of race and identity in eighteenth-century Florida, Georgia, and Alabama.

HARRY W. FRITZ, Ph.D., is Professor of History and Chairman of the Department of History at The University of Montana in Missoula. Professor Fritz teaches courses in early American history, American military history, and Montana history. He was the University of Montana's Teacher of the Year in 1972 and 1999 and a Distinguished Service Award winner in 1985; he also won the Governor's Humanities Award in 2003. He has written several articles and lectured widely on the Lewis and Clark Expedition. He is the author of *Montana: Land of Contrast* (1984; rev. ed., 2001) and co-editor of *Montana and the West* (1984), *The Montana Heritage* (1992), and *The Montana Legacy* (2002). In 1985 and 1987, he served in the Montana house of representatives and, in 1991 and 1993, in the Montana senate.

WILLIAM S. HANABLE, Ph.D., is Principal of Research North and Visiting Researcher at Western Oregon University. He is the author of numerous books and articles on the history of Alaska.

SAMUEL B. HAND is Professor of History Emeritus at the University of Vermont. He has lectured and published widely on the history of Vermont. Generally regarded as the dean of Vermont historians, his recent monograph, *The Star That Set: The Vermont Republican Party, 1854–1974* , appeared in 2002. He has co-edited *The Encyclopedia of Vermont*, published in 2003.

PETER HEYRMAN has been writing nonfiction and fiction for over two decades. His published work includes articles and book reviews for *The Washington Post*, *The Delaware State News*, and several other newspapers, and short stories in a dozen different books and magazines.

M. H. HOEFLICH holds a B.A. and M.A. from Haverford College, an M.A. and Ph.D. from Cambridge University, a J.D. from the Yale Law School, and an LL.D. (h.c.) from Baker University. He is the John H. & John M. Kane Distinguished Professor of Law at the University of Kansas and Courtesy Professor of History. In 2002–2003, he served as the President of the Kansas

Historical Society, Inc. He is the author or editor of seven books, including *The Gladsome Light of Jurisprudence*, *Learning the Law in England and the United States in the 18th and 19th Centuries*, *Roman and Civil Law and the Development of Anglo-American Jurisprudence in the Nineteenth Century*, and *Tall Grass Essays* (with Davis and Hoy), and of more than seventy articles in learned journals. He is also a columnist for the Lawrence, Kansas, *Journal-World*.

ARTHUR HOLST is Legislative and Regulatory Affairs Manager for the Philadelphia Water Department. He previously served as Executive Director of the Betsy Ross House and Chief of Staff to Philadelphia Councilman Joseph C. Vignola. He earned his Ph.D. in political science at Temple University where he also earned a master's in public administration and a bachelor's in business administration. Dr. Holst has contributed to a number of reference works on various subjects related to political science, history, and the environment. He is also an adjunct faculty member at Widener University in the Master of Public Administration Program. He has taught at Temple University and the Community College of Philadelphia and was a Fulbright Scholar in the Ukraine during the 2001–2002 academic year.

ADAM R. HORNBUCKLE is an independent historian and freelance writer living in College Park, Maryland. A contributor to several other Greenwood Press reference books, such as the *Biographical Dictionary of American Sport*, his contribution to this volume is his first outside his specialty of sports history. A civilian employee of the Department of the Air Force, Mr. Hornbuckle is the Branch Chief of the Air Force Declassification Office at the National Archives in College Park, Maryland.

JOHN P. HUNDLEY is an expatriate Hoosier living in Chicago. He formerly held the position of Cultural History Program Developer at the Indiana State Museum.

FRANKIE HUTTON is a former journalist and Associate Professor of Mass Media at Hampton University. She was awarded a Ph.D. in American history at Rutgers State University in 1990 and has since been Visiting Associate Professor of History at Howard University, Washington, D.C., and Montclair State University, New Jersey. She is the author of *The Early Black Press in America, 1827–1860* and co-author of *Outsiders in Nineteenth Century Press History: Multicultural Perspectives*. In 1999, she was awarded a Salzburg Fellowship. She gratefully acknowledges the assistance of the Greenbrier (West Virginia) Historical Society and Tara Curtis in the completion of this article.

MATTHEW H. JENNINGS is a Ph.D. candidate in history at the University of Illinois, Urbana-Champaign. His dissertation treats violence in the colonial Southeast from a cross-cultural perspective and is titled "This Country Is Worth the Trouble of Going to War to Keep It: Colonization, Communities and Conflict in South Carolina to 1740." His research and teaching interests include Native American history, early American history, slavery, and violence.

MELINDA MARIE JETTÉ is a native-born Oregonian, the descendant of interethnic French Canadian and Indian families who settled the Willamette Valley in the 1840s. She received her M.A. in history from Université Laval in Quebec City. She is currently completing a Ph.D. in history at the University of British Columbia. Her doctoral research examines intercultural relations in the Willamette Valley on the eve of large-scale American migration to Oregon (1812–1843).

JONATHAN KASPAREK received a Ph.D. from the University of Wisconsin—Madison. His dissertation on Philip F. La Follette and the Wisconsin Progressive Party won the 2003 UW Baensch Prize for best dissertation on a topic in Wisconsin history. He is the author of several articles and reviews on Wisconsin history published in the *Wisconsin Magazine of History*, and he lectures at Edgewood College.

JOHN R. KEMP is Deputy Director of the Louisiana Endowment for the Humanities and the former Associate Commissioner for Public Affairs at the Louisiana Board of Regents for Higher Education. Mr. Kemp also served as a staff writer for the New Orleans *Times-Picayune* daily newspaper and was former chief curator of the Louisiana State Museum's Louisiana Historical Center. He has taught Louisiana history and currently writes about New Orleans, its history, visual arts, and historic preservation for a number of national and regional magazines. Among his many books are *Alan Flattmann's French Quarter Impressions* (2002), *Manchac Swamp: Louisiana's Undiscovered Wilderness* (1996), and *New Orleans: An Illustrated History* (1997). Mr. Kemp also has contributed chapters and sections to the *Encyclopedia of Urban America: The Cities and Suburbs* (1998) and to *More Conversations with Walker Percy* (1993).

JEFFREY M. KINTOP has an M.A. in history and is currently the State Archives Manager for the Nevada State Library and Archives. His historical interests include U.S. territorial history and the political history of Nevada. He is the author of several books and articles on Nevada history.

MAXINE N. LURIE has a Ph.D. from the University of Wisconsin. She is currently Associate Professor and Chair of the History Department at Seton Hall University, where she specializes in teaching courses on colonial and Revolutionary America. She has edited several books and written articles on New Jersey history.

MICHAEL MANGUS received his doctoral degree from The Ohio State University in 1998. A specialist in nineteenth-century U.S. history, his research focuses on the interaction of Union soldiers and Confederate civilians during the American Civil War. He currently serves as a Lecturer at The Ohio State University at Newark.

SUSAN MANGUS received her Ph.D. from The Ohio State University in 1999. She is Assistant Professor of History at Muskingum College and Director of Educational Programs at the John and Annie Glenn Historic Site in New Concord, Ohio. A specialist in twentieth-century U.S. history, her research focuses upon American historical identity.

ROLAND MARDEN is a Lecturer in American Studies at the University of Sussex, England. He graduated from the City University of New York in 2001 and has since written articles on eighteenth-century Anglo-American political thought. He is currently working on a book that examines the understanding of natural rights in political discourse during the American Revolution.

JOHN McCORMICK received his Ph.D. from the University of Utah and is Associate Professor of History at Salt Lake Community College.

MICHAEL E. MEAGHER received his Ph.D. from Southern Illinois University in 1993 and is currently Associate Professor of Political Science at the University of Missouri—Rolla. He teaches courses in American government and the American presidency. His research areas are American political thought and the American presidency.

JOHN E. MILLER, Professor of History at South Dakota State University, received his Ph.D. in history from the University of Wisconsin and teaches courses in twentieth-century American history, economic history, South Dakota history, and historical methods. He has published a number of books and articles on South Dakota and Midwestern politics and culture.

NICOLE MITCHELL received her M.A. in history from Georgia College and State University in 2003. She is currently Assistant Archivist for Special Collections at the university and is a member of the Society for Georgia Archivists, the Georgia Historical Society, and the Southern Historical Association.

CHAD MORGAN received his Ph.D. in history from the University of North Carolina at Chapel Hill in 2003. His work has appeared in *Civil War History* and *The Georgia Historical Quarterly*.

H. NICHOLAS MULLER III is a former Professor of History at the University of Vermont, where he taught the history of Vermont. He has edited *Vermont History* and served as senior editor for *Vermont Life Magazine*. He left Vermont to serve consecutively as President of Colby-Sawyer College, Director of the Wisconsin Historical Society, and President and CEO of the Frank Lloyd Wright Foundation. Dr. Muller has recently returned to the Champlain Valley and resumed writing about Vermont's past. He and Dr. Hand have previously collaborated on *In a State of Nature*, published in 1982 and developed to help teach the history of Vermont.

DEANNE STEPHENS NUWER, Ph.D., is an Associate Professor of History at the University of Southern Mississippi. She specializes in southern history and currently is researching coastal seafood strikes and southern diseases such as yellow fever and hookworm.

WILLIAM L. OLBRICH, Jr., received an M.L.S. from the University of Texas at Austin and is a Ph.D. candidate in history at the University of Missouri—Columbia. He teaches local history in Ucollege at Washington University in St. Louis and is a Fellow of the American Cultural Studies Program and a member of the Native American Social Work Institute.

ELLEN HOLMES PEARSON holds a Ph.D. in colonial British American history from The Johns Hopkins University. She is an Assistant Professor of History at the University of North Carolina, Asheville. Dr. Pearson's research interests include early American cultural history and American legal culture, and she is currently completing a manuscript about early American legal educators and the creation of American identities.

JOHN DAVID RAUSCH, Jr., is Assistant Professor of Political Science at West Texas A&M University. A native of Pennsylvania, he holds degrees from the University of Alaska—Fairbanks and the University of Oklahoma, and he has studied at Webster University in Vienna, Austria, and at the University of Michigan. His primary teaching and research areas are American political institutions, state and local government, direct democracy, and religion and politics. He is co-editor of *The Test of Time: Coping with Legislative Term Limits* (2003).

AGNESA REEVE received her Ph.D. from the University of New Mexico and has been President of the Historical Society of New Mexico since 1991. She is the author of numerous books and articles.

WILLIAM ROBA received his Ph.D. in American studies from the University of Iowa in 1979. He currently is an Instructor of History at Scott Community College in Bettendorf, Iowa, and is the author of several books and essays dealing with German-American studies in the nineteenth century. He served as Commissioner for the Iowa Sesquicentennial Commission, 1992–1997.

PHIL ROBERTS, a native of Wyoming, holds a law degree from the University of Wyoming (1977) and a Ph.D. in history from the University of Washington. He joined the history faculty at the University of Wyoming in 1990. A veteran of the U.S. Marine Corps, he edited newspapers in Arizona and Wyoming before earning his law degree. Prior to his current position, he practiced law in Wyoming, worked in public history, and published a city magazine. He is author of *A Penny for the Governor, A Dollar for Uncle Sam: Taxation in Washington* (2002) and has served as editor of *Annals of Wyoming* since 1995.

JONATHAN S. RUSS, Ph.D., is Professor of History at the University of Delaware. A specialist in American history, he received his bachelor's degree from Colby College and his M.A. and Ph.D. from the University of Delaware.

His recent publications include *Young, Conaway, Stargatt & Taylor* (1999) and *Global Motivation: Honda, Toyota, and the Drive Toward American Manufacturing* (forthcoming), in addition to numerous articles, essays, and reviews. He regularly teaches courses in U.S. history, the history of Delaware, and the history of American business.

JIM SCHWARTZ spent more than a decade in journalism and has recently completed his doctorate at Wayne State University in Detroit, Michigan.

WILLIAM VIRDEN is a Lecturer in History at the University of Northern Colorado in Greeley, Colorado, where he has taught for the last fifteen years. He is also Director of the Colorado Institute for Historical Study in Fort Collins, Colorado. The institute is a nonprofit, educational and research organization that promotes the research and study of local, state, and regional history. Over the last three years, Mr. Virden has published three books. The first two, *Go to the Source* and *My Colorado*, are supplementary textbooks for teaching U.S. history and Colorado history using original sources. Both were written in conjunction with a colleague at the University of Northern Colorado, Ms. Mary Borg. The third publication, *Cornerstones and Communities: A Historical Overview of Colorado's County Seats and County Courthouses*, is a public history that combines anecdotes and folklore with history to tell the story of local government in early Colorado. It emphasizes the continuity of community as carried forward in Colorado's county courthouses.

ANNE WOO-SAM received her Ph.D. in history from the University of California—Berkeley in 1999 and is currently a Visiting Scholar at U.C. Berkeley's Institute of Governmental Studies. Her work looks at the interplay of political institutions, racial and ethnic relations, and domestic and foreign policy to understand the development of immigration policy in California and other heavily immigrant-impacted states as part of a larger book project, *Integrating the Immigrant: California's Immigrant Integration Policy from the Progressive Era to the Present.*

KERRY WYNN is a Ph.D. candidate in American history at the University of Illinois at Urbana-Champaign. She is currently writing her dissertation, "The Embodiment of Citizenship: Sovereignty and the Body in the Cherokee Nation, 1880–1920."

TIM ZACHARIAS is a high school social sciences teacher, possessing a B.A. in history from Oregon State University (1979) and an M.A. in history from Washington State University (2003). He has taught for nineteen years in three school districts in rural eastern Oregon. Despite the rural isolation, he supervised a student project that became one of six nationally recognized by NATO in 1987. In 1994, he was Oregon's first runner-up for the Christa McAuliffe fellowship and was named Oregon's James Madison Memorial Senior Fellow for 2000.